THE Ultimate Soup COOKBOOK

Reader's Digest

THE READER'S DIGEST ASSOCIATION, INC.
PLEASANTVILLE, NEW YORK | MONTREAL

PROJECT STAFF

Recipe Editor
Nancy Shuker

Editors
Neil Wertheimer
Suzanne G. Beason
Don Earnest
Marianne Wait

Designer
Elizabeth Tunnicliffe

Production Associate
Erick Swindell

Copy Editors
Jane Sherman
Jeanette Gingold
Delilah Smittle

Indexer
Nanette Bendyna

Editorial Assistants
William DeMott
Alison Palmer Dupree
Joanne Stewart

READER'S DIGEST BOOKS

Editor in Chief
Neil Wertheimer

Managing Editor
Suzanne G. Beason

Creative Director
Michele Laseau

Production Technology Director
Douglas A. Croll

Manufacturing Manager
John L. Cassidy

Marketing Director
Dawn Nelson

President and Publisher,
Trade Publishing
Harold Clarke

President, U.S. Books & Home
Entertainment
Dawn Zier

READER'S DIGEST
ASSOCIATION, INC.

President &
Chief Executive Officer
Eric Schrier

Copyright © 2006 by The Reader's Digest Association, Inc.
Copyright © 2006 by The Reader's Digest Association (Canada) Ltd.
Copyright © 2006 by The Reader's Digest Association Far East Ltd.
Philippine Copyright © 2006 by The Reader's Digest Association Far East Ltd.

Library of Congress Cataloging-in-Publication Data

The ultimate soup cookbook : Over 900 family-friendly recipes / The Reader's
Digest Association, Inc. ; [editor, Neil Wertheimer].

   p. cm.

Includes index.

ISBN 0-7621-0727-8

ISBN 978-0-7621-0886-2 (trade edition)

1. Soups. 2. One-dish meals. I. Wertheimer, Neil. II. Reader's Digest
Association.

TX757.U48 2006

641.8'13--dc22

                                2006001068

Address any comments about *The Ultimate Soup Cookbook* to:

The Reader's Digest Association, Inc.
Editor-in-Chief, Books
Reader's Digest Road
Pleasantville, NY 10570-7000

For more Reader's Digest products and information, visit our website:
www.rd.com (in the United States)
www.readersdigest.ca (in Canada)

Printed in the United States of America

3 5 7 9 10 8 6 4

THE Aroma of Home

My wife and I have a lot of cooking gear. But none provoke as many memories or are as cherished as our soup pots.

Each one has a story. There's the 70-year-old, impossibly heavy Griswold cast-iron pot, pulled from a hidden, hay-covered corner of an old Pennsylvania barn (the owner, a friend of ours, was moving and let us search her barn for old furniture and castoffs). After much cleaning and conditioning, the pot has become the perfect host for short ribs and chili—what must be hundreds of gallons over the years.

Then there's the sturdy 12-quart aluminum pot my parents bought themselves shortly after their marriage in 1950 and which I nearly destroyed in my youth by repeatedly burning popcorn in it. They recently passed the pot to me—along with the original lid and a few remaining specks of diamond-hard popcorn carbon on the bottom. Somehow it seems morally wrong to cook chicken soup in any other vessel.

There's another one. My father had a short, failed venture in the restaurant business back in the '70s. One of the only remnants is a professional stockpot he gave me from the place that is so massive it comfortably holds gumbo for 40, crab legs whole. It looks awkwardly large on my home stove top, sitting atop two separate burners, but nothing makes me as happy as seeing it up there.

It might be my imagination, but the soups and stews that emerge from our favorite old pots seem to have more flavor, more personality, more love than almost anything else my wife and I cook. Some of that is our romantic attachment to the pots. But even more are the aromas, textures, and colors of the foods they contain. What is more satisfying for a cook than to look into a gently simmering pot of soup—carrots and onions and barley in constant motion, herbs and oils bubbling thinly at the top, a well-cooked bone sticking out above all else? Even *serving* soup seems special—dipping a ladle deep into the pot, searching out a nice morsel of meat or fish, and pouring its rich, chunky contents into a wide, worn ceramic bowl.

Soup is extraordinary food. It is rich with history, culture, and personality. It is fast to make and soulfully good to eat. Good cooks can work subtle magic with the flavors, and new cooks are all but guaranteed to be successful—what is more forgiving for a beginning chef than a big pot of soup? Best of all, soup fills a home with blessed aromas that cheer you up on even the coldest, most gray day of winter.

Reader's Digest has always celebrated the family, and with *The Ultimate Soup Cookbook*, we particularly have family in mind. These 943 recipes, gathered from sources far and wide, are all well tested and proven to fill your house with the aromas of home. Children will love them, spouses will cherish them, and friends and visitors will be comforted by them. So get out your favorite pot and start cooking up some new family memories today. With *The Ultimate Soup Cookbook,* a happy, well-fed, even-better-loved family is only the next meal away.

Neil Wertheimer
Editor in Chief, Reader's Digest Books

TABLE OF
contents

Let us celebrate the unique pleasures and virtues of soup.

This page: Mediterranean Roasted Vegetable Soup, page 354.
Opposite page, clockwise from top left: Turkey, Spinach, and Rice in Roasted Garlic Broth, page 125; Classic Veal Stew, page 205; Corn Chowder with Soda Crackers, page 323.

6

For many, soup is a robust steaming bowl for a cold winter night.

Opposite page, clockwise from top left: Cheddar Cheese and Broccoli Soup, page 340; Green Pork Chili, page 234; Oven-Roasted Onion Soup, page 382; Spiced Butternut Squash Soup, page 404. *This page, clockwise from top left:* Portuguese Kale Soup with Beans, page 442; Beef-Vegetable Soup, page 142; Santa Fe Chicken Chili, page 254.

But soup is so much more. It is a **welcoming start** to a holiday meal.

Opposite page: Pumpkin Bisque, page 329. *This page, clockwise from top left:* Asparagus Soup, page 358; Tomato Egg Drop Soup, page 412; Shrimp and Fennel Bisque, page 312.

This page, clockwise from top left: Crostini with Artichokes and Tomato, page 515; Carrot Soup with Dill, page 60; Easy Borscht, page 362. *Opposite page:* Simple Gazpacho, page 65.

Soup is cool
freshness
on a summer day.

13

14

This page, clockwise from bottom left: Sausage Potato Soup, page 190; Root Vegetable Chowder with Bacon Bits, page 330; Chile-Cheese Quesadillas with Tomatoes, page 515; Ham, Barley, and Bean Soup, page 185. *Opposite page, clockwise from left:* Summer Garden Soup, page 348; Creamy Asparagus Soup, page 359; Minestrone with Turkey Meatballs, page 128.

Soup is light and healthy nutrition for an energetic day.

And soup is a .
near-instant
meal on a time-harried
weekday.

TIPS FOR QUICK FLAVOR

Use fresh garlic or fresh ginger for an instantly bold aroma.

Add frozen vegetables to the pot for easy, tasty nutrition.

Quickly heat dry spices in a skillet to release their aromas.

Freeze herbs in ice cubes for instant freshness year-round.

17

This page, clockwise from top left: Barley Soup with Lean Beef,
page 499; White Bean Soup with Spinach, page 434;
Quick Goulash, page 181; All-Day Beef-Vegetable Soup, page 143

We love soups rich with bold, chunky meats.

Sauté onions before adding to soup for sweetness and texture.

Brown meat first to cook off fat, seal in flavor, and improve color.

Add wine for heartier flavor; the alcohol will evaporate.

And we love light soups filled with the
colors of nature.

Opposite page: Pumpkin Soup with Muffins, page 398. *This page, clockwise from top left:* Spinach and Onion Soup with Tomato Crostini, page 401; Vegetable Soup with Pesto, page 354; Ham and Fresh Pea Soup, page 183; Manhattan Shrimp Chowder, page 309.

Of course, chicken soup is the queen of all soups.

TIPS FOR BETTER STOCK

Boil chicken pieces alone at first; skim off the gray foam.

Add vegetables and aromatics after the broth is skimmed.

For a clear stock, strain through a cheesecloth-lined sieve.

It's easiest to remove fat that has hardened in the refrigerator.

Opposite page, from top: Chicken-Tortilla Soup with Cheese, page 102; Chicken-Kale Soup, page 100.
This page: Country-Style Chicken-Vegetable Soup, page 97.

And who can resist the textures of barley, beans, and dumplings?

Opposite page, clockwise from top left: Chinese Beef Soup with Barley and Spinach, page 500; Mushroom-Barley Soup, page 498; Quick Cassoulet, page 444; Black Bean Soup with Green Pepper, page 451. *This page:* Tuscan Three-Bean Soup, page 430.

25

Fruit soups sparkle with
surprise and delight.

27

This page, clockwise from top right: Quick Fish Chowder with Tomato and Fennel, page 295; Hearty Mussel Soup, page 286; Shrimp and Barley Gumbo, page 279.
Opposite page: Cod and Vegetable Stew, page 271.

And what better usage for
fresh seafood
than a fine chowder or stew?

TIPS FOR THICKER SOUPS

Pureeing some of the vegetables makes soup thicker.

Mix cornstarch and cold water before adding to the pot.

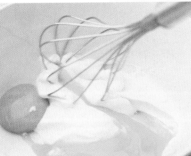

Whisk egg yolks and cream and add for richer soup.

Finely grated bread crumbs will add texture to broth.

Let soup fill your
kitchen
with fine smells
and eager eaters...

Opposite page: Chunky Turkey Chili, page 255.
This page, clockwise from top left: Monkfish Ragout, page 272; Speedy Chicken Noodle Soup, page 93;
Crispy Seed-Topped Flatbreads, page 512; Beef Stock with Tomatoes, page 46.

For few foods say love as does soup.

Clockwise from top left: Turkey Chili with Salsa, page 241; Oven Cheese Chowder, page 335;
Piquant Cod Chowder, page 297.

32

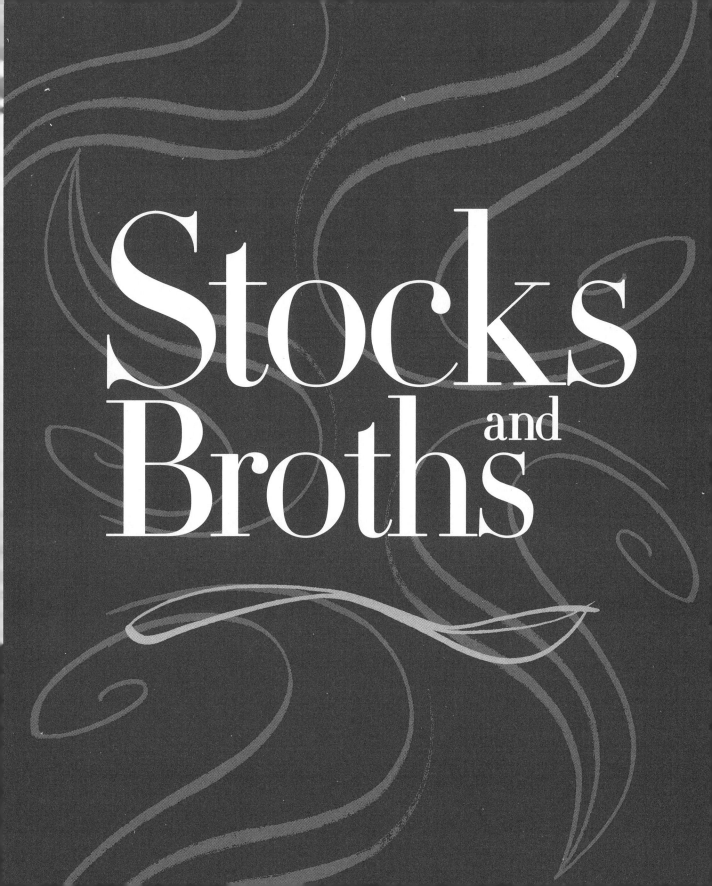

Stocks and Broths

STOCKS AND BROTHS

recipe list

 EASY: 10 minutes to prepare

QUICK: Ready to eat in 30 minutes

ONE-DISH: contains protein, vegetables, and good carbohydrates (beans, whole-grains, etc.) for a complete healthy meal

HEALTHY: High in nutrients, low in bad fats and empty carbohydrates

SLOW COOKER: Easily adapted for slow cooker by cutting down on liquids

BASIC CHICKEN STOCK

This is the kind of chicken stock you'll want to keep as a staple. If you freeze it in 1-cup containers, you can thaw just what you need for a recipe.

MAKES 5 CUPS

1 chicken carcass, bones from 4 chicken pieces, or 1 leg with thigh (about 8 ounces)
1 onion, quartered
1 large carrot, coarsely chopped
1 celery stalk, cut into chunks
1 bay leaf
1 parsley sprig
1 thyme sprig
8 whole black peppercorns
1/2 teaspoon salt

1 Break up chicken carcass or bones; leave leg whole. In a large saucepan over medium-high heat, combine bones or chicken, onion, carrot, and celery. Add 7 cups water and bring to boil, skimming off foam.

2 Add bay leaf, parsley, thyme, peppercorns, and salt, then reduce heat, cover, and simmer 2 hours.

3 Strain stock through a sieve into a heatproof bowl, discarding solids. Let cool, then refrigerate until cold and remove fat with a spoon. Use refrigerated stock within 3 days or frozen stock within 3 months.

CHICKEN STOCK WITH GARLIC

Garlic not only has its own distinct flavor, it also brings out the flavor of other ingredients.

MAKES 9 CUPS

3 pounds chicken wings, necks, and gizzards
2 celery stalks, cut into 2-inch pieces
1 large onion, unpeeled, quartered
1 garlic clove
Parsley sprigs
2 bay leaves
2 large carrots, cut into 2-inch pieces
10 whole black peppercorns

1 Remove all fat and skin from chicken. Rinse chicken, place in a large soup pot over medium heat, and cover with 12 cups water. Bring to boil, skimming off foam.

2 Add celery, onion, garlic, parsley, bay leaves, carrots, and peppercorns and return to boil. Reduce heat, partially cover, and simmer, skimming occasionally, 1 1/2 to 2 hours.

3 Strain through a cheesecloth-lined or very fine mesh sieve into a large heatproof bowl, discarding solids. Skim off fat by drawing a sheet of paper towel across the surface or let cool, refrigerate until cold, and remove fat with a spoon. Use refrigerated stock within 3 days or frozen stock within 3 months.

CHICKEN STOCK WITH PARSNIPS

The secret to rich-tasting stock is long simmering over low heat to draw out all the flavor of the ingredients.

MAKES 8 CUPS

1 roasting or stewing chicken (5 pounds)
    or 5 pounds chicken parts
1 large yellow onion, quartered
2 medium celery stalks, quartered
2 medium carrots, quartered
1 parsnip or turnip, quartered
6 parsley sprigs
2 bay leaves
12 whole black or green peppercorns
1/2 teaspoon salt
1 teaspoon dried rosemary, crumbled
1 teaspoon dried thyme, crumbled
2 garlic cloves *(optional)*

1 In a large soup pot over high heat, combine 12 cups water, chicken, onion, celery, carrots, parsnip, parsley, bay leaves, peppercorns, salt, rosemary, thyme, and garlic, if desired. Bring to boil, then reduce heat and simmer, partially covered, occasionally skimming off foam.

2 After 1 1/2 hours or when juices run clear when meat is pierced with a knife, transfer chicken to a plate. When cool enough to handle, remove meat (reserve for another use, if desired) and return bones to pot. Simmer 30 minutes or more, then remove from heat.

3 When stock is cool, strain through a fine mesh sieve or cheesecloth-lined colander into a large heatproof bowl, discarding solids. Cover and refrigerate until cold, then remove fat with a spoon. Use refrigerated stock within 3 days or frozen stock within 3 months.

CHICKEN STOCK WITH CLOVES

Roasting the chicken parts before making the stock adds extra flavor and color.

MAKES 8 CUPS

4 pounds chicken wings, necks, and backs
2 medium yellow onions, quartered
3 celery stalks with leaves, cut into
    2-inch chunks
2 medium carrots, scrubbed and cut into
    2-inch chunks
4 garlic cloves, minced
10 parsley sprigs
4 thyme sprigs or 1 teaspoon dried thyme
2 bay leaves
12 whole black peppercorns
4 whole cloves

1 Preheat oven to 450°F. Arrange chicken in a large shallow pan and roast, turning occasionally, 40 minutes or until browned.

2 Using a slotted spoon, transfer to an 8-quart soup pot. Add 14 cups water, onions, celery, carrots, garlic, parsley, thyme, bay leaves, peppercorns, and cloves. Pour 2 cups water into roasting pan and stir with a wooden spoon to loosen browned bits. Add to pot and bring to boil, skimming off foam. Reduce heat and simmer, uncovered, 2 hours, skimming occasionally.

3 Strain stock through a sieve into a large heatproof bowl, discarding solids. When cool, cover and refrigerate until cold, then remove fat with a spoon. Use refrigerated stock within 3 days or frozen stock within 3 months.

BROWN CHICKEN STOCK

MAKES 12 CUPS

4 pounds bony chicken pieces
   (backs, necks, and wings)
4 celery stalks with leaves, cut up
4 large carrots, cut up
2 large yellow onions, thickly sliced
2 medium tomatoes, cut up *(optional)*
 1 large all-purpose potato, white turnip,
   or parsnip, peeled and thickly sliced
1 cup thickly sliced scallion or leek tops
4 garlic cloves, halved
4 bay leaves
1 tablespoon dried basil
1 tablespoon dried thyme
2 teaspoons salt
1 teaspoon whole black peppercorns
1/2 teaspoon whole cloves

1 Preheat oven to 425°F. Arrange chicken in a large shallow pan and roast 25 minutes. Turn and roast until well browned, about 15 minutes. Transfer to a 10-quart soup pot.

2 Pour 2 cups water into roasting pan and stir with a wooden spoon to loosen browned bits. Add to pot over medium heat, then add 12 cups water, celery, carrots, onions, tomatoes, if desired, potato, scallions, garlic, bay leaves, basil, thyme, salt, peppercorns, and cloves. Bring to boil, then reduce heat and simmer, covered, 3 1/2 hours.

3 Using a slotted spoon, remove chicken. When cool enough to handle, remove meat (reserve for another use, if desired).

4 Strain stock through a large sieve lined with 2 layers of cheesecloth into a large heatproof bowl, discarding solids.

5 To clarify stock, if desired, pour into a clean saucepan. In a cup, stir together 1/4 cup cold water and 1 egg white. Pour into stock and bring to a boil, then remove from heat and let stand 5 minutes. Strain through a sieve lined with clean, damp cheesecloth.

6 When stock is cool, cover and refrigerate until cold, then remove fat with a spoon. Use refrigerated stock within 3 days or frozen stock within 3 months.

This is the rich, aromatic chicken stock that makes homemade soups and sauces come alive with flavor.

LARGE-POT CHICKEN STOCK

Homemade chicken stock is delicious, fat-free, and low in sodium. Making a large amount is efficient and, if you freeze it in small containers, will enrich your soups and stews for several months.

MAKES 20 CUPS

4 whole cloves

2 medium yellow onions

5 pounds chicken parts, preferably dark meat

3 celery stalks with leaves, coarsely chopped

2 large carrots, scrubbed and coarsely chopped

6 garlic cloves

4 thyme sprigs or 2 teaspoons dried thyme

2 bay leaves

12 parsley sprigs

12 whole black peppercorns

1/2 teaspoon salt

1 Insert 2 cloves into each onion. In a 10- or 12-quart soup pot, bring 24 cups cold water and chicken to boil over high heat, skimming off foam. Add onions, celery, carrots, garlic, thyme, bay leaves, parsley, peppercorns, and salt and return to boil. Reduce heat and simmer, uncovered, 3 hours.

2 Strain stock through a large sieve into a large heatproof bowl, discarding solids. When cool, cover and refrigerate until cold, then remove fat with a spoon. Use refrigerated stock within 3 days or frozen stock within 3 months.

CHICKEN CONSOMMÉ

This shortcut recipe is as good as any that Grandma ever made. Egg whites and eggshells are added to make the broth sparkling clear.

SERVES 4

6 cups canned low-sodium chicken broth

3 large egg whites, lightly beaten

3 eggshells, crushed

3 scallions with tops, thinly sliced

1 medium tomato, chopped

1 small carrot, peeled and sliced

1/2 cup chopped fresh parsley

1/2 teaspoon dried thyme

1/2 teaspoon dried basil

6 whole black peppercorns

1 bay leaf

1 In a large heavy saucepan over medium-high heat, combine broth, egg whites, eggshells, scallions, tomato, carrot, parsley, thyme, basil, peppercorns, and bay leaf. Bring to boil, whisking constantly 6 minutes, then reduce heat and simmer, uncovered, 30 minutes.

2 Strain through a large fine mesh sieve lined with a dampened kitchen towel or 2 layers of dampened cheesecloth into a heatproof bowl. Discard solids, skim off fat, and ladle into bowls.

CONSOMMÉ WITH VEGETABLES

This clear consommé with added vegetables is a healthy starter soup for any meal.

SERVES 4

6 cups canned low-sodium chicken broth

3 large egg whites, lightly beaten

3 eggshells, crushed

3 scallions with tops, thinly sliced

1 medium tomato, chopped

1 small carrot, peeled and sliced

1/2 cup chopped fresh parsley

1/2 teaspoon dried thyme

1/2 teaspoon dried basil

6 whole black peppercorns

1 bay leaf

1 small carrot, peeled and finely chopped

1 small celery stalk, finely chopped

1 small white turnip, peeled and finely chopped

1 small yellow onion, finely chopped

1 In a large heavy saucepan over medium-high heat, combine broth, egg whites, eggshells, scallions, tomato, carrot, parsley, thyme, basil, peppercorns, and bay leaf. Bring to boil, whisking constantly 6 minutes, then reduce heat and simmer, uncovered, 30 minutes.

2 Strain consommé through a large fine mesh sieve lined with a dampened kitchen towel or 2 layers of dampened cheesecloth into another large heavy saucepan. Discard solids and skim off fat. Add carrot, celery, turnip, and onion and bring to boil. Reduce heat and simmer, uncovered, 5 minutes or until vegetables are just tender.

CONSOMMÉ MADRILÈNE

This version of consommé has more tomato than most, and a nice red color.

SERVES 4

6 cups chicken stock

3 large egg whites, lightly beaten

3 eggshells, crushed

3 scallions with tops, thinly sliced

5 medium tomatoes, chopped

1 small carrot, peeled and sliced

1/2 cup chopped fresh parsley

1/2 teaspoon dried thyme

1/2 teaspoon dried basil

6 whole black peppercorns

1 bay leaf

1 In a large heavy saucepan over medium-high heat, combine broth, egg whites, eggshells, scallions, 3 tomatoes, carrot, parsley, thyme, basil, peppercorns, and bay leaf. Bring to boil, whisking constantly 6 minutes, then reduce heat and simmer, uncovered, 30 minutes.

2 Strain consommé through a large fine mesh sieve lined with a dampened kitchen towel or 2 layers of dampened cheesecloth into a heatproof bowl. Discard solids, skim off fat, and ladle into bowls. Top with remaining tomatoes.

JELLIED CONSOMMÉ

This is a refreshing summer version of consommé.

SERVES 4

6 cups canned low-sodium chicken broth
3 large egg whites, lightly beaten
3 eggshells, crushed
3 scallions with tops, thinly sliced
1 medium tomato, chopped
1 small carrot, peeled and sliced
1/2 cup chopped fresh parsley
1/2 teaspoon dried thyme
1/2 teaspoon dried basil
6 whole black peppercorns
1 bay leaf
1 envelope unflavored gelatin
2 tablespoons Madeira wine or sherry

1 In a large heavy saucepan over medium-high heat, combine broth, egg whites, eggshells, scallions, tomato, carrot, parsley, thyme, basil, peppercorns, and bay leaf. Bring to boil, whisking constantly 6 minutes, then reduce heat and simmer, uncovered, 30 minutes.

2 Strain consommé through a large fine mesh sieve lined with a dampened kitchen towel or 2 layers of dampened cheesecloth into another large heavy saucepan. Discard solids and skim off fat. Transfer 1 cup stock to a small bowl, sprinkle gelatin on top, and let stand 5 minutes. Bring remaining consommé to boil, then reduce heat and simmer, uncovered.

3 Stir gelatin mixture and Madeira into pot and cook, stirring, 2 minutes or until gelatin dissolves. Transfer to a large heatproof bowl, let cool to room temperature, cover, and refrigerate 2 hours or until lightly set. Beat briskly with a fork and serve in chilled bowls.

SIMPLE CHICKEN SOUP

This easy, quick soup is a healthy starter for any lunch or dinner. It's also very tasty.

SERVES 4

4 cups chicken stock
1 small skinless, boneless chicken breast, thinly sliced
1 small carrot, thinly sliced
1/2 small leek, thinly sliced
1 small celery stalk, thinly sliced
Salt and black pepper

1 In a large saucepan over high heat, bring stock to boil. Add chicken, carrot, leek, and celery. Reduce heat and simmer, covered, 2 minutes or until chicken is cooked through and vegetables are crisp-tender. Season to taste with salt and pepper.

ASIAN CHICKEN SOUP

Shiitake mushrooms, lettuce, cayenne pepper, and cilantro flavor this soup, based on chicken stock and made substantial with vermicelli and threads of beaten egg.

SERVES 4

5 cups chicken stock
1/4 teaspoon cayenne pepper
3 1/2 ounces shiitake mushrooms, thinly sliced
1 1/2 ounces vermicelli
1 small head Bibb lettuce, finely shredded
1 large egg, beaten
1 tablespoon chopped fresh cilantro

1 In a large saucepan over high heat, bring stock and cayenne to boil. Add mushrooms, reduce heat, and simmer 2 minutes. Break up vermicelli, add to pan, and simmer 3 minutes until just barely cooked. Add lettuce, increase heat to high, and bring to rolling boil.

2 Remove from heat and slowly add egg, stirring gently (it will cook very quickly, forming threads). Stir in cilantro and serve immediately.

CHINESE NOODLE SOUP

A traditional Chinese American meal usually begins with a hot, light soup. Often the soup includes noodles because in Chinese culture, eating noodles is thought to ensure long life.

SERVES 6

6 dried Chinese mushrooms

2 ounces Chinese egg noodles or
    fine egg noodles

3 1/2 cups chicken stock

1/2 cup bite-size pieces cooked chicken,
    pork, or low-sodium ham

1 cup thinly sliced Napa cabbage

1/8 teaspoon black pepper

1 large scallion with top, finely sliced

2 tablespoons minced fresh parsley

1 In a small bowl, cover mushrooms with warm water and let stand 30 minutes. Rinse well and squeeze out water. Slice thinly, discarding stems.

2 Meanwhile, in a large saucepan, cook noodles according to package directions, then drain and transfer to a bowl.

3 Add stock to pan and bring to boil over medium heat. Stir in mushrooms, chicken, cabbage, and pepper. Reduce heat and simmer, covered, 10 minutes.

4 To serve, divide noodles among 6 soup bowls. Using a slotted spoon, lift mushroom mixture out of broth and place equal portions on top of noodles. Carefully pour in broth and sprinkle with scallion and parsley.

SUPREME CHINESE SOUP BROTH

There is an expression from China that "broth to a cook is voice to a singer." By combining pork with chicken, this broth makes your soups sing with flavor.

MAKES 12 CUPS

1 whole chicken (3 pounds)

1 pound shoulder or loin of pork

4 scallions, white part only

2 ounces fresh ginger, peeled and slightly
    crushed

1 teaspoon peppercorns

2 tablespoons rice wine or dry sherry

1 Place whole chicken and pork in a stockpot and add cold water to cover. Bring to boil over high heat and skim off foam. Add scallions, ginger, peppercorns, and rice wine. Reduce heat, cover, and simmer, 2 hours.

2 Remove solid ingredients. Pull cooked chicken breasts off bones and discard remaining solids. Lightly mash chicken breasts and set aside. Strain broth through dampened gauze or fine-mesh cheesecloth. Let broth cool to room temperature.

3 Add mashed chicken breasts to cooled broth. Place over high heat and stir continually in one direction (either clockwise or counter-clockwise, but do not change direction) until boiling. Reduce heat and gently boil broth, 15 minutes.

4 Any remaining impurities in broth will adhere to chicken breast. Remove breasts and strain broth again. Use broth immediately or store in refrigerator up to 3 days. Broth can be frozen up to 3 months.

TOFU-VEGETABLE SOUP

You can make this light soup, packed with protein and vitamin C, in 20 minutes or less.

SERVES 4

1 1/2 cups chicken stock

2 tablespoons rice vinegar

2 tablespoons ketchup

1 tablespoon sesame oil

3/4 teaspoon salt

1/2 teaspoon ground ginger

1 pound firm tofu, cut into 1-inch chunks

3 cups Napa cabbage, shredded

2 carrots, thinly sliced

6 scallions, sliced

1 In a medium saucepan over medium-high heat, bring 1 1/2 cups water, stock, vinegar, ketchup, oil, salt, and ginger to boil. Add tofu, cabbage, carrots, and scallions. Reduce heat and simmer, covered, 5 minutes or until carrots are tender.

MATZO BALL SOUP

Eating matzo (unleavened bread) and the matzo meal made from it is traditional at Passover, the spring holiday that celebrates the liberation of Jews from slavery in Egypt millennia ago.

SERVES 6 ☀

2 large egg whites

1 large egg

1 tablespoon vegetable oil

1/4 cup unflavored seltzer

2/3 cup matzo meal

2 tablespoons chopped fresh parsley

3/4 teaspoon salt

1/4 teaspoon black pepper

6 1/4 cups chicken stock

1 In a medium bowl, whisk together egg whites, egg, and oil, then whisk in seltzer. Add matzo meal, 1 tablespoon parsley, salt, and pepper and stir until smooth. Cover and refrigerate 30 minutes.

2 Meanwhile, half-fill a large saucepan with cold water and bring to boil over high heat. Using your hands, roll matzo mixture into 1-inch balls (about 22) and drop into pan. Reduce heat, cover, and simmer 40 minutes or until cooked through.

3 In another large saucepan, bring stock to boil over high heat, adding more salt to taste. Using a slotted spoon, transfer several matzo balls to each soup bowl, then ladle in hot stock. Garnish with remaining parsley.

GREEK EGG AND LEMON SOUP

This classic soup from Greece is a lovely first course for lunch or dinner.

SERVES 6

1 tablespoon olive oil

1 yellow onion, finely chopped

8 cups homemade chicken stock or canned low-sodium chicken broth

2 eggs, well beaten

1/3 cup fresh lemon juice

1 1/2 teaspoons salt

1/4 cup fresh dill

Snipped dill sprigs

6 lemon slices

1 Heat oil in a 4-quart saucepan over medium heat. Add onion and sauté 3 minutes. Add stock and bring to boil, then reduce heat and simmer, covered, 20 minutes. Remove from heat and let cool slightly.

2 Place eggs in a medium bowl and whisk in 1 cup stock mixture, lemon juice, and salt. Stir into pan and cook until heated through (do not boil, or soup may curdle).

3 Stir in dill. Garnish each serving with snipped dill and lemon.

GREEK EGG AND LEMON SOUP WITH RICE

Greek cooks say that when preparing this soup, making a kissing sound as you stir the broth and lemon juice into the eggs prevents the mixture from curdling.

SERVES 4

3 1/2 cups canned low-sodium chicken broth
1/4 cup long-grain white rice
3 large eggs
3 tablespoons fresh lemon juice
2 tablespoons minced fresh mint or parsley

1 In a large saucepan over medium heat, bring broth to boil. Stir in rice, then reduce heat and simmer, covered, until almost tender, about 15 minutes.

2 Meanwhile, in a large howl, using an electric mixer on high speed, beat eggs until light yellow and slightly thickened. Gradually add 1/4 cup hot broth mixture and lemon juice and beat 2 minutes.

3 Slowly pour egg mixture into pan in a thin stream, beating constantly with a fork until eggs cook and shred very finely (do not boil, or eggs will curdle). Sprinkle each serving with mint.

BASIC BEEF STOCK

Nothing makes soup or stew taste better than really well-seasoned, homemade stock. It's worth the effort to always have some on hand in the freezer.

MAKES 5 CUPS

1 tablespoon sunflower oil
1 piece lean stewing beef (4 ounces)
1 onion, quartered
1 carrot, coarsely chopped
1 celery stalk, coarsely chopped
2 bay leaves
1 parsley sprig
1 thyme sprig
10 whole black peppercorns
1/2 teaspoon salt

1 Heat oil in a large saucepan over high heat. Add beef and cook until browned on all sides, then transfer to a plate. Reduce heat, add onion, carrot, and celery, and sauté 5 minutes or until browned. Add 7 cups water, increase heat to high, and bring to boil.

2 Return beef to pan, return to boil, and skim off foam. Add bay leaves, parsley, thyme, peppercorns, and salt. Reduce heat and simmer, covered, 2 hours.

3 Strain stock through a sieve into a heatproof bowl, discarding solids. When cool, refrigerate until cold, then remove fat with a spoon. Use refrigerated stock within 3 days or frozen stock within 3 months.

ROASTED BEEF STOCK

Roasting both the bones and the vegetables gives this stock rich flavor as well as beautiful color.

MAKES 8 CUPS

4 pounds beef shinbones

2 large yellow onions, cut into slim wedges

3 medium carrots, scrubbed and cut into
    2-inch chunks

1 medium white turnip,
    scrubbed and quartered

1 parsnip, scrubbed and cut into 2-inch chunks

2 celery stalks with leaves, cut into
    2-inch chunks

4 garlic cloves, bruised

6 parsley sprigs

8 whole black peppercorns

2 thyme sprigs or 1/2 teaspoon
    dried thyme, crumbled

1 Preheat oven to 450°F. Place bones in a large shallow pan and roast, turning occasionally, until beginning to brown, about 30 minutes. Stir in onions, carrots, turnip, parsnip, and celery and roast 30 minutes or until bones are well browned.

2 Using a slotted spoon, transfer bones and vegetables to an 8-quart soup pot. Add 14 cups water, garlic, parsley, peppercorns, and thyme. Drain off excess fat from roasting pan, pour in 2 cups water, and stir with a wooden spoon to loosen browned bits. Add to pot.

3 Bring stock to boil over high heat, skimming off foam. Reduce heat to medium-low and simmer 3 hours, skimming occasionally.

4 Strain stock through a large sieve lined with 2 layers of cheesecloth into a large heatproof bowl, discarding solids. When stock is cool, cover and refrigerate until cold, then remove fat with a spoon. Use refrigerated stock within 3 days or frozen stock within 3 months.

BEEF STOCK WITH ROASTED VEGETABLES

Here's a great technique for adding extra flavor to homemade stock: Roast the vegetables before putting them in the pot.

MAKES 12 CUPS

3 pounds beef bones

1 1/2 pounds meaty crosscut beef shanks,
    1 inch thick

1 pound boneless beef chuck,
    cut into large chunks

1 extra-large yellow onion, unpeeled,
    quartered

1 large white turnip, peeled and cut
    into 1-inch cubes

3 large carrots, scrubbed and coarsely
    chopped

1 large parsnip, peeled and thickly sliced

1 1/2 cups low-sodium vegetable juice cocktail

1 can (16 ounces) whole tomatoes, undrained

2 large leeks with tops, rinsed and thickly sliced

1 celery stalk with leaves, thickly sliced

8 parsley sprigs

4 garlic cloves, crushed with the flat of a knife

2 thyme sprigs or 1 teaspoon dried thyme

2 bay leaves

1/2 teaspoon salt

1 Preheat oven to 500°F. Arrange bones, shanks, and chuck in a large shallow pan and roast 45 minutes or until well browned, turning occasionally. Transfer to an 8-quart soup pot. Stir onion, turnip, carrots, and parsnip into pan juices and roast 15 minutes or until browned, stirring occasionally. Transfer to pot.

2 Pour 2 cups cold water into roasting pan, stir with a wooden spoon to loosen browned bits, and add to pot. Add 12 cups water, vegetable juice, tomatoes, leeks, celery, parsley, garlic, thyme, bay leaves, and salt. Bring to boil over high heat, skimming off foam. Reduce heat and simmer, uncovered, 5 hours, skimming occasionally.

3 Strain stock through a large sieve into a heatproof bowl, discarding solids. When cool, cover and refrigerate until cold, then remove fat with a spoon. Use refrigerated stock within 3 days or frozen stock within 3 months.

BEEF STOCK WITH TOMATOES

Adding tomatoes to basic beef stock enriches the color, flavor, and nutrition of this soup-making essential. (Photograph on page 31)

MAKES 9 CUPS

3 pounds beef or veal bones,
    cut into 2-inch pieces
2 large onions, unpeeled, halved
2 garlic cloves
10 whole black peppercorns
2 bay leaves
Parsley sprigs
2 large carrots, cut into 2-inch pieces
2 celery stalks, cut into 2-inch pieces
1 cup canned crushed tomatoes

1 Rinse bones under cold water. In a large soup pot over medium-high heat, combine bones and 12 cups water and bring to boil, skimming off foam.

2 Add onions, garlic, peppercorns, bay leaves, parsley, carrots, and celery and return to boil. Reduce heat, partially cover, and simmer, skimming occasionally, 1 hour. Add tomatoes and simmer 30 minutes.

3 Strain stock through a cheesecloth-lined sieve into a large heatproof bowl, discarding solids. Skim off fat by drawing a sheet of paper towel across the surface or let cool, refrigerate until cold, and remove fat with a spoon. Use refrigerated stock within 3 days or frozen stock within 3 months.

VIETNAMESE BROTH WITH NOODLES

Punchy flavors and aromatic ingredients transform this light broth into an exotic dish. Unlike many Asian soups, the ingredients in this one are not fried first, so fat content remains low. Select prime-quality lean steak, which has good flavor when poached.

SERVES 2

1 ounce dried shiitake mushrooms
3 ounces fine rice noodles, such as vermicelli
6 ounces lean top round steak, diced
1 1/4 cups beef stock
2 tablespoons fish sauce
1 heaping teaspoon grated fresh ginger
1 ounce bean sprouts
1/2 small onion, thinly sliced
2 scallions, thinly sliced
2 small fresh red bird's-eye chiles or 1 medium
    red chile, seeded and finely chopped
    (wear gloves when handling; they burn)
1 tablespoon shredded fresh mint
1 tablespoon shredded fresh cilantro
1 tablespoon shredded fresh basil
Lime wedges
Soy sauce *(optional)*

1 Rinse mushrooms and place in a small bowl. Place noodles in a large bowl. Cover mushrooms with boiling water and soak 20 minutes. Cover noodles with boiling water and soak 4 minutes or according to package directions; drain.

2 Drain mushrooms and pour soaking liquid into a large saucepan. Trim tough stems from mushrooms, then slice caps and add to pan. Add steak, stock, fish sauce, and ginger and bring to boil. Reduce heat and simmer, skimming off foam, 10 to 15 minutes, or until steak is tender.

3 Divide noodles, bean sprouts, and onion between 2 large deep soup bowls. Using a slotted spoon, remove steak and mushrooms from broth and divide between bowls. Ladle in broth, then scatter scallions, chiles, mint, cilantro, and basil over each serving. Garnish with lime wedges and soy sauce, if desired.

BROWN MEAT STOCK

Nothing ensures the success of a homemade soup as much as a base of good, homemade stock. This recipe can make rich beef, veal, or lamb stock.

MAKES 12 CUPS

4 pounds meaty beef, lamb, or veal bones (neck bones, shank crosscuts, short ribs, knuckles, or leg bones with marrow)

1/2 cup low-sodium tomato sauce *(optional)*

4 celery stalks with leaves, cut up

4 large carrots, cut up

2 large yellow onions, thickly sliced

2 medium tomatoes, cut up *(optional)*

1 large all-purpose potato, white turnip, or parsnip, peeled and thickly sliced

1 cup thickly sliced scallion or leek tops

4 garlic cloves, halved

4 bay leaves

1 tablespoon dried basil

1 tablespoon dried thyme

2 teaspoons salt

1 teaspoon whole black peppercorns

1/2 teaspoon whole cloves

1 Preheat oven to 425°F. Arrange bones in a large shallow pan and roast 25 minutes, then turn and roast 15 minutes. If desired, use a pastry brush to spread tomato sauce over bones. Roast 10 minutes or until well browned. Transfer to a 10-quart soup pot.

2 Pour 2 cups water into pan, stir with a wooden spoon to loosen browned bits, and add to pot. Add

12 cups water, celery, carrots, onions, tomatoes, if desired, potato, scallions, garlic, bay leaves, basil, thyme, salt, peppercorns, and cloves. Bring to boil, then reduce heat and simmer, covered, 3 1/2 hours.

3 Using a slotted spoon, remove bones. When cool enough to handle, remove meat (reserve for another use, if desired). Strain stock through a large sieve lined with 2 layers of cheesecloth into a large heatproof bowl, discarding solids.

4 To clarify stock, if desired, pour into a clean saucepan over medium-high heat. In a cup, stir together 1/4 cup cold water and 1 egg white. Pour into stock and bring to a boil, then remove from heat and let stand 5 minutes. Strain through a sieve lined with clean, damp cheesecloth.

5 When stock is cool, cover and refrigerate until cold, then remove fat with a spoon. Use refrigerated stock within 3 days or frozen stock within 3 months.

LAMB STOCK

You can use lean lamb to make stock. Always chill and remove fat from the surface before using finished stock.

MAKES 5 CUPS

1 tablespoon sunflower oil

4 ounces lamb stew meat or leg-of-lamb bone

1 onion, quartered

1 carrot, coarsely chopped

1 celery stalk, coarsely chopped

2 bay leaves

1 parsley sprig

1 thyme sprig

10 whole black peppercorns

1/2 teaspoon salt

1 Heat oil in a large saucepan over high heat. Add lamb or bone and cook until browned on all sides, then transfer to a plate. Reduce heat, add onion, carrot, and celery, and sauté 7 minutes or until browned. Add 7 cups water and bring to boil.

2 Return lamb to pan and bring to boil, skimming off foam. Add bay leaves, parsley, thyme, peppercorns, and salt. Reduce heat and simmer, covered, 2 hours.

3 Strain stock through a sieve into a heatproof bowl, discarding solids. When stock is cool, cover and refrigerate until cold, then remove fat with a spoon. Use refrigerated stock within 3 days or frozen stock within 3 months.

HAM STOCK

This is an excellent liquid for cooking beans or making ham- or pork-based soups.

MAKES ABOUT 7 CUPS

1 meaty knucklebone from cooked ham
1 onion, quartered
1 carrot, coarsely chopped
1 celery stalk, coarsely chopped
1 bay leaf
1 parsley sprig
2 fresh sage leaves
4 whole cloves
8 whole black peppercorns

1 In a large saucepan, combine hambone, onion, carrot, and celery. Add 9 cups cold water and bring to boil, skimming off foam. Add bay leaf, parsley, sage, cloves, and peppercorns, then reduce heat and simmer, covered, 2 hours.

2 Strain stock through a sieve into a heatproof bowl, discarding solids. When cool, cover and refrigerate until cold, then remove fat with a spoon. Use refrigerated stock within 3 days or frozen stock within 3 months.

BASIC FISH STOCK

Trimmings from lean fresh fish, such as cod, sole, or flounder, are the base of this light, rich-tasting broth.

MAKES 8 CUPS

2 pounds heads, bones, and trimmings from cod, flounder, or other lean fish, rinsed and cut into 3-inch pieces
2 carrots, cut into 2-inch pieces
1 large onion, unpeeled, quartered
1 strip lemon rind, 2 inches long
1 strip orange rind, 2 inches long
8 whole black peppercorns
1 bay leaf
Parsley stems

1 Place fish trimmings in a large soup pot over medium heat, cover with 12 cups water, and bring to boil, skimming off foam.

2 Add carrots, onion, lemon and orange rind, peppercorns, bay leaf, and parsley and return to boil. Reduce heat to low, partially cover, and simmer, skimming occasionally, 30 minutes.

3 Strain stock a through cheesecloth-lined sieve into a heatproof bowl, discarding solids. Use refrigerated stock within 3 days, frozen stock within 3 months.

EASY FISH STOCK

MAKES 4 CUPS

1 onion, thinly sliced
4 parsley sprigs
2 bay leaves
2 carrots, peeled and thinly sliced
2 celery stalks, thinly sliced
4 whole black peppercorns
2 pounds white fish skin, bones, and heads without gills, rinsed

1 In a large saucepan over high heat, combine onion, parsley, bay leaves, carrots, celery, peppercorns, and fish trimmings. Add 5 cups boiling water and bring to boil, skimming off foam. Reduce heat and simmer, uncovered, 30 minutes.

2 Remove from heat and let cool 10 minutes, then strain through a fine sieve into a heatproof bowl, discarding solids. When cool, cover and refrigerate until cold, then remove fat with a spoon. Use refrigerated stock within 3 days or frozen stock within 3 months.

FISH STOCK WITH WINE

Wine adds an extra dimension to the flavor of fish stock; you can use this homemade brew for wonderful soups and sauces.

MAKES 16 CUPS ☼

6 pounds heads and bones from lean
    white fish, such as flounder, haddock,
    halibut, sea bass, cod, or sole, rinsed
4 medium yellow onions, unpeeled,
    coarsely chopped
4 celery stalks with leaves, coarsely chopped
2 cups dry white wine or cold water
16 parsley sprigs
16 whole black peppercorns
2 bay leaves

1 In an 8-quart soup pot over high heat, combine fish trimmings, onions, celery, wine, parsley, peppercorns, and bay leaves. Add 14 cups cold water and bring to boil, skimming off foam. Reduce heat and simmer, uncovered, 30 minutes.

2 Strain stock through a sieve into a heatproof bowl, discarding solids. When cool, cover and refrigerate until cold, then remove fat with a spoon. Use refrigerated stock within 3 days or frozen stock within 3 months.

FISH STOCK WITH LEEKS

A fragrant fish stock such as this one can make the difference between a great fish soup and a so-so one.

MAKES 6 CUPS

2 tablespoons olive oil
1 medium yellow onion,
    halved and thinly sliced
1 medium leek, halved lengthwise
    and thinly sliced
1 garlic clove, crushed
1 celery stalk, thinly sliced
2 medium carrots, thinly sliced
2 1/2 pounds heads and bones from
    flounder, cod, or halibut, rinsed,
    cut up, and gills removed
1/2 cup dry white wine
6 flat-leaf parsley sprigs
1/2 teaspoon dried thyme, crumbled
1/2 teaspoon salt

1 Heat oil in a 5-quart Dutch oven or soup pot over medium heat. Add onion, leek, and garlic and sauté 7 minutes or until softened. Add celery and carrots and sauté 6 minutes or until carrots are softened.

2 Add fish trimmings and stir to coat. Add wine and cook 2 minutes or until slightly evaporated. Increase heat to high, add 6 cups cold water, and bring to boil, skimming off foam. Reduce heat to medium-low, add parsley, thyme, and salt, and simmer, partially covered, 40 minutes or until broth is richly flavored.

3 Strain stock through a sieve into a heatproof bowl, discarding solids. When cool, cover and refrigerate until cold, then remove fat with a spoon. Use refrigerated stock within 3 days or frozen stock within 3 months.

SEAFOOD BROTH

Delicate seafood is complemented by saffron, tomatoes, and zucchini in a clear, flavorful broth. (Photograph on page 4)

SERVES 4

3 1/2 cups fish stock

1/4 teaspoon saffron threads

1 pound mussels in shells,
    scrubbed and beards removed

4 ounces shrimp, peeled and deveined

4 ounces scallops, shelled and sliced

1 pound flounder fillet, skin removed
    and cut into 3/4 x 2-inch pieces

2 tomatoes, cored, seeded, and diced

1 zucchini, finely diced

Salt and black pepper

1 tablespoon fresh chives, minced

1 In a large saucepan over medium-high heat, bring stock to boil. Crumble in saffron, stir well, and remove from heat.

2 Discard any broken mussel shells or those that do not close when tapped. Place mussels in a clean saucepan over medium heat and cover tightly; do not add water. Cook 4 minutes or until shells open, shaking pan occasionally.

3 Set a colander over stock pan and tip mussels into it to drain juices into stock. When mussels are cool, remove from shells, discarding any that did not open.

4 Bring stock to boil, then reduce heat and simmer. Add mussels, shrimp, scallops, flounder, tomatoes, and zucchini. Return to boil, then reduce heat and simmer 3 minutes. Season to taste with salt and pepper.

5 Ladle soup into warm bowls and garnish with chives.

ASIAN-STYLE FISH SOUP

This is a tasty soup you can prepare with ingredients from a well-stocked pantry and have on the table in minutes.

SERVES 4

4 cups fish stock

4 scallions, sliced

1 garlic clove, minced

1 piece fresh ginger, 1/2 inch long,
    finely chopped

1 teaspoon soy sauce

1 teaspoon hot red pepper flakes

1/2 cup cooked shrimp, chopped

1 can (6 1/2 ounces) chopped clams, drained

Chopped fresh cilantro

1 In a medium soup pot over medium heat, bring stock to boil. Add scallions, garlic, ginger, soy sauce, red pepper flakes, shrimp, and clams. Reduce heat and simmer, uncovered, 2 minutes or until heated through. Garnish with cilantro.

BASIC VEGETABLE STOCK

Making your own vegetable stock gives you a delicious base for many vegetarian soups and stews and it's far less salty than commercial versions.

MAKES ABOUT 4 CUPS

2 large carrots, coarsely chopped

1 large onion, coarsely chopped

2 celery stalks, coarsely chopped

1 large tomato, cut into 1-inch chunks

1 medium turnip, coarsely chopped

1 small parsnip, coarsely chopped

1 cup shredded Romaine lettuce

6 parsley sprigs

1 garlic clove

1 bay leaf

3/4 teaspoon dried thyme

1 In a large soup pot over medium heat, combine carrots, onion, celery, tomato, turnip, parsnip, lettuce, parsley, garlic, bay leaf, and thyme. Add 7 cups water and bring to boil, skimming off foam. Reduce heat to low and simmer, partially covered, 1 hour.

2 Strain stock through a sieve lined with 2 layers of dampened cheesecloth into a large heatproof bowl, discarding solids. When cool, cover and refrigerate up to 3 days or freeze up to 3 months.

ROASTED VEGETABLE STOCK

Roasting vegetables enriches the flavor of vegetable stock just as much as roasting bones does for meat and poultry stocks.

MAKES 5 1/2 CUPS

2 tablespoons olive oil
3 large carrots
2 medium parsnips, peeled
2 medium leeks, halved lengthwise
2 celery stalks with leaves, halved
1 large yellow onion, halved
4 garlic cloves, unpeeled
3 plum tomatoes, halved
6 parsley sprigs
3 slices fresh ginger, each about the
    size of a quarter, unpeeled
3/4 teaspoon dried rosemary, crumbled
1 teaspoon salt

1 Preheat oven to 400°F. Pour oil into a 13 x 9 x 2-inch roasting pan and add carrots, parsnips, leeks, celery, onion, and garlic. Stir to coat, then roast, uncovered, 30 minutes or until lightly colored.

2 Transfer vegetables to a 5-quart Dutch oven or soup pot over high heat and add 7 cups water, tomatoes, parsley, and ginger. Bring to boil and stir in rosemary and salt. Reduce heat to medium-low

and simmer, partially covered, 1 hour or until vegetables are very tender and stock is richly flavored.

3 Strain stock through a sieve into a heatproof bowl, discarding solids. Add salt. When cool, cover and refrigerate up to 3 days or freeze up to 3 months.

LIGHT VEGETABLE STOCK

This stock is a necessity for vegetarian dishes, but it's also very good for fish and poultry recipes that require delicate flavor.

MAKES 6 CUPS

1 tablespoon sunflower oil
8 ounces leeks, chopped
1 large onion, chopped
1 large bay leaf
Thyme sprigs
Parsley sprigs
8 ounces carrots, diced
3 large celery stalks with leaves, diced
1 teaspoon salt
5 whole black peppercorns

1 Heat oil in a large heavy saucepan or soup pot over medium heat. Add leeks and onion, stir, and reduce heat to low. Cover tightly and cook 20 minutes, shaking pan occasionally.

2 Add bay leaf, thyme, parsley, carrots, celery, and salt. Add 7 cups cold water, increase heat to high, and bring to boil, skimming off foam. Add peppercorns, reduce heat to low, and simmer, covered, 35 minutes.

3 Strain stock through a sieve into a large heatproof bowl, discarding solids. When cool, cover and refrigerate up to 3 days or freeze up to 3 months.

VEGETABLE STOCK WITH CELERY ROOT

Celery root brings a rich, deep flavor to this vegetarian vegetable stock.

MAKES 12 CUPS

2 tablespoons vegetable oil

3 large leeks with tops, rinsed and sliced

2 large carrots, scrubbed and
    coarsely chopped

1 medium onion, coarsely chopped

4 garlic cloves, crushed with the flat of a knife

8 ounces fresh mushrooms, halved

1 small celery root, peeled and sliced

3 celery stalks with leaves, coarsely chopped

2 medium parsnips, peeled and thickly sliced

10 parsley sprigs

1 1/2 tablespoons minced fresh ginger

2 bay leaves

3/4 teaspoon dried marjoram

3 tablespoons tomato paste

1/2 teaspoon salt

1 Heat oil in a 6-quart stockpot over medium-high heat. Add leeks, carrots, onion, and garlic and sauté, stirring occasionally, 10 minutes or just until tender.

2 Add 14 cups water, mushrooms, celery root, celery, parsnips, parsley, ginger, bay leaves, marjoram, tomato paste, and salt. Increase heat to high and bring to boil, then reduce heat and simmer, uncovered, 1 hour. Strain stock through a large sieve into a heatproof bowl, discarding solids. When cool, cover and refrigerate up to 3 days or freeze up to 3 months.

VEGETABLE STOCK WITH ROASTED WHEAT

This stock is excellent in meat soups and casseroles as well as in vegetarian recipes. You can find wheat grains at health food stores.

MAKES 6 CUPS

4 1/2 ounces whole wheat grains

1 tablespoon sunflower oil

4 ounces dark flat mushrooms, chopped

2 onions, chopped

3 carrots, peeled and chopped

3 celery stalks, chopped

1 parsley sprig

1 thyme sprig

1 marjoram sprig

2 bay leaves

8 whole black peppercorns

1 teaspoon salt

1 Preheat oven to 350°F. Place wheat in roasting pan and roast 30 minutes or until grains are dark brown.

2 Heat oil in a large heavy saucepan over low heat. Add mushrooms and onions, stir to coat, and cook, covered, 5 minutes, shaking pan occasionally. Stir in wheat, carrots, and celery. Add 7 cups water and bring to boil, skimming off foam. Reduce heat, add parsley, thyme, marjoram, bay leaves, peppercorns, and salt, and simmer, covered, 45 minutes.

3 Strain stock through a fine sieve into a heatproof bowl, discarding solids. When cool, cover and refrigerate up to 3 days or freeze up to 3 months.

QUICK VEGETABLE CONSOMMÉ

Here's a healthy, pretty, tasty soup that you can whip up in no time. Offer a sandwich with it for lunch or use it as a starter for dinner.

SERVES 4

6 parsley sprigs

2 garlic cloves

2 bay leaves

1 teaspoon whole black peppercorns

1 tablespoon butter

1 medium leek, white part only, rinsed and sliced

4 cups vegetable stock

2 medium celery stalks, cut into matchsticks

2 medium carrots, peeled and cut into matchsticks

4 ounces snow peas, trimmed

1 Tie parsley, garlic, bay leaves, and peppercorns in a piece of cheesecloth to make a bouquet garni.

2 In a large saucepan over low heat, melt butter. Add leek and sauté 5 minutes or until soft. Add stock and bouquet garni, increase heat to high, and bring to boil.

3 Add celery and carrots, reduce heat, and simmer, covered, 5 minutes or until vegetables are just tender. Remove bouquet garni, stir in snow peas, and cook 1 minute or until heated through.

SHREDDED SPINACH SOUP

This is an impressive homemade soup that will take no time at all to put before your family or friends.

SERVES 4

4 cups vegetable stock

1 cup tender spinach leaves, rolled and cut crosswise into narrow strips

Salt and black pepper

Ground nutmeg

Toasted slivered almonds

1 In a medium saucepan over medium heat, bring stock to boil. Add spinach and cook 1 minute. Season to taste with salt, pepper, and nutmeg and sprinkle with almonds.

VEGETARIAN VEGETABLE PASTA SOUP

Here's a light soup that is quick to make and very tasty. Put it in a thermos to enjoy away from home.

SERVES 4

4 cups vegetable stock

1/4 cup pastina or other tiny pasta shapes

2 fresh mushrooms, sliced

1/4 leek, sliced

1 small tomato, peeled, cored, seeded, and diced

1 tablespoon parsley, chopped

Salt and black pepper

1 In a large saucepan over medium-high heat, bring stock to boil. Add pastina, reduce heat, and simmer, uncovered, 4 minutes or until pasta is partially cooked.

2 Add mushrooms, leek, and tomato and simmer 3 minutes or until crisp-tender. Stir in parsley and season to taste with salt and pepper.

JAPANESE MISO SOUP

Shiitake mushrooms, ginger, miso, and stock made with dried kombu seaweed bring rich, savory flavors to this Asian broth, which is quick and easy to make. You can find dried kombu and miso (soybean paste) in Asian markets, health food stores, or specialty food stores. Although they're relatively high in sodium, a small amount provides a lot of flavor.

SERVES 4

1 packet (about 14 ounces)
   dried kombu seaweed

1 tablespoon sake, Chinese rice wine,
   or dry sherry

2 teaspoons superfine sugar

1/2 teaspoon finely grated fresh ginger

2 tablespoons miso paste

4 scallions, sliced at an angle

6 fresh shiitake mushrooms, thinly sliced

3 ounces tofu, diced

1 bunch watercress, trimmed

1 In a medium saucepan, combine 2 1/2 cups water and kombu. Bring to boil, then remove from heat, cover, and let stand 5 minutes. Using a slotted spoon, remove kombu.

2 Stir sake, sugar, and ginger into pan and bring to boil. Reduce heat and stir in miso until dissolved.

3 Add scallions, mushrooms, tofu, and watercress and cook, stirring, over low heat 2 minutes (do not boil). Ladle soup into small bowls.

MISO SOUP WITH CABBAGE AND ROOT VEGETABLES

This soup is very nourishing yet light.

SERVES 6

2 teaspoons vegetable oil

1 medium yellow onion, finely chopped

1 small celery stalk, finely chopped

2 garlic cloves, minced

2 teaspoons minced fresh ginger

1 large carrot, peeled and thinly sliced

1 large parsnip, peeled and thinly sliced

3 turnips, peeled and cut into 1/2-inch cubes

1 1/2 cups coarsely chopped Savoy cabbage

6 cups vegetable stock

1 tablespoon miso paste

1/4 teaspoon salt

1/8 teaspoon red pepper flakes

2 tablespoons minced fresh cilantro
   or parsley (*optional*)

1 Heat oil in a large saucepan over medium heat. Add onion, celery, garlic, and ginger and sauté, stirring occasionally, 5 minutes.

2 Add carrot, parsnip, turnips, cabbage, stock, miso, salt, and red pepper flakes. Bring to boil, stirring to dissolve miso. Reduce heat, cover, and simmer 20 minutes or until vegetables are tender. Garnish with cilantro, if desired.

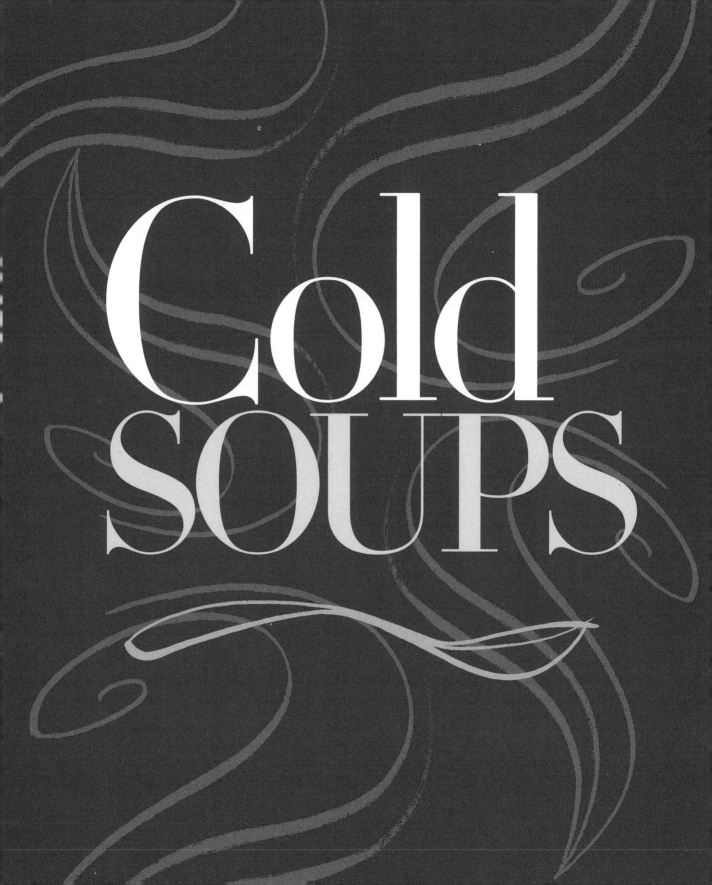

Cold
SOUPS

COLD SOUPS
recipe list

EASY: 10 minutes to prepare

QUICK: Ready to eat in 30 minutes

ONE-DISH: contains protein, vegetables, and good carbohydrates (beans, whole-grains, etc.) for a complete healthy meal

HEALTHY: High in nutrients, low in bad fats and empty carbohydrates

SLOW COOKER: Easily adapted for slow cooker by cutting down on liquids

Gazpacho with French Bread, *70*

White Gazpacho with Potatoes and Yogurt, *70*

White Gazpacho with Grapes and Chicken Stock, *71*

Green Gazpacho, *71*

Chickpea Gazpacho, *72*

Black Bean Gazpacho, *72*

Spiced Rhubarb Soup, *72*

Cream of Watercress Soup, *73*

Apricot-Buttermilk Soup, *73*

Blackberry Soup, *73*

Spicy Blueberry Soup, *74*

Cool Blueberry Soup, *74*

Chilled Cantaloupe Soup, *74*

Cantaloupe and Orange Soup, *75*

Honeydew Soup, *75*

Hungarian Cream of Cherry Soup, *75*

Tart Cherry Soup, *76*

Black Cherry Soup, *76*

Peach Soup with Almonds, *76*

Pretty Peach Soup, *77*

Cool Raspberry Soup, *77*

Danish Fruit Soup, *78*

Chilled Strawberry Soup, *78*

Fresh Fruit Vegetable Soup, *78*

Mixed Fruit Soup, *79*

Iced Melon and Berry Soup, *80*

Summer Fruit Soup, *80*

Summer Pudding Soup, *81*

Chilled Trout Soup, *81*

Cold Shrimp and Cucumber Soup, *82*

AVOCADO SOUP

SERVES 6

2 tablespoons unsalted butter

1 medium yellow onion, chopped

2 large fresh or pickled jalapeño peppers with seeds, minced (wear gloves when handling; they burn)

2 tablespoons all-purpose flour

3 1/2 cups homemade chicken stock or low-sodium canned chicken broth

2 medium ripe avocados, peeled, halved, and pitted

1/2 cup low-fat plain yogurt

1/4 cup chopped fresh cilantro or 1/4 cup chopped fresh parsley plus 2 teaspoons ground coriander

Fresh lemon juice to taste

Garnish (optional):
2 tablespoons vegetable oil

1/4 teaspoon chili powder

3 corn tortillas (6-inch diameter)

1 In a large heavy saucepan over medium-high heat, melt butter. Add onion and jalapeños and sauté 5 minutes or until tender. Stir in flour and cook, stirring constantly, until bubbly. Whisk in stock and 1/2 cup water and bring to boil. Reduce heat and simmer, covered, 15 minutes. Strain mixture into a large bowl, reserving vegetables. Return stock to pan.

2 Cut 1 1/2 avocados into chunks. Dice remaining avocado half and set aside. In a food processor or blender, puree vegetables, yogurt, and avocado chunks 45 seconds or until smooth.

3 Bring stock to simmer over medium heat. Whisk in avocado puree and heat through (do not boil). Remove from heat, stir in cilantro and diced avocado, and season to taste with lemon juice. Ladle into small bowls and refrigerate at least 3 hours.

4 About 15 minutes before serving, prepare tortilla chips, if desired. Preheat oven to 400°F. In a cup, mix oil and chili powder and brush on both sides of tortillas. Using scissors, cut each tortilla into 8 wedges and bake on an ungreased baking sheet 10 minutes or until crisp and golden. Garnish soup with tortilla chips.

This Southwestern soup combines avocado with Mexican spices and a French velouté, or white sauce made with stock.

LEEK AND AVOCADO SOUP

Cilantro and lime juice accentuate the delicate avocado flavor in this refreshing soup.

SERVES 4

1 tablespoon extra-virgin olive oil

1 pound leeks, halved lengthwise and sliced

1 garlic clove, minced

2 1/2 cups vegetable or chicken stock

1 large ripe avocado, halved and pitted

1/2 cup low-fat plain yogurt

1 tablespoon lime juice

2 tablespoons chopped fresh cilantro

Salt and black pepper

Lime slices

Cilantro sprigs

1 Heat oil in a medium saucepan over medium heat. Add leeks and garlic and sauté 10 minutes or until leeks are softened. Add stock and bring to boil. Reduce heat and simmer, covered, 10 minutes or until leeks are cooked.

2 Remove from heat and let cool. Puree in a blender or food processor or in pan with a hand-held blender. Pour into a bowl and refrigerate at least 3 hours.

3 Just before serving, scoop flesh from avocado and puree until smooth. Stir puree, yogurt, lime juice, and cilantro into soup. Season with salt and pepper. Ladle into 4 bowls and garnish with lime and cilantro.

AVOCADO AND COCONUT SOUP

Tropical flavors of chile pepper, coconut, and cilantro characterize this cold soup, which gets its silky texture and rich flavor from ripe avocados and smooth, creamy Greek yogurt.

SERVES 4

1/2 vegetable stock cube

2 medium avocados

4 scallions, chopped

1 large garlic clove, minced

1 fresh green chile, seeded and chopped (wear gloves when handling; chiles burn)

1 small bunch cilantro, rinsed, dried, and chopped

1 cup Greek yogurt

2/3 cup coconut milk

1 tablespoon olive oil

Pinch of sugar

1 tablespoon lemon juice

Salt and black pepper

Fresh cilantro leaves

1 In a measuring cup, dissolve stock cube in a small amount of boiling water, then add chilled water to make 1 1/4 cups.

2 Halve and pit avocados and scoop flesh into a blender or food processor. Add stock, scallions, garlic, chile, cilantro, yogurt, coconut milk, oil, sugar, and lemon juice and process until smooth.

3 Season with salt and pepper and refrigerate at least 3 hours. Serve in chilled bowls and garnish with cilantro leaves and freshly ground black pepper.

AVOCADO AND SHRIMP SOUP

On a hot summer day, this soup is quite refreshing.

SERVES 8

1 bottle (8 ounces) clam juice

1 package (8 ounces) cream cheese, softened

1 garlic clove, minced

1 package (5 ounces) frozen cooked salad shrimp, thawed

1 bottle (32 ounces) tomato juice

1 medium ripe avocado, peeled, halved, pitted, and diced

1/2 cup chopped cucumber

1/3 cup chopped scallions

2 tablespoons red wine vinegar

2 teaspoons sugar

1 teaspoon dill weed

1/2 teaspoon salt

1/4 teaspoon hot red pepper sauce

1/8 teaspoon black pepper

1 In a blender, combine clam juice and cream cheese and process until smooth. Pour into a large bowl.

2 Add garlic, shrimp, tomato juice, avocado, cucumber, scallions, vinegar, sugar, dill, salt, red pepper sauce, and pepper and mix well. Cover and refrigerate at least 2 hours before serving.

CARROT SOUP WITH DILL

Carrots and dill are a perfect taste combination; this lovely soup is as good hot as it is cold. (Photograph on page 12)

SERVES 4

1 tablespoon vegetable oil

1 onion, coarsely chopped

1 garlic clove, minced

2 cans (14 1/2 ounces each) low-sodium fat-free chicken broth

1 1/4 pound carrots, peeled and coarsely chopped

1/2 teaspoon dried thyme, crumbled

1/4 teaspoon salt

1/4 teaspoon white pepper

1/4 cup low-fat plain yogurt

1 tablespoon finely chopped dill

1 In a medium saucepan over medium heat, heat oil. Add onion and garlic and sauté 5 minutes or until softened. Add broth, carrots, and thyme. Bring to boil, reduce heat, and simmer, uncovered, 40 minutes or until vegetables are tender.

2 Transfer in batches to a food processor or blender, cover, and puree until smooth. Add salt and pepper. To serve hot, ladle into bowls and garnish each with yogurt and dill. To serve cold, remove from heat and let cool to room temperature. Cover and refrigerate 3 hours. Garnish just before serving.

COOL CUCUMBER SOUP

This is a great soup to make on a steamy summer day, since it requires no cooking. Just assemble the cold ingredients, mix them together, and ladle out.

SERVES 4

1 large cucumber

4 bushy mint sprigs

1 2/3 cups plain yogurt

2/3 cup light cream

2 tablespoons white wine vinegar

Salt and black pepper

Ice cubes *(optional)*

4 small mint sprigs

1 Place 4 soup bowls in refrigerator. Trim, rinse, and dry cucumber, then grate coarsely into a large bowl.

2 Rinse and dry mint. Strip leaves from stalks and shred enough to give 4 tablespoons. Add to cucumber.

3 Stir in yogurt, cream, and vinegar. Season with salt and pepper and stir again. Divide among chilled bowls. Add one or two ice cubes to each, if desired, and garnish with mint.

CUCUMBER SOUP WITH BUTTERMILK

Nothing is more cooling on a sultry summer day than this chilled cucumber soup.

SERVES 4

2 medium cucumbers, peeled, seeded, and chopped
1 medium red onion, thinly sliced
1/3 cup fresh dill, minced,
    or 1 1/2 teaspoons dill weed
2 tablespoons fresh mint, minced,
    or 2 teaspoons mint flakes
2 cups buttermilk
1/2 cup low-fat plain yogurt
1/2 cup low-sodium chicken broth
1 1/2 tablespoons chopped walnuts
3 tablespoons red wine vinegar
1/4 teaspoon salt
1/4 teaspoon black pepper
1/8 teaspoon cayenne pepper

1 In a food processor or blender, process cucumbers, onion, dill, and mint 30 seconds. Add buttermilk, yogurt, broth, and walnuts and process 20 seconds or until blended.

2 Transfer to a medium bowl and stir in vinegar, salt, black pepper, and cayenne. Cover and refrigerate at least 2 hours before serving.

YELLOW SQUASH AND PEPPER SOUP

Yellow squash and bell peppers are part of summer's bounty that can be united for a delightful cold soup.

SERVES 8

2 large yellow bell peppers, cored,
    seeded, and coarsely chopped
2 garlic cloves, finely chopped
1 teaspoon tomato paste
6 cups vegetable stock
1 pound yellow squash, sliced
1 cup low-fat (1%) milk
1 tablespoon chopped fresh chives or parsley
1/8 teaspoon salt
1/8 teaspoon black pepper

1 In a 4-quart saucepan, combine bell peppers, garlic, and tomato paste. Add stock and bring to boil. Reduce heat and simmer, partially covered, about 8 minutes, stirring occasionally, until peppers are tender. Add squash and simmer, partially covered, 10 minutes or until squash and pepper are soft.

2 Remove from heat and strain stock into a large bowl. Stir puree into stock and allow to cool, then then stir in milk, chives, salt, and pepper. Refrigerate at least 3 hours.

YELLOW SQUASH SOUP WITH ROSEMARY

The inspired combination of rosemary and yellow squash in this soup is made more piquant with a dash of parsley pesto.

SERVES 6

3 tablespoons olive oil

1 large yellow onion, chopped

8 medium yellow squash, chopped

1/4 cup snipped fresh rosemary or
    1 teaspoon dried rosemary

3 cups homemade chicken stock or canned
    low-sodium chicken broth

1/4 teaspoon salt

1/8-1/4 teaspoon black pepper

Pesto:

1 cup fresh parsley leaves

1 scallion, trimmed and cut into chunks

1 tablespoon fresh rosemary

2 teaspoons lemon juice

2 tablespoons softened butter

2 tablespoons olive oil

1/8 teaspoon salt

1 For soup, heat oil in a large saucepan, over medium heat. Add onion and sauté 5 minutes or until limp. Add squash, rosemary, and stock and bring to boil. Reduce heat and simmer, uncovered, 10 minutes or until squash is tender. Remove from heat and let cool slightly.

2 Transfer in batches to a blender or food processor, cover, and puree until smooth. Stir in salt and pepper. Pour into a large bowl, cover, and refrigerate at least 3 hours.

3 For pesto, combine parsley, scallion, rosemary, lemon juice, and salt in a blender or food processor. Cover and chop finely. Add butter and oil and puree until smooth. To serve, ladle soup into bowls and top with small dollops of pesto.

CREAM OF ZUCCHINI SOUP

Chilled cream of zucchini soup, decorated with a pretty swirl of yogurt, tastes as good as it looks.

SERVES 8

1 tablespoon olive or canola oil

1 large onion, coarsely chopped

2 garlic cloves, minced

6 cups vegetable stock

8 ounces all-purpose potatoes,
    peeled and diced

1 pound zucchini, trimmed and thinly sliced

1 1/2 cups flat-leaf parsley leaves

1 cup low-fat (1%) milk

1/8 teaspoon salt

1/8 teaspoon black pepper

1 cup fat-free plain yogurt

1 In a 4-quart saucepan over medium heat, heat oil. Add onion and garlic, then about 1/4 cup stock. Sauté until softened but not browned. Add potatoes and stir to coat. Pour in remaining stock and bring to boil.

2 Add zucchini, reduce heat, and simmer, partially covered, 10 minutes or until vegetables are tender. Remove from heat and stir in parsley. Strain into a large bowl. Transfer vegetables to a blender or food processor, cover, and puree until very smooth.

3 Stir puree into stock and let cool, then stir in milk, salt, and pepper. Refrigerate soup 3 hours. Before serving, spoon a large dollop of yogurt into each bowl of soup.

COLD ZUCCHINI SOUP

A wonderful start to a summer meal, this velvety soup is as lovely to look at as it is to eat.

SERVES 6

Soup:

3 tablespoons olive oil

1 large yellow onion, chopped

8 medium zucchini, chopped

1/4 cup snipped fresh dill or
    1 teaspoon dill weed

3 cups homemade chicken stock or canned
    low-sodium chicken broth

1/4 teaspoon salt

1/8-1/4 teaspoon black pepper

Croutons:

2 tablespoons butter

2 teaspoons olive oil

2 slices firm-textured bread, cut into 1/2-inch
    cubes

1 For soup, heat oil in a large saucepan over medium heat. Add onion and sauté 5 minutes or until limp. Add zucchini, dill, and stock and bring to boil. Reduce heat and simmer, uncovered, 8 minutes or until zucchini is tender. Remove from heat and let cool slightly.

2 Transfer in batches to a blender or food processor, cover, and puree until smooth. Stir in salt and pepper. Pour into a large bowl, cover, and refrigerate at least 3 hours.

3 Meanwhile, for croutons, melt butter in a large skillet over medium heat. Stir in oil and heat until bubbling. Add bread cubes in a single layer. As croutons brown, turn with tongs. When browned on all sides, transfer to paper towels to drain.

4 To serve, ladle soup into 6 bowls and top with croutons.

CHIVE VICHYSSOISE

Here's a low-calorie version of the classic chilled potato soup. Buttermilk replaces heavy cream.

SERVES 4

1 tablespoon unsalted butter

1 medium yellow onion, chopped

1 medium leek, chopped

1 medium celery stalk, chopped

2 medium all-purpose potatoes,
    peeled and diced

1 3/4 cups low-sodium chicken broth

1 cup buttermilk

1 tablespoon minced fresh or freeze-dried
    chives

2 teaspoons lemon juice

1/4 teaspoon hot red pepper sauce

1 In a large heavy saucepan over medium heat, melt butter. Add onion, leek, and celery and sauté 6 minutes or until tender. Add potatoes and sauté 3 minutes.

2 Stir in broth and bring to boil. Reduce heat and simmer, covered, 20 minutes or until potatoes are tender.

3 Transfer soup in batches to a blender or food processor, cover, and process 30 seconds. Stir in buttermilk, chives, lemon juice, and red pepper sauce. Cover and refrigerate at least 3 hours before serving.

WHITE BORSCHT

Potatoes, not beets, are the basis for this popular Central European soup.

SERVES 4

3/4 pound small red potatoes, thinly sliced

3 cups buttermilk

1 large cucumber, peeled, seeded, and thinly sliced

1 small red onion, thinly sliced

1/3 cup walnuts

3/4 teaspoon salt

1/2 teaspoon black pepper

3/4 cup thinly sliced radishes, cut into thin matchsticks

1/4 cup snipped fresh dill

1 In a medium saucepan, cook potatoes in boiling water for 10 minutes or until tender. Drain well and set aside to cool to room temperature.

2 Meanwhile, in a food processor, combine 2 cups buttermilk, cucumber, onion, walnuts, salt, and pepper. Process until well blended.

3 Transfer to a large bowl and whisk in remaining buttermilk. Add potatoes, radishes, and dill. Cover and refrigerate 3 hours or until well chilled.

CREAMY CHILLED TOMATO SOUP

This is an ideal soup for a hot summer day and a perfect way to enjoy your homegrown tomatoes.

SERVES 4

1 1/2 tablespoons unsalted butter

1 medium yellow onion, chopped

1 medium carrot, peeled and grated

3 large tomatoes (about 1 1/2 pounds), peeled, cored, seeded, and chopped, or 2 cans (1 pound each) low-sodium crushed tomatoes

1 cup low-sodium chicken broth

2 tablespoons minced fresh basil or 1/4 teaspoon dried basil, crumbled

1 cup low-fat plain yogurt

1 teaspoon lemon juice

1/4 teaspoon black pepper

1 Melt butter over low heat in a large heavy saucepan. Add onion and carrot and sauté 5 minutes or until soft. Add tomatoes, broth, and basil and bring to boil. Reduce heat and simmer, uncovered, stirring occasionally, 10 minutes. Let cool.

2 Transfer in 3 batches to a blender or food processor, cover, and puree until very smooth. Stir in yogurt, lemon juice, and pepper. Cover and refrigerate at least 3 hours.

CHILLED TOMATO AND FENNEL SOUP

The slightly licorice taste of fennel combines with the tartness of tomatoes to make a refreshing cold soup.

SERVES 8

1 1/2 tablespoons olive or canola oil

1 1/4 pounds fennel, coarsely chopped, and fronds reserved

3 cups vegetable stock

1 can (28 ounces) crushed tomatoes

1 cup low-sodium tomato juice

1/2 cup dry white wine or vegetable stock

1 bay leaf

1/3 cup low-fat sour cream

1/8 teaspoon salt

1/8 teaspoon black pepper

1 In a large saucepan over medium heat, heat oil. Add fennel and 1/4 cup stock and sauté until softened but not browned.

2 Stir in tomatoes, tomato juice, wine, and remaining stock. Add bay leaf and bring to boil. Reduce heat and simmer, partially covered, 25 minutes or until fennel is soft and mixture has thickened slightly.

3 Remove from heat and discard bay leaf. Transfer to a blender or food processor, cover, and puree until very smooth. Let cool, then stir in sour cream, salt, and pepper. Refrigerate 3 hours. Serve garnished with reserved fennel fronds.

CLASSIC GAZPACHO

This traditional chilled Spanish soup is full of wonderfully fresh flavors and packed with vitamins and minerals.

SERVES 4

1 pound ripe tomatoes, quartered and seeded

1/4 large cucumber, peeled and coarsely chopped

1 red bell pepper, cored, seeded, and coarsely chopped

2 garlic cloves, sliced

1 small onion, quartered

1 slice bread, torn into pieces

2 tablespoons red wine vinegar

1/2 teaspoon salt

2 tablespoons extra-virgin olive oil

1 can (17 ounces) tomato juice

1 tablespoon tomato puree

Salt and black pepper

Garnishes:

1 red bell pepper

4 scallions

1/4 cucumber

1/2 cup garlic croutons

1 In a large bowl, combine tomatoes, cucumber, bell pepper, garlic, onion, bread, vinegar, salt, oil, tomato juice, and tomato puree. Transfer in batches to a food processor or blender, cover, and puree until smooth. Pour soup into a large clean bowl, cover, and refrigerate at least 2 hours.

2 Toward end of chilling time, prepare garnishes. Core, seed, and finely dice bell pepper. Then thinly slice scallions and finely dice cucumber. Place vegetables and croutons in separate serving dishes. Season soup to taste with salt and pepper. Ladle into bowls and pass vegetables and croutons.

SIMPLE GAZPACHO

Packed with vitamins and other healthy ingredients, this slightly spicy cold soup is a true summer refresher. (Photograph on page 13)

SERVES 4

4 cups tomato juice

4 plum tomatoes, cored, seeded, and coarsely chopped

1 cucumber, peeled, seeded, and coarsely chopped

1 small yellow bell pepper, cored, seeded, and coarsely chopped

3 scallions, finely chopped

1/4 cup fresh lemon juice

1/4 cup coarsely chopped fresh basil

1 garlic clove, minced

1/4 teaspoon salt

1/4 teaspoon black pepper

1/4 teaspoon hot red pepper sauce

1 In a large bowl or pitcher, combine tomato juice, tomatoes, cucumber, bell pepper, scallions, lemon juice, basil, garlic, salt, pepper, and red pepper sauce. Refrigerate at least 2 hours.

CHUNKY GAZPACHO

Serve this soup from Andalusia, in southern Spain, in sipping cups as an appetizer or in bowls for a summery supper. (Photograph on page 27)

SERVES 4

Croutons:

2 garlic cloves, peeled
4 slices French bread (1 inch thick)
1/2 teaspoon black pepper
1/4 teaspoon salt

Soup:

1/2 cup coarsely chopped red onion
1 can (28 ounces) low-sodium tomatoes, undrained
1/4 cup seasoned dry bread crumbs
1/4 cup chopped parsley
3 tablespoons red wine vinegar
1 tablespoon olive oil
1/2 teaspoon black pepper
1/4 teaspoon salt
2 medium cucumbers, peeled and chopped
2 medium green bell peppers, cored, seeded, and chopped
2 medium red bell peppers, cored, seeded, and chopped

1 For croutons, preheat oven to 350°F. Cut 1 garlic clove in half and rub cut sides on inside of a large bowl and both sides of bread slices. Tear bread into 1-inch pieces. Place in bowl and lightly coat with cooking spray. Sprinkle with pepper and salt and toss to coat. Transfer to a baking sheet and bake until golden, about 15 minutes. Cool completely.

2 For soup, pulse onion and remaining garlic in a food processor or blender until finely chopped. Add half of tomatoes and all their juice and puree. Add bread crumbs, parsley, vinegar, oil, pepper, and salt. Process just until blended and pour into a large nonreactive bowl.

3 Chop remaining tomatoes. Stir into tomato puree with half of cucumbers and half of bell peppers. Refrigerate at least 2 hours. Ladle into bowls and top with remaining cucumber, peppers, and croutons.

GAZPACHO WITH AVOCADO

A perfect summer starter, this chilly gazpacho is topped with creamy avocado and crunchy croutons.

SERVES 5

2 1/2 cups tomato juice
3 tablespoons wine vinegar
1/2 teaspoon Worcestershire sauce
2 tablespoons vegetable or olive oil
1 teaspoon minced garlic
2 teaspoons snipped fresh parsley
1/8 teaspoon hot red pepper sauce
1/2 teaspoon salt
1/8 teaspoon black pepper
1 tablespoon lemon juice
1 cup finely chopped tomatoes
1/2 cup finely chopped celery
1/2 cup finely chopped green bell pepper
1/2 cup finely chopped onion
1 small cucumber, peeled, seeded, and finely chopped
1 avocado, peeled, halved, pitted, and chopped
Croutons

1 In a large bowl, combine tomato juice, vinegar, Worcestershire sauce, oil, garlic, parsley, red pepper sauce, salt, pepper, and lemon juice and mix well. Stir in tomatoes, celery, bell pepper, onion, and cucumber and refrigerate at least 2 hours or overnight.

2 Ladle into bowls and garnish with avocado and croutons.

GAZPACHO WITH PAPRIKA

SERVES 4 TO 6

Soup:

1 thick slice dry-textured bread

6 tablespoons extra-virgin olive oil

4 tablespoons red wine vinegar

Salt and black pepper

1 tablespoon paprika or hot or sweet
    Spanish paprika

1 can (19 ounces) chopped tomatoes,
    undrained

1 red onion

4 large garlic cloves

1 large cucumber

1 red bell pepper

1 yellow bell pepper

1 green bell pepper

1 fresh or dried red chile
    or 1 fresh green chile

6 large basil and/or mint leaves,
    rinsed, dried, and chopped

1 1/4 cups ice-cold water

Croutons:

2 teaspoons olive oil

1 garlic clove, sliced

3 slices day-old bread, crusts removed,
    cut into 1/2-inch cubes

1 For soup, remove crusts from bread, place slice in a food processor, and process into crumbs.

2 Place oil in a large serving bowl and whisk in vinegar and salt to make a creamy emulsion. Add paprika and bread crumbs and stir until thoroughly combined (it will have a sloppy consistency). Stir in tomatoes and set aside.

3 Peel onion, garlic, and cucumber. Rinse, halve, and seed bell peppers and chile (wear gloves; chiles burn), then cut into squares. In a food processor or blender, coarsely chop onion and garlic and add to bread crumb mixture. One by one, coarsely chop cucumber, bell peppers, and chile, and add to soup.

4 Add basil or mint, stir well, and season to taste with salt and pepper. Stir in enough ice-cold water to give mixture a dense soup-like consistency. Refrigerate 2 hours or stir in 12 ice cubes and serve immediately.

5 For croutons, heat oil in a skillet over medium heat. Add garlic and sauté 1 to 2 minutes. Add bread and sauté, turning often, until browned. Transfer to paper towels to drain. Discard garlic. Serve croutons with soup.

This crunchy, floating salad, one of many versions of the celebrated Spanish soup, is incomparable on a hot day.

BLENDER RED GAZPACHO

It takes a little peeling and chopping, but this is an easy way to make a refreshing summer soup.

SERVES 4

1 small yellow onion, quartered

1 clove garlic, chopped

1 small red or green bell pepper, cored, seeded, and chopped

1/2 medium cucumber, peeled, halved, seeded, and thinly sliced

2 medium tomatoes, peeled, cored, seeded, and chopped

1 1/2 cups low-sodium chicken broth

2 tablespoons lemon juice

1 tablespoon olive oil

1/8 teaspoon cayenne pepper

1/8 teaspoon hot red pepper sauce

Garnishes:

1 small red or green bell pepper, cored, seeded, and chopped

2 scallions with tops, sliced thin

1 medium tomato, cored, seeded, and chopped

1/2 medium cucumber, peeled, halved, seeded, and chopped

1/4 cup minced fresh parsley or basil

1 In a blender or food processor combine onion, garlic, bell pepper, cucumber, tomatoes, broth, lemon juice, oil, cayenne, and red pepper sauce. Cover and puree until smooth. Pour into a large bowl, cover, and refrigerate at least 2 hours.

2 To serve, add vegetable garnishes and ladle into 4 chilled bowls.

GAZPACHO WITH CELERY AND CORIANDER

To make gazpacho in a food processor, chop one vegetable at a time, using quick on-and-off pulses so that the vegetables are coarsely chopped, not pureed. Add each vegetable in turn to a large bowl, then stir in the remaining ingredients.

SERVES 4

2 pounds tomatoes, coarsely chopped

1 red bell pepper, cut into 1/4-inch dice

1 green bell pepper, cut into 1/4-inch dice

1 small red onion, finely chopped

1 celery stalk, cut into 1/4-inch dice

1/4 cup red wine vinegar

3/4 teaspoon salt

1/2 teaspoon ground coriander

1/2 teaspoon hot red pepper sauce

1 In a large bowl, combine tomatoes, bell peppers, onion, celery, vinegar, salt, coriander, and red pepper sauce.

2 Refrigerate 2 hours or until well chilled. Ladle into soup bowls.

GAZPACHO WITH VEGETABLE JUICE

This is certainly an easy way to make this cooling soup—keep it around the house on hot summer days.

SERVES 6

2 cans (14 1/2 ounces each) tomatoes, undrained, minced

2 cups vegetable juice

2 tablespoons red wine vinegar

1 garlic clove, minced

1 teaspoon salt

1/2 teaspoon black pepper

8-10 drops hot red pepper sauce

Garnishes:

1 package (6 ounces) seasoned croutons

1 medium cucumber, peeled and diced

1 medium green bell pepper, cored, seeded, and diced

1 bunch scallions with tops, sliced

1 In a large bowl, combine tomatoes, vegetable juice, vinegar, garlic, salt, pepper, and red pepper sauce. Cover and refrigerate overnight.

2 To serve, stir well, ladle into soup bowls, and garnish as desired with croutons, cucumber, bell pepper, and scallions.

TOMATO-APPLE GAZPACHO

Tomato juice, full of the antioxidant lycopene, provides a base for this takeoff on traditional gazpacho. Both spicy and sweet, this is a colorful and healthy summer soup.

SERVES 4

3 cups tomato juice

3 tablespoons tomato paste

1 large apple, cut into chunks

3/4 cup chopped red onion

2 garlic cloves, peeled

1/3 cup unblanched almonds

1/4 cup red wine vinegar

2 teaspoons hot red pepper sauce

1 teaspoon chili powder

3/4 teaspoon ground coriander

1/4 teaspoon salt

4 plum tomatoes, cored, seeded, and cut into 1/2-inch chunks

1 Hass avocado, peeled, halved, pitted, and cut into 1/2-inch chunks

1 In a medium bowl, combine tomato juice, tomato paste, apple, 1/2 cup onion, garlic, almonds, vinegar, red pepper sauce, chili powder, coriander, and salt. Transfer to a blender or food processor and process just until chunky.

2 Return mixture to bowl and stir in 1/2 cup water and tomatoes. Cover and refrigerate 2 hours. Serve topped with remaining onion and avocado.

HERBED GAZPACHO

Chilled vegetable juice rather than straight tomato juice is the base for this soup. You can garnish each bowl with cold cooked shrimp for a fancy finish.

SERVES 10

1 can (46 ounces) vegetable juice, chilled

1 can (14 1/2 ounces) Italian stewed tomatoes

3 medium tomatoes, cored, seeded, and chopped

1 medium green bell pepper, cored, seeded, and chopped

1 medium cucumber, chopped

1/2 cup Italian dressing

1/4 cup minced fresh parsley

4 garlic cloves, minced

1 teaspoon Italian seasoning

1 teaspoon salt

1/4 teaspoon black pepper

Chopped cooked shrimp

1 In a large bowl, combine vegetable juice, tomatoes, bell pepper, cucumber, dressing, parsley, garlic, Italian seasoning, salt, and black pepper and mix well.

2 Cover and refrigerate at least 2 hours. Garnish each serving with shrimp.

GAZPACHO WITH FRENCH BREAD

This soup allows you to enjoy the vitamin benefits of raw vegetables plus a great fresh taste.

SERVES 4

3 ounces French or Italian bread

1 large red or green bell pepper, cored, seeded, and coarsely chopped

1 red onion, coarsely chopped

1 small cucumber, peeled, seeded, and sliced

8 ounces plum tomatoes, cored, seeded, and quartered

1/4 cup packed fresh basil or parsley

1 garlic clove, finely chopped

2 tablespoons olive oil

2 tablespoons red or white wine vinegar

3 cups reduced-sodium tomato juice

1/8 teaspoon black pepper

1 Remove crusts from bread and tear bread into pieces. Place in a small bowl, cover with water, and let stand at least 5 minutes. Drain some water from bowl and squeeze most of remaining water from bread. Set aside.

2 Place bell pepper, onion, and cucumber in a food processor and process until very finely chopped. Pour mixture into a large bowl. Add tomatoes and basil to food processor and process until very finely chopped but not pureed. Add to bowl.

3 Add garlic, oil, vinegar, bread, and tomato juice to food processor and process until blended. Stir into soup until thoroughly combined. Add black pepper, cover, and refrigerate at least 2 hours before serving.

WHITE GAZPACHO WITH POTATOES AND YOGURT

This is an interesting change from the traditional tomato-based cold soup.

SERVES 4

2 medium all-purpose potatoes, peeled and cut into 1-inch cubes

2 large cucumbers, peeled, halved lengthwise, seeded, and coarsely chopped

9 scallions with tops, cut into 1/4-inch-thick slices

1/2 cup walnuts

2 cups buttermilk

1 cup low-fat plain yogurt

2 tablespoons olive or vegetable oil

1 teaspoon prepared horseradish

1/4 teaspoon hot red pepper sauce

1/4 teaspoon salt

1 red bell pepper, cored, seeded, and finely chopped

4 plum tomatoes, cored and finely chopped

4 hard-cooked large eggs, 3 chopped (white part only), 1 thinly sliced

1 In a large saucepan of boiling water, cook potatoes, uncovered, 10 minutes or until tender. Drain and let cool.

2 Meanwhile, in a food processor or blender, puree cucumbers, half of scallions, walnuts, buttermilk, yogurt, oil, horseradish, red pepper sauce, and salt until smooth.

3 Transfer to a large bowl and stir in red bell pepper, tomatoes, and potatoes. Cover with plastic wrap and refrigerate 3 hours or until well chilled.

4 To serve, adjust salt and red pepper sauce to taste, then stir in chopped eggs. Garnish with egg slices and remaining scallions.

WHITE GAZPACHO WITH GRAPES AND CHICKEN STOCK

This is an exotic take on gazpacho, with grapes, almonds, and milk replacing many of the vegetables.

SERVES 4

3 ounces French or Italian bread

1 cup low-fat (1%) milk

1 cup coarsely chopped blanched almonds

1 cucumber, peeled, seeded, and sliced

1 1/2 cups seedless green grapes, halved

1 garlic clove

2 cups vegetable or chicken stock

2 tablespoons white or red wine vinegar

1/8 teaspoon salt

1/8 teaspoon black pepper

Fresh mint leaves

1 Remove crusts from bread and tear bread into pieces. Place in a bowl, cover with milk, and let stand at least 5 minutes. Transfer to a food processor with almonds and process until very finely chopped and almost pureed. Transfer to a large bowl.

2 Place cucumber, grapes, and garlic in food processor and process until finely chopped. Add to almond mixture and stir in stock, vinegar, salt, and pepper. Cover and refrigerate at least 2 hours. Serve soup garnished with mint leaves.

GREEN GAZPACHO

Green and white vegetables make up this variation on the classic cold vegetable soup from Spain.

SERVES 4 TO 6

3 ounces French or Italian bread

1 cucumber, peeled, seeded, and sliced

1/2 cup packed watercress leaves

1/4 cup packed fresh parsley leaves

2 green bell peppers, cored, seeded, and coarsely chopped

2 celery stalks, sliced

2 scallions, white and green parts, sliced

3 cups vegetable stock

2 tablespoons olive oil

2 tablespoons white or red wine vinegar

1/8 teaspoon salt

1/8 teaspoon black pepper

1 Remove crusts from bread and tear bread into pieces. Place in a bowl, cover with water, and let stand at least 5 minutes. Drain off water from bowl and squeeze out most of remaining water from bread.

2 Place cucumber in a food processor with watercress and parsley and process until very finely chopped but not pureed. Pour into a large bowl.

3 Place bell peppers, celery, and scallions in food processor and process until finely chopped. Add to bowl.

4 Place soaked bread in food processor with stock, oil, and vinegar and process until blended. Add salt and black pepper, then stir into bowl. Cover and refrigerate at least 2 hours.

CHICKPEA GAZPACHO

This version of gazpacho has chickpeas for a little more heft, as well as the usual cold vegetables.

SERVES 6

1 can (15 ounces) chickpeas, drained and rinsed

1 can (14 1/2 ounces) Italian diced tomatoes, undrained

1 1/4 cups vegetable juice

1 cup beef stock

1 cup quartered cherry tomatoes

1/2 cup chopped seeded cucumber

1/4 cup chopped red onion

1/4 cup minced fresh cilantro

3 tablespoons lime juice

1 garlic clove, minced

1/2 teaspoon salt

1/4 teaspoon hot red pepper sauce

1 In a large bowl, combine chickpeas, diced tomatoes, vegetable juice, stock, cherry tomatoes, cucumber, onion, cilantro, lime juice, garlic, salt, and red pepper sauce. Cover and refrigerate at least 2 hours.

BLACK BEAN GAZPACHO

This colorful chilled soup has a garden-fresh flavor and makes a wonderful cold meal for summer.

SERVES 8

3 cans (11 1/2 ounces each) vegetable juice

4 medium tomatoes, cored, seeded, and chopped

1 can (15 ounces) black beans, drained and rinsed

1 cup cubed fully cooked ham

1/2 cup chopped green bell pepper

1/2 cup chopped yellow bell pepper

1/2 cup chopped red bell pepper

1/2 cup chopped cucumber

1/2 cup chopped zucchini

1/4 cup finely chopped scallions

2 tablespoons Italian dressing

3/4 teaspoon salt

1/8-1/4 teaspoon hot red pepper sauce

1 In a large bowl, combine vegetable juice, tomatoes, beans, ham, bell peppers, cucumber, zucchini, scallions, dressing, salt, and red pepper sauce. Cover and refrigerate at least 2 hours.

SPICED RHUBARB SOUP

Rhubarb, cinnamon, and lemon combine in this zesty but sweet soup that can be a dessert as well as a first course. (Photograph on page 27)

SERVES 4

8 cups diced fresh or thawed frozen rhubarb

1 cup sugar

4 cinnamon sticks (3 inches long)

1/4 teaspoon salt

3 tablespoons plus 1 1/2 teaspoons cornstarch

1 lemon slice

4 tablespoons reduced-fat sour cream

1 In a large saucepan, bring 3 1/4 cups water, rhubarb, sugar, cinnamon, and salt to a boil. Reduce heat and simmer, uncovered, until rhubarb is tender, about 20 minutes. Remove cinnamon sticks.

2 Strain rhubarb mixture and discard pulp. Return liquid to pan and bring to boil. In a small bowl, whisk cornstarch into 1/4 cup water until smooth. Stir into pan and cook, stirring, until thickened, about 3 minutes. Remove from heat and add lemon. Let cool.

3 Cover and refrigerate at least 3 hours. Remove lemon slice. Garnish each serving with 1 tablespoon sour cream.

CREAM OF WATERCRESS SOUP

What better starter is there to a summer meal on a hot, hot day than cold cream of watercress soup?

SERVES 8

1 tablespoon olive or canola oil

2 large onions, coarsely chopped

6 cups vegetable stock

1 pound all-purpose potatoes, peeled and diced

2 cups watercress, stems removed

1 cup low-fat (1%) milk

1/8 teaspoon salt

1/8 teaspoon black pepper

Pinch of grated nutmeg

1 In a 4-quart saucepan over medium heat, heat oil. Add onions, 2 tablespoons stock and sauté 5 minutes or until softened but not browned. Add potatoes and remaining stock and bring to boil. Reduce heat, partially cover, and simmer, stirring occasionally, 10 minutes or until potatoes are tender.

2 Remove from heat and stir in watercress. Strain soup into a large bowl. Transfer vegetables to a blender or food processor, cover, and puree until very smooth. Stir puree into stock and let cool, then stir in milk, salt, pepper, and nutmeg. Refrigerate 3 hours.

APRICOT-BUTTERMILK SOUP

So good and so easy to make, this refreshing, light soup can be served as a first course or for lunch, accompanied by rolls and a salad.

SERVES 4

3 cups apricot nectar

1 cup buttermilk

2 teaspoons grated orange zest

Juice of 1 orange

1 tablespoon honey

1 teaspoon lemon juice

1/4 teaspoon ground allspice

1/8 teaspoon ground nutmeg

Mint sprigs *(optional)*

1 In a large bowl, stir together apricot nectar, buttermilk, orange zest, orange juice, honey, lemon juice, allspice, and nutmeg until thoroughly blended. Cover and refrigerate at least 2 hours. Garnish with mint, if desired.

BLACKBERRY SOUP

This cooler combines blackberries with pear juice, honey, cinnamon, vanilla, and nutmeg as well as vanilla yogurt.

SERVES 4

4 cups frozen blackberries, thawed

1 cup pear juice

1/2 cup honey

1 lime or lemon wedge

1/4 teaspoon ground cinnamon

1/4 teaspoon vanilla extract

Dash of ground nutmeg

1 cup fat-free vanilla yogurt

1 In a large heavy saucepan over low heat, combine 1/4 cup water, blackberries, pear juice, honey, lime wedge, cinnamon, vanilla, and nutmeg. Cook, uncovered, until berries are soft, about 20 minutes.

2 Remove and discard lime wedge. Strain berry mixture into a bowl, reserving juice. Press berry mixture through a fine-mesh sieve and discard seeds. Add pulp to bowl, cover, and refrigerate at least 3 hours.

3 Set aside 2 tablespoons yogurt for garnish. Place berry mixture and remaining yogurt in a food processor or blender, cover, and puree until smooth. Top each serving with a dollop of yogurt.

SPICY BLUEBERRY SOUP

Start off a light summer supper in healthy Scandinavian style with a jewel-colored blueberry soup.

SERVES 4

3 tablespoons sugar
1 teaspoon grated lemon zest
1/8 teaspoon ground allspice
2 bags (12 ounces each) frozen blueberries
1 1/4 cups fat-free plain yogurt
2 tablespoons fresh lemon juice

1 In a small skillet, combine sugar, lemon zest, allspice, and 1 cup water over medium heat. Bring to a boil and cook 1 minute to dissolve sugar.

2 Place frozen blueberries, 1 cup yogurt, and lemon juice in a food processor or blender. Remove syrup from heat, add to food processor, and puree until smooth.

3 Refrigerate at least 3 hours. Top each serving with 1 tablespoon yogurt.

COOL BLUEBERRY SOUP

Here's an easy cooler for a summer lunch or dinner. (Photograph on page 27)

SERVES 4

1 bag (16 ounces) frozen blueberries, partially thawed
2/3 cup sour cream
1/3 cup orange juice
3 tablespoons sugar
1 lemon, thinly sliced

1 Place blueberries in a food processor or blender and add sour cream, orange juice, and sugar. Cover and puree until smooth, occasionally scraping sides of container with a rubber spatula.

2 Pour directly from food processor into bowls and garnish each serving with 2 or 3 lemon slices.

CHILLED CANTALOUPE SOUP

This cold melon soup, spiced with cinnamon, is a light and colorful summer meal starter. (Photograph on page 4)

SERVES 6

1 medium cantaloupe, peeled, seeded, and cut into cubes
2 cups orange juice
1 tablespoon lime juice
1/4-1/2 teaspoon ground cinnamon
Fresh mint leaves (*optional*)

1 Place cantaloupe and 1/2 cup orange juice in a blender or food processor, cover, and puree until smooth.

2 Transfer to a large bowl and stir in lime juice, cinnamon, and remaining orange juice. Cover and chill at least 2 hours. Garnish with mint, if desired.

CANTALOUPE AND ORANGE SOUP

These two orange fruits combine delectably for a cold summer appetizer bursting with vitamins and minerals.

SERVES 6

3 large oranges
1 large cantaloupe, halved and seeded
2 cups orange juice
Juice of 1 lime
1 tablespoon honey
1 cup fat-free plain yogurt
1 cup fresh raspberries

1 Finely grate zest from 1 or 2 oranges, according to taste, and reserve. With a sharp knife, peel melon. Cut flesh into chunks and place in a food processor or blender. Peel and section oranges, then cut sections into pieces and add to melon. Puree until smooth.

2 Strain puree through a medium-gauge sieve into a large bowl, pressing fruit through sieve with the back of a wooden spoon.

3 Stir in orange juice, lime juice, honey, and yogurt until blended. Cover bowl and refrigerate at least 2 hours.

4 Serve soup garnished with orange zest and fresh raspberries.

HONEYDEW SOUP

This delicate cold soup has only three ingredients, so it's easy to keep on hand for summer's hottest days.

SERVES 3

3 cups cubed honeydew
1/2 cup white grape juice
1 tablespoon sugar

1 Place the melon, juice, and sugar in a blender or food processor, cover, and puree until smooth. Transfer to a bowl. Cover and refrigerate at least 2 hours.

HUNGARIAN CREAM OF CHERRY SOUP

Immigrants from Eastern Europe and the Scandinavian countries served this creamy, chilled soup as a hot-weather first course or as a light dessert.

SERVES 6

1/4 cup sugar
1 cinnamon stick (4 inches long)
1 teaspoon cornstarch
2 cups fresh or thawed and frozen pitted dark sweet and/or tart cherries
1 cup reduced-fat sour cream
1/2 cup dry red wine or orange juice

1 In a medium saucepan, bring 1 cup water, sugar, and cinnamon to a boil. Reduce heat and simmer, uncovered, 5 minutes. Discard cinnamon.

2 In a small bowl, whisk together 2 tablespoons cold water and cornstarch, then whisk into sugar mixture. Cook 2 minutes or until thickened, whisking constantly. Stir in cherries. Pour into a bowl and cool to room temperature. Cover and refrigerate at least 3 hours. To serve, stir in sour cream and wine. Ladle into chilled bowls.

TART CHERRY SOUP

Serve this refreshing soup as a first course with a dollop of yogurt or topped with whipped cream for dessert.

SERVES 4

2 cans (14 1/2 ounces each) water-packed
    pitted tart cherries
1/2 cup orange juice
1/2 cup sugar
2 tablespoons lime juice
1 teaspoon grated lime zest
1/2 teaspoon ground cinnamon
4 lime slices

1 Place cherries in a blender or food processor, cover, and process until finely chopped.

2 Transfer to a saucepan and add orange juice, sugar, lime juice, lime zest, and cinnamon. Bring to a boil, reduce heat, and simmer, covered, 10 minutes. Cool to room temperature, then refrigerate at least 3 hours. Garnish with lime slices.

BLACK CHERRY SOUP

This is a spicy, rich fruit soup that is quite filling. Follow with a light main course of poached fish or grilled chicken breast.

SERVES 4

3 whole cloves
Finely grated zest and juice of 1 lemon
1 cinnamon stick
2 cans (1 pound each) pitted black cherries
    in heavy syrup
1 cup reduced-fat sour cream
Fresh mint leaves for garnish

1 In a medium saucepan, combine 1 cup water, cloves, lemon zest, lemon juice, and cinnamon.

Bring to boil over medium heat, stir in cherries and return to boil.

2 Reduce heat and simmer, stirring occasionally, 10 minutes or until very soft. Remove from heat and discard spices. Strain contents of saucepan into a large bowl, transfer cherries to a food processor or blender and puree until smooth. Stir puree into bowl, mix, and strain into another large bowl.

3 Stir in sour cream until combined. Cover bowl and refrigerate at least 3 hours. Garnish with mint.

PEACH SOUP WITH ALMONDS

This soup may taste like dessert, but each serving is rich in fiber and vitamins and has 4 to 7 grams of protein.

SERVES 4

1 1/2 pounds fresh peaches or 1 package
    (20 ounces) frozen peaches, thawed
2 tablespoons sugar
Grated zest of 1 lemon
2 cups buttermilk or low-fat (1%) milk
Pinch of ground nutmeg
1 cup peach nectar
1/4 cup sliced almonds

1 Bring a large saucepan of water to boil. If using fresh peaches, add a few at a time to pan and return to boil (this makes them easier to peel). After a minute of boiling, transfer to a bowl of cold water. Repeat until all peaches are parboiled. When cool enough, peel with a small knife and cut into chunks, discarding pits.

2 In a medium saucepan, bring 1 cup water, sugar, and lemon zest to boil. Add peaches, reduce heat, and simmer, covered, stirring occasionally, 5 minutes or until very soft. Remove from heat and discard lemon zest.

3 Pour 1 cup buttermilk into a food processor or blender. Use a slotted spoon to add peaches, reserving syrup, and puree. Transfer puree to a bowl, add remaining buttermilk, nutmeg, and peach nectar. Stir in reserved syrup. Cover and refrigerate at least 3 hours.

4 Preheat oven to 350°F. Spread almonds on a baking sheet in a single layer and toast 10 minutes or until golden. Let cool and sprinkle on soup before serving.

PRETTY PEACH SOUP

Peaches and yogurt are dressed up with raspberry puree in this smooth cold soup.
(Photograph on page 27)

SERVES 4

1 cup fresh or thawed frozen raspberries
3 cups fresh or thawed frozen peaches
3 tablespoons lemon juice
1 cup peach nectar
1 cup plain yogurt
1/4 cup sugar *(optional)*
1 teaspoon almond extract

1 Place raspberries in a blender or food processor, cover, and puree until smooth. Strain into a bowl and discard seeds. Cover and refrigerate.

2 Place peaches and lemon juice in blender or food processor, cover, and puree until smooth. Transfer to a bowl and stir in peach nectar, yogurt, sugar, if desired, and almond extract. Cover and refrigerate 3 hours. Garnish each serving by drizzling 1 tablespoon raspberry puree on top.

COOL RASPBERRY SOUP

Cold fruit soups are perfect appetizers for summer meals. This one mixes raspberries with cranberry juice, cinnamon, and cloves.

SERVES 4

1 package (20 ounces) frozen raspberries, thawed
1/4 cup white wine *(optional)*
1 cup cranberry-raspberry juice
1/2 cup sugar
1 1/2 teaspoons ground cinnamon
3 whole cloves
1 tablespoon lemon juice
1 cup raspberry yogurt
1/2 cup sour cream

1 Place 1 1/4 cups water, raspberries, and wine, if desired, in a blender or food processor, cover, and puree until smooth.

2 Transfer to a large saucepan and add cranberry-raspberry juice, sugar, cinnamon, and cloves. Bring just to a boil over medium heat.

3 Remove from heat, strain into a bowl, and cool. Whisk in lemon juice and yogurt. Refrigerate at least 3 hours. Top each serving with a dollop of sour cream.

DANISH FRUIT SOUP

Love raspberries? Here's one more way to enjoy these favorite berries.

SERVES 6

1 package (3 ounces) raspberry gelatin

1/8 teaspoon salt

1 cup boiling water

1 package (12 ounces) frozen raspberries without syrup

2 tablespoons lemon juice

Sour cream (*optional*)

Ground nutmeg (*optional*)

1 In a large bowl, combine gelatin and salt. Gradually stir in boiling water until dissolved.

2 Add 1 1/2 cups cold water, raspberries, and lemon juice and mix well. Refrigerate at least 20 minutes. Stir just before serving. Garnish with sour cream and nutmeg, if desired.

CHILLED STRAWBERRY SOUP

This pretty red fruit soup can start or end a meal on a steamy hot day.

SERVES 6

1 cup apple juice

2/3 cup sugar

1/2 teaspoon ground cinnamon

1/8 teaspoon ground cloves

2 cups fresh strawberries

2 cups strawberry yogurt

2 drops red food coloring (*optional*)

Strawberry halves

1 In a medium saucepan over medium heat, combine 3/4 cup water, apple juice, sugar, cinnamon, and cloves. Bring to boil, then remove from heat and let cool.

2 Place strawberries and 1/4 cup water in a blender or food processor, cover, and puree until smooth. Pour into a large bowl and add apple juice mixture, yogurt, and food coloring, if desired. Cover and refrigerate until well chilled, at least 3 hours. Garnish with strawberry halves.

FRESH FRUIT VEGETABLE SOUP

Not only is this refreshing soup perfect for sweltering summer days, it can also give you a boost in winter when you feel slightly under the weather. (*Photograph on page 26*)

SERVES 4

2 cups pineapple juice

2 cups orange juice

1/2 cucumber, peeled, seeded, and diced

1/4 red onion, diced

1 small red bell pepper, cored, seeded, and chopped

1/2 fresh red chile, seeded and chopped (wear gloves when handling; chiles burn)

Juice of 1 lime

1/2 teaspoon superfine sugar

2 passionfruits

1 large mango, peeled and diced

10 cape gooseberries or grapes, peeled and quartered

1 firm pear, cored and diced

1 tablespoon chopped fresh mint

2 teaspoons chopped fresh cilantro

Mint sprigs (*optional*)

1 In a large bowl, mix pineapple and orange juices. Add cucumber, onion, bell pepper, chile, lime juice, and sugar and stir. Cover and refrigerate at least 2 hours.

2 Meanwhile, halve and scoop flesh from passionfruits. Stir into soup along with mango, gooseberries, pear, mint, and cilantro. Ladle into bowls and garnish with mint.

MIXED FRUIT SOUP

SERVES 6

Soup:

6 cups cranberry-apple juice

1 large tart green apple, peeled, cored, and diced (1 1/2 cups)

3/4 cup pitted prunes, quartered

3/4 cup dried apricots, quartered

1/4 cup dark raisins

1/4 cup golden raisins

1 cinnamon stick (3 inches long)

1/2 teaspoon grated orange zest

3 tablespoons instant tapioca

2 tablespoons sugar

Topping:

1 cup low-fat plain yogurt

2 teaspoons sugar

1/2 teaspoon vanilla extract

1 For soup, in a large saucepan, bring 4 cups juice, apple, prunes, apricots, raisins, cinnamon, and orange zest to boil. Reduce heat and simmer, uncovered, 15 minutes or until fruits are tender.

2 In a small saucepan, stir together remaining juice, tapioca, and sugar. Let stand 5 minutes, then cook over medium heat until mixture boils and turns translucent. Stir into fruit mixture, cover, and refrigerate 3 hours. Remove cinnamon stick.

3 For topping, line a strainer with cheesecloth or a paper coffee filter and place over a medium bowl. Spoon in yogurt, cover, and refrigerate 30 minutes.

4 Discard liquid, transfer yogurt to a small bowl and stir in sugar and vanilla. Spoon soup into small bowls and garnish each with a swirl of topping.

Scandinavians brought their own unique food traditions to America, such as beginning a meal with a tart, cold fruit soup.

ICED MELON AND BERRY SOUP

Almost any variety of green-fleshed melon, such as Galia or honeydew, can be used for this refreshing soup, but the melon must be ripe and sweet. (Photograph on page 26)

SERVES 4

1 large ripe green-fleshed melon
(about 2 3/4 pounds), halved and seeded
Juice of 1 lime
1 1/2 inch piece fresh ginger,
peeled and grated
1/2 cup fresh blueberries
1/2 cup fresh orange juice
2 tablespoons yogurt
1/2 cup raspberries or strawberries

1 Scoop melon flesh into a blender or food processor. Add lime juice and ginger and puree until smooth, stopping occasionally to push pieces of melon to bottom. Pour into a medium bowl, cover, and refrigerate 2 hours.

2 Place blueberries into blender or food processor, add orange juice and yogurt, and puree until smooth. Transfer to a second bowl, cover, and refrigerate 2 hours.

3 Divide soup among 4 chilled bowls. Spoon blueberry puree into center of each in a decorative pattern and scatter raspberries or strawberries on top.

SUMMER FRUIT SOUP

You can make this soup any time of year with frozen or canned ingredients, but it's at its best when you use fresh fruit. (Photograph on page 27)

SERVES 6

1/2 cup sugar
3 tablespoons quick-cooking tapioca
1 can (6 ounces) frozen orange juice concentrate
1 package (10 ounces) frozen sliced sweetened strawberries, thawed
2 cups fresh or thawed frozen sliced peaches, cut into bite-size pieces
1 can (11 ounces) mandarin oranges, drained
2 medium ripe bananas, sliced

1 In a medium saucepan over medium heat, combine 1 1/2 cups water, sugar, and tapioca. Cook until thickened and clear, about 5 minutes.

2 Remove from heat, add 1 cup water and orange juice concentrate, and stir until concentrate is thawed. Stir in strawberries, peaches, and oranges. Cover and refrigerate 2 hours. Just before serving, stir in bananas.

SUMMER PUDDING SOUP

Almost like ice cream made from your three favorite berries, this lovely summer delight can set you up for a light meal or elegantly finish one off.

SERVES 4

2 tablespoons sugar
Zest of 1 lemon
1 cup fresh or thawed frozen blueberries
1 cup fresh or thawed frozen strawberries
1 cup fresh or thawed frozen raspberries
1/2 cup reduced-fat sour cream
1/2 cup low-fat (1%) milk

1 In a medium saucepan, combine 1 cup water, sugar, lemon zest, and blueberries. Bring to boil, reduce heat, and simmer, uncovered, 2 minutes or until berries begin to split.

2 Remove from heat and discard lemon zest. Add strawberries and raspberries. Transfer to a food processor or blender and puree until smooth. Strain puree into a large bowl, pressing fruit through sieve with the back of a wooden spoon.

3 Add sour cream and milk to blender and process until smooth. Add about 2 cups fruit puree and blend. Stir mixture back into remaining puree. Cover bowl and refrigerate at least 3 hours.

CHILLED TROUT SOUP

This elegant, pale pink dish is perfect for summer-time dining. Low-fat cream cheese makes it creamy and keeps it low in fat at the same time.

SERVES 6

1 fennel bulb, quartered lengthwise
2 slices raw, unpeeled beet
    (about 1/2 inch thick)
2 bay leaves
1/2 teaspoon black peppercorns
1/2 teaspoon salt
1 cup medium-dry white wine
2 fresh tarragon sprigs
1 large fresh cleaned trout (about 12 ounces)
1 packet (4 ounces) low-fat cream cheese
1 tablespoon grated horseradish or
    2 tablespoons horseradish sauce
3 ounces smoked trout fillet, flaked

1 Put fennel in a saucepan large enough to hold whole trout. Add beet, bay leaves, peppercorns, salt, wine, and 3 1/2 cups cold water. Pick leaves off tarragon and reserve. Add stems to pan.

2 Bring to boil, reduce heat, and simmer 10 minutes. Add whole trout and return to boil. Reduce heat and simmer 7 to 8 minutes until flesh is opaque throughout. Transfer to plate and let cool.

3 Skin and bone trout and return head, tail, skin, and bones to saucepan, reserving flesh. Return to boil, reduce heat, and simmer, partially covered, 15 minutes, then strain liquid into a large bowl and let cool.

4 Puree reserved trout, cream cheese, and horseradish in a blender or food processor. Transfer to bowl and add cooking liquid. Season with salt and pepper to taste, then refrigerate at least 3 hours. Ladle into cold soup bowls and sprinkle with smoked trout, tarragon leaves, and black pepper.

COLD SHRIMP AND CUCUMBER SOUP

*Nothing could be more welcome on a warm day
than this cool, delicious combination of shrimp,
cucumbers, and buttermilk with hints of dill
and fennel.*

SERVES 4

1/2 pound medium raw shrimp

1 teaspoon salt

1 cup peeled, seeded, diced cucumber

1/2 teaspoon ground fennel seed

1 garlic clove, minced

1 tablespoon grated onion

1 teaspoon fresh chopped dill

4 cups buttermilk

Salt and ground white pepper

1 In a large saucepan bring 6 cups water to boil. Add 1 teaspoon salt and shrimp. Boil 3 minutes or until shrimp are pink, then drain shrimp, let cool, peel and devein. Save and refrigerate 4 whole shrimp for garnish and finely chop remaining shrimp. Set aside.

2 In a large bowl, stir together cucumber, fennel, garlic, onion, dill, buttermilk, and chopped shrimp. Adjust seasoning with salt and white pepper. Cover and refrigerate at least 2 hours. Divide among 4 chilled bowls and top each with whole shrimp.

Chicken and Turkey SOUPS

CHICKEN AND TURKEY SOUPS

recipe list

 EASY: 10 minutes to prepare

QUICK: Ready to eat in 30 minutes

ONE-DISH: contains protein, vegetables, and good carbohydrates (beans, whole-grains, etc.) for a complete healthy meal

HEALTHY: High in nutrients, low in bad fats and empty carbohydrates

SLOW COOKER: Easily adapted for slow cooker by cutting down on liquids

CHICKEN AND TURKEY SOUPS

recipe list CONTINUED

CHICKEN-RICE SOUP

The simplicity of this recipe makes it extremely versatile. You can begin easily by experimenting with different herbs or other seasonings to suit your taste.

SERVES 4

1 tablespoon butter

1 tablespoon vegetable oil

1 pound skinless, boneless chicken breast, cut into 3/4-inch cubes

4 cups chicken stock

2 medium carrots, peeled and thinly sliced

2 medium celery stalks, thinly sliced

1 large yellow onion, finely chopped

1/2 cup long-grain white rice

2 tablespoons minced fresh parsley

1/4 teaspoon salt

1/8 teaspoon black pepper

1 In a 5-quart Dutch oven over medium heat, melt butter and heat oil. Add chicken and sauté 5 minutes or until lightly browned.

2 Add stock, carrots, celery, onion, rice, parsley, salt, and pepper. Bring to boil, reduce heat, and simmer, covered, 20 minutes or until rice is tender.

COCK-A-LEEKIE SOUP

This chicken and leek soup is a staple comfort food in Scottish households.

SERVES 6

1 stewing chicken (3-4 pounds), giblets removed

6 large leeks with tops, washed and sliced

1 bay leaf

1/2 teaspoon salt

1/2 teaspoon black pepper

1/2 cup long-grain white rice

1/4 cup chopped parsley

1 In a 6-quart Dutch oven or soup pot, bring 8 cups water, chicken, half of leeks, bay leaf, salt, and pepper to boil over high heat, skimming off any foam. Reduce heat, cover, and simmer, skimming surface occasionally, 2 hours or until chicken is very tender and falls away from bone.

2 Using a slotted spoon, transfer chicken to a plate. When cool enough to handle, remove skin and bones and tear meat into shreds, then return to pot.

3 Add rice and remaining leeks and bring to boil. Reduce heat and simmer, covered, 20 minutes or until rice is tender. Remove bay leaf and stir in parsley.

SOUTHERN CHICKEN-RICE SOUP

A wonderful dish for potluck dinners, this nutritious soup has spicy Creole roots.

SERVES 10

1 broiler/fryer chicken (about 3 pounds)

2 teaspoons salt

1/2 cup long-grain rice

1/2 cup chopped onion

1/2 cup chopped celery

1/2 cup thinly sliced carrots

1/2 cup sliced fresh or frozen okra

1 can (14 1/2 ounces) stewed tomatoes, diced

1 tablespoon chopped green chiles (wear gloves when handling; they burn)

1 garlic clove, minced

1 1/2 teaspoons chili powder

1 teaspoon seasoned salt

1/2 teaspoon lemon-pepper seasoning

1/2 teaspoon Creole seasoning

1 In a Dutch oven or soup pot, combine 10 cups water, chicken, and salt. Bring to boil and skim off foam. Reduce heat and simmer, covered, 1 1/2 hours or until tender.

2 Transfer chicken to a plate. When cool enough to handle, remove skin and bones and dice meat. Skim fat from stock and add rice, onion, celery, carrots, okra, tomatoes, chiles, garlic, chili powder, salt, lemon-pepper seasoning, and Creole seasoning. Bring to boil, then reduce heat and simmer, uncovered, 30 minutes.

3 Return chicken to pot and simmer 30 minutes or until vegetables are tender.

SPICY CHICKEN-RICE SOUP

This recipe comes from Arkansas, a top rice-producing state, where chicken soup without rice is unthinkable.

SERVES 8

2 cans (14 1/2 ounces each) chicken broth

3 cups cooked rice

2 cups diced cooked chicken

1 can (15 1/4 ounces) whole-kernel corn, undrained

1 can (11 1/2 ounces) vegetable juice

1 cup salsa

1 can (4 ounces) chopped green chiles, drained

1/2 cup chopped scallions

2 tablespoons minced fresh cilantro

1/2 cup shredded Monterey Jack cheese *(optional)*

1 In a large saucepan over medium-high heat, combine broth, rice, chicken, corn, vegetable juice, salsa, chiles, scallions, and cilantro. Bring to boil, then reduce heat and simmer, covered, 15 minutes or until heated through. Garnish with cheese, if desired.

MEDITERRANEAN CHICKEN SOUP

This colorful soup is just as delicious made with skinless, boneless turkey.

SERVES 4

1 tablespoon olive oil

1 medium yellow onion, coarsely chopped

1 medium green bell pepper, cored, seeded, and coarsely chopped

2 garlic cloves, minced

1 can (14 1/2 ounces) low-sodium tomatoes, undrained, chopped

4 cups chicken stock

1/2 cup long-grain white rice

1 tablespoon minced fresh basil or 1 teaspoon dried basil, crumbled

6 medium carrots, peeled and cut into 1/2-inch-thick slices

1 pound skinless, boneless chicken breasts, cut into 3/4-inch cubes

1 package (10 ounces) frozen green beans

1/2 cup chopped pitted black olives

1/4 teaspoon black pepper

1 Heat oil in a soup pot or 5-quart Dutch oven over medium heat. Add onion, bell pepper, and garlic and sauté 5 minutes or until soft.

2 Stir in 2 cups water, tomatoes, stock, rice, and basil. Bring to boil, then reduce heat and simmer, covered, 10 minutes. Add carrots and cook 5 minutes.

3 Add chicken, beans, and olives and cook, uncovered, until chicken is just cooked through, about 5 minutes. Stir in black pepper.

CHICKEN-RICE SOUP WITH SPINACH

Greens can perk up a healthy soup that might otherwise be bland.

SERVES 6

3/4 cup long-grain white rice

8 cups chicken stock

2 skinless, boneless chicken breast halves (8 ounces), cut into 1/4-inch pieces

12 ounces fresh spinach leaves or 1 small head escarole, washed and shredded

1 tablespoon fresh lemon juice

1/8 teaspoon salt

1/8 teaspoon black pepper

1 In a 4-quart saucepan, combine rice and stock and bring to boil, then reduce heat and simmer, covered, 10 minutes.

2 Add chicken and simmer, partially covered, 5 minutes. Stir in spinach and simmer 5 minutes or until rice is tender and chicken and spinach are cooked. Season with lemon juice, salt, and pepper.

CHICKEN SOUP WITH PARMESAN

Spinach and piquant Parmesan give a flavor twist to this chicken soup.

SERVES 4

1 tablespoon butter

1 tablespoon vegetable oil

1 pound skinless, boneless chicken breasts, cut into 3/4-inch cubes

4 cups chicken stock

2 medium carrots, peeled and thinly sliced

3 cups chopped fresh spinach

2 medium celery stalks, thinly sliced

1 large yellow onion, finely chopped

1/2 cup long-grain white rice

2 tablespoons minced fresh parsley

1/4 teaspoon salt

1/8 teaspoon black pepper

2 eggs

1/4 cup grated Parmesan cheese

1 In a 5-quart Dutch oven over medium heat, melt butter and heat oil. Add chicken and sauté 5 minutes or until lightly browned.

2 Add stock, carrots, spinach, celery, onion, rice, parsley, salt, and pepper. Bring to boil, then reduce heat and simmer, covered, 20 minutes or until rice is tender.

3 In a small bowl, lightly beat eggs. When soup is done, drizzle in eggs, whisking constantly. Cook, whisking occasionally, just until soup returns to a simmer. Remove from heat and stir in cheese.

CHICKEN-RICE SOUP WITH LEMON

Here's a simple, quick version of a classic Greek soup. Lemon juice makes the delicious difference.

SERVES 4

1 can (11 1/2 ounces) condensed chicken rice soup

1 can (10 3/4 ounces) condensed cream of chicken soup

1 cup diced cooked chicken

1-2 tablespoons fresh lemon juice

Black pepper

Minced fresh parsley *(optional)*

1 In a 3-quart saucepan over medium heat, combine 2 1/4 cups water, chicken rice soup, and cream of chicken soup and stir to mix well. Cook until heated through.

2 Add chicken and lemon juice and season to taste with pepper. Garnish with parsley, if desired.

CHICKEN SOUP WITH RICE, MINT, AND LEMON

This is a refreshing version of chicken soup with rice.

SERVES 4

8 cups homemade chicken stock or canned low-sodium chicken broth

1 whole chicken breast

1 large yellow onion, coarsely chopped

4 strips lemon rind, 2 x 1/2 inch

3 mint sprigs

2 parsley sprigs

1 thyme sprig or 1/4 teaspoon dried thyme, crumbled

1 garlic clove, minced

4 whole black peppercorns, crushed

1 cup cooked long-grain rice

2 teaspoons fresh lemon juice

1 teaspoon salt

1/4 cup chopped fresh mint

Extra mint sprigs (*optional*)

Lemon slices (*optional*)

1 In a 4-quart saucepan over high heat, bring stock, chicken, onion, lemon rind, mint sprigs, parsley, thyme, garlic, and peppercorns to a boil. Reduce heat and simmer, covered, 30 minutes or until chicken is tender.

2 Using a slotted spoon, transfer chicken to a cutting board to cool. Strain soup into a large heatproof bowl, discarding vegetables and seasonings.

3 Return soup to pan over high heat and bring to boil. Cook, uncovered, 10 minutes or until slightly reduced.

4 Meanwhile, remove skin and bones from cooled chicken and shred meat. Add to soup along with rice, lemon juice, salt, and chopped mint. Heat 2 minutes, ladle into soup bowls, and garnish with mint and lemon slices, if desired.

GREEK-STYLE LEMON CHICKEN SOUP

This delicate yet rich-tasting soup is packed with good nutrition and makes a warming and sustaining main course.

SERVES 4

3 small skinless, boneless chicken breasts

1 large onion, thinly sliced

2 celery stalks, chopped

1 large carrot, thinly sliced

6 whole black peppercorns

1 strip lemon rind

1 small bunch fresh dill or flat-leaf parsley

5 1/2 ounces long-grain white rice

Juice of 1 lemon

2 eggs, beaten

Salt and black pepper

Fresh dill or flat-leaf parsley sprigs

1 In a large saucepan over medium heat, combine 3 cups water, chicken, onion, celery, carrot, peppercorns, lemon rind, and dill. Bring to boil, skimming off any foam. Reduce heat and simmer, partially covered, 15 minutes or until chicken is cooked through.

2 Using a slotted spoon, transfer chicken to a plate. Strain stock into another saucepan, discarding vegetables and seasonings. Return stock to boil and stir in rice. Reduce heat and simmer, covered, 8 minutes or until almost tender.

3 Meanwhile, shred cooled chicken. In a small bowl, mix lemon juice and eggs. Add chicken to pan and cook over medium heat until almost boiling. Remove from heat and add egg mixture, stirring constantly. Season to taste with salt and pepper and garnish with dill.

CHICKEN AND DUMPLING SOUP

Serving this soup with thyme-flavored dumplings on Christmas Eve is a tradition in many parts of the Midwest.

SERVES 16

Soup:
1 broiler/fryer chicken (about 3 pounds)
1/4 cup chicken bouillon granules
1 bay leaf
1 teaspoon whole black peppercorns
1/8 teaspoon ground allspice
6 cups (12 ounces) wide noodles
4 cups sliced carrots
1 package (10 ounces) frozen mixed vegetables
3/4 cup sliced celery
1/2 cup chopped onion
1/4 cup long-grain rice
2 tablespoons minced fresh parsley

Dumplings:
1 1/3 cups all-purpose flour
2 teaspoons baking powder
1 teaspoon dried thyme
1/2 teaspoon salt
2/3 cup milk
2 tablespoons vegetable oil

1 For soup, combine 12 cups water, chicken, bouillon, bay leaf, peppercorns, and allspice in a soup pot or Dutch oven. Bring to boil, then reduce heat and simmer, covered, 1 1/2 hours.

2 Using a slotted spoon, transfer chicken to a plate. Strain stock into a heatproof bowl, discarding bay leaf and peppercorns, and skim off fat. When chicken is cool enough to handle, remove skin and bones and cut meat into chunks. Return chicken and stock to pot and add noodles, carrots, mixed vegetables, celery, onion, rice, and parsley. Bring to boil, then reduce heat and simmer, uncovered, until dumplings are added.

3 For dumplings, combine flour, baking powder, thyme, and salt in a small bowl. In another small bowl, combine milk and oil. Stir into flour mixture until a soft dough forms. Drop by teaspoons into soup and simmer, covered, 15 minutes or until a toothpick inserted in a dumpling comes out clean.

SOUTHWESTERN CHICKEN-BARLEY SOUP

Barley gives this chicken soup both texture and heft.

SERVES 12

1 tablespoon olive oil
1 medium onion, chopped
1 garlic clove, minced
1 can (15 1/4 ounces) whole-kernel corn, drained
1 can (15 ounces) black beans, drained and rinsed
1 can (15 ounces) tomato sauce
1 can (14 1/2 ounces) diced tomatoes, undrained
1 can (14 1/2 ounces) chicken broth
1/2 cup medium pearl barley
1 can (4 ounces) chopped green chiles, drained
1 tablespoon chili powder
1 teaspoon ground cumin
3 cups cubed cooked chicken

1 Heat oil in a Dutch oven or soup pot over medium heat. Add onion and garlic and sauté 4 minutes or until tender.

2 Add 3 cups water, corn, beans, tomato sauce, tomatoes, broth, barley, chiles, chili powder, and cumin. Bring to boil, reduce heat, and simmer, covered, 45 minutes. Stir in chicken and cook 15 minutes or until chicken is heated through and barley is tender.

OLD-FASHIONED CHICKEN NOODLE SOUP

SERVES 4

Stock:

1 chicken, about 3 pounds,
    cut up and skin removed,
    or 4 chicken quarters, skin removed

2 onions, halved

3 carrots, chopped

3 celery stalks, chopped

Bouquet garni (2 sprigs parsley, 2 sprigs
    thyme, and 1 bay leaf tied together)

4 whole black peppercorns

1 teaspoon salt

Soup:

4 ounces spaghetti or linguine,
    broken into 2-inch pieces

1 carrot, halved lengthwise and thinly sliced

1 celery stalk, thinly sliced

1/2 cup small broccoli florets

1 can (11 ounces) whole-kernel corn, drained

2 tablespoons fresh parsley, finely chopped

2 teaspoons fresh thyme

1 For stock, place chicken in a large heavy soup pot or saucepan and add 8 cups water, onions, carrots, and celery. Bring to boil, skimming off any foam.

2 Reduce heat to low and add bouquet garni, peppercorns, and salt. Simmer, partially covered, skimming foam as necessary, 30 minutes or until juices run clear when chicken is pierced with a knife. Transfer chicken to a plate.

3 Strain stock into a large heatproof bowl, discarding vegetables and seasonings. Rinse out pot. Skim fat from stock and return 6 cups stock to pot (cool and freeze any remaining stock for later use). When chicken is cool enough to handle, remove bones and cut enough meat into bite-size pieces to pack a cup (refrigerate any remaining chicken for sandwiches or other uses).

4 For soup, bring stock to boil, then reduce heat to simmer. Add spaghetti and carrot and simmer 4 minutes. Add celery, broccoli, and corn and simmer 5 minutes or until just tender. Stir in chicken and heat through. Sprinkle in parsley and thyme.

It's easy to see why this soup—packed with fresh flavors, pasta, chicken, and a bounty of just-tender vegetables—is traditionally eaten as a restorative.

CHICKEN NOODLE SOUP

Here's the classic soup to heal what ails you—or just to make a lovely lunch.

SERVES 4

1 small stewing chicken (2-3 pounds)
3 teaspoons salt
1/8 teaspoon pepper
2 chicken bouillon cubes
1/2 medium onion, chopped
1/4 teaspoon dried marjoram
1/4 teaspoon dried thyme
1 bay leaf
1 cup diced carrots
1 cup diced celery
1 1/2 cups fine noodles

1 In a large soup pot, combine 2 1/2 quarts water, chicken, salt, pepper, bouillon, onion, marjoram, thyme, bay leaf, carrots, and celery. Cover and bring to boil, skimming off foam. Reduce heat and simmer, covered, 1 1/2 hours or until chicken is tender.

2 Transfer chicken to a plate. When cool enough to handle, remove skin and bones and cut meat into chunks. Skim fat from stock and bring to boil. Add noodles and cook 8 minutes or until tender. Return chicken to pot and heat through. Remove bay leaf before serving.

SPEEDY CHICKEN NOODLE SOUP

This is a fast and easy way to get the benefit of real, home-style chicken soup when you're feeling under the weather. (Photograph on page 31)

SERVES 4

1 cup chicken stock
1 celery stalk, sliced
1 carrot, sliced

1 garlic clove, minced
1/4 teaspoon salt
1/3 cup ditalini or other small pasta
1 pound skinless, boneless chicken thighs, cut into 1/2-inch chunks.

1 In a medium saucepan, combine 2 cups water, stock, celery, carrot, garlic, and salt and bring to boil. Add pasta and chicken, reduce heat, and simmer, covered, 10 minutes or until done.

CHICKEN NOODLE SOUP WITH ROSEMARY

Brimming with chicken and a variety of vegetables, this rosemary-flavored soup gets better as it simmers. (Photograph on page 4)

SERVES 6

1 tablespoon olive oil
1 chicken (3 1/2 pounds), cut up and skin removed
1 large onion, chopped
1 bay leaf
1/2 teaspoon dried rosemary
1 teaspoon salt
1/4 teaspoon black pepper
2 garlic cloves, minced
3 carrots, cut into matchsticks
2 leeks, cut unto matchsticks
1 parsnip, cut into matchsticks
1 white turnip, cut into matchsticks
1 red bell pepper, corded, seeded, and cut into strips
2 celery stalks, thinly sliced
6 ounces linguine

1 Heat oil in a large saucepan over medium-high heat. Add chicken in a single layer, then add onion and sauté until chicken is browned on both sides and onion is opaque. Add bay leaf, rosemary, salt, and black pepper.

2 Meanwhile, in a soup pot, bring 12 cups water to boil. Carefully pour over chicken and return to boil. Reduce heat and simmer, partially covered, 1 hour or until stock is richly flavored. Transfer chicken to a plate. Strain stock into a large heat-proof bowl, discarding onion and bay leaf. Skim off fat and return to pan.

3 Add garlic, carrots, leeks, parsnip, turnip, bell pepper, and celery and bring to boil. Reduce heat and simmer, uncovered, 5 minutes. When chicken is cool enough to handle, remove bones and cut meat into bite-size pieces. Add to pot, stir in linguine, and simmer, uncovered, 15 minutes or until tender.

CHICKEN NOODLE SOUP WITH PEAS AND BEANS

Garlic and green vegetables add to this soup's healing power.

SERVES 6 TO 8

Stock:
1 broiler/fryer chicken
    (about 3 1/2 pounds), cut up
1 large carrot, sliced
1 large onion, sliced
1 celery stalk, sliced
1 garlic clove, minced
1 bay leaf
1 teaspoon dried thyme
1 teaspoon salt
1/4 teaspoon black pepper

Soup:
2 large carrots, sliced
2 celery stalks, sliced
1 medium onion, chopped
2 cups fine egg noodles
1 cup frozen peas
1/2 cup frozen cut green beans

1 For stock, combine 10 cups water, chicken, carrot, onion, celery, garlic, bay leaf, thyme, salt, and pepper in a Dutch oven or soup pot. Bring to boil, then reduce heat and simmer, covered, until chicken is tender, about 1 1/2 hours.

2 Transfer chicken to a plate. When cool enough to handle, remove skin and bones and cut meat into bite-size pieces. Strain stock, discarding vegetables and bay leaf.

3 For soup, return stock to pot and add carrots, celery, and onion. Bring to boil, then reduce heat and simmer, covered, until tender, about 10 minutes.

4 Add noodles and chicken and bring to boil. Reduce heat and simmer, covered, 6 minutes. Stir in peas and beans and cook until beans and noodles are tender, about 4 minutes.

FEEL-GOOD CHICKEN SOUP

Every grandmother believes that nothing cures the sniffles better than homemade soup.

SERVES 4

3 1/2 cups canned low-sodium
    chicken broth
1 package (10 ounces) frozen peas
    and carrots
1 cup chopped cooked chicken
1 1/2 teaspoons dried oregano
1/4 teaspoon salt
1/4 teaspoon black pepper
1/2 cup fine egg noodles

1 In a large saucepan over medium heat, combine broth, vegetables, chicken, oregano, salt, and pepper. Bring to boil, then reduce heat and stir in noodles. Cover and simmer, stirring occasionally, until noodles are tender, about 6 minutes.

CHICKEN NOODLE SOUP WITH DILL AND PEAS

Many traditional chicken soups use dill for flavor.

SERVES 6

8 cups homemade chicken stock or
    canned low-sodium chicken broth

3/4 teaspoon salt

3 large carrots, peeled and thickly sliced

1 celery stalk, diced

1/4 teaspoon black pepper

1 cup fine egg noodles

2 cups diced cooked chicken

1 cup frozen peas

1 tablespoon chopped fresh parsley

1 tablespoon snipped fresh dill

1 In a large saucepan over high heat, bring stock and salt to boil. Add carrots, celery, and pepper, then reduce heat and simmer, uncovered, 10 minutes.

2 Stir in noodles and simmer, stirring occasionally, 8 minutes or until tender. Add chicken, peas, parsley, and dill and simmer, uncovered, 5 minutes or until heated through.

CHINESE CHICKEN NOODLE SOUP

A simple and tasty soup that makes a good dinner appetizer or a light lunch.

SERVES 4

2 cups chicken stock

2 teaspoons soy sauce

1 tablespoon sesame oil

1 tablespoon rice vinegar

8 ounces chicken breast, diced

6 ounces fresh linguine

2 cups watercress leaves

1 scallion, minced

1 In a medium saucepan, bring 3 cups water, stock, soy sauce, sesame oil, and vinegar to boil. Add chicken and cook 2 minutes.

2 Add linguine, watercress, and scallion and cook 2 minutes, or until pasta is done.

ROOT VEGETABLE-CHICKEN SOUP

Carrots, sweet potato, and parsnip add an earthy note to this rich-tasting chicken noodle soup.

SERVES 10

1 chicken (4-5 pounds), quartered

3 carrots, peeled

1 small sweet potato, peeled

4 celery stalks with leaves, cut up

1 small parsnip, peeled and sliced

1 large onion, peeled and quartered

Dill sprigs

Salt and black pepper

8 ounces thin egg noodles, cooked and drained

1 In a soup pot, combine chicken, carrots, sweet potato, celery, parsnip, onion, and dill. Add water to cover, about 10 cups. Cover and bring to boil over high heat, skimming off foam. Add salt and pepper, reduce heat, and simmer, covered, 2 hours.

2 Transfer chicken to a plate. Strain stock into a large heatproof bowl, discarding all vegetables except carrots. When chicken is cool enough to handle, remove skin and bones and dice meat. Return to pot. Slice carrots and return to stock.

3 Add noodles and cook until heated through.

FRENCH CHICKEN SOUP

This hearty soup can also be made with 2 1/2 cups cubed cooked chicken or turkey. Simply reduce the cooking time in Step 3 to 2 minutes so the meat is heated through.

SERVES 6

2 tablespoons olive oil

1 medium yellow onion, coarsely chopped

3 garlic cloves, thinly sliced

1 large red bell pepper, cored, seeded, and diced

1 small green bell pepper, cored, seeded, and diced

2 medium zucchini, halved lengthwise and cut into 3/4-inch-thick slices

1/2 teaspoon dried marjoram, crumbled

1 can (8 ounces) tomato sauce

2 3/4 cups canned chicken broth

1 1/2 cups broad egg noodles

1 1/4 pounds skinless, boneless chicken thighs or turkey drumsticks, cut into 1/2-inch cubes

1/4 teaspoon salt

1 Heat oil 1 minute in a large saucepan over medium heat. Add onion and sauté 5 minutes or until limp. Add garlic and sauté 1 minute.

2 Stir in bell peppers, cover, and cook over medium-low heat, stirring occasionally, 5 minutes or until glossy and crisp-tender. Add zucchini and marjoram, cover, and cook, stirring occasionally, 7 minutes or until tender.

3 Add tomato sauce and simmer, covered, 5 minutes. Add 2 cups water and broth and bring to boil over high heat. Add noodles and cook, covered, 5 minutes. Add chicken and salt, reduce heat to medium, and simmer, covered, 5 minutes or until chicken is cooked through.

CHICKEN-TORTELLINI SOUP

This soup uses leftover chicken to fine effect. If you don't have any leftovers, you can poach a few chicken breasts for 10 minutes.

SERVES 8

7 3/4 cups chicken stock

1 can (14 1/2 ounces) stewed tomatoes, cut up

1 package (10 ounces) frozen chopped spinach, thawed

1/4 cup grated Parmesan cheese

1/2 teaspoon salt

1/4 teaspoon black pepper

1 package (9 ounces) refrigerated cheese tortellini

2 1/2 cups cubed cooked chicken

1 In a Dutch oven or soup pot over medium-high heat, combine stock, tomatoes, spinach, cheese, salt, and pepper. Bring to boil, reduce heat, and simmer, covered, 10 minutes.

2 Add pasta and chicken. Bring to boil, reduce heat, and simmer, covered, until heated through, about 5 minutes.

QUICK CHICKEN-VEGETABLE SOUP

This recipe is perfect for a quick lunch or supper. Red bell pepper, corn, and a sprinkling of fresh greens bring color and texture to a simple chicken soup base. Adding sherry deepens the flavor. (Photograph on page 16)

SERVES 4

3 cups chicken stock

1 red bell pepper, cored, seeded, and cut into strips

1/2 cup frozen whole-kernel corn

8 ounces skinless, boneless chicken breast, cut into 1/2-inch strips

4 ounces beet greens, chard, escarole,
   or spinach, shredded
2 tablespoons dry sherry
3 tablespoons snipped fresh chives
3 tablespoons chopped fresh tarragon
Salt and black pepper

1 In a large saucepan over high heat, bring stock to boil. Add bell pepper, corn, and chicken. Return to boil, reduce heat, and simmer, covered, 5 minutes.

2 Uncover and return to boil. Sprinkle greens into soup, letting them cook on surface, uncovered, until just tender, about 3 minutes.

3 Remove from heat and stir in sherry, chives, tarragon, and salt and black pepper to taste.

COUNTRY-STYLE CHICKEN-VEGETABLE SOUP

The root vegetables carrot and turnip add an earthy flavor to this traditional soup.
(Photograph on page 23)

SERVES 4

1 tablespoon vegetable oil
1 medium onion, coarsely chopped
3 carrots, peeled and diced
1 medium celery stalk, diced
2 cans (14 1/2 ounces each) fat-free low-
   sodium chicken broth
1 can (14 1/2 ounces) diced tomatoes, undrained
8 ounces chicken breast, skin removed
1 small turnip, peeled and diced
1 teaspoon dried basil, crumbled
1 1/2 cups thin noodles
1/4 teaspoon black pepper

1 Heat oil in a large saucepan over medium heat. Add onion, carrots, and celery and sauté 5 minutes or until softened. Add broth, tomatoes, chicken,
turnip, and basil. Simmer, uncovered, 30 minutes or until chicken is cooked through.

2 Transfer chicken to a plate. When cool enough to handle, remove bones and coarsely chop meat. Return to pan, add noodles, and cook 4 minutes or until tender. Add pepper.

CHICKEN-VEGETABLE SOUP WITH TARRAGON

This is a light, delicious, one-dish meal that even children will love.

SERVES 4

3 tablespoons butter
3 medium all-purpose potatoes,
   peeled and cut into 1-inch chunks
8 ounces carrots, sliced
3 scallions, cut diagonally into 1/2-inch pieces,
   white and green parts separated
2 tablespoons all-purpose flour
1/2 teaspoon sugar
1/4 teaspoon dried tarragon, crumbled
1/8 teaspoon black pepper
4 cups canned low-sodium chicken broth
8 ounces skinless, boneless chicken breast, cut
   into 1/2-inch pieces

1 In a large saucepan over medium heat, melt butter. Add potatoes and carrots and stir to coat with butter. Add white parts of scallions and sauté 1 minute.

2 Add flour, sugar, tarragon, and pepper and stir to combine. Add broth and bring to boil over high heat. Add chicken, reduce heat, and simmer, covered, 20 minutes or until vegetables are tender and chicken is cooked through. Stir in scallion greens.

HEARTY CHICKEN-VEGETABLE SOUP

This is an easy, sweet-sour chicken soup to serve a crowd any time of the year.

SERVES 20

2 tablespoons vegetable oil

3 large green bell peppers, cored, seeded, and chopped

3 large onions, chopped

3 cans (two 28 ounces, one 14 1/2 ounces) whole tomatoes, undrained

4 cups fresh or frozen whole-kernel corn

3 cups cubed cooked chicken

3 large all-purpose potatoes, diced

1 can (16 ounces) butter beans, drained and rinsed

1 cup frozen peas

1 cup frozen chopped okra

1/2 cup sugar

3 jalapeño peppers, seeded, deveined, and chopped (wear gloves when handling; they burn)

1/4 cup vinegar

3 tablespoons salt

1 Heat oil in a Dutch oven or soup pot over medium heat. Add bell peppers and onions and sauté until tender, about 4 minutes.

2 Add 2 cups water, tomatoes, corn, chicken, potatoes, beans, peas, okra, sugar, jalapeños, vinegar, and salt. Bring to boil, cover, and reduce heat. Simmer, stirring occasionally, until potatoes are tender, about 40 minutes.

PHILADELPHIA PEPPER POT SOUP

Women selling soup from carts in Philadelphia used to cry, "Pepper pot, pepper pot! Makes backs strong; makes lives long. All hot! Pepper pot!"

SERVES 6

1 tablespoon unsalted butter

1 tablespoon vegetable oil

1 1/2 cups chopped, seeded green bell pepper

1 cup chopped onion

1/2 cup chopped celery

2 cups diced all-purpose potatoes

2 tablespoons all-purpose flour

5 1/2 cups homemade chicken stock or canned low-sodium chicken broth

1 bay leaf

1/2 teaspoon salt

1/2 teaspoon crushed red pepper flakes

1/2 teaspoon dried thyme

1/8 teaspoon ground allspice

1/8 teaspoon ground cloves

8 ounces skinless, boneless chicken breasts or cooked tripe, cut into 1-inch pieces

1/2 cup light cream *(optional)*

1/4 teaspoon black pepper

1/4 cup chopped fresh parsley

1 In a large heavy saucepan over medium-high heat, melt butter and heat oil. Stir in bell pepper, onion, and celery and sauté 5 minutes or until tender. Stir in potatoes and flour and cook until bubbling. Stir in stock, bay leaf, salt, red pepper flakes, thyme, allspice, and cloves. Bring to boil, then cover, reduce heat, and simmer, stirring occasionally, 20 minutes or until potatoes are tender.

2 Add chicken and cream, if desired, cover, and simmer, stirring occasionally, 5 minutes or until chicken is cooked through. Remove bay leaf, add black pepper, and stir in parsley.

CHINESE CHICKEN SOUP

Sherry and ginger give this delightful chicken soup its distinctive taste.

SERVES 4

8 ounces skinless, boneless chicken breast

2 tablespoons dry sherry

4 cups low-sodium chicken broth

4 ounces mushrooms, sliced

1 teaspoon minced fresh ginger
 or 1/8 teaspoon ground ginger

1 tablespoon light soy sauce

3 scallions, cut diagonally into
 1/2-inch thick slices

4 ounces Napa cabbage, shredded
 1/2 inch thick

1/2 cup canned whole water chestnuts,
 thinly sliced

1 Cut chicken crosswise into 1/4-inch-thick slices. In a medium bowl, combine chicken and sherry and let stand 10 minutes.

2 In a large saucepan over high heat, combine broth, mushrooms, ginger, and soy sauce. Bring to boil, then reduce heat, add chicken, and simmer 1 minute. Stir in scallions, cabbage, and water chestnuts and cook 5 minutes or until chicken is cooked through and cabbage is crisp-tender.

CHICKEN AND ESCAROLE SOUP

For an even heartier soup, add a cup of cooked noodles or rice to this main-course recipe.

SERVES 4

2 cups low-sodium chicken broth

8 ounces skinless, boneless chicken breast

2 medium carrots, peeled and chopped

2 medium celery stalks, chopped

1 medium yellow onion, chopped

1/4 cup fresh parsley, minced

1/8 teaspoon black pepper

8 ounces escarole, spinach,
 or Swiss chard, trimmed

1 large tomato, peeled, cored,
 seeded, and chopped

1 In a large heavy saucepan over medium heat, bring 2 cups water and broth to boil. Add chicken, carrots, celery, onion, parsley, and pepper and return to boil. Reduce heat and simmer, covered, 20 minutes or until chicken is tender.

2 Transfer chicken to a plate. Stir escarole and tomato into pan and simmer, uncovered, 5 minutes or until escarole is tender.

3 Cut cooled chicken into 1/2-inch cubes, return to pan, and simmer until heated through, about 1 minute.

CHICKEN-LIMA BEAN SOUP

Enlivened by spinach and parsley, this soup is a delightful combination of subtle flavors.

SERVES 12

1 pound dry large lima beans,
 sorted and rinsed

1 broiler/fryer chicken (3-3 1/2 pounds)

2 celery stalks with leaves, sliced

4 chicken bouillon cubes

2 1/2 teaspoons salt

1/2 teaspoon black pepper

3 medium carrots, chopped

4 cups chopped fresh spinach

2 tablespoons minced fresh parsley

1 In a Dutch oven or soup pot, combine 12 cups water, beans, chicken, celery, bouillon, salt, and pepper. Bring to boil, reduce heat, and simmer, covered, 2 hours or until beans are tender.

2 Transfer chicken to a plate. When cool enough to handle, remove skin and bones and cut meat into chunks. Return to pot, add carrots, and simmer 30 minutes or until carrots are tender. Stir in spinach and parsley and heat through.

TEX-MEX CHICKEN SOUP

In the Southwest, even chicken soup has to have hot chiles, corn, and some form of tortillas.

SERVES 4

1 tablespoon butter

1 tablespoon vegetable oil

1 pound skinless, boneless chicken breasts, cut into 3/4-inch cubes

4 cups chicken stock

2 medium carrots, peeled and thinly sliced

2 medium celery stalks, thinly sliced

1 large yellow onion, finely chopped

2 cups fresh corn or thawed frozen whole-kernel corn

1 cup canned crushed tomatoes

1/4 cup drained canned green chiles

2 tablespoons minced fresh parsley

1/4 teaspoon salt

1/8 teaspoon black pepper

2 cups crumbled tortilla chips

1 In a 5-quart Dutch oven over medium heat, melt butter and heat oil. Add chicken and sauté 5 minutes or until lightly browned.

2 Add stock, carrots, celery, onion, corn, tomatoes, chiles, parsley, salt, and pepper. Bring to boil, then reduce heat and simmer, covered, 20 minutes. Sprinkle with tortilla chips.

CHICKEN-KALE SOUP

Nutty-flavored flaxseed oil, high in omega-3 fatty acids, is available in the refrigerated section of many health food stores. If you can't find it, substitute dark sesame oil in this recipe. (Photograph on page 22)

SERVES 4

1 1/4 pounds skinless, boneless chicken thighs, cut into 1-inch chunks

4 carrots, thinly sliced

3 large red onions, cut into 1/2-inch chunks

6 garlic cloves (5 minced, 1 whole)

2 tablespoons finely chopped fresh ginger

1 teaspoon cayenne pepper

3/4 teaspoon salt

2 red bell peppers, cored, seeded, and cut lengthwise into flat pieces

1 tablespoon hulled roasted pumpkin seeds

1 tablespoon flaxseed oil

1/4 cup orzo pasta

8 cups shredded kale

1 In a large saucepan or soup pot over high heat, combine 4 cups water, chicken, carrots, onions, minced garlic, ginger, cayenne, and salt. Bring to boil, then reduce heat and simmer, partially covered, 25 minutes.

2 Preheat broiler. Place peppers skin side up on a broiler pan and broil 6 inches from heat 10 minutes or until skin is well charred. Transfer to a plate. When cool enough to handle, peel and transfer to a food processor or blender with pumpkin seeds, oil, and whole garlic clove. Cover and puree until smooth.

3 Add orzo to pot and cook, uncovered, 5 minutes. Stir in kale and cook 5 minutes or until tender. Serve with roasted pepper puree.

CHICKEN-TOMATO SOUP

This chicken soup has a sweet tomato base that complements the broccoli, corn, and two kinds of beans.

SERVES 12

1 package (10 ounces) frozen chopped broccoli

3/4 cup chopped onion

1 garlic clove, minced

12 ounces skinless, boneless chicken breast, cut into 1-inch chunks

1/2 teaspoon seasoned salt

1/4 teaspoon black pepper

1 can (46 ounces) tomato juice

1 can (15 1/2 ounces) great Northern beans, drained and rinsed

1 can (15 ounces) black beans, drained and rinsed

1 can (11 ounces) whole-kernel corn, drained

1 tablespoon ketchup

1 teaspoon brown sugar

Crumbled bacon *(optional)*

Shredded cheddar cheese *(optional)*

1 In a Dutch oven or soup pot over medium-high heat, combine 1 1/2 cups water, broccoli, onion, and garlic. Bring to boil and cook, stirring frequently, 8 to 10 minutes.

2 Meanwhile, in a nonstick skillet over medium heat, cook chicken until no longer pink, about 6 minutes. Sprinkle with seasoned salt and pepper and add to pot.

3 Stir in tomato juice, great Northern and black beans, corn, ketchup, and brown sugar. Bring to boil, then reduce heat and simmer, covered, 10 to 15 minutes, stirring occasionally. Garnish with bacon and cheese, if desired.

CHICKEN-TOMATO SOUP WITH TORTILLAS

Scallions, tomatoes, chiles, and lime juice team up to make this zesty soup a good source of vitamin C.

SERVES 6

1 whole chicken breast, skin removed

8 cups fat-free low-sodium chicken broth

3 garlic cloves

1 teaspoon salt

1 teaspoon black pepper

1 teaspoon dried oregano, crumbled

1 tablespoon olive oil

5 scallions, coarsely chopped

1 can (4 1/2 ounces) green chiles, drained

4 medium tomatoes, cored, seeded, and coarsely chopped

1/2 cup fresh lime juice

4 corn tortillas (6 inches), cut into 3 x 1/4-inch strips and toasted

3 tablespoons chopped fresh cilantro

1 In a medium saucepan, combine chicken, broth, 2 garlic cloves, salt, pepper, and oregano. Bring to boil, then reduce heat and simmer, uncovered, 25 minutes. Transfer chicken to a plate. When cool enough to handle, remove bones and cut meat into large chunks. Strain stock into a large heatproof bowl, discarding garlic.

2 Heat oil in a large saucepan over medium heat. Mince remaining garlic and add to pan. Add scallions and sauté 5 minutes or until softened. Add chiles, tomatoes, and stock and bring to boil. Reduce heat and simmer, partially covered, 15 minutes. Add chicken, lime juice, and tortilla strips and simmer 5 minutes. Garnish with cilantro.

SALSA CHICKEN SOUP

This lively chicken soup gets its zip from chili powder and a healthy portion of salsa.

SERVES 6

8 ounces skinless, boneless
   chicken breasts, cut into cubes
1 can (14 1/2 ounces) low-sodium chicken broth
1 1/2 teaspoons chili powder
1 cup frozen whole-kernel corn
1 cup salsa
Shredded Monterey Jack or pepper
   Jack cheese *(optional)*

1 In a Dutch oven or soup pot over medium-high heat, combine 1 3/4 cups water, chicken, broth, and chili powder. Bring to boil, then reduce heat and simmer, covered, 5 minutes.

2 Add corn and return to boil. Reduce heat and simmer, uncovered, 5 minutes or until chicken is no longer pink and corn is tender. Add salsa and heat through. Garnish with cheese, if desired.

CHICKEN-TORTILLA SOUP WITH CHEESE

Instead of rice or noodles, crispy tortilla ribbons go into this soup. (Photograph on page 22)

SERVES 4

6 corn tortillas (6 inches)
2 teaspoons olive oil
1 green bell pepper, cored, seeded,
   and cut into 1/2-inch squares
3 scallions, thinly sliced
3 garlic cloves, minced
2 large tomatoes, cored, seeded, and cubed
1 1/2 cups canned fat-free low-sodium
   chicken broth
1 1/2 teaspoons ground cumin
1 1/2 teaspoons ground coriander

1/2 teaspoon salt
6 ounces skinless, boneless chicken breast,
   cut into thin strips
1/4 cup shredded Monterey Jack cheese

1 Preheat oven to 400°F. Cut tortillas into 1/2-inch-wide strips, place on a baking sheet, and bake until crisp, about 5 minutes.

2 Meanwhile, heat oil in a medium nonstick saucepan over medium heat. Add bell pepper, scallions, and garlic and sauté 2 minutes or until scallions are tender. Stir in tomatoes and cook 2 minutes or until beginning to collapse.

3 Add 1/2 cup water, broth, cumin, coriander, and salt and bring to boil. Add chicken, reduce heat, and simmer, covered, 3 minutes or until cooked through.

4 Ladle soup into 4 bowls and top with tortilla strips and cheese.

MINTY CHICKEN SOUP

Mint and lemon zest give this chicken soup its zip.

SERVES 4

1 tablespoon unsalted butter
2 tablespoons all-purpose flour
5 cups canned low-sodium chicken broth
1 teaspoon grated lemon zest
2 tablespoons fresh lemon juice
1 cup cubed cooked chicken breast
2 tablespoons minced fresh mint

1 Melt butter in a large heavy saucepan over medium heat. Blend in flour and cook, stirring, 4 minutes. Slowly whisk in broth, add lemon zest and juice, and bring to boil, stirring constantly.

2 Reduce heat and simmer, stirring occasionally, 5 minutes. Add chicken and simmer 1 minute. Stir in mint.

CHINESE HOT-AND-SOUR SOUP

This spicy soup makes a fine prelude to a stir-fry or stands alone for a satisfying lunch.

SERVES 4

3/4 cup drained canned bamboo shoots

4 large dried shiitake mushrooms

2 teaspoons dark sesame oil

8 ounces skinless, boneless chicken breast, cut into 2 x 1/4 x 1/4-inch strips

7 ounces fresh mushrooms, sliced

3 scallions with tops, sliced

2 1/2 cups chicken stock

2-3 tablespoons reduced-sodium soy sauce

2 teaspoons honey

1 1/2 tablespoons cornstarch

8 ounces firm tofu, cut into 1/2 x 1/2 x 2-inch strips

2 tablespoons rice vinegar or white wine vinegar

1/4 teaspoon hot red pepper sauce

1 In a small saucepan, bring 1 cup water to a boil. Place bamboo shoots in a small heatproof bowl and add 1/2 cup boiling water. Soak 5 minutes, then drain.

2 Meanwhile, add dried mushrooms to remaining water in pan and soak 15 minutes. Set a sieve lined with cheesecloth or paper towels over a bowl and drain, reserving liquid. Slice mushrooms, discarding stems.

3 Heat oil in a large saucepan over medium heat. Add chicken and sauté 4 minutes or until no longer pink. Add soaked mushrooms, fresh mushrooms, scallions, stock, soy sauce, honey, and soaking liquid. Bring to boil, then reduce heat and simmer.

4 Meanwhile, in a small bowl, mix cornstarch with 1/4 cup water. Stir into soup and cook 5 minutes. Stir in tofu, vinegar, and red pepper sauce and cook until tofu is heated through.

CHICKEN-BROCCOLI SOUP

Using packaged broccoli in cheese sauce simplifies this recipe and makes it a speedy and delicious lunch or supper.

SERVES 6

1/4 cup butter

1/2 cup chopped onion

1/2 cup chopped celery

3 tablespoons all-purpose flour

1 tablespoon dry mustard

1/2 teaspoon salt

1/4 teaspoon black pepper

3 cups milk

2 teaspoons fresh lemon juice

1 1/2 cups diced cooked chicken

2 packages (10 ounces each) cut broccoli in cheese sauce, thawed and chopped

Seasoned croutons *(optional)*

1 In a large saucepan over medium heat, melt butter. Add onion and celery and sauté 4 minutes or until crisp-tender. Stir in flour, mustard, salt, and pepper and cook until smooth and bubbling.

2 Gradually add milk, cooking and stirring until mixture boils and thickens. Stir in lemon juice, chicken, and broccoli and simmer, stirring occasionally, until heated through. Top with croutons, if desired.

CURRIED CHICKEN SOUP

SERVES 4

1 1/2 pounds skinless, boneless chicken breasts

1/4 teaspoon salt

1/8 teaspoon black pepper

3 tablespoons unsalted butter

1 medium yellow onion, finely chopped

1 large celery stalk, sliced

1 medium carrot, peeled and sliced

2 garlic cloves, minced

1 to 2 teaspoons curry powder

5 cups chicken stock

1 bay leaf

1/3 cup long-grain white rice

1 tablespoon arrowroot blended with 1 cup heavy cream or low-fat plain yogurt

4 teaspoons chutney (optional)

1/2 teaspoon paprika (optional)

1 Sprinkle chicken with salt and pepper. In a large saucepan over medium heat, melt butter. Add chicken and sauté 1 minute on each side, then transfer to a plate. Add onion, celery, carrot, and garlic to pan and sauté 2 minutes. Blend in curry powder and stir 1 minute.

2 Add stock and bay leaf and bring to boil. Return chicken to pan, reduce heat, and simmer, partially covered, 7 minutes or until chicken is no longer pink. Transfer to a plate. When cool enough to handle, cut into bite-size pieces.

3 Bring stock to boil and add rice, then reduce heat and simmer, partially covered, 12 minutes or until tender. Remove bay leaf.

4 Return stock to boil, stir in arrowroot mixture, and cook, stirring constantly, 2 minutes or until slightly thickened. Return chicken to pan, reduce heat, and simmer, uncovered, 2 minutes or until heated through.

5 Ladle soup into bowls and garnish each serving with 1 teaspoon chutney and a sprinkling of paprika, if desired.

This curry soup has a rich, satisfying flavor. You can heat it up with extra curry powder.

MULLIGATAWNY SOUP

Mulligatawny is a thick, curry-flavored soup of Indian origin.

SERVES 4

1 tablespoon unsalted butter

1 medium yellow onion, chopped

1 medium carrot, peeled and sliced

1 medium tart apple, peeled, cored, and chopped

1 medium celery stalk, sliced

1 small green bell pepper, cored, seeded, and chopped

2 tablespoons all-purpose flour

1 tablespoon curry powder

4 cups canned low-sodium chicken broth

1 can (14 1/2 ounces) low-sodium tomatoes, drained and chopped

3 whole cloves

1/4 teaspoon ground mace

1/4 teaspoon ground nutmeg

1/8 teaspoon black pepper

1 cup cubed cooked chicken

1/2 cup cooked rice

1/4 cup low-fat plain yogurt

4 teaspoons chopped fresh parsley *(optional)*

1 In a large heavy saucepan over medium heat, melt butter. Add onion, carrot, apple, celery, and bell pepper. Sauté, uncovered, 5 minutes or until onion is soft. Blend in flour and curry powder and cook, stirring, 1 minute.

2 Add broth, tomatoes, cloves, mace, nutmeg, and black pepper and bring to boil. Reduce heat and simmer, covered, 30 minutes. Remove from heat and let stand 10 minutes. Remove cloves.

3 Transfer soup in 3 batches to a food processor, cover, and puree until smooth. Return to pan, add chicken and rice, and cook, stirring, over medium heat until heated through. Ladle into bowls, top each with 1 tablespoon yogurt, and sprinkle with parsley.

QUICK CHICKEN-CURRY SOUP

If you like curry, this quick soup should be a welcome addition to your repertoire.

SERVES 5

2 tablespoons butter

1 cup chopped onion

3/4 teaspoon curry powder

2 chicken bouillon cubes

1 can (14 1/2 ounces) diced tomatoes, undrained

1 can (10 3/4 ounces) condensed cream of celery soup

1 cup half-and-half

1 can (5 ounces) white chicken, drained

1 In a 3-quart saucepan over medium heat, melt butter. Add onion and curry and sauté until onion is tender, about 3 minutes.

2 In a small bowl, dissolve bouillon in 1 cup hot water, then add to pan. Stir in tomatoes, soup, half-and-half, and chicken and cook until heated through.

SPICY CHICKEN SOUP

Start with a small amount of hot sauce when you first make this soup, then add more if your palate can take it.

SERVES 8

6 cups milk

3 cans (10 3/4 ounces each) condensed cream of chicken soup

3 cups shredded cooked chicken

1 cup sour cream

1/4-1/2 cup hot red pepper sauce

1 In a slow cooker, combine milk, soup, chicken, sour cream, and red pepper sauce. Cover and cook on low 4 to 5 hours.

CREAMED CHICKEN SOUP

For many people, this is a comfort food: a velvety soup with chicken, rice, and just a touch of nutmeg.

SERVES 4

1 tablespoon butter

1 tablespoon vegetable oil

1 pound skinless, boneless chicken breast, cut into 3/4-inch cubes

4 cups chicken stock

2 medium carrots, peeled and thinly sliced

2 medium celery stalks, thinly sliced

1 large yellow onion, finely chopped

1/2 cup long-grain white rice

2 tablespoons minced fresh parsley

1/4 teaspoon salt

1/8 teaspoon black pepper

2 tablespoons cornstarch

1 cup milk or half-and-half

Pinch of ground nutmeg

1 In a 5-quart Dutch oven over medium heat, melt butter and heat oil. Add chicken and sauté 5 minutes or until lightly browned.

2 Add stock, carrots, celery, onion, rice, parsley, salt, and pepper. Bring to boil, then reduce heat and simmer, covered, 20 minutes or until rice is tender.

3 In a small bowl, blend cornstarch, milk, and nutmeg, then stir into soup. Cook, stirring, until soup returns to simmer and thickens.

CHICKEN-SUCCOTASH SOUP

This protein-packed soup gets its flavor from the American Indian combination of lima beans and corn.

SERVES 4

1 tablespoon olive or vegetable oil

1 large yellow onion, coarsely chopped

1 broiler/fryer chicken (3-3 1/2 pounds) with giblets, cut into 8 pieces

5 parsley sprigs, 6 whole black peppercorns, 1 teaspoon dried marjoram, and 1 teaspoon thyme, crumbled and tied in cheesecloth

4 cups chicken stock

3/4 teaspoon salt

1/4 teaspoon black pepper

2 cups fresh or 1 package (10 ounces) frozen baby lima beans

2 cups fresh or 1 package (10 ounces) frozen whole-kernel corn

1 cup half-and-half or light cream

1/3 cup minced fresh parsley

1 Heat oil 1 minute in a large saucepan over medium heat. Add onion and sauté 3 minutes or until slightly softened but not browned.

2 Add chicken, giblets, spice bag, stock, salt, and pepper and bring to boil over high heat. Reduce heat and simmer, covered, 30 minutes or until chicken is done and juices run clear when meat is pierced with a knife.

3 Transfer chicken to a plate. Remove spice bag and giblets and skim fat from stock. When chicken is cool enough to handle, remove skin and bones and cut meat into bite-size pieces.

4 Meanwhile, add lima beans to stock and bring to boil over high heat. Reduce heat and simmer, covered, 10 minutes. Add corn and return to boil, then reduce heat and simmer, covered, 1 minute. Add chicken and half-and-half, cover, and simmer until just heated through. Stir in parsley.

CHICKEN STEW WITH APPLES

There's an Old World feeling to this dish, which is made with apples, cabbage, and potatoes. When fresh cider is out of season, you can use apple juice or hard cider instead.

SERVES 4

2 tablespoons unsalted butter

1 chicken (about 3 1/2 pounds), cut into 8 pieces and skin removed

1/4 cup all-purpose flour

1 small onion, finely chopped

1 1/2 pounds all-purpose potatoes, peeled and thickly sliced

1 small head green cabbage, halved and cut into 1-inch wedges

2 Granny Smith apples, peeled and cut into 1/2-inch chunks

1/2 cup apple cider

3/4 teaspoon salt

1/2 teaspoon black pepper

1 Preheat oven to 350°F. In a Dutch oven or soup pot over medium heat, melt butter. Place flour in a shallow dish and dredge chicken, shaking off excess. Add chicken to pot and sauté until golden, about 4 minutes on each side. Using a slotted spoon, transfer to a plate.

2 Add onion to pot, reduce heat to low, and sauté until soft, about 5 minutes. Add potatoes, cabbage, and apples, then cover and cook, stirring occasionally, until cabbage is wilted, about 10 minutes. Add cider, salt, and pepper, increase heat to high, and cook until liquid is slightly reduced, about 2 minutes.

3 When chicken is cool enough to handle, remove bones and cut meat into bite-size pieces. Return to pot and bring to boil. Cover and bake until chicken is cooked through, about 50 minutes.

CHICKEN STEW WITH PEARS

This is an unusual but delightful pairing of fowl and fruit.

SERVES 4

2 tablespoons unsalted butter

1 chicken (about 3 1/2 pounds), cut into 8 pieces and skin removed

1/4 cup all-purpose flour

2 cups frozen pearl onions

1 tablespoon sugar

2 firm-ripe pears, peeled and sliced

3/4 cup chicken stock

1/4 cup balsamic vinegar

1/2 teaspoon salt

1/2 teaspoon black pepper

1/2 teaspoon dried tarragon

1/4 cup heavy cream

1/4 cup chopped fresh parsley

1 Preheat oven to 350°F. In a Dutch oven over medium heat, melt butter. Place flour in a shallow dish and dredge chicken, shaking off excess. Add to Dutch oven and sauté until golden, about 4 minutes on each side. Using a slotted spoon, transfer to a plate.

2 Add onions to Dutch oven, reduce heat to low, sprinkle with sugar, and sauté until golden, about 5 minutes. Add pears and sauté until crisp-tender, about 5 minutes. Add stock, vinegar, salt, and pepper, increase heat to high, and cook until liquid is slightly reduced, about 2 minutes.

3 When chicken is cool enough to handle, remove bones and cut meat into bite-size pieces. Return to Dutch oven and bring to boil. Cover and bake until chicken is cooked through, about 50 minutes. Return Dutch oven to stove, add cream, and cook over high heat until slightly reduced. Stir in parsley.

CHICKEN GUMBO

This Louisiana stew, full of peppers and okra, is a favorite one-dish meal.

SERVES 4

1 tablespoon unsalted butter

1 large yellow onion, chopped

1 garlic clove, minced

1/2 small green bell pepper, cored, seeded, and chopped

1 medium celery stalk, chopped

2 tablespoons all-purpose flour

1 can (16 ounces) low-sodium crushed tomatoes

1 cup canned low-sodium chicken broth

1/4 teaspoon hot red pepper sauce

2 cups sliced fresh okra or 1 package (10 ounces) frozen sliced okra

1 1/2 cups cubed cooked chicken or turkey

1/2 teaspoon fresh lemon juice

1 In a large heavy saucepan over medium heat, melt butter. Add onion, garlic, bell pepper, and celery and sauté 5 minutes or until softened.

2 Blend in flour and cook, stirring, 3 minutes. Slowly stir in tomatoes and broth, then add red pepper sauce. Cook, stirring constantly, until mixture thickens and comes to boil, about 3 minutes. Add okra and return to boil, then reduce heat and simmer, covered, 6 minutes. Add chicken and heat through, stirring occasionally, about 4 minutes. Stir in lemon juice.

HERBED CHICKEN STEW

This chicken and vegetable stew is heart-healthy as well as heartwarming because it's flavored with lean turkey bacon instead of fatty pork.

SERVES 4

3 turkey bacon slices, cut crosswise into thin strips

1 teaspoon olive oil

1 small onion, chopped

2 garlic cloves, minced

2 red bell peppers, cored, seeded, and cut into thick slices

6 ounces fresh mushrooms, quartered

1/3 cup dry sherry or chicken broth

1 1/4 cups canned fat-free low-sodium chicken broth

3/4 teaspoon dried thyme

1/2 teaspoon salt

1/4 teaspoon black pepper

1 pound skinless, boneless chicken thighs, cut into 1-inch chunks

1/4 cup fat-free sour cream

2 tablespoons all-purpose flour

1 In a nonstick Dutch oven over medium heat, cook bacon in oil until slightly crisp, about 3 minutes.

2 Add 1/4 cup water, onion, and garlic and sauté 3 minutes or until onion begins to brown. Add bell peppers and mushrooms, cover, and cook, stirring occasionally, until crisp-tender, about 4 minutes.

3 Stir in sherry and cook 2 minutes. Add broth, thyme, salt, and black pepper and bring to boil. Add chicken, reduce heat, and simmer, covered, 20 minutes or until cooked through.

4 In a small bowl, stir together sour cream and flour. Whisk into soup and cook, stirring, until slightly thickened, about 2 minutes.

CHICKEN STEW WITH SPRING VEGETABLES

Scallions, carrots, tiny red potatoes, and peas give this stew a fresh flavor made piquant with rosemary.

SERVES 4

1 tablespoon olive oil

4 skinless, boneless chicken breast halves (about 1 1/2 pounds total)

1/4 cup all-purpose flour

6 scallions, cut into 1-inch lengths

3 carrots, cut into 2-inch lengths

8 garlic cloves

1 pound small red potatoes, quartered

3/4 cup chicken stock

1/2 teaspoon salt

1/2 teaspoon dried rosemary

1 cup frozen peas

1 Heat oil in a nonstick Dutch oven over medium heat. Place flour in a shallow dish and dredge chicken, reserving excess. Add to Dutch oven and sauté until golden, about 4 minutes on each side. Using a slotted spoon, transfer to a plate.

2 Preheat oven to 350°F. Add scallions, carrots, and garlic to Dutch oven and sauté until garlic is lightly colored, about 5 minutes. Add potatoes, broth, salt, and rosemary and bring to boil. Return chicken to Dutch oven and bring to boil. Cover and bake until chicken is cooked through and potatoes are tender, about 45 minutes.

3 Return Dutch oven to stove. Using a slotted spoon, transfer chicken to a platter. Add peas to Dutch oven. In a small bowl, combine reserved flour and 1/2 cup cooking liquid. Stir into stew, bring to boil over high heat, and cook until slightly thickened, about 1 minute. Spoon over chicken.

CHICKEN STEW WITH BUTTERNUT SQUASH

This chicken and winter squash combination makes an appealing autumn dinner.

SERVES 4

1 tablespoon vegetable oil

3 tablespoons all-purpose flour

1 1/4 pounds skinless, boneless chicken breast, cut into 1-inch chunks

1 onion, cut into 1/2-inch chunks

4 garlic cloves, slivered

1 large butternut squash (2 1/2 pounds), peeled and cut into 1-inch chunks

2 cups canned low-sodium chopped tomatoes

1 cup chicken stock

1/2 cup apple juice

2 tablespoons low-sodium tomato paste

1/2 teaspoon dried sage

1/2 teaspoon salt

1/4 teaspoon black pepper

1 Heat 1 1/2 teaspoons oil in a large nonstick Dutch oven, soup pot, or flameproof baking dish over medium heat. Place flour in a shallow dish and dredge chicken, shaking off excess. Add half of chicken to pot and sauté 3 minutes or until lightly browned on both sides. Transfer to a plate. Repeat with remaining oil and chicken.

2 Add onion and garlic to pot and sauté 7 minutes or until onion is softened. Add squash and stir to coat. Add tomatoes, stock, apple juice, tomato paste, sage, salt, and pepper and bring to boil. Reduce heat and simmer, covered, 7 minutes.

3 Return chicken to pot and simmer, covered, 10 minutes or until chicken is cooked through and squash is tender.

CHICKEN AND CARROT STEW

Here's a simple low-fat stew packed with protein and beta-carotene as well as flavor.

SERVES 4

1 tablespoon olive oil

2 tablespoons all-purpose flour

4 skinless, boneless chicken breast halves
    (1 pound total), quartered crosswise

1 large onion, cut into 1-inch chunks

3 garlic cloves, minced

1 pound peeled baby carrots

2/3 cup chicken stock

1/2 teaspoon dried marjoram

1/2 teaspoon salt

1/4 teaspoon ground ginger

1/4 teaspoon black pepper

1 Heat oil in a large nonstick skillet over medium heat. Place flour in a shallow dish and dredge chicken, shaking off excess. Add chicken to skillet and sauté 2 minutes per side or until lightly browned. Using a slotted spoon, transfer to a plate.

2 Add onion and garlic to skillet and sauté 7 minutes or until onion is tender. Add carrots and toss to coat. Add 2/3 cup water, stock, marjoram, salt, ginger, and pepper and bring to boil. Reduce heat and simmer, covered, 7 minutes or until carrots are crisp-tender. Add chicken, cover, and simmer 4 minutes or until chicken and carrots are tender.

CHICKEN AND LENTIL STEW

Even though the lentils simmer for 45 minutes, they won't turn mushy because the acid in the tomatoes slows the rate at which lentils cook.

SERVES 4

1 tablespoon olive oil

4 large skinless, boneless chicken thighs
    (4 ounces each), quartered

1 onion, finely chopped

1 yellow or red bell pepper, cored, seeded,
    and diced

4 garlic cloves, minced

3/4 cup lentils

1 1/4 cups chicken stock

3/4 cup canned low-sodium tomatoes,
    undrained, chopped

1 teaspoon ground coriander

1 teaspoon ground ginger

1/2 teaspoon salt

10 ounces red potatoes, cut into
    1/2-inch chunks

1 Heat oil in a large nonstick skillet over medium heat. Add chicken and cook 6 minutes or until browned on both sides. Using a slotted spoon, transfer to a plate.

2 Add onion, bell pepper, and garlic to skillet and sauté 5 minutes or until softened. Add 1/2 cup water, lentils, stock, tomatoes, coriander, ginger, and salt. Bring to boil, then reduce heat and simmer, covered, 20 minutes or until lentils are just barely tender.

3 Return chicken to skillet, add potatoes, and return to boil. Reduce heat and simmer, covered, 25 minutes or until chicken is cooked through and potatoes are tender.

LATIN AMERICAN CHICKEN STEW

Turmeric—in place of costly saffron—tints the rice a rich golden yellow in this adaptation of arroz con pollo.

SERVES 4

2 tablespoons olive oil
1 chicken (about 3 1/2 pounds), cut into
    8 pieces and skin removed
1/4 cup all-purpose flour
3 scallions, thinly sliced
1 cup rice
1/2 teaspoon ground turmeric
1 1/4 cups chicken stock
1 can (19 ounces) black beans,
    drained and rinsed
1 teaspoon grated lemon zest
1/2 teaspoon salt

1 Preheat oven to 350°F. Heat oil in a Dutch oven over medium-high heat. Place flour in a shallow dish and dredge chicken, shaking off excess. Add chicken to Dutch oven and sauté until golden, about 4 minutes on each side. Using a slotted spoon, transfer to a plate. When cool enough to handle, remove bones and cut into bite-size pieces.

2 Add scallions to Dutch oven and sauté until soft, about 1 minute. Stir in 3/4 cup water, rice, turmeric, stock, beans, lemon zest, and salt and bring to boil. Add chicken and return to boil. Cover and bake until chicken and rice are tender, about 40 minutes.

THAI CHICKEN STEW

Thai cooking balances tastes and textures. Here, a bland, creamy sauce is made interesting with garlic, ginger, and lime juice as well as fresh herbs and peanut butter.

SERVES 4

2 teaspoons vegetable oil
1 red bell pepper, cored, seeded,
    and cut into 1/2-inch squares
2 garlic cloves, minced
1 tablespoon minced fresh ginger
1 pound all-purpose potatoes, peeled
    and cut into 1/2-inch chunks
1 cup chicken stock
1 pound skinless, boneless chicken breast,
    cut into 1-inch chunks
2 cups unflavored soy milk
1/3 cup chopped fresh basil
1/4 cup chopped fresh cilantro
2 tablespoons fresh lime juice
2 tablespoons reduced-sodium soy sauce
1 tablespoon reduced-fat peanut butter
2 teaspoons dark brown sugar
1/4 teaspoon coconut extract

1 Heat oil in a large nonstick skillet over medium heat. Add bell pepper, garlic, and ginger and sauté 4 minutes or until pepper is crisp-tender. Add potatoes and stock and bring to boil. Reduce heat and simmer, covered, 7 minutes or until potatoes are firm-tender.

2 Add chicken, soy milk, basil, cilantro, lime juice, soy sauce, peanut butter, brown sugar, and coconut extract. Bring to boil, then reduce heat and simmer, covered, 5 minutes or until chicken and potatoes are cooked through.

OLD ENGLISH STEWED ROSEMARY CHICKEN

Mace, ginger, and rosemary are savory seasonings for chicken in this appealing dish.

SERVES 4

4 shallots, finely chopped
2 teaspoons grated fresh ginger
1/2 teaspoon ground mace
Pinch of cayenne pepper
1 cup red wine or chicken stock
1 tablespoon fresh rosemary leaves
4 chicken quarters or 8 thighs, skin removed
2 tablespoons all-purpose flour
1 tablespoon butter
1 tablespoon sunflower oil
Salt and black pepper
Rosemary sprigs

1 In a large bowl, combine shallots, ginger, mace, cayenne, wine, rosemary leaves, and chicken. Turn to coat evenly, then cover and refrigerate several hours or overnight.

2 Drain chicken, reserving marinade, and pat dry with paper towels. Sprinkle evenly with flour.

3 In a Dutch oven over medium heat, melt butter and heat oil. Add chicken and cook until lightly browned. Add marinade and bring to boil. Reduce heat, cover, and simmer, turning occasionally, 30 minutes or until chicken is tender and juices run clear when meat is pierced with a knife. Season to taste with salt and pepper and top with rosemary sprigs.

COUNTRY CAPTAIN CHICKEN STEW

Here's a simple curried chicken dish that would honor any guest. Serve it over hot cooked rice.

SERVES 4 TO 6

2 1/2-3 pounds chicken breasts, thighs, and drumsticks
3/4 teaspoon salt
1 tablespoon vegetable oil
3 large green bell peppers, cored, seeded, and cut into bite-size strips
3 large yellow onions, chopped
3 cans (14 1/2 ounces each) low-sodium tomatoes, undrained, cut up
1 cup golden raisins
2 teaspoons curry powder
1 1/2 teaspoons dried thyme
1/4 teaspoon cayenne pepper
1/4 teaspoon black pepper
1/8 teaspoon ground cloves

1 Remove chicken skin. Rinse and drain chicken and pat dry with paper towels.

2 In a soup pot or Dutch oven, combine chicken, enough cold water to cover, and 1/4 teaspoon salt. Bring to boil and skim off foam. Reduce heat, cover, and simmer until chicken is tender and no longer pink, about 30 minutes. Transfer to a plate. When cool enough to handle, remove bones and cut meat into bite-size pieces.

3 Heat oil in a 12-inch skillet over medium-high heat. Add bell peppers and onions and cook until tender, about 5 minutes. Stir in tomatoes, raisins, curry powder, thyme, cayenne, black pepper, cloves, and remaining salt. Bring to boil, then reduce heat and simmer, covered, 15 minutes. Stir in chicken and cook until heated through.

FRENCH-STYLE CHICKEN IN WINE

SERVES 4

1 1/2 tablespoons garlic-flavored olive oil

2 ounces Canadian bacon, cut into thin strips

12 shallots or pearl onions, peeled

12 cremini or white mushrooms

4 chicken pieces, such as boneless, skinless
    breast halves (about 6 ounces each)

Parsley sprigs, stems bruised

Thyme sprigs

1 bay leaf

2/3 cup chicken stock

1 1/2 cups full-bodied red wine

Salt and black pepper

2 carrots, cut into chunks

Pinch of sugar

1 tablespoon cornstarch

Chopped fresh parsley

This updated and low-fat version of a classic bistro dish requires the addition of only a baguette of fresh French bread for a truly satisfying meal.

1 Heat 1 tablespoon oil in a Dutch oven or soup pot over medium heat. Add Canadian bacon and sauté 3 minutes or until crisp. Using a slotted spoon, transfer to a plate.

2 Add shallots and sauté 5 minutes or until browned. Using a slotted spoon, transfer to a plate. Add mushrooms and remaining oil, if needed, and sauté 3 minutes or until golden.

3 Return half of bacon and shallots to pot. Place chicken on top and sprinkle with remaining bacon and shallots. Tie herbs into a bouquet garni and add to pot with stock and wine. Season generously with salt and pepper.

4 Bring to boil, then reduce heat and simmer, covered, 15 minutes. Add carrots and simmer until chicken juices run clear when meat is pierced with a knife and carrots are fork-tender.

5 Arrange chicken on a warm serving platter. Strain stock into a saucepan, adding Canadian bacon, mushrooms, shallots, and carrots to platter and reserving bouquet garni. Cover and keep warm.

6 Return bouquet garni to stock and add sugar, then bring to boil and cook until sauce is reduced to about 1 1/2 cups. Meanwhile, in a cup, combine cornstarch with a little water until a smooth paste forms. Stir into sauce and simmer until thickened. Remove bouquet garni, spoon sauce over chicken and vegetables, and sprinkle with parsley.

CORONATION CHICKEN STEW

SERVES 6

1 chicken (about 3 1/2 pounds)
1 can (14 1/2 ounces) chicken broth
1 bay leaf
1 large parsley sprig
1 large thyme sprig
8 whole black peppercorns
2 teaspoons sunflower oil
2 shallots, finely chopped
1 tablespoon medium Madras
    curry paste or powder
1/2 cup red wine
1 tablespoon tomato puree
1 tablespoon apricot jam
1 tablespoon fresh lemon juice
5 1/2 ounces low-fat mayonnaise
5 1/2 ounces low-fat yogurt
Salt and black pepper
1 bunch watercress, washed and trimmed

1 Place chicken in a large soup pot and add enough broth to cover. Add bay leaf, parsley, thyme, and peppercorns. Bring to boil, then reduce heat and simmer, covered, until chicken is cooked through, about 1 hour 20 minutes. Remove from heat and let cool in stock 30 minutes.

2 Heat oil in a saucepan over medium heat. Add shallots and sauté 4 minutes or until softened. Add curry paste and stir 30 seconds, then add wine, tomato puree, jam, and lemon juice. Bring to boil, then reduce heat and simmer, uncovered, 5 minutes or until reduced by half. Remove from heat and let cool.

3 Transfer chicken to a plate. Strain stock, discarding spices, and reserve for another use. When chicken is cool enough to handle, remove skin and bones and cut meat into thick slices

4 In a blender or food processor, puree curry mixture with mayonnaise and yogurt until smooth. Add salt and pepper to taste and stir in chicken. Serve on a bed of watercress.

Originally created by Constance Spry for the coronation of England's Queen Elizabeth II in 1953, this now-classic dish is made lighter by using yogurt instead of cream. It's usually served on a bed of watercress with wild rice as an accompaniment.

CHICKEN STEW WITH LEEKS AND APPLE DUMPLINGS

Leeks and apple dumplings complement this stew, which is simmered in cider with root vegetables and mustard.

SERVES 4

Stew:

2 tablespoons vegetable oil

4 skinless, boneless chicken breasts, cut into 1-inch cubes

2 bay leaves

1 large onion, chopped

2 large carrots, peeled and cut into chunks

2 parsnips, peeled and cut into chunks

1/2 turnip, peeled and coarsely diced

1 celery stalk, diced

1 tablespoon whole-grain mustard

2 1/2 cups dry cider

Salt and black pepper

Dumplings:

1 tablespoon olive oil

1 small leek, finely chopped

1 tart apple, peeled and coarsely grated

1 cup self-rising flour

4 tablespoons butter, softened

1/2 cup low-fat (1%) milk

1 For soup, heat oil in a large Dutch oven or soup pot over medium heat. Increase heat, add chicken, and cook until browned, about 5 minutes. Transfer to a plate.

2 Reduce heat to medium and add bay leaves, onion, carrots, parsnips, turnip, and celery. Stir well, cover, and cook 5 minutes. Return chicken to pot and stir in mustard and cider. Bring to boil, then reduce heat and simmer, covered, 20 minutes. Season to taste with salt and pepper.

3 For dumplings, heat oil in a small saucepan over medium heat. Add leek and sauté 5 minutes or until softened. Transfer to a medium bowl and stir in apple. Add flour and butter, then stir in milk to make a soft dough. Using floured hands, shape into 16 balls.

4 Arrange dumplings on top of stew, cover, and simmer 25 minutes or until dumplings rise and are fluffy and shiny on top. Ladle stew and dumplings into bowls.

CHICKEN STEW WITH MARSALA WINE AND FENNEL

Cooking with wine gives depth to a sauce without adding alcohol or calories. Both burn away, leaving only lovely flavor behind.

SERVES 4

1 chicken (about 3 pounds) cut up

2 tablespoons all-purpose flour

Salt and black pepper

2 tablespoons extra-virgin olive oil

1 large leek, cleaned and coarsely chopped

1 tablespoon chopped fresh parsley

1 teaspoon fennel seed

6 tablespoons Marsala wine

2 1/4 cups chicken stock

2 medium fennel bulbs, trimmed and cut into chunks

2 cups shelled fresh or frozen peas

Juice of 1 lemon

1 large egg, lightly beaten

Chopped fresh parsley

Shredded lemon rind

1 Remove skin from chicken. Season flour with salt and pepper and dust over chicken.

2 Heat 1 tablespoon oil in a large skillet over medium heat. Add leek, parsley, and fennel seed and sauté 5 minutes or until leek is softened. Using a slotted spoon, transfer to a plate.

3 Heat remaining oil, add chicken, and sauté 6 minutes or until golden. Transfer to a plate. Add wine to skillet, bring to boil, and cook until reduced to 2 tablespoons glaze. Pour in stock and add leek mixture and dark meat chicken (wait to add breasts to avoid overcooking). Add fennel and bring to boil, then reduce heat and simmer, covered, 10 to 15 minutes. Add breasts and simmer, covered, 15 minutes or until chicken is tender and juices run clear when meat is pierced with a knife. Add peas during last 5 minutes of cooking.

4 Using a slotted spoon, transfer chicken and vegetables to a serving bowl and keep warm.

5 In a small bowl, mix lemon juice into egg. Slowly stir in 4 tablespoons hot stock, then slowly stir back into skillet. Return chicken and vegetables to skillet and warm through over low heat so sauce does not curdle. Season to taste with salt and pepper and return to serving bowl. Garnish with parsley and lemon rind.

MOROCCAN CHICKEN STEW

Moroccans traditionally cook this spicy dish in a pot called a couscoussier, which allows the moisture from the stew to steam the couscous.

SERVES 6

2 cups reduced-sodium tomato juice

1/4 teaspoon cumin seed or 1/8 teaspoon ground cumin

1/4 teaspoon coriander seed or 1/8 teaspoon ground coriander

1/8 teaspoon hot red pepper flakes

1/8 teaspoon salt

1/8 teaspoon black pepper

1 1/2 cups couscous

1 can (14 ounces) chickpeas, drained and rinsed

1 tablespoon olive or canola oil

2 large onions, coarsely chopped

4 boneless, skinless chicken breast halves (about 1 pound), thickly sliced

4 zucchini, diced

1 can (14 ounces) crushed tomatoes

1 In a large nonstick saucepan, combine tomato juice and 1/4 cup water and bring to boil over medium-high heat.

2 Meanwhile, in a small bowl, crush cumin and coriander seed with red pepper flakes, salt, and pepper. Add to pan, reduce heat, and simmer 10 minutes.

3 Preheat oven to 375°F. Add couscous to pan and stir just to combine. Cover, remove from heat, and let stand 5 minutes or until couscous is tender and liquid is absorbed. Add chickpeas and, using a fork, lightly stir to fluff up couscous. Spoon in an even layer into a 13 x 9 x 2-inch baking dish.

4 Meanwhile, in a nonstick skillet, heat oil. Add onions and sauté 5 minutes or until wilted. Add chicken and sauté 5 minutes. Add zucchini and tomatoes and bring to boil. Remove from heat and spoon chicken and vegetables over couscous. Bake 20 minutes or until chicken and zucchini are tender.

CHICKEN STEW WITH LEMONGRASS

A cross between a soup and a stew, this dish captures the exciting spicy and sour flavors of Southeast Asia.

SERVES 4

1 small fresh hot chile, split lengthwise but left whole (wear gloves when handling; they burn)

1 garlic clove, halved

1/2-inch piece fresh ginger, peeled and cut into 4 slices

2 stalks lemongrass, bruised and halved
Note: "bruised" means just what it says and is a legitimate cooking term. Bruising of herbs like lemongrass releases flavor.

4 chicken pieces, such as breasts or thighs, (about 6 ounces each), skin removed

1 shallot, finely chopped

9 ounces *haricots verts* or young green beans, trimmed and cut into bite-size pieces

1 zucchini, sliced lengthwise with a vegetable peeler into thin strips

2 1/2 ounces creamed coconut, crumbled

Juice and finely grated zest of 1 lime

Salt and black pepper

2 tablespoons fresh cilantro, chopped

1 Place 3 1/2 cups water in a medium saucepan over high heat. Thread chile, garlic, and ginger onto a wooden toothpick (this makes them easy to remove later) and add to pan. Add lemongrass, bring to boil, and cook 1 minute. Remove from heat, cover, and let stand 30 minutes.

2 Return to boil, then reduce heat to low. Add chicken, shallot, and beans and simmer 12 to 15 minutes or until juices run clear when meat is pierced with a knife. Add zucchini during last 2 minutes of cooking.

3 Using a slotted spoon, transfer chicken, beans, and zucchini to a warm bowl. Add a little stock to keep them moist, then cover tightly and keep warm. Return stock to boil and add coconut, stirring until dissolved. Cook, uncovered, 5 to 6 minutes or until liquid is reduced by a third.

4 When chicken is cool enough to handle, remove bones and coarsely shred meat. Return meat, beans, and zucchini to soup and stir, then reheat briefly. Stir in lime zest and juice and season to taste with salt and pepper. Divide chicken and vegetables among 4 soup bowls. Discard lemongrass and toothpick of chili, garlic, and ginger and ladle broth into bowls. Sprinkle with cilantro.

NANA'S CHICKEN STEW

Farm-fresh cream made old-fashioned chicken stews wonderfully rich. This version uses half-and-half to cut the fat while keeping the luscious flavor.

SERVES 4

2 1/2-3 pounds chicken breasts, thighs, and drumsticks

2 teaspoons dill weed

1/2 teaspoon salt

1/4 teaspoon black pepper

4 carrots, cut into 1/2-inch-thick slices

2 medium all-purpose potatoes, cut into 1-inch cubes

2 parsnips, peeled and cut into 1/2-inch-thick slices

3 tablespoons all-purpose flour

1/3 cup half-and-half

1 Remove chicken skin. Rinse and drain chicken and pat dry with paper towels.

2 In a soup pot or Dutch oven over medium-high heat, combine 3 1/2 cups water, chicken, dill, salt, and pepper. Bring to boil, then reduce heat and simmer, covered, 5 minutes. Stir in carrots, potatoes, and parsnips and return to boil. Reduce heat and simmer, covered, until chicken is tender and no longer pink, about 25 minutes. Transfer chicken and vegetables to a serving bowl.

3 In a small bowl, whisk 1/2 cup cold water and flour. Whisk into pot and cook, whisking constantly, 2 minutes. Stir in half-and-half, bring to boil, and cook 1 minute. Serve over chicken and vegetables.

FAMILY BRUNSWICK STEW

This thrifty Southern dish originated with American Indian women, who used rabbit and squirrel instead of chicken. The stew can be made a day or two ahead without any loss of flavor.

SERVES 4

1 chicken (2 1/2-3 pounds), excess
    fat removed

5 large parsley sprigs

6 whole black peppercorns

1 bay leaf, crumbled

4 cups canned low-sodium
    chicken broth or water

1 1/2 teaspoons ground poultry seasoning

1 1/2 teaspoons ground sage

2 medium carrots, peeled and cut into
    1-inch-thick slices

2 large celery stalks, cut into 1-inch-thick slices

2 medium all-purpose potatoes,
    peeled and cut into 1-inch cubes

1 can (14 1/2 ounces) low-sodium
    tomatoes, undrained

1 medium yellow onion, chopped

1 cup fresh or frozen lima beans

1 cup fresh or frozen whole-kernel corn

1/2 teaspoon black pepper

1 Place chicken and giblets in a 6-quart Dutch oven or soup pot. Tie parsley, peppercorns, and bay leaf in cheesecloth and add to pot along with broth, 1/2 teaspoon poultry seasoning, and 1/2 teaspoon sage.

2 Bring to boil, then reduce heat and simmer, covered, 1 hour or until chicken is tender. Transfer chicken and giblets to a platter and skim fat from broth.

3 Add carrots, celery, potatoes, tomatoes, onion, beans, and another 1/2 teaspoon poultry seasoning and 1/2 teaspoon sage to pot. Simmer, covered, 30 minutes, stirring occasionally.

4 When chicken is cool enough to handle, remove skin and bones. Cut meat and giblets into bite-size pieces, return to pot, and add corn. Simmer, covered, 30 minutes, stirring occasionally. Stir in pepper and remaining poultry seasoning and sage. Remove cheesecloth bag.

BRUNSWICK STEW FOR A CROWD

This Brunswick stew, ideal for a potluck supper, is thickened with okra.

SERVES 10

2 broiler/fryer chickens (3 pounds each),
    skin removed and cut into 16 pieces

1 teaspoon salt

2 large yellow onions, sliced

1 1/2 pounds all-purpose potatoes,
    peeled and diced

1 can (28 ounces) low-sodium chopped
    tomatoes, undrained

1 tablespoon sugar

1 teaspoon black pepper

4 cups fresh corn or 2 packages (10 ounces
    each) frozen whole-kernel corn

2 cups shelled fresh lima beans or 1 package
    (9 ounces) frozen lima beans

2 cups sliced fresh okra or 1 package
    (10 ounces) frozen cut okra

1 In an 8-quart Dutch oven or soup pot over high heat, bring 8 cups cold water, chicken, and

1/2 teaspoon salt to boil. Reduce heat and simmer, uncovered, 45 minutes or until chicken is tender, skimming off foam occasionally. Using a slotted spoon, transfer chicken to a plate.

2 Add onions, potatoes, tomatoes, sugar, pepper, and remaining salt and return to boil. Reduce heat, cover, and simmer 15 minutes. Add corn and beans, cover, and simmer 5 minutes.

3 When chicken is cool enough to handle, remove bones and cut meat into bite-size pieces. Stir okra and chicken into pot, cover, and simmer 5 minutes or until okra is tender and chicken is heated through.

ONE-POT JAPANESE CHICKEN

Based on Japanese-style fondues, in which food is cooked at the table in savory broth, this chicken and vegetable stew makes a satisfying main course all in one pot. You can dip chicken pieces from your bowl into ponzu sauce at the table. The sauce can be made a day or more in advance.

SERVES 4

Sauce:
3 tablespoons mirin (sweet rice wine)
Juice of 1 lemon
Juice of 1 1/2 limes
3 tablespoons rice vinegar
3 ounces dark soy sauce

Stew:
8 ounces fine rice noodles
2 cups chicken stock
1 1/4 pounds skinless, boneless chicken breasts, thinly sliced
4 medium carrots, sliced
8 ounces snow peas

1 can (5 1/2 ounces) sliced bamboo shoots, drained
4 ounces shiitake mushrooms, sliced
4 ounces Napa cabbage, shredded

1 For sauce, pour mirin into a small saucepan over high heat, bring to boil, and cook 30 seconds to evaporate alcohol. Stir in lemon juice, lime juice, vinegar, and soy sauce and remove from heat. Pour into a dish and cover.

2 For stew, place noodles in a bowl, add enough cold water to cover, and soak 10 minutes, then drain. In a large Dutch oven over medium heat, bring stock to boil. Add chicken, reduce heat, and simmer, covered, 10 minutes.

3 Add carrots and simmer 5 minutes. Add snow peas and bamboo shoots and simmer 3 minutes. Stir in mushrooms and cabbage and bring to boil. Reduce heat and simmer, covered, 3 minutes. Stir in noodles and simmer until hot, about 2 minutes.

4 Divide sauce among 4 small bowls. Ladle stew into warm serving bowls and serve ponzu on the side.

CHICKEN AND DUMPLINGS

SERVES 4

Soup:

1 broiler/fryer chicken (2 1/2-3 pounds), skin removed and cut into 8 pieces

1/4 teaspoon salt

1/4 teaspoon black pepper

1 tablespoon olive oil

2 cups chopped leeks

1 1/2 cups chopped carrots

1/2 cup chopped celery

1/2 teaspoon dried marjoram

1/2 teaspoon dried thyme

1/4 cup all-purpose flour

5 1/2 cups homemade chicken stock or canned low-sodium chicken broth

1/2 cup milk

1 teaspoon fresh lemon juice

3 tablespoons chopped fresh parsley

Dumplings:

1 3/4 cups all-purpose flour

1/2 teaspoon baking soda

1/4 teaspoon salt

3 tablespoons vegetable shortening

2/3-3/4 cup low-fat buttermilk

1 For soup, sprinkle chicken with salt and pepper. Heat oil in a deep nonstick 12-inch skillet over medium-high heat. Add chicken and cook 4 minutes on each side or until browned. Using a slotted spoon, transfer to a plate. When cool enough to handle, remove bones and cut meat into bite-size pieces.

2 Add leeks, carrots, celery, marjoram, and thyme to skillet and sauté 5 minutes. Stir in flour and cook until bubbling, then stir in stock and milk. Add chicken and bring to boil, then reduce heat and simmer, covered, 20 minutes. Stir in lemon juice.

3 For dumplings, combine flour, baking soda, and salt in a medium bowl. Using 2 knives or a pastry cutter, cut in shortening, then stir in enough buttermilk to form a soft dough. Turn out onto a floured surface and roll into an 8 x 8 x 1/2-inch square, then cut into sixteen 2-inch squares.

4 Slide dumplings into skillet and simmer 10 minutes, covered, or until a toothpick inserted in a dumpling comes out clean. Top with parsley.

For many Americans with Northern European backgrounds, this is pure comfort food.

POACHED CHICKEN

Somewhere between a soup and a stew, poached chicken offers a delicate balance of flavors in a one-dish meal.

SERVES 4

1 chicken (3 1/2 pounds)

6 cups chicken stock

8 parsley sprigs

2 bay leaves

4 carrots, cut into 1-inch pieces

2 leeks, white parts only, or onions, sliced

2 large all-purpose potatoes, peeled and cut into cubes

6 garlic cloves

1 tablespoon fresh lemon juice

1/8 teaspoon salt

1/8 teaspoon black pepper

1 Cut fat from both ends of chicken and wipe inside with paper towels. Tuck wings under body, fold skin over body cavity opening, and tie legs together with string. Place in a 4-quart Dutch oven or soup pot over medium heat, and add stock and 5 cups water. Bring to boil and skim off any foam.

2 Tie parsley and bay leaves together to make a bouquet garni. Add to pot with carrots, leeks, potatoes, and garlic; return to boil. Reduce heat and simmer, partially covered, 1 1/4 hours or until chicken and vegetables are cooked through. Transfer chicken to a platter and cover with foil to keep warm. Strain stock into a large heatproof bowl and skim off fat. Reserve vegetables and discard bouquet garni.

3 In a blender or food processor, puree half the vegetables and 1 1/2 cups stock. Pour into a saucepan, add lemon juice, salt, and pepper, and bring to a simmer. Remove skin and bones from chicken and carve meat. Place chicken and remaining vegetables on a platter and pour on sauce.

POACHED CHICKEN BREASTS WITH TOMATO SAUCE

When you are poaching chicken, keep it simmering. Boiling toughens the meat.

SERVES 4

4 skinless, boneless chicken breast halves (1 1/2 pounds)

3 cups chicken stock

8 ounces plum tomatoes, peeled and chopped

4 large carrots, diced

2 parsnips, peeled and diced

3 garlic cloves, finely chopped

1 bay leaf

1 tablespoon fresh lemon juice

1/8 teaspoon salt

1/8 teaspoon black pepper

1 Remove any fat from chicken. In a deep skillet or wide flameproof baking dish over medium heat, combine stock and 1 cup water and bring to boil.

2 Add tomatoes, carrots, parsnips, garlic, and bay leaf and return to boil. Reduce heat and simmer, covered, 10 minutes or until tender. Add chicken, making sure to cover with vegetables and stock. Cover and simmer 10 minutes or until cooked through.

3 Using a slotted spoon, transfer chicken to a plate, cover with foil, and keep warm. Transfer vegetables to a blender or food processor, cover, and puree until smooth. Add 1 cup stock and process until combined.

4 Remove bay leaf from pot and simmer remaining stock, uncovered, until reduced to about 1 1/2 cups. Stir in vegetable puree, lemon juice, salt, and pepper. Return to boil and add chicken, then reduce heat and simmer about 3 minutes or until heated through.

GREEK POACHED CHICKEN AND LEMON STEW

Here is the Greek version of a poached chicken dinner.

SERVES 4

1 chicken (3 1/2 pounds), cut into
    serving-size pieces
6 cups chicken stock
8 parsley sprigs
2 bay leaves
2 carrots, cut into 1-inch pieces
2 leeks, white parts only,
    or small onions, sliced
6 garlic cloves
Juice and grated zest of 1 lemon
1 teaspoon dried oregano
1/3 cup orzo or long-grain rice
2 teaspoons cornstarch
1 cup fat-free plain yogurt
1/8 teaspoon black pepper

1 Place chicken in a 4-quart Dutch oven over medium heat and add stock and 5 cups water. Bring to boil and skim off any foam. Tie parsley and bay leaves together to make a bouquet garni. Add to pot along with carrots, leeks, and garlic and return to boil. Reduce heat and simmer, partially covered, 40 minutes or until chicken and vegetables are cooked through.

2 Transfer chicken to a plate. Strain stock into a large saucepan and skim off fat. Reserve vegetables and discard bouquet garni. Add lemon zest and oregano to pan and bring to boil, then reduce heat and simmer, uncovered, 40 minutes or until reduced to 6 cups. Meanwhile, remove skin and bones from chicken and cut meat into 1-inch pieces. Add orzo to pan and simmer, covered, 15 minutes or until tender.

3 In a small bowl, whisk cornstarch into 1/4 cup stock until smooth, then stir into pan. Simmer 1 minute or until thickened. Add chicken, vegetables, and lemon juice and return to boil. Remove from heat, stir in yogurt, and season with pepper.

COCK-A-LEEKIE STEW

The name gives it away—this is a chicken and leek stew popular all over the British Isles and beyond.

SERVES 6

1 small chicken (about 2 1/2 pounds)
6 thick leeks, slit, washed, and coarsely
    chopped, green and white parts separated
6 whole black peppercorns
2 fresh bay leaves
12 prunes, coarsely chopped
2 tablespoons chopped fresh parsley

1 In a large saucepan, combine chicken, green leeks, peppercorns, bay leaves, and just enough water to cover chicken. Bring to boil, then reduce heat and simmer, covered, 20 minutes. Remove from heat, cover tightly, and let stand until chicken is cooked through and tender, about 1 hour.

2 Transfer chicken to a colander set over a bowl. When cool enough to handle, remove skin and bones and shred meat.

3 Remove green leeks, peppercorns, and bay leaves and return stock to pan. Add white leeks and bring to boil. Reduce heat and simmer, covered, 10 minutes or until tender. Add chicken and prunes and heat through. Serve sprinkled with parsley.

POST-THANKSGIVING TURKEY SOUP

First, make a rich stock using the turkey carcass. Then add your favorite vegetables for a soup that becomes a meal.

SERVES 8

Stock:
1 turkey carcass
1 chicken bouillon cube
1 celery stalk with leaves
1 small onion, halved
1 carrot
3 whole black peppercorns
1 garlic clove
1 teaspoon seasoned salt
1/4 teaspoon dried thyme

Soup:
2 chicken bouillon cubes
1/2-3/4 teaspoon black pepper
4 cups sliced carrots, celery, and/or other vegetables
3/4 cup chopped onion
4 cups diced cooked turkey

1 For stock, combine 8 cups water, carcass, bouillon, celery, onion, carrot, peppercorns, garlic, seasoned salt, and thyme in a Dutch oven or soup pot over medium-high heat. Bring to boil, then reduce heat and simmer, covered, 25 minutes. Strain stock into a large heatproof bowl, discarding bones and vegetables. When cool, skim off fat.

2 For soup, return 8 cups stock to pot and add bouillon, pepper, vegetables, and onion. Bring to boil, then reduce heat and simmer, covered, until tender, about 15 minutes. Add turkey and heat through.

OLD VIRGINIA TURKEY SOUP

This is a glorious, creamy soup that is a worthy end for a Thanksgiving turkey.

SERVES 16

1 turkey carcass
3 large onions, finely chopped
3 celery stalks, finely chopped
2 large carrots, finely chopped
1/4 cup long-grain rice
1 cup butter
1 1/2 cups all-purpose flour
1 pint half-and-half
1/2 teaspoon poultry seasoning
Salt and black pepper

1 Place carcass and 16 cups water in a large soup pot. Bring to boil, then reduce heat and simmer, uncovered, 1 hour. Remove from heat and transfer carcass to a plate. When cool enough to handle, remove bones and reserve meat. Strain stock into a large heatproof bowl.

2 In a large saucepan, combine onions, celery, carrots, rice, and 4 cups stock. Bring to boil, then reduce heat and simmer, covered, 20 minutes. Remove from heat.

3 In a large soup pot over medium heat, melt butter. Blend in flour and cook several minutes. Add half-and-half and 8 cups stock and cook, stirring, until beginning to thicken. Stir in vegetable mixture, turkey, poultry seasoning, and salt and pepper to taste. Simmer 4 to 5 minutes or until heated through.

TURKEY-WILD RICE SOUP

Turkey, wild rice, and mushrooms in a warming bowl of soup is a combination to take the edge off raw winter evenings.

SERVES 6

2 tablespoons butter

1 medium onion, chopped

1 can (4 ounces) sliced mushrooms, drained

2 cups chicken stock

1 package (6 ounces) long-grain and wild rice mix

2 cups diced cooked turkey

1 cup heavy cream

Chopped fresh parsley

1 In a large saucepan over low heat, melt butter. Add onion and mushrooms and sauté until onion is tender, about 4 minutes.

2 Add 3 cups water, stock, and rice mix with its seasonings. Bring to boil, then reduce heat and simmer, covered, 20 to 25 minutes or until rice is tender. Stir in turkey and cream and heat through. Sprinkle with parsley.

HARVEST TURKEY SOUP

Here is a delicious and healthy supper dish for lots and lots of people; all your guests will love it.

SERVES 20

1 turkey carcass (from 12-pound or larger turkey)

2 large carrots, shredded

1 cup chopped celery

1 large onion, chopped

4 chicken bouillon cubes

1 can (28 ounces) stewed tomatoes

3/4 cup fresh or frozen peas

3/4 cup long-grain rice

1 package (10 ounces) frozen chopped spinach

1 tablespoon salt *(optional)*

3/4 teaspoon black pepper

1/2 teaspoon dried marjoram

1/2 teaspoon dried thyme

1 Place turkey carcass and 20 cups water in a Dutch oven or soup pot. Bring to boil, then reduce heat and simmer, covered, 1 1/2 hours. Transfer carcass to a plate. When cool enough to handle, remove meat from bones and cut into bite-size pieces.

2 Strain stock and return to pot. Add carrots, celery, onion, and bouillon and bring to boil. Reduce heat and simmer, covered, 30 minutes. Add tomatoes, peas, rice, spinach, salt, if desired, pepper, marjoram, thyme, and turkey. Return to boil, then reduce heat and cook, uncovered, 20 minutes or until rice is tender.

TURKEY SOUP WITH RICE

Many Americans look forward to this soup as much as they do the roast turkey on Thanksgiving Day.

SERVES 8

1 turkey carcass (from 14-pound turkey)
1/2 cup long-grain rice
1 medium onion, finely chopped
4 celery stalks, finely chopped
2 carrots, grated
1 bay leaf
Dash of poultry seasoning
Salt *(optional)*
Black pepper
Onion powder
Garlic powder

1 Place carcass and 12 cups water in a large soup pot. Bring to boil, then reduce heat and simmer, covered, 4 to 5 hours.

2 Transfer carcass to a plate. When cool enough to handle, cut off and dice any meat. Return to pot and add rice, onion, celery, carrots, bay leaf, and poultry seasoning. Add salt, if desired, pepper, onion powder, and garlic powder to taste. Return to boil, then reduce heat and simmer, covered, until rice is cooked, about 20 minutes.

LEMONY TURKEY RICE SOUP

Lemon and cilantro add a deliciously different twist to turkey soup.

SERVES 8

6 cups chicken broth, divided
1 can (10 3/4 ounces) condensed cream
    of chicken soup
2 cups cooked rice
2 cups diced cooked turkey
1/4 teaspoon black pepper

2 tablespoons cornstarch
1/4 cup lemon juice
1/4 cup minced fresh cilantro

1 In a large saucepan, combine 5 1/2 cups broth, soup, rice, turkey, and pepper. Bring to boil and boil 3 minutes.

2 In a small bowl, combine cornstarch and remaining broth until smooth. Gradually stir mixture into hot soup.

3 Cook and stir 1 to 2 minutes or until thickened and heated through.

4 Remove from heat. Stir in lemon juice and cilantro.

TURKEY, SPINACH, AND RICE IN ROASTED GARLIC BROTH

A combination of garlic, enriched rice, fresh spinach, and lean turkey makes this a particularly healthy soup. (Photograph on page 7)

SERVES 4

2 medium whole heads garlic, unpeeled
2 tablespoons tomato paste
2 cans (14 1/2 ounces each) fat-free low-sodium
    chicken or turkey broth
1 cup cubed cooked turkey
1 cup cooked long-grain white rice
12 ounces spinach, trimmed
    and coarsely chopped
1/4 teaspoon black pepper
1/4 teaspoon hot red pepper flakes
1 tablespoon fresh lemon juice

1 Preheat oven to 400°F.

2 Cut top off top third of garlic heads and wrap each in foil. Bake until very soft, about 50 minutes. Let cool, remove foil, and squeeze pulp into a small bowl.

3 In a large saucepan, stir together garlic and tomato paste. Stir in broth and bring to boil. Add turkey, rice, spinach, pepper, and red pepper flakes and simmer, uncovered, 8 minutes. Just before serving, stir in lemon juice.

TURKEY SOUP WITH GREEN BEANS

Making soup from leftover Thanksgiving turkey is as traditional as the dinner itself.

SERVES 10

2 tablespoons unsalted butter

3 cups sliced fresh mushrooms

1 1/2 cups chopped yellow onions

1 cup sliced carrots

1 cup sliced celery

3 garlic cloves, minced

10 cups homemade turkey stock or canned low-sodium chicken broth

2/3 cup long-grain white rice

1 bay leaf

1 teaspoon salt

1/2 teaspoon black pepper

1 tablespoon chopped fresh thyme or 1/2 teaspoon dried thyme

1 tablespoon chopped fresh rosemary or 1/2 teaspoon dried rosemary

2 cups diced white turnips

2 cups bite-size pieces fresh or frozen green beans

2 cups diced cooked turkey

2 tablespoons fresh lemon juice

1/4 cup chopped fresh parsley

1 In an 8-quart soup pot over medium-high heat, melt butter. Add mushrooms, onions, carrots, celery, and garlic and sauté 5 minutes or until tender.

2 Add stock, rice, bay leaf, salt, pepper, thyme, and rosemary. Increase heat to high and bring to boil. Reduce heat and simmer, uncovered, 20 minutes, stirring and skimming the surface occasionally.

3 Add turnips and beans and simmer 7 minutes. Stir in turkey and simmer 5 minutes or until vegetables are tender. Remove bay leaf and stir in lemon juice and parsley.

TURKEY SOUP WITH VEGETABLES

Wise cooks leave a little meat on the turkey bones so the soup is both hearty and delicious.

SERVES 6

Stock:

1 meaty turkey carcass, broken up

2 medium yellow onions or rutabagas, quartered

2 cups loosely packed parsley sprigs or celery leaves

4 garlic cloves, quartered

4 bay leaves

2 teaspoons whole black peppercorns

1 teaspoon salt

Soup:

1 large yellow onion, chopped

1/2 cup long-grain white rice

4 cups fresh vegetables, such as sliced carrots or celery, chopped broccoli, cauliflower florets, sliced mushrooms, chopped green bell pepper, peas, or lima beans

1 teaspoon dried tarragon

1/2 teaspoon salt

1/2 teaspoon black pepper

1 For stock, combine 8 cups water, carcass, onions, parsley, garlic, bay leaves, peppercorns, and salt in a 12-quart soup pot. Bring to boil, then reduce heat and simmer, covered, 2 hours.

2 Transfer carcass to a plate. Set a cheesecloth-lined sieve over a large saucepan and strain stock, discarding vegetables and seasonings. Skim off fat. When carcass is cool enough to handle, remove meat from bones.

3 For soup, bring stock to boil over medium heat and stir in onion and rice. Reduce heat, cover, and simmer 15 minutes. Stir in turkey, vegetables, tarragon, salt, and pepper. Cover and simmer, stirring occasionally, until vegetables are crisp-tender, about 15 minutes.

TURKEY MINESTRONE

Here's a lovely leftover turkey and pasta soup made in the blink of an eye with pantry staples.

SERVES 4

1 can (13 3/4 ounces) chicken broth
1 can (14 1/2 ounces) low-sodium stewed tomatoes
1 cup cooked small pasta shells
1 cup frozen peas
2 cups cubed cooked turkey breast
2 tablespoons grated Parmesan cheese

1 In a medium saucepan, combine 2 cups water, broth, tomatoes, pasta, peas, and turkey. Bring to boil, then reduce heat and simmer 5 minutes to heat through.

2 Ladle into individual bowls and sprinkle each serving with Parmesan.

TURKEY MINESTRONE FOR A CROWD

Italian turkey sausage gives this savory soup just the right amount of spiciness.

SERVES 16

2 tablespoons vegetable oil
2/3 cup chopped onion
8 ounces ground turkey
8 ounces hot Italian turkey sausage links, casings removed
1/2 cup minced fresh parsley
2 garlic cloves, minced
1 teaspoon dried oregano
1 teaspoon dried basil
2 cans (14 1/2 ounces each) Italian stewed tomatoes
6 cups chicken stock
1 medium zucchini, sliced
1 package (10 ounces) frozen mixed vegetables
1 can (16 ounces) kidney beans, drained and rinsed
1 1/2 cups cooked elbow macaroni
2 tablespoons cider vinegar
1/2 teaspoon salt *(optional)*
Pinch of black pepper

1 Heat oil in a Dutch oven or soup pot over medium heat. Add onion and sauté 4 minutes or until tender. Add turkey, sausage, parsley, garlic, oregano, and basil and cook until meat is no longer pink.

2 Add tomatoes, stock, zucchini, and vegetables. Bring to boil, then reduce heat and simmer, covered, 5 minutes. Add beans, macaroni, vinegar, salt, if desired, and pepper and simmer until heated through, about 3 minutes.

MINESTRONE WITH TURKEY MEATBALLS

In Italian, a minestra is a soup, but a minestrone is a big soup, one that's a meal in itself.
(Photograph on page 15)

SERVES 4

1 teaspoon olive oil

1 small onion, finely chopped

3 garlic cloves, minced

8 ounces skinless, boneless turkey breast,
    cut into chunks

3 tablespoons old-fashioned rolled oats

1/4 cup low-fat (1%) milk

1/4 cup grated Parmesan cheese

1/2 cup chopped fresh basil

3/4 teaspoon salt

2 cups fat-free low-sodium chicken broth

1 1/2 cups chopped undrained canned tomatoes

2/3 cup small bowtie pasta

4 cups kale, shredded

1 yellow squash, quartered lengthwise
    and thickly sliced

1 Heat oil in a medium nonstick saucepan over low heat. Add onion and garlic and sauté 5 minutes or until onion is tender. Transfer to a medium bowl and let cool to room temperature.

2 Meanwhile, in a blender or food processor, grind turkey with on-off pulses until fine. Add to onion mixture. Add oats, milk, 2 tablespoons Parmesan, 2 tablespoons basil, and 1/4 teaspoon salt and stir to combine. Gently shape into 24 small meatballs.

3 In a Dutch oven over high heat, combine 2 cups water, remaining salt, broth, and tomatoes and bring to boil. Add pasta and kale and cook 5 minutes, then reduce heat and simmer.

4 Add remaining basil and meatballs and cook 1 minute. Add squash and simmer, covered, 5 minutes or until meatballs are cooked through and kale is tender. Serve sprinkled with remaining Parmesan.

TURKEY NOODLE SOUP

There are probably as many recipes for turkey noodle soup as there are cooks in the United States. This one has the flavor of sage and cloves to distinguish it.

SERVES 6

9 cups chicken or turkey stock

4 medium carrots, shredded

3 celery stalks, sliced

1 medium onion, chopped

1 teaspoon rubbed sage

1/2 teaspoon black pepper

3 whole cloves

1 bay leaf

2 cups diced cooked turkey

1 cup macaroni

1/4 cup chopped fresh parsley

1 In a Dutch oven or soup pot over medium-high heat, combine stock, carrots, celery, onion, sage, and pepper. Tie cloves and bay leaf in cheesecloth and add to pot. Bring to boil, reduce heat, and simmer, covered, 1 hour.

2 Add turkey, macaroni, and parsley and simmer, covered, until macaroni is tender and soup is heated through, about 15 minutes. Remove spice bag before serving.

HEARTY TURKEY-VEGETABLE SOUP

Potatoes, corn, and lima beans bulk up this turkey soup that will fuel an afternoon of touch football or soccer.

SERVES 12

6 cups turkey or chicken stock

3 medium all-purpose potatoes, peeled and chopped

2 carrots, chopped

2 celery stalks, chopped

2 medium onions, chopped

2 cans (15 ounces each) cream-style corn

2 cans (8 1/2 ounces each) lima beans, drained

2 cups chopped cooked turkey

1/2–1 teaspoon chili powder

Salt and black pepper to taste

1 In a large soup pot or Dutch oven, combine stock, potatoes, carrots, celery, and onions. Bring to boil, then reduce heat, cover, and simmer 30 minutes or until tender.

2 Add corn, beans, turkey, chili powder, salt, and pepper and simmer, covered, 10 minutes.

TURKEY MEATBALL SOUP WITH MUSHROOMS, ALMONDS, AND SHERRY

This is a dressed-up, savory version of turkey soup with meatballs that may be a surprise hit with guests.

SERVES 4

Meatballs:

2 slices day-old bread, cubed

2 tablespoons low-fat (1%) milk

12 ounces ground turkey

2 tablespoons minced fresh parsley

1 large egg white

1/4 teaspoon salt

1/4 teaspoon ground sage

3 dashes of hot red pepper sauce

Soup:

3 3/4 cups chicken stock

1 medium celery stalk, diced

2 medium carrots, peeled, halved lengthwise, and thinly sliced

3 1/2 ounces fresh mushrooms, sliced

1 tablespoon dry sherry

1/4 teaspoon salt

1/8 teaspoon dried thyme, crumbled

1/8 teaspoon ground sage

1/4 teaspoon black pepper

3 scallions with tops, sliced

1 tablespoon slivered almonds *(optional)*

1 tablespoon minced fresh parsley *(optional)*

1 For meatballs, soak bread in milk in a medium bowl until soft, about 3 minutes. Mash with a fork, stir in turkey, parsley, egg white, salt, sage, and red pepper sauce and mix well. With moistened hands, form into balls, using 1 tablespoon for each, and place on wax paper.

2 For soup, combine stock, celery, carrots, mushrooms, sherry, salt, thyme, sage, and pepper in a large saucepan or 4-quart Dutch oven over medium heat. Bring to boil, then reduce heat and simmer, covered, 15 minutes.

3 Uncover pan and drop in meatballs. Add scallions and simmer, covered, 15 minutes or until meatballs are cooked through. Garnish with almonds or parsley, if desired.

TURKEY MEATBALL SOUP

Ground turkey makes healthy, low-fat baked meatballs. This soup can feed a crowd or give you a second fuss-free meal from the freezer at a later date.

SERVES 12

Meatballs:
1/4 cup cooked rice
1/4 cup finely chopped onion
1/4 cup finely chopped celery
2 tablespoons all-purpose flour
1/2 teaspoon ground cumin
1/2 teaspoon salt *(optional)*
1/8 teaspoon black pepper
12 ounces ground turkey breast

Soup:
6 cups chicken stock
1 cup fine egg noodles
1/2 teaspoon black pepper
1/4 teaspoon garlic salt
1/8 teaspoon dill weed
1 tablespoon minced fresh parsley

1 For meatballs, preheat oven to 450°F. Coat 2 baking sheets with cooking spray.

2 In a medium bowl, combine 2 tablespoons water, rice, onion, celery, flour, cumin, salt, if desired, and pepper. Add turkey and mix well. Shape into 1-inch balls and place on baking sheets. Bake until turkey is no longer pink, about 15 minutes.

3 For soup, bring stock to boil in a large Dutch oven or soup pot. Add meatballs, noodles, pepper, garlic salt, and dill and return to boil. Reduce heat and simmer, uncovered, until noodles are tender, about 5 minutes. Stir in parsley.

ZESTY TURKEY SOUP

Lemon rind and parsley enliven the taste of this light turkey and vegetable soup, while carrots, celery, and broccoli provide essential vitamins.

SERVES 4

1 lemon
1 small bunch parsley
3 1/2 cups chicken stock
2 carrots, sliced
2 celery stalks, sliced
8 ounces turkey cutlets, cut into
    1/2 x 1 1/2-inch strips
4 ounces small broccoli florets
Salt and black pepper

1 Using a vegetable peeler, peel half of lemon in 1 long strip and place strip in a large saucepan. Cut thickest parsley stalks, tie together with string, and add to pan. Reserve remaining lemon and parsley. Pour stock into pan and bring to boil. Add carrots and celery and return to boil, then reduce heat and simmer, covered, 5 minutes.

2 Add turkey and simmer, covered, 5 minutes. Bring to boil, add broccoli, and cook, uncovered, 3 minutes or until just tender.

3 Peel rest of reserved lemon in long shreds. Halve lemon and juice it. Chop reserved parsley. Remove strip of lemon rind and parsley from soup. Stir in lemon juice with most of shredded rind and chopped parsley. Season to taste with salt and pepper and garnish with remaining rind and parsley.

TURKEY, TOMATO, AND BARLEY SOUP

This is a robust soup that practically cooks itself. The dark meat on drumsticks makes it flavorful.

SERVES 6

2 tablespoons olive or vegetable oil

2 pounds turkey or chicken drumsticks

4 medium celery stalks, cut into 1/2-inch-thick slices

3 medium carrots, peeled and cut into 1/2-inch-thick slices

1 large yellow onion, coarsely chopped

2 cans (14 1/2 ounces) tomatoes, undrained, broken up

1/3 cup medium pearl barley

1 teaspoon salt

1 teaspoon dried marjoram, crumbled

1 teaspoon dried thyme, crumbled

1/2 teaspoon black pepper

1/4 cup minced fresh parsley

1 Heat oil in a large saucepan or 5-quart Dutch oven over medium heat. Add drumsticks and cook until browned on all sides, about 10 minutes.

2 Add 3 cups water, celery, carrots, onion, tomatoes, barley, salt, marjoram, thyme, and pepper. Bring to boil, then reduce heat and simmer, covered, until meat is tender, about 1 1/2 hours for turkey or 1 hour for chicken.

3 Stir in parsley and serve, or let soup cool and refrigerate 2 hours, then skim off fat, remove skin and bones, and cut meat into bite-size chunks. Reheat when ready to serve.

CREAMY TURKEY SOUP

Leftover turkey has no finer destination than this rich, herb-flavored soup with carrots and peas.

SERVES 6 TO 8

6 tablespoons butter

1 large onion, chopped

3 celery stalks with leaves, cut into 1/4-inch slices

6 tablespoons all-purpose flour

1 teaspoon salt

1/4 teaspoon black pepper

1/4 teaspoon garlic powder

1/2 teaspoon dried thyme

1/2 teaspoon savory

1/2 teaspoon parsley flakes

1 1/2 cups milk

4 cups cubed cooked turkey

5 medium carrots, cut into 1/4-inch slices

1 1/2 cups turkey or chicken stock

1 package (10 ounces) frozen peas

1 In a Dutch oven or soup pot over medium heat, melt butter. Add onion and celery and sauté 4 minutes or until tender. Stir in flour, salt, pepper, garlic powder, thyme, savory, and parsley and cook until bubbling. Gradually add milk, stirring constantly until thickened.

2 Add turkey and carrots, then add stock until soup is desired consistency and bring to boil. Reduce heat and simmer, covered, 15 minutes. Add peas and simmer, covered, 5 minutes or until vegetables are tender.

TURKEY DUMPLING SOUP

SERVES 16

Stock:

1 turkey carcass (from 11-pound or larger turkey)
6 cups chicken stock
2 celery stalks, cut into 1-inch slices
1 medium carrot, cut into 1-inch slices
1 tablespoon poultry seasoning
1 bay leaf
1/2 teaspoon salt
1/2 teaspoon black pepper

Soup:

1 medium onion, chopped
2 celery stalks, chopped
2 medium carrots, sliced
1 cup cut fresh or frozen green beans
1 package (10 ounces) frozen corn
1 package (10 ounces) frozen peas
2 cups biscuit/baking mix
2/3 cup milk

1 For stock, combine 6 cups water, carcass, stock, celery, carrot, poultry seasoning, bay leaf, salt, and pepper in a Dutch oven or soup pot over medium-high heat. Bring to boil, then reduce heat and simmer, covered, 3 hours.

2 Transfer carcass to a plate. When cool enough to handle, remove meat from bones and cut into chunks, reserving 4 cups (refrigerate any remaining meat for another use). Strain stock into a large bowl, discarding vegetables and bay leaf, and skim off fat.

3 For soup, return stock to pot and add onion, celery, carrots, and beans. Bring to boil, then reduce heat and simmer, covered, 10 minutes or until vegetables are tender. Add corn, peas, and turkey and bring to boil, then reduce heat and simmer, uncovered.

4 In a small bowl, combine biscuit mix and milk. Drop by teaspoons into simmering soup. Cover and simmer until a toothpick inserted in a dumpling comes out clean, about 10 minutes.

Some people think turkey soup is just an excuse to have their favorite dumplings; this soup pleases both soup and dumpling lovers.

TURKEY, CHESTNUT, AND BARLEY SOUP

This turkey leftovers dish is packed with vegetables, barley, and chestnuts—a really satisfying treat.

SERVES 6

Stock:

1 turkey carcass
1 onion, quartered
1 carrot, chopped
2 celery stalks, chopped
Parsley sprigs
Thyme sprigs
1 bay leaf

Soup:

1 large carrot, chopped
1 large parsnip, peeled and chopped
3 celery stalks, chopped
4-6 Brussels sprouts, chopped
1 large leek, chopped
3 1/2 ounces freshly cooked or vacuum-packed chestnuts, coarsely chopped
2 1/2 ounces pearl barley
3 tablespoons chopped fresh parsley
3 1/2 ounces cooked skinless turkey, chopped or shredded
Salt and black pepper

1 For stock, break up carcass, discarding any skin, and place in a very large saucepan. Add onion, carrot, and celery. Tie parsley and thyme sprigs and bay leaf together to make a bouquet garni and add to pan. Cover with water and bring to boil, skimming off any foam. Reduce heat and simmer, covered, 1 1/2 hours. Strain stock into a large heatproof bowl, discarding bones and vegetables. Wipe out pan.

2 For soup, measure stock and, if necessary, add water to make 6 cups. Skim off fat and return stock to pan.

3 Return stock to boil and add carrot, parsnip, celery, Brussels sprouts, leek, chestnuts, and barley. Reduce heat and simmer, covered, 35 minutes or until barley is tender. Add parsley and turkey and simmer 4 minutes or until heated through. Season to taste with salt and pepper.

TOMATO-TURKEY SOUP

Tomatoes and okra give this turkey soup a Southern touch.

SERVES 14

6 cups chicken or turkey stock
2 cans (14 1/2 ounces each) diced tomatoes, undrained
1/3 cup quick-cooking barley
1 tablespoon parsley flakes
1 teaspoon salt
1/2 teaspoon garlic powder
1/2 teaspoon dried oregano
1/2 teaspoon dried basil
1/4 teaspoon black pepper
2 cups cubed cooked turkey
1 1/2 cups sliced carrots
1 1/2 cups sliced celery
1 medium onion, chopped
1 cup chopped seeded green bell pepper
1 package (10 ounces) frozen chopped okra

1 In a Dutch oven or soup pot over medium-high heat, combine stock, tomatoes, barley, parsley, salt, garlic powder, oregano, basil, and black pepper. Bring to boil, then reduce heat and simmer, covered, 50 minutes.

2 Add turkey, carrots, celery, onion, bell pepper, and okra and return to boil. Reduce heat and simmer, covered, until vegetables are tender, about 10 minutes.

THAI-STYLE TURKEY SOUP

Lime zest, lime leaves, lemongrass, red chiles, fish sauce, and cilantro flavor this turkey and vegetable soup, while carrots, celery, and snow peas provide essential vitamins.

SERVES 4

1 lime

3 lime leaves

1 stalk lemongrass, cut into 3 pieces

1 garlic clove, halved

1 small fresh red chile, halved and seeded
   (wear gloves when handling; they burn)

1 bunch cilantro stalks

1-inch piece fresh ginger, sliced

3 1/2 cups chicken stock

2 carrots, sliced

2 celery stalks, sliced

8 ounces turkey cutlets, cut into
   1/2 x 1 1/2-inch strips

4 ounces snow peas, cut into pieces

1-2 tablespoons fish sauce

Salt and black pepper

1 Using a vegetable peeler, peel half of lime in 1 long strip and place strip in a large saucepan. Reserve lime. Place lime leaves, lemongrass, garlic, chile, 3 stalks cilantro, and ginger in a square of muslin and tie with string. Reserve remaining cilantro. In a saucepan over medium-high heat, bring stock and spice bag to boil. Add carrots and celery and return to boil, then reduce heat and simmer, covered, 5 minutes.

2 Add turkey and simmer, covered, 5 minutes. Bring to boil, add snow peas, and cook, uncovered, 3 minutes or until just tender.

3 Peel rest of reserved lime in long shreds. Halve lime and juice it. Chop reserved cilantro. Remove strip of lime rind and spice bag from soup. Stir in lime juice and fish sauce with most of shredded rind and chopped cilantro. Season to taste with salt and pepper and garnish with remaining rind and parsley.

TURKEY SAUSAGE SOUP WITH KALE

Tart greens play off against the hot sausage and mild potatoes in this soup from Southern Europe.

SERVES 4

1 pound all-purpose potatoes, peeled
   and thinly sliced

6 cups chicken stock

4 ounces chorizo sausage or turkey sausage,
   thinly sliced

1 garlic clove, finely chopped

12 ounces kale leaves or collard greens,
   washed and shredded

1/8 teaspoon black pepper

1 In a large saucepan over medium heat, combine potatoes and stock and bring to boil. Reduce heat and simmer 10 minutes or until very soft. With a fork, mash about half of potatoes against side of pan. Remove from heat.

2 Add sausage to a nonstick skillet over medium heat and cook, stirring, about 5 minutes or until slices are crisp and fat is rendered. Drain off fat.

3 Add garlic and sauté 3 minutes or until softened. Add kale and stir to combine. Add 1/4 cup water and cook, covered, 5 minutes or until kale is wilted.

4 Stir kale and chorizo into potatoes. Return to heat and simmer about 5 minutes or until heated through. Season to taste with pepper.

TURKEY GUMBO

Gumbos are thickened by a substance released from okra, which is always included in the ingredients.

SERVES 4

2 teaspoons olive oil

1 pound skinless, boneless turkey breast, cut into 1-inch chunks

2 ounces smoked ham, chopped

1 onion, finely chopped

2 scallions, thinly sliced

1 red bell pepper, cored, seeded, and coarsely chopped

1 tablespoon all-purpose flour

1/2 package (10 ounces) frozen sliced okra

1 cup chicken stock

4 cups kale or spinach, shredded

1/2 teaspoon dried thyme

1/2 teaspoon dried marjoram

1/4 teaspoon salt

1/8 teaspoon cayenne pepper

1 Heat oil in a nonstick Dutch oven or flame-proof baking dish over medium-high heat. Add turkey and ham and cook 5 minutes or until turkey is lightly browned. Transfer to a plate.

2 Add onion and scallions to Dutch oven and sauté 5 minutes. Add bell pepper and sauté 4 minutes, then stir in flour until vegetables are well coated. Add okra and stir until well combined. Gradually add stock and 2/3 cup water, stirring constantly until smooth.

3 Add kale, thyme, marjoram, salt, and cayenne and bring to boil. Reduce heat and simmer, covered, stirring occasionally, 30 minutes or until thickened. Return turkey and ham to Dutch oven and cook 2 minutes or until turkey is heated through.

TURKEY STROGANOFF

The carrots and green peas in this updated classic add color and nutritional value.

SERVES 4

8 ounces medium egg noodles

2 tablespoons olive oil

1 pound skinless, boneless turkey breast, cut into 2 x 1/2-inch strips

2 carrots, thinly sliced

8 ounces small fresh mushrooms, halved

3/4 cup canned low-sodium chicken broth

1 cup frozen peas

1/2 teaspoon salt

1/2 teaspoon black pepper

1/4 teaspoon dried rosemary, crumbled

1/2 cup reduced-fat sour cream

1 tablespoon all-purpose flour

1 In a large pot of boiling water, cook noodles according to package directions until firm-tender; drain.

2 Meanwhile, heat 1 tablespoon oil in a large skillet over medium heat. Add turkey and sauté 3 minutes or until just cooked through. Using a slotted spoon, transfer to a plate.

3 Add remaining oil to skillet, add carrots and mushrooms, and sauté 3 minutes or until mushrooms begin to release their liquid. Add 1/2 cup water, broth, peas, salt, pepper, and rosemary and bring to boil. Reduce heat and simmer, uncovered, 2 minutes or until carrots are tender.

4 In a small bowl, combine sour cream and flour, then whisk into skillet. Return turkey and any juices to skillet and cook 2 minutes or until sauce is thickened. Serve over hot egg noodles.

HEARTY BROCCOLI, POTATO, AND SMOKED TURKEY STEW

This is a warm and welcoming one-dish meal for chilly evenings or potluck suppers.

SERVES 4

1 tablespoon olive oil

1 large onion, finely chopped

3 garlic cloves, minced

2 carrots, cut into 1-inch lengths

12 ounces all-purpose potatoes, peeled and cut into 1/2-inch chunks

3/4 cup chicken stock

1/2 teaspoon dried tarragon

1/4 teaspoon black pepper

1 bunch broccoli

8 ounces unsliced smoked turkey, cut into 1/2-inch chunks

1 cup frozen whole-kernel corn

1 Heat oil in a large saucepan over medium heat. Add onion and garlic and sauté 7 minutes. Add carrots and potatoes and stir to coat.

2 Add 1 cup water, stock, tarragon, and pepper and bring to boil. Reduce heat and simmer, covered, 17 minutes or until potatoes and carrots are almost tender.

3 Meanwhile, trim tough stem ends from broccoli and cut tops into small florets. Peel stalks and slice thinly. Add florets and stalks to pan and simmer, covered, 5 minutes.

4 Add turkey and corn and cook 3 minutes or just until heated through.

PHEASANT STEW WITH GINGER

Casseroling is an excellent way to cook pheasant, since it produces succulent pieces of both breast and dark meat, and the goodness from both creates a rich sauce.

SERVES 4

1 tablespoon sunflower oil

1 pheasant (about 2 1/4 pounds), cut into 4 or 8 pieces

2/3 cup shallots or pearl onions, peeled and halved

1 large fennel bulb, cut into 8 wedges and leaves reserved

4 pieces preserved ginger (about 4 ounces total), cut into thin strips

4 tablespoons white Zinfandel or other white wine

1 1/4 cups chicken stock

Salt and black pepper

1 Preheat oven to 375°F. Heat oil in a large Dutch oven over medium-high heat. Add pheasant and shallots and sauté until browned on all sides.

2 Add fennel. Turn pheasant skin side up and sprinkle with ginger. Add wine and enough stock to come halfway up pheasant but not cover completely. Season to taste with salt and pepper and bring to boil.

3 Cover and bake until pheasant is tender, 1 to 1 1/4 hours. Garnish with reserved fennel leaves.

Meat
SOUPS

MEAT SOUPS

recipe list

 EASY: 10 minutes to prepare

 QUICK: Ready to eat in 30 minutes

ONE-DISH: contains protein, vegetables, and good carbohydrates (beans, whole-grains, etc.) for a complete healthy meal

HEALTHY: High in nutrients, low in bad fats and empty carbohydrates

SLOW COOKER: Easily adapted for slow cooker by cutting down on liquids

MEAT SOUPS

recipe list CONTINUED

BEEF-VEGETABLE SOUP

(Photograph on page 9)

SERVES 16

2 tablespoons vegetable oil

3 1/2 pounds meaty cross-cut beef shanks
   or oxtails, 1 inch thick

6 large carrots, peeled and sliced

4 celery stalks, sliced

2 medium yellow onions, coarsely chopped

3 garlic cloves, minced

2 cans (28 ounces each) crushed tomatoes

1 teaspoon salt

1/2 teaspoon black pepper

1 teaspoon dried oregano

1 teaspoon dried marjoram

1 teaspoon dried thyme

2 medium all-purpose potatoes,
   peeled and diced

2 medium parsnips, peeled and diced

3 medium white turnips, peeled and diced

1 pound green beans, trimmed and cut
   into bite-size pieces

1 1/2 cups fresh corn

1 cup fresh peas

1/4 cup chopped fresh parsley

1 Heat oil in an 8-quart soup pot over medium-high heat. Add beef and cook, turning frequently, about 10 minutes or until browned. Transfer to a plate.

2 Add carrots, celery, onions, and garlic and sauté 15 minutes or until tender. Stir in 12 cups water, tomatoes, salt, pepper, oregano, marjoram, and thyme.

3 Return beef to pot, increase heat to high, and bring to boil. Reduce heat and simmer, uncovered, 2 1/2 hours or until meat is tender, stirring and skimming the surface occasionally. Using a slotted spoon, transfer beef to a cutting board. When cool enough to handle, remove bones and cut meat into bite-size pieces. Return beef to pot.

4 Add potatoes, parsnips, turnips, and beans and simmer, uncovered, 10 minutes. Stir in corn and peas and simmer 5 minutes or until vegetables are tender. Stir in parsley.

This recipe comes from the family of Adele Kaffer, one of the first women settlers in Wyoming.

ALL-DAY BEEF-VEGETABLE SOUP

It's a treat to come home from work and have this savory soup ready to eat. Pair it with crusty rolls topped with melted mozzarella cheese. (Photograph on page 18)

SERVES 8 TO 10

1 pound boneless round steak,
    cut into 1/2-inch cubes
1 can (14 1/2 ounces) diced tomatoes,
    undrained
2 medium all-purpose potatoes,
    peeled and cut into cubes
2 medium onions, diced
3 celery stalks, sliced
2 carrots, sliced
3 beef bouillon cubes
1/2 teaspoon dried basil
1/2 teaspoon dried oregano
1/2 teaspoon salt
1/4 teaspoon black pepper
1 1/2 cups frozen mixed vegetables

1 In a slow cooker, combine 3 cups water, meat, tomatoes, potatoes, onions, celery, carrots, bouillon, basil, oregano, salt, and pepper. Cover and cook on high 6 hours.

2 Add mixed vegetables, cover, and cook on high until meat is tender, about 2 hours.

QUICK BEEF-VEGETABLE SOUP

Brimming with beef, potatoes, carrots, green beans, and mushrooms, this soup and some crusty breads are all you need to serve a crowd.

SERVES 12

2 cans (14 1/2 ounces each) beef broth
1 tablespoon Worcestershire sauce
1 teaspoon coarse-grain mustard
1/2 teaspoon salt
1/4 teaspoon black pepper

3 medium all-purpose potatoes, peeled
    and cut into cubes
6 medium carrots, cut into 1/2-inch slices
3 cups cubed cooked beef
2 cups frozen cut green beans, thawed
2 cups sliced fresh mushrooms
1 cup frozen peas, thawed
1 can (15 ounces) tomato sauce
2 tablespoons minced fresh parsley

1 In a Dutch oven or soup pot, combine broth, Worcestershire sauce, mustard, salt, and pepper. Stir in potatoes and carrots and bring to boil. Reduce heat, cover, and simmer until carrots are crisp-tender, about 12 minutes.

2 Stir in beef, beans, mushrooms, peas, tomato sauce, and parsley. Return to boil, reduce heat, and simmer, uncovered, until vegetables are tender, about 5 minutes.

EASY BEEF-VEGETABLE SOUP

A fast, delicious way to use up the last of a big beef roast.

SERVES 6

3 cups cubed cooked roast beef
1 cup diced carrots
1 cup diced peeled all-purpose potatoes
1 cup fresh, canned, or frozen
    whole-kernel corn
1 cup cut green beans
1/2 cup chopped onion
1 quart tomato sauce
1/2 teaspoon salt
1 teaspoon dried basil
1 teaspoon dried oregano
1 tablespoon chopped fresh parsley

1 In a large saucepan, combine beef, carrots, potatoes, corn, beans, onion, tomato sauce, salt, basil, oregano, and parsley. Bring to boil, then reduce heat and simmer, covered, 30 minutes or until vegetables are tender. If soup is too thick, add 1/2 to 1 cup water.

BEEF-VEGETABLE SOUP WITH CABBAGE

Serve this hearty soup as a main course accompanied by crusty whole wheat rolls or breadsticks.

SERVES 4

2 teaspoons vegetable oil
1 pound boneless beef chuck,
    cut into 1-inch cubes and patted dry
1/2 teaspoon salt
1/4 teaspoon black pepper
1 large yellow onion, sliced
1 medium celery stalk, thinly sliced
2 garlic cloves, minced
1 can (14 1/2 ounces) tomatoes,
    undrained, chopped
4 cups beef stock
1/2 teaspoon dried thyme, crumbled
1/2 teaspoon dried marjoram, crumbled
1 bay leaf
2 large Idaho or russet potatoes,
    peeled and cut into 1-inch cubes
2 small carrots, peeled and cut into
    1-inch-thick slices
2 cups shredded cabbage

1 Heat oil in a 10-inch nonstick skillet over medium heat. Add beef, 1/4 teaspoon salt, and 1/8 teaspoon pepper and cook until beef is browned on all sides, about 5 minutes. Using a slotted spoon, transfer to a soup pot or 5-quart Dutch oven.

2 Add onion and celery to skillet and sauté in drippings, stirring occasionally, until soft, about 5 minutes. Transfer to pot.

3 Add garlic, tomatoes, stock, thyme, marjoram, bay leaf, and remaining salt and pepper. Bring to boil, reduce heat, and simmer, covered, 30 minutes. Add potatoes, carrots, and cabbage, increase heat, and return to boil. Reduce heat, cover, and simmer until vegetables and meat are tender, about 25 minutes. Remove bay leaf before serving.

SHORT-RIB SOUP

This soup has it all—aromatic broth, tender beef, and flavorful barley and vegetables.

SERVES 6 TO 8

1 can (15 1/4 ounces) lima beans
1 can (14 1/2 ounces) cut green beans
2 pounds beef short ribs
1 can (14 1/2 ounces) diced tomatoes,
    undrained
1 cup coarsely chopped carrot
3/4 cup chopped onion
1/3 cup medium pearled barley
1 tablespoon salt
1 tablespoon sugar
1/2 teaspoon dried basil
1 bay leaf

1 Drain lima and green beans, reserving liquid, and set aside. Pour liquid into a Dutch oven or soup pot and add 4 cups water, beef, tomatoes, carrot, onion, barley, salt, sugar, basil, and bay leaf. Bring to boil, then reduce heat and simmer, covered, until beef is tender, about 2 hours.

2 Remove beef from pot. When cool enough to handle, remove meat from bones, cut into bite-size pieces, and return to pot. Add beans and cook until heated through, about 10 minutes. Remove bay leaf before serving.

STEAK SOUP

This is an elegant but hearty soup for special occasions.

SERVES 6

2 tablespoons butter

2 tablespoons vegetable oil

1 1/2-2 pounds lean round steak, cut into 1/2-inch cubes

1/4 cup chopped onion

3 tablespoons all-purpose flour

1 tablespoon paprika

1 teaspoon salt

1/4 teaspoon black pepper

4 cups beef stock

1 bay leaf

4 parsley sprigs, chopped

2 sprigs celery leaves, chopped

1/2 teaspoon dried marjoram

1 1/2 cups cubed peeled all-purpose potatoes

1 1/2 cups sliced carrots

1 1/2 cups chopped celery

1 can (6 ounces) tomato paste

1 In a Dutch oven or soup pot over medium heat, melt butter, then add oil. Add steak and onion and cook until browned.

2 In a small bowl, combine flour, paprika, salt, and pepper. Sprinkle over beef and mix well. Stir in 2 cups water, stock, bay leaf, parsley, celery leaves, and marjoram. Bring to boil, then reduce heat and simmer, covered, about 1 hour or until tender.

3 Add potatoes, carrots, and celery and simmer, covered, 30 to 45 minutes or until vegetables are tender and soup begins to thicken. Stir in tomato paste and simmer, uncovered, 15 minutes. Remove bay leaf before serving.

BEEF-TOMATO SOUP

This soup is good any time of year but especially in winter, served with grilled cheese sandwiches. It's also a nice lunch with a side salad or homemade cornbread.

SERVES 6 TO 8

1 pound beef stew meat, cut into 1/2-inch cubes

1 small meaty beef soup bone

2 tablespoons vegetable oil

1 can (28 ounces) diced tomatoes, undrained

1 cup chopped carrots

1 cup chopped celery

1/4 cup chopped celery leaves

1 tablespoon salt

1/2 teaspoon dried marjoram

1/2 teaspoon dried basil

1/4 teaspoon dried savory

1/4 teaspoon dried thyme

1/8 teaspoon ground mace

1/8 teaspoon hot red pepper sauce

1 Heat oil in a Dutch oven or soup pot over medium heat. Add beef and soup bone and sauté until browned.

2 Add 4 cups water, tomatoes, carrots, celery, celery leaves, salt, marjoram, basil, savory, thyme, mace, and red pepper sauce. Bring to boil, then reduce heat and simmer, covered, until beef is tender, about 4 hours.

3 Skim off fat and remove soup bone. When cool enough to handle, remove meat from bone and cut into 1/2-inch cubes. Return to pot and heat through.

SPICY ITALIAN BEEF SOUP

This is an easy, aromatic soup with plenty of meat, vegetables, and seasonings.

SERVES 8

2 tablespoons olive or vegetable oil

1 pound beef stew meat, cut into 1-inch cubes

1 small soup bone *(optional)*

1 can (28 ounces) stewed tomatoes

1 cup chopped celery

1 cup sliced carrots

1/4 cup snipped celery leaves

1 tablespoon salt

1/2 teaspoon dried marjoram

1/2 teaspoon dried basil

1/2 teaspoon Italian seasoning

1/4 teaspoon dried savory

1/4 teaspoon dried thyme

1/8 teaspoon ground mace

Hot peppers, seeded and minced
(wear gloves when handling; they burn),
or red pepper flakes

1 cup elbow macaroni

1 Heat oil in a Dutch oven or soup pot over medium-high heat. Add beef and soup bone, if desired, and cook until browned. Stir in tomatoes, celery, carrots, celery leaves, salt, marjoram, basil, Italian seasoning, savory, thyme, and mace. Add hot peppers to taste.

2 Add 4 cups water and bring to boil. Reduce heat and simmer, covered, 3 hours or until meat is tender.

3 If using soup bone, remove from pot. When cool enough to handle, remove meat from bone, dice, and return to pot. Add macaroni and simmer, covered, 20 minutes or until tender.

BIG RED SOUP

Here's a hearty soup for a crowd that simmers all day while you are doing other things.

SERVES 10

2 tablespoons vegetable oil

2 pounds beef stew meat, trimmed

3/4 cup chopped onion

2 garlic cloves, minced

2 cans (14 1/2 ounces each) tomatoes

1 can (10 1/2 ounces) beef broth

1 can (10 1/2 ounces) chicken broth

1 can (10 3/4 ounces) condensed tomato soup

1 teaspoon ground cumin

1 teaspoon chili powder

1 teaspoon salt

1/2 teaspoon lemon pepper

2 teaspoons Worcestershire sauce

1/3 cup mild salsa

8 corn tortillas, cut into quarters

4 ounces mild cheddar cheese, grated

1 Heat oil in a large skillet over medium heat. Add beef and cook until browned.

2 Transfer to a slow cooker. Add 1/4 cup water, onion, garlic, tomatoes, beef broth, chicken broth, soup, cumin, chili powder, salt, lemon pepper, Worcestershire sauce, and salsa. Cover and cook on low for 10 hours.

3 Place 3 tortilla quarters in each of 10 bowls. Pour in soup and sprinkle with cheese.

CHUNKY BEEF AND ONION SOUP

Be sure to serve biscuits or French bread to sop up the rich, delicious broth.

SERVES 4

3 tablespoons olive or vegetable oil

1 1/4 pounds boneless beef chuck, cut into 1/2-inch cubes

5 large Spanish onions, halved and thinly sliced

1 1/2 tablespoons sugar

2 medium carrots, peeled, halved lengthwise, and cut into 1/4-inch-thick slices

1 3/4 cups beef stock

1 cup canned crushed tomatoes

1/4 teaspoon salt

1 Heat 2 tablespoons oil in a 5-quart Dutch oven or soup pot over medium-high heat. Working in batches if necessary, add beef and cook until browned on all sides, about 5 minutes.

2 Add remaining oil, onions, and sugar. Reduce heat to medium and sauté until onion is soft, about 3 minutes. Add carrots and sauté 3 minutes.

3 Stir in 2 cups water, stock, tomatoes, and salt and bring to boil. Reduce heat and simmer, covered, until beef is tender, about 40 minutes.

BEEF SOUP WITH ZUCCHINI

This soup is a wonderful way to use extra zucchini at the end of the season.

SERVES 8

1 tablespoon vegetable oil

1 pound beef stew meat, cut into 1-inch cubes

1 can (8 ounces) tomato sauce

1 medium onion, chopped

1 1/2 teaspoons salt

3/4 teaspoon dried oregano

1/4 teaspoon black pepper

2 cups thinly sliced zucchini

1 cup broken spaghetti

1 Heat oil in a Dutch oven or soup pot over medium heat. Add beef and cook until browned; drain off fat.

2 Add 6 cups water, tomato sauce, onion, salt, oregano, and pepper. Bring to boil, then reduce heat and simmer, covered, 2 hours.

3 Add zucchini and spaghetti and return to boil. Reduce heat and simmer, covered, until tender, about 15 minutes.

RUSSIAN BORSCHT

SERVES 8

1 pound beef shanks

5 whole black peppercorns

2 bay leaves

1 teaspoon salt

1/2 teaspoon dill weed

3 medium beets, peeled and shredded

2 tablespoons vegetable oil

2 teaspoons white vinegar

2 medium all-purpose potatoes,
    peeled and cut into cubes

2 medium carrots, sliced

1 cup shredded cabbage

2 tablespoons minced fresh parsley

1 medium onion, chopped

1 tablespoon all-purpose flour

2 medium tomatoes, cored, seeded,
    and chopped

1/2 cup sour cream

1 In a Dutch oven or soup pot, combine 8 cups water, beef, peppercorns, bay leaves, salt, and dill. Bring to boil, then reduce heat and simmer, covered, until beef is tender, about 1 1/2 hours.

2 Meanwhile, heat 1 tablespoon oil in a skillet over medium heat. Add beets and sauté 3 minutes. Stir in vinegar and set aside.

3 Using a slotted spoon, remove beef from pot. When cool enough to handle, remove meat from bones, cut into chunks, and set aside. Strain stock, discarding peppercorns and bay leaves, and skim off fat. Add enough water to stock to measure 6 cups and return to pot. Add potatoes, carrots, cabbage, parsley, and beets and bring to boil.

4 Heat remaining oil in a skillet over medium heat. Add onion and sauté until tender, about 5 minutes. Sprinkle with flour and stir until blended. Whisk onion into pot, reduce heat, and simmer, covered, until vegetables are tender, about 30 minutes. Add tomatoes.

5 Transfer soup in small batches to a blender or food processor, cover, and puree until smooth. Pour into a large saucepan, add beef, and heat through. Garnish with sour cream.

This authentic recipe came to the United States in 1998 with a cook from Belarus, who has shared it often with appreciative friends.

BORSCHT WITH LEFTOVER BEEF

You can make a quick and easy version of this hearty soup by substituting 1 package (10 ounces) of frozen chopped spinach, thawed, for the beet tops and 2 cans (15 ounces each) of julienne beets, drained, for the fresh beets.

SERVES 8

6 medium beets with tops

2 tablespoons butter

1 large yellow onion, chopped

5 cups canned low-sodium beef broth

1 3/4 cups chopped tomatoes or 1 can (14 1/2 ounces) low-sodium tomatoes, undrained, cut up

2 teaspoons dried marjoram

1 teaspoon salt

1 teaspoon dill weed

1/2 teaspoon black pepper

2 cups shredded cabbage

2 cups bite-size pieces cooked beef, pork, or low-sodium ham

2 tablespoons vinegar

1 tablespoon sugar

1 Trim leaves from beets, leaving 1 inch of stem attached. Reserve beet tops. In a 6-quart soup pot or Dutch oven over medium heat, cover beets with lightly salted water. Bring to boil, then reduce heat and simmer, covered, until tender, about 45 minutes. Drain well and let cool slightly. Peel beets by slipping off skins while still warm, then cut into 1 1/2 x 1/4-inch sticks. Measure 4 cups.

2 Meanwhile, wash beet tops, chop finely, and measure 2 cups.

3 Add butter to pot and melt over medium-high heat. Add onion and sauté until tender, about 5 minutes. Add beet tops, broth, tomatoes, marjoram, salt, dill, and pepper. Bring to boil, then reduce heat and simmer, covered, until beet tops are tender, about 5 minutes. Stir in cabbage, beef, vinegar, and sugar. Carefully stir in beets and simmer, covered, until heated through, about 5 minutes.

MEATBALL-VEGETABLE SOUP

Meatballs, carrots, spinach, and tomatoes float with pasta tubes and white beans in a rich thyme-flavored beef broth, making a refreshing and healthy meal.

SERVES 6

1 pound ground beef

1 egg, lightly beaten

1/2 cup small fresh bread cubes

3/4 cup onion, finely chopped

1 teaspoon salt

2 tablespoons vegetable oil

3 1/2 cups beef stock

1 can (14 1/2 ounces) stewed tomatoes

2 carrots, coarsely chopped

1/2 teaspoon dried crushed thyme

1/2 teaspoon freshly ground black pepper

1 cup cooked small tube macaroni

1 can (14 1/2 ounces) white kidney beans

2 small zucchini, coarsely chopped

1/2 pound fresh spinach, washed and stemmed

1 In a large bowl, mix beef, egg, bread, 1/4 cup onion, and 1/2 teaspoon salt. Shape the mixture into 36 meatballs.

2 In a soup pot or Dutch oven over medium heat, heat oil. Add meatballs and remaining onion and sauté 5 minutes or until browned. Add stock, tomatoes, carrots, remaining salt, thyme, and pepper. Bring to boil, reduce heat, and simmer 10 minutes or until meatballs are cooked through and carrots are almost tender. Add macaroni, beans, and spinach and simmer 5 minutes or until macaroni and beans are heated through.

MEATBALL SOUP WITH THYME

Thyme is a classic flavoring for beef, onion, carrots, and mushrooms. Once you try this soup, you'll know why.

SERVES 10

1 egg
1/4 cup dry bread crumbs
2 tablespoons minced fresh thyme
    or 2 teaspoons dried thyme
1/2 teaspoon salt
1 1/2 pounds ground beef
1 small onion, chopped
2 medium carrots, chopped
12 ounces fresh mushrooms, sliced
1 tablespoon olive oil
1 1/4 pounds red potatoes, cubed
2 cans (14 1/2 ounces each) beef broth
1 can (14 1/2 ounces) stewed tomatoes

1 In a large bowl, combine egg, bread crumbs, 1 tablespoon thyme, and salt. Crumble beef over mixture, mix well, and shape into 1-inch balls. Add to a Dutch oven or soup pot over medium heat and cook until no longer pink. Transfer to a plate and drain fat from pot.

2 Add oil to pot and heat over medium heat. Add onion, carrots, and mushrooms and sauté until onion is tender, about 4 minutes. Stir in potatoes, broth, tomatoes, meatballs, and remaining thyme. Bring to boil, then reduce heat and simmer, covered, until potatoes are tender, about 25 minutes.

.

MEATBALL-ESCAROLE SOUP

Escarole gives an interesting, sharp taste to this healthful soup with its tiny meatballs.

SERVES 16

Soup:
15 chicken wings
4 medium carrots, cut into 1/2-inch pieces
1 large all-purpose potato, cut into
    1/2-inch cubes
4 celery stalks, sliced
1 large tomato, cored, seeded, and diced
1 large onion, diced
1 tablespoon salt
1 teaspoon black pepper
1 small (5-6 ounces) head escarole

Meatballs:
1 egg, beaten
8 ounces ground beef
1/2 cup dry bread crumbs
1 tablespoon chopped fresh parsley
1/2 teaspoon salt
1 garlic clove, minced
1 teaspoon grated Parmesan cheese

1 For soup, combine 4 quarts water, chicken wings, carrots, potato, celery, tomato, onion, salt, and pepper in a large Dutch oven or soup pot over medium-high heat. Bring to boil, then reduce heat and simmer, covered, 1 hour or until chicken and vegetables are tender. Remove chicken, debone, and return to pot. Add escarole and simmer 15 minutes.

2 For meatballs, combine egg, beef, bread crumbs, parsley, salt, garlic, and cheese in a medium bowl and mix well. Shape into marble-size balls and add to soup. Simmer 10 minutes or until cooked through.

SWEDISH MEATBALL SOUP

This is a warm, homey soup that can surely qualify as comfort food.

 SERVES 9

1 egg
2 cups half-and-half
1 cup soft bread crumbs
1 small onion, finely chopped
1 3/4 teaspoons salt
1 1/2 pounds ground beef
1 tablespoon butter
3 tablespoons all-purpose flour
3/4 teaspoon beef bouillon granules
1/2 teaspoon black pepper
1/4 teaspoon garlic salt
1 pound red potatoes, cut into cubes
1 package (10 ounces) frozen peas, thawed

1 In a medium bowl, beat egg, then add 1/3 cup half-and-half, bread crumbs, onion, and 1 teaspoon salt. Add beef, mix well, and shape into 1/2-inch balls.

2 In a Dutch oven or soup pot over medium heat, melt butter. Add meatballs half at a time and sauté until no longer pink. Transfer to a plate and drain fat from pot.

3 Add flour, bouillon, pepper, garlic salt, and remaining salt to pot and stir until smooth. Gradually stir in 3 cups water and bring to boil, stirring often. Add potatoes and meatballs. Reduce heat and simmer, covered, 25 minutes or until potatoes are tender. Stir in peas and remaining half-and-half and heat through.

MEATBALL MUSHROOM SOUP

This creamy, super-thick mushroom soup is made heartier with meatballs, barley, macaroni, and rice.

 SERVES 6

8 ounces ground beef
2 cans (10 3/4 ounces each) condensed cream of mushroom soup
1 1/3 cups milk
1 teaspoon Italian seasoning
1 teaspoon dried minced onion
1/2 teaspoon dried minced garlic
1/4 cup quick-cooking barley
1/4 cup elbow macaroni
1/4 cup long-grain rice
1 medium carrot, shredded
1 jar (4 1/2 ounces) sliced mushrooms, drained
2 tablespoons grated Parmesan cheese

1 Shape beef into 1-inch balls and set aside.

2 In a large saucepan over medium heat, combine 1 1/3 cups water, soup, and milk and bring to boil. Add Italian seasoning, onion, garlic, barley, macaroni, and rice. Reduce heat and simmer, uncovered, 15 minutes.

3 Meanwhile, in a nonstick skillet over medium heat, cook meatballs until no longer pink.

4 Stir carrot into pan, cover, and simmer 5 minutes. Using a slotted spoon, transfer meatballs to pan. Stir in mushrooms and cheese and heat through.

SPICY CHEESEBURGER SOUP

Most cheeseburgers don't have the zip that this soup gets from jalapeño pepper—a fine tradeoff for a bun.

SERVES 6

2 cups cubed peeled all-purpose potatoes

2 small carrots, grated

1 small onion, chopped

1/4 cup seeded and chopped green
    bell pepper

1 jalapeño pepper, seeded, deveined,
    and chopped (wear gloves when
    handling; they burn)

1 garlic clove, minced

1 tablespoon beef bouillon granules

1/2 teaspoon salt

1 pound ground beef, browned and drained

2 1/2 cups milk

3 tablespoons all-purpose flour

8 ounces process American cheese,
    cut into cubes

1/2 teaspoon cayenne pepper (*optional*)

8 ounces sliced bacon, cooked and crumbled

1 In a large saucepan, combine 1 1/2 cups water, potatoes, carrots, onion, bell pepper, jalapeño, garlic, bouillon, and salt. Bring to boil, then reduce heat and simmer, covered, until potatoes are tender, about 15 minutes. Stir in beef and 2 cups milk and heat through.

2 In a small bowl, combine flour and remaining milk and stir until smooth. Gradually stir into pan. Bring to boil and cook, stirring, until thickened and bubbling, about 2 minutes.

3 Reduce heat and stir in cheese until melted. Add cayenne, if desired. Top with bacon just before serving.

HEARTY HAMBURGER SOUP

This soup has the robust flavor of hamburger plus plenty of good-for-you vegetables.

SERVES 8

1 pound ground beef

1 can (14 1/2 ounces) diced tomatoes,
    undrained

3 medium carrots, sliced

2 medium all-purpose potatoes,
    peeled and cut into cubes

1 medium onion, chopped

1/2 cup chopped celery

4 beef bouillon cubes

1 1/2 teaspoons salt

1/4 teaspoon black pepper

1/4 teaspoon dried oregano

1 cup cut fresh or frozen green beans

1 In a large saucepan over medium heat, cook beef until no longer pink; drain off fat.

2 Add 4 cups water, tomatoes, carrots, potatoes, onion, celery, bouillon, salt, pepper, and oregano. Bring to boil, then reduce heat and simmer, covered, until potatoes and carrots are tender, about 15 minutes. Add beans, cover, and simmer until tender, about 15 minutes.

CREAMED HAMBURGER SOUP

This cream of hamburger soup with potatoes and carrots is unexpectedly delicious.

SERVES 8

1 pound ground beef

1 medium onion, chopped

2 cups tomato juice

1 cup diced carrots

1 cup diced peeled all-purpose potato

1 1/2 teaspoons salt

1/4 teaspoon black pepper

1 teaspoon seasoned salt

1/4 cup butter

1/3 cup all-purpose flour

4 cups milk

1 In a medium skillet over medium heat, cook beef and onion until beef is browned and onion is soft; drain off fat.

2 Add tomato juice, carrots, potato, salt, pepper, and seasoned salt. Bring to boil, then reduce heat and simmer, covered, 10 minutes or until vegetables are tender.

3 Meanwhile, melt butter in a saucepan over low heat. Stir in flour and cook, stirring, until smooth. Slowly add milk and whisk over medium heat until thickened, about 5 minutes. Stir in vegetable mixture and cook until heated through.

GROUND BEEF SOUP WITH POTATOES AND CABBAGE

This wonderful, nourishing soup appeals to just about everybody.

SERVES 8

1 pound ground beef

1 cup chopped onion

1 cup diced peeled all-purpose potatoes

1 cup sliced carrots

1 cup shredded cabbage

1 cup sliced celery

2 cans (16 ounces each) tomatoes, undrained, cut up

1/4 cup long-grain rice

2 teaspoons salt

1/4 teaspoon dried basil

1/4 teaspoon dried thyme

1 bay leaf

1 In a large soup pot or Dutch oven over medium heat, cook beef and onion until beef is no longer pink and onion is soft; drain off fat.

2 Add 3 cups water, potatoes, carrots, cabbage, celery, tomatoes, rice, salt, basil, thyme, and bay leaf. Bring to boil, then reduce heat and simmer, covered, 1 hour, stirring occasionally. Remove bay leaf before serving.

GROUND ROUND SOUP FOR A CROWD

This is a one-pot meal that you might serve after an afternoon of football—as spectator or participant.

SERVES 10

1/2 cup butter

1 cup all-purpose flour

2 pounds ground round steak, browned and drained

1 cup chopped onion

1 cup chopped celery

1 package (20 ounces) frozen mixed vegetables, thawed

1 can (28 ounces) tomatoes, undrained, cut up

1 teaspoon salt

1 teaspoon black pepper

2 tablespoons bottled browning sauce *(optional)*

1 In a large saucepan over low heat, melt butter. Stir in flour to make a smooth paste and cook 2 minutes. Add 6 cups water and cook, stirring, over medium heat until thickened.

2 Add beef, onion, celery, mixed vegetables, tomatoes, salt, pepper, and browning sauce, if desired. Bring to boil, then reduce heat and simmer, covered, 20 minutes or until vegetables are tender.

CHEESY HAMBURGER-BROCCOLI SOUP

This soup very cleverly substitutes broccoli for the bun in a cheeseburger, making a delicious meal with fewer carbohydrates.

SERVES 6

2 chicken bouillon cubes
1 package (10 ounces) frozen broccoli
2 tablespoons butter or margarine
1/4 cup finely chopped onion
3 tablespoons all-purpose flour
1/4 teaspoon salt
1/8 teaspoon black pepper
2 cups milk
1 cup cubed process cheese
1 pound ground beef, browned and drained

1 In a medium saucepan, bring 1 1/2 cups water to boil. Add bouillon and stir until dissolved. Add broccoli and cook according to package directions, then remove from heat (do not drain).

2 In a large saucepan over medium heat, melt butter. Add onion and sauté 4 minutes or until tender. Add flour, salt, and pepper and stir until well blended.

3 Remove from heat and stir in enough milk to make a smooth paste, then stir in remaining milk. Return to heat, bring to boil, and cook 1 minute, stirring constantly. Add cheese, beef, and broccoli and cooking liquid. Cook, stirring occasionally, until heated through and cheese is melted.

BEEF SOUP WITH CABBAGE

This is delicious, hearty fare that you can put together in a hurry and enjoy the good smells while it simmers.

SERVES 8

1 pound lean ground beef
1/2 teaspoon garlic salt
1/4 teaspoon garlic powder
1/4 teaspoon black pepper
2 celery stalks, chopped
1 can (16 ounces) kidney beans, undrained
1/2 medium head cabbage, chopped
1 can (28 ounces) tomatoes, drained
    (liquid reserved) and chopped
4 beef bouillon cubes
 Chopped fresh parsley

1 In a Dutch oven over medium heat, cook beef until browned. Add 1 tomato can water, garlic salt, garlic powder, pepper, celery, beans, cabbage, tomatoes, and bouillon. Bring to boil, then reduce heat and simmer, covered, 1 hour. Garnish with parsley.

AUTUMN BEEF SOUP

Rutabaga gives this rich soup its distinctive flavor.

SERVES 8

1 can (28 ounces) stewed tomatoes
1 pound ground beef
1 cup chopped onion
1 cup diced carrots
1 cup diced celery
1 cup diced peeled all-purpose potato
1 cup diced peeled rutabaga
1 bay leaf
1/8 teaspoon dried basil

1 In a blender or food processor, puree tomatoes; set aside.

2 In a skillet over medium heat, cook beef until browned; drain off fat. Stir in 4 cups water, tomatoes, onion, carrots, celery, potato, rutabaga, bay leaf, and basil. Bring to boil, then reduce heat and simmer, covered, 25 minutes or until vegetables are tender. Remove bay leaf before serving.

BEEF-CARROT SOUP

Carrots and beef have complementary flavors and are the basis of a fine soup combination.

SERVES 8

1 pound ground beef, browned
    and drained
1/2 cup chopped celery
1/2 cup chopped onion
1 cup seeded and chopped green bell pepper
2 1/2 cups grated carrots
1 can (32 ounces) tomato juice
2 cans (10 3/4 ounces each) condensed
    cream of celery soup
1/2 teaspoon garlic salt
1/2 teaspoon dried marjoram
1 teaspoon sugar
1/2 teaspoon salt
 Shredded Monterey Jack cheese

1 In a large Dutch oven or soup pot, combine beef, celery, onion, bell pepper, carrots, tomato juice, soup, garlic salt, marjoram, sugar, and salt. Add 1 1/2 cups water and bring to boil. Reduce heat and simmer, uncovered, about 1 hour or until vegetables are tender. Sprinkle each serving with cheese.

CREAMY BEEF-CARROT SOUP

This simple but nourishing soup can be made in 30 minutes, so it appears on many busy-day menus.

SERVES 6

1 pound ground beef
1/4 cup chopped onion
2 cans (10 3/4 ounces each) condensed
    cream of celery soup
3 cups tomato juice
2 cups grated carrots
1 bay leaf
1/2 teaspoon sugar
1/2 teaspoon dried marjoram
1/2 teaspoon salt
1/4 teaspoon garlic powder
1/4 teaspoon black pepper

1 In a large saucepan over medium heat, cook beef and onion until beef is no longer pink; drain off fat.

2 Add 1 cup water, soup, tomato juice, carrots, bay leaf, sugar, marjoram, salt, garlic powder, and pepper. Bring to boil, then reduce heat and simmer, covered, until carrots are tender, about 15 minutes. Remove bay leaf before serving.

CHUCKWAGON SOUP

This is a warming and quick-to-make soup for an after-the-game supper with friends.

SERVES 8

1 1/2 pounds ground beef

1 small onion, diced

1 package (10 ounces) frozen peas, thawed

3 cans (14 1/2 ounces each) tomatoes, undrained, cut up

1 quart plus 1 cup tomato juice

1 pound noodles

1 teaspoon salt

1/2 teaspoon dried basil

1/4 teaspoon black pepper

1 cup (4 ounces) cheddar cheese, shredded

1 In a skillet over medium heat, sauté beef and onion until beef is browned and onion is translucent, about 5 minutes; drain off fat.

2 Stir in peas, tomatoes, and tomato juice. Add noodles, salt, basil, and pepper. Bring to boil, then reduce heat and simmer, covered, 25 minutes or until noodles are tender. Ladle into bowls and sprinkle cheese on top.

GERMAN BEEF-VEGETABLE SOUP

This delectable beef soup has 10 different vegetables for flavor and health.

SERVES 16

1 1/2 pounds ground beef

2 medium onions, diced

2 tablespoons beef bouillon granules

Salt and black pepper

1/2-1 teaspoon garlic powder

1 bay leaf

1 can (46 ounces) tomato or vegetable juice

3 celery stalks, diced

6 carrots, sliced

3 medium all-purpose potatoes, peeled and diced

3 cups shredded cabbage

1 small green bell pepper, cored, seeded, and chopped

1 can (8 ounces) cut green beans, drained

1 can (8 1/2 ounces) sweet peas, drained

1 can (15-16 ounces) whole-kernel corn, drained

1 In a large soup pot or Dutch oven over medium heat, cook beef and onions until beef is browned and onions are soft, about 5 minutes; drain off fat.

2 Dissolve bouillon in 1 cup boiling water and add to pot. Add salt, pepper, garlic, bay leaf, tomato juice, celery, carrots, potatoes, cabbage, and bell pepper. Bring to boil, then reduce heat and simmer, covered, until vegetables are tender, about 25 minutes.

3 Stir in beans, peas, and corn and heat through. Remove bay leaf before serving.

CORNY TOMATO DUMPLING SOUP

Corn has a major role in both the broth and the dumplings in this main course soup that gets its protein from ground beef and cheddar cheese.

SERVES 8

Soup:

1 pound ground beef

3 cups fresh or frozen whole-kernel corn

1 can (28 ounces) diced tomatoes, undrained

2 cans (14 1/2 ounces each) beef broth

1 cup chopped onion

1 garlic clove, minced

1 1/2 teaspoons dried basil

1 1/2 teaspoons dried thyme

1/2 teaspoon dried rosemary, crushed

Salt and black pepper

Dumplings:

1 cup all-purpose flour

1/2 cup cornmeal

2 1/2 teaspoons baking powder

1/2 teaspoon salt

1 egg

2/3 cup milk

1 cup fresh or frozen whole-kernel corn

1/2 cup (2 ounces) shredded cheddar cheese

1 tablespoon minced fresh parsley

1 For soup, add beef to a Dutch oven or soup pot over medium heat and cook until no longer pink; drain off fat. Stir in corn, tomatoes, broth, onion, garlic, basil, thyme, rosemary, salt, and pepper. Bring to boil, then reduce heat and simmer, covered, 30 minutes.

2 For dumplings, combine flour, cornmeal, baking powder, and salt in a medium bowl. In another medium bowl, beat egg, then stir in milk, corn, cheese, and parsley. Stir into flour mixture just until moistened. Drop by tablespoonfuls into soup. Cover and simmer until a toothpick inserted in a dumpling comes out clean, about 15 minutes (do not uncover while simmering).

SPICY BEEF-POTATO SOUP

Tomato sauce and hot peppers enliven this basic meat-and-potatoes soup designed to satisfy big appetites.

SERVES 6

1 pound ground beef

4 cups cubed peeled all-purpose potatoes (1/2-inch cubes)

1 small onion, chopped

3 cans (8 ounces each) tomato sauce

2 teaspoons salt

1 1/2 teaspoons black pepper

1/2-1 teaspoon hot red pepper sauce

1 In a Dutch oven or soup pot over medium heat, cook beef until browned; drain off fat.

2 Add potatoes, onion, and tomato sauce. Stir in 4 cups water, salt, pepper, and red pepper sauce. Bring to boil, then reduce heat and simmer, covered, 1 hour or until potatoes are tender and soup has thickened.

OLD-FASHIONED BEEF STEW

SERVES 4

2 tablespoons all-purpose flour

1/2 teaspoon salt

1/4 teaspoon black pepper

1 pound boneless beef chuck or bottom
    round, cut into 1-inch cubes

2 tablespoons vegetable oil

2 large yellow onions, coarsely chopped

6 ounces small whole mushrooms

1 pound all-purpose potatoes,
    peeled and cut into 3/4-inch cubes

8 medium carrots, peeled and cut into
    1/2-inch-thick slices

2 1/4 cups beef stock

1 cup dry red wine

1 bay leaf

1/2 teaspoon dried thyme, crumbled

3 medium parsnips, peeled and quartered

1 pint fresh Brussels sprouts or 1 package
    (10 ounces) frozen Brussels sprouts

1/4 cup minced fresh parsley

1 Place flour, salt, and pepper in a small paper bag and shake to mix. Add beef in two batches and shake until well coated.

2 Heat oil in a soup pot or 5-quart Dutch oven over medium-high heat. Add half of beef and cook, turning frequently, until browned on all sides, 5 to 8 minutes. Transfer to a plate and repeat with remaining beef.

3 Add onions to pot and sauté until slightly soft, about 3 minutes. Add mushrooms and sauté until golden, about 2 minutes.

4 Return beef to pot and add potatoes, carrots, stock, wine, bay leaf, and thyme. Bring to boil, then reduce heat to low and simmer, covered, 1 hour. Add parsnips, cover, and cook 15 minutes. Add Brussels sprouts, cover, and cook until vegetables are tender, about 15 minutes. Remove bay leaf and stir in parsley.

Not only does this classic stew have the carrots, potatoes, and mushrooms you expect, it also includes parsnips and Brussels sprouts for more vegetable power.

BEEF STEW WITH BLACK BEANS

This traditional beef stew offers extra fiber—and taste—with the addition of black beans.

SERVES 6

1 1/2 pounds boneless lean beef chuck steak

1 1/2 tablespoons olive or canola oil

6 carrots, thickly sliced diagonally

2 green or red bell peppers, cored, seeded, and cubed

8 ounces frozen pearl onions, thawed

1 tablespoon all-purpose flour

1-2 cups beef stock

1 cup dark beer or beef stock

1 can (28 ounces) crushed tomatoes

1 bay leaf

1 can (16 ounces) black beans, drained and rinsed

1/8 teaspoon salt

1/8 teaspoon black pepper

1 Using a sharp knife, trim all fat and cartilage from beef. Cut meat into 1-inch cubes.

2 Heat 1 tablespoon oil in a soup pot or Dutch oven over medium heat. Add carrots, peppers, and onions and sauté about 10 minutes or until browned. Remove from heat and, using a slotted spoon, transfer vegetables to a plate.

3 Add remaining oil to pot and heat. Add beef and sauté, stirring, about 3 minutes or until well browned on all sides. Sprinkle flour over beef and cook 1 to 2 minutes.

4 Return vegetables to pot and add 1 cup stock, beer, tomatoes, and bay leaf. Bring to boil, cover, and gently simmer 2 to 2 1/2 hours or until beef is fork-tender. Add up to 1 cup additional stock if stew becomes too thick. Remove bay leaf, stir in beans, and cook about 5 minutes or until heated through. Season with salt and pepper.

BEEF STEW WITH BEER

Beer was first added to beef stew by the Belgians. It adds a distinctive nutty flavor.

SERVES 8

3 pounds boneless beef chuck, cut into 2-inch cubes

1/2 teaspoon salt

1/4 teaspoon black pepper

2 tablespoons vegetable oil

3 large yellow onions, thickly sliced

1 teaspoon sugar

1 can (12 ounces) lager beer

1 1/2 cups beef stock

1 1/2 teaspoons dried thyme, crumbled

1 bay leaf

8 medium carrots, peeled and cut into 1 1/2-inch lengths

1 pound small new potatoes

2 tablespoons arrowroot or cornstarch with 1/4 cup cold water

1 1/2 tablespoons white wine vinegar

1 Season beef with 1/4 teaspoon salt and 1/8 teaspoon pepper. Heat oil in a Dutch oven or 5-quart flameproof baking dish over medium-high heat. Working in batches, add beef and cook until browned on all sides, about 7 minutes per batch. Transfer to a plate.

2 Reduce heat to medium, add onions and remaining salt and pepper, and sauté until golden. Add sugar and cook, stirring, 1 minute.

3 Return beef to pot and add beer, stock, thyme, and bay leaf. Bring to boil, then reduce heat to medium-low and simmer, covered, until beef is tender, about 1 1/2 hours. Add carrots and potatoes, cover, and simmer 20 to 30 minutes.

4 Uncover, increase heat to medium-high, and bring to boil. Blend in arrowroot mixture and cook, stirring constantly, until thickened, 2 to 3 minutes. Stir in vinegar and remove bay leaf.

BURGUNDY BEEF STEW

This slow-cooked stew, the French boeuf bour-guignon, is a tantalizing amalgam of rich, warming flavors—perfect for a midwinter dinner party. (Photograph on page 4)

SERVES 4

12 ounces eye round of beef, trimmed and cut into 1/2-inch chunks

3 turkey bacon slices, coarsely chopped

1 1/2 cups frozen pearl onions, thawed

3 carrots, thinly sliced

4 garlic cloves, slivered

1 tablespoon sugar

12 ounces mushrooms, quartered

2 tablespoons all-purpose flour

1/2 cup dry red wine or chicken stock

3/4 teaspoon thyme

3/4 teaspoon salt

1/2 teaspoon black pepper

1 Preheat oven to 350°F. Coat a nonstick Dutch oven or flameproof baking dish with nonstick cooking spray. Add beef and cook until browned, about 5 minutes. Using a slotted spoon, transfer to a plate.

2 Add bacon, onions, carrots, and garlic to Dutch oven. Sprinkle with sugar and cook until onions are golden, about 7 minutes. Add mushrooms and cook until tender, about 4 minutes.

3 Return beef and any juices to Dutch oven. Sprinkle with flour and cook, stirring, until flour is absorbed, about 3 minutes.

4 Add wine and bring to boil. Add 3/4 cup water, thyme, salt, and pepper and return to boil. Cover and bake until meat is tender, about 1 hour.

QUICK-COOK BEEF BURGUNDY STEW

Using tender beef sirloin cuts down on the cooking time for this classic stew.

SERVES 4

2 ounces bacon, coarsely chopped

2 tablespoons all-purpose flour

1 pound beef sirloin, trimmed and cut into 1/2-inch chunks

1 cup frozen pearl onions, thawed

4 garlic cloves, peeled and halved

2 carrots, halved lengthwise and cut into 2-inch lengths

8 ounces small button mushrooms, quartered

4 ounces fresh shiitake mushrooms or button mushrooms, trimmed and thickly sliced

2/3 cup dry red wine

2/3 cup chicken stock

1 tablespoon tomato paste

1/2 teaspoon dried thyme

1/2 teaspoon salt

1 In a Dutch oven or flameproof baking dish over medium heat, heat bacon and 1/4 cup water 4 minutes or until bacon renders its fat. Place flour in a shallow dish and dredge beef, shaking off excess. Add to Dutch oven and sauté 3 minutes or until lightly browned on all sides. Transfer to a plate.

2 Add onions and garlic to Dutch oven and sauté 5 minutes. Add carrots and sauté 7 minutes. Add button and shiitake mushrooms and cook 4 minutes.

3 Add wine, increase heat to high, and cook 5 minutes or until reduced by half. Add stock, tomato paste, thyme, and salt and simmer 10 minutes. Return beef to Dutch oven and simmer 3 minutes.

BEEF STEW WITH BASIL-TOMATO PASTE

This stew has a delicious Italian bias with its basil, fennel, and garlic seasonings, as well as a full spectrum of vegetables from tomatoes to snow peas.

SERVES 4

1 tablespoon olive oil

1 pound boneless lean chuck steak, cut into 1 1/2-inch cubes

1/4 teaspoon black pepper

1/2 cup dry red wine

2 cups canned low-sodium beef broth

1 can (16 ounces) low-sodium tomatoes, pureed with juice

1 medium celery stalk, sliced

4 garlic cloves, minced

2 strips orange rind, 3 inches long

1/2 teaspoon fennel seed, crushed

1/2 teaspoon dried basil, crumbled

1/2 teaspoon dried thyme, crumbled

1 bay leaf

2 medium yellow onions, quartered

4 medium turnips, peeled and quartered

4 medium carrots, peeled and cut into 1-inch-thick slices

3 tablespoons fresh basil, minced, or 2 tablespoons fresh parsley, minced, plus 1 teaspoon dried basil, crumbled

2 tablespoons low-sodium tomato paste

6 ounces fresh or thawed frozen snow peas

1 Heat oil 1 minute in a heavy 10-inch skillet over medium heat. Season beef with pepper, add to skillet, and cook until browned, about 4 minutes. Transfer to a 4-quart Dutch oven.

2 Add wine to skillet and bring to boil. Cook, uncovered, 2 minutes, scraping up browned bits. Add broth, tomatoes, celery, half of garlic, orange zest, fennel seed, basil, thyme, and bay leaf and bring to boil. Pour into Dutch oven, then reduce heat and simmer, covered, 1 1/4 hours.

3 Remove bay leaf and add onions, turnips, and carrots. Simmer, covered, until vegetables are tender, about 45 minutes.

4 In a small bowl, mash remaining garlic and basil with a fork, blend in tomato paste, and set aside. Cook snow peas 1 minute in boiling water, then drain. Stir basil-tomato paste into stew along with snow peas and heat 1 minute.

LOUISIANA BEEF STEW

The tomatoes that enliven this stew are a rich source of disease-fighting lycopene.

SERVES 4

2 tablespoons all-purpose flour

1 pound bottom round of beef, trimmed and cut into 1/2-inch chunks

1 tablespoon vegetable oil

1 small onion, finely chopped

2 garlic cloves, minced

2 carrots, thinly sliced

1 pound all-purpose potatoes, peeled and cut into 1/2-inch chunks

3 cups canned low-sodium tomatoes, undrained, chopped

3 tablespoons molasses

3 tablespoons red wine vinegar

3/4 teaspoon ground ginger

3/4 teaspoon salt

1 Place flour in a shallow dish and dredge beef, shaking off excess. In a Dutch oven or flameproof baking dish, heat oil over medium-high heat. Add beef and cook 3 minutes or until lightly browned. Transfer to a plate.

2 Reduce heat to medium, add onion and garlic to Dutch oven, and sauté 5 minutes. Add carrots and cook 3 minutes. Add potatoes, tomatoes, molasses, vinegar, ginger, and salt and bring to boil.

Reduce heat and simmer, covered, 30 minutes or until potatoes are tender.

3 Return beef to Dutch oven and simmer, covered, 5 minutes or until cooked through.

SUNDOWN STEW

The aroma of beef simmering in gravy will summon hikers to dinner long before it's even time to add the dumplings. This stew is as good at home as it is by the campfire.

SERVES 4

2 tablespoons vegetable oil

1 pound lean boneless chuck steak, 1 inch thick, cut crosswise into 1/4-inch-wide strips

1 envelope (3/4 ounce) mushroom gravy mix

4 medium carrots, peeled and thickly sliced

2 cups fresh green peas or 1 package (10 ounces) frozen green peas

2 cups biscuit mix

2/3 cup low-fat (1%) milk

1 Heat oil in a large saucepan over medium heat. Add beef and cook until browned on all sides, about 10 minutes.

2 In a small bowl or resealable plastic bag, combine gravy mix and 1 cup water. Stir into pan and simmer, stirring occasionally, 2 minutes. Add carrots and bring to boil. Reduce heat, cover, and simmer until beef is almost tender, about 1 hour. Stir in peas.

3 In a small bowl or plastic bag, combine biscuit mix and milk, then drop by tablespoons into stew. Cover and cook 10 minutes, then uncover and cook 10 minutes.

COWBOY STEAK STEW

To quote Colorado cowboys about the secret of cooking good beef: "Don't mess with it—the simpler, the better!"

SERVES 8

2 1/4 pounds boneless beef round or chuck steak, trimmed and cut into 1-inch pieces

1 teaspoon black pepper

1/4 teaspoon salt

1 medium yellow onion, thinly sliced

4 medium all-purpose potatoes, peeled and cut into bite-size pieces

6 large carrots, peeled and cut diagonally into 1/2-inch-thick slices

1 celery stalk, chopped

8 ounces green beans, trimmed and cut into 2-inch pieces

2 cans (14 1/2 ounces each) low-sodium stewed tomatoes, undrained

1 can (10 3/4 ounces) condensed tomato soup

2 tablespoons quick-cooking tapioca

1 On a piece of wax paper, toss beef with pepper and salt. Place in a 5-quart slow cooker and layer onion, potatoes, carrots, celery, and green beans on top.

2 In a medium bowl, stir together tomatoes, soup, and tapioca and pour over beef and vegetables. Cover and cook on high 5 to 6 hours or on low 9 to 10 hours or until tender, stirring once during last hour of cooking. Serve with freshly baked cornbread.

BEEF SHORT-RIB STEW WITH CHILI BISCUIT TOPPING

SERVES 6

Stew:

1/4 cup all-purpose flour

3 pounds lean beef short ribs

3 tablespoons vegetable oil

4 medium carrots, peeled and cut into
   1/2-inch rounds

1 large yellow onion, chopped

1 garlic clove, minced

4 cups homemade beef stock or canned
   low-sodium beef broth

1 can (16 ounces) Italian plum tomatoes,
   undrained

1/2 teaspoon salt

1/2 teaspoon dried thyme, crumbled

1/4 teaspoon black pepper

1 cup pearl onions

1/4 cup chopped fresh parsley

Topping:

2 cups all-purpose flour

1 tablespoon baking powder

2 teaspoons chili powder

1/2 teaspoon baking soda

1/2 teaspoon salt

1/3 cup vegetable shortening

2 tablespoons butter or margarine

1 cup coarsely shredded sharp cheddar cheese

3/4 cup buttermilk

1 For stew, preheat oven to 350°F. Place flour in a large resealable plastic bag and, working in batches, dredge beef. Set aside.

2 Heat 1 tablespoon oil 1 minute in a 6-quart Dutch oven over medium-high heat. Add carrots, onion, and garlic and sauté until onion is limp, about 5 minutes. Transfer to a small bowl.

3 Add remaining oil to Dutch oven and heat 2 minutes. Add beef, in batches if necessary, and sauté, turning frequently, until browned, about 5 minutes. Add stock, tomatoes, salt, thyme, and pepper and bring to boil over high heat. Cover and bake until beef is almost tender, 1 1/2 to 2 hours. Stir in reserved vegetables and pearl onions, cover, and bake until meat is fork-tender, 30 to 40 minutes.

4 For topping, combine flour, baking powder, chili powder, baking soda, and salt in a large bowl. Using a pastry blender, cut in shortening and butter until mixture resembles coarse crumbs. Using a fork, add cheese and then buttermilk, mixing until a soft dough forms. Turn out onto a lightly floured surface and pat into a circle 3/4 inch thick. Using a floured 3-inch biscuit cutter, cut into 6 rounds.

5 Remove stew from oven and increase oven temperature to 450°F. Skim fat from stew. Place biscuits evenly on top of bubbling stew and bake, uncovered, until golden, 12 to 15 minutes. Sprinkle stew and topping with parsley.

This stew with its savory biscuit topping is hearty and delicious and perfect for a cold winter night.

BEEF POTPIE

English colonists brought potpies to America. This one has a Southern touch; it's topped with buttermilk biscuits instead of piecrust.

SERVES 8

Potpie:

2 pounds boneless beef chuck, trimmed and cut into 3/4-inch cubes

1/4 cup all-purpose flour

1 tablespoon vegetable oil

1 cup chopped onion

3 garlic cloves, minced

3 cups homemade beef stock or canned low-sodium beef broth

1 tablespoon tomato paste

1/2 teaspoon dried thyme

1/2 teaspoon salt

1/2 teaspoon black pepper

4 large carrots, peeled and cut into 1/4-inch rounds

1 large all-purpose potato, peeled and cut into 1/2-inch cubes

2 medium parsnips, peeled and cut into 1/2-inch cubes

Biscuits:

1 1/2 cups all-purpose flour

1 3/4 teaspoons baking powder

1/2 teaspoon sugar

1/2 teaspoon dried thyme

1/4 teaspoon salt

1/4 teaspoon baking soda

1/4 cup (1/2 stick) cold unsalted butter, cut up

3/4 cup low-fat buttermilk

1 For potpie, preheat oven to 350°F. Place flour in a shallow dish and dredge beef, shaking off excess. In a 6-quart nonstick Dutch oven, heat oil over medium-high heat. Add beef and sauté, turning frequently, 5 minutes or until browned. Transfer to a bowl.

2 Add onion and garlic to Dutch oven and sauté 5 minutes or until tender. Stir in beef and any juices, stock, tomato paste, thyme, salt, and pepper and bring to boil over high heat. Cover and bake 30 minutes. Stir in carrots, potato, and parsnips and bake, covered, 40 minutes or until meat is tender.

3 For biscuits, combine flour, baking powder, sugar, thyme, salt, and baking soda in a large bowl. Using a pastry blender or two knives, cut in butter until mixture resembles coarse crumbs. Using a fork or your hands, mix in buttermilk just until a dough forms. Turn out onto a lightly floured surface and pat into a circle 1/2 inch thick. Using a floured 2-inch biscuit cutter, cut out about 16 biscuits and place on top of beef mixture. Bake, uncovered, 15 minutes or until biscuits are golden.

HUNGARIAN GOULASH

Over the years, many American families have adopted this stew as their own. Serve it with egg noodles.

SERVES 4

1 pound boneless beef chuck, trimmed and cut into 1 1/2-inch cubes

1/2 teaspoon black pepper

1/4 teaspoon salt

2 tablespoons olive oil

1 large yellow onion, thinly sliced

1 tablespoon all-purpose flour

1 tablespoon sweet Hungarian paprika

1 tablespoon tomato paste

1 tablespoon red wine vinegar

2 garlic cloves, minced

1/2 teaspoon caraway seed

1/2 teaspoon dried marjoram

1 1/4-1 3/4 cups homemade beef stock or canned low-sodium beef broth

8 ounces red potatoes, scrubbed and cut into 3/4-inch cubes

4 ounces mushrooms, quartered

2 tablespoons chopped fresh parsley

1/2 teaspoon grated lemon zest

1 Season beef with pepper and salt. Heat 1 tablespoon oil in a 5-quart nonstick Dutch oven over medium-high heat. Add beef and sauté 6 minutes, then transfer to a plate.

2 Add onion to Dutch oven and sauté 5 minutes or until golden and tender. Stir in beef and any juices, flour, paprika, tomato paste, vinegar, garlic, caraway seed, and marjoram. Cook 3 minutes, stirring constantly.

3 Stir in stock and bring to boil. Reduce heat and simmer, covered, 1 hour. Add potatoes and more stock if needed. Simmer, uncovered, 25 minutes or until beef and potatoes are tender.

4 Meanwhile, heat remaining oil in an 8-inch skillet over medium-high heat. Add mushrooms and sauté 6 minutes or until browned. Stir into goulash with parsley and lemon zest.

GOULASH STEW WITH DUMPLINGS

This rich meal-in-a-bowl combines beef with vegetables, dumplings, and three essential ingredients of an authentic goulash: paprika, onions, and caraway seed.

SERVES 4

Goulash:

1 1/2 tablespoons sunflower oil

2 large onions, sliced

2 garlic cloves, finely chopped

1 pound 2 ounces lean chuck steak, trimmed and cut into 3/4-inch cubes

2 large carrots, diced

1 tablespoon paprika

1/4 teaspoon caraway seed

1 can (14 1/2 ounces) chopped tomatoes, undrained

2 1/2 cups beef stock

1/2 small head white cabbage, finely shredded

Salt and black pepper

Chopped fresh parsley

Dumplings:

1 tablespoon sunflower oil

1 onion, finely chopped

1 egg

3 tablespoons low-fat (1%) milk

3 tablespoons fresh parsley, chopped

4 1/2 ounces fresh bread crumbs

Salt and black pepper

1 For goulash, heat oil in a large saucepan over medium-low heat. Add onions and garlic and sauté just until beginning to brown, about 10 minutes.

2 Add beef and sauté until browned, about 5 minutes. Add carrots, paprika, caraway seed, tomatoes, and stock. Season to taste with salt and pepper. Bring to boil, then reduce heat and simmer, covered, until beef is just tender, about 1 hour.

3 For dumplings, heat oil in a skillet over low heat. Add onion and sauté until softened but not colored, about 10 minutes. In a small bowl, beat egg and milk, then add onion, parsley, and bread crumbs. Season to taste with salt and pepper and mix well.

4 Add cabbage to pan and stir to mix. Using wet hands, shape dumpling mixture into 12 walnut-size balls. Add to pan and simmer, covered, until dumplings are cooked, about 15 minutes. Ladle into warm soup bowls and sprinkle with parsley.

CLASSIC BEEF STROGANOFF

Named for a Russian diplomat, this dish is fast and easy to prepare. Reduced-fat sour cream makes it healthy, too. Serve with rice or noodles.

SERVES 4

1 tablespoon vegetable oil

1 pound beef sirloin, trimmed and cut into 3 x 1-inch strips

3 scallions, thinly sliced

8 ounces mushrooms, thinly sliced

1/3 cup canned low-sodium tomatoes, undrained, chopped

1 tablespoon tomato paste

1/2 teaspoon dried tarragon

1/4 teaspoon salt

1/4 teaspoon black pepper

1/8 teaspoon cayenne pepper

1/4 cup reduced-fat sour cream

1 Heat 2 teaspoons oil in a large nonstick skillet over medium-high heat. Add beef and sauté 2 to 3 minutes or until lightly browned and just cooked through. Using a slotted spoon, transfer to a plate.

2 Add remaining oil, scallions, and mushrooms to skillet and cook, stirring frequently, 3 minutes or until mushrooms begin to release their juice. Add tomatoes, tomato paste, tarragon, salt, black pepper, and cayenne. Bring to boil and cook 1 minute. Remove from heat and stir in sour cream. Return beef to skillet and stir.

BEEF STROGANOFF WITH GREEN PEPPERCORNS AND GHERKINS

This is a twist on classic stroganoff; the peppercorns and gherkins offset the richness of the sour cream.

SERVES 4

3 tablespoons olive oil

1 large red onion, thinly sliced

1/2 pound small mushrooms, halved

1 1/4 pounds beef fillet, cut into thin strips

2 teaspoons fresh green peppercorns in brine

2 tablespoons Dijon mustard

1 1/4 cups sour cream

3 ounces drained cocktail gherkins

Snipped fresh chives

1 Heat 1 tablespoon oil in a large skillet over medium-high heat. Add onion and sauté 3 minutes or until softened. Add mushrooms and sauté 5 minutes or until softened and liquid has evaporated. Transfer to a bowl.

2 Add another 1 tablespoon oil to skillet and increase heat to high. Add half of beef and stir-fry 2 to 3 minutes or until lightly browned. Transfer to a plate. Add remaining oil and stir-fry remaining beef 2 to 3 minutes.

3 Return onion, mushrooms, and first batch of beef with juice to pan. Crush peppercorns, add to skillet, and cook, stirring, 2 minutes or until heated through.

4 In a medium bowl, combine mustard and sour cream. Stir into beef mixture, add gherkins, and heat through (do not boil). Garnish with chives.

POT-AU-FEU

Enjoy this classic French country dish in a low-fat recipe that preserves its homey goodness and fabulous flavor.

SERVES 8

4 medium leeks

6 flat-leaf parsley sprigs plus 1/4 cup chopped flat-leaf parsley

6 thyme sprigs

1 bay leaf

3 pounds bone-in chicken pieces

1 garlic head, separated into cloves and peeled

1 teaspoon salt

1 teaspoon black pepper

5 cans (14 1/2 ounces each) low-sodium chicken broth

1 medium head green cabbage (about 2 pounds), cut into eight wedges

1 pound carrots, peeled and cut into 2-inch pieces

1 pound small red potatoes, scrubbed and halved

1 pound beef tenderloin, tied with string

1 Cut roots and dark green tops from leeks. Cut white parts in half lengthwise and rinse well, swishing to remove sand. Tie leek tops, parsley and thyme sprigs, and bay leaf into a bouquet garni with kitchen string.

2 In a large soup pot, combine chicken, bouquet garni, white parts of leeks, garlic, 1/2 teaspoon salt, and 1/2 teaspoon pepper. Pour in broth and add enough water to cover. Bring to boil, then reduce heat and simmer, uncovered, 30 minutes.

3 Submerge cabbage, carrots, potatoes, and beef in liquid. Simmer 30 minutes or until beef is done to taste (135° to 140°F for medium-rare). Add remaining salt and pepper.

4 Remove bouquet garni and skim fat from broth. Transfer beef to cutting board, remove string, cover with foil, and let stand 5 minutes. Cut across grain into thin slices. Debone chicken and remove skin. Divide chicken, beef, and vegetables among 8 large soup bowls and ladle hot broth over each portion. Sprinkle with chopped parsley.

SPICED BEEF STEW WITH DRIED FRUIT

This British-inspired stew combines beef, fruit, and spices with delicious results.

SERVES 6

1 1/2 pounds lean chuck steak

1 1/2 tablespoons olive or canola oil

2 large onions, thinly sliced

1 tablespoon all-purpose flour

1/2 teaspoon ground cumin

1/2 teaspoon ground coriander

1 1/2-2 1/2 cups beef stock

1 can (28 ounces) crushed tomatoes

1/2 cup pearled barley

1/2 cup pitted dried apricots, halved

1/2 cup pitted prunes, halved

1/8 teaspoon salt

1/8 teaspoon black pepper

1 Using a sharp knife, trim all fat and cartilage from beef. Cut beef into 1-inch cubes.

2 Heat 1 tablespoon oil in a Dutch oven or soup pot over medium heat. Add onions and sauté 10 minutes or until well browned. Using a slotted spoon, transfer to a plate.

3 Add remaining oil to pot and heat. Add beef and sauté 3 minutes or until well browned on all sides. Sprinkle with flour, cumin, and coriander and cook 1 to 2 minutes or until flour and spices are absorbed.

4 Return onions to pot with 1 1/2 cups stock and tomatoes. Bring to boil, then reduce heat and gently simmer, covered, about 1 hour or until beef is half cooked. Stir in barley, apricots, prunes, salt, and pepper. Cover and cook 1 to 1 1/2 hours or until meat is very tender when pierced with a fork. Add up to 1 cup additional stock if stew becomes too thick.

MOROCCAN BEEF STEW WITH SWEET POTATOES, CHICKPEAS, AND DRIED FRUIT

A provocative mix of Middle Eastern spices, sweet potatoes, and fruit makes this beef hotpot exotic and delectable.

SERVES 6

1 tablespoon vegetable oil

1 pound beef bottom round steak, cut into 1-inch cubes

1 onion, finely chopped

4 garlic cloves, minced

1/2 teaspoon ground ginger

1/2 teaspoon ground cinnamon

1/2 teaspoon ground nutmeg

1/2 teaspoon ground turmeric

1/2 teaspoon salt

1/4 teaspoon black pepper

1/2 cup chopped dried apricots

1/4 cup golden or dark seedless raisins

2 sweet potatoes, peeled and cut into 3/4-inch chunks

3 cups canned fat-free low-sodium chicken broth

1 can (15 ounces) chickpeas, drained and rinsed

Thinly sliced strips scallion greens

Thin strips orange rind

1 Heat oil in a large nonstick saucepan or pot over medium-high heat. Working in batches, add beef and cook until browned on all sides, 3 to 4 minutes per batch, and transfer to a plate. Add onion to pan and cook 5 minutes or until softened, adding a spoonful of water if necessary to prevent sticking.

2 Add garlic, ginger, cinnamon, nutmeg, turmeric, salt, and pepper and cook 1 minute. Add apricots, raisins, sweet potatoes, beef, and broth. Cover and simmer 1 1/2 hours or until meat is very tender.

3 Stir in chickpeas and heat through. Garnish with scallions and orange zest.

BAKED BEEF STEW

Here's a beef stew that will let you do other things while it gets more and more savory in the oven.

SERVES 6

2 pounds lean beef stew meat, cut into 1-inch cubes

1 cup canned tomatoes, cut up

6 carrots, cut into strips

3 medium all-purpose potatoes, peeled and quartered

1/2 cup thickly sliced celery

1 medium onion, sliced and separated into rings

3 tablespoons quick-cooking tapioca

1 slice bread, crumbled

1 Preheat oven to 325°F. Grease a 3-quart baking dish.

2 In a large bowl, combine 1 cup water, beef, tomatoes, carrots, potatoes, celery, onion, tapioca, and bread. Spoon into baking dish, cover, and bake 3 1/2 hours.

NEW ENGLAND BOILED BEEF STEW

SERVES 4

Stew:

1 1/2 pounds lean chuck steak, trimmed

3 thyme sprigs

3 parsley sprigs

1 large bay leaf

2 large garlic cloves, sliced

10 whole black peppercorns, lightly crushed

8 ounces leeks, sliced

1 celery stalk, cut into 3-inch pieces

8 ounces baby new potatoes, scrubbed

12 small shallots

8 ounces baby turnips

8 ounces baby carrots

1 small head Savoy cabbage, cored and finely shredded

1/2 teaspoon salt

Minced parsley

Relish:

3 medium beets, cooked, peeled, and finely diced

6 scallions, minced

3 tablespoons fresh parsley, minced

Salt and black pepper

1 For stew, place beef in a Dutch oven or soup pot and add 5 cups water. Bring to boil over high heat, skimming surface to remove foam. As soon as liquid boils, reduce heat to very low.

2 Tie thyme, parsley, bay leaf, garlic, and peppercorns in a muslin bag and add to pan with leeks and celery. Partially cover and simmer, skimming as necessary, 2 hours or until beef is very tender when pierced with a sharp knife.

3 Meanwhile, for relish, combine beets, scallions, parsley, salt, and pepper in a medium bowl. Cover and refrigerate.

4 Preheat oven to 200°F. When beef is done, transfer to an ovenproof serving dish and spoon in broth to cover. Cover with foil and place in oven to keep warm.

5 Remove muslin bag from pot. Add potatoes, shallots, and salt, increase heat to medium, and cook 5 minutes. Add turnips and carrots, reduce heat, and simmer, covered, 15 minutes or until tender. Using a slotted spoon, transfer to dish with meat.

6 Add cabbage to broth and simmer 3 minutes or until tender. Remove with a slotted spoon and add to other vegetables.

7 Slice beef against grain and place in soup bowls. Top with a selection of vegetables, spoon in broth, and sprinkle with parsley. Pass relish at table.

This traditional American dish is a one-pot meal of succulent beef and crisp-tender vegetables in tasty broth.

BEEF AND BISCUIT STEW

This inviting beef stew wears a cap of biscuits.

SERVES 8

Stew:

All-purpose flour

2 pounds beef stew meat, cut into
    1-inch cubes

2 tablespoons cooking oil

2 beef bouillon cubes

Salt and black pepper

6-8 small all-purpose potatoes,
    peeled and quartered

3 small onions, quartered

4 carrots, sliced

1 package (10 ounces) frozen green beans,
    thawed

2 tablespoons cornstarch

Biscuits:

2 cups all-purpose flour

4 teaspoons baking powder

1/2 teaspoon salt

2 tablespoons vegetable oil

3/4-1 cup milk

Melted butter

1 For stew, place flour in a shallow dish and dredge beef cubes. Heat oil in a large Dutch oven over medium heat. Add beef and cook until browned on all sides.

2 Dissolve bouillon in 2 cups boiling water and add to Dutch oven. Season with salt and pepper. Bring to boil, then reduce heat and simmer, covered, 1 1/2 hours or until tender.

3 Add potatoes, onions, carrots, and beans and cook 30 to 45 minutes or until tender. In a small bowl, combine cornstarch and 1/4 cup water. Stir into stew and cook until thickened and bubbling.

4 For biscuits, preheat oven to 350°F. In a large bowl, combine flour, baking powder, salt, oil, and milk. Stir until a light, soft dough forms, adding more milk if necessary. Drop by tablespoons on top of stew and brush tops with melted butter. Bake, uncovered, 20 to 30 minutes or until biscuits are done.

GONE-ALL-DAY STEW

This quick-to-prepare but long-cooking stew has Italian roots. Serve over noodles or with crusty French bread.

SERVES 8

1 can (10 3/4 ounces) condensed
    tomato soup

1/4 cup all-purpose flour

2 pounds beef chuck, trimmed and
    cut into 1- to 2-inch cubes

3 medium carrots, cut diagonally into
    1-inch-thick slices

6 white boiling onions or yellow onions,
    quartered

4 medium all-purpose potatoes,
    cut into 1 1/2-inch chunks

1/2 cup celery, cut into 1-inch chunks

12 whole large fresh mushrooms

2 beef bouillon cubes

1 tablespoon Italian herb seasoning mix or
    1 teaspoon each dried oregano, thyme,
    and rosemary

1 bay leaf

1/4 teaspoon black pepper

1 Preheat oven to 275°F. In a Dutch oven, stir together 1 cup water, soup, and flour until smooth. Add beef, carrots, onions, potatoes, celery, mushrooms, bouillon, Italian seasoning, bay leaf, and pepper. Cover and bake 4 to 5 hours or until meat is tender. Remove bay leaf before serving.

HUNTER'S STEW

A wonderful recipe for venison, this healthy stew is also a hit with beef as the main ingredient.

SERVES 8

2 tablespoons vegetable oil

2 pounds beef chuck or venison,
    cut into 1-inch cubes

1/2 cup tomato juice

2 medium onions, cut into wedges

2 celery stalks, sliced

1 teaspoon Worcestershire sauce

2 bay leaves

2-3 teaspoons salt

1/2 teaspoon black pepper

6 carrots, peeled and quartered

1 rutabaga, peeled and cubed

6 medium all-purpose potatoes,
    peeled and quartered

1 cup frozen peas

1 tablespoon cornstarch

1 Heat oil in a cast-iron Dutch oven over medium heat. Add beef and cook until browned. Add 4 cups water and scrape up browned bits.

2 Add tomato juice, onions, celery, Worcestershire sauce, bay leaves, salt, and pepper. Cover tightly, reduce heat, and simmer, stirring occasionally, 2 hours.

3 Remove bay leaves and add carrots, rutabaga, and potatoes. Cover and cook 40 minutes. Stir in peas and cook 10 minutes. In a small bowl, combine cornstarch with 1/2 cup water, then stir into stew. Cook, stirring, until thickened.

BEEF AND PASTA STEW

Slim pasta spirals called fusilli are delicious in a stew with beef and vegetables.

SERVES 4

1 tablespoon extra-virgin olive oil

12 ounces chuck steak, cut into
    1/2-inch cubes

1 onion, chopped

1 can (14 1/2 ounces) chopped tomatoes,
    undrained

2 tablespoons tomato puree

2 garlic cloves, minced

4 cups beef or vegetable stock

3 large carrots, sliced

4 celery stalks, sliced

1 small turnip, chopped

Salt and black pepper

1 tablespoon chopped fresh oregano or
    1 teaspoon dried oregano

8 ounces fusilli

1 Heat oil in a large flameproof baking dish over medium heat. Add beef and cook, stirring frequently, until browned. Using a slotted spoon, transfer to a plate.

2 Add onion to baking dish and cook, stirring often, about 5 minutes or until softened. Add tomatoes, tomato puree, garlic, and 2 cups stock. Stir well and bring to boil.

3 Return beef to baking dish and add carrots, celery, turnip, salt, and pepper. Reduce heat and simmer, covered, 1 hour or until beef is tender.

4 Add pasta, oregano, and remaining stock and bring to boil. Reduce heat and simmer, covered, 20 to 25 minutes or until pasta is tender. Serve immediately.

BEEF AND BARLEY STEW

Here, beef is simmered until meltingly tender, while nourishing pot barley thickens the gravy to make a hearty stew.

SERVES 4

1 pound 2 ounces beef chuck or
    lean braising steak, trimmed and
    cut into 2-inch cubes

2 garlic cloves, halved

3 bay leaves

6 juniper berries, lightly crushed

1 thyme sprig

1 cup full-bodied red wine

12 pearl onions

1 tablespoon extra-virgin olive oil

1/4 cup pot barley

1 3/4 cups beef stock

Salt and black pepper

3 large carrots, cut into large chunks

2 celery stalks, sliced

1 medium rutabaga, peeled and cut into
    1/2-inch chunks

1 In a medium bowl, combine beef, garlic, bay leaves, juniper berries, and thyme. Pour in wine, cover, and refrigerate at least 8 hours or overnight.

2 Preheat oven to 325°F. In a small bowl, cover pearl onions with boiling water. Let stand 2 minutes, then drain. When cool enough to handle, remove skins and set aside.

3 Remove beef from marinade and pat dry with paper towels. Heat oil in a large Dutch oven over medium-high heat. Working in batches if necessary, add beef and cook until browned on all sides. Transfer to a plate.

4 Add onions to Dutch oven and sauté 4 minutes or until lightly colored. Add barley and cook, stirring, 1 minute. Return beef and any juices to Dutch oven, add stock, and bring to boil. Strain marinade

into Dutch oven, adding bay leaves and thyme from sieve. Season to taste with salt and pepper. Cover tightly and bake 45 minutes.

5 Stir in carrots, celery, and rutabaga. Cover and bake 1 hour or until beef, barley, and vegetables are tender. Remove bay leaves and thyme before serving.

ASIAN BEEF AND CAULIFLOWER STEW

This lovely stew is flavored with ginger, soy sauce, and green bell peppers. Serve with rice.

SERVES 6

2 tablespoons vegetable oil

1 1/2 pounds lean round steak, cut into
    1-inch cubes

3 cups beef stock

1 small head cauliflower, separated into florets

1 green bell pepper, cored, seeded, and
    cut into chunks

1/4 cup soy sauce

1 garlic clove, minced

1 1/2 teaspoons grated fresh ginger *(optional)*

2-3 tablespoons cornstarch

1/2 teaspoon sugar

1 cup sliced scallions

1 Heat oil in a skillet over medium-high heat. Add beef and cook until browned on all sides. Add stock and bring to boil, then reduce heat and simmer, covered, until tender, about 1 hour.

2 Add cauliflower, bell pepper, soy sauce, garlic, and ginger, if desired. Simmer, covered, 5 minutes or until vegetables are tender.

3 In a small bowl, combine cornstarch, sugar, and 1/4 cup water, then stir into skillet. Bring to boil, stirring constantly, and cook 2 minutes or until thickened. Stir in scallions.

SHIPWRECK STEW

This is the dish you make with all the leftovers in your galley after a shipwreck—or your pantry after a too-busy week. It's delicious, and your friends will love it.

SERVES 10

1 pound ground beef

1 cup chopped onion

3 cups cubed peeled all-purpose potatoes

3 medium carrots, peeled and sliced

1 cup chopped celery

1/4 cup minced fresh parsley

1 package (9 ounces) frozen cut green beans, thawed

1 can (15 ounces) kidney beans, drained and rinsed

1 can (8 ounces) tomato sauce

1/4 cup long-grain rice

1 teaspoon salt

1 teaspoon Worcestershire sauce

1/2-1 teaspoon chili powder

1/4 teaspoon black pepper

1 Preheat oven to 350°F. Add beef and onion to a medium skillet and cook over medium heat until beef is browned and onion is softened. Drain off fat.

2 In a 3-quart baking dish, combine beef mixture with 1 cup water, potatoes, carrots, celery, parsley, green beans, kidney beans, tomato sauce, rice, salt, Worcestershire sauce, chili powder, and pepper. Cover and bake for 1 hour or until rice and potatoes are tender.

BOLOGNESE BEEF POT

Lemon and fennel bring fresh flavors to familiar ground beef in this Italian-inspired stew.

SERVES 4

1 pound extra-lean ground beef

1 onion, chopped

2 garlic cloves, crushed

1 1/2 pounds all-purpose potatoes, scrubbed and cubed

2 cans (14 1/2 ounces) chopped tomatoes, undrained

1/2 cup chicken stock

Grated zest and juice of 1 lemon

1 tablespoon light brown sugar

1 fennel bulb, thinly sliced

1/2 cup frozen green beans

Salt and black pepper

Minced fennel leaves

Minced flat-leaf parsley

1 In a large saucepan over medium heat, combine beef, onion, and garlic and sauté 5 minutes or until beef is browned.

2 Stir in potatoes, tomatoes, stock, half of lemon zest, and sugar. Bring to boil, then reduce heat, and simmer, covered, 10 minutes.

3 Stir in fennel, beans, and lemon juice and simmer, covered, 5 minutes or until potatoes are tender and fennel and beans are crisp-tender.

4 Season to taste with salt and pepper. Pour into soup bowls and garnish with remaining lemon zest, fennel, and parsley.

QUICK BEEF STEW

Rich and delicious, this stew takes only minutes to prepare.

SERVES 4

2 cups diced cooked roast beef

1 can (16 ounces) mixed vegetables, drained and liquid reserved

1 can (10 3/4 ounces) condensed cream of celery soup

1 can (10 3/4 ounces) condensed cream of mushroom soup

1/2 teaspoon dried thyme *(optional)*

1/4 teaspoon dried rosemary *(optional)*

Black pepper

1 In a large saucepan, combine beef, vegetables, celery soup, mushroom soup, thyme, if desired, rosemary, if desired, and pepper. Cook 4 to 5 minutes or until heated through. If desired, add reserved vegetable liquid to thin stew.

SOUTHWEST STEW

This is a rugged, stick-to-your ribs dish for healthy appetites.

SERVES 8

2 pounds ground beef

1 1/2 cups diced onion

1 can (28 ounces) tomatoes, undrained, chopped

1 can (15 ounces) pinto beans, drained and rinsed

1 can (17 ounces) whole-kernel corn, drained

1 cup prepared salsa

1 teaspoon ground cumin

1/2 teaspoon garlic powder

1/2 teaspoon black pepper

Salt

Shredded cheddar cheese *(optional)*

1 In a large skillet over medium heat, cook beef and onions until browned; drain off fat. Add 3/4 cup water, tomatoes, beans, corn, salsa, cumin, garlic powder, pepper, and salt and bring to boil. Reduce heat and simmer, covered, 15 to 20 minutes. Garnish with cheese, if desired.

SOUTHWEST STEW WITH HOMINY

This makes a satisfying dinner that can be put together quickly with items from your pantry.

SERVES 4

1 pound ground beef or turkey

1 medium onion, diced

1 can (16 ounces) tomatoes, undrained

1 can (15 ounces) chili beans, undrained

1 can (4 ounces) diced green chiles, undrained

1 can (15 1/2 ounces) hominy, drained

1 can (16 ounces) whole-kernel corn, drained

Salt and pepper to taste

1 tablespoon cornstarch *(optional)*

1 In a large skillet over medium heat, cook beef and onion until browned; drain off fat. Stir in tomatoes, beans, chiles, hominy, corn, salt, and pepper. If desired, combine cornstarch and 1/4 cup water in a small bowl, then stir into stew to thicken. Cook, stirring, until heated through.

HOT-AND-SOUR SOUP WITH PORK AND TOFU

This Chinese restaurant favorite is surprisingly easy to make at home.

SERVES 4

1/4 cup dried porcini or other
    dried mushrooms

2 tablespoons light soy sauce

1 tablespoon cornstarch

1 teaspoon dark brown sugar

6 ounces pork tenderloin, trimmed, thinly
    sliced, and cut into 1/4-inch-wide strips

2 teaspoons vegetable oil

8 ounces fresh mushrooms, sliced

4 scallions, thinly sliced

1 1/2 cups chicken stock

1/4 cup rice vinegar or cider vinegar

2 tablespoons low-sodium tomato paste

1 teaspoon ground ginger

1/4 teaspoon cayenne pepper

1 pound firm tofu, cut into chunks

1 In a medium bowl, combine dried mushrooms and 1 cup boiling water. Let stand 20 minutes. Scoop out mushrooms, rinse, and slice thinly. Place a sieve lined with cheesecloth over a small bowl and strain liquid.

2 Meanwhile, in a medium bowl, combine soy sauce, cornstarch, and brown sugar. Add pork and toss to coat.

3 In a large saucepan, heat oil over medium heat. Add fresh mushrooms and scallions and sauté 4 minutes or until mushrooms are soft. Then stir in 1 cup water, stock, mushroom soaking liquid, vinegar, sliced mushrooms, tomato paste, ginger, and cayenne and bring to boil. Reduce heat and simmer, covered, 7 minutes.

4 Return to boil, add pork mixture and tofu, and cook, stirring, 2 minutes or until pork is just cooked through and soup is slightly thickened.

PORK EGG DROP SOUP

This is a classic Chinese soup that you can make at home. Browning the bones with the meat adds flavor to the soup.

SERVES 4

2 pork loin rib chops, 1/2 inch thick
    (about 1 1/4 pounds)

1 tablespoon vegetable oil

2 cups canned beef broth

3 scallions, sliced

1/2 cup canned sliced bamboo shoots,
    drained

1 tablespoon minced fresh ginger or
    1 teaspoon ground ginger

1 package (10 ounces) frozen peas

2 large eggs

Salt

1 Remove bones from chops and set aside. Trim and discard visible fat from pork and cut into strips. Heat oil in a 5-quart Dutch oven or soup pot over high heat. Add bones and pork and sauté 8 minutes or until pork is well browned.

2 Add 2 cups water, broth, scallions, bamboo shoots, and ginger. Bring to boil, then reduce heat and simmer, covered, 10 minutes. Place peas in a colander under warm running water 2 minutes to thaw.

3 Remove bones from pot. Add peas, increase heat, and cook 4 minutes or until tender.

4 In a small bowl, beat eggs. Slowly stir into soup and cook 1 minute or until just set. Remove from heat and add salt.

ASIAN MEATBALL SOUP

SERVES 4

Meatballs:

1 cup long-grain rice

12 ounces lean minced pork

1 piece fresh ginger, 1 inch long,
    peeled and grated

6 scallions, sliced

1 garlic clove, minced

2 tablespoons soy sauce

1/2 teaspoon toasted sesame oil

1/2 teaspoon five-spice powder

Pinch of chili powder

8 ounces bok choy, leaves removed and
    finely chopped and stalks reserved

Soup:

8 ounces red chard

5 cups chicken stock

1 piece fresh ginger, 1 inch long, peeled
    and cut into thin strips

3 tablespoons dry sherry

2 tablespoons light soy sauce

1 jar (7 ounces) baby corn, each ear sliced
    diagonally into 2 or 3 pieces

4 ounces shiitake mushrooms, thinly sliced

8 ounces snow peas, each cut diagonally
    into 2 or 3 pieces

1 can (8 ounces) sliced bamboo shoots,
    drained

6 scallions, thinly sliced diagonally

1 For meatballs, place rice in a medium sauce-pan, add water to cover, and bring to boil. Cook 1 minute, then drain and set aside.

2 In a large bowl, stir together pork, ginger, scallions, garlic, soy sauce, sesame oil, five-spice powder, chili powder, and chopped bok choy.

3 Place rice in a large shallow bowl and separate grains with a fork. Using moistened hands, roll small lumps of pork mixture into walnut-size balls. Roll meatballs in rice, pressing firmly into grains to coat thickly, then place on a plate.

4 For soup, cover bottom of a steamer rack with a single layer of chard, leaving gaps between leaves. (If using stacking bamboo steamer baskets, you will need two.) Add meatballs in one layer, leaving space between them for rice to swell. Add stock and ginger to steamer base and bring to boil, then reduce heat to simmer. Set rack on top, cover, and steam 35 minutes.

5 Meanwhile, cut bok choy stalks into 1/2-inch pieces. Transfer rack to a plate. Add sherry, soy sauce, corn, mushrooms, snow peas, remaining chard, bamboo shoots, and scallions to base. Return to boil, reduce heat, and simmer. Replace rack, cover, and steam 5 minutes.

6 Transfer meatballs to a warm serving bowl and add chard leaves from rack to broth. Season with soy sauce to taste, ladle broth and vegetables into 4 warm bowls, and add a few meatballs to each.

Aromatic rice, pork meat-balls, and lots of interesting vegetables bring Asian flavors to this satisfying main-meal soup.

STIR-FRIED PORK SOUP

This soup combines stir-fried pork and crisp stir-fry vegetables with chicken stock and a "dropped" egg.

SERVES 6

2 tablespoons vegetable oil
11 ounces boneless pork loin, cut into thin strips
1 cup sliced fresh mushrooms
1 cup chopped celery
1/2 cup diced carrots
6 cups chicken stock
1/2 cup chopped fresh spinach
2 tablespoons cornstarch
1 egg, lightly beaten
Black pepper

1 Heat oil in a 3-quart saucepan over medium-high heat. Add pork, mushrooms, celery, and carrots and stir-fry until pork is browned and vegetables are tender. Add stock and spinach and bring to boil, then reduce heat and simmer, covered, 5 minutes.

2 In a small bowl, combine cornstarch and 3 tablespoons cold water to make a thin paste, then stir into soup. Return to boil and cook 1 minute. Quickly stir in egg. Add pepper and serve.

ASIAN PORK NOODLE SOUP

If you put the pork in the freezer until partially frozen (about 45 minutes), it will be much easier to cut into strips.

SERVES 4

2 tablespoons vegetable oil
1 pound boneless pork shoulder, trimmed and cut into thin strips
1 garlic clove, minced
1 tablespoon minced fresh ginger
8 cups chicken stock

1 pound kale, mustard greens, or spinach, trimmed, rinsed, and cut into bite-size pieces
8 scallions with tops, thinly sliced
2 cups fine egg noodles
1/2 teaspoon salt
1/8 teaspoon black pepper
1 tablespoon Oriental sesame oil *(optional)*

1 Heat oil in a large saucepan over medium heat. Add pork, garlic, and ginger and stir-fry until pork is no longer pink, about 2 minutes. Add stock and bring to boil, then reduce heat and simmer, covered, 15 minutes.

2 Stir in kale and scallions and simmer, covered, 10 minutes. Add noodles and cook, covered, until kale and noodles are tender, about 5 minutes. Stir in salt, pepper, and sesame oil, if desired.

HOMINY-PORK SOUP

Using tender pork instead of beef and hominy instead of beans makes this chili-flavored soup a bit different.

SERVES 7

1 pound pork loin, cut into 1/2-inch cubes
2 cans (15 ounces each) chili without beans
1 can (15 1/2 ounces) hominy, drained
1 can (8 ounces) tomato sauce
1 medium onion, chopped
1 bay leaf
1 tablespoon chili powder
1 teaspoon dried basil
1 teaspoon dried oregano
1 teaspoon parsley flakes
1 teaspoon ground cumin
Warmed flour tortillas
Shredded Monterey Jack cheese
Sliced scallions
Lime wedges

1 In a slow cooker, combine pork, chili, hominy, tomato sauce, onion, bay leaf, chili powder, basil, oregano, parsley, and cumin. Cover and cook on high until meat is tender, about 4 hours. Remove bay leaf.

2 Spoon into tortillas, sprinkle with cheese and scallions, and add a squeeze of lime juice.

PORK AND SAUERKRAUT SOUP

Bluish-gray juniper berries, available in specialty shops, are often used when cooking game. In this tame pork stew, however, the berries add a pleasant tart-sweet flavor to the sauerkraut.

SERVES 4

1 lean bacon slice, chopped

12 ounces lean boneless pork, trimmed and cut into 3/4-inch cubes

1 large yellow onion, chopped

2 garlic cloves, minced

1 can (16 ounces) sauerkraut or 1 package (16 ounces) refrigerated sauerkraut, undrained

2 medium all-purpose potatoes, peeled and chopped

1 3/4 cups canned low-sodium beef broth

1 can (12 ounces) lite beer

6 juniper berries

3 bay leaves

1 teaspoon paprika

1 teaspoon fennel seed, crushed

1/2 teaspoon caraway seed

1/4 teaspoon black pepper

1/4 cup reduced-fat sour cream

1 In a large saucepan over medium heat, cook bacon until crisp. Remove from pan, reserving drippings, and transfer to paper towels to drain.

2 Add pork, onion, and garlic to pan and sauté in drippings until pork is browned and onion is softened. Add sauerkraut, potatoes, broth, beer, juniper berries, bay leaves, paprika, fennel seed, caraway seed, and pepper. Bring to boil, then reduce heat and simmer, covered, until pork is tender, about 1 hour. Remove bay leaves and juniper berries. Serve soup topped with sour cream and bacon.

ROAST PORK SOUP

This satisfying soup has rich apple-flavored broth brimming with tender chunks of pork, potatoes, and navy beans.

SERVES 9

3 cups cubed cooked pork roast

2 medium all-purpose potatoes, peeled and chopped

1 large onion, chopped

1 can (15 ounces) navy beans, drained and rinsed

1 can (14 1/2 ounces) Italian diced tomatoes, undrained

1/2 cup unsweetened apple juice

1/2 teaspoon salt *(optional)*

1/2 teaspoon black pepper

Minced fresh basil

1 In a Dutch oven or soup pot over medium-high heat, combine 4 cups water, pork, potatoes, onion, beans, tomatoes, apple juice, salt, if desired, and pepper. Bring to boil, then reduce heat and simmer, covered, until vegetables are crisp-tender, about 45 minutes. Sprinkle with basil.

GOULASH SOUP WITH JERUSALEM ARTICHOKES

Give homely Jerusalem artichokes, also called sun chokes, a chance. They are full of vitamin C, calcium, iron, and fiber, plus nutty flavor and a bit of crunch.

SERVES 4

2 tablespoons vegetable oil

1 small yellow onion, chopped

2 small Jerusalem artichokes, peeled and diced

1 small carrot, sliced

1 garlic clove, finely chopped

2 knackwurst, sliced

1 1/2 teaspoons paprika

1/2 teaspoon dill weed

Salt and black pepper

1 can (14 1/2 ounces) whole peeled tomatoes, drained and coarsely chopped

1/2 cup medium-width egg noodles

1 Heat oil in a large saucepan over medium heat. Add onion, Jerusalem artichokes, carrot, and garlic and sauté 10 minutes or until onions are softened. Add knackwurst, paprika, dill, salt, and pepper and stir until well mixed.

2 Add 4 cups water and tomatoes. Bring to boil over high heat, then reduce heat and simmer, covered, 10 minutes. Increase heat to high and return to boil. Stir in noodles and cook 5 minutes or until just tender, about 5 minutes.

HUNGARIAN PORK GOULASH

This robust stew with pork tenderloin and peas in a creamy pink sauce is best when you use real Hungarian sweet paprika.

SERVES 4

1 tablespoon olive oil

1 pound pork tenderloin, cut into 1-inch chunks

1 large onion, halved and thinly sliced

4 garlic cloves, slivered

1 tablespoon sweet paprika

1 teaspoon caraway seed

1/2 teaspoon salt

1 cup frozen peas

8 ounces wide yolkless noodles

1/2 cup bottled roasted red peppers, drained and rinsed

1/4 cup fat-free sour cream

2 tablespoons tomato paste

2 tablespoons all-purpose flour

1 Preheat oven to 350°F. Heat oil in a medium nonstick Dutch oven over medium heat. Add pork and sauté 4 minutes or until lightly browned. Using a slotted spoon, transfer to a plate.

2 Add onion and garlic to Dutch oven and sauté 5 minutes or until onion is tender. Stir in paprika and sauté 1 minute or until fragrant. Add 2 cups water, caraway seed, and salt and bring to boil. Return pork to Dutch oven, cover, and bake 30 minutes or until tender. Remove from oven and stir in peas.

3 Meanwhile, cook noodles according to package directions and drain.

4 In a food processor or blender, combine peppers, sour cream, tomato paste, and flour, cover, and puree until smooth. Stir into Dutch oven and cook over medium heat 2 minutes or until slightly thickened. Serve over noodles.

PORK AND RED CABBAGE STEW

This dish tastes even better if prepared a day ahead; the flavors develop more fully with time. Serve with mustard on the side.

SERVES 4

2 tablespoons flour

12 ounces boneless lean pork butt, cut into 1-inch cubes

1 medium yellow onion, thinly sliced

1 medium carrot, sliced

3 garlic cloves, minced

1 large apple, peeled, cored, quartered, and thinly sliced

1/2 small head red cabbage, cored and coarsely shredded

3 tablespoons red wine vinegar

1/2 cup canned low-sodium chicken broth

2 bay leaves

7 allspice berries

6 whole black peppercorns

1/4 teaspoon dried sage, crumbled

1 Place flour in a shallow dish and dredge pork, shaking off any excess. Lightly coat a heavy 6-quart Dutch oven with nonstick cooking spray, set over medium heat 30 seconds, and add pork. Cook until browned on all sides, about 10 minutes. Transfer to a bowl and set aside.

2 Preheat oven to 350°F. Add onion, carrot, and garlic to Dutch oven and sauté over medium heat 5 minutes or until softened. Add apple and cabbage and cook, covered, 15 minutes or just until cabbage is wilted.

3 Stir in vinegar, broth, bay leaves, allspice berries, peppercorns, sage, and pork. Bring to boil, then cover and bake 1 hour. Remove bay leaves, allspice berries, and peppercorns before serving.

PORK AND ROOT VEGETABLE STEW

Gingersnap cookies work as both thickeners and flavor enhancers in this winter stew. Rutabaga adds a sweet, peppery taste. If only huge rutabagas are available, save leftovers for other uses, such as mashed rutabaga.

SERVES 4

1 tablespoon olive oil

3 leeks, rinsed, halved lengthwise, and thinly sliced crosswise

3 garlic cloves, thinly sliced

2 carrots, halved lengthwise and thinly sliced crosswise

2 medium parsnips, halved lengthwise and thinly sliced crosswise

1 small rutabaga, peeled and cut into 1/2-inch chunks

1 1/4 cups canned crushed tomatoes

6 gingersnap cookies, crumbled

3 tablespoons cider vinegar

2 teaspoons light brown sugar

3/4 teaspoon salt

1 pound pork tenderloin, trimmed and cut into 1-inch chunks

1 Heat oil in a nonstick Dutch oven or flame-proof baking dish over medium heat. Add leeks and garlic and sauté 5 minutes or until tender.

2 Stir in carrots, parsnips, and rutabaga and sauté 7 minutes or until crisp-tender. Add 1 cup water, tomatoes, gingersnaps, vinegar, brown sugar, and salt and bring to boil. Add pork, reduce heat, and simmer, covered, 30 minutes or until pork and vegetables are tender.

QUICK GOULASH

This shortcut version of classic Hungarian goulash is still rich and delicious. (Photograph on page 18)

SERVES 4

2 tablespoons extra-virgin olive oil

1 large onion, chopped

2 garlic cloves, crushed

3 thick lean pork loin steaks (about 10 1/2 ounces total), cut into thin strips

1 tablespoon all-purpose flour

1 can (14 1/2 ounces) tomatoes, undrained

1/2 cup dry white vermouth

2 tablespoons paprika

1 teaspoon caraway seed

1 teaspoon superfine sugar

1 cube chicken stock, crumbled

1 large green bell pepper, cored, seeded, and chopped

8 ounces red cabbage, shredded

Salt and black pepper

Garnishes:

4 tablespoons plain yogurt

Paprika

Minced chives

1 Heat oil in a large saucepan over medium heat. Increase heat to high, add onion, garlic, and pork, and sauté 3 minutes or until meat is no longer pink and onion is softened. In a small bowl, blend flour with 4 tablespoons juice from tomatoes to make a smooth paste.

2 Stir vermouth, paprika, caraway seed, and sugar into pan. Stir in tomatoes and remaining juice, breaking them up with a spoon. Stir in stock cube and flour mixture, bring to boil, and cook, stirring, 2 minutes or until juices thicken.

3 Stir in bell pepper and cabbage until thoroughly coated with juices. Reduce heat and simmer,

covered, 15 minutes or until meat is done and vegetables are tender. Season to taste with salt and pepper. Top each portion with a spoonful of yogurt, a dash of paprika, and a bit of chives.

MEXICAN PORK STEW

The secret ingredient in this stew is a touch of chocolate, which blends with other spices to create a dark, rich flavor.

SERVES 6

1 1/2 pounds boneless pork shoulder

1 dried hot or mild chile, such as ancho or pasilla

1 1/2 tablespoons olive or canola oil

2 green bell peppers, cored, seeded, and diced

2 large onions, coarsely chopped

2 garlic cloves, minced

1/2 teaspoon ground cumin

1 tablespoon all-purpose flour

1 can (28 ounces) crushed tomatoes

2 cups chicken or beef stock

1 tablespoon unsweetened cocoa

1 can (16 ounces) red kidney beans, drained and rinsed

1/8 teaspoon salt

1/8 teaspoon black pepper

1 Using a sharp knife, trim all fat and cartilage from pork. Cut meat into 1-inch strips, then cut crosswise into 1-inch cubes.

2 Place chile in a small bowl, cover with boiling water, and soak at least 20 minutes or until very soft; drain. Wearing rubber gloves, remove core and seeds and chop finely.

3 Heat 1 tablespoon oil in a Dutch oven over medium-high heat. Add bell peppers, onions, and garlic and sauté 10 minutes or until golden. Stir in cumin and cook 1 to 2 minutes or until fragrant. Using a slotted spoon, transfer vegetables to a plate. Add remaining oil and heat over medium-high heat. Sauté pork 5 to 7 minutes or until well browned on all sides. Sprinkle with flour and cook, stirring, 2 minutes.

4 Return vegetables to Dutch oven and add chile, tomatoes, and stock. Bring to boil, then reduce heat and simmer, covered, 2 hours or until pork is fork-tender. In a small bowl, combine cocoa with 1/2 cup cooking liquid and whisk until blended. Stir into Dutch oven, add beans, and season with salt and pepper. Simmer 5 minutes or until heated through.

HAM AND BEAN SOUP

Bacon enlivens this basic, comforting bean soup that is delicately flavored and designed to stick to your ribs.

SERVES 6

2 bacon slices

1 large yellow onion, chopped

2 medium carrots, peeled and sliced

2 cans (19 ounces each) cannellini beans, drained and rinsed

1 can (8 ounces) tomato sauce

8 ounces baked ham, cubed

1 bay leaf

Salt and black pepper

1 In a large saucepan over medium-high heat, cook bacon until lightly browned on both sides. Transfer to paper towels to drain. Reduce heat to medium, add onion and carrots, and sauté in drippings 5 minutes.

2 Stir in 4 cups water, half of beans, tomato sauce, ham, and bay leaf. Increase heat to high,

cover, and bring to boil. Reduce heat and simmer, covered, 20 minutes, stirring occasionally.

3 Remove bay leaf. Stir in remaining beans, season to taste with salt and pepper, and bring to boil. Remove from heat, ladle into bowls, and crumble an equal amount of bacon on each.

HAM AND POTATO SOUP

This traditional German soup gets its distinctive flavor from sauerkraut.

SERVES 4

1 tablespoon olive or vegetable oil

1 tablespoon butter

1 large yellow onion, coarsely chopped

8 ounces baked or boiled ham, cut into 1/2-inch cubes

1 can or package (1 pound) sauerkraut, drained and rinsed

1 pound all-purpose potatoes, peeled and cut into 1/2-inch cubes

3 1/2 cups beef stock

1 teaspoon caraway seed

1/4 teaspoon black pepper

1 Heat oil and melt butter in a 5-quart Dutch oven over medium heat. Add onion and sauté 3 minutes or until softened.

2 Add ham and sauté 5 minutes. Add sauerkraut, potatoes, stock, caraway seed, and pepper and bring to boil. Reduce heat and simmer, covered, 20 minutes or until potatoes are tender.

HAM AND FRESH PEA SOUP

A hint of cream makes this fresh green soup seem delightfully indulgent. The high proportion of peas fills the soup with vitamins and fiber, while a modest amount of lean cooked ham adds protein and depth of flavor. (Photograph on page 21)

SERVES 4

1 tablespoon extra-virgin olive oil

1 onion, chopped

1 small carrot, peeled and diced

2 garlic cloves, sliced

1 leek, chopped

1 celery stalk, diced

2 tablespoons fresh parsley, chopped

1 all-purpose potato, peeled and diced

3 1/2 ounces lean boiled or baked ham, diced

1 1/8 pounds shelled fresh or frozen peas

1/2 teaspoon dried *herbes de Provence*

3 1/2 cups vegetable stock

3 large lettuce leaves, finely shredded

Salt and black pepper

2 tablespoons whipping cream

1 Heat oil in a large saucepan over medium heat. Add onion, carrot, garlic, leek, celery, parsley, potato, and ham and stir well. Cover, reduce heat, and cook, stirring occasionally, 30 minutes or until vegetables are softened.

2 Add peas, *herbes de Provence,* and stock and bring to boil. Reduce heat and simmer, covered, until peas are just tender (10 minutes for fresh peas or 5 minutes for frozen). Add lettuce and simmer 5 minutes.

3 Transfer half of soup to a blender or food processor and puree, then return to pan (or use a handheld blender to partially puree soup in pan). Heat through and season to taste with salt and pepper. Ladle into warm bowls and swirl a little cream into each serving.

HAM AND BLACK BEAN SOUP WITH SWEET POTATOES

The perfect end to a long day may be this hearty one-dish meal made all the tastier with sweet potatoes, spices, and lime juice.

SERVES 4

2 tablespoons olive oil

3 medium red or yellow onions, coarsely chopped

4 garlic cloves, thinly sliced

1 large green bell pepper, cored, seeded, and diced

2 medium sweet potatoes, peeled and cut into 1-inch cubes

1 1/2 cups canned crushed tomatoes

3/4 teaspoon ground cumin

3/4 teaspoon ground coriander

1/2 teaspoon ground ginger

1/2 teaspoon salt

1/4 teaspoon cayenne pepper

1 cup cooked white or brown rice

4 cups cooked black beans or 2 cans (15 ounces each) black beans, drained and rinsed

6 ounces boiled or baked ham, cut into thin strips

3 tablespoons lime juice

2 limes, cut into wedges *(optional)*

1 Heat oil in a soup pot or 5-quart Dutch oven over medium heat. Add onions and garlic and sauté 5 minutes or until soft. Add bell pepper and sauté 5 minutes. Stir in sweet potatoes and tomatoes and cook, uncovered, 4 minutes or until slightly thickened.

2 Stir in cumin, coriander, ginger, salt, and cayenne. Add 3 1/2 cups water, increase heat to high, and bring to boil. Reduce heat and simmer, covered, 20 minutes or until sweet potatoes are tender.

3 Stir in rice, beans, and ham and cook, uncovered, 5 minutes or until heated through. Stir in lime juice. Garnish each serving with lime wedges, if desired.

HAM AND VEGETABLE SOUP

Leftover ham combines with fresh zucchini, mushrooms, corn, and tomatoes to make a delightful main-dish soup.

SERVES 8

1 tablespoon olive oil
1 medium onion, thinly sliced and separated into rings
1 medium zucchini, cut into cubes
1 pound fresh mushrooms, sliced
3 cups fresh or frozen corn
3 cups cubed fully cooked ham
6 medium tomatoes, cored, peeled, seeded, and chopped
1/2 cup chicken stock
1 1/2 teaspoons salt
1/2 teaspoon black pepper
1/2 teaspoon garlic powder
Shredded mozzarella cheese

1 Heat oil in a large saucepan over medium heat. Add onion and zucchini and sauté 5 minutes or until onion is tender. Add mushrooms, corn, and ham and sauté 5 minutes.

2 Stir in tomatoes, stock, salt, pepper, and garlic powder and bring to boil. Reduce heat and simmer, covered, 5 minutes. Uncover and simmer 5 minutes. Garnish with cheese.

HAM AND GREENS SOUP

A small ham hock gives this soup rich flavor. If you like, you can dice the meat from the bone and add it to the soup when it has finished cooking. Spinach or kale can be substituted for collards.

SERVES 10

1 tablespoon vegetable oil
1 large yellow onion, finely chopped
3 scallions with tops, thinly sliced
3 garlic cloves, slivered
8 ounces mushrooms, thickly sliced
1 large yam or sweet potato, peeled and cut into 1-inch cubes
6 plum tomatoes, chopped
1 1/2 pounds collard greens, thick stems removed and leaves shredded, or 2 bags (10 ounces each) collard greens
1 small smoked ham hock (1/2 pound)
3/4 teaspoon salt
1/2 teaspoon dried savory, crumbled
1/4 teaspoon cayenne pepper
2 tablespoons red wine vinegar

1 Heat oil in a soup pot or 5-quart Dutch oven over low heat. Add onion, scallions, and garlic and sauté 5 minutes or until onions are softened. Add mushrooms and sauté 2 minutes. Stir in yam, tomatoes, and collard greens and cook 2 minutes.

2 Add 9 cups water, ham hock, salt, savory, and cayenne and bring to boil. Reduce heat, then simmer, covered, 35 minutes or until yam and greens are tender. Remove ham hock and, if desired, remove and dice meat and return to pot. Skim fat from surface of soup and stir in vinegar.

HAM, BARLEY, AND BEAN SOUP

This is a hearty, flavorful soup that can satisfy the biggest appetite. (Photograph on page 14)

SERVES 4

2 tablespoons olive oil

1 ham steak (5 1/2 ounces), cut into 1/2-inch pieces

1 onion, chopped

2 large thick leeks, sliced

4 thyme sprigs

2 bay leaves

4 ounces pearled barley

5 1/2 cups vegetable stock

8 ounces fava beans, shelled

Salt and black pepper

3 tablespoons flat-leaf parsley, minced

1 Heat oil in a large saucepan over medium-low heat. Add ham and sauté until heated through. Add onion and leeks and cook, stirring occasionally, until softened and golden, about 10 minutes. Add thyme and bay leaves toward end of cooking.

2 Add barley and cook 2 minutes, then pour in stock. Bring to boil, then reduce heat and simmer, uncovered, until barley is tender and stock is a soupy consistency, about 30 minutes.

3 Add beans and simmer 5 minutes. Season to taste with salt and pepper, ladle into warm bowls, and sprinkle with parsley.

HAM SOUP WITH TOMATOES AND HOMINY

Hominy gives this soup an appealing tortilla-like flavor.

SERVES 6

1 can (16 ounces) white or yellow hominy, drained and rinsed

1 can (14 1/2 ounces) low-sodium tomatoes, drained and juice reserved

1 tablespoon olive oil

1 medium yellow onion, coarsely chopped

1 medium red bell pepper, core, seeded, and finely chopped

1 teaspoon chili powder

4 cups chicken stock

1 package (10 ounces) frozen whole-kernel corn

1/2 teaspoon dried oregano, crumbled

1 cup finely diced 95% fat-free smoked ham

1 tablespoon lemon juice

1/4 teaspoon black pepper

1 In a blender or food processor, coarsely chop hominy and tomatoes.

2 Heat oil in a soup pot or 5-quart Dutch oven over medium heat. Add onion and bell pepper and sauté 2 to 3 minutes. Stir in chili powder, stock, corn, oregano, hominy mixture, and reserved tomato juice. Bring to boil, then reduce heat and simmer, covered, 10 minutes.

3 Stir in ham, lemon juice, and black pepper and cook, uncovered, 1 minute or until ham is heated.

HUNGARIAN HAM AND CABBAGE SOUP

The typical Hungarian seasonings of caraway seed and paprika are combined with sour cream in this savory soup.

SERVES 4

1/2 teaspoon caraway seed, crushed

1 1/2 teaspoon paprika

1/2 cup sour cream

2 tablespoons (1/4 stick) butter

1 large yellow onion, chopped

4 cups canned beef broth

8 ounces baked ham, diced

 Salt and black pepper

1/2 small head cabbage, cored and shredded

1 tablespoon chopped fresh parsley

1 In a small bowl, combine caraway seed, paprika, and sour cream and refrigerate until soup is ready to serve.

2 Melt butter in a large saucepan over medium heat. Add onion and sauté 5 minutes or until softened. Add broth, ham, and salt and pepper to taste and bring to boil. Stir in cabbage, reduce heat, and simmer 5 minutes or until crisp-tender. Stir in parsley, ladle into bowls, and top each serving with a dollop of sour cream mixture.

QUICK HAM STEW

This stew just may hit the spot when you are very busy and very hungry.

SERVES 4

4 carrots, cut into 1-inch pieces

1 1/2 cups peeled and diced potatoes

2 medium onions, cut into chunks

1 package (10 ounces) frozen peas, thawed

2 cups cubed ham

1 can (10 3/4 ounces) condensed cream
    of celery soup

1 jar (8 ounces) process cheese spread

1 In a large saucepan or Dutch oven, combine carrots, potatoes, onions, and just enough water to cover. Bring to boil, then reduce heat, and simmer, covered, 10 minutes or until vegetables are tender.

2 Add peas and ham and cook 5 minutes, then drain off excess water. Stir in soup and cheese and heat through.

BACON, LETTUCE, AND TOMATO SOUP

This is a soup version of the beloved BLT sandwich.

SERVES 8

3 tablespoons butter

2 teaspoons vegetable oil

3 cups cubed French bread

1 pound sliced bacon, diced

2 cups finely chopped celery

1 medium onion, finely chopped

2 tablespoons sugar

6 tablespoons all-purpose flour

5 cups chicken stock

1 jar (16 ounces) salsa

1 can (8 ounces) tomato sauce

1/8 teaspoon black pepper

3 cups shredded lettuce

1 Melt butter and heat oil in a Dutch oven or soup pot over medium heat. Add bread cubes and sauté until crisp and golden. Transfer to paper towels.

2 Add bacon and cook until crisp. Drain, reserving 1/4 cup drippings, and transfer to paper towels.

3 Add drippings, celery, and onion to pot and sauté 4 minutes or until tender. Add sugar and cook, stirring, 1 minute. Stir in flour and cook, stirring, 1 minute. Add stock, salsa, tomato sauce, and pepper. Bring to boil and cook, stirring, 2 minutes.

4 Just before serving, add lettuce and heat through. Garnish with croutons and bacon.

PUREED BACON, LETTUCE, AND TOMATO SOUP WITH ORANGE

This mixture of flavors and textures may change your preference from the popular sandwich to this soup variation.

SERVES 6

4 bacon slices

2 medium carrots, peeled and chopped

1 large yellow onion, chopped

1 celery stalk, chopped

1 large garlic clove, minced

1 can (28 ounces) whole tomatoes, undrained

3 cups homemade beef stock or canned low-sodium beef broth

2 tablespoons chopped fresh basil or 2 teaspoons dried basil

1 strip orange rind, 1 x 1/2 inch

1 teaspoon salt

1/2 teaspoon sugar

1/4 teaspoon black pepper

4 cups shredded romaine lettuce

1 Stack bacon slices and, using sharp kitchen scissors, cut crosswise into 1/4-inch strips. In a 4-quart saucepan over medium-high heat, cook until crisp, 4 to 5 minutes. Transfer to paper towels.

2 Add carrots, onion, celery, and garlic to drippings and sauté over medium heat 7 to 8 minutes or until tender. Stir in tomatoes, stock, basil, orange rind, salt, sugar, and pepper. Bring to boil, then reduce heat and simmer, covered, 25 to 30 minutes. Remove from heat and let cool.

3 Transfer in batches to a blender or food processor, cover, and puree until smooth. Return to pan and cook over medium heat 5 minutes or until heated through. Stir in lettuce and cook 1 minute or until wilted. Ladle into bowls and garnish with bacon.

PORTUGUESE GREENS SOUP WITH SPICY SAUSAGES

This recipe calls for fresh chorizo, a spicy Mexican pork sausage. If you can't find chorizo, use a second Italian sausage link.

SERVES 4

1 teaspoon olive oil

1 sweet Italian sausage link (2 1/2 ounces), cut into 1/2-inch-thick slices

1 large onion, finely chopped

2 garlic cloves, minced

1 can (10 ounces) red kidney beans, drained and rinsed

1 fresh chorizo sausage link (3 ounces), cut into 1/2-inch-thick slices

1 cup chicken stock

2 tablespoons low-sodium tomato paste

1/2 teaspoon black pepper

10 cups firmly packed kale and Swiss chard leaves, torn into bite-size pieces

1 tablespoon red wine vinegar

1 Heat oil in a nonstick Dutch oven over medium heat. Add Italian sausage and cook, turning occasionally, 4 minutes or until sausage is browned and fat has been rendered.

2 Add onion and garlic and sauté 7 minutes or until softened. Add 3 cups water, beans, chorizo, stock, tomato paste, and pepper. Bring to boil, then reduce to simmer and add greens. Cook, uncovered, 30 minutes or until sausage is cooked through and greens are as tender as you like them. Stir in vinegar.

PORTUGUESE GREEN SOUP WITH KIELBASA

Caldo verde, or green soup, is a specialty handed down by the Portuguese fishermen who settled in New England.

SERVES 4

1 tablespoon olive or vegetable oil

1 large yellow onion, finely chopped

2 garlic cloves, minced

3 1/2 cups canned low-sodium chicken broth

3 medium all-purpose potatoes, peeled and chopped

1 package (10 ounces) frozen chopped spinach, thawed

6 ounces turkey kielbasa, sliced

1/4 teaspoon salt

1/4 teaspoon black pepper

1 Heat oil in a large saucepan over medium heat. Add onion and garlic and sauté 5 minutes or until onion is tender.

2 Add broth and potatoes and bring to boil. Reduce heat, cover, and simmer 30 minutes or until potatoes are very soft. Using a potato masher or large spoon, slightly mash potatoes to thicken soup.

3 Stir in spinach, kielbasa, salt, and pepper and simmer, uncovered, 5 minutes or until heated.

KIELBASA AND CABBAGE SOUP

Cruciferous vegetables like cabbage (and broccoli and kale) are nutritional superstars that can raise the healthy status of almost any dish.

SERVES 6

1 tablespoon vegetable oil

8 ounces reduced-fat kielbasa, diced

1 medium onion, coarsely chopped

4 garlic cloves, minced

2 cans (14 1/2 ounces each) fat-free low-sodium beef broth

1/2 medium head Savoy cabbage, coarsely chopped (about 4 1/2 cups)

2 medium red potatoes, diced

2 medium carrots, peeled and diced

1 medium beet, peeled and diced

3 tablespoons finely chopped fresh dill

1 bay leaf

1 tablespoon red wine vinegar

1 Heat oil in a large saucepan over medium-high heat. Add kielbasa and sauté 5 minutes or until browned. Add onion and garlic and sauté 5 minutes or until tender.

2 Add 1 1/4 cups water, broth, cabbage, potatoes, carrots, beet, dill, and bay leaf. Simmer, covered, 45 minutes or until tender. Stir in vinegar and remove bay leaf.

KIELBASA VEGETABLE SOUP

This is a hearty, quick soup for healthy appetites.

SERVES 6

8 ounces fully cooked kielbasa
  or Polish sausage, diced
6 medium all-purpose potatoes,
  peeled and cut into cubes
2 cups frozen whole-kernel corn
1 1/2 cups chicken stock
1 celery stalk, sliced
1/4 cup sliced carrot
1/2 teaspoon garlic powder
1/2 teaspoon onion powder
1/2 teaspoon salt
1/4 teaspoon black pepper
1 1/2 cups milk
2/3 cup shredded cheddar cheese
1 teaspoon minced fresh parsley

1 In a large saucepan over medium heat, cook kielbasa until browned. Transfer to a plate and drain fat from pan.

2 Add potatoes, corn, stock, celery, carrot, garlic powder, onion powder, salt, and pepper to pan. Bring to boil, then reduce heat and simmer, covered, 15 minutes or until tender.

3 Add milk, cheese, parsley, and sausage. Cook, stirring, over low heat until cheese is melted and soup is heated through.

KIELBASA STEW

This sausage stew can add a warming note to a chilly evening.

SERVES 4

1 pound kielbasa, cut into
  1 1/4-inch chunks
8 small white onions
8 small red potatoes, quartered
4 medium carrots, cut into
  1/2-inch-thick slices
1 teaspoon dried marjoram or thyme,
  crumbled
1 bay leaf
1 teaspoon cornstarch
1 cup frozen green peas or cut green beans

1 In a 5-quart Dutch oven or soup pot, cook kielbasa, turning frequently, until browned on all sides. Using a slotted spoon, transfer to paper towels to drain.

2 Add onions, potatoes, and carrots to pot and sauté in drippings until lightly browned, about 10 minutes.

3 Return sausage to pot and add 2 cups minus 1 tablespoon water, marjoram, and bay leaf. Increase heat to high and bring to boil. Reduce heat to low and simmer, covered, until potatoes and carrots are tender, about 20 minutes. In a cup, combine 1 tablespoon water and cornstarch until smooth.

4 Stir cornstarch mixture and peas into pot. Increase heat to high, bring to boil, stirring constantly, and cook until peas are tender, about 5 minutes. Remove bay leaf before serving.

SAUSAGE-POTATO SOUP

There's no question that sausage and potatoes are a dynamite combination; this soup proves it again. (Photograph on page 14)

SERVES 6

1 pound pork sausage links, cut into
    1/4-inch pieces
1 cup sliced celery
1/2 cup chopped onion
1/2 teaspoon dried thyme
1/2 teaspoon salt
2 tablespoons all-purpose flour
1 can (14 1/2 ounces) chicken broth
4 medium all-purpose potatoes,
    peeled and diced
1 cup milk
1 cup sliced green beans, partially cooked
 Chopped fresh parsley

1 In a heavy skillet over medium heat, cook sausage until browned. Transfer to paper towels and drain all but 1 tablespoon drippings from pan. Add celery, onion, thyme, and salt and sauté 3 minutes or until onion is tender.

2 Stir in flour and cook 1 minute. Gradually add 1/2 cup water and broth, stirring until mixture comes to boil. Add potatoes and return to boil. Reduce heat and simmer, covered, 25 minutes or until potatoes are tender. Remove from heat and let cool.

3 Transfer 2 cups soup to a blender or food processor, cover, and puree until smooth. Return to pot. Add milk, beans, and sausage, and heat through. Garnish with parsley.

SAUSAGE, CABBAGE, AND POTATO SOUP

This version of a Portuguese soup, caldo verde, features the traditional potato and shredded cabbage.

SERVES 4

3 medium all-purpose potatoes,
    peeled and thinly sliced
2 garlic cloves, sliced
2 cups green or Savoy cabbage, shredded
1 teaspoon dill weed
3 ounces chorizo sausage, thinly sliced
 Salt and black pepper
4 tablespoons extra-virgin olive oil

1 In a medium saucepan, cover potatoes with 4 cups cold water and bring to boil. Add garlic and return to boil. Skim off foam, reduce heat, and simmer, partially covered, 7 to 10 minutes or until potatoes are almost tender.

2 Remove from heat and mash potatoes in cooking water to break them up as much as possible. Add cabbage and dill and return to boil. Reduce heat and simmer 4 to 7 minutes or until cabbage is cooked.

3 Remove from heat and mash potatoes again. Season to taste with salt and pepper, then ladle into soup bowls. Add sausage slices to each serving, trickle on oil in a zigzag pattern, and add freshly ground black pepper.

SAUSAGE STROGANOFF SOUP

This rich soup starts with a scalloped potato mix and brown-and-serve breakfast sausages. It never gets any harder than that to make.

SERVES 6

1 package (12 ounces) brown-and-serve sausage links, cut into 1/2-inch slices

1 garlic clove, minced

1 package (5 ounces) scalloped potatoes

1 can (14 1/2 ounces) chicken broth

1 jar (4 1/2 ounces) sliced mushrooms, drained

1 cup half-and-half

1 cup sour cream

2 tablespoons Dijon mustard

Paprika *(optional)*

1 In a large saucepan over medium heat, sauté sausage and garlic 6 minutes or until sausage is golden. Stir in contents of potato and sauce packets.

2 Add 3 cups water, broth, and mushrooms and bring to boil. Reduce heat and simmer, uncovered, 14 minutes or until potatoes are tender.

3 Stir in half-and-half, sour cream, and mustard and heat through (do not boil). Sprinkle with paprika, if desired.

ITALIAN SAUSAGE-VEGETABLE SOUP

If you love Italian sausage—and who doesn't?—you will enjoy whipping up this soup for a quick dinner.

SERVES 6

1 pound bulk Italian sausage

1 medium onion, sliced

1 can (16 ounces) whole tomatoes, undrained, chopped

1 can (15 ounces) chickpeas, drained and rinsed

1 can (14 1/2 ounces) beef broth

2 medium zucchini, cut into 1/4-inch slices

1/2 teaspoon dried basil

Grated Parmesan cheese

1 In a 3-quart saucepan over medium heat, cook sausage and onion until sausage is no longer pink and onion is softened. Drain off fat.

2 Stir in 1 1/2 cups water, tomatoes, chickpeas, broth, zucchini, and basil. Bring to boil, then reduce heat and simmer, covered, 5 minutes or until zucchini is tender. Sprinkle each serving with cheese.

SAUSAGE AND CORN SOUP

This soup is easy to make and will be a big hit with family and guests.

SERVES 16

6 tablespoons butter

2 1/2 cups chopped onions

1/2 cup chopped seeded green bell pepper

1/2 cup chopped seeded red bell pepper

1/2 cup chopped celery

1 1/2 pounds fully cooked smoked sausage, cut into 1/4-inch pieces

3 garlic cloves, minced

4 cans (15 ounces each) Italian-style tomato sauce

3 packages (16 ounces each) frozen whole-kernel corn

2 cans (14 1/2 ounces each) Italian diced tomatoes, undrained

3 bay leaves

1 1/2 teaspoons dried basil

1 1/2 teaspoons dried oregano

1 1/2 teaspoons dried thyme

1/2 teaspoon black pepper

1/4 teaspoon dried marjoram

1/4 teaspoon hot red pepper sauce *(optional)*

1 In a Dutch oven or soup pot over medium heat, melt butter. Add onions, bell peppers, and celery and sauté 5 minutes or until tender. Add sausage and garlic and sauté 5 minutes or until heated through.

2 Stir in 2 cups water, tomato sauce, corn, tomatoes, bay leaves, basil, oregano, thyme, pepper, marjoram, and red pepper sauce, if desired. Bring to boil, then reduce heat and simmer, uncovered, 1 hour, stirring occasionally. Remove bay leaves before serving.

SMOKED SAUSAGE SOUP

This is a thick, stew-like soup that combines prepared ingredients to good effect.

SERVES 8

1 can (28 ounces) diced tomatoes, undrained

1 envelope onion soup mix

1 package (9 ounces) frozen cut green beans

3 small carrots, halved and thinly sliced

2 celery stalks, thinly sliced

1 tablespoon sugar

1/2 teaspoon salt

1/2 teaspoon dried oregano

1/8 teaspoon hot red pepper sauce

1 pound fully cooked smoked sausage, halved and thinly sliced

2 1/2 cups frozen shredded hash brown potatoes

1 In a Dutch oven or soup pot, combine 4 1/2 cups water, tomatoes, soup mix, beans, carrots, celery, sugar, salt, oregano, and red pepper sauce. Bring to boil, then reduce heat and simmer, covered, 20 minutes or until vegetables are tender.

2 Stir in sausage and potatoes and bring to boil. Reduce heat and cook, covered, 5 minutes or until heated through.

SLOW-COOK SAUSAGE-SAUERKRAUT SOUP

This soup, a favorite in Pennsylvania Dutch country, has German roots that are evident in its sausage, bacon, chicken, potato, mushrooms, and sauerkraut.

SERVES 10 TO 12

1 medium all-purpose potato, cut into 1/4-inch cubes

1 pound fully cooked kielbasa or Polish sausage, cut into 1/2-inch cubes

1 can (32 ounces) sauerkraut, drained and rinsed

4 cups chicken stock

1 can (10 3/4 ounces) condensed cream of mushroom soup

8 ounces fresh mushrooms, sliced

1 cup cubed cooked chicken

2 medium carrots, cut into 1/4-inch slices

2 celery stalks, sliced

2 tablespoons vinegar

2 teaspoons dill weed

1/2 teaspoon black pepper

3-4 bacon slices, cooked and crumbled

1 In a 5-quart slow cooker, combine potato, kielbasa, sauerkraut, stock, soup, mushrooms, chicken, carrots, celery, vinegar, dill, and pepper. Cover and cook on high 5 hours or until vegetables are tender. Skim off fat. Garnish each serving with bacon.

PIZZA SOUP WITH SAUSAGE

Anyone who likes pizza topping better than the crust will probably love this soup.

SERVES 4

1 teaspoon vegetable oil
1 1/4 cups sliced fresh mushrooms
1/2 cup finely chopped onion
1 can (15 ounces) pizza sauce
1 cup chopped pepperoni
1 cup chopped seeded fresh tomatoes
1/2 cup cooked Italian sausage
1/4 teaspoon Italian seasoning
1/4 cup grated Parmesan cheese
Shredded mozzarella cheese

1 Heat oil in a large saucepan over medium heat. Add mushrooms and onion and sauté until tender, about 3 minutes.

2 Add 2 cups water, pizza sauce, pepperoni, tomatoes, sausage, and Italian seasoning. Bring to boil, then reduce heat, cover, and simmer, stirring occasionally, 20 minutes. Before serving, stir in Parmesan. Garnish with mozzarella.

SAUSAGE BEAN STEW

A satisfying stew that's simple to prepare and perfect for campsite consumption.

SERVES 4

1 tablespoon vegetable oil
1 medium yellow onion, thinly sliced
1 pound kielbasa, frankfurters, or knockwurst, cut into 3/4-inch-thick slices
2 cans (16 ounces each) barbecue baked beans, drained
2 tablespoons tomato paste
2 tablespoons Dijon mustard
1/2 teaspoon dried thyme, crumbled

1/4 teaspoon salt
1/4 teaspoon black pepper
2 medium yellow squash or 1 zucchini and 1 yellow squash, halved lengthwise and cut into 1/2-inch-thick slices

1 Heat oil in a large saucepan over medium heat. Add onion and kielbasa, cover, and cook, stirring occasionally, 5 minutes.

2 Add 2/3 cup water, beans, tomato paste, mustard, thyme, salt, and pepper. Bring to boil, then reduce heat, cover, and simmer, stirring occasionally, 8 minutes. Add squash and simmer, covered, 5 minutes or until tender.

PORK SAUSAGE STEW

This stew combines several food favorites for a tasty one-dish meal.

SERVES 4

1 pound bulk sausage
1 medium yellow onion, sliced
1 can (14 1/2 or 16 ounces) diced tomatoes, undrained
1 can (8 ounces) whole-kernel corn
1 can (8 ounces) tomato sauce
2 cups elbow macaroni
2 cups thinly sliced green cabbage
Salt and black pepper

1 In a 5-quart Dutch oven or soup pot over medium-high heat, cook sausage and onion until sausage is well browned and onion is softened, about 7 minutes. Drain off fat.

2 Stir in 1 cup water, tomatoes, corn, and tomato sauce and bring to boil. Stir in macaroni and cabbage and return to boil. Reduce heat and simmer, covered, 8 minutes or until macaroni is tender and most of liquid has been absorbed. Season to taste with salt and pepper.

LEMON SOUP WITH LAMB

Light yet filling, this tasty, lemony soup offers protein from meat and eggs, vitamins and minerals from greens, and carbohydrates from pasta.

SERVES 4

2 pounds boneless lamb shoulder or
  stew meat, cut into 1 1/2-inch cubes

1 large yellow onion, coarsely chopped

1 medium celery stalk, coarsely chopped

1 small carrot, peeled and coarsely chopped

6 cups chicken stock

1 teaspoon minced fresh rosemary or
  1/2 teaspoon dried rosemary, crumbled

1 teaspoon minced fresh thyme or
  1/2 teaspoon dried thyme, crumbled

1/4 teaspoon salt

1/8 teaspoon black pepper

1/2 cup orzo or other small pasta,
  such as tubettini

3 large eggs

1/3 cup fresh lemon juice

2 cups fresh spinach, collard greens,
  or escarole, trimmed, rinsed, and cut
  crosswise into thin strips

1/2 cup heavy cream *(optional)*

3 tablespoons snipped fresh dill

Dill sprigs *(optional)*

1 In a large saucepan over high heat, bring 2 cups water, lamb, onion, celery, carrot, stock, rosemary, thyme, salt, and pepper to boil. Reduce heat, partially cover, and simmer 30 minutes, occasionally skimming off any foam. Strain stock into a large heatproof bowl, discarding vegetables and reserving lamb.

2 Return lamb and stock to pan, increase heat to medium-high, and bring to boil. Add orzo and cook, stirring occasionally, 10 minutes or until pasta is just tender. Remove from heat.

3 In a medium bowl, beat eggs until frothy, then beat in lemon juice. Gradually whisk in 1 cup hot stock, then slowly stir mixture into pan. Cook over low heat, stirring constantly, 2 minutes or until slightly thickened.

4 Stir in spinach, then blend in cream, if desired, and dill. Garnish each serving with dill sprigs, if desired.

SCOTCH BROTH

This is a traditional robust lamb soup from Scotland that must be a national comfort food.

SERVES 6

1 pound boneless lamb shoulder,
  trimmed and cut into 3/4-inch cubes

2 large leeks with tops, washed and sliced

2 large carrots, peeled and chopped

1 cup chopped peeled rutabaga

1 celery stalk, finely chopped

1/4 cup dry green split peas

2 tablespoons medium pearled barley

3/4 teaspoon salt

1/2 teaspoon black pepper

1/4 cup chopped fresh parsley

1 In a 6-quart Dutch oven or soup pot over medium-high heat, bring 8 cups cold water, lamb, leeks, carrots, rutabaga, celery, peas, barley, salt, and pepper to boil. Reduce heat and simmer, covered, 1 1/2 hours or until lamb and peas are tender. Stir in parsley.

SPRING LAMB AND VEGETABLE STEW

This stew is based on a classic French dish called navarin, made in spring to celebrate the new season's lamb and delicate young vegetables.

SERVES 4

2 teaspoons extra-virgin olive oil

1 large onion, chopped

1 garlic clove, finely chopped

1 pound lean boneless leg of lamb, trimmed and cut into cubes

1 cup dry white wine

2 cups lamb or chicken stock

1 bay leaf

1 thyme sprig

2 pounds baby new potatoes, scrubbed

8 ounces baby carrots, scrubbed

8 ounces pearl onions

1 small turnip, diced

8 ounces shelled fresh peas or 3/4 cup frozen peas

2 tablespoons fresh parsley, chopped

Salt and black pepper

1 Preheat oven to 350°F. Heat oil in a large Dutch oven over medium heat. Add chopped onion and garlic and sauté 5 minutes or until softened. Add lamb and sauté 5 minutes or until browned on all sides.

2 Add wine, stock, bay leaf, thyme, potatoes, carrots, and pearl onions and bring to boil. Cover tightly and bake 1 hour.

3 Add turnip and stir, then cover and bake 35 minutes or until meat and vegetables are tender. Add peas during last 10 minutes of cooking. Remove bay leaf, season to taste with salt and pepper, and top with parsley.

LAMB AND BARLEY SOUP

Full of tender lamb cubes, nutty pearled barley, and chunky vegetables, this substantial soup is a meal in a bowl. It's often served with savory scones.

SERVES 4

1 tablespoon extra-virgin olive oil

12 ounces lean boneless lamb, cut into 3/4-inch cubes

1 onion, chopped

2 carrots, peeled and chopped

8 ounces turnips, peeled and cut into 1/2-inch cubes

8 ounces rutabaga, cut into 1/2-inch cubes

3 1/2 ounces pearled barley

4 cups lamb or chicken stock

2 teaspoons fresh rosemary, chopped

1 teaspoon fresh thyme, chopped

1/2 package (10 ounces) frozen peas

Salt and black pepper

1 Heat oil in a large saucepan over high heat. Add lamb and sauté 5 minutes or until browned. Transfer to a plate.

2 Add onion, carrots, turnips, and rutabaga to pan and sauté 2 minutes or until beginning to soften. Return lamb to pan and stir in barley, stock, rosemary, and thyme. Bring to boil, then reduce heat and simmer, covered, 40 minutes. Add peas and simmer 10 minutes. Season to taste with salt and pepper to taste and ladle into bowls.

PIQUANT LAMB STEW

Green chiles and garlic add spice to this lamb and zucchini stew. You can make it with either yogurt or sour cream. Yogurt is slightly tart and is lower in fat; sour cream is a bit mellower.

SERVES 6

2 tablespoons butter

1 tablespoon vegetable oil

1 large yellow onion, coarsely chopped

1 can (4 ounces) green chiles, drained and coarsely chopped (wear gloves when handling; chiles burn)

1 garlic clove, minced

1/2 teaspoon salt

1/2 teaspoon ground cinnamon

Pinch of ground cloves

1/4 teaspoon black pepper

3 pounds boneless lamb shoulder, cut into 1-inch cubes

1 1/2 cups long-grain white rice

2 medium zucchini, cut into 1/4-inch-thick slices

1 tablespoon cornstarch

1 cup low-fat plain yogurt or sour cream

2 tablespoons minced fresh cilantro or flat-leaf parsley

1 In a soup pot or 5-quart Dutch oven over medium heat, melt butter and heat oil. Add onion and sauté 5 minutes or until softened.

2 Add chiles, garlic, salt, cinnamon, cloves, and pepper and sauté 5 minutes. Add lamb and sauté 10 minutes or until golden.

3 Stir in 1 cup water, reduce heat to low, and simmer, covered, 1 1/2 hours or until lamb is tender. About 20 minutes before lamb is done, cook rice according to package directions.

4 Skim fat from surface of stew and stir in zucchini, cover, and cook 5 minutes. In a small bowl, blend cornstarch with 2 tablespoons yogurt. Whisk in remaining yogurt, then stir into pot and cook, stirring constantly, until heated through (do not boil). Sprinkle with cilantro and serve over rice.

LANCASHIRE LAMB STEW

In mining areas of Britain, cheap coal made hotpots popular, as affordable cuts of meat often required long cooking in a coal-fired oven. With its lean meat and vegetables, this modern hotpot is a nutritious family dish.

SERVES 4

8 lamb cutlets, trimmed

1 pound onions, sliced

1 pound carrots, peeled and sliced

Salt and black pepper

4 tablespoons chopped fresh parsley

1 tablespoon fresh thyme

2 pounds all-purpose potatoes, peeled and thinly sliced

1 1/2 cups chicken stock

2 tablespoons olive oil

1 Heat oven to 350°F. Layer lamb, onions, and carrots in a large Dutch oven, sprinkling each layer with salt, pepper, parsley, and thyme. Arrange potatoes in an overlapping layer on top.

2 Add stock, cover, and bake 2 hours, then increase temperature to 450°F. Remove lid, drizzle oil over potatoes, and bake, uncovered, 30 minutes or until potatoes are golden.

LAMB HOTPOT WITH PARSNIPS

The influence of the Middle East brings beans, eggplant, apricots, garlic, and warm spices to this delicious lamb stew.

SERVES 6

1 cup dry black-eyed peas, soaked overnight

1 tablespoon extra-virgin olive oil

2 onions, sliced

1 garlic clove, minced

1 pound boneless leg of lamb, cut into
   1-inch cubes

1 large eggplant, cubed

1 cup quartered dried apricots

2 carrots, diced

2 turnips, peeled and diced

1/2 teaspoon ground cinnamon

1 teaspoon ground cumin

1 teaspoon ground coriander

1 1/2 pounds parsnips, peeled and thinly sliced

4 cups vegetable stock

Salt and black pepper

Flat-leaf parsley sprigs

1 Preheat oven to 325°F. Drain peas and place in a saucepan. Add cold water to cover, bring to boil, and boil rapidly 10 minutes. Drain well and set aside.

2 Heat 2 teaspoons oil in a large Dutch oven over medium heat. Add onions and garlic and sauté 2 minutes. Add lamb and sauté 5 minutes or until browned. Stir in eggplant, apricots, carrots, turnips, cinnamon, cumin, coriander and salt and pepper to taste. Add peas and stir well.

3 Arrange parsnips in a thick layer on top of stew, slightly overlapping slices. Add enough stock to come just below surface of parsnips and bring to boil. Cover and bake 1 1/2 hours.

4 Preheat broiler. Uncover stew and brush remaining oil over parsnips. Broil 4 inches from heat until top is crisp. Garnish with parsley.

MOROCCAN LAMB STEW

Based on a North African dish called a tagine, this stew can be served with couscous or rice.

SERVES 4

2 teaspoons olive oil

1 pound boneless lamb shoulder,
   trimmed and cut into 1/2-inch chunks

1 large onion, finely chopped

3 garlic cloves, minced

1 teaspoon ground coriander

3/4 teaspoon paprika

3/4 teaspoon salt

1/2 teaspoon black pepper

2 tablespoons low-sodium tomato paste

1 1/2 pounds sweet potatoes,
   peeled and cut into 1-inch chunks

1/2 cup pitted prunes, coarsely chopped

1 Preheat oven to 350°F. Heat oil in a nonstick Dutch oven or flameproof baking dish over medium-high heat. Add lamb and sauté 4 minutes or until lightly browned. Using a slotted spoon, transfer to a plate. Add onion and garlic to pan and sauté 7 minutes or until onion is tender.

2 Return lamb to pan and add coriander, paprika, salt, and pepper, stirring to coat. Add 1 cup water and tomato paste and bring to boil. Cover and bake 30 minutes.

3 Add 1/3 cup water, sweet potatoes, and prunes. Cover and bake 30 minutes or until lamb and sweet potatoes are tender.

LAMB, BUTTERNUT, AND BARLEY STEW

This stew is simple to make, and it comes out of the oven smelling and tasting absolutely wonderful.

SERVES 4

1 tablespoon extra-virgin olive oil

4 lamb chops (about 1 pound total), trimmed

2 onions, quartered

2 large leeks, cut into 1-inch pieces

1 butternut squash (about 1 1/2 pounds), peeled, seeded, cut into 1-inch chunks

2 turnips, quartered

3 1/2 ounces pearled barley

3 cups hot lamb stock

2 bay leaves

2 large thyme sprigs

Salt and black pepper

2 tablespoons fresh parsley, chopped

1 Preheat oven to 325°F. Heat oil in a large Dutch oven over medium-high heat. Add chops and cook until browned on both sides, then transfer to a plate.

2 Add onions to Dutch oven and sauté until browned on all sides, about 5 minutes. Stir in leeks, squash, and turnips, reduce heat, and cook, covered, 5 minutes.

3 Sprinkle in barley and cook, stirring, 1 minute, then pour in stock. Return chops to Dutch oven, tucking them among vegetables. Add bay leaves, thyme, and salt and pepper to taste and bring to boil. Cover and bake until meat and vegetables are very tender, about 1 1/4 hours.

4 Remove from oven and let stand 10 minutes to let barley soak up stock. Remove bay leaves and sprinkle with parsley.

LAMB STEW WITH SPINACH

Warmly spiced rather than fiery hot thanks to the cooling effect of the yogurt, this curry has a wonderful flavor. The lamb is infused with spices, and Basmati rice, chapattis, and tomato-and-cucumber chutney make this an irresistible meal that's also low in calories.

SERVES 4

2 tablespoons sunflower oil

2 onions, minced

4 garlic cloves, crushed

1 piece fresh ginger, 2 inches long, peeled and chopped

1 red chile, seeded, deveined, and sliced (wear gloves when handling; chiles burn)

2 teaspoons paprika

2 teaspoons ground cumin

2 teaspoons ground coriander

1 teaspoon ground white pepper

1/2 teaspoon ground cinnamon

Seeds from 8 green cardamom pods, crushed

2 bay leaves

1/2 teaspoon salt

1/2 cup plain yogurt

1/4 cup fat-free sour cream

1 pound lean boneless lamb, cubed

2 large tomatoes, cored, seeded, and chopped

1 bag (10 ounces) fresh baby spinach

4 tablespoons chopped fresh cilantro

Fresh cilantro sprigs

1 Heat oil in a large saucepan or Dutch oven over medium heat. Add onions, garlic, and ginger and sauté 10 minutes or until onions are golden.

2 Stir in chile, paprika, cumin, coriander, white pepper, cinnamon, cardamom seed, bay leaves, and salt. In a small bowl, combine yogurt and sour cream and stir into pan along with 2/3 cup water. Add lamb and mix well, then cover and simmer 1 1/4 hours or until lamb is tender.

3 Add tomatoes, spinach, cilantro and cook, stirring, until tomatoes are softened and spinach wilts. Remove bay leaves and garnish with cilantro.

TRADITIONAL IRISH STEW

This classic celebratory dish gets a nutrition update—the proportion of vegetables to meat has been increased considerably, adding flavor as well as vitamins and antioxidants.

SERVES 4

2 teaspoons vegetable oil

1 pound boneless lamb shoulder, cut into 1-inch chunks

4 red or Yukon Gold potatoes, coarsely chopped

3 carrots, peeled and cut into bite-size chunks

2 onions, coarsely chopped

2 leeks, rinsed and white and pale green parts coarsely chopped

1 large turnip, peeled and coarsely chopped

2 tablespoons all-purpose flour

1 bay leaf

1/2 teaspoon dried rosemary

1 teaspoon salt

1/4 teaspoon black pepper

1 cup fresh or frozen green peas

1 Heat oil in a large nonstick saucepan or deep skillet over medium-high heat. Working in batches, add meat and cook until browned on all sides, about 5 minutes per batch. Transfer to a medium bowl.

2 Add potatoes, carrots, onions, leeks, and turnip to pan and sauté 10 minutes. Stir in flour until blended. Add 3 cups water, bay leaf, rosemary, salt, and pepper and bring to boil. Reduce heat, add meat, and simmer, uncovered and stirring occasionally, 50 to 60 minutes or until meat is tender. Add peas and simmer 5 minutes. Remove bay leaf before serving.

WHITE IRISH STEW

This simple lamb dish is called a "white" stew because the meat isn't browned before it's simmered.

SERVES 4

1 pound lean boneless lamb, trimmed and cut into 1-inch cubes

4 1/2 cups canned low-sodium beef broth

3 medium leeks, sliced, or 1 large yellow onion, thinly sliced

1 bay leaf

1/2 teaspoon salt

1/4 teaspoon black pepper

4 medium carrots, sliced

3 medium parsnips, peeled and cut into 1/2-inch pieces

1 teaspoon dill weed

1/4 cup all-purpose flour

1 In a soup pot or Dutch oven over medium heat, combine lamb, 4 cups broth, leeks, bay leaf, salt, and pepper. Bring to boil, then reduce heat and simmer, covered, 45 minutes.

2 Increase heat to medium, stir in carrots and parsnips, and bring to boil. Reduce heat and simmer, covered, 30 minutes or until meat and vegetables are tender. Stir in dill.

3 In a small bowl, stir together flour and remaining broth. Add to pan and cook over medium heat, stirring constantly, until liquid starts to thicken. Continue to cook, stirring, 2 minutes or until thickened. Remove bay leaf before serving.

LAMB COBBLER

If you enjoy hearty stews topped with dumplings or crumbly pastry, you'll love this low-fat version with many more vegetables than cubes of meat.

SERVES 4

Cobbler:

1 pound lean lamb steak, trimmed and cut into 1-inch cubes

1 pound carrots, thickly sliced

4 large celery stalks, thickly sliced

1 pound leeks, thickly sliced

12 ounces strong dry cider

1 can (14 1/2 ounces) fat-free low-sodium chicken broth

Salt and black pepper

1 package (10 ounces) frozen peas, thawed

Bouquet garni (several fresh rosemary, sage, and thyme sprigs tied together)

Topping:

1 cup sifted self-rising white flour

1/4 cup chopped fresh parsley and sage

1/2 teaspoon salt

1/8 teaspoon black pepper

1/2 cup reduced-fat sour cream

1-2 teaspoons low-fat milk *(optional)*

1 For cobbler, fry lamb in a large flameproof baking dish over medium-high heat, stirring frequently, 8 minutes or until lightly browned. Add carrots, celery, and leeks and sauté 4 minutes.

2 Add cider, broth, and salt and pepper to taste and bring to boil. Reduce heat, cover, and simmer 20 minutes or until vegetables are tender.

3 For topping, heat oven to 400°F. In a medium bowl, stir together flour, parsley and sage, salt, and pepper. Stir in sour cream and mix until a firm dough forms; if dough is too dry, add milk. Turn out onto a lightly floured surface, roll to 1/2-inch thickness, and cut into 16 triangles.

4 Add peas and bouquet garni to baking dish. Arrange dough on top, covering surface. Bake 25 to 30 minutes or until topping has risen and is golden.

LAMB STEAK IRISH STEW

Traditional Irish stew uses a tough, fatty cut of lamb, with only potatoes, onions, and herbs. This up-to-date version, which calls for leg of lamb and carrots, is leaner but still comforting.

SERVES 4

4 boneless lean leg-of-lamb steaks (about 1 pound 2 ounces total), trimmed and each cut into 4 pieces

2 large baking potatoes, peeled and thickly sliced

1 large onion, sliced

10 medium carrots, thickly sliced

2 tablespoons chopped parsley

1 teaspoon fresh thyme

1 tablespoon snipped fresh chives

2 cups lamb or vegetable stock

Salt and black pepper

Chopped fresh thyme and parsley

1 Preheat oven to 325°F. Layer lamb, potatoes, onion, and carrots in a large Dutch oven, sprinkling each layer with parsley, thyme, chives, salt, and pepper and ending with a layer of potatoes. Pour stock over all, cover tightly, and bake 2 hours or until meat and vegetables are tender when tested with a skewer.

2 Increase oven temperature to 400°F. Uncover and bake 20 minutes or until potatoes on top are golden and crisp. Sprinkle with thyme and parsley.

MEDITERRANEAN LAMB STEW

Rosemary, basil, and garlic provide the seasoning in this aromatic and savory stew.

SERVES 6

1 1/2 pounds boned lean lamb shoulder

1 1/2 tablespoons olive or canola oil

2 large onions, sliced

2 garlic cloves, minced

1 tablespoon all-purpose flour

2 teaspoons chopped fresh rosemary
or 1 teaspoon dried rosemary

1-2 cups beef stock

1 1/2 cups reduced-sodium tomato juice

1 can (16 ounces) chickpeas, drained
and rinsed

2 zucchini, cubed

1 pint cherry tomatoes, halved

1/8 teaspoon salt

1/8 teaspoon black pepper

2 teaspoons chopped fresh basil or
1 teaspoon dried basil

1 Using a sharp knife, trim all fat and cartilage from lamb. Cut meat into 1-inch cubes.

2 Heat 1 tablespoon oil in a Dutch oven or soup pot over medium heat. Add onions and garlic and sauté 10 minutes or until well browned. Using a slotted spoon, transfer to a plate.

3 Add remaining oil to pot and heat over medium-high heat. Add lamb and sauté 3 minutes or until well browned on all sides. Sprinkle flour and rosemary over meat and cook about 1 1/2 minutes or until flour is absorbed.

4 Return onions to pot and add 1 cup stock and tomato juice. Bring to boil, then reduce heat to simmer, covered, 1 hour or until lamb is half cooked. Stir in chickpeas and simmer 1 to 1 1/4 hours or

until meat is almost tender. Stir in zucchini, tomatoes, salt, pepper, and basil. If stew is too thick, add up to 1 cup additional stock. Simmer 15 minutes or until meat is fork-tender.

LAMB STEW WITH SWEET POTATOES

Okra and peanut butter contribute to the thickness and heartiness of this flavorful West African-inspired stew.

SERVES 4

1 tablespoon olive oil

1 pound lean leg of lamb, trimmed and
cut into 1-inch chunks

1 medium onion, finely chopped

4 garlic cloves, minced

1 cup canned crushed tomatoes

1 pound sweet potatoes, peeled and cut
into 1/2-inch chunks

2 tablespoons creamy peanut butter

1 teaspoon salt

1/2 teaspoon cayenne pepper

1 package (10 ounces) frozen cut or whole
okra, thawed

1 Preheat oven to 350°F. Heat 2 teaspoons oil in a large nonstick Dutch oven or flameproof baking dish over medium-high heat. Add lamb and sauté 5 minutes or until browned. Transfer to a plate.

2 Reduce heat to medium, add remaining oil, onion, and garlic, and sauté 2 minutes. Stir in 1/3 cup water and cook until onion is golden and tender.

3 Stir in 1 1/2 cups water, tomatoes, sweet potatoes, peanut butter, salt, and cayenne and bring to boil. Add lamb, cover and bake 25 minutes. Stir in okra and bake 15 minutes or until lamb and okra are tender.

LAMB CHOP STEW

6 tablespoons olive oil

1 medium eggplant, cut into 1-inch cubes

1 medium zucchini, cut into 1/4-inch-thick slices

1 large green bell pepper, cored, seeded, and cut into 1-inch-square pieces

1 medium yellow onion, thinly sliced

1 can (14 1/2 ounces) tomatoes, drained and chopped

1 tablespoon minced garlic

1/2 teaspoon dried rosemary, crumbled

1/2 teaspoon dried thyme, crumbled

1/2 teaspoon dried basil, crumbled

1/2 teaspoon salt

1/4 teaspoon black pepper

2 tablespoons tomato paste

4 shoulder lamb chops (8 ounces each)

1/4 cup all-purpose flour

2 tablespoons minced fresh basil or parsley

2 tablespoons grated Parmesan cheese

1 Heat 2 tablespoons oil in a 12-inch skillet over medium-high heat. Add eggplant and sauté 6 minutes or until golden on all sides. Transfer to an ungreased shallow 2-quart baking dish.

2 Add another 2 tablespoons oil to skillet and heat. Add zucchini and sauté 3 minutes or until golden. Transfer to baking dish.

3 Preheat oven to 375°F. Add bell pepper and onion to skillet and sauté 5 minutes or until softened. Stir in tomatoes, garlic, rosemary, thyme, basil, 1/4 teaspoon salt, and 1/8 teaspoon black pepper. Cook, uncovered and stirring occasionally, 2 minutes or until thickened. Stir in tomato paste, transfer to baking dish, and toss lightly.

4 Place flour in a shallow dish and dredge lamb, shaking off any excess. Sprinkle with remaining salt and pepper. Add remaining oil to skillet and heat, then add lamb and cook 5 minutes on each side or until browned. Transfer to baking dish and spoon some vegetable mixture on top. Cover with foil and bake 30 minutes or until lamb is tender. Sprinkle with basil and cheese.

You can serve this succulent casserole with pasta, couscous, or polenta on the side.

LAMB, CARROT, AND GREEN BEAN STEW

You can double the recipe for this savory winter stew, refrigerate half of it, and enjoy it later in the week.

SERVES 4

2 tablespoons unsalted butter

1 pound boneless lean lamb shoulder, cut into 1-inch cubes

4 small white onions

1 garlic clove, minced

2 cups canned low-sodium beef broth

1 tablespoon snipped fresh dill or 1 teaspoon dill weed

1/4 teaspoon black pepper

2 medium carrots, peeled and cut into 1-inch cubes

2 small baking potatoes, peeled and cut into 1-inch cubes

2 tablespoons all-purpose flour

1 cup fresh or frozen cut green beans

1 In a large heavy saucepan over high heat, melt butter. When bubbling, add lamb and sauté 5 minutes or until browned on all sides. Transfer to paper towels to drain.

2 Reduce heat to medium, add onions, and sauté 8 minutes or until softened. Stir in garlic during last 2 minutes of cooking. Add broth to pan and stir 1 minute, scraping up browned bits. Return lamb to pan, add dill and pepper, and bring to boil. Reduce heat and simmer, covered, 20 minutes. Add carrots and potatoes and bring to boil. Reduce heat and simmer, covered, 15 minutes.

3 In a small bowl, blend flour with enough hot cooking liquid to make a smooth paste. Add to pan and cook, stirring, 3 minutes or until slightly thickened. Add beans and simmer, covered, 5 minutes or until crisp-tender.

HUNGARIAN LAMB STEW

Paprika and caraway give special zing to this savory and satisfying lamb dish.

SERVES 6

3 bacon slices, cut into 1-inch pieces

2 medium onions, thinly sliced

2 pound boneless lamb for stew

2 tablespoons Hungarian paprika

1 1/2 teaspoons salt

1 teaspoon caraway seed

1 garlic clove, crushed

1 large tomato, cored, seeded, and sliced

1 green bell pepper, cored, seeded, and sliced

1 red bell pepper, cored, seeded, and sliced

3 medium all-purpose potatoes, peeled and cut into eighths

1 In a heavy Dutch oven or soup pot over medium-high heat, cook bacon until browned. Transfer to paper towels to drain. Add onions to pot, reduce heat, and cook 4 minutes or until tender. Transfer to a plate.

2 Increase heat slightly, add lamb, and cook until browned. Add bacon, onions, paprika, salt, caraway seed, garlic, and half the tomato and bell peppers. Add 1/2 cup water and bring to boil. Reduce heat and simmer, covered, 1 1/2 to 2 hours or until meat is tender. Add more water to thin stew if necessary.

3 Stir in potatoes and remaining tomato and peppers. Bring to boil, then reduce heat and simmer, covered, 25 minutes or until tender.

SKILLET LAMB STEW WITH OKRA

Okra helps fight heart disease because it contains pectin and other soluble fibers that lower cholesterol; it also thickens gravy better than flour does.

SERVES 4

1 tablespoon olive oil

2 onions, finely chopped

2 garlic cloves, minced

8 ounces ground lamb

1 tomato, cored, seeded, and finely chopped

1/4 cup tomato paste

3/4 teaspoon salt

1/8 teaspoon black pepper

1 pound okra, trimmed

2 tablespoons fresh lemon juice

1 tablespoon finely chopped fresh cilantro
     (optional)

1 Heat oil in a large nonstick skillet over medium heat. Add onions and sauté 5 minutes or until softened. Add garlic and sauté 1 minute. Add lamb and cook, breaking up meat with wooden spoon, 5 minutes or until browned. Drain off fat.

2 Stir in 1 cup water, tomato, tomato paste, salt, and pepper. Top with okra and sprinkle with lemon juice. Bring to boil, then reduce heat and simmer, covered, 15 minutes or until okra is tender. Uncover and simmer 5 minutes to reduce liquid. Sprinkle with cilantro before serving, if desired.

LIVER AND BACON HOTPOT

This dish is a great choice for everyday healthy eating. It's bursting with flavor from bacon, coarse-grain mustard, peppery sage, carrots, and rutabaga.

SERVES 4

1 1/2 pounds all-purpose potatoes,
     peeled and sliced

2 tablespoons sunflower oil

14 ounces calf's liver, sliced

2 bacon slices, chopped

2 onions, chopped

1 small rutabaga, diced

4 medium carrots, peeled and diced

2 tablespoons all-purpose flour

2 cups lamb or chicken stock

1 tablespoon chopped fresh sage

1 tablespoon coarse-grain mustard

1 tablespoon butter

Salt and black pepper

1 Preheat oven to 375°F. Place potatoes in a large saucepan with enough water to cover and bring to boil. Cook 5 minutes or until just tender; drain.

2 Meanwhile, heat oil in a nonstick skillet over medium-high heat. Add liver and cook 1 minute on each side, turning once. Transfer to Dutch oven.

3 Reduce heat to medium, add bacon, onions, rutabaga, and carrots to skillet, and sauté 10 minutes or until bacon and onions are golden. Sprinkle with flour and stir. Stir in stock. Add sage, 2 teaspoons mustard, and salt and pepper to taste. Bring to boil, stirring.

4 Pour bacon and vegetable mixture over liver. Arrange potatoes on top, overlapping slices neatly and covering vegetables and liver completely. In a small saucepan over low heat, melt butter and stir in remaining mustard. Brush over potatoes and season with salt and pepper. Bake 45 minutes or until potatoes are browned and tender.

CLASSIC VEAL STEW

This heart-healthy main dish—high in vitamins, minerals, and fiber and low in saturated fat—is also a mouthwatering take on traditional beef carbonara, popular in Belgium.
(Photograph on page 7)

SERVES 4

1 pound stewing veal, cut into
    1-inch pieces
1/4 teaspoon black pepper
3/4 teaspoon salt
2 tablespoons vegetable oil
2 portobello mushrooms, stems removed
    and caps cut into 1-inch dice
8 large shallots or 1 onion, finely chopped
2 tablespoons all-purpose flour
1 bottle dark beer
1 tablespoon white wine vinegar
1/2 teaspoon dried thyme, crumbled
1 pound large carrots, peeled and cut into
    2-inch lengths

1 Pat veal dry and season with pepper and 1/4 teaspoon salt.

2 Heat oil in a large flameproof baking dish over high heat. Working in batches, add veal and cook until browned on all sides, 3 to 4 minutes per batch. Transfer to a plate.

3 Reduce heat to medium and add mushrooms and shallots to baking dish. Sauté 5 minutes or until shallots are just golden. Stir in flour. Add veal, beer, vinegar, thyme, and remaining salt and bring to boil. Add carrots, reduce heat, and simmer, covered, 1 1/4 hours or until veal is tender.

4 Transfer veal, carrots, and mushrooms to a warm serving dish. Boil liquid until reduced to about 1 1/4 cups and pour over veal.

VEAL AND ORANGE STEW

The orange flavor gives zest to this fresh-tasting stew.

SERVES 4

2 teaspoons olive oil
1 pound veal stew meat, cut into
    1/2-inch chunks
2 tablespoons all-purpose flour
1 onion, finely chopped
2 garlic cloves, minced
8 ounces small mushrooms, quartered
1 cup canned low-sodium tomatoes,
    undrained, chopped
1 teaspoon grated orange zest
1/2 cup orange juice
1/2 teaspoon salt
1 cup frozen peas
1/4 cup chopped fresh basil

1 Preheat oven to 350°F. Heat oil in a nonstick Dutch oven or flameproof baking dish over medium heat. Place flour in a shallow dish and dredge veal, shaking off excess. Working in batches if necessary, add veal to Dutch oven and sauté 4 minutes or until golden. Using a slotted spoon, transfer to a plate.

2 Add onion and garlic to Dutch oven and sauté 3 minutes or until onion is crisp-tender. Add mushrooms and sauté 5 minutes or until they begin to release their juices.

3 Add tomatoes, orange zest, orange juice, and salt and bring to boil. Add veal, cover, and bake 45 minutes or until tender. Stir in peas and basil and cook 5 minutes or until peas are heated through.

VENISON SOUP

Soup:

2 tablespoons extra-virgin olive oil

1 large onion, chopped

1 garlic clove, crushed

1 pound ground venison

8 juniper berries, crushed

1/2 cup red wine

1 large all-purpose potato, peeled and cut into 1-inch chunks

1 large celery root, peeled and cut into 1-inch chunks

1 large rutabaga, peeled and cut into 1-inch chunks

3 large carrots, peeled and cut into 1-inch chunks

3 1/2 cups beef stock

Salt and black pepper

Chopped fresh parsley or cilantro

Relish:

1 tablespoon extra-virgin olive oil

3 large shallots, each cut into 8 wedges

16 juniper berries, crushed

3 tablespoons superfine sugar

1 tablespoon red wine vinegar

1 pint fresh or 1 package (5 1/2 ounces) frozen black currants

1 For soup, heat oil in a large saucepan over medium heat. Add onion and garlic and sauté 5 minutes or until onion has softened and is starting to brown.

2 Increase heat to high and add venison and juniper berries. Cook, stirring and breaking up meat, 5 minutes or until browned. Stir in wine, potato, celery root, rutabaga, carrots, stock, and salt and pepper to taste. Bring to boil, then reduce heat and simmer, covered, 30 minutes.

3 For relish, heat oil in a small saucepan over medium heat. Add shallots and sauté 5 minutes or until softened. Stir in 4 tablespoons water, juniper berries, sugar, and vinegar. Boil rapidly 5 minutes or until liquid is reduced. Stir in currants and cook 2 minutes or until mixture forms a pulpy relish. Remove from heat and let cool.

4 Transfer soup to a food processor or blender, cover, and puree until smooth. Return to pan and reheat. Ladle into warm bowls and top each serving with a spoonful of relish. Scatter parsley or cilantro on top.

This soup has a rich, meaty flavor, which is deliciously complemented by piquant and fruity black currant relish. Juniper berries and black currants are available at health food and specialty stores.

VENISON CHESTNUT STEW

Full of flavor but low in fat, venison is a healthy substitute for beef in a stew. Port and beets enhance the richness, color, and flavor of the venison, and chestnuts add texture and body to the stew.

SERVES 4

2 tablespoons butter

2 tablespoons extra-virgin olive oil

1 pound boneless venison haunch or shoulder, cut into 1 1/2-inch cubes

2 medium onions, sliced

2 garlic cloves, crushed

2 medium beets, cooked and cut into 6 wedges

Grated zest and juice of 1/2 large orange

1/2 cup port

1 1/4 cups beef stock

1 jar (3 1/2 ounces) vacuum-packed peeled whole chestnuts

3 carrots, halved lengthwise and cut into 1-inch chunks

1 piece fresh ginger, 1 inch long, grated

4 shallots, unpeeled, roots removed

1 tablespoon all-purpose flour

Salt and black pepper

1 Preheat oven to 350°F. In a large Dutch oven over medium heat, melt 1 tablespoon butter and heat 1 tablespoon oil. Working in batches if necessary, add venison in one layer and cook 5 minutes, turning once, until browned. Using a slotted spoon, transfer to a plate.

2 Add onions to Dutch oven and sauté until softened and just beginning to brown, about 10 minutes. Add garlic, beets, orange zest and juice, and stir well. Return venison and juices to pan, add port and stock, and bring to boil. Cover and bake until tender, about 1 1/4 hours, adding chestnuts during last 15 minutes of cooking.

3 Place carrots, ginger, and shallots in a roasting pan, add remaining oil, and stir until evenly coated. Place on oven rack above Dutch oven and roast 1 hour, turning halfway through cooking time.

4 Return Dutch oven to stove over medium heat. In a cup, blend remaining butter with flour and add a little at a time, whisking constantly. Cook until gravy thickens and season to taste with salt and pepper. Serve stew with roasted vegetables on the side.

HASENPFEFFER

German families often served hasenpfeffer, which means "peppered hare." Originally, the spicy marinade helped tenderize wild rabbit. Today, cooks use it for more tender domestic rabbit—or chicken—to add a rich, sweet-sour flavor.

SERVES 4

1 skinned domestic rabbit (2 1/2 to 3 pounds) or 2 1/2 to 3 pounds chicken breasts, thighs, and drumsticks, skin removed

1 1/2 cups canned low-sodium beef broth

1 cup dry red wine or tomato juice

1/2 cup red wine vinegar or cider vinegar

1/4 cup firmly packed light brown sugar

2 bay leaves

3 inches cinnamon stick, broken

1 teaspoon whole cloves

1 teaspoon whole allspice berries

1/4 teaspoon salt

1/4 teaspoon black pepper

1 tablespoon vegetable oil

1 medium yellow onion, sliced

2 tablespoons all-purpose flour

1 Cut rabbit into 8 pieces, then rinse, drain, and pat dry. In a large heavy-duty plastic bag, combine rabbit, broth, wine, vinegar, brown sugar, bay leaves, cinnamon, cloves, allspice, salt, and pepper. Refrigerate 1 to 2 days, turning bag periodically.

2 Remove rabbit from bag and strain marinade into a large bowl, discarding whole spices. Pat rabbit dry with paper towels.

3 Heat oil in a soup pot or Dutch oven over medium heat. Add rabbit and cook, turning occasionally, 7 to 8 minutes or until browned. Add marinade and onion and bring to boil. Reduce heat and simmer, covered, 45 minutes or until rabbit is tender. Transfer to a platter and cover with foil to keep warm.

4 Skim fat from marinade, measure out 1 1/2 cups (discard remainder), and return to pot. In a small bowl, stir together 1/4 cup cold water and flour. Add to pot, bring to boil over medium heat, and cook 1 minute, stirring constantly, to thicken sauce. Serve with rabbit.

RABBIT SOUP WITH OATCAKES

A wholesome meal in a bowl, this soup is similar to Scotch broth but is made with lean chunks of rabbit rather than lamb. It is traditionally served with oatcakes.

SERVES 4

Soup:
2 tablespoons extra-virgin olive oil
1 onion, peeled and coarsely chopped
2 celery stalks, chopped
1 large leek, sliced
2 carrots, peeled and sliced
1 pound lean boneless rabbit, cut into
    1-inch cubes
4 cups chicken stock
2 teaspoons red wine vinegar

1 tablespoon red currant jelly
1 tablespoon chopped fresh tarragon or
    1 teaspoon dried tarragon
1/2 cup mixed long-grain and wild rice
4 ounces green beans, cut into short lengths,
    or frozen cut green beans
Salt and black pepper

Oatcakes:
1 cup old-fashioned rolled oats
1 tablespoon chopped fresh tarragon or
    1 teaspoon dried tarragon
1/4 teaspoon salt
1/4 teaspoon baking powder
2 tablespoons butter, melted

1 For soup, heat oil in a large heavy saucepan over medium heat. Add onion, celery, leek, and carrots and sauté 5 minutes or until onion and leek begin to soften. Stir in rabbit and sauté 2 minutes or until browned. Add stock, vinegar, jelly, tarragon, and salt and pepper to taste. Bring to boil, then reduce heat and simmer, covered, 30 minutes.

2 For oatcakes, preheat oven to 325°F. Sprinkle a baking pan with flour. In a medium bowl, combine oats, tarragon, salt, and baking powder. Add 4 tablespoons boiling water to melted butter and stir into oats to make a stiff paste. Roll dough into a ball, place on pan, and press or roll into a 9-inch circle, pressing cracks together with your fingertips. Using a sharp knife, cut into 8 wedges. Bake 30 minutes or until lightly browned. Transfer to a wire rack to cool.

3 Stir rice into soup and simmer, covered, 15 minutes or until tender. Add beans and simmer, uncovered, 5 minutes or until tender. Ladle into warm bowls and serve with warm oatcakes.

MUSTARD AND RABBIT COBBLER

This lively rabbit stew, seasoned with mustard, is topped with savory biscuit rounds.

SERVES 6

Cobbler:
1 tablespoon sunflower oil
2 pounds rabbit meat, diced
4 lean bacon slices, diced
1 large onion, sliced
1 garlic clove, crushed
2 carrots, peeled and sliced
1/2 cup dry white wine
1 cup chicken stock
1/3 cup red lentils
1 large thyme sprig
1 bay leaf
2 tablespoons white wine vinegar
Salt and black pepper
2 tablespoons coarse-grain mustard

Topping:
1 cup self-rising flour
1/4 teaspoon celery salt
2 tablespoons butter
2 tablespoons chives, minced
1/2 cup fat-free milk

1 For cobbler, preheat oven to 425°F. Heat oil in a soup pot over medium heat. Add rabbit and bacon and cook, stirring, until golden. Add onion and garlic and sauté 2 minutes. Stir in carrots, wine, stock, lentils, thyme, bay leaf, and vinegar. Bring to boil, then reduce heat and simmer, covered, 20 minutes. Season to taste with salt and pepper.

2 For topping, sift flour into a medium bowl, then add celery salt and cut in butter. Stir in chives and milk and mix into a firm dough. Knead briefly, turn out onto a lightly floured surface, and roll into a circle 1/2 inch thick. Using a biscuit cutter, cut out 20 rounds.

3 Remove bay leaf from stew. Add mustard and spoon into an ovenproof dish. Top with rounds of dough, brush with milk, and bake 15 minutes or until topping is golden.

BEEF AND SAUSAGE SOUP

This soup combines spicy sausage and seasonings with plain old meat and potatoes to make a satisfying meal.

SERVES 6

1 tablespoon cooking oil
1 pound beef stew meat, cut into
    1/2-inch cubes
1 pound bulk Italian sausage,
    shaped into balls
1 can (28 ounces) tomatoes, undrained,
    chopped
1 cup chopped onion
1 teaspoon salt
1/2 teaspoon Italian seasoning
1 tablespoon Worcestershire sauce
2 cups cubed peeled all-purpose potatoes
1 cup sliced celery

1 Heat oil in a Dutch oven or soup pot over medium-high heat oil. Add beef and cook until browned on all sides. Using a slotted spoon, transfer to a plate. Add sausage and cook until browned on all sides. Transfer to a plate and drain fat from pot.

2 Return beef and sausage to pot and add 3 1/2 cups water, tomatoes, onion, salt, Italian seasoning, and Worcestershire sauce. Bring to boil, then reduce heat and simmer, covered, 1 1/2 hours or until beef is tender.

3 Add potatoes and celery and simmer, covered, 30 minutes or until tender.

BASQUE SOUP

This is a one-dish meal from the mountains of northern Spain.

12 ounces Polish sausage, sliced
1 broiler-fryer chicken (2-3 pounds)
2 leeks, sliced
2 carrots, sliced
1 large turnip, peeled and cubed
1 large onion, chopped
1 large all-purpose potato, peeled and cubed
1 garlic clove, minced
1 1/2 teaspoons salt
1/2 teaspoon black pepper
1 tablespoon snipped fresh parsley
1 teaspoon dried thyme
1 cup shredded cabbage
2 cups cooked navy or great Northern beans

1 In a skillet over medium heat, brown sausage. Transfer to paper towels to drain.

2 In a large Dutch oven, combine 8 cups water and chicken and bring to boil. Reduce heat and simmer, covered, 30 minutes or until tender. Transfer to a plate and let cool. Strain stock and skim off fat.

3 Return stock to Dutch oven and add leeks, carrots, turnip, onion, potato, garlic, salt, pepper, parsley, and thyme. Bring to boil, then reduce heat and simmer, covered, 30 minutes.

4 Meanwhile, remove chicken from bones, cut into bite-size pieces, and add to Dutch oven. Add cabbage, beans, and sausage and simmer, uncovered, 30 minutes or until vegetables are tender.

PEPPERONI-BEEF SOUP

All the ingredients of a good pizza are combined in this soup; serve it with crisp bread.

SERVES 6

1 pound ground beef
1 small onion, chopped
1 cup sliced mushrooms
1 green bell pepper, cored, seeded, and cut into strips
1 can (28 ounces) tomatoes, undrained, cut up
1 cup beef stock
1 cup sliced pepperoni
1 teaspoon dried basil
Shredded mozzarella cheese

1 In a large saucepan over medium heat, sauté beef, onion, mushrooms, and bell pepper until beef is browned and vegetables are almost tender. Drain off fat.

2 Stir in tomatoes, stock, pepperoni, and basil and cook until heated through. Ladle into oven-proof bowls and top with cheese. Broil or microwave until cheese is melted and bubbling.

HAM, BEEF, AND BACON SOUP

This soup is a meat lover's dream, but there are plenty of vegetables to add vitamins and minerals.

SERVES 10

8 ounces ground beef, browned and drained
8 ounces bacon, diced, cooked, and drained
8 ounces fully cooked ham, cubed
2 cans (15 ounces each) lima beans, drained and rinsed
1 medium onion, chopped
1 package (20 ounces) frozen mixed vegetables, thawed
1 can (10 1/2 ounces) beef broth

1 can (10 3/4 ounces) condensed tomato soup

1 teaspoon sugar

3/4 teaspoon salt

1/4 teaspoon black pepper

1-2 cups tomato juice (optional)

1 In a Dutch oven or soup kettle, combine beef, bacon, ham, beans, onion, mixed vegetables, broth, soup, sugar, salt, and pepper. Bring to boil, then reduce heat and simmer, covered, 30 minutes or until vegetables are heated through and flavors blended. Season with additional salt and pepper if desired. For thinner soup, stir in tomato juice.

BEEF AND SAUSAGE GOULASH

Goulash is Hungarian for a meat stew with vegetables. This is a spicy version, made almost sweet by the cabbage.

SERVES 8

1 pound bulk pork sausage

1 pound ground beef

1 large onion, chopped

1 can (28 ounces) tomatoes, undrained, chopped

1 can (6 ounces) tomato paste

2 tablespoons vinegar

1 tablespoon chili powder

1 teaspoon garlic powder

1/4 teaspoon crushed red pepper flakes (optional)

10 cups shredded cabbage

1 In a large soup pot over medium heat, brown sausage, beef, and onion; drain off fat.

2 Add tomatoes, tomato paste, vinegar, chili powder, garlic powder, and red pepper flakes and mix well. Stir in cabbage and bring to boil. Reduce heat and simmer, covered, 15 minutes or until cabbage is tender.

BACON-CHICKEN HOT-AND-SOUR SOUP

This is a Szechuan soup that uses chicken instead of pork. Try to find rice vinegar at an Asian market; it's milder than other vinegars.

SERVES 4

1 cup dried shiitake mushrooms

2 cups canned chicken broth

1/4 cup rice vinegar

1 teaspoon sugar

1 teaspoon black pepper

1/2 teaspoon salt

2 cups shredded Napa cabbage

3/4 pound boneless skinless chicken breasts, cut crosswise into 1/4-inch-wide strips

2 ounces Canadian bacon, cut into matchsticks

2 tablespoons cornstarch blended with 1/4 cup water

2 scallions, thinly sliced

2 teaspoons sesame oil

1 In a small bowl, combine 1 1/2 cups boiling water and mushrooms. Let stand 20 minutes or until softened. With your fingers, lift mushrooms from liquid and rinse under warm running water. Cut off tough stems and thinly slice caps. Line a sieve with a paper towel, set over a bowl, and strain soaking liquid.

2 In a large saucepan over medium heat, combine 2 cups water, broth, vinegar, sugar, pepper, salt, mushrooms, and soaking liquid. Bring to boil, then reduce heat and simmer. Add cabbage, chicken, and Canadian bacon and cook 2 minutes or until chicken is cooked through. Return to boil, stir in cornstarch mixture, and cook, stirring, 1 minute or until thickened. Remove from heat and stir in scallions and sesame oil.

BEEF, PORK, AND CHICKEN *BOOYAH*

Belgian by origin, booyah is bouillon, which is the base for this Midwestern stew-like soup of beef, pork, and chicken.

SERVES 12

1 stewing chicken (about 4 pounds), giblets removed

2 1/2 pounds meaty cross-cut beef shanks, 1 inch thick

1 1/2 pounds bone-in pork shoulder

3 cups homemade chicken stock or canned low-sodium chicken broth

4 garlic cloves, 3 whole and 1 minced

2 bay leaves

1 tablespoon vegetable oil

2 medium yellow onions, chopped

3 large carrots, peeled and sliced

2 celery stalks, chopped

6 medium all-purpose potatoes, peeled and cut into 1/2-inch cubes

1 1/2 cups bite-size pieces fresh or frozen green beans

1 can (14 1/2 ounces) whole tomatoes, drained

1 1/2 teaspoons salt

1 teaspoon dried rosemary

1/2 teaspoon black pepper

1/2 dried thyme

1/2 cup frozen peas

1 1/2 teaspoons grated lemon zest

Hot red pepper sauce

1/2 cup chopped fresh parsley

1 In an 8-quart soup pot over high heat, bring 7 cups water, chicken, beef, pork, stock, 3 whole garlic cloves, and bay leaves to boil, skimming off any foam. Reduce heat, cover, and simmer 2 hours or until meat is tender. Uncover pot for last 40 minutes of cooking.

2 Transfer meat to a plate. When cool enough to handle, remove meat from bones, cut into bite-size pieces, and set aside. Strain stock and measure 8 cups, adding water if necessary. Discard skin, bones, garlic, and bay leaves.

3 Heat oil in pot over medium-high heat. Add onions, carrots, celery, and minced garlic and sauté 5 minutes or until tender. Add stock, potatoes, beans, tomatoes, salt, rosemary, pepper, and thyme and bring to boil. Reduce heat and simmer, uncovered, 10 minutes or until potatoes and beans are tender.

4 Add peas, meat, lemon zest, and red pepper sauce. Simmer 5 minutes or until peas are tender. Ladle into large soup bowls and garnish with parsley.

EASY GUMBO

The flavor of the southern United States has never been more pronounced than in this version of Louisiana's favorite stew.

SERVES 4

1 1/2 tablespoons butter

1 tablespoon olive oil

1 medium onion, sliced

1 small green bell pepper, cored, seeded, and chopped

2 celery stalks, chopped

Salt

1 3/4 cups long-grain white rice

2 tablespoons all-purpose flour

1 can (19 ounces) chopped tomatoes

1 1/4 cups fish or vegetable stock

1 bay leaf

1/2-1 teaspoon cayenne pepper

1/2 teaspoon paprika

2/3 pound fresh okra, trimmed and cut into 1/2-inch pieces

8 ounces smoked hotdogs, cut into
1/2-inch pieces

2 cans (4 ounces each) crabmeat, drained

9 ounces canned mussels, smoked or
unsmoked, drained

1 In a large saucepan over medium heat, melt butter and heat oil. Add onion and sauté 5 minutes or until translucent. Add bell pepper and celery and sauté 3 minutes.

2 In another large saucepan, bring water to a boil, then add salt and rice. Return to boil, then reduce heat and simmer, covered, 15 minutes or until tender.

3 Add flour to pan, stirring to make a roux, and cook 2 minutes. Add tomatoes, stock, bay leaf, cayenne, and paprika. Bring to boil, reduce heat, and simmer, covered, 15 minutes, or until slightly thickened. Add okra and cook until heated through. Remove bay leaf

4 Add hotdogs, crabmeat, and mussels and simmer 2 to 3 minutes or until heated through. Drain rice, divide among four warm bowls, and spoon gumbo on top.

GUMBO Z'HERBES

Gumbo is the Angolan word for okra—the one ingredient that is shared by nearly all gumbos.

SERVES 4

1/4 cup olive oil

1 pound beef brisket or chuck steak,
cut into 1/2-inch chunks

6 ounces baked ham, cut into 1/2-inch chunks

1 large yellow onion, finely chopped

6 scallions with tops, thinly sliced

1 large red bell pepper, cored, seeded,
and diced

3 tablespoons all-purpose flour

1 cup thinly sliced fresh okra or 1/2 package
(10 ounces) frozen okra

4 cups homemade chicken stock or canned
low-sodium chicken broth

8 ounces cabbage, cored and cut into
1/2-inch chunks

4 cups thinly sliced mustard greens

3 cups thinly sliced turnip greens

1/2 teaspoon salt

1/4 teaspoon black pepper

1 bay leaf

1/2 teaspoon dried thyme, crumbled

1/2 teaspoon dried marjoram, crumbled

4 allspice berries

2 whole cloves

1/8 teaspoon cayenne pepper

6 cups trimmed, washed, and coarsely
chopped spinach

1 bunch watercress, tough stems removed
and leaves coarsely chopped

1 Heat oil 2 minutes in an 8-quart Dutch oven over medium heat. Add beef and ham and sauté 5 minutes or until lightly browned. Transfer to a bowl.

2 Add onion and scallions to Dutch oven and sauté 5 minutes or until softened. Add bell pepper and sauté 4 minutes or until crisp-tender. Stir in flour until vegetables are well coated. Add okra and cook, stirring constantly. Gradually add stock, stirring until well combined.

3 Add cabbage, mustard greens, turnip greens, salt, pepper, bay leaf, thyme, marjoram, allspice, cloves, cayenne, and meat. Bring to boil, then reduce heat and simmer, covered and stirring occasionally, 1 1/2 hours or until gumbo is thickened and beef is tender.

4 Add spinach and watercress and simmer, covered, 15 minutes or until tender. Remove bay leaf.

LOUISIANA GUMBO STEW WITH SAUSAGE, HAM, AND SHRIMP

SERVES 12

1 broiler/fryer chicken (about 3 pounds), cut up

3/4 cup all-purpose flour

1/2 cup vegetable oil

1/2 cup sliced scallions

1/2 cup chopped onion

1/2 cup chopped seeded green bell pepper

1/2 cup chopped seeded red bell pepper

1/2 cup chopped celery

2 garlic cloves, minced

8 ounces fully cooked smoked sausage, cut into 1-inch cubes

8 ounces fully cooked ham, cut into 3/4-inch cubes

8 ounces fresh or frozen shrimp, peeled and deveined

1 cup cut fresh or frozen okra (3/4-inch pieces)

1 can (15 ounces) kidney beans, drained and rinsed

1/2 teaspoon salt

1/4 teaspoon black pepper

1/4 teaspoon hot red pepper sauce

Hot cooked rice (optional)

1 In a Dutch oven or soup pot, bring 8 cups water and chicken to boil. Skim off fat, reduce heat, and simmer, covered, 30 minutes or until tender. Transfer chicken to a plate, reserving 6 cups broth. When chicken is cool enough to handle, debone and cut meat into bite-size pieces.

2 Add flour and oil to pot and stir until smooth. Cook, stirring, over medium-low heat 2 to 3 minutes or until browned. Stir in scallions, onion, bell peppers, celery, and garlic and sauté 5 minutes or until tender. Stir in sausage, ham, broth, and chicken. Bring to boil, reduce heat, and simmer, covered, 45 minutes.

3 Add shrimp, okra, beans, salt, black pepper, and red pepper sauce. Cover and simmer until shrimp are pink, about 5 minutes. Serve over rice, if desired.

This traditional Creole dish is hot, hearty, and delicious.

ANDOUILLE SAUSAGE AND CHICKEN GUMBO

Gumbo king John Noel advises, "Stir your roux constantly so it doesn't stick, and keep stirring until it turns a deep mahogany brown."

SERVES 8

1/4 cup plus 1 tablespoon vegetable oil

1/2 cup flour

4 pounds skinless chicken parts

1/4 teaspoon salt

3/4 teaspoon black pepper

2 cups chopped onions

1 cup chopped celery

1 cup chopped seeded green bell pepper

3 garlic cloves, minced

1 pound andouille or other smoked sausage, cut diagonally into 1/2-inch slices

1/2 teaspoon cayenne pepper

1/2 teaspoon dried thyme

2 cups okra, cut into 1-inch pieces, or 1 package (10 ounces) sliced frozen okra

2 tablespoons sliced scallions

1/4 cup chopped fresh parsley

Hot red pepper sauce

4 cups cooked long-grain white rice

1 Heat 1/4 cup oil in a heavy 6-inch skillet over medium-low heat. Add flour and cook, stirring constantly, 10 minutes or until deep brown. Remove from heat.

2 Heat remaining oil in a 6-quart Dutch oven or soup pot over medium-high heat. Season chicken with salt and 1/4 teaspoon black pepper, add to pot, and cook 4 minutes on each side or until golden. Transfer to a platter.

3 Add onions, celery, bell pepper, and garlic to pot and sauté 5 minutes or until tender. Stir in roux and heat until bubbling. Gradually whisk in 8 cups cold water, mixing until smooth.

4 Add chicken and sausage, remaining black pepper, cayenne, and thyme. Bring to boil, then reduce heat and simmer, uncovered, 1 1/2 hours, skimming off foam occasionally. Stir in okra and scallions and simmer 10 minutes. Stir in parsley and season to taste with red pepper sauce (don't be timid!). Ladle over rice.

ITALIAN SAUSAGE AND CHICKEN STEW

Serve this Cajun-style dish over hot cooked rice or noodles.

SERVES 4

2 large green bell peppers, halved, cored, seeded, and thinly sliced

1 large yellow onion, halved and thinly sliced

4 ounces bulk sweet Italian sausage

4 garlic cloves, minced

2 1/2-3 pounds chicken breasts, thighs, and drumsticks, skin removed

1 tablespoon vegetable oil

1 can (28 ounces) plum tomatoes, undrained, coarsely chopped

2 tablespoons red wine vinegar or cider vinegar

1/4 teaspoon salt

1 In a soup pot or Dutch oven over medium heat, combine bell peppers, onion, sausage, and garlic. Cook, stirring, until sausage is cooked through. Transfer to a bowl, drain fat from pot, and wipe out.

2 Rinse chicken and pat dry with paper towels. Add oil to pot and heat over medium-high heat. Add chicken and cook, turning often, 10 minutes or until browned. Stir in sausage mixture, tomatoes, vinegar, and salt and bring to boil. Reduce heat, cover, and simmer, stirring often, 30 minutes or until chicken is cooked through.

ALGARVE PORK AND CLAM
CATAPLANA

The Algarve is a Portuguese province where fish stews are made in a cataplana, a copper pot that looks like a giant hinged clamshell. A Dutch oven will do.

SERVES 4

2 tablespoons olive oil

1 large yellow onion, finely chopped

4 garlic cloves, minced

2 large green bell peppers, cored, seeded, and diced

4 ounces *linguiça* or chorizo sausage, halved lengthwise and thinly sliced

3 ounces prosciutto, chopped

1 can (28 ounces) tomatoes, drained and chopped

1 cup homemade fish stock or 1/2 cup each bottled clam juice and water

1 cup chopped flat-leaf parsley

1/2 teaspoon hot red pepper sauce

24 littleneck clams, well scrubbed

1 Heat oil 1 minute in a 5-quart Dutch oven over medium heat. Add onion and garlic and sauté 6 minutes or until softened.

2 Add bell peppers and sauté 5 minutes or until softened. Add sausage and prosciutto and cook, stirring often, 4 minutes or until fat is rendered.

3 Stir in tomatoes, stock, parsley, and red pepper sauce and bring to boil. Add clams, reduce heat to medium, and cook, covered, 10 minutes or just until clams open. Discard any that do not open.

CHINESE FIRE POT

SERVES 6

Dipping Items:

1 pound skinless, boneless chicken breasts, put in freezer until almost frozen, about 45 minutes

1 pound beef tenderloin, top sirloin, or flank steak, put in freezer until almost frozen, about 45 minutes

2 tablespoons soy sauce

2 tablespoons rice wine or dry sherry

2 teaspoons Oriental sesame oil

1 pound fresh spinach, trimmed, rinsed, and dried

1 pound large shrimp, peeled and deveined

4 ounces snow peas, trimmed and rinsed

Dipping Sauce:

1/2 cup soy sauce

1/4 cup rice wine or dry sherry

1/4 cup rice vinegar or cider vinegar

2 tablespoons Oriental sesame oil

1 tablespoon chili oil or peanut oil blended with 1/2 teaspoon hot red pepper sauce

2 teaspoons sugar

2 garlic cloves, minced

1 tablespoon minced fresh ginger

4 scallions with tops, thinly sliced

Soup:

6 cups chicken stock

2 ounces fine transparent noodles, soaked in hot water 30 minutes, drained, and cut into 2-inch lengths, or 2 ounces fine noodles, cooked and drained

8 ounces Napa cabbage or green cabbage, cut into 1 1/2-inch-thick slices

6 ounces firm tofu, cut into 1/2-inch cubes

2 tablespoons rice wine or dry sherry

1/4 teaspoon salt

3 tablespoons minced fresh cilantro or flat-leaf parsley

1 For dipping items, use a sharp knife to cut chicken and beef across grain into very thin slices, then arrange on a platter. In a small bowl, combine soy sauce, wine, and sesame oil, then brush on meat. Cover with plastic wrap and refrigerate until ready to serve.

2 Place spinach in a small bowl, cover with moist paper towels and plastic wrap, and refrigerate. Arrange shrimp and peas on separate platters, cover with plastic wrap, and refrigerate.

3 For dipping sauce, combine soy sauce, wine, vinegar, sesame oil, chili oil, sugar, garlic, and ginger in a food processor or blender and process 10 to 15 seconds. Transfer to a bowl, cover with plastic wrap, and refrigerate. Place scallions in a small bowl and refrigerate.

4 For soup, just before serving, combine stock, noodles, cabbage, tofu, wine, and salt in a large saucepan over medium-high heat. Bring to boil, remove from heat, cover, and let stand 5 to 10 minutes.

5 Set a Chinese fire pot (available at Asian specialty stores), large fondue pot, chafing dish, or electric skillet in center of table. Arrange platters of beef and chicken, shrimp, and vegetables around it. Divide dipping sauce equally among 6 small bowls and top each with scallions. Set a bowl at each place, along with a plate, fondue fork or long-handled kitchen fork, dinner knife, and fork.

6 Return soup to boil, stir in cilantro, and ladle 2/3 into fire pot. Adjust flame so soup simmers gently. Let guests use forks to dip chicken, beef, shrimp, and vegetables into soup for 30 to 60 seconds, then into dipping sauce before placing on their plates. When all food is eaten, add remaining soup to pot, heat through, and divide equally among guests' bowls.

Despite its long list of ingredients, this impressive party dish is easy to prepare. Let your guests do the cooking themselves. The beef, chicken, shrimp, vegetables, and dipping sauce can be prepared up to 4 hours ahead.

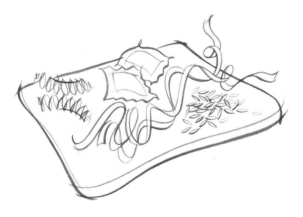

KENTUCKY BURGOO

From Owensboro, Kentucky, comes this recipe featuring the three burgoo basics: beef, lamb, and chicken.

SERVES 14

1 tablespoon vegetable oil

2 pounds meaty cross-cut beef shanks, 1 inch thick

2 pounds meaty cross-cut lamb shanks, 1 inch thick

1 stewing chicken (4 pounds)

1 1/2 teaspoons salt

1/2 teaspoon black pepper

1 large head green cabbage, shredded

6 large russet potatoes (3 pounds), peeled and diced

1 can (28 ounces) low-sodium whole tomatoes, undrained

1 bag (20 ounces) frozen baby lima beans

3 medium yellow onions, chopped

1/2 cup low-sodium ketchup

1/3 cup tomato puree

1 1/2 tablespoons Worcestershire sauce

1 1/4 teaspoons hot red pepper sauce

1/2 teaspoon crushed red pepper flakes

2 packages (10 ounces each) frozen whole-kernel corn

3 tablespoons cider vinegar

2 tablespoons fresh lemon juice

1 Heat oil in a heavy 12-inch skillet over medium-high heat. Working in batches, add beef and lamb and cook, turning frequently, 3 to 4 minutes or until browned.

2 In an 8-quart soup pot, combine 3 1/2 quarts cold water, beef, lamb, chicken, salt, and pepper. Bring to boil over high heat, skimming off any fat. Reduce heat and simmer, uncovered, 2 hours or until meat is tender. Transfer to a plate and let cool.

3 Add cabbage, potatoes, tomatoes, lima beans, onions, ketchup, tomato puree, Worcestershire sauce, red pepper sauce, and red pepper flakes to pot. Bring to boil, reduce heat, and simmer, uncovered, 2 hours, stirring occasionally.

4 Meanwhile, remove skin and bones from chicken and bones from beef and lamb. Cut meat into bite-size pieces and add to pot. Stir in corn, vinegar, and lemon juice and simmer 10 minutes or until heated through.

Chilies

CHILIES

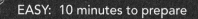

recipe list

🤏 **EASY:** 10 minutes to prepare

⏰ **QUICK:** Ready to eat in 30 minutes

🥣 **ONE-DISH:** contains protein, vegetables, and good carbohydrates (beans, whole-grains, etc.) for a complete healthy meal

☀ **HEALTHY:** High in nutrients, low in bad fats and empty carbohydrates

🍲 **SLOW COOKER:** Easily adapted for slow cooker by cutting down on liquids

CHILI IN BREAD BOWLS

SERVES 9

1 tablespoon all-purpose flour

1/4 teaspoon salt

1/8 teaspoon black pepper

8 ounces lean beef stew meat, cubed

8 ounces skinless, boneless chicken breast, cubed

8 ounces boneless pork, cubed

1 tablespoon vegetable oil

1 medium onion, chopped

1 medium green bell pepper, cored, seeded and chopped

1 jalapeño pepper, seeded, deveined, and chopped (wear gloves when handling; they burn)

1 can (28 ounces) diced tomatoes, drained

1 can (16 ounces) kidney beans, drained and rinsed

1 can (15 1/2 ounces) navy or great Northern beans, drained and rinsed

1 can (8 ounces) tomato sauce

1 tablespoon chili powder

1 garlic clove, minced

1 1/2 teaspoons ground cumin

1/2 teaspoon dried basil

1/2 teaspoon cayenne pepper

9 large hard rolls

Sour cream (optional)

Chopped scallions (optional)

Chopped seeded red bell pepper (optional)

1 In a large resealable plastic bag, combine flour, salt, and black pepper. Add beef, chicken, and pork in batches and shake to coat.

2 Heat oil in a large skillet over medium heat. Add beef, chicken, and pork in batches and cook until browned.

3 Using a slotted spoon, transfer meat to a 5-quart slow cooker. Stir in onion, green bell pepper, jalapeño, tomatoes, beans, tomato sauce, chili powder, garlic, cumin, basil, and cayenne. Cover and cook on low until meat is tender, about 7 hours.

4 Cut tops off rolls, carefully hollow out bottom halves, and spoon about 1 cup chili into each. Garnish with sour cream, scallions, and bell pepper, if desired.

Here's a wonderful, spicy chili that comes in its own edible dishes—a festive presentation for parties.

CALIFORNIA PEPPER CHILI

This chili uses four kinds of hot peppers and three kinds of meat. The result is dynamite.

SERVES 8

8 ounces bacon, diced

2 1/2 pounds beef stew meat, cut into 3/4-inch cubes

1 1/2 pounds pork stew meat, cut into 3/4-inch cubes

2 medium onions, chopped

6-8 garlic cloves, minced

1-2 tablespoons chopped seeded fresh Serrano chiles

1-2 tablespoons chopped seeded fresh poblano chiles

1-2 tablespoons chopped, seeded, and deveined fresh jalapeño peppers (wear gloves when handling; they burn)

2-3 teaspoons cayenne pepper

1 1/2 teaspoons dried oregano

1 teaspoon salt

1 teaspoon ground cumin

1 can (15 ounces) tomato puree

1 can (14 1/2 ounces) beef broth

7 plum tomatoes, cored, seeded, and chopped

Shredded cheddar cheese *(optional)*

1 In a Dutch oven or soup pot over medium heat, cook bacon until crisp. Transfer to paper towels to drain. Drain fat from pot, reserving 3 tablespoons.

2 Add beef, pork, and onions to pot and sauté in drippings until meat is browned and onions are softened. Drain off fat. Add garlic, Serrano, poblano, and jalapeño peppers, cayenne, oregano, salt, and cumin and sauté 2 minutes.

3 Stir in tomato puree, broth, and tomatoes and bring to boil. Reduce heat and simmer, covered, until meat is tender, about 1 hour. Garnish with bacon and cheese, if desired.

ROUND STEAK CHILI

Using chunks of round steak instead of ground beef gives this chili a different texture that many people prefer.

SERVES 6

1 1/2 tablespoons vegetable oil

1 pound round steak, cut into 1/2-inch cubes

1 large onion, chopped

2 garlic cloves, minced

1 can (46 ounces) vegetable juice

1 can (28 ounces) crushed tomatoes

2 cups sliced celery

1 can (16 ounces) kidney beans, drained and rinsed

1 medium green bell pepper, cored, seeded, and chopped

1 bay leaf

2 tablespoons chili powder

1 1/2 teaspoons salt

1 teaspoon dried oregano

1/2 teaspoon celery seed

1/2 teaspoon paprika

1/2 teaspoon ground cumin

1/4 teaspoon cayenne pepper

1/4 teaspoon dried basil

1/2 teaspoon coarse-grain mustard

1 teaspoon brown sugar

1 Heat oil in a Dutch oven or soup pot over medium heat. Add steak, onion, and garlic and sauté until steak is browned and vegetables are softened.

2 Add vegetable juice, tomatoes, celery, beans, bell pepper, bay leaf, chili powder, salt, oregano, celery seed, paprika, cumin, cayenne, basil, mustard, and brown sugar. Bring to boil, then reduce heat and simmer, uncovered, 3 hours. Remove bay leaf before serving.

CLASSIC CHILI CON CARNE WITH CORNBREAD

Slow-cooked beef and beans in a rich tomato sauce spiced with chiles and cumin make this an inviting meal on a wintry day. Warm, crumbly, moist cornbread studded with corn kernels and mild green chiles makes the perfect accompaniment.

SERVES 6

Chili:

1 tablespoon extra-virgin olive oil

3/4 pound lean stewing beef, trimmed and cut into small cubes

1 large onion, finely chopped

2 garlic cloves, crushed

1/2 teaspoon cumin seed

1 teaspoon crushed dried chiles

1 tablespoon tomato puree

1 can (14 1/2 ounces) chopped tomatoes, undrained

2 cans (14 1/2 ounces) red kidney beans, drained and rinsed

1 1/4 cups beef stock

Cornbread:

Butter

1 cup cornmeal

3/4 cup flour

2 teaspoons baking powder

1/2 teaspoon salt

1 large egg

1 cup low-fat (1%) milk

1 cup fresh corn or thawed frozen whole-kernel corn

1 small mild fresh green chile, seeded and finely chopped

1 For chili, heat oil in a large Dutch oven or soup pot over medium-high heat. Add beef and sauté 4 minutes or until well browned. Using a slotted spoon, transfer to a plate.

2 Reduce heat to low, add onion to pot, and sauté 10 minutes. Add garlic, cumin seed, and chiles and sauté 1 minute, then return beef to pan. Add tomato puree, tomatoes, beans, and stock and stir well. Bring to boil, then reduce heat, cover, and simmer, stirring occasionally, 1 hour or until meat is tender.

3 For cornbread, preheat oven to 400°F. Grease a shallow 8-inch-square pan with butter. In a medium bowl, mix cornmeal, flour, baking powder, and salt. In a small bowl, combine egg and milk, then stir into cornmeal mixture until evenly moist. Fold in corn and chile. Spoon into prepared pan and bake 25 minutes or until firm to the touch.

4 Turn cornbread out of pan onto a wire rack, then cut into large squares. Serve chili in warm bowls with warm cornbread.

CHUNKY STEAK CHILI

Some cooks like to serve this chili in bread baskets made by scooping out round hard rolls.

SERVES 6

1 tablespoon vegetable oil

1 1/2 pounds lean chuck or round steak, cut into bite-size pieces

2 garlic cloves, minced

2 green bell peppers, cored, seeded, and chopped

1 large onion, chopped

2 tablespoons chili powder

2 teaspoons ground cumin

1 teaspoon dried oregano

1 can (28 ounces) low-sodium tomatoes, undrained, chopped

1 can (15-16 ounces) kidney beans, rinsed and drained

1 Heat oil in a large heavy saucepan over medium heat. Add beef and sauté until lightly browned. Add garlic, bell peppers, onion, chili powder, cumin, oregano, and tomatoes. Bring to boil, then reduce heat and simmer, covered, 2 1/2 hours or until meat is tender.

2 Stir in beans and simmer 30 minutes.

SANTA FE CHILI

Here is a hot, satisfying Southwestern main dish that takes very little effort to put together.

SERVES 8

2 tablespoons cooking oil

1 lean beef roast (2-3 pounds), cut into 1/2-inch cubes

2 medium onions, sliced

1 can (10 ounces) tomatoes with jalapeños or 1 can (16 ounces) tomatoes, undrained, cut up

1 can (15 ounces) pinto beans, drained and rinsed

2 cans (4 ounces each) chopped green chiles

1 can (10 1/2 ounces) beef broth

1 tablespoon sugar

1 garlic clove, minced

2 teaspoons ground cumin

1 green bell pepper, cored, seeded, and chopped

Salt

Shredded Monterey Jack cheese

1 Heat oil in a Dutch oven or soup pot over medium heat. Add beef and cook until browned on all sides. Add 1 cup water, onions, tomatoes, beans, chiles, broth, sugar, garlic, cumin, bell pepper, and salt to taste. Bring to boil, then reduce heat and simmer, covered, 1 1/2 hours or until meat is tender.

2 Spoon into bowls and top with cheese.

HOT, HOT CHILI

This spicy-hot chili is not for the meek. Aficionados of hot chiles will love it.

SERVES 8

2 tablespoons vegetable oil

2 pounds beef stew meat, cut into 3/4-inch cubes

1 medium onion, chopped

3 garlic cloves, minced

1 jar (16 ounces) hot banana peppers

2 cans (14 1/2 ounces each) diced tomatoes, undrained

1 can (10 ounces) diced tomatoes and green chiles, undrained

1 can (6 ounces) tomato paste

1 can (16 ounces) kidney beans, drained and rinsed

1 can (4 ounces) chopped green chiles

1 fresh jalapeño or hot banana pepper, seeded, deveined, and chopped (wear gloves when handling; they burn)

2 tablespoons chili powder

1 1/2 tablespoons hot red pepper sauce

1 teaspoon salt

1/8 teaspoon ground cumin

Whole banana peppers *(optional)*

1 Heat oil in a large saucepan over medium heat. Add beef, onion, and garlic and sauté until meat is browned. Drain off fat.

2 Remove stems and seeds from 10 banana peppers and chop peppers. Add to pan with diced tomatoes, tomatoes and chiles, tomato paste, beans, green chiles, jalapeño, chili powder, red pepper sauce, salt, and cumin.

3 Bring to boil, then reduce heat and simmer, covered, until meat is tender, about 2 hours. Uncover and simmer until chili reaches desired consistency. Garnish with whole peppers, if desired.

ONE-POT CHILI

This one has all the spice and heft chili should have—without all the mess.

SERVES 4

2 teaspoons vegetable oil

3 scallions, thinly sliced

2 garlic cloves, minced

1 tablespoon chili powder

1 teaspoon ground cumin

1/2 teaspoon oregano

1 pound lean ground round

1 can (16 ounces) red kidney beans,
   drained and rinsed

1 can (14 1/2 ounces) low-sodium
   stewed tomatoes

1 cup whole-kernel corn

1 Heat oil in a medium saucepan over medium heat. Add scallions, garlic, chili powder, cumin, and oregano and sauté 1 minute. Add beef and stir until browned.

2 Add beans, tomatoes, and corn and simmer 5 minutes.

HAMBURGER CHILI

This is a well-seasoned chili with a high ratio of meat to tomatoes and beans.

SERVES 8

2 pounds ground beef

2 tablespoons olive oil

2 garlic cloves, minced

2 medium onions, chopped

1 green bell pepper, cored, seeded,
   and chopped

1 1/2 teaspoons salt

2 tablespoons chili powder

1/8 teaspoon cayenne pepper

1/4 teaspoon ground cinnamon

1 teaspoon ground cumin

1 teaspoon dried oregano

2 cans (16 ounces each) tomatoes,
   undrained, chopped

3 beef bouillon cubes

1 can (16 ounces) kidney
   beans, undrained

1 In a large soup pot over medium heat, cook beef until browned, then transfer to a plate. Drain off fat.

2 Add oil to pot and heat. Reduce heat to low. Add garlic and onions, and sauté until onions are tender. Stir in bell pepper, salt, chili powder, cayenne, cinnamon, cumin, and oregano and cook, stirring, 2 minutes.

3 Add beef and tomatoes. In a small bowl, dissolve bouillon in 1 cup boiling water and add to pot. Bring to boil, then reduce heat and simmer, covered, about 1 hour. Add beans and simmer 30 minutes.

CHILI-IN-A-HURRY

This simple chili is no less tasty for being put together quickly.

SERVES 6

1 pound ground beef

1 cup diced onion

2 cans (15 ounces each) kidney beans,
   partially drained

2 cans (16 ounces each) tomatoes,
   undrained, cut up

1 celery stalk, diced

1 teaspoon salt

1 teaspoon black pepper

1/2 teaspoon chili powder

1/4-1/2 teaspoon crushed red pepper flakes

1 In a large saucepan or skillet over medium heat, cook beef and onion until beef is browned and onion is translucent. Drain off fat.

2 Add beans, tomatoes, celery, salt, pepper, chili powder, and red pepper flakes. Bring to boil, then reduce heat and simmer, covered, 30 minutes.

TRULY TEXAN CHILI

This chili is better the second day, so it's refrigerated overnight and served some 24 hours after being made.

SERVES 6

2 tablespoons vegetable oil
3 pounds ground beef
2-3 garlic cloves, minced
3 tablespoons chili powder
1 tablespoon ground cumin
1/4 cup all-purpose flour
1 tablespoon dried oregano
2 cans (14 1/2 ounces each) beef broth
1 teaspoon salt
1/4 teaspoon black pepper
1 can (15 ounces) pinto beans,
   drained and rinsed *(optional)*

Garnishes *(optional)*:
Shredded cheddar cheese
Tortilla chips
Sour cream
Lime wedges

1 Heat oil in a large soup pot or heavy saucepan over medium heat. Add beef and cook, stirring frequently, until browned. Drain off fat. Reduce heat, stir in garlic, and cook 1 minute.

2 In a small bowl, combine chili powder, cumin, flour, and oregano. Sprinkle over beef and stir until evenly coated. Add broth, salt, and pepper and bring to boil. Reduce heat and simmer, covered, 1 1/2 to 2 hours, stirring occasionally.

3 Let chili cool, then cover and refrigerate overnight. Remove coagulated fat and reheat in a heavy saucepan, double boiler, or slow cooker over low heat. If desired, add beans and cook until heated through. Garnish each serving with cheese, tortilla chips, sour cream, or lime wedges, if desired.

SIMPLE CHILI

This is as basic and mild as chili can be—a good choice for young children or finicky eaters.

SERVES 4

1 pound lean ground beef
1 can (15 1/2 ounces) red kidney
   beans, undrained
1 can (14 1/2 ounces) low-sodium
   stewed tomatoes, undrained, cut up
1 can (8 ounces) low-sodium
   tomato sauce
1 tablespoon chili powder
1 1/2 teaspoons onion powder
1/4 cup (1 ounce) shredded reduced-
   fat cheddar cheese

1 In a large saucepan over medium-high heat, cook ground beef until browned. Drain off fat.

2 Stir in beans, tomatoes, tomato sauce, chili powder, and onion powder. Bring to boil, then reduce heat and simmer, covered, 10 minutes, stirring occasionally.

3 Ladle into soup bowls and sprinkle with cheese.

PRONTO TACO CHILI

This is a savory, filling meal that you can put together quickly for unexpected dinner guests.

SERVES 8

1 pound ground beef

1 medium onion, chopped

2 garlic cloves, minced

2 cans (14 1/2 ounces each) beef broth

1 can (14 1/2 ounces) diced tomatoes, undrained

1 1/2 cups salsa

1 cup spiral or small shell pasta

1 medium green bell pepper, cored, seeded, and chopped

2 teaspoons chili powder

1 teaspoon parsley flakes

Shredded cheddar cheese

Tortilla chips

1 In a large saucepan over medium heat, cook beef, onion, and garlic until beef is browned. Drain off fat.

2 Add broth, tomatoes, salsa, pasta, bell pepper, chili powder, and parsley and bring to boil, stirring occasionally. Reduce heat and simmer, covered, until pasta is tender, about 10 minutes. Garnish with cheese and tortilla chips.

BAKED CHILI

The advantage of baking chili is that you can cook a batch of cornbread right on top.

SERVES 8

Chili:

1 pound ground beef

1 large onion, chopped

1 large green bell pepper, cored, seeded, and chopped

1 can (16 ounces) kidney beans, drained and rinsed

1 can (15 1/4 ounces) whole-kernel corn, drained

1 can (15 ounces) tomato sauce

1 can (14 1/2 ounces) diced tomatoes, undrained

1 can (4 ounces) chopped green chiles

2 teaspoons chili powder

1 teaspoon salt

1 teaspoon ground cumin

1/2 teaspoon sugar

1/2 teaspoon garlic powder

Cornbread:

1 cup all-purpose flour

1 cup cornmeal

2 teaspoons baking powder

1/8 teaspoon salt

1 egg

1/2 cup milk

1/2 cup sour cream

1 For chili, cook beef, onion, and bell pepper in a Dutch oven or soup pot over medium heat until beef is browned. Drain off fat.

2 Add beans, corn, tomato sauce, tomatoes, chiles, chili powder, salt, cumin, sugar, and garlic powder to pot. Bring to boil, stirring occasionally, then reduce heat, cover, and simmer 10 minutes.

3 For cornbread, combine flour, cornmeal, baking powder, and salt in a medium bowl. In a small bowl, beat egg, milk, and sour cream until smooth. Stir into flour mixture just until moistened.

4 Preheat oven to 400°F. Transfer chili to an ungreased 13 x 9 x 2-inch baking dish. Drop cornbread batter by heaping teaspoons on top and bake, uncovered, until golden, about 15 minutes.

CHUCKWAGON CHILI

Whether you're feeding hungry kids after a game or cowboys on the range, this is a quick chili that can be cooked indoors or out. Over an open fire, lower the heat by raising the rack that the saucepan sits on.

SERVES 4

12 ounces lean ground beef
1 medium yellow onion, chopped
1 can (16 ounces) pork and beans
    in tomato sauce
1 can (14 1/2 ounces) low-sodium
    tomatoes, undrained, cut up
1 1/2 cups canned low-sodium beef broth
1 tablespoon chili powder
1/4 teaspoon salt
1/4 teaspoon black pepper
1/2 cup wagon-wheel pasta
    or elbow macaroni
1/4 cup (1 ounce) shredded
    cheddar cheese

1 In a large saucepan over medium-high meat, cook beef and onion until beef is browned. Drain off fat.

2 Stir in pork and beans, tomatoes, broth, chili powder, salt, and pepper. Bring to boil, reduce heat, and stir in pasta. Cover and simmer, stirring frequently, 15 minutes or until pasta is tender. Serve with cheese.

DRY-BEAN CHILI WITH BEEF

Dry beans add more flavor and better texture than canned; this recipe uses the quick-soak method of preparing them.

SERVES 6

1 pound dry kidney beans
1 1/2 pounds ground beef
1 large onion, chopped
3 cans (16 ounces each) stewed tomatoes
1 can (29 ounces) tomato puree
2 cans (4 ounces each) green chiles
3 garlic cloves, minced
2 tablespoons parsley flakes
1 tablespoon red pepper flakes
1 tablespoon dried oregano
2 teaspoons ground cumin
Salt and black pepper

1 Rinse beans, place in a Dutch oven or soup pot, and cover with water. Bring to boil and cook 2 minutes, then remove from heat, let stand 1 hour and drain.

2 Add 9 cups water to beans in pot and bring to boil. Reduce heat and simmer, covered, 1 1/2 to 2 hours or until tender; drain (beans should measure 6 cups).

3 In a large skillet over medium heat, brown beef and sauté onion. Drain off fat.

4 Add beef mixture to beans in pot. Combine with tomatoes, tomato puree, chiles, garlic, parsley, red pepper flakes, oregano, cumin, and pepper. Bring to boil, then reduce heat and simmer, covered, 1 hour.

CALICO CHILI

This chili has rice and beans, as well as corn and zucchini, to complement the ground beef.

SERVES 8

1 pound ground beef

1 medium onion, chopped

2 garlic cloves, minced

1 celery stalk, chopped

1 green bell pepper, cored, seeded, and chopped

1 cup diced zucchini (*optional*)

1 tablespoon chili powder

1 tablespoon parsley flakes

1/4 teaspoon dried oregano

1/4 teaspoon dried thyme

1/4 teaspoon dried rosemary

Salt and black pepper

1 can (30 ounces) kidney beans, drained and rinsed

1 can (15-16 ounces) whole-kernel corn, drained

1 can (28 ounces) tomatoes, undrained, cut up

1 cup cooked rice

2 tablespoons vinegar

1 tablespoon Worcestershire sauce

1 In a large soup pot or Dutch oven over medium heat, cook beef until browned. Drain off fat. Add onion, garlic, celery, bell pepper, and zucchini, if desired, and sauté until onion is transparent, about 5 minutes.

2 Add chili powder, parsley, oregano, thyme, rosemary, and salt and black pepper to taste. Stir in 1 cup water, beans, corn, tomatoes, rice, vinegar, and Worcestershire sauce. Bring to boil, then reduce heat and simmer, stirring occasionally, until thickened and all ingredients are heated through, about 20 minutes.

PRONTO CHILI

Pronto Chili is both quick and delicious. Extra chili powder and cumin will make it spicier.

SERVES 4

1 pound ground beef

1 small onion, chopped

1 can (6 ounces) tomato paste

2 teaspoons chili powder

1 teaspoon salt

1/2 teaspoon cumin (*optional*)

1/4 teaspoon black pepper

2 tablespoons brown sugar

1 can (16 ounces) kidney beans, drained and rinsed

Shredded cheddar cheese (*optional*)

1 In a medium saucepan over medium heat, cook beef and onion until beef is browned. Drain off fat.

2 Stir in tomato paste, 2 tomato paste cans water, chili powder, salt, cumin, if desired, pepper, sugar, and beans. Bring to boil, then reduce heat and simmer, covered, 20 minutes. Top each serving with cheese, if desired.

MEATY MUSHROOM CHILI

For chili lovers who don't like beans, here's a recipe that uses mushrooms instead to delicious effect.

SERVES 8

1 pound bulk Italian sausage

1 pound ground beef

1 cup chopped onion

1 pound fresh mushrooms, sliced

1 can (46 ounces) vegetable juice

1 can (6 ounces) tomato paste

1 teaspoon sugar

1 teaspoon salt

1 teaspoon garlic powder
1 teaspoon dried oregano
1 teaspoon Worcestershire sauce
1/2 teaspoon dried basil
1/2 teaspoon black pepper
Sour cream *(optional)*

1 In a large saucepan over medium heat, cook sausage, beef, and onion until meat is browned. Drain off fat.

2 Stir in mushrooms, vegetable juice, tomato paste, sugar, salt, garlic powder, oregano, Worcestershire sauce, basil, and pepper. Bring to boil, then reduce heat and simmer, covered, 1 hour. Garnish with sour cream, if desired.

CHILI WITH CORN

Fresh meat, onion, and celery add some serious flavor to the canned ingredients that make up this chili.

SERVES 6

1 pound ground beef
1 medium onion, chopped
1/4 cup chopped celery
1 can (16 ounces) pork and
    beans, undrained
1 can (15 1/2 ounces) kidney beans,
    drained and rinsed
1 can (12 ounces) whole-kernel corn
1 can (10 3/4 ounces) condensed
    tomato soup
1 can (10 3/4 ounces) condensed
    vegetable soup
1/4 cup packed brown sugar *(optional)*
1 tablespoon vinegar
2 1/2 tablespoons chili powder

1 In a Dutch oven or soup pot over medium heat, cook beef, onion, and celery until beef is browned and vegetables are softened, about 5 minutes. Drain off fat.

2 Add 1/4 cup water, pork and beans, kidney beans, corn, tomato soup, vegetable soup, sugar, if desired, vinegar, and chili powder. Bring to boil, then reduce heat and simmer, covered, 4 minutes or until heated through.

CHILI WITH TORTILLA DUMPLINGS

Southwestern cooking is popular in Texas, and this chili is a special favorite.

SERVES 6

1 tablespoon vegetable oil
1 medium onion, chopped
2 garlic cloves, minced
2 pounds ground beef
2 cans (16 ounces each) kidney
    beans, drained and rinsed
1 can (28 ounces) diced
    tomatoes, undrained
1 can (14 1/2 ounces) chicken broth
2 tablespoons chili powder
1 teaspoon ground cumin
1 teaspoon dried oregano
1/2 teaspoon salt
4 flour tortillas (7 inches)

1 Heat oil in a 3-quart saucepan over medium heat. Add onion and garlic and sauté until softened, about 3 minutes. Add beef and cook until browned, about 6 minutes. Drain off fat.

2 Add beans, tomatoes, broth, chili powder, cumin, oregano, and salt. Bring to boil, then reduce heat and simmer, covered, 50 minutes.

3 Halve each tortilla, cut into 1/4-inch strips, and gently stir into soup. Cover and simmer until soft, about 8 minutes.

PEPPERONI PIZZA CHILI

This chili is a little like a pizza without the crust!

SERVES 8

1 pound ground beef
1 can (16 ounces) kidney beans,
    drained and rinsed
1 can (15 ounces) pizza sauce
1 can (14 1/2 ounces) Italian
    stewed tomatoes
1 can (8 ounces) tomato sauce
1 package (3 1/2 ounces) sliced pepperoni
1/2 cup chopped seeded green bell pepper
1 teaspoon pizza seasoning
    or Italian seasoning
1 teaspoon salt
Shredded mozzarella cheese *(optional)*

1 In a large saucepan over medium heat, cook beef until browned. Drain off fat.

2 Stir in 1 1/2 cups water, beans, pizza sauce, tomatoes, tomato sauce, pepperoni, bell pepper, pizza seasoning, and salt. Bring to boil, then reduce heat and simmer, uncovered, until chili reaches desired consistency, about 30 minutes. Garnish with cheese, if desired.

HEARTY ITALIAN CHILI

Here's a traditional chili with Italian touches—spaghetti sauce, mushrooms, and pepperoni.

SERVES 8

1 pound ground beef
8 ounces bulk Italian sausage
1 medium onion, chopped
1/2 cup chopped seeded green
    bell pepper
1 can or jar (about 28 ounces) spaghetti sauce
1 can (16 ounces) kidney beans,
    drained and rinsed

1 can (14 1/2 ounces) diced tomatoes, undrained
1 jar (4 1/2 ounces) sliced
    mushrooms, drained
1/3 cup halved sliced pepperoni
5 teaspoons chili powder
1/2 teaspoon salt
Pinch of black pepper

1 In a 3-quart saucepan over medium heat, cook beef, sausage, onion, and bell pepper until meat is browned and vegetables are softened. Drain off fat.

2 Add 1 cup water, spaghetti sauce, beans, tomatoes, mushrooms, pepperoni, chili powder, salt, and black pepper. Bring to boil, then reduce heat and simmer, uncovered, 30 minutes.

ALOHA CHILI

This chili comes from Hawaii, complete with meat, beans, and pineapple!

SERVES 8

2 pounds ground beef
1 large onion, finely chopped
1 can (16 ounces) kidney beans,
    drained and rinsed
1 can (16 ounces) pork and
    beans, undrained
1 can (20 ounces) pineapple
    chunks, undrained
1 cup ketchup
1/4 cup packed brown sugar
1/4 cup vinegar

1 In a large saucepan over medium heat, sauté beef and onion until meat is browned and onion is tender. Drain off fat.

2 Stir in kidney beans, pork and beans, pineapple, ketchup, sugar, and vinegar. Bring to boil, then reduce heat and simmer, covered, until heated through, about 20 minutes.

CABBAGE PATCH CHILI

Cabbage adds a slightly sweet note to conventional chili.

SERVES 4

8 ounces ground beef

1 1/2 cups chopped onion

1/2 cup sliced celery

1 can (16 ounces) kidney beans, drained and rinsed

1 can (14 1/2 ounces) stewed tomatoes

1 cup shredded cabbage

1 teaspoon chili powder

1/2 teaspoon salt

Hot mashed potatoes *(optional)*

1 In a medium saucepan over medium heat, cook beef, onion, and celery until beef is browned and vegetables are tender. Drain off fat.

2 Add 2 cups water, beans, tomatoes, cabbage, chili powder, and salt and bring to boil. Reduce heat and simmer, covered, until cabbage is tender, about 20 minutes. Top each serving with mashed potatoes, if desired.

ELK MEAT CHILI

Don't hurry this chili. The longer it simmers, the better it tastes.

SERVES 8

2 pounds ground elk or buffalo meat

1/2 cup chopped onion

3 garlic cloves, minced

2 cans (14 1/2 ounces each) diced tomatoes, undrained

1 can (28 ounces) pork and beans, undrained

3 tablespoons salsa

1 tablespoon brown sugar

1 tablespoon chili powder

1/2 teaspoon garlic salt

1/2 teaspoon black pepper

1 In a Dutch oven or soup pot over medium heat, cook elk, onion, and garlic until meat is browned and vegetables are tender. Drain off fat.

2 Stir in tomatoes, pork and beans, salsa, brown sugar, chili powder, garlic salt, and pepper. Bring to boil, reduce heat, and simmer, covered, 2 hours.

BUFFALO CHILI

In some parts of the United States, you can buy buffalo meat at the local supermarket. Elsewhere, you can try specialty meat markets. The meat is leaner than beef and, to many, tastier.

SERVES 8

2 pounds ground buffalo meat

1 tablespoon vegetable oil

1 large onion, chopped

2 green bell pepper, cored, seeded, and chopped

2 cloves garlic, minced

1-2 tablespoons chili powder

3 cans (10 ounces each) diced tomatoes with green chiles, undrained

1 can (10 ounces) tomato sauce

1 cup hot salsa

1 teaspoon salt

1 teaspoon black pepper

1 can (16 ounces) black beans, undrained

1 can (16 ounces) kidney beans, undrained

1 cup (4 ounces) grated cheddar cheese

1 In a large skillet over medium heat, cook buffalo until browned. Remove from heat and drain off fat.

2 Heat oil in a large soup pot or Dutch oven over medium heat. Add onion and sauté 5 minutes or until softened. Add bell pepper, garlic, and chili powder and sauté 3 minutes. Add buffalo, tomatoes, tomato sauce, salsa, salt, and black pepper and bring to boil. Reduce heat and simmer, covered, 30 minutes.

3 Add black beans and kidney beans and simmer 10 minutes or until heated through. Sprinkle each serving with cheese.

GREEN PORK CHILI

Although 1 1/2 cups may seem like a lot, cilantro lends distinctive Southwestern flavor and color to chili. Stirring in half of this pungent herb just before serving gives it a final, fresh burst of flavor. (Photograph on page 8)

SERVES 4

2 tablespoons olive oil

1 pound pork tenderloin, cut into
    1-inch chunks

2 tablespoons all-purpose flour

6 scallions, thinly sliced

3 cloves garlic, minced

1 large green bell pepper, cored,
    seeded, and cut into 1/2-inch chunks

1 pickled jalapeño pepper, finely chopped
    (wear gloves when handling; they burn)

1 can (4 1/2 ounces) chopped
    mild green chiles

1 1/2 cups packed cilantro
    sprigs, chopped

3/4 teaspoon salt

1/2 teaspoon ground coriander

1 1/2 cups thawed frozen peas

2 tablespoons fresh lime juice

1 red bell pepper, cored,
    seeded, and slivered

1 Preheat oven to 350°F. Heat oil in a nonstick Dutch oven or flameproof baking dish over medium heat. Place flour in a shallow dish and dredge pork, shaking off excess. Add pork to Dutch oven and sauté 4 minutes or until golden. Using a slotted spoon, transfer to a plate.

2 Add scallions and garlic to Dutch oven and sauté 1 minute or until scallions are tender. Add green bell pepper and jalapeño and sauté 4 minutes or until bell pepper is crisp-tender. Stir in 1 1/4 cups water, green chiles, half of cilantro, salt, and coriander and bring to boil.

3 Return pork to Dutch oven, cover, and bake 25 minutes or until tender. Stir in peas, lime juice, and remaining cilantro. Cover and let stand 3 minutes. Garnish with red bell pepper.

SOUTHWESTERN CHILI

This is a surprising chili from Arizona that has no tomatoes and uses hominy instead of beans.

SERVES 8

1 pork shoulder roast (2-3 pounds)

1 tablespoon vegetable oil

1/2 cup chopped onion

1 garlic clove, minced

4 cups chicken stock

2 cans (4 ounces each) chopped
    green chiles

2 tablespoons chili powder

1/2 teaspoon dried oregano

1/2 teaspoon salt

1/2 teaspoon black pepper

2 cans (15 1/2 ounces each)
    hominy, drained

Warm flour tortillas *(optional)*

1 Trim pork and cut into 1/2-inch cubes. Heat oil in a 3-quart saucepan over medium heat. Add pork and sauté until browned. Drain off fat. Add onion and garlic and sauté until softened, about 2 minutes.

2 Add stock, chiles, chili powder, oregano, salt, and pepper and bring to boil Reduce heat and simmer, covered, 1 hour. Add hominy and simmer until pork is tender, about 30 minutes. Serve with tortillas, if desired.

MEXICAN PORK STEW

The secret ingredient in this stew is a touch of chocolate, which blends with other spices to create a dark, rich flavor.

SERVES 6

1 1/2 pounds boneless pork shoulder

1 dried hot or mild chile pepper, such as ancho or pasilla

1 1/2 tablespoons olive or canola oil

2 green bell peppers, diced

2 large onions, coarsely chopped

2 garlic cloves, minced

1/2 teaspoon ground cumin

1 tablespoon all-purpose flour

1 can (28 ounces) crushed tomatoes

2 cups chicken or beef stock

1 tablespoon unsweetened cocoa

1 can (16 ounces) red kidney beans, drained and rinsed

1/8 teaspoon salt

1/8 teaspoon black pepper

1 Using a sharp knife, trim all fat and cartilage from pork. Cut meat into 1-inch strips, then cut strips across into 1-inch cubes.

2 Place chile pepper in a small bowl and cover with boiling water. Allow to soak 20 minutes or until very soft. Drain chile pepper and, wearing rubber gloves, remove core and seeds and finely chop.

3 In a Dutch oven over medium-high heat, heat 1 tablespoon oil. Sauté green peppers, onions, and garlic 10 minutes or until golden. Stir in cumin and cook 1 to 2 minutes longer or until fragrant. Using a slotted spoon, transfer vegetables to a plate. Heat remaining oil over medium high heat. Sauté pork 5 to 7 minutes or until well browned on all sides. Sprinkle with flour and cook, stirring 2 minutes.

4 Return vegetables to Dutch oven with chile pepper, tomatoes, and stock. Bring to boil, reduce heat, and simmer, covered, 2 hours or until pork is tender when pierced with a fork. In a small bowl combine cocoa with 1/2 cup cooking liquid and whisk to blend well. Stir mixture into Dutch oven, add beans, and season with salt and pepper. Simmer 5 minutes to heat through.

PORK AND BEAN CHILI

This Tex-Mex treat is mild, but you can heat it up with more chili powder (or hotter chiles) if you wish.

SERVES 4

1 tablespoon vegetable oil

8 ounces pork tenderloin, trimmed and cut into 1/2-inch chunks

2 tablespoons all-purpose flour

1 large onion, chopped

3 garlic cloves, minced

1 green bell pepper, cored, seeded, and cut into 1/2-inch squares

1 can (14 1/2 ounces) low-sodium tomatoes, undrained, chopped

1 can (4 ounces) chopped mild green chiles

1 1/2 teaspoons mild chili powder

1/2 teaspoon dried oregano

1/2 teaspoon salt

3 cups cooked black beans

1 tablespoon lime juice

1 Heat oil in a large nonstick skillet over medium-high heat. Dust pork with flour, shaking off excess. Add to skillet and sauté 2 minutes or until lightly browned. Using a slotted spoon, transfer to a plate.

2 Add onion and garlic to skillet and sauté 5 minutes or until softened. Add bell pepper and sauté 4 minutes or until softened.

3 Add 1/4 cup water, tomatoes, chiles, chili powder, oregano, and salt. Bring to boil, reduce heat, and simmer. Return pork to skillet, add beans, and cook, covered, 7 minutes or until pork is tender. Stir in lime juice.

pork and cook until browned, about 4 minutes. Using a slotted spoon, transfer to a plate.

2 Reduce heat to medium. Add scallions and garlic and sauté until scallions are tender, about 2 minutes. Stir in bell peppers and jalapeños and cook until bell peppers are tender, about 4 minutes.

3 Return pork to Dutch oven. Add cumin, coriander, and salt and stir to coat. Add 1 cup water and bring to boil, then reduce heat and simmer, covered, 20 minutes.

4 Stir in chickpeas and cook, covered, until heated through, about 5 minutes. Stir in cilantro just before serving.

NEW MEXICAN GREEN CHILI

A change of pace from red chili, this Southwestern specialty uses lean pork, chickpeas, green bell peppers, jalapeños, and a good fistful of fresh cilantro.

SERVES 4

1 tablespoon olive oil

1 pound pork tenderloin, trimmed and cut into 1-inch chunks

5 scallions, thinly sliced

4 garlic cloves, minced

2 large green bell peppers, cored, seeded, and cut into 1/2-inch squares

2 pickled jalapeño peppers, seeded and minced (wear gloves when handling; they burn)

2 teaspoons ground cumin

2 teaspoons ground coriander

1/2 teaspoon salt

1 can (15 ounces) chickpeas, drained and rinsed

1/2 cup chopped fresh cilantro

1 Heat oil in a nonstick Dutch oven or flame-proof baking dish over medium-high heat. Add

CHILI VERDE

This chili is named for the green chiles used in making it, but it also lacks the familiar red of tomatoes.

SERVES 6

4 tablespoons vegetable oil

4 pounds boneless pork, cut into 3/4-inch cubes

1/4 cup all-purpose flour

1 can (4 ounces) chopped green chiles

1/2 teaspoon ground cumin

1/4 teaspoon salt

1/4 teaspoon black pepper

3 garlic cloves, minced

1/2 cup chopped fresh cilantro or parsley

1/2-1 cup salsa

1 can (14 1/2 ounces) chicken broth

Flour tortillas

1 Heat 1 tablespoon oil in a Dutch oven over medium-high heat. Add 1 pound pork and cook, stirring, until lightly browned, then transfer to a plate. Repeat with remaining pork, adding more oil as needed.

2 Return all pork to Dutch oven, sprinkle with flour, and mix well. Add chiles, cumin, salt, pepper, garlic, cilantro, salsa, and broth. Bring to boil, then reduce heat, cover, and simmer 1 1/2 hours or until pork is tender and chili reaches desired consistency. Serve with warm tortillas.

BLACK BEAN AND SAUSAGE CHILI

Spicy sausage and earthy black beans make this chili particularly rich and satisfying.

SERVES 5

1 pound bulk Italian sausage

3 garlic cloves, minced

1/2 cup chopped seeded green
    bell pepper

1/2 cup chopped onion

1 can (15 ounces) black beans,
    drained and rinsed

1 can (14 1/2 ounces) diced
    tomatoes, undrained

1 can (11 ounces) whole-kernel
    corn, drained

1 can (8 ounces) tomato sauce

1 can (6 ounces) tomato paste

1 tablespoon chili powder

1 teaspoon dried oregano

3/4 teaspoon salt

1/2 teaspoon dried basil

1/4 teaspoon black pepper

Shredded cheddar cheese *(optional)*

1 In a 3-quart saucepan over medium heat, cook sausage until no longer pink. Drain off fat. Add garlic, bell pepper, and onion and sauté until tender.

2 Add 1/2 cup water, beans, tomatoes, corn, tomato sauce, tomato paste, chili powder, oregano, salt, basil, and black pepper. Bring to boil, then reduce heat and simmer, covered, 30 minutes. Garnish with cheese, if desired.

SPICY CHICKEN CHILI

The inspiration for this recipe is pozole, a classic Mexican soup made with pork.

SERVES 4

1 can (4 ounces) green chiles,
    undrained, or 3 dried ancho chiles

4 cloves garlic, 1 sliced and 3 minced

2 pounds skinless, boneless chicken breasts

6 cups chicken stock

1 large yellow onion, finely chopped

2 teaspoons ground cumin

1 bay leaf

1/2 teaspoon dried thyme, crumbled

1/4 teaspoon salt

1 can (16 ounces) hominy, undrained, or
    1 can (16 ounces) shoepeg corn, undrained

1/4 cup minced fresh cilantro or
    flat-leaf parsley

Garnishes *(optional)*:

2 cups crumbled tortilla chips

1 avocado, halved, pitted, peeled,
    and diced

2 scallions with tops, thinly sliced

1 In a food processor or blender, puree chiles and sliced garlic. (If using dried chiles, place in a small saucepan, add 1 cup boiling water, and soak 15 minutes. Drain soaking liquid into processor, then, wearing gloves, halve chiles and remove seeds, stems, veins, and skins. Add to processor with sliced garlic and puree.)

2 In a 4-quart Dutch oven over medium-high heat, combine chicken, stock, onion, cumin, bay leaf, thyme, minced garlic, and salt. Bring to boil, then reduce heat and simmer, covered, 15 minutes. Transfer chicken to a plate. When cool enough to handle, cut into bite-size pieces.

3 Add hominy and chili mixture to Dutch oven over medium heat and bring to boil. Reduce heat and simmer, uncovered, 15 minutes. Add chicken and simmer, uncovered, 4 minutes or until heated through. Remove bay leaf and stir in cilantro.

4 Ladle into bowls and top each serving with tortilla chips, avocado, and scallions, if desired.

CREAMY WHITE CHILI

This is a change-of-pace chicken and white bean chili that's held together with two kinds of cream.

SERVES 7

1 tablespoon vegetable oil

1 pound skinless, boneless chicken
   breasts, cut into 1/2-inch cubes

1 medium onion, chopped

1 1/2 teaspoons garlic powder

2 cans (15 1/2 ounces each) great
   Northern beans, drained and rinsed

1 can (14 1/2 ounces) chicken broth

2 cans (4 ounces each) chopped
   green chiles

1 teaspoon salt

1 teaspoon ground cumin

1 teaspoon dried oregano

1/2 teaspoon black pepper

1/4 teaspoon cayenne pepper

1 cup sour cream

1/2 cup heavy whipping cream

1 Heat oil in a large saucepan over medium heat. Add chicken, onion, and garlic powder and sauté 3 minutes or until chicken is no longer pink.

2 Add beans, broth, chiles, salt, cumin, oregano, black pepper, and cayenne. Bring to boil, then reduce heat and simmer, uncovered, 30 minutes. Remove from heat and stir in sour cream and whipping cream.

SPICY WHITE CHILI

Substituting chicken for beef, great Northern beans for pinto beans, and Monterey Jack for cheddar cheese are the keys to keeping this chili light in color.

SERVES 6

1 tablespoon vegetable oil

2 medium onions, chopped

4 garlic cloves, minced

2 cans (4 ounces each) chopped green chiles

2 teaspoons ground cumin

1 teaspoon dried oregano

1/4 teaspoon cayenne pepper

1/4 teaspoon ground cloves

2 cans (14 1/2 ounces each) chicken broth

4 cups cubed cooked chicken

3 cans (15 1/2 ounces each) great
   Northern beans, drained and rinsed

2 cups (8 ounces) shredded
   Monterey Jack cheese

Sour cream *(optional)*

Sliced jalapeños *(optional)*

1 Heat oil in a 3-quart saucepan over medium heat. Add onions and sauté until tender, about 5 minutes. Stir in garlic, chiles, cumin, oregano, cayenne, and cloves and sauté until chiles are tender, about 2 minutes.

2 Add broth, chicken, and beans. Bring to boil, reduce heat, and simmer, uncovered, 15 minutes. Remove from heat and stir in cheese until melted. Garnish with sour cream and jalapeños, if desired.

TURKEY CHILI WITH SPAGHETTI

This chili is an ideal cook-ahead dish, as the flavor of the sauce improves when made a day in advance and reheated.

SERVES 4

Topping:
5 1/2 ounces plain low-fat yogurt

1 scallion, finely chopped

4 tablespoons mixed fresh herbs,
    such as parsley, cilantro, and chives,
    finely chopped

Chili:
1 tablespoon sunflower oil

1 large garlic clove, crushed

1 onion, finely chopped

2 red or green bell peppers, cored,
    seeded, and finely chopped

1 1/2 teaspoons cayenne pepper

2 teaspoons ground cumin

1 teaspoon dried oregano

1 pound ground turkey

2 cans (14 1/2 ounces each) chopped
    tomatoes, undrained

1 can (14 1/2 ounces) red kidney beans,
    drained and rinsed

8 ounces spaghetti

Salt and black pepper

1 For topping, combine yogurt, scallion, and herbs, then cover and refrigerate.

2 For chili, heat oil in a large skillet or heavy saucepan over medium heat. Add garlic and sauté 30 seconds. Add onion and bell peppers and sauté 5 minutes or until softened.

3 Stir in cayenne, cumin, and oregano and sauté 2 minutes. Add turkey and sauté until browned and crumbly.

4 Stir in tomatoes and beans. Bring to boil, then reduce heat and simmer 15 minutes.

5 Meanwhile, cook spaghetti according to package directions until al dente; drain. Divide among 4 plates and spoon on equal amounts of chili. Top with herb-flavored yogurt.

ZESTY TURKEY CHILI

In stews, turkey often has less fat than beef and more flavor than chicken. This tasty, healthy chili also has cloves and hot spices.

SERVES 8

1 teaspoon vegetable oil

1 large onion, chopped

3 garlic cloves, minced

1 can (4 ounces) green chiles, undrained

2 teaspoons ground cumin

1 1/2 teaspoons dried oregano

1/4 teaspoon ground cloves

1/8 teaspoon hot red pepper sauce

1/8 teaspoon cayenne pepper

2 cans (15 1/2 ounces each) great
    Northern beans, drained and rinsed

3 cups chicken stock

3 cups cubed cooked turkey breast

1 Heat oil in a 3-quart saucepan over medium heat. Add onion and garlic and sauté until tender, about 5 minutes. Add chiles, cumin, oregano, cloves, red pepper sauce, and cayenne and sauté 3 minutes. Stir in beans, stock, and turkey and bring to boil. Reduce heat, cover, and simmer 15 minutes.

TURKEY AND BLACK BEAN CHILI

Chili made with skinless turkey breast and lots of veggies has clear health advantages over standard beef-only chili. (Photograph on page 4)

SERVES 4

1 tablespoon plus 1 teaspoon olive oil

1 pound skinless, boneless turkey breast,
     cut into 1/2-inch chunks

1 large onion, cut into 1/2-inch chunks

3 garlic cloves, minced

1 green bell pepper, cored, seeded,
     and cut into 1/2-inch-wide strips

1 pound sweet potatoes, peeled
     and cut into 1/2-inch chunks

1 tablespoon chili powder

1 teaspoon ground coriander

1/2 teaspoon dried oregano

1/2 teaspoon salt

1 can (15 ounces) crushed tomatoes

1 can (15 ounces) black beans,
     drained and rinsed

1 Heat 1 tablespoon oil in a Dutch oven or soup pot over medium-high heat. Add turkey and cook until lightly browned, about 4 minutes. Transfer to a plate.

2 Add remaining oil, onion, and garlic and sauté 5 minutes or until onion is golden. Add bell pepper and sauté 4 minutes until crisp-tender.

3 Add sweet potatoes, chili powder, coriander, oregano, and salt and stir to coat. Add 1 1/2 cups water and bring to boil, then reduce heat and simmer, covered, 5 minutes. Add tomatoes and beans and simmer, covered, 5 minutes or until sweet potatoes are tender.

4 Return turkey to Dutch oven and cook, covered, 3 minutes or until cooked through.

TURKEY CHILI

Turkey cuts down on the fat in this delicious chili. Serve with warm cornbread or tortillas.

SERVES 4

1 tablespoon vegetable oil

1 onion, finely chopped

3 garlic cloves, minced

1 green bell pepper, cored, seeded,
     and cut into 1/2-inch squares

1 red bell pepper, cored, seeded,
     and cut into 1/2-inch squares

2 teaspoons chili powder

3/4 teaspoon dried oregano

3/4 teaspoon ground cumin

3/4 teaspoon ground coriander

1 pound lean ground turkey breast

1 can (14 1/2 ounces) low-sodium stewed
     tomatoes, undrained, chopped

1 can (8 ounces) low-sodium tomato sauce

2 tablespoons low-sodium tomato paste

1/2 teaspoon salt

1/4 teaspoon black pepper

1 can (15 ounces) red kidney beans,
     drained and rinsed

1 Heat oil in a Dutch oven or flameproof baking dish over medium heat. Add onion and garlic and sauté 5 minutes or until onion is softened. Add bell peppers and sauté 5 minutes or until softened.

2 Stir in chili powder, oregano, cumin, and coriander and cook 1 minute. Add turkey and sauté 3 minutes or until no longer pink. Add tomatoes, tomato sauce, tomato paste, salt, and black pepper and bring to simmer. Add beans and cook 3 minutes or until heated through.

TURKEY CHILI WITH SALSA

(Photograph on page 32)

SERVES 6

Chili:

2 teaspoons extra-virgin olive oil

1 pound ground turkey

1 onion, chopped

2 celery stalks, sliced

1 red or yellow bell pepper, cored, seeded, and chopped

3 garlic cloves, minced

1 can (14 1/2 ounces) diced tomatoes, undrained

3 1/2 cups turkey or chicken stock

1/4 teaspoon ground coriander

1/4 teaspoon ground cumin

1/4 teaspoon dried oregano

1/2 teaspoon chili powder

8 ounces zucchini, diced

1 1/2 cups fresh or thawed frozen whole-kernel corn

1 can (14 1/2 ounces) kidney beans, drained and rinsed

Salt and black pepper

12 flour tortillas

Salsa:

2 tablespoons fresh lime juice

2 avocados, halved, pitted, peeled, and diced

1 cup cherry tomatoes, quartered

6 scallions, finely sliced

1 cup arugula, chopped

Salt and black pepper

1 For chili, heat oil in a large saucepan over high heat. Add turkey and sauté 4 minutes or until lightly browned. Reduce heat to medium and add onion, celery, bell pepper, and garlic. Sauté 2 minutes or until onion begins to soften. Stir in tomatoes, stock, coriander, cumin, oregano, and chili powder and bring to boil. Reduce heat and simmer, covered, 20 minutes.

2 Preheat oven to 325°F. Add zucchini, corn, and beans to pan and return to boil. Reduce heat and simmer, covered, 10 minutes or until zucchini is just tender. Wrap tortillas tightly in foil and heat in oven 10 minutes or until warm and softened.

3 For salsa, place lime juice in a medium bowl, add avocado, and toss. Mix in tomatoes, scallions, and arugula without mashing avocado. Season to taste with salt and pepper.

4 Season chili to taste with salt and pepper. Ladle into warm bowls and pass salsa and tortillas.

This low-fat chili comes with its own avocado salsa. It can either be spooned on top of the chili or wrapped in warm tortillas and served as an accompaniment.

GARDEN HARVEST CHILI

Quick, healthy, and full of good flavors, this has to be a favorite chili recipe.

SERVES 6

2 tablespoons vegetable oil

2 garlic cloves, minced

1 medium green bell pepper, cored, seeded, and chopped

1 medium red bell pepper, cored, seeded, and chopped

1 1/2 cups sliced fresh mushrooms

1/2 cup chopped onion

1 can (28 ounces) whole tomatoes, undrained, cut up

1 can (15 ounces) tomato sauce

2 tablespoons chili powder

2 teaspoons sugar

1 teaspoon ground cumin

1 can (16 ounces) kidney beans, drained and rinsed

2 cups sliced zucchini

1 package (10 ounces) frozen corn, thawed

1 1/2 cups (6 ounces) shredded cheddar cheese *(optional)*

1 Heat oil in a medium skillet over medium-high heat. Add garlic, bell peppers, mushrooms, and onion and sauté until tender, about 5 minutes. Add tomatoes, tomato sauce, chili powder, sugar, and cumin and bring to boil.

2 Add beans, zucchini, and corn, reduce heat to low, and simmer, uncovered, 10 minutes or until zucchini is tender.

3 Spoon into bowls and sprinkle with cheese, if desired.

BEAN AND BULGUR CHILI

Because bulgur has a distinctly meaty texture, it makes a good substitute for ground beef in vegetarian dishes.

SERVES 4

1 tablespoon olive oil

1 large onion, finely chopped

3 garlic cloves, minced

1 red bell pepper, cored, seeded, and diced

1 pickled jalapeño pepper, seeded, deveined, and finely chopped (wear gloves when handling; they burn)

1 cup coarse bulgur

1 can (14 1/2 ounces) low-sodium stewed tomatoes, undrained, chopped

1 teaspoon mild chili powder

1 teaspoon ground coriander

3/4 teaspoon salt

1 can (15 1/2 ounces) pinto beans, drained and rinsed

1 Heat oil in a Dutch oven over medium heat. Add onion and garlic and sauté 7 minutes or until onion is tender. Add bell pepper and jalapeño and cook 5 minutes or until bell pepper is tender.

2 Stir in 2 cups water, bulgur, tomatoes, chili powder, coriander, and salt. Bring to boil, then reduce heat and simmer, covered, 15 minutes or until water has almost evaporated.

3 Stir in beans and cook, uncovered, 10 minutes or until heated through.

MEATLESS CHILI POTS
CON QUESO

Chunks of vegetables, a bounty of beans, and low-fat cheddar make this chili healthier but just as hearty as others you may have tried. (Photograph on page 16)

SERVES 4

1 large green bell pepper, cored, seeded, and finely chopped

1 large onion, finely chopped

2 large garlic cloves, minced

2 cans (15 ounces each) red kidney beans, drained and rinsed

1 can (28 ounces) low-sodium crushed tomatoes in puree

1/2 teaspoon chili powder

1/2 teaspoon black pepper

1/2 teaspoon ground cumin

1/4 teaspoon ground cinnamon

3/4 cup (3 ounces) shredded low-sodium low-fat cheddar cheese

1 Lightly coat a large nonstick skillet with cooking spray and set over medium-high heat. Add bell pepper, onion, and garlic and sauté until onion is browned, about 5 minutes. Stir in beans, tomatoes, chili powder, black pepper, cumin, and cinnamon. Reduce heat and simmer 5 minutes.

2 Preheat broiler. Line a broiler pan with foil. Divide chili among four 2-cup ovenproof bowls and place on broiler pan. Mound 2 tablespoons cheese in center of each serving.

3 Broil 6 inches from heat until cheese melts, about 1 minute (watch closely!).

CHIPOTLE PEPPER CHILI

If you can't find chipotle peppers in adobo sauce (they're sold in cans in the international section of many supermarkets), substitute 1 teaspoon hot chili powder in this recipe.

SERVES 4

1 cup dry red kidney beans, sorted and rinsed

1 tablespoon olive oil

1 large onion, finely chopped

3 cloves garlic, minced

1 large red bell pepper, cored, seeded, and cut into 1/2-inch chunks

1 large green bell pepper, cored, seeded, and cut into 1/2-inch chunks

2 cups 1-inch chunks butternut squash

2 tablespoons unsweetened cocoa powder

1 tablespoon light brown sugar

1 teaspoon dried marjoram

1/2 teaspoon salt

1 1/2 cups canned crushed tomatoes

1 chipotle pepper in adobo, minced (about 2 teaspoons)

1 In a large saucepan, cover beans with 3 inches water and bring to boil. Reduce heat and simmer, covered, 2 1/4 hours or until tender. Drain, reserving 1 cup liquid.

2 Heat oil in a Dutch oven or flameproof baking dish over medium heat. Add onion and garlic and sauté 7 minutes or until tender. Stir in bell peppers and squash and sauté 4 minutes or until peppers are crisp-tender. Add cocoa, brown sugar, marjoram, and salt and stir to coat.

3 Stir in beans, reserved cooking liquid, tomatoes, and chipotle pepper. Bring to boil, then reduce heat and simmer, covered, 30 minutes.

HARVEST CHILI

As its name implies, this chili is designed to use up—in a tasty way—the produce from your garden or farmers' market.

SERVES 7

2 tablespoons vegetable oil

1 medium red bell pepper, cored, seeded, and chopped

1 medium onion, chopped

4 garlic cloves, minced

1 tablespoon chili powder

1 teaspoon ground cumin

1 teaspoon dried oregano

2 cups cubed peeled butternut squash

1 can (28 ounces) diced tomatoes, undrained

2 cups diced zucchini

1 can (15 ounces) black beans, drained and rinsed

1 can (8 3/4 ounces) whole-kernel corn, drained

1/4 cup minced fresh parsley

1 Heat oil in a Dutch oven or soup pot over medium heat. Add bell pepper, onion, and garlic and sauté until tender, about 5 minutes.

2 Stir in chili powder, cumin, oregano, squash, and tomatoes. Bring to boil, then reduce heat and simmer, uncovered, until squash is almost tender, about 10 minutes. Stir in zucchini, beans, corn, and parsley and simmer, covered, 10 minutes.

SWEET POTATO-CORN CHILI

The rainbow assortment of vegetables in this recipe provides a full spectrum of good nutrients.

SERVES 4

1 tablespoon olive oil

6 scallions, thinly sliced

2 garlic cloves, minced

1 red bell pepper, cored, seeded, and cut into 1/2-inch squares

1 1/2 cups chicken stock

12 ounces sweet potatoes, peeled and cut into 1/2-inch cubes

1 1/2 cups chopped plum tomatoes

1 can (4 1/2 ounces) chopped mild green chiles, drained

2 fresh jalapeño peppers, seeded, deveined, and finely chopped (wear gloves when handling; they burn)

1/2 teaspoon dried oregano

1 cup frozen whole-kernel corn

1 tablespoon fresh lime juice

1 Heat oil in a large saucepan over medium heat. Add scallions and garlic and sauté 2 minutes or until tender. Add bell pepper and sauté 4 minutes or until crisp-tender.

2 Stir in 1 1/2 cups water, stock, sweet potatoes, tomatoes, chiles, jalapeños, and oregano. Bring to boil, then reduce heat and simmer, covered, 20 minutes or until sweet potatoes are tender. Stir in corn and lime juice and cook, uncovered, 3 minutes or until corn is heated through.

As good as chili can be as a family meal, it is the American favorite for feeding a crowd. These recipes are for 10 or more hungry guests.

ZESTY COLORADO CHILI

In this mountain state, chili is a winter staple for warming up skiers and others who love the outdoors.

SERVES 12

1 pound Italian sausage links

1 pound pork shoulder

2 pounds ground beef

2 medium onions, chopped

1 large green bell pepper, cored, seeded, and chopped

1 tablespoon minced garlic

1 can (29 ounces) tomato puree

1 can (28 ounces) diced tomatoes, undrained

1 cup beef stock

1 jalapeño pepper, seeded, deveined, and minced (wear gloves when handling; they burn)

2 tablespoons brown sugar

1 tablespoon vinegar

2 teaspoons chili powder

2 teaspoons ground cumin

1 1/2 teaspoons crushed red pepper flakes

1 teaspoon dried basil

1 teaspoon dried oregano

1/2 teaspoon hot red pepper sauce

2 cans (16 ounces each) kidney beans, drained and rinsed

1 Cut sausage into 1/2-inch pieces. Trim fat from pork and cut meat into 1/2-inch pieces. In a Dutch oven or soup pot over medium heat, cook sausage, pork, and beef until browned. Transfer meat to a plate. Drain pot, discarding all but 1 tablespoon drippings.

2 Add onions, bell pepper, and garlic to pot and sauté in drippings until tender, about 5 minutes. Add tomato puree, tomatoes, stock, jalapeño, brown sugar, vinegar, chili powder, cumin, red pepper flakes, basil, oregano, and red pepper sauce. Return meat to pan and bring to boil, then reduce heat and simmer, covered, 1 hour. Add beans and cook until heated through.

MEATY VEGETABLE CHILI

This chili gives you the best of both worlds—plenty of good, chunky beef and lots of fresh-picked vegetables.

SERVES 12

1-2 tablespoons vegetable oil

1 pound beef stew meat, cut into 1/2-inch cubes

8 ounces skinless, boneless chicken, cut into 1/2-inch cubes

3 medium carrots, cubed

2 zucchini, cubed

2 tomatoes, cored, seeded, and cubed

1 medium onion, chopped

1 medium turnip, cubed

1 green or red bell pepper, cored, seeded, and chopped

2 cans (30 ounces each) dark red kidney beans, drained and rinsed

1 bottle (12 ounces) chili sauce

1 Heat oil in a large Dutch oven over medium-high heat. Add beef and chicken and cook until browned on all sides. Drain off fat.

2 Add 3 1/2 cups water, carrots, zucchini, tomatoes, onion, turnip, and bell pepper. Bring to boil, then reduce heat and simmer, covered, 1 hour or until beef is tender.

3 Add kidney beans and chili sauce and simmer 15 minutes.

CHUNKY BEEF CHILI

Your family's bound to love this extra-beefy chili.

SERVES 10

1/2 cup all-purpose flour

1 1/2 teaspoons dried thyme

1 1/2 teaspoons dried rosemary, crushed

1 1/2 pounds beef stew meat, cut into 1-inch cubes

8 ounces ground beef

1 can (14 1/2 ounces) beef broth

1 large onion, finely chopped

1/2 cup chopped seeded green bell pepper

1 garlic clove, minced

1 can (4 ounces) chopped green chiles

1-2 jalapeño peppers, seeded, deveined, and minced (wear gloves when handling; they burn)

1 can (16 ounces) crushed tomatoes

2 cans (15 1/2 ounces each) chili beans, undrained

1 can (15 1/2 ounces) pinto beans, drained and rinsed

1 can (15 ounces) white or red kidney beans, drained and rinsed

1 can (6 ounces) tomato paste

2 tablespoons ground cumin

1 teaspoon dried oregano

1/2 teaspoon black pepper

1/2 teaspoon white pepper

1/2 teaspoon cayenne pepper

3-4 drops hot red pepper sauce

Shredded cheddar cheese (*optional*)

1 In a resealable plastic bag, combine flour, thyme, and rosemary, then add beef cubes and shake to coat.

2 In a Dutch oven or soup pot over medium heat, cook ground beef and beef cubes until browned. Drain off fat.

3 Add broth, onion, bell pepper, garlic, chiles, jalapeños, tomatoes, chili beans, pinto beans, kidney beans, tomato paste, cumin, oregano, black pepper, white pepper, cayenne, and red pepper sauce. Bring to boil, then reduce heat and simmer 5 hours. Garnish each serving with cheese, if desired.

WEST COAST CHILI

The secret ingredients in this rich chili, designed for a crowd, are honey and cocoa.

SERVES 14

1 pound bacon, diced

2 pounds beef stew meat, cut into 1/4-inch cubes

2 medium onions, chopped

4 cloves garlic, minced

1 cup bottled barbecue sauce

1 cup chili sauce

1/2 cup honey

3 cans (16 ounces each) whole tomatoes, chopped

4 beef bouillon cubes

1 bay leaf

1 tablespoon chili powder

1 tablespoon unsweetened cocoa powder

1 tablespoon Worcestershire sauce

1 tablespoon Dijon mustard

1 1/2 teaspoons ground cumin

1/4 teaspoon cayenne pepper (*optional*)

3 cans (16 ounces each) kidney beans, drained and rinsed

1 cup (4 ounces) shredded cheddar cheese

1 In a large Dutch oven or soup pot over medium heat, cook bacon until crisp. Transfer to paper towels to drain. Discard all but 3 tablespoons drippings. Add beef to pot and cook in drippings until browned. Add onion and garlic and sauté until onions are softened.

2 Return bacon to pot. Add barbecue sauce, chili sauce, honey, tomatoes, bouillon, bay leaf, chili powder, cocoa, Worcestershire sauce, mustard, cumin, and cayenne, if desired. Bring to boil, then reduce heat and simmer, covered, until beef is tender, about 3 hours.

3 Add beans and cook until heated through. Top each serving with cheese.

PEORIA CHILI

This is a simple, long-cooking chili that is hearty and satisfying.

SERVES 10

2 pounds ground beef

1 medium onion, chopped

1 can (28 ounces) whole tomatoes, undrained, chopped

1 can (46 ounces) tomato juice

1 1/2 tablespoons chili powder

1 tablespoon sugar

Salt and black pepper to taste

2 cans (15 ounces each) red kidney beans, drained and rinsed

Shredded cheddar cheese *(optional)*

1 In a large soup pot or Dutch oven over medium heat, cook beef and onion until browned. Drain off fat.

2 Add tomatoes, tomato juice, chili powder, sugar, salt, and pepper. Bring to boil, then reduce heat and simmer, covered, 2 to 3 hours.

3 Stir in beans and heat through. Garnish each serving with cheese, if desired.

TEXICAN CHILI

This flavorful, meaty chili takes care of itself in the slow cooker while you take care of other things.

SERVES 16

8 bacon slices, diced

2 1/2 pounds beef stew meat, cut into 1/2-inch cubes

2 cans (one 28 ounces, one 14 1/2 ounces) stewed tomatoes

2 cans (8 ounces each) tomato sauce

1 can (16 ounces) kidney beans, drained and rinsed

2 cups sliced carrots

1 medium onion, chopped

1 cup chopped celery

1/2 cup chopped seeded green bell pepper

1/4 cup minced fresh parsley

1 tablespoon chili powder

1 teaspoon salt *(optional)*

1/2 teaspoon ground cumin

1/4 teaspoon black pepper

1 In a medium skillet over medium heat, cook bacon until crisp. Transfer to paper towels to drain. Add beef to skillet and cook in drippings until browned. Drain off fat.

2 Transfer beef to a 5-quart slow cooker and add bacon, tomatoes, tomato sauce, beans, carrots, onion, celery, bell pepper, parsley, chili powder, salt, if desired, cumin, and black pepper. Cover and cook on low, stirring occasionally, until meat is tender, 9 to 10 hours.

BARBECUED BEEF CHILI

Served with a loaf of hot bread and a side salad, this slow-cooker chili makes a hearty meal for a hungry mob.

SERVES 12

7 teaspoons chili powder

1 tablespoon garlic powder

2 teaspoons celery seed

1 teaspoon coarsely ground black pepper

1/4–1/2 teaspoon cayenne pepper

1 fresh beef brisket (3 to 4 pounds)

1 medium green bell pepper, cored, seeded, and chopped

1 large onion, chopped

1 bottle (12 ounces) chili sauce

1 cup ketchup

1/2 cup barbecue sauce

1/3 cup packed brown sugar

1/4 cup cider vinegar

1/4 cup Worcestershire sauce

1 teaspoon coarse-grain mustard

1 can (15 1/2 ounces) hot chili beans

1 can (15 1/2 ounces) great Northern beans, drained and rinsed

1 In a small bowl, combine chili powder, garlic powder, celery seed, black pepper, and cayenne, then rub over beef. Cut beef into 8 pieces and place in a 5-quart slow cooker.

2 In a medium bowl, combine bell pepper, onion, chili sauce, ketchup, barbecue sauce, brown sugar, vinegar, Worcestershire sauce, and mustard, then pour over beef. Cover and cook on high until meat is tender, about 5 hours.

3 Transfer meat to a plate. Skim fat from cooking liquid. When meat is cool enough to handle, shred with two forks and return to slow cooker. Reduce heat to low, stir in beans and cook, covered, until heated through, about 1 hour.

CHILI FOR A CROWD

Chili is a great dish to serve company. You can make it ahead of time, it's filling, and everyone loves it.

SERVES 20

3 pounds ground beef

2 cans (28 ounces each) diced tomatoes, undrained

4 cans (15-16 ounces each) kidney, pinto, and/or black beans, drained and rinsed

1 pound fully cooked kielbasa, halved and sliced

2 large onions, halved and thinly sliced

2 cans (8 ounces each) tomato sauce

2/3 cup hickory-flavored barbecue sauce

1/2 cup packed brown sugar

5 fresh banana peppers, seeded, deveined, and sliced

2 tablespoons chili powder

2 teaspoons coarse-grain mustard

2 teaspoons instant coffee granules

1 teaspoon dried oregano

1 teaspoon dried thyme

1 teaspoon dried sage

1/2 teaspoon cayenne pepper

1/2 teaspoon crushed red pepper flakes

2 garlic cloves, minced

1 In an 8-quart Dutch oven or soup pot over medium heat, cook beef until browned. Drain off fat.

2 Add 1 1/2 cups water, tomatoes, beans, kielbasa, onions, tomato sauce, barbecue sauce, brown sugar, peppers, chili powder, mustard, coffee, oregano, thyme, sage, cayenne, red pepper flakes, and garlic. Bring to boil, then reduce heat and simmer, covered, 1 hour, stirring occasionally.

GROUND BEEF CHILI

This is an all-around, all-American chili recipe that should please almost any palate.

SERVES 16

3 pounds ground beef

1 large onion, chopped

1 medium green bell pepper, cored, seeded, and chopped

2 celery stalks, chopped

2 cans (16 ounces each) kidney beans, drained and rinsed

1 can (29 ounces) tomato puree

1 jar (16 ounces) salsa

1 can (14 1/2 ounces) diced tomatoes, undrained

1 can (10 1/2 ounces) condensed beef broth

1/4 cup chili powder

2 tablespoons Worcestershire sauce

1 tablespoon dried basil

2 teaspoons ground cumin

2 teaspoons steak sauce

1 teaspoon garlic powder

1 teaspoon salt

1 teaspoon coarsely ground black pepper

1 1/2 teaspoons browning sauce *(optional)*

Chopped onion *(optional)*

1 In a Dutch oven or soup pot over medium heat, cook beef, onion, bell pepper, and celery until beef is browned and vegetables are tender. Drain off fat.

2 Stir in 1 cup water, beans, tomato puree, salsa, tomatoes, broth, chili powder, Worcestershire sauce, basil, cumin, steak sauce, garlic powder, salt, black pepper, and browning sauce, if desired. Bring to boil, then reduce heat and simmer, uncovered, until chili reaches desired consistency, about 30 minutes. Garnish with chopped onion, if desired.

CHURCH SUPPER CHILI

This popular chili can be fixed ahead and reheated when you need it—a perfect contribution to a potluck supper.

SERVES 20

2 1/2 pounds ground beef

1/2 cup chopped seeded green bell pepper

1 cup chopped celery

2 cups chopped onion

1 garlic clove, minced

3 tablespoons chili powder

2 teaspoons salt

1/2 teaspoon black pepper

1 can (16 ounces) tomatoes, undrained, cut up

1 can (46 ounces) tomato juice

1 can (30 ounces) vegetable juice

1 can (30 ounces) kidney beans, drained and rinsed

1 can (30 ounces) hot chili beans, drained and rinsed

1 In a large Dutch oven or soup pot over medium heat, cook beef until browned. Drain off fat. Add bell pepper, celery, onion, and garlic and sauté until tender, about 5 minutes.

2 Add chili powder, salt, black pepper, tomatoes, and juices and bring to boil. Reduce heat and simmer, covered, 20 minutes. Add beans and simmer, covered, 20 minutes.

KENTUCKY CHILI

This meaty chili includes spaghetti as well as beans.

 SERVES 10

1 1/2 pounds ground beef
1 medium onion, chopped
2 cans (32 ounces each) tomato juice
1 can (15 ounces) chili beans, undrained
1 tablespoon chili powder
1 teaspoon salt
1/2 teaspoon black pepper
8 ounces spaghetti, broken in half

1 In a medium skillet over medium heat, cook beef and onion until browned. Drain off fat and transfer mixture to a large bowl.

2 In a large soup pot, combine 1 cup water, tomato juice, beans, chili powder, salt, and pepper. Bring to boil, then reduce heat and simmer, covered, 10 to 15 minutes.

3 Stir in beef mixture and simmer 10 minutes.

4 Meanwhile, cook spaghetti according to package directions. Drain and stir into chili.

HOOSIER CHILI

This is a solid, hunger-quenching chili with pasta as well as beans to give it heft.

 SERVES 12

2 pounds extra-lean ground beef
2 cups chopped onion
3/4 cup chopped celery
1/2 cup chopped seeded green bell pepper
3 garlic cloves, minced
1 teaspoon salt *(optional)*
1/4 teaspoon black pepper
1 tablespoon brown sugar
3 tablespoons chili powder

2 cans (16 ounces each) stewed tomatoes
1 can (46 ounces) tomato juice
1 can (10 1/2 ounces) beef broth
1/2 cup elbow macaroni
1 can (15 ounces) kidney beans,
    drained and rinsed

1 In a large Dutch oven or soup pot over medium heat, cook beef until browned. Add onion, celery, bell pepper, and garlic and sauté 7 minutes or until tender.

2 Add salt, if desired, black pepper, brown sugar, chili powder, tomatoes, tomato juice, and broth. Bring to boil, then reduce heat and simmer, covered, 1 hour.

3 Add macaroni and simmer, covered 30 minutes. Stir in beans and cook until heated through.

PUMPKIN CHILI

Pumpkin and pumpkin pie spice give a third dimension to this conventionally hot beef chili recipe.

 SERVES 10

3 pounds ground beef
1 medium onion, chopped
1 cup canned pumpkin
1 teaspoon salt
1 teaspoon pepper
2 teaspoons pumpkin pie spice
2 cans (10 3/4 ounces each) condensed
    tomato soup
2 cans (16 ounces each) chili sauce
1 teaspoon sugar
1 teaspoon chili powder

1 In a large Dutch oven or soup pot over medium heat, cook beef and onion until browned, about 5 minutes. Drain off fat.

2 Add pumpkin, salt, pepper, pie spice, soup, chili sauce, sugar, and chili powder and stir to mix well (if chili is too thick, add some water). Bring to boil, then reduce heat and simmer, covered, 1 hour.

SWEET SUCCOTASH CHILI

This recipe deliciously combines two all-American dishes—succotash and chili.

SERVES 12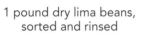

1 pound dry lima beans,
    sorted and rinsed
3 tablespoons olive oil
2 pounds ground beef
4 medium onions, chopped
1/4 cup hot Hungarian paprika
3 tablespoons ground cumin
3 garlic cloves, minced
1 teaspoon salt
1 can (49 1/2 ounces) chicken broth
1 can (28 ounces) crushed tomatoes
2 packages (10 ounces each)
    frozen whole-kernel corn

1 In a large saucepan or soup pot, cover beans with water, bring to boil, and cook 2 minutes. Remove from heat and let stand 1 hour; drain.

2 Heat oil in a 6-quart Dutch oven or soup pot over medium heat. Add beef and onions and sauté until beef is browned and onions are tender. Drain off fat.

3 Add beans, paprika, cumin, garlic, and salt. Stir in broth and tomatoes and bring to boil. Reduce heat and simmer, covered, 1 hour. Add corn and simmer, covered, until beans are tender, about 1 hour.

HUNTER'S CHILI

This is a great meal to come home to after a long day outdoors.

SERVES 14

1 pound fresh bratwurst
1 pound ground beef
2 cups chopped onion
1 large green bell pepper, cored,
    seeded, and chopped
2 garlic cloves, minced
1 can (6 ounces) tomato paste
1 can (28 ounces) diced tomatoes, undrained
1 can (8 ounces) tomato sauce
1 can (15 1/4 ounces) whole-kernel
    corn, drained
2 cans (16 ounces each) kidney beans,
    drained and rinsed
1 can (15 ounces) pinto beans,
    drained and rinsed
2 cans (4 ounces each) mushroom stems
    and pieces, drained
3 tablespoons chili powder
1 tablespoon paprika
1 teaspoon ground cumin
1 teaspoon dried oregano
1 teaspoon salt
1/2 teaspoon black pepper
1/4 teaspoon cayenne pepper
1/4 teaspoon crushed red pepper flakes
2 bay leaves

1 In a Dutch oven or soup pot over medium heat, cook bratwurst until browned. Remove, let cool, and slice thinly, then return to pot over medium heat. Add beef, onion, and bell pepper and sauté until beef is browned. Drain off fat.

2 Add 4 cups water, garlic, tomato paste, tomatoes, tomato sauce, corn, kidney beans, pinto beans, mushrooms, chili powder, paprika, cumin, oregano, salt, black pepper, cayenne, red pepper flakes, and bay leaves. Bring to boil, then reduce heat and simmer, covered, until meat is tender, about 1 1/2 hours. Remove bay leaves before serving.

BEEF-PORK CHILI

Beef and pork make a tasty combination in this chili without beans, just as they do in a good meat loaf.

SERVES 10

2 pounds ground beef
1 pound ground pork
1 can (8 ounces) tomato sauce
Salt and black pepper to taste
1 tablespoon instant dried onion
4 tablespoons chili powder
2 teaspoons ground cumin
1/4 teaspoon cayenne pepper
1 teaspoon dried minced garlic
1 teaspoon paprika
1 teaspoon dried oregano
1/4 cup white cornmeal
2 tablespoons all-purpose flour

1 In a large Dutch oven or soup pot over medium heat, cook beef and pork until browned. Drain off fat.

2 Add 4 cups water, tomato sauce, salt, and pepper and bring to boil. Reduce heat and simmer, covered, 1 1/2 to 2 hours, adding more water if necessary. Stir in onion, chili powder, cumin, cayenne, garlic, paprika, and oregano and simmer 30 minutes.

3 In a small bowl, combine cornmeal, flour, and enough water to make a thin paste. Stir into chili and simmer 10 minutes or until slightly thickened.

HAM AND BEAN CHILI

Leftover ham, ripe olives, and three kinds of beans distinguish this unusual and savory chili.

SERVES 10

1 tablespoon olive oil
2 cups cubed fully cooked ham
1 medium onion, chopped
1 medium green bell pepper, cored, seeded, and chopped
1 garlic clove, minced
1 can (28 ounces) diced tomatoes, undrained
1 can (16 ounces) kidney beans, drained and rinsed
1 can (15 ounces) black beans, drained and rinsed
1 can (15 ounces) pinto beans, drained and rinsed
1 jar (8 ounces) salsa
1 can (8 ounces) tomato sauce
1 can (2 1/4 ounces) sliced black olives, drained
1 teaspoon beef bouillon granules
1 teaspoon dried thyme
1 teaspoon salt
1/4 teaspoon black pepper
Shredded cheddar cheese

1 Heat oil in a Dutch oven or soup pot over medium heat. Add ham, onion, bell pepper, and garlic and sauté 5 minutes or until tender.

2 Stir in tomatoes, kidney beans, black beans, pinto beans, salsa, tomato sauce, and 1/2 cup water, if desired, and bring to boil. Stir in olives, bouillon, thyme, salt, and pepper. Reduce heat and simmer, uncovered, 15 minutes. Garnish with cheese.

BOLD BEAN AND PORK CHILI

This tempting chili is big on flavor and very simple to make. Prepare it ahead of time up to the point of adding the beans, then refrigerate and finish it the next day.

SERVES 15

3 tablespoons olive oil

1 pork shoulder (4 to 5 pounds), trimmed and cut into 3/4-inch cubes

2 large onions, chopped

8 garlic cloves, minced

4 cans (14 1/2 ounces each) chicken broth

1 can (28 ounces) crushed tomatoes

1/2 cup chili powder

3 tablespoons dried oregano

2-3 tablespoons ground cumin

4 1/2 teaspoons salt

2 teaspoons cayenne pepper

4 cans (15 ounces each) black beans, drained and rinsed

Minced fresh cilantro *(optional)*

1 Heat oil in a 6-quart Dutch oven or soup pot over medium heat. Add pork and sauté until browned. Drain off fat. Add onions and sauté until softened, about 3 minutes. Add garlic and sauté 2 minutes.

2 Stir in broth, tomatoes, chili powder, oregano, cumin, salt, and cayenne and bring to boil. Reduce heat, cover, and simmer, stirring occasionally, at least 1 hour.

3 Skim off fat. Stir in beans and simmer, uncovered, until chili reaches desired consistency, about 15 minutes. Garnish with cilantro, if desired.

PUEBLO GREEN CHILI

Green chiles, pork, and chicken stock distinguish this lighter-colored but lively chili.

SERVES 10

2 pounds lean boneless pork, cut into 1 1/2-inch cubes

1 tablespoon vegetable oil

3 cans (12 ounces each) whole-kernel corn, drained

2 celery stalks, chopped

2 medium all-purpose potatoes, peeled and chopped

2 medium tomatoes, cored, seeded, and coarsely chopped

3 cans (4 ounces each) chopped green chiles

4 cups chicken stock

2 teaspoons ground cumin

1 teaspoon dried oregano

1 teaspoon salt *(optional)*

1 Heat oil in a large Dutch oven or soup pot over medium heat oil. Add half of pork and stir until browned. Transfer to a plate and cook remaining pork.

2 Return reserved pork to pot and add corn, celery, potatoes, tomatoes, chiles, stock, cumin, oregano, and salt, if desired. Bring to boil, then reduce heat and simmer, covered, 1 hour or until pork is tender.

SANTA FE CHICKEN CHILI

Lots of vegetables and seasonings make this low-fat chicken chili lively and satisfying.
(Photograph on page 9)

SERVES 14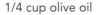

1/4 cup olive oil

2 pounds skinless, boneless chicken breasts, cut into 1/2-inch cubes

4 medium red bell peppers, cored, seeded, and diced

4 garlic cloves, minced

2 large onions, chopped

3 tablespoons chili powder

2 teaspoons ground cumin

1/4 teaspoon cayenne pepper

1 can (28 ounces) diced tomatoes, undrained

2 cans (14 /2 ounces each) chicken broth

2 cans (16 ounces each) kidney beans, drained and rinsed

1 jar (12 ounces) salsa

1 package (10 ounces) frozen whole-kernel corn

1/2 teaspoon salt

1/2 teaspoon black pepper

1 Heat oil in a Dutch oven or soup pot over medium heat. Add chicken, peppers, garlic, and onions and sauté until chicken is no longer pink and vegetables are tender, about 8 minutes.

2 Add chili powder, cumin, and cayenne and cook, stirring, 1 minute. Add tomatoes and broth and bring to boil. Reduce heat, cover, and simmer 15 minutes.

3 Stir in beans, salsa, corn, salt, and pepper and bring to boil. Reduce heat and simmer, uncovered, until chicken is tender, about 10 minutes.

PARTY CHICKEN CHILI

You can roast or stew a large chicken a day ahead to get 3 pounds of cooked chicken for this wonderful recipe that easily feeds a crowd.

SERVES 16

2 tablespoons butter

1/2 celery stalk, chopped

3 carrots, chopped

3 medium onions, chopped

3 green bell peppers, cored, seeded, and chopped

3 pounds cooked chicken, cubed

3 cans (14 1/2 ounces) diced tomatoes, undrained

12 cups chicken stock

1 cup chopped fresh cilantro

3 tablespoons ground cumin

3 tablespoons ground coriander

3 tablespoons ground unsweetened chocolate

3 cans (16 ounces) black beans

Salt and black pepper

Hot red pepper sauce *(optional)*

2 cups (8 ounces) shredded cheddar cheese

1 In a large soup pot or Dutch oven over medium heat, melt butter. Add celery, carrots, onions, and bell peppers and sauté 7 minutes or until softened. Add chicken and sauté 2 minutes.

2 Add tomatoes, stock, cilantro, cumin, coriander, and chocolate and bring to boil. Reduce heat and simmer, covered, 30 minutes. Add beans and simmer 20 minutes or until thickened. Season to taste with salt and pepper and red pepper sauce, if desired. Sprinkle each serving with cheese.

CHUNKY TURKEY CHILI

Canned beans are convenient, but the flavor and texture of dry beans are better in a party-size batch of chili. If you like, soak and cook the beans ahead of time and refrigerate until ready to use.
(Photograph on page 30)

SERVES 12

1 pound dry pinto beans,
    sorted and rinsed

3 tablespoons olive oil

2 pounds skinless, boneless turkey breast,
    cut into 1/2-inch chunks

1 large onion, finely chopped

6 garlic cloves, minced

2 green bell peppers, cored, seeded,
    and cut into 1/2-inch squares

2 carrots, thinly sliced

1/2 cup chili powder

1 tablespoon ground cumin

1 tablespoon ground coriander

1 can (28 ounces) crushed tomatoes

2 teaspoons salt

2 cans (15 ounces each) hominy,
    drained and rinsed

1 Place beans in a large soup pot with enough water to cover by several inches and soak overnight.

2 Drain beans, place in a large saucepan with enough water to cover by 2 inches, and bring to boil. Reduce heat and simmer, partially covered, until tender, about 1 1/4 hours. Drain, reserving 2 cups cooking liquid.

3 Heat oil in a Dutch oven or soup pot over medium heat. Working in batches, add turkey and sauté until golden, about 4 minutes. Using a slotted spoon, transfer to a plate. Add onion and garlic to pot and sauté until onion is softened, about 5 minutes.

4 Add 1/2 cup water, bell peppers, and carrots and cook, stirring frequently, until carrots are crisp-tender, about 7 minutes. Stir in chili powder, cumin, and coriander.

5 Add beans, reserved cooking liquid, tomatoes, and salt and bring to boil. Reduce heat and simmer, covered, 30 minutes or until sauce is richly flavored.

6 Stir in turkey and hominy and simmer, uncovered, until turkey is cooked through, about 10 minutes.

SPICY TURKEY CHILI

This peppery chili is saucy and satisfying for lovers of hot food.

SERVES 12

2 pounds ground turkey or turkey sausage

1 large onion, chopped

4 garlic cloves, minced

2 cans (15 3/4 ounces each) chili beans,
    undrained

2 cans (15 ounces each) tomato sauce

1 can (28 ounces) crushed tomatoes

1 1/2 cups beef stock or beer

2 1/2 tablespoons chili powder

2 teaspoons Italian seasoning

1/2 teaspoon ground cinnamon

1 jalapeño pepper, seeded, deveined,
    and finely chopped (wear gloves
    when handling; they burn)

Dash of cayenne pepper

1 In a Dutch oven or soup pot over medium heat, cook turkey, onion, and garlic until meat is browned and vegetables are tender. Drain off fat.

2 Add beans, tomato sauce, tomatoes, stock, chili powder, Italian seasoning, cinnamon, jalapeño, and cayenne. Bring to boil, then reduce heat and simmer, uncovered, 45 minutes, stirring occasionally.

MEATY THREE-BEAN CHILI

With three types of beans and two kinds of meat, this chili is a many flavored, delightful party meal.

SERVES 10

12 ounces Italian sausage links, cut into 1/2-inch chunks

12 ounces ground beef

1 large onion, chopped

1 medium green bell pepper, cored, seeded, and chopped

1 jalapeño pepper, seeded, deveined, and minced (wear gloves when handling; they burn)

2 garlic cloves, minced

1 cup beef stock

1/2 cup Worcestershire sauce

1 1/2 teaspoons chili powder

1 teaspoon black pepper

1 teaspoon coarse-grain mustard

1/2 teaspoon celery seed

1/2 teaspoon salt

6 cups chopped fresh plum tomatoes

6 bacon slices, cooked and crumbled

1 can (16 ounces) kidney beans, drained and rinsed

1 can (15 ounces) pinto beans, drained and rinsed

1 can (15 ounces) chickpeas, drained and rinsed

Chopped onions *(optional)*

1 In a Dutch oven or soup pot over medium heat, cook sausage and beef until browned. Drain off fat, discarding all but 1 tablespoon, and transfer meat to a bowl.

2 Add onion, bell pepper, jalapeño, and garlic to pot and sauté in drippings until softened, about 3 minutes. Add stock, Worcestershire sauce, chili powder, black pepper, mustard, celery seed, and salt. Bring to boil, then reduce heat and simmer, covered, 10 minutes.

3 Add tomatoes, bacon, sausage, and beef and return to boil. Reduce heat and simmer, covered, 30 minutes. Add kidney beans, pinto beans, and chickpeas, cover, and simmer, stirring occasionally, 1 hour. Garnish with chopped onion, if desired.

SPICY PINTO BEAN CHILI

Here's a vegetarian chili that will satisfy any appetite.

SERVES 12

2 cups dry pinto beans, sorted and rinsed

1 large sweet onion, chopped

2 garlic cloves, minced

1 can (28 ounces) tomatoes, undrained, chopped

1 can (4 ounces) chopped green chiles

2 carrots, shredded

1 tablespoon chili powder

1 tablespoon ground cumin

1 tablespoon dried oregano

1 tablespoon paprika

2 teaspoons salt

1/2 teaspoon cayenne pepper

Shredded cheddar cheese *(optional)*

1 In a large saucepan, cover beans with water and soak overnight; drain.

2 Add 4 cups water to pan and bring to boil. Reduce heat and simmer, covered, until almost tender, about 1 hour. Add onion, garlic, tomatoes, chiles, carrots, chili powder, cumin, oregano, paprika, salt, and cayenne.

3 Simmer, covered, stirring occasionally, 2 hours or until beans are tender. Garnish with cheese, if desired.

BEAN AND BARLEY CHILI

This is hearty chili with just the right amount of heat. If you use vegetable broth rather than chicken broth, it's a prime vegetarian dish.

SERVES 12

1 cup medium pearl barley

1 tablespoon vegetable oil

2 cups chopped onion

2 cups chopped seeded red bell pepper

1 tablespoon minced garlic

2 tablespoons chili powder

1 1/2 teaspoons ground cumin

1/8 teaspoon cayenne pepper

1 can (14 1/2 ounces) chicken broth

1 can (14 1/2 ounces) stewed tomatoes

1 can (16 ounces) kidney beans, drained and rinsed

1 can (15 ounces) black beans, drained and rinsed

1 can (15 1/2 ounces) black-eyed peas, drained and rinsed

1 Cook barley according to package directions with the exception of adding salt; drain.

2 Heat oil in a 3-quart saucepan over medium heat. Add onions and bell pepper and sauté 5 minutes or until tender. Add barley, garlic, chili powder, cumin, cayenne, broth, tomatoes, kidney beans, black beans, and peas. Bring to boil, then reduce heat and simmer, uncovered, 20 minutes.

VEGETABLE-BEAN CHILI

This is a delicious vegetarian chili with ingredients that require some serious chopping. Once the chopping is done, though, the rest of the preparation is quick.

SERVES 16

1/4 cup olive oil

4 medium zucchini, chopped

2 medium onions, chopped

1 medium green bell pepper, cored, seeded, and chopped

1 medium red bell pepper, cored, seeded, and chopped

4 garlic cloves, minced

2 cans (28 ounces each) Italian stewed tomatoes, cut up

1 can (15 ounces) tomato sauce

1 can (15 ounces) pinto beans, drained and rinsed

1 can (15 ounces) black beans, drained and rinsed

1 jalapeño pepper, seeded, deveined, and chopped (wear gloves when handling; they burn)

1/4 cup minced fresh cilantro

1/4 cup minced fresh parsley

2 tablespoons chili powder

1 tablespoon sugar

1 teaspoon salt

1 teaspoon ground cumin

1 Heat oil in a large Dutch oven or soup pot over medium heat. Add zucchini, onions, bell peppers, and garlic and sauté until tender.

2 Stir in tomatoes, tomato sauce, pinto beans, black beans, jalapeño, cilantro, parsley, chili powder, sugar, salt, and cumin. Bring to boil, then reduce heat and simmer, covered, 30 minutes, stirring occasionally.

ROASTED VEGGIE CHILI

SERVES 24

2 cups fresh or frozen whole-kernel corn

2 cups cubed zucchini

2 cups cubed yellow squash

2 cups cubed eggplant

2 medium green bell peppers, cored, seeded, and cut into 1-inch pieces

2 medium red bell peppers, cored, seeded, and cut into 1-inch pieces

2 large onions, chopped

1/2 cup garlic cloves

1/4 cup olive oil

16 cups chicken stock

2 cans (14 1/2 ounces each) stewed tomatoes

2 cans (14 1/2 ounces each) tomato puree

1/4 cup fresh lime juice

4 teaspoons chili powder

1 1/4 teaspoons cayenne pepper

1 teaspoon ground cumin

1/2 cup (1 stick) butter

1/2 cup all-purpose flour

3 cans (15 ounces each) cannellini or white kidney beans, drained and rinsed

1/2 cup minced fresh cilantro

Sour cream (optional)

Chopped scallions (optional)

1 Preheat oven to 400°F. Place corn, zucchini, squash, eggplant, bell peppers, onions, and garlic in a roasting pan, drizzle with oil, and toss to coat. Cover and roast until tender, about 20 minutes. Let cool slightly, then remove and chop garlic.

2 In an 8-quart Dutch oven or soup pot over medium-high heat, combine stock, tomatoes, tomato puree, lime juice, chili powder, cayenne, and cumin. Bring to boil, then reduce heat and simmer, uncovered, until reduced by a quarter, about 25 minutes.

3 In a small saucepan, melt butter and stir in flour until smooth. Cook, stirring, until bubbling and beginning to brown. Slowly whisk into pot. Add vegetables, garlic, beans, and cilantro, mix well, and simmer until thickened. Garnish with sour cream and scallions, if desired.

This is a delightfully different chili with lots of spice but also lots of mellow, slow-cooked vegetables. You can make it vegetarian by using vegetable stock instead of chicken stock.

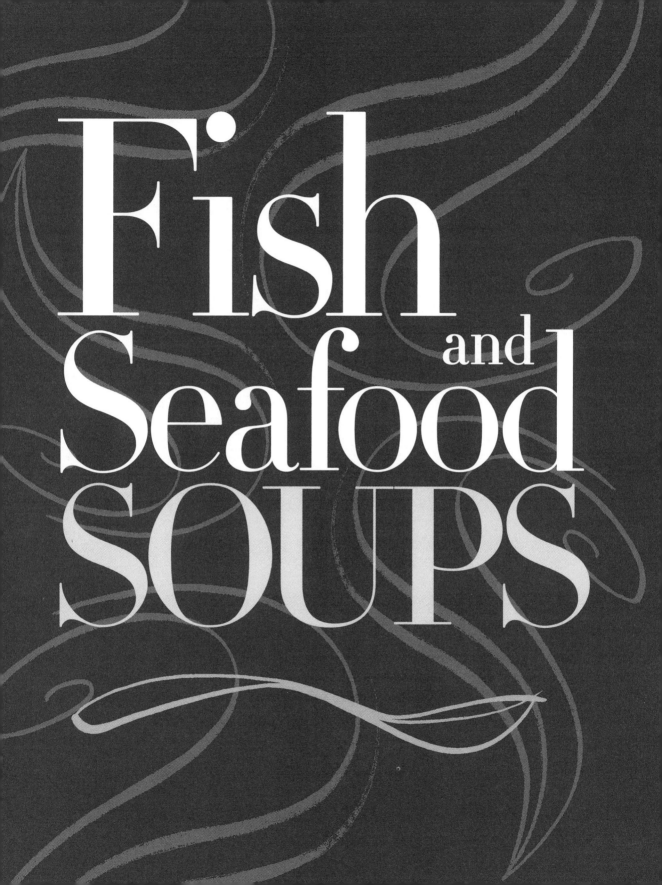

Fish and Seafood SOUPS

FISH AND SEAFOOD SOUPS

recipe list

 EASY: 10 minutes to prepare

QUICK: Ready to eat in 30 minutes

ONE-DISH: contains protein, vegetables, and good carbohydrates (beans, whole-grains, etc.) for a complete healthy meal

HEALTHY: High in nutrients, low in bad fats and empty carbohydrates

SLOW COOKER: Easily adapted for slow cooker by cutting down on liquids

CLASSIC BOUILLABAISSE

SERVES 6

8 ounces fresh or thawed frozen sole, flounder, or halibut fillets

8 ounces fresh or thawed frozen sea scallops

1 frozen small rock lobster tail (8 ounces), partially thawed, or 8 ounces lobster meat

1 tablespoon olive oil

1 large yellow onion, chopped

2 garlic cloves, minced

3 1/2 cups low-sodium chicken broth

1 3/4 cups chopped tomatoes or 1 can (14 1/2 ounces) low-sodium tomatoes, undrained, cut up

1 cup dry white wine or low-sodium chicken broth

2 tablespoons minced fresh parsley

2 bay leaves

1 teaspoon dried thyme

1 teaspoon fennel seed or celery seed

1/2 teaspoon salt

1/4 teaspoon saffron threads, crushed (optional)

1/8 teaspoon cayenne pepper

1 can (6 1/2 ounces) minced clams

1 Rinse fish, scallops, and lobster and pat dry. Cut fish into 2-inch pieces, halve large scallops, halve lobster tail lengthwise, then cut crosswise into 6 portions.

2 In a large saucepan heat oil over medium heat. Add onion and garlic and sauté 5 minutes or until onion is tender. Stir in broth, tomatoes, wine, parsley, bay leaves, thyme, fennel seed, salt, saffron, if desired, and cayenne. Bring to boil, reduce heat, and simmer, covered, 30 minutes.

3 Line a large sieve with 2 layers of cheesecloth and set in a large saucepan. Strain vegetable mixture, discarding vegetables and seasonings.

4 Bring liquid to boil, add fish, scallops, lobster, and clams. Return to boil, reduce heat and simmer, uncovered, stirring, 4 minutes or until fish flakes easily and scallops and lobster are opaque.

In France, this classic fish soup is made with as many as a dozen different kinds of Mediterranean seafood, including sea bass, eel, and scallops. Americans can adapt the recipe to use local seafood, such as rock lobster, sole, and clams. Serve with French bread.

AMERICAN BOUILLABAISSE

This version uses fewer herbs and skips the fennel, which is standard in classic bouillabaisse recipes. But it has extra seafood, giving it more flavors of the ocean.

SERVES 8

1 onion, chopped

2 carrots, peeled and thinly sliced

1 leek, halved lengthwise, washed, and thinly sliced

2 tomatoes, cored, seeded, and chopped

2 garlic cloves, minced

1 cup dry white wine

4 bottles (8 ounces each) clam juice

6 cups fish stock

2 pinches of saffron threads, crumbled

2 pounds mussels, scrubbed and beards removed

12 clams, scrubbed

8 ounces boneless halibut, cut into 1 1/2-inch pieces

8 ounces boneless scrod, cut into 1 1/2-inch pieces

8 ounces bay scallops

8 ounces large shrimp, peeled and deveined

1 In an 8-quart Dutch oven, combine onion, carrots, leek, tomatoes, garlic, wine, clam juice, fish stock, and saffron. Bring to boil over medium-high heat, then reduce heat and simmer, uncovered, 30 minutes.

2 Strain stock, discarding vegetables, and return to Dutch oven. Bring to boil, add clams and mussels. Reduce heat, cover, and simmer 5 minutes or until mussels and clams open (discard any that do not open). Add halibut, scrod, scallops, and shrimp and simmer, uncovered, 5 minutes.

3 Divide fish and shellfish among 8 large, warm soup bowls and ladle in stock.

ITALIAN FISH SOUP

Serve this easy Italian-style fish soup with garlic bread or Parmesan toast.

SERVES 4

1 tablespoon olive oil

2 medium leeks, coarsely chopped

2/3 cup chopped fennel or celery

3 garlic cloves, minced

1/8 teaspoon salt

1/8 teaspoon black pepper

4 1/2 cups chicken stock

1/2 cup dry white wine or chicken stock

1 can (14 1/2 ounces) low-sodium tomatoes, undrained

1/2 teaspoon dried thyme, crumbled

1/4 teaspoon crumbled saffron *(optional)*

1 bay leaf

12 clams or mussels, scrubbed and beards removed from mussels

8 ounces large shrimp, peeled and deveined

8 ounces firm white fish fillets, such as cod, monkfish, or halibut, cut into 2-inch pieces

Minced fresh basil or parsley *(optional)*

1 In a large saucepan over medium heat, heat oil. Add leeks, fennel, garlic, salt, and pepper and sauté, stirring occasionally, 3 minutes or until leeks are soft. Add stock, wine, tomatoes, thyme, saffron, if desired, and bay leaf. Bring to boil, reduce heat, and simmer, covered, 20 minutes.

2 Add clams and simmer, covered, 5 minutes or until opened (discard any that do not open). Using a slotted spoon, transfer to a bowl and cover loosely with foil.

3 Add shrimp and fish to pan and simmer, stirring occasionally, 3 minutes or until cooked through. Remove bay leaf. Garnish each serving with 3 clams and basil, if desired.

FISH MUDDLE

Order fish stew for supper in North Carolina and you're likely to be served fish muddle. But, to quote a North Carolinian, "Never, oh never, put milk in the pot!"

SERVES 4

1 teaspoon vegetable oil

2 strips reduced-salt bacon, diced

6 scallions with tops, sliced

1 medium green bell pepper, cored, seeded, and chopped

1 large carrot, peeled and chopped

2 1/2 cups homemade fish stock or canned low-sodium chicken broth

2 medium all-purpose potatoes, peeled and cut into bite-size pieces

1 medium tomato, cored, seeded, and chopped

1/2 teaspoon dried thyme

8 ounces cod or scrod fillets, cut into 2-inch chunks

8 ounces sea scallops, trimmed and halved

3 tablespoons chopped parsley

1 In a large saucepan over medium low heat, heat oil. Add bacon and sauté 2 minutes or just until it sweats. Stir in scallions, pepper, and carrot. Cover and cook, stirring once, 5 minutes or until vegetables are tender.

2 Add stock, potatoes, tomato, and thyme. Increase heat to high and bring to boil. Reduce heat and simmer, uncovered, 15 minutes or until potatoes are tender. Stir in cod and scallops. Cover and cook 5 minutes or just until seafood is opaque. Stir in parsley.

CARIBBEAN SEAFOOD CURRY STEW

Ginger, curry powder, hot red pepper flakes, ground allspice, bell peppers, and scallions contribute a unique blend of health-protective phytochemicals to this delicious stew.

SERVES 4

2 teaspoons olive oil

6 thin scallions, finely chopped

1 yellow bell pepper, cored, seeded, and coarsely chopped

1 tablespoon finely chopped peeled fresh ginger

1 1/2 teaspoons curry powder

1/4-1/2 teaspoons hot red pepper flakes

1/4 teaspoon ground allspice

2 tablespoons reduced-sodium soy sauce

1 1/2 tablespoons brown sugar

1/4 teaspoon salt

1 can (14 ounces) reduced-fat coconut milk

3 plum tomatoes, quartered lengthwise and seeded

8 ounces halibut steaks, skin removed and steaks cut into 2-inch chunks

8 ounces medium shrimp, peeled and deveined

2 tablespoons chopped fresh cilantro

1 tablespoon fresh lime juice

1 In a large saucepan over medium heat, heat oil. Add scallions, bell pepper, and ginger and sauté until softened, about 5 minutes. Add curry powder, red pepper flakes to taste, and allspice and sauté 2 minutes. Stir in soy sauce, brown sugar, salt, coconut milk and tomatoes. Gently simmer, uncovered, 15 minutes.

2 Add halibut and shrimp and gently simmer, uncovered, just until fish is cooked through, 5 to 8 minutes. Stir in cilantro and lime juice.

PROVENÇAL FISH STEW

The inspiration for this dish is bouillabaisse, a classic French stew. You can vary the combination of fish and shellfish to suit your preference, but there should be 2 pounds in all.

SERVES 6

3 tablespoons olive oil

1 large yellow onion, thinly sliced

1 can (14 1/2 ounces) tomatoes, undrained, coarsely chopped

2 cups dry white wine or 1 cup clam juice or fish stock plus 1 cup chicken broth

1 bottle (8 ounces) clam juice or 1 cup fish stock

2 garlic cloves, minced

1 bay leaf

1 teaspoon dried basil, crumbled

1/2 teaspoon dried thyme, crumbled

1/2 teaspoon grated orange zest

1/8 teaspoon black pepper

1/8 teaspoon cayenne pepper

1 pound whitefish fillets, such as halibut, cod, sea bass, or preferably a combination, cut into 1-inch-square pieces

8 ounces medium shrimp, peeled and deveined

12 clams or mussels, scrubbed and beards removed from mussels

2 medium zucchini, cut into 3/4-inch-thick slices

12 slices (about 3/4 inch thick) French bread, toasted

1/4 cup olive oil mixed with 1 crushed garlic clove

2 tablespoons minced fresh parsley

1 In a soup pot or 6-quart Dutch oven over medium heat, heat oil. Add onion and sauté until very soft, about 10 minutes.

2 Stir in 1 cup water, tomatoes, wine, clam juice, garlic, bay leaf, basil, thyme, orange zest, black pepper, and cayenne. Bring to boil, reduce heat, and simmer, partially covered, 15 minutes. Add fish, shrimp, clams, and zucchini and cook, covered, until fish is just opaque and clams have opened, 8 to 10 minutes. Discard any unopened clams and remove bay leaf.

3 Brush bread with garlic oil and place 2 slices in bottom of each of 6 soup bowls. Ladle stew on top and sprinkle with parsley.

WEST COAST SEAFOOD STEW

Here is a delicious stew that you can make in minutes after you purchase the fresh fish.

SERVES 6

3 tablespoons olive oil

1 medium yellow onion, sliced

1 small green bell pepper, cored, seeded, and chopped

1 cup sliced mushrooms

2 garlic cloves, minced

1 can (14 1/2 or 16 ounces) whole peeled tomatoes, undrained

1 can (8 ounces) tomato sauce

1/2 cup dry white wine

1 bay leaf

12 littleneck clams or 1 can (10 ounces) whole clams, drained

1 pound monkfish or halibut, cut into chunks

8 ounces cooked crabmeat or imitation crabmeat chunks

1 In a large saucepan or soup pot, heat oil over medium heat. Add onion, bell pepper, mushrooms, and garlic and sauté 5 minutes.

2 Stir in 1 cup water, tomatoes, tomato sauce, wine, and bay leaf. Bring to boil, stirring to break up tomatoes. Reduce heat and simmer, covered, 10 minutes.

3 Scrub fresh clams under cold running water to remove sand. Add to tomato mixture, cover, increase heat to high, and bring to boil. (If using canned clams, skip this step and add them with crabmeat in Step 4.)

4 Add fish. Reduce heat and simmer, covered, 5 minutes or until clams open and fish flakes easily. Stir in crabmeat and heat through. Remove any clams that did not open and bay leaf.

ITALIAN SEAFOOD STEW WITH POLENTA

Any fish or shellfish is delicious in this Italian fisherman's stew—pick your favorites at the market.

SERVES 4

Stew:

2 tablespoons extra-virgin olive oil

1 medium leek, coarsely chopped

1 onion, chopped

4 garlic cloves, chopped

1/2 green bell pepper, cored, seeded, and chopped

1/2 medium fennel bulb, diced

12 ounces dry white wine

1 1/4 cups fish stock

1 can (14 1/2 ounces) chopped tomatoes, undrained

2 tablespoons tomato paste

1/4 teaspoon dried *herbes de Provence*

1 medium zucchini, sliced

3 tablespoons coarsely chopped fresh parsley

2 ounces shelled fresh peas or frozen peas

3 ounces baby chard or spinach leaves

8 ounces skinless cod fillet, cut into chunks

1 pound mixed seafood, such as shrimp, scallops, squid rings, and mussels

Salt and black pepper

Polenta:

2 teaspoons extra-virgin olive oil

8 ounces instant polenta

Salt and black pepper

1 In a large saucepan over medium heat, heat oil. Add leek and onion and sauté 2 minutes or until starting to soften. Add garlic, bell pepper, and fennel and sauté 5 minutes or until softened.

2 Add wine, stock, tomatoes, and salt and pepper to taste. Bring to boil, reduce heat, and simmer, covered, 30 minutes or until slightly thickened. Stir in tomato paste, *herbes de Provence*, and zucchini and simmer 10 minutes, adding a little water if mixture becomes too thick.

3 Meanwhile, lightly oil a shallow 7 x 11-inch baking pan. Cook polenta according to package directions until thick. Season with salt and pepper to taste. Pour into pan and let cool until firm. Cut into triangles. Preheat broiler.

4 Stir parsley, peas, chard, fish, and shellfish into tomato mixture. Cover and simmer 5 minutes or until seafood is just cooked.

5 Lightly brush polenta triangles with oil and broil until lightly browned. Serve with stew.

MALAY FISH STEW

Braising keeps fish moist and succulent. Spiced with care and simmered in a little coconut milk, this stew is delicious with plain noodles or rice.

SERVES 4

1 tablespoon sunflower oil

4 scallions, chopped

1 red chile, seeded and sliced (wear gloves when handling; chiles burn)

2 celery stalks, sliced

1 red bell pepper, cored, seeded, and sliced

1 garlic clove, crushed

1/2 teaspoon fennel seed

2 teaspoons ground coriander

1/2 teaspoon ground cumin

1/4 teaspoon turmeric

1 can (14 1/2 ounces) chopped tomatoes

1/2 cup coconut milk

1 1/4 cups fish stock

2 tablespoons fish sauce or light soy sauce

1 can (6 ounces) sliced bamboo shoots, drained

1 1/2 pounds thick skinless white fish fillets, such as cod or haddock, cut into chunks

16 tiger shrimp, peeled

Juice of 1/2 lime

2 scallions, chopped

1 tablespoon chopped fresh cilantro

1 In a large skillet over medium heat, heat oil. Add scallions, chile, celery, and pepper and sauté 5 minutes or until slightly softened.

2 Stir in garlic, fennel seed, coriander, cumin, and turmeric and sauté 1 minute. Add tomatoes, coconut milk, stock, and fish sauce. Bring to boil, reduce heat, and simmer, covered, 5 minutes.

3 Stir in bamboo shoots, fish, and shrimp. Simmer, covered, 5 minutes or until fish flakes easily and shrimp is pink. Stir in lime juice. Garnish with scallions and cilantro.

SEAFOOD GUMBO

Lucky is the guest invited to share this magnificent party dish!

SERVES 24

1 cup all-purpose flour

1 cup vegetable oil

4 cups chopped onion

2 cups chopped celery

2 cups chopped green bell pepper

1 cup sliced scallions and tops

4 cups chicken stock

4 cups sliced okra

2 tablespoons paprika

2 tablespoons salt

2 teaspoons dried oregano

1 teaspoon black pepper

12 cups mixed shrimp, scallops, and crayfish

1 cup snipped fresh parsley

2 tablespoons gumbo filé

1 In a heavy Dutch oven over medium-high heat, combine flour and oil until smooth. Cook 5 minutes, stirring constantly. Reduce heat to medium and cook, stirring about 10 minutes, or until mixture is reddish-brown (the color of a penny).

2 Add onion, celery, bell pepper, and scallions and sauté 5 minutes. Add 8 cups water, stock, okra, paprika, salt, oregano, and black pepper. Bring to boil, then reduce heat and simmer, covered, 10 minutes.

3 Add seafood and parsley. Simmer, uncovered, 5 minutes or until seafood is done. Remove from heat and stir in filé.

CHINESE SEAFOOD NOODLE SOUP

In China, soups are served between courses. That is why they are made with light stock, which makes them appropriate starters for Western meals.

SERVES 6

2 ounces fine stir-fry rice noodles, broken into 4-inch lengths

2 teaspoons peanut oil

1-inch piece fresh ginger, peeled and finely chopped

2 1/2 ounces shiitake mushrooms, stalks removed and caps thinly sliced

4 cups chicken stock

1 tablespoon dry sherry

2 tablespoons light soy sauce

4 1/2 ounces cooked mixed seafood, such as shrimp, squid, and scallops

1 cup Napa cabbage, shredded

4 scallions, thinly sliced

1/4 cup bean sprouts

Fresh cilantro leaves

Chili sauce

1 Place noodles in a small bowl, cover with boiling water, and soak 4 minutes.

2 In a large saucepan over medium heat, heat oil. Add ginger and mushrooms and sauté 2 minutes or until softened. Add stock, sherry, and soy sauce and bring to boil.

3 Halve scallops if they are large. Add seafood, cabbage, scallions, and sprouts to boiling stock. Return to boil and cook 1 minute or until seafood is heated through.

4 Drain noodles and add to soup. Return to boil and turn off heat. Ladle soup into bowls and sprinkle with cilantro. Serve with chili sauce.

CARIBBEAN FISH SOUP

Peppers—hot and sweet—and lime juice and zest distinguish this lovely fish soup.

SERVES 6

2 onions, coarsely chopped

1 large red or green bell pepper, cored, seeded and coarsely chopped

2 cups canned crushed tomatoes

Dash of hot red pepper sauce

1/2 teaspoon dried thyme

1 bay leaf

5 cups fish stock

1 cup white wine or fish stock

8 ounces all-purpose potatoes, peeled and thinly sliced

Finely grated zest and juice of 1 lime

1 pound firm white fish fillets, cut into 2-inch pieces

1/8 teaspoon pepper

1 In a 4-quart saucepan, combine onions, bell pepper, tomatoes, hot pepper sauce, thyme, bay leaf, stock, and wine. Bring to boil.

2 Stir in potatoes. Reduce heat, partially cover, and simmer, stirring occasionally, 15 minutes.

3 Stir in lime zest and juice and simmer 5 minutes. Add fish, cover, and simmer 5 minutes or until potatoes are tender and fish flakes easily. Remove bay leaf and season with pepper.

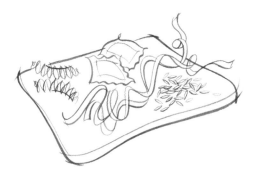

FISH SOUP WITH PEPPER POLENTA STICKS

SERVES 4

Polenta Sticks:

2 red bell peppers, halved lengthwise and seeded

1 teaspoon salt

7 ounces instant polenta

3 tablespoons freshly grated Parmesan cheese

Soup:

3 cups fish stock

1 bay leaf

1 parsley sprig

1 thyme sprig

2 celery stalks, thinly sliced

1 fennel bulb, quartered lengthwise and thinly sliced

2 carrots, halved lengthwise and thinly sliced

Grated zest of 1 lemon

1 shallot, chopped

1 garlic clove, minced

1 fresh red chile, halved and seeded (optional) (wear gloves when handling; chiles burn)

8 ounces monkfish fillet, cut into bite-size chunks

8 ounces skinless white fish fillet, such as cod or haddock, cut into bite-size chunks

Salt and black pepper

Fennel leaves or fresh dill

Quality fish stock provides the base for this lovely fish soup that goes well with polenta sticks.

1 For polenta sticks, preheat grill to high. Place pepper halves on grill rack, cut sides down, and grill until skin is charred. Transfer to brown paper bag until cool enough to handle, about 15 minutes. Peel peppers and cut lengthwise into 1/4-inch-wide strips. Set aside.

2 Cook polenta with salt according to package directions, stirring constantly, until thick. Sprinkle a plastic cutting board or tray with water and turn polenta out onto it. Using a spatula, spread polenta into a rectangle about 1/2 inch thick. Arrange pepper strips diagonally on top, gently pressing into polenta. Trim and neaten edges of rectangle with a sharp knife. Let cool.

3 Preheat oven to 400°F and grease a baking sheet. Sprinkle cheese over polenta and cut it into 16 sticks. Transfer to baking sheet and bake 15 minutes or until cheese is melted and bubbling. Cool 2 minutes on baking sheet, then transfer sticks to a wire rack and cool completely.

4 For soup, pour stock into a saucepan. Tie bay leaf, parsley, and thyme together into a bouquet garni, and add to pan with celery, fennel, carrots, lemon zest, shallot, garlic, and chile, if desired. Bring to boil, reduce heat, and simmer, covered, 5 minutes or until vegetables are just tender. Remove from heat and let stand, covered, 10 minutes.

5 Remove bouquet garni and chile halves, then return liquid to boil. Reduce heat, add monkfish and white fish and simmer, uncovered, 4 minutes or until fish chunks are opaque and flake easily. Season to taste with salt and pepper.

6 Transfer polenta sticks to serving plate. Ladle soup into warmed bowls and sprinkle with fennel leaves or dill.

CHUNKY FISH SOUP

This is an elegantly simple soup. Cubes of fresh white fish are flavored with herbs, tomatoes, and wine, and a little cream gives the soup richness.

SERVES 4 TO 6

2 1/2 cups fish stock

2 tablespoons olive oil

1 medium onion, finely chopped

1 medium fennel bulb, finely chopped

2/3 cup dry white wine or vermouth

1 can (19 ounces) chopped tomatoes

1 bay leaf

1 teaspoon sugar

Salt and black pepper

1 pound firm fish fillets, such as cod
    or scrod, cut into 1-inch cubes

3 or 4 parsley sprigs, chopped

1 tablespoon cornstarch

2 tablespoons milk

3 tablespoons whipping cream

Fennel tops

1 In a large saucepan over medium heat, heat stock. In another large saucepan over medium heat, heat oil. Add onion and fennel and sauté 5 minutes or until softened.

2 Pour off any surplus oil from saucepan, then add warm stock, wine, tomatoes, bay leaf, sugar, salt, and pepper. Bring to boil, reduce heat, and simmer, covered, 10 minutes. Add fish and parsley and simmer, covered, 5 minutes.

3 In a small bowl, blend cornstarch and milk. When fish is tender, remove bay leaf, stir in cornstarch mixture, and simmer until soup thickens slightly. Stir in cream and simmer 2 minutes to heat through. Garnish with fennel and parsley.

MEDITERRANEAN FISH SOUP

Garlic, bell pepper, fennel, bay leaf, and tomatoes give this lively fish soup its Mediterranean flavor.

SERVES 8

1 tablespoon olive or canola oil

2 garlic cloves, finely chopped

1 large onion, coarsely chopped

2 fennel bulbs or celery stalks, coarsely
    chopped

1 large red bell pepper, cored, seeded,
    and diced

6 cups fish stock

2 cups canned crushed tomatoes

1 bay leaf

1 pound firm white fish, such as flounder, cod,
    grouper, or perch, cut into 2-inch pieces

8 ounces medium shrimp, peeled and
    deveined

1/8 teaspoon salt

1/8 teaspoon black pepper

1 Heat oil in a 4-quart saucepan over medium heat. Add garlic, onion, fennel, and bell pepper and sauté 5 minutes or until softened.

2 Add stock, tomatoes, and bay leaf. Bring to boil, reduce heat, and simmer 25 minutes.

3 Add fish and shrimp, cover, and simmer 4 minutes or until fish flakes easily and shrimp are cooked through. Remove bay leaf and season with salt and pepper.

SPICY FISH SOUP

Salsa packs a punch in this recipe. It's delicious served with slices of oven-fresh bread.

SERVES 8

2 cans (14 1/2 ounces each) low-sodium chicken broth

2/3 cup instant rice

1 1/2 cups salsa

1 package (10 ounces) frozen whole-kernel corn

1 pound frozen cod, thawed and cut into 2-inch pieces

Fresh lime wedges (*optional*)

1 In a large saucepan, bring 2 1/2 cups water, broth, and rice to boil. Reduce heat and simmer, covered, 5 minutes.

2 Add salsa and corn and return to boil. Add fish, then reduce heat and simmer, covered, 5 minutes or until fish flakes easily. Serve with lime wedges, if desired.

COD AND VEGETABLE STEW

This simple fish stew, made with chunks of white, firm-fleshed cod, is a powerhouse of nutrition-rich beta-carotene, B vitamins, selenium, potassium, and magnesium. (Photograph on page 29)

SERVES 4

2 tablespoons olive oil

2 medium onions, chopped

3 cloves garlic, sliced

1 large red bell pepper, cored, seeded, and cut into matchsticks

1 pound sweet potatoes, peeled and cut into 1/2-inch chunks

3/4 teaspoon salt

1/2 teaspoon dried thyme

1 1/2 cups frozen peas

1 cup frozen whole-kernel corn

1 1/2 pounds skinless, boneless cod fillets, cut into bite-size pieces

1 In a large skillet or Dutch oven over medium heat, heat oil. Add onions and garlic and sauté 5 minutes or until onion is golden.

2 Add bell pepper and sweet potatoes and cook, covered, 5 minutes or until sweet potatoes begin to soften. Stir in 1 1/3 cups water, salt, and thyme. Bring to boil, reduce heat, and simmer, covered, 5 minutes or until sweet potatoes are tender. Stir in peas and corn.

3 Place cod on top of vegetables, cover, and simmer 7 minutes or until fish is cooked through and flakes easily.

FISH SOUP WITH SAFFRON

Saffron gives soup a delicate flavor and a bright yellow color.

SERVES 4

Pinch of saffron threads

2 teaspoons extra-virgin olive oil

2 strips bacon, chopped

1/4 pound waxy potatoes, diced

1/4 pound parsnips, diced

2 celery stalks, chopped

1 medium onion, chopped

1 bay leaf

1 strip lemon zest

Salt and black pepper

2 1/2 cups fish stock

8 ounces skinless haddock fillet, cut into bite-size pieces

4 scallions, finely chopped

1 In a small skillet over medium heat, stir saffron until it just begins to give off its aroma. Immediately transfer to a small plate and set aside.

2 In a large nonstick saucepan over medium heat, heat oil. Add bacon and cook, stirring often, 2 minutes. Add potatoes, parsnips, celery, and onion and sauté 1 minute.

3 Add saffron threads, bay leaf, and lemon zest, and season with salt and pepper to taste. Add stock and bring to boil. Reduce heat, partially cover, and simmer, stirring occasionally, 8 minutes or until vegetables are almost tender when pierced with the tip of a knife.

4 Lay haddock on top of vegetables, reduce heat to low, and cover pan tightly. Simmer 7 minutes or until fish flakes easily and vegetables are tender. Remove bay leaf and lemon zest.

5 Ladle into bowls and sprinkle with scallions.

SMOKED HADDOCK SOUP

Modest ingredients make this a delicious and healthy family soup.

SERVES 4 TO 6

2 1/2 cups fish, chicken, or vegetable stock
2 tablespoons extra-virgin olive oil
1 medium onion, chopped
5 medium leeks, sliced
1 can (19 ounces) flageolet beans, undrained
1 pound undyed smoked haddock, skinned, boned, and cut into pieces
Black pepper
Small handful fresh parsley, chopped
4-6 tablespoons whipping cream (*optional*)

1 Heat stock in a medium saucepan over medium heat.

2 Heat oil in another medium saucepan over medium heat. Add onion and leeks and sauté 5 minutes. Add warm stock, bring to boil, reduce heat, and simmer, covered, 5 minutes.

3 Add beans to pan and mash roughly. Return to boil, reduce heat, and simmer, covered, 3 minutes. Add fish and cook 5 minutes or until flesh becomes opaque and flakes easily.

4 Season to taste with pepper (the smoked fish should provide enough salt). Sprinkle with parsley and swirl a spoonful of whipping cream into each bowl, if desired.

MONKFISH RAGOUT

Monkfish retains its shape, texture, and flavor in a stew, making it a favorite fish in European kitchens. (Photograph on page 31)

SERVES 4

1 pound trimmed monkfish
Salt and black pepper
3 tablespoons olive oil
1 small onion, chopped
2 garlic cloves, minced
1 pound tomatoes, peeled, cored, seeded, and chopped
1/3 cup white wine or vermouth
1 tarragon sprig, rinsed, dried, and stripped
Grated zest of 1 lemon
2 tablespoons whipping cream

1 Cut fish into cubes and season lightly with salt and pepper. In a skillet over high heat, heat oil and fry half the fish 2 minutes on each side or until it turns white and looks cooked on the outside. Remove and set aside. Fry the second batch of fish and set aside.

2 Reduce heat to medium, add onion and garlic, and sauté 3 minutes or until softened. Add tomatoes and wine and increase heat. Add tarragon and lemon zest, bring to rapid boil, and boil 5 minutes.

3 Return fish to pan and stir in whipping cream. Reduce heat and simmer 5 minutes or until fish is cooked through.

BROCCOLI SOUP WITH SALMON CAKES

Salmon goes well with broccoli and watercress, both in flavor and color. Here the fish is combined with potato and dill in miniature cakes that are delicious served in this fresh, green vegetable soup.

SERVES 4

Salmon Cakes:
1 1/2 pounds all-purpose potatoes, peeled and cut into cubes
1 salmon fillet (about 10 ounces)
1 cup low-fat (1%) milk
3 scallions, sliced
2 tablespoons chopped fresh dill
Grated zest of 1 lemon
Salt and black pepper
2 ounces semolina
3 tablespoons sunflower oil

Soup:
2 tablespoons butter
1 potato, peeled and cut into cubes
2 broccoli stalks, coarsely chopped
1 large leek, sliced
1 large bunch watercress
3 1/2 cups vegetable stock
Salt and black pepper
Watercress leaves
Finely shredded lemon zest

1 For salmon cakes, add potatoes to a saucepan of boiling water and cook about 10 minutes or until tender. Drain and mash until smooth.

2 Meanwhile, place salmon in a sauté pan over medium-low heat. Add milk and heat until bubbles appear around edges and milk is simmering. Cover and simmer 3 minutes or until salmon flakes easily. Remove from pan, reserving milk, and flake, discarding any bones and skin. Add to mashed potatoes and mix in scallions, dill, lemon zest, salt, and pepper.

3 Place semolina on a large plate. Shape salmon mixture into 20 balls, flatten into neat patties, and coat lightly on both sides with semolina. Cover and refrigerate.

4 For soup, melt butter in a large saucepan over medium heat. Add potato, broccoli, and leek and sauté 10 minutes or until softened. Stir in watercress. Add stock and bring to boil, then reduce heat and simmer, covered, 10 minutes or until vegetables are just tender. Let cool slightly, then transfer to a blender or food processor and puree until smooth. Return to pan, stir in reserved milk, and season to taste with salt and pepper. Heat over low heat until simmering.

5 While soup heats, heat 1 1/2 tablespoons oil in a large skillet over medium-high heat. Add half of the cakes and cook 3 minutes on each side or until golden. Transfer to paper towels to drain. Heat remaining oil and cook remaining cakes.

6 Ladle into warm bowls and float 2 or 3 salmon cakes in each. Garnish with watercress and lemon zest and serve with remaining salmon cakes.

SEA BASS AND FENNEL SOUP

This healthful soup combines sea bass, shrimp, and small pasta shells with the full flavors of fennel and leeks.

SERVES 6

2 tablespoons extra-virgin olive oil

1 leek, cleaned and sliced

1 fennel bulb, chopped

10 ounces dry white wine

6 cups fish stock

6 ounces conchigliette or other soup pasta

1 pound sea bass fillets, skinned and cut into chunks

2 tomatoes, peeled, cored, seeded, and chopped

1 tablespoon cornstarch

4 ounces peeled cooked shrimp

1/2 teaspoon chili sauce

2 tablespoons cream

2 tablespoons chopped fresh parsley

Salt and black pepper

1 In a large heavy saucepan over medium heat, heat oil. Add leek and fennel and sauté 5 minutes.

2 Add wine and stock and bring to boil. Add pasta and stir once, then cook 8 minutes or until pasta is almost tender.

3 Stir in fish, tomatoes, and salt and pepper to taste. Reduce heat and simmer 3 minutes or until fish is just firm.

4 Meanwhile, in a small bowl, blend cornstarch and 2 tablespoons water into a smooth paste. Stir into soup and bring to boil, stirring constantly. Add shrimp and simmer 1 minute to heat through.

5 Stir in chili sauce, then cream and parsley.

SHRIMP JAMBALAYA

Always a Louisiana favorite, this shrimp-and-sausage stew is now popular everywhere.

SERVES 4

1 tablespoon olive oil

5 scallions, thinly sliced

3 garlic cloves, minced

1 celery stalk, thinly sliced

1 green bell pepper, cut into 1/2-inch squares

1 red bell pepper, cut into 1/2-inch squares

4 ounces fresh chorizo sausage, thinly sliced

1 1/4 cups rice

1 cup chicken stock

1/2 teaspoon dried thyme

1/2 teaspoon salt

1/2 teaspoon black pepper

1 pound medium shrimp, peeled and deveined

1 Heat oil in a large saucepan over medium heat. Add scallions and garlic and sauté 1 minute or until soft. Add celery and bell peppers and sauté 5 minutes or until peppers are crisp-tender. Stir in chorizo.

2 Add rice, stirring to coat. Add 1 3/4 cups water, stock, thyme, salt, and black pepper, and bring to boil. Reduce heat and simmer, covered, 17 minutes or until rice is tender. Stir in shrimp, cover, and cook 3 minutes or until firm and pink.

CAJUN SHRIMP SOUP

You can cut corn off the cob to make this soup or use canned cream-style corn. Red pepper gives it heat to warm you up on a chilly night.

SERVES 8

2 tablespoons vegetable oil

2 tablespoons all-purpose flour

3 celery stalks, thinly sliced

1 medium onion, chopped

1 small green bell pepper, cored, seeded, and chopped

2 scallions, thinly sliced

2 garlic cloves, minced

4 cups fresh corn or 4 cans (14 3/4 ounces each) cream-style corn

1 can (10 ounces) diced tomatoes and green chiles, undrained

1 bay leaf

1/8 teaspoon white pepper

1/8 teaspoon cayenne pepper

Dash of hot red pepper sauce

3 cups cooked small shrimp

1/3 cup chopped fresh parsley

1 In a heavy saucepan over medium heat, heat oil. Add flour and carefully cook, stirring, 6 to 8 minutes or until golden brown. Reduce heat to low.

2 Add celery, onion, bell pepper, scallions, and garlic and sauté 5 minutes.

3 Add corn, tomatoes, bay leaf, white pepper, cayenne, and red pepper sauce. Bring to boil, reduce heat, and simmer, covered, 30 to 40 minutes. Stir in shrimp and parsley and heat through. Remove bay leaf before serving.

CAJUN SHRIMP AND CORN SOUP

This is another variation on a classic Cajun soup. It calls for a dark roux, the flour-oil basis of many Cajun dishes, and raw shrimp.

SERVES 12

1/2 cup vegetable oil

1/2 cup all-purpose flour

1 small onion, chopped

1/3 cup chopped scallion

2 quarts hot water or chicken stock

2 cans (14 1/2 ounces) stewed tomatoes, cut up

8 cups corn or 4 cans (16 ounces each) whole-kernel corn, drained

2 pounds peeled deveined shrimp

Salt and black pepper

1 In a heavy 8-quart soup pot over medium-high heat, combine oil and flour until smooth. Cook 5 minutes, stirring constantly, to create a roux. Reduce heat to medium and cook, stirring 5 minutes more or until roux is reddish-brown (the color of a penny).

2 Add onion and scallion and cook 5 minutes, stirring often. Increase heat to high and add hot water, tomatoes, and corn. Bring to boil, reduce heat, and simmer, covered, 15 minutes. Add shrimp and simmer 5 minutes or until pink. Season with salt and pepper.

CREOLE SHRIMP SOUP

This delicious soup comes from Louisiana, where shrimp is plentiful, spices are hot, and herbs are pungent.

SERVES 4

1 bag (12 ounces) frozen peeled
    and deveined shrimp
2 tablespoons (1/4 stick) butter
1 medium white onion, chopped
1 medium green bell pepper, cored,
    seeded, and chopped
1 teaspoon fresh parsley, finely chopped
1/2 teaspoon dried thyme, crumbled
1 small bay leaf
1/4 teaspoon hot red pepper sauce
2 1/2 teaspoons all-purpose flour
1 can (14 1/2 or 16 ounces) whole peeled
    tomatoes, undrained, coarsely chopped
Salt

1 Thaw shrimp in colander under cool running water.

2 In a large saucepan over medium heat, melt butter. Add onion and sauté 5 minutes or until soft. Stir in bell pepper, parsley, thyme, bay leaf, and hot pepper sauce and sauté 1 minute. Stir in flour until well mixed.

3 Add 1 1/2 cups water and tomatoes and bring to boil. Reduce heat, cover, and simmer 5 minutes. Add shrimp and simmer, covered, 5 minutes or until cooked through. Remove bay leaf and season to taste with salt.

HOT-AND-SOUR SHRIMP SOUP

The homemade version of this soup, a favorite from Chinese restaurants, is a snap to make and very tasty.

SERVES 5

6 cups fish stock
1 tablespoon finely chopped lemongrass or
    1/2 teaspoon finely grated lime zest
1 garlic clove, minced
1 fresh hot red or green chile, seeded
    and finely chopped (wear gloves when
    handling; chiles burn)
8 ounces mushrooms, sliced
4 ounces medium shrimp, peeled
    and deveined
2 tablespoons rice vinegar or white vinegar
1 tablespoon reduced-sodium soy sauce
1 tablespoon cornstarch
2 scallions, thinly sliced

1 In a large saucepan, combine stock, lemongrass, garlic, and chile. Bring to boil, reduce heat, and simmer, partially covered, about 5 minutes.

2 Stir in mushrooms and shrimp and simmer, partially covered, 3 minutes or until mushrooms are soft and shrimp turn pink.

3 In a small bowl, combine rice vinegar and soy sauce with cornstarch, stirring until smooth. Stir into simmering soup and return to boil. Remove from heat and stir in scallions.

CHINESE SHRIMP SOUP

The exotic ingredients called for in this recipe can be found at Asian markets and in many larger supermarkets.

SERVES 4

Stock:

1 ounce dried shrimp

1-inch piece fresh ginger, peeled and sliced

4 scallions

1 whole star anise

Soup:

6 dried Chinese mushrooms (about 1/2 ounce)

1 teaspoon toasted sesame oil

1-inch piece fresh ginger, peeled and finely chopped

2 scallions, thinly sliced

2 ounces bamboo shoots, cut into fine matchsticks

4 1/2 ounces cooked peeled shrimp

2 tablespoons light soy sauce

1 tablespoon fish sauce

3 ounces fine Chinese egg noodles

Fresh cilantro leaves

1 For stock, combine 6 cups water, shrimp, ginger, scallions, and anise in a large saucepan over high heat. Bring to boil and skim off any scum. Reduce heat, cover, and simmer 1 hour. Strain stock, discarding flavorings.

2 Meanwhile, for soup, rinse mushrooms in cold water and put in a bowl. Pour in boiling water to cover and soak 20 minutes. Drain, then discard tough stalks and cut mushroom caps into thin slices.

3 In a large saucepan over medium heat, heat sesame oil. Add ginger and stir-fry 30 seconds. Add stock and mushrooms, bring to boil, and cook 3 minutes. Add scallions, bamboo shoots, shrimp, soy sauce, and fish sauce and bring to boil. Add noodles and cook 3 minutes or until softened. Ladle into bowls and sprinkle with cilantro.

SHRIMP AND PEA SOUP WITH MINT

Fresh-picked peas in the pod are available in summer, and they should be eaten while they still have their natural sweetness. The high vitamin and fiber content of peas is also found in the pods, and this healthy soup makes the most of both.

SERVES 4

1 1/2 pounds fresh peas, in pods

1 pound cooked, unpeeled shrimp

2 tablespoons vegetable oil

5-6 scallions, trimmed and sliced

1 large garlic clove, coarsely chopped

1-inch piece fresh ginger, peeled and coarsely grated

2 mint sprigs

1 teaspoon black peppercorns

1 large baking potato, peeled and grated

Salt and black pepper

Sugar *(optional)*

Small bunch chives, minced

1 Shell peas into bowl. Reserve and coarsely chop pods. Peel and devein shrimp, reserving shells.

2 Heat oil in a large saucepan over medium heat. Add scallions and sauté 2 minutes or until soft. Add garlic, pea pods, and shrimp shells and cook, stirring frequently, 4 minutes or until shells release a powerful aroma.

3 Add 3 1/2 cups water, ginger, mint, and peppercorns and bring to boil. Skim off any scum, reduce heat, and simmer 15 minutes. Strain through a large sieve into a deep bowl, pressing with a spoon to extract liquid. Discard flavorings.

4 Rinse saucepan and return liquid to it. Add potato and half of peas. Bring to boil, reduce heat, and simmer 5 minutes. Puree, using a handheld blender or a food processor. Return to heat, add remaining peas, and simmer 4 minutes or until tender.

5 Season with salt, pepper, and sugar to taste and transfer to warm soup bowls. Add shrimp and top with chives.

HOUSTON SHRIMP GUMBO

SERVES 8

1/4 cup all-purpose flour
4 thick slices lean bacon, diced
1 pound fresh or frozen okra, sliced
1 cup chopped onion
1 cup chopped celery
1/2 cup chopped green bell pepper
2 garlic cloves, minced
1 can (28 ounces) low-sodium whole
    tomatoes, undrained
3 cups mixed vegetable juice
1 bay leaf
1 teaspoon dried thyme
1/2 teaspoon black pepper
4 pounds medium fresh shrimp,
    peeled and deveined
1 cup (4 ounces) dried shrimp (optional)
1/4 cup chopped fresh parsley
1 teaspoon hot red pepper sauce
4 cups cooked long-grain white rice

1 In a 6-inch skillet, stir flour constantly over medium heat 5 minutes or until brown. Remove from heat.

2 In a 6-quart Dutch oven, cook bacon over medium-high heat 3 minutes or until crisp. Transfer to paper towels. Add okra and sauté 10 minutes. Stir in onion, celery, bell pepper, and garlic and sauté 5 minutes or until tender.

3 Add 3 cups cold water, roux, tomatoes, vegetable juice, bay leaf, thyme, and black pepper. Bring to boil and add shrimp, parsley, and red pepper sauce. Reduce heat and simmer, uncovered, 1 1/2 hours or until gumbo turns rich brown. Remove bay leaf. Ladle gumbo over rice and sprinkle with bacon.

One Texas cook says the secret to good gumbo is to make the roux by browning dry flour and to use both fresh and dried shrimp.

SHRIMP GUMBO

From Louisiana country kitchens straight to yours, this hearty stew has an authentically Cajun blend of flavors.

SERVES 8

6 ounces andouille or chorizo sausage, finely chopped

1/4 cup all-purpose flour

1 package (10 ounces) frozen cut okra

1 large onion, chopped

1 green bell pepper, cored, seeded, and chopped

3 celery stalks, chopped

1 can (48 ounces) low-sodium vegetable juice

2 cans (14 1/2 ounces each) diced Cajun-seasoned tomatoes

1 teaspoon Cajun or Creole seasoning

1 1/2 pounds medium shrimp, peeled and deveined

4 cups cooked long-grain white rice

1 In a small skillet over medium-high heat, cook sausage until brown, about 6 minutes. Transfer to paper towels with a slotted spoon.

2 Stir flour into pan drippings and cook, stirring frequently, over low heat until flour turns deep mahogany brown, about 8 minutes. Remove from heat.

3 Lightly coat a large Dutch oven with nonstick cooking spray. Add okra and sauté until very tender, about 10 minutes. Add onion, bell pepper, and celery and sauté until vegetables begin to soften, about 8 minutes. Stir in roux, coating vegetables well.

4 Stir in vegetable juice, tomatoes, and Cajun seasoning and bring to boil. Reduce heat and simmer, stirring occasionally, 45 minutes. Stir in shrimp and cook until pink, about 3 minutes. Serve in shallow bowls, topped with rice.

SHRIMP AND BARLEY GUMBO

The combination of collard greens, butternut squash, red and green peppers, and tomatoes makes this Louisiana-influenced stew rich in vitamin C, beta-carotene, and calcium.
(Photograph on page 28)

SERVES 4

1 tablespoon olive oil

1 large onion, finely chopped

3 garlic cloves, minced

1 green bell pepper, cored, seeded, and diced

1 red bell pepper, cored, seeded, and diced

1 small butternut squash (about 1 1/2 pounds), peeled and cut into 1/2-inch chunks

1 cup quick-cooking barley

1 1/4 teaspoons hot red pepper sauce

1 teaspoon salt

1/2 teaspoon dried thyme

2 packages (9 ounces each) frozen chopped collard greens

1 cup canned crushed tomatoes

1 pound medium shrimp, peeled and deveined

1 Heat oil in a Dutch oven over medium-low heat. Add onion and garlic and sauté 7 minutes or until onion is tender. Add bell peppers and squash and sauté 5 minutes or until peppers are crisp-tender.

2 Add 3 1/2 cups water, barley, pepper sauce, salt, and thyme and bring to boil. Stir in collards and tomatoes and return to boil. Reduce heat and simmer, covered, 10 minutes or until barley is tender.

3 Place shrimp on top of stew, cover, and simmer 4 minutes or until shrimp are cooked through.

SPICY SHRIMP AND RICE STEW

Here's a quick and healthy stew you can make in the microwave. For sharper flavor, increase the hot red pepper sauce to 3/4 teaspoon.

SERVES 4

1 large yellow onion, coarsely chopped

1 small green bell pepper, cored, seeded, and coarsely chopped

2 garlic cloves, minced

2 tablespoons olive oil

1 can (14 1/2 ounces) no-salt-added stewed tomatoes, undrained

1 cup chicken stock

1 package (10 ounces) frozen sliced okra

1/2 teaspoon hot red pepper sauce

1/4 teaspoon dried oregano, crumbled

1 pound medium shrimp, peeled and deveined

1 cup quick-cooking white rice

2 tablespoons minced fresh parsley

1 teaspoon lemon juice

1 In an ungreased 2 1/2-quart microwavable baking dish with a lid, combine onion, pepper, garlic, and oil. Cover and microwave on high 4 to 5 minutes or until onion is glassy, stirring midway.

2 Break up tomatoes with a fork and stir into baking dish. Add stock, okra, red pepper sauce, and oregano. Cover and microwave 12 minutes or until okra is tender, stirring every 4 minutes. Add shrimp, cover, and microwave 2 1/2 to 3 minutes or until cooked through and pink.

3 Add rice and stir until well moistened. Cover and microwave 2 minutes. Let stand, covered, in microwave oven 3 minutes, then stir in parsley and lemon juice.

FRENCH SHRIMP STEW

Stews from the Mediterranean basin are frequently accented with the licorice-like taste of fennel. You can substitute celery, if necessary.

SERVES 4

1 red bell pepper, cored, seeded, and cut lengthwise into flat panels

1/2 teaspoon hot red pepper sauce

1 tablespoon olive oil

1 small onion, finely chopped

2 garlic cloves, minced

1 small trimmed fennel bulb or 1 large celery stalk, cut into 1/2-inch pieces

2/3 cup canned low-sodium chopped tomatoes, undrained

1/2 cup chicken stock

3/4 teaspoon grated orange zest

1/2 teaspoon salt

1 pound medium shrimp, peeled and deveined

4 slices French or Italian bread, toasted

1 Preheat broiler. Place bell pepper pieces skin-side up on broiler rack and broil 4 inches from heat 12 minutes or until skin is blackened. When peppers are cool enough to handle, peel and transfer to a food processor or blender. Add hot pepper sauce and 1 teaspoon oil and puree.

2 Meanwhile, in a large nonstick skillet, heat remaining oil over medium heat. Add onion and garlic and sauté 5 minutes or until soft. Add fennel and cook 7 minutes or until tender. Stir in tomatoes, stock, orange zest, and salt. Bring to boil, reduce heat, and simmer, covered, 5 minutes.

3 Add shrimp and cook 4 minutes or until just cooked through. Stir roasted pepper puree into skillet. Serve with toast.

TOMATO AND CRAB SOUP

Forget about time-consuming crab preparation. Just buy cooked lump crabmeat to make this easy luxury soup.

SERVES 4

1 tablespoon butter

2 teaspoons extra-virgin olive oil

1 large onion, finely chopped

1 pound all-purpose potatoes, peeled and finely diced

3/4 pound ripe tomatoes, peeled, cored, seeded, and diced

2 anchovy fillets, drained and chopped

2 cups fish stock

1 glass dry white wine

1 tablespoon tomato paste

Salt and black pepper

1 pound cooked lump crabmeat

3/4 cup reduced-fat (2%) milk

Garnishes:

3 tablespoons sour cream

2 anchovy fillets, drained and cut into thin strips

Paprika

1 In a large saucepan over medium heat, melt butter and heat oil. Add onion and potatoes and sauté 5 minutes or until onion is softened.

2 Stir in tomatoes and anchovies. Add stock, wine, and tomato paste. Season with salt and pepper to taste. Bring to boil, then reduce heat and simmer, covered, 15 minutes, stirring occasionally.

3 Add three-quarters of crabmeat to pan and stir in milk. Cover and heat through.

4 Ladle soup into bowls and swirl sour cream over top. Garnish with remaining crabmeat, anchovies, and paprika.

EAST COAST CRAB SOUP

Here's a quick and absolutely wonderful crab soup that will make any meal a special occasion.

SERVES 4

1/4 cup (1/2 stick) butter

3 tablespoons finely chopped onion

1 garlic clove, minced

1/4 cup all-purpose flour

1/2 teaspoon salt

1/8 teaspoon black pepper

2 1/2 cups half-and-half

2 cups tomato juice

1/4 teaspoon Worcestershire sauce

1/4 teaspoon ground savory

Dash of hot red pepper sauce

2 cans (6 ounces each) lump crabmeat, drained and rinsed

Sour cream (*optional*)

Minced fresh parsley (*optional*)

1 In a 2-quart saucepan over medium heat, melt butter. Add onion and garlic and sauté 3 minutes or until onion is tender. Stir in flour, salt, and pepper and stir until bubbling.

2 Gradually add half-and-half, tomato juice, Worcestershire sauce, savory, and red pepper sauce. Bring to boil and cook, stirring constantly, until thick and smooth. Add crab and heat through. Garnish each serving with sour cream and parsley, if desired.

VEGETABLE CRAB SOUP

This tasty crab soup takes advantage of packaged ingredients, so it comes to the table quickly.

SERVES 8

1 can (19 ounces) ready-to-serve New England clam chowder

1 can (11 ounces) condensed cheddar cheese soup

3 cups half-and-half

1/4 cup white wine or chicken broth

1 tablespoon Worcestershire sauce

1 package (16 ounces) frozen stir-fry vegetables

2 cans (6 ounces each) crabmeat, drained, flaked, and cartilage removed

1 medium tomato, cored, seeded, and chopped

2/3 cup shredded cheddar cheese

2 tablespoons minced fresh parsley

1/2 teaspoon black pepper

1 In a large saucepan, combine chowder, soup, half-and-half, wine, and Worcestershire sauce and bring to boil. Stir in vegetables and return to boil. Reduce heat, cover, and simmer, 6 minutes or until vegetables are crisp-tender.

2 Stir in crab, tomato, cheese, parsley, and pepper. Cook, stirring, until heated through.

CRAB AND BLACK MUSHROOM SOUP

Black mushrooms can be found in the Asian foods section of most supermarkets and in specialty food stores.

SERVES 4

1/2 cup long-grain white or brown rice

1 package (1 ounce) dried Chinese black mushrooms

2 tablespoons vegetable oil

3 scallions with tops, finely chopped

1 tablespoon minced fresh ginger

8 ounces fresh or thawed and drained frozen crabmeat, picked over

1/4 teaspoon salt

1/8 teaspoon black pepper

4 cups chicken stock

2 tablespoons soy sauce

1 tablespoon dry sherry

1 cup frozen green peas, thawed

2 tablespoons cornstarch blended with 1/4 cup cold water

2 large eggs beaten with a pinch of salt

1 teaspoon Oriental sesame oil, or to taste

4 scallion tops, thinly sliced (*optional*)

1 Cook rice according to package directions, then drain and set aside. Meanwhile, in a small heatproof bowl, soak mushrooms in 1 cup boiling water 15 minutes. Drain, reserving soaking water, and slice mushrooms, discarding stems.

2 In a wok or large saucepan over medium-high heat, heat oil. Add scallions and ginger and stir-fry 30 seconds. Add crab, mushrooms, salt, and pepper and stir-fry 1 minute.

3 Add stock, soy sauce, sherry, and reserved soaking water and bring to boil. Add peas, reduce heat, and simmer, uncovered, about 3 minutes or until tender.

4 Increase heat to high and bring to boil. Blend in cornstarch mixture, reduce heat, and simmer, stirring constantly, about 1 minute or until slightly thick. Remove from heat and slowly add eggs in a thin stream. Stir in sesame oil. Divide reserved rice among 4 bowls, ladle in soup, and sprinkle with scallion tops, if desired.

CRAB NOODLE SOUP

You can quickly kick packaged soup up to the next level with some snow peas and imitation crabmeat.

SERVES 4

2 packages (3 ounces) chicken-flavored
    ramen noodle soup
1 package (6 ounces) frozen snow peas
8 ounces imitation crabmeat

1 In a large saucepan, bring 4 1/2 cups water and seasoning from one package noodle soup to boil. Add noodles from both packages and snow peas.

2 Cook, stirring frequently, 3 minutes or until noodles are tender and snow peas are thawed. Add crab and cook until just heated through.

MUSSELS IN BROTH

There is no more delightful start to any meal than fresh mussels cooked in this aromatic and spicy broth. (Photograph on page 4)

SERVES 4

4 1/2 pounds mussels
1 tablespoon olive oil
1 large onion, sliced
1 garlic clove, minced
3/4-inch piece fresh ginger, peeled
    and chopped
Pinch of saffron threads
1/2 cup dry cider
1/2 cup fish stock
1 tablespoon fresh dill, minced
Salt and black pepper
1 tablespoon fresh parsley, minced

1 Wash mussels in a few changes of cold water, scrubbing to remove any beards attached to shells. Discard damaged ones and those with open shells that do not close when tapped. Drain.

2 Heat oil in a soup pot or large saucepan over medium-low heat. Add onion and garlic and sauté 5 minutes or until translucent. Add ginger and sauté 3 minutes without browning.

3 Add saffron, cider, stock, dill, and salt and pepper to taste. Bring to boil and add mussels, then cover and cook 4 minutes, shaking pan occasionally, or until shells open. Transfer to serving bowls, discarding any that did not open. Stir parsley into broth and spoon broth over mussels.

BILLI BI

4 pounds mussels, scrubbed and
    beards removed

1 tablespoon dry mustard

1 1/2 cups dry white wine, fish stock,
    or clam juice

1/3 cup finely chopped washed leeks,
    white parts only

2 tablespoons chopped fresh parsley

1 1/2 teaspoons fresh thyme or
    1/2 teaspoon dried thyme

1 bay leaf

2 cups light cream or whole milk

2 cups whole milk

1/4 teaspoon salt

1/4 teaspoon turmeric

1/8 teaspoon cayenne pepper

1 large egg yolk

1 tablespoon cornstarch

2 tablespoons fresh lemon juice

Paprika to taste

1 Discard mussels with broken shells and those that do not close when tapped. Place in a large bowl, cover with cold water, and stir in mustard, which helps them disgorge any sand. Let stand 15 minutes. Drain and rinse with cold running water.

2 In a covered 6-quart Dutch oven, bring mussels, wine, leeks, parsley, thyme, and bay leaf to boil over high heat. Reduce heat and simmer, covered, 5 minutes or until mussels open (discard any that do not open).

3 Line a large strainer or colander with cheesecloth and place over a large heat-resistant bowl. Pour broth mixture through strainer, catching mussels. Remove bay leaf. Shuck mussels and cover to keep warm; discard shells. Return broth to Dutch oven and stir in 1 1/2 cups cream, milk, salt, turmeric, and cayenne. Bring just to a simmer over medium heat, stirring often.

4 Meanwhile, in a medium bowl, whisk egg yolk and cornstarch with remaining 1/2 cup cream. Whisk in about 1 cup hot soup, then, whisking constantly, pour in yolk mixture. Continue cooking, stirring constantly, 5 minutes or until soup thickens slightly (do not boil). Season with lemon juice. Divide mussels among 6 large, warm soup bowls, ladle in soup, and sprinkle with paprika.

This recipe substitutes whole milk and light cream for the heavy cream used traditionally. The resulting soup is lower in fat, yet still plenty creamy.

MUSSEL AND FENNEL SOUP

The delicate anise flavor of fennel complements mineral-rich mussels in this tasty broth.

SERVES 4

4 tablespoons olive oil
1 fennel bulb, chopped
2 leeks, thinly sliced
1 large garlic clove, minced
1 cup medium-dry white wine
1 cup fish stock
2 1/4 pounds mussels
1/2 cup low-fat *crème fraîche* or
    sour cream
Black pepper
2 tablespoons chopped parsley

1 In a large saucepan over medium heat, heat oil. Add fennel, leeks, and garlic and sauté 5 minutes or until leeks wilt. Add wine and stock and remove from heat.

2 Scrub mussels if necessary, scraping off barnacles and pulling away beards. Discard any with damaged shells and any that do not close when tapped sharply.

3 Return pan to heat and bring broth to boil. Add mussels and cook, covered, over high heat 3 minutes or until shells open, shaking pan from time to time.

4 Using a slotted spoon, transfer mussels to a bowl. Discard any that did not open.

5 Shuck mussels, leaving a few in for garnish, if desired. Return to broth and heat over low heat. Whisk in *crème fraîche* and season to taste with pepper. Transfer to warm bowls and sprinkle with parsley.

THAI-STYLE MUSSEL SOUP

Pomegranate molasses, a sweet and tangy Middle Eastern condiment, is available in specialty food stores. If you can't find it, substitute 2 tablespoons currant jelly and increase lime juice to 3 tablespoons.

SERVES 4

3 tablespoons flaked coconut
3/4 cup boiling water
2 teaspoons olive oil
5 scallions, thinly sliced
3 garlic cloves, minced
2 tablespoons minced fresh ginger
1/2 cup canned crushed tomatoes
1 tablespoon reduced-sodium soy sauce
2 tablespoons pomegranate molasses
1/2 cup chopped fresh cilantro
1/2 teaspoon salt
3 pounds mussels, scrubbed and beards
    removed
2 tablespoons fresh lime juice

1 Combine coconut and boiling water in a small bowl. Let stand 30 minutes or until coconut is very soft and water tastes of coconut. Strain into another small bowl, pressing coconut to extract liquid. Discard solids.

2 In a large saucepan over low heat, heat oil. Add scallions, garlic, and ginger and sauté 3 minutes or until ginger is tender. Add coconut water, tomatoes, soy sauce, molasses, cilantro, and salt and bring to boil.

3 Add mussels, cover, and boil 5 minutes or until mussels open (discard any that do not open). With a slotted spoon, divide mussels among 4 large bowls. Stir lime juice into broth and spoon broth over mussels.

HEARTY MUSSEL SOUP

Potatoes complement mussels and make this soup more filling than many mussel soups. (Photograph on page 28)

SERVES 4

2 1/4 pounds mussels, scrubbed

2 tablespoons extra-virgin olive oil

1 onion, finely chopped

2 garlic cloves, minced

2 leeks, thinly sliced

3 celery stalks, thinly sliced

2 carrots, peeled and diced

1 pound all-purpose potatoes, peeled and cut into small cubes

3 cups vegetable stock

1/2 cup dry white wine

1 tablespoon lemon juice

1 bay leaf

1 thyme sprig

4 tablespoons fresh parsley, chopped

2 tablespoons fresh chives, snipped

Salt and black pepper

1 Discard mussels with broken shells and those that do not close when tapped. Put wet mussels into a clean saucepan and cover tightly (do not add water). Cook over medium heat 4 minutes or until mussels open, shaking pan occasionally.

2 Drain, reserving juices. Reserve a few mussels in shells for garnish, then shuck remainder and set aside. Discard shells and unopened mussels. Rinse out pan.

3 Add oil and heat over medium heat. Add onion, garlic, leeks, celery, and carrots and sauté 5 minutes or until vegetables are soft. Add potatoes, stock, wine, reserved juices, lemon juice, bay leaf, thyme, and salt and pepper to taste. Bring to boil, reduce heat, and simmer, covered, 20 minutes or until vegetables are tender.

4 Remove bay leaf and thyme. Add shelled mussels, parsley, and chives and heat 1 minute (do not boil).

5 Ladle soup into warm bowls and garnish with reserved mussels.

CLASSIC OYSTER STEW

If you love seafood, this will be a favorite recipe—rich and delicious to eat and quick and easy to make.

SERVES 4

1 large yellow onion, finely chopped

1/4 cup low-sodium chicken broth

1 pint shucked oysters, undrained

1/2 teaspoon salt

1/8 teaspoon cayenne pepper

1 3/4 cups low-fat (1%) milk

1 cup half-and-half

1/2 teaspoon low-sodium Worcestershire sauce *(optional)*

1 In a large saucepan over medium heat, combine onion and broth. Bring to boil, reduce heat and simmer, covered, 5 minutes or until onion is tender. Add oysters, salt, and cayenne. Cook 3 minutes or until oysters are plump and opaque.

2 Add milk, half-and-half, and Worcestershire sauce, if desired. Cook over medium heat, stirring often, until heated through.

CREAMY OYSTER STEW

When you shuck oysters, work over a bowl to catch the liquid. You'll need a half cup of this "liquor" for the stew. If you have too little liquid, add some clam juice.

SERVES 4

4 large slices (2 ounces) unseeded Italian bread
2 teaspoons unsalted butter
3 cups low-fat (1%) milk
1/4 cup all-purpose flour
3/4 teaspoon salt
1/4 teaspoon cayenne pepper
24 oysters, shucked, and liquor reserved
1/4 cup chopped fresh parsley

1 Toast bread, spread with butter, and set aside.

2 In a large saucepan over low heat, whisk milk into flour until smooth. Add salt and cayenne and cook, stirring frequently, 3 minutes or until slightly thickened and no floury taste remains.

3 Stir in 1/2 cup reserved oyster liquor. Bring to a simmer and add oysters. Cook 3 minutes, covered, just until edges of oysters begin to curl. Stir in parsley.

4 Spoon stew into individual soup bowls and serve with buttered toast.

NEW YEAR'S OYSTER STEW

This dish greets the New Year—and your friends—with delicious good cheer.

SERVES 12

1/4 cup butter or margarine
3 leeks, white part only, chopped
2 all-purpose potatoes, peeled and diced
3 chicken bouillon cubes
2 cups milk
2 cups half-and-half
1/4 teaspoon cayenne pepper
4 cans (16 ounces each) oysters, drained
Salt and black pepper
Chopped fresh parsley

1 In a large soup pot or Dutch oven over medium heat, melt butter and leeks and sauté 10 minutes or until tender.

2 Add 2 cups water, potatoes, and bouillon and bring to boil. Reduce heat and simmer, covered, 20 minutes or until potatoes are tender.

3 Allow mixture to cool, then transfer to a blender or food processor and puree. Return to pot and add milk, half-and-half, cayenne, and oysters. Heat slowly to serving temperature (do not boil). Season with salt and pepper and garnish with parsley.

CAJUN CRAYFISH ÉTOUFFÉE

SERVES 4

12 ounces peeled fresh or thawed frozen crayfish tails or large shrimp

3 tablespoons all-purpose flour

3 tablespoons olive or vegetable oil

1 large yellow onion, chopped

1 medium green bell pepper, cored, seeded, and chopped

2 celery stalks, sliced

4 large scallions with tops, sliced

3 garlic cloves, minced

1/2 teaspoon salt

1/2 teaspoon hot red pepper sauce

4 medium tomatoes, peeled and chopped

1 Rinse crayfish and pat dry. In a large heavy saucepan over medium heat, stir together flour and oil until smooth. Cook, stirring constantly, 5 minutes or until roux is dark brown.

2 Add onion, bell pepper, celery, scallions, garlic, salt, and hot pepper sauce. Sauté 8 minutes or until vegetables are just tender. Gradually stir in tomatoes. Bring to boil and add crayfish. Reduce heat and simmer, covered, stirring occasionally, 5 minutes or just until crayfish are opaque. Serve with hot cooked rice.

Crayfish are freshwater shellfish that taste like slightly sweet shrimp. If crayfish aren't available, substitute shrimp.

Chowders and Cheese SOUPS

CHOWDERS AND CHEESE SOUPS

recipe list

 EASY: 10 minutes to prepare

QUICK: Ready to eat in 30 minutes

ONE-DISH: contains protein, vegetables, and good carbohydrates (beans, whole-grains, etc.) for a complete healthy meal

HEALTHY: High in nutrients, low in bad fats and empty carbohydrates

SLOW COOKER: Easily adapted for slow cooker by cutting down on liquids

CHOWDERS AND CHEESE SOUPS

recipe list CONTINUED

SEAFOOD CHOWDER WITH MUSHROOMS

The original recipe for Seafood Chowder with Mushrooms won a prize at the Seafood Festival in Charlestown, Rhode Island. This lighter version is also a winner.

SERVES 6

3 tablespoons unsalted butter

2 tablespoons all-purpose flour

4 ounces mushrooms, sliced (1 1/4 cups)

1/3 cup finely chopped white onion

1 1/2 cups low-fat (1%) milk

12 ounces fresh, canned, or thawed frozen crabmeat, picked over for bits of shell

8 ounces medium fresh or thawed frozen shrimp, shelled and deveined, halved

1 cup regular or fat-free half-and-half

1/4 teaspoon salt

1/4 teaspoon white pepper

1/4 cup chopped parsley

3 tablespoons dry sherry *(optional)*

1 In a large heavy saucepan, melt butter over medium heat. Stir in flour and cook, stirring constantly, until bubbly. Add mushrooms and onion and sauté 5 minutes or until tender. Add milk, reduce heat, and simmer, uncovered, 10 minutes.

2 Stir in crabmeat, shrimp, and half-and-half. Simmer 5 minutes longer or just until shrimp are cooked through. Season with salt and pepper. Stir in parsley, plus sherry, if desired. (This recipe may easily be doubled for parties.)

MANHATTAN SEAFOOD CHOWDER

Manhattan-style chowder, made with tomatoes, is lower in fat and calories than cream-based New England chowders.

SERVES 4

1 onion, finely chopped

1/2 cup dry white wine or chicken stock

1 dozen littleneck clams, well scrubbed

3/4 pound all-purpose potatoes, peeled and cut into 1/2-inch cubes

1 red bell pepper, cut into 1/2-inch squares

1 celery stalk, cut into 1/4-inch dice

3 cups low-sodium canned tomatoes, chopped, undrained

1 cup chicken stock

1/2 teaspoon dried thyme

1/2 teaspoon salt

1 pound cod steak, cut into 1/2-inch cubes

1 In a Dutch oven or flameproof casserole, combine onion, wine, and clams. Bring to boil over medium heat, cover, and cook 5 minutes or until clams have opened. Remove clams from pan (discard any that have not opened). Remove clam meat from shells and discard shells.

2 Add potatoes, bell pepper, celery, and 1 cup water to pan and bring to boil. Reduce heat and simmer, covered, 5 minutes. Add tomatoes and their juice, stock, thyme, and salt, and return to boil. Reduce heat and simmer, covered, 15 minutes or until potatoes are tender.

3 Add cod to pan, cover, and cook 5 minutes or until fish is almost cooked through. Return clams to pan and cook just until heated through.

SLOW-COOK
SEAFOOD CHOWDER

This is a special dish that almost makes itself. It's great for busy holidays.

SERVES 8

1 can (10 3/4 ounces) condensed
    cream of potato soup
1 can (10 3/4 ounces) condensed
    cream of mushroom soup
2 1/2 cups milk
4 medium carrots, finely chopped
2 medium potatoes, peeled and cut into
    1/4-inch cubes
1 large onion, finely chopped
2 celery stalks, finely chopped
1 can (6 1/2 ounces) chopped clams, drained
1 can (6 ounces) medium shrimp, drained
4 ounces imitation crabmeat, flaked
5 bacon strips, cooked and crumbled

1 In a slow cooker, combine potato soup, mushroom soup, and milk. Stir in carrots, potatoes, onion, and celery. Cover and cook on low 4 to 5 hours.

2 Stir in clams, shrimp, and crab. Cover and cook until heated through, about 20 minutes. Garnish each serving with bacon.

CHUNKY SEAFOOD CHOWDER

This creamy chowder is brimming with crab, tender potatoes, clams, and onion.

SERVES 8

2 tablespoons butter
1 medium onion, chopped
2 pints half-and-half
1 can (10 3/4 ounces) condensed
    New England clam chowder

3 medium potatoes, peeled and cut into cubes
1 teaspoon salt
1/4 teaspoon white pepper
1 package (8 ounces) imitation
    crabmeat, flaked

1 In a saucepan over medium-low heat, melt butter. Add onion and sauté until tender.

2 Add half-and-half and canned chowder and bring to boil. Stir in potatoes, salt, and pepper. Reduce heat and simmer, uncovered, 15 minutes or until potatoes are tender. Stir in crab and heat through.

SEAFOOD BISQUE

This rich, creamy bisque can be made in no time—to the delight of family and guests.

SERVES 10

2 cans (10 3/4 ounces each) condensed
    cream of mushroom soup
1 can (10 3/4 ounces) condensed
    cream of celery soup
2 2/3 cups milk
4 scallions, chopped
1/2 cup finely chopped celery
1 garlic clove, minced
1 teaspoon Worcestershire sauce
1/4 teaspoon hot red pepper sauce
1 1/2 pounds medium shrimp,
    peeled and deveined
1 can (6 ounces) crabmeat, drained, flaked,
    and cartilage removed
1 jar (4 1/2 ounces) whole mushrooms, drained
3 tablespoons Madeira wine or chicken broth
1/2 teaspoon salt
1/2 teaspoon black pepper
Minced fresh parsley

1 In a Dutch oven or soup pot, combine mushroom soup, celery soup, milk, scallions, celery, garlic, Worcestershire sauce, and red pepper sauce. Bring to boil.

2 Reduce heat and add shrimp, crab, and mushrooms. Simmer, uncovered, 10 minutes. Stir in wine, salt, and pepper and cook 2 to 3 minutes. Garnish with parsley.

MEDITERRANEAN SEAFOOD CHOWDER

This creamy chowder combines shrimp and cod, a popular combination with just about everybody.

SERVES 10

2 tablespoons olive oil

1 1/2 cups chopped seeded yellow
    or red bell peppers

1 large onion, quartered and thinly sliced

3 garlic cloves, minced

1 can (28 ounces) crushed tomatoes

1 can (14 1/2 ounces) chicken broth

1 cup long-grain rice

1/2 cup white wine or chicken broth

1/2 teaspoon dried thyme

1/2 teaspoon dried basil

1/2 teaspoon salt

1/8 teaspoon crushed red pepper flakes

8 ounces medium shrimp,
    peeled and deveined

8 ounces cod fillets, cut into pieces

1 In a Dutch oven or soup pot over medium heat, heat oil. Add peppers, onion, and garlic and sauté 4 minutes or until tender.

2 Add tomatoes, 2 1/4 cups water, broth, rice, wine, thyme, basil, salt, and red pepper flakes. Bring to boil, reduce heat, and simmer, covered, 15 minutes or until rice is tender.

3 Add shrimp and cod. Cover and simmer 4 minutes or until shrimp is pink and fish flakes easily with a fork.

QUICK FISH CHOWDER WITH TOMATO AND FENNEL

An easy dish to make and an easy dish to enjoy, this chowder has the barest hint of licorice from the fennel seed. (Photograph on page 28)

SERVES 4

1 tablespoon olive oil

1 medium onion, coarsely chopped

2 garlic cloves, minced

1 teaspoon fennel seed

2 cups bottled clam juice

1 can (14 1/2 ounces) stewed tomatoes

1/2 cup dry white wine

1/2 pound red potatoes, unpeeled,
    cut into small dice

1 pound firm fish fillets, such as cod or scrod,
    cut into 8 pieces

1/4 cup coarsely chopped parsley

1 In a large saucepan over medium-high heat, heat oil. Add onion and garlic. Sauté 5 minutes or until softened. Add fennel seed. Sauté 30 seconds. Add clam juice, tomatoes, wine, and potatoes. Simmer, uncovered, 15 minutes or until potatoes are tender.

2 Add fish and parsley. Bring to a gentle boil. Remove from heat and serve.

GONE FISHIN' CHOWDER

This classic chowder is a wonderful way to serve up a day's catch.

SERVES 12

4 bacon strips

1 cup chopped onion

1 teaspoon dried thyme

3 cups diced peeled potatoes

1 1/2 cups coarsely chopped carrots

1/2 cup chopped celery

2 teaspoons salt *(optional)*

1/4 teaspoon black pepper

1 can (28 ounces) diced tomatoes, undrained

1 tablespoon parsley flakes

1 1/2 cups cubed whitefish

1 In a Dutch oven or soup pot over medium heat, cook bacon until crisp. Crumble onto paper towels and set aside. Drain pot, reserving 1 teaspoon drippings. Return drippings to pot, add onion and thyme, and sauté over medium heat.

2 Add 5 cups water, potatoes, carrots, celery, salt, if desired, and pepper. Bring to boil, reduce heat, and simmer, covered, 20 minutes or until vegetables are tender. Add tomatoes, parsley, bacon, and fish and simmer 10 minutes or until fish flakes easily with a fork.

FISH BISQUE

A simple white-fleshed fish like orange roughy can be the basis for a lovely first-course or lunch soup.

SERVES 4

1 large yellow onion, finely chopped

1 celery stalk, finely chopped

1/4 cup low-sodium chicken broth

2 3/4 cups low-fat (1%) milk

1 cup half-and-half

3 tablespoons all-purpose flour

1/2 teaspoon salt

1/2 teaspoon ground mace

1/4 teaspoon white or black pepper

8 ounces fresh or thawed frozen orange roughy fillets, cut into 3/4-inch pieces

1/4 cup dry sherry, dry white wine, or half-and-half

1 In a large saucepan over medium heat, combine onion, celery, and broth. Bring to boil, reduce heat, and simmer, covered, until vegetables are tender, about 5 minutes. Stir in milk.

2 In a small bowl, whisk together half-and-half, flour, salt, mace, and pepper. Stir into pan and cook, stirring constantly, over medium heat until thickened and bubbling, about 10 minutes. Stir in fish and bring to boil. Reduce heat and simmer, uncovered, until fish flakes easily with a fork, 3 to 5 minutes. Stir in sherry.

SPICY TOMATO FISH CHOWDER

Here is a speedy main dish that is hearty and healthy. All it needs to make it a meal is some crisp bread.

SERVES 4

4 teaspoons olive oil

2 cloves garlic, minced

3 medium tomatoes (about 1 pound), peeled, cored, seeded, and chopped, or 1 can (1 pound) low-sodium tomatoes, chopped, with juice

1 teaspoon dried basil, crumbled

1/2 teaspoon dried oregano, crumbled

Pinch of cayenne pepper

1/2 cup dry white wine or chicken broth

1/2 pound cod or other white fish fillets, cut into bite-size pieces

2 tablespoons minced parsley

1 In a large heavy saucepan, heat olive oil over medium heat. Add garlic, tomatoes, basil, oregano, cayenne pepper, and wine, and cook, uncovered, 10 minutes.

2 Add 3 cups water, bring to boil, reduce heat, and simmer. Mix in cod and simmer, uncovered, 5 minutes. Ladle into bowls and sprinkle with parsley.

PIQUANT COD CHOWDER

A variety of vegetables ensures that this wonderful soup is as healthy as it is delicious.
(Photograph on page 32)

SERVES 4

2 parsley sprigs

2 thyme sprigs

1 bay leaf

1 celery stalk, 3-inch-long piece

1 can (14 1/2 ounces) chopped
    tomatoes, undrained

2 1/2 cups fish stock

4 tablespoons cider

1 large onion, chopped

1 pound waxy potatoes (thin-skinned)
    cut into large chunks

1/2 pound carrots, thickly sliced

1/2 pound zucchini, thickly sliced

1/2 pound green beans cut into short lengths

1 yellow or red bell pepper, cored,
    seeded, and sliced

Salt and pepper

1 1/4 pounds cod fillet, skinned and cut into
    large pieces

2 tablespoons finely chopped parsley

1 tablespoon snipped fresh chives

Finely shredded zest of 1 lemon

1 Tie parsley, thyme, bay leaf, and celery into a bundle to make a bouquet garni. Put bouquet garni in a large saucepan. Add tomatoes and juice, stock, cider, and onion. Bring to boil, reduce heat, and simmer, partially covered, 15 minutes.

2 Add potatoes and carrots. Increase heat to medium and cook, covered, 15 minutes or until vegetables are almost tender. Stir in zucchini, green beans, and bell pepper. Continue simmering, covered, 5 minutes or until all vegetables are tender. Discard bouquet garni.

3 Season with salt and pepper to taste. Add cod to simmering broth. Cover and cook 3 minutes or until fish is opaque, just firm, and flakes easily.

4 Ladle fish and vegetables into warm bowls and add broth. Sprinkle with parsley, chives, and lemon zest.

CAPE ANN HADDOCK CHOWDER

A hearty dish that can hold its own for dinner, this soup is made with haddock, a favorite chowder fish among Yankee fishermen.

SERVES 4

1 ounce salt pork, finely chopped

1 large yellow onion, coarsely chopped

1 1/2 tablespoons all-purpose flour

1 bottle (8 ounces) clam juice

1 1/2 cups milk

1/2 teaspoon black pepper

1/4 teaspoon salt

1 large all-purpose potato, peeled and chopped

12 ounces skinned and boned haddock,
    cut into 1 1/2-inch chunks

1 In a large saucepan over high heat, cook salt pork 2 minutes, stirring occasionally. Add onion and continue cooking 2 minutes or until softened.

2 Blend in flour, then gradually pour in clam juice, whisking to combine. Add milk, pepper, salt, and potato and bring to simmer. Reduce heat to medium low and simmer, uncovered, 20 minutes or until potato is tender and soup is nicely thickened.

3 Add haddock and cook 5 minutes or just until fish flakes at the touch of a fork.

NEW ENGLAND HADDOCK CHOWDER

Haddock, with its firm meat and delicate flavor, makes a superior fish chowder.

SERVES 10

1/2 cup butter

3 medium onions, sliced

5 medium potatoes, peeled and diced

4 teaspoons salt

1/2 teaspoon black pepper

2 pounds fresh or frozen haddock fillets, cut into large chunks

1 quart milk, scalded

1 can (12 ounces) evaporated milk

1 In a 6-quart soup pan over medium heat, melt 1/4 cup butter. Add onions and sauté 4 minutes or until tender but not browned.

2 Add potatoes, salt, pepper, and 3 cups boiling water. Top with fish. Bring to boil again, reduce heat, and simmer, covered, 25 minutes or until potatoes are fork-tender.

3 Stir in scalded milk, evaporated milk, and remaining butter and heat through. Season with additional salt and pepper, if desired.

HALIBUT CHOWDER

This rich, creamy chowder features tender chunks of halibut, but salmon or other white fish will do as well.

SERVES 8 TO 10

2 tablespoons butter

8 scallions, thinly sliced

2 garlic cloves, minced

4 cans (10 3/4 ounces each) condensed cream of potato soup

2 cans (10 3/4 ounces each) condensed cream of mushroom soup

4 cups milk

2 packages (8 ounces each) cream cheese, cut into cubes

1 1/2 pounds halibut or salmon fillets, cut into cubes

1 1/2 cups frozen sliced carrots

1 1/2 cups frozen corn

1/4 teaspoon cayenne pepper *(optional)*

1 In a Dutch oven or soup pot over medium heat, melt butter. Add scallions and garlic and sauté 4 minutes or until tender.

2 Add potato soup, mushroom soup, milk, and cream cheese. Cook, stirring, until cheese is melted. Bring to boil and stir in fish, carrots, and corn. Reduce heat and simmer, uncovered, 5 minutes or until fish flakes easily with a fork and vegetables are tender. Add cayenne, if desired.

HERRING CHOWDER

With a few fresh ingredients, pantry staples can be transformed into this great, quick dish. Canned smoked herring and corn make delicious chowder when combined with fresh leeks, potatoes, and herbs.

SERVES 4

1 tablespoon extra-virgin olive oil

1 leek, thinly sliced

1/2 pound small new potatoes,
    peeled and quartered

1 cube of fish stock, crumbled

1 bay leaf

1 1/4 cups whole milk

1 can (14 1/2 ounces) creamed corn

2 tablespoons fresh chives, minced

2 tablespoons parsley, chopped

1 can (6 ounces) smoked herring in oil,
    drained and skinned

Salt and pepper

1 In a large saucepan over medium heat, heat oil. Add leek and sauté 2 minutes or until just softened. Add potatoes and sauté 2 minutes. Add 2 cups boiling water, fish stock cube, and bay leaf and bring to boil. Reduce heat and simmer, covered, 15 minutes.

2 Remove and discard bay leaf. Stir in milk, corn, and half of chives and parsley. Use fork to break herring into chunks and add to soup. Season with salt and pepper to taste. Bring soup to boil and remove pan from heat to prevent overcooking fish.

3 Ladle soup into bowls and garnish with sprinkling of chives and parsley.

TROUT CHOWDER

This hearty chowder conveniently cooks in a slow cooker, but only for a short time.

SERVES 6

1 tablespoon butter

1 medium onion, chopped

2 cups milk

1 cup ranch dressing

1 pound boneless trout fillets, skin removed

1 package (10 ounces) frozen broccoli
    cuts, thawed

1 cup cubed or shredded cheddar cheese

1 cup cubed or shredded Monterey Jack cheese

1/4 teaspoon garlic powder

Paprika *(optional)*

1 In a skillet over medium heat, melt butter. Add onion and sauté 3 minutes or until tender. Transfer to a slow cooker, then add milk, dressing, fish, broccoli, cheddar cheese, Jack cheese, and garlic powder.

2 Cover and cook on high until soup is bubbling and fish flakes easily with a fork, about 1 1/2 hours. Sprinkle each serving with paprika, if desired.

LICKETY-SPLIT TUNA CHOWDER

You can put together this kid-pleasing soup in no time.

SERVES 4

1 can (10 3/4 ounces) condensed
    cream of potato or cream of celery soup

1 can (10 3/4 ounces) condensed
    Manhattan-style clam chowder

2 cups low-fat (1%) milk

1 can (6 ounces) water-packed chunk light
    tuna, rinsed, drained, and flaked

1 jar (2 ounces) sliced pimientos,
    undrained *(optional)*

1 1/2 teaspoons dried thyme

1/4 teaspoon black pepper

1 In a large saucepan over medium heat, combine soup, chowder, milk, tuna, pimientos, if desired, thyme, and pepper. Bring to boil, reduce heat, and simmer, covered, 5 minutes, stirring occasionally.

TUNA CHOWDER WITH BUTTERY CRUMB TOPPING

A sprinkling of deliciously flavored bread crumbs makes this a particularly warm and nourishing lunch soup.

SERVES 4

Chowder:
2 tablespoons butter

2 medium yellow onions, finely chopped

1 large red bell pepper, cored, seeded, and finely chopped

1 large green bell pepper, cored, seeded, and finely chopped

1 cup canned tomatoes, chopped

2 bottles (8 ounces each) clam juice

1/4 cup chopped pimiento

1 large all-purpose potato, peeled and diced

1/2 teaspoon salt

1/4 teaspoon black pepper

1/2 teaspoon dried thyme, crumbled

1 can (6 1/2 ounces) water-packed chunk-light tuna, drained and flaked

Buttery Crumb Topping:
1 large garlic clove

4 slices white bread, torn into small pieces

1 tablespoon butter, softened and cut into small pieces

1 tablespoon chopped parsley

1 For the chowder, in a 2-quart saucepan over medium heat, melt butter. Add onions and sauté 2 minutes or until limp. Add bell peppers and sauté 2 minutes. Add tomatoes, clam juice, pimiento, potato, salt, pepper, and thyme.

2 Bring to boil, reduce heat to medium-low, and simmer, uncovered, 30 minutes or until potato is tender.

3 For the buttery crumb topping, preheat oven to 350°F. Drop garlic into a blender or the feed tube of a food processor. Add bread, butter, and parsley. Process until uniformly fine. Spread topping in a thin layer on an ungreased baking sheet and bake, uncovered, 15 minutes, turning every 5 minutes, until golden brown. Set aside.

4 Mix tuna into pot mixture and heat 1 minute. Ladle into 4 bowls and top with crumb topping.

NORTHWEST SALMON CHOWDER

This is the chowder that people make in the land of salmon.

SERVES 8

3 tablespoons butter

1/2 cup chopped celery

1/2 cup chopped onion

1/2 cup chopped seeded green bell pepper

1 garlic clove, minced

1 can (14 1/2 ounces) chicken broth

1 cup diced peeled potatoes

1 cup shredded carrots

1 1/2 teaspoons salt

1/2 teaspoon black pepper

1/2 teaspoon dill weed

1 can (14 3/4 ounces) cream-style corn

2 cups half-and-half

2 cups fully cooked salmon chunks or 1 can (14 3/4 ounces) salmon, drained, flaked, and bones and skin removed

1 In a large saucepan over medium heat, melt butter. Add celery, onion, bell pepper, and garlic and sauté 4 minutes or until tender.

2 Add broth, potatoes, carrots, salt, pepper, and dill. Bring to boil, reduce heat, and simmer, covered, 40 minutes or until vegetables are nearly tender. Stir in corn, half-and-half, and salmon and cook 15 minutes or until heated through.

SALMON AND TOMATO CHOWDER

SERVES 4

1 fillet (7 ounces) skinless salmon

1 bay leaf

1 1/4 cups fish or vegetable stock

2 1/2 cups low-fat (1%) milk

1 tablespoon unsalted butter

1 teaspoon sunflower oil

1 large onion, finely chopped

1 leek, chopped

1 thick slice Canadian bacon, about 1 ounce, rind removed and chopped

2 medium potatoes, peeled and diced

2 large tomatoes, skinned, seeded, and diced

3 tablespoons chopped parsley

4 tablespoons nonfat sour cream

Salt and black pepper

Chowder is a classic meal-in-a-bowl soup. This version is flavored with lean bacon, leeks, and tomatoes and thickened with potatoes, all of which provide the perfect background for the protein-packed salmon.

1 Put salmon fillet and bay leaf in a large saucepan. Pour stock over and add some milk, if needed, to cover fish with liquid. Slowly bring to boil over medium heat. Reduce heat, cover, and simmer 6 minutes or until fish flakes easily. Remove salmon with slotted spoon, break into large flakes, discard any bones, and set meat aside. Pour cooking liquid (with bay leaf) into a measuring jug or large bowl and reserve.

2 In saucepan over low heat, melt butter with oil. Add onion, leek, and bacon, and sauté 10 minutes or until soft. Add potatoes and sauté mixture 2 minutes.

3 Add reserved cooking liquid and remaining milk. Bring to boil, half-cover saucepan, and simmer, stirring occasionally, 8 minutes. Add diced tomatoes and simmer 4 minutes or until potatoes have become tender, but have not started to disintegrate.

4 To thicken soup, remove a ladleful or two and puree it in a bowl with a handheld blender, or in a food processor. Return to soup in saucepan and mix well. Stir in flaked salmon and 2 tablespoons parsley. Simmer until soup is piping hot, 1 to 2 minutes longer. Discard bay leaf and season with salt and pepper to taste.

5 Ladle soup into warmed serving bowls. Top each with 1 tablespoon nonfat sour cream, swirling it around, and add a sprinkling of remaining chopped parsley.

SALMON CHOWDER

Salmon's popularity in the Pacific Northwest began with local Indians, for whom the words fish and salmon were synonymous.

SERVES 6

1 tablespoon vegetable oil

1 large yellow onion, finely chopped

1 garlic clove, minced

2 medium all-purpose potatoes, peeled and diced

1 cup canned crushed tomatoes, undrained

1/2 fish bouillon cube or 1 teaspoon fish bouillon granules

12 ounces boned and skinned fresh or canned salmon fillets, cut into 1/2-inch pieces

2 tablespoons snipped fresh dill or 2 teaspoons dried dill weed

1/4 teaspoon salt

1/4 teaspoon black pepper

2 cups low-fat (1%) milk

2 teaspoons fresh lemon juice

1 In a large heavy saucepan, heat oil over medium-high heat. Add onion and garlic and sauté 5 minutes or until tender. Stir in potatoes, tomatoes, bouillon cube, and 3 cups cold water and bring to boil. Reduce heat and simmer, covered, stirring occasionally, 15 minutes or until the potatoes are tender.

2 Stir in salmon, dill, salt, and pepper. Simmer, uncovered, 3 minutes or just until salmon is opaque. Stir in milk and simmer 2 minutes or until heated through. Remove from heat and stir in lemon juice.

SALMON CHOWDER WITH BUTTERY CRUMB TOPPING

A tasty and good-for-you main dish, this salmon chowder also has the healthy fish oils your body needs.

SERVES 4

Chowder:

2 tablespoons butter

2 medium yellow onions, finely chopped

1 large green bell pepper, cored, seeded, and finely chopped

1/4 cup chopped pimiento

2 bottles (8 ounces each) clam juice

1 large all-purpose potato, peeled and diced

1/2 teaspoon salt

1/4 teaspoon black pepper

1 can (7 1/2 ounces) boned and skinned salmon

Buttery Crumb Topping:

1 large garlic clove

4 slices white bread, torn into small pieces

1 tablespoon butter, softened and cut into small pieces

1 tablespoon chopped parsley

1 For the chowder, in a 2-quart saucepan over medium heat, melt butter. Add onions and sauté 2 minutes or until limp. Add bell pepper and pimiento and sauté 2 minutes. Add clam juice, potato, salt, and pepper.

2 Bring to boil, reduce heat and simmer, uncovered, 30 minutes or until potato is tender.

3 For the buttery crumb topping, preheat oven to 350°F. Drop garlic into a blender or the feed tube of a food processor. Add bread, butter, and parsley. Process until uniformly fine. Spread topping in a thin layer on an ungreased baking sheet and bake, uncovered, 15 minutes, turning with a spatula every 5 minutes, until golden brown. Set aside while chowder is prepared. Mix salmon into soup and heat 1 minute. Ladle into 4 bowls and top with crumb topping.

PUGET SOUND FISH CHOWDER

Here is a delightful salmon chowder that is as good for you as it tastes.

SERVES 4

2 tablespoons (1/4 stick) butter

1 medium yellow onion, chopped

1 large unpeeled baking potato, scrubbed and diced

1/2 teaspoon salt

1/4 teaspoon ground white pepper

1 pound salmon fillets or steaks, skinned, boned, and cut into 1-inch chunks

2 cups milk

2 teaspoons fresh dill or parsley, chopped

1 In a large saucepan, melt butter over medium heat. Add onions and sauté 5 minutes or until soft.

2 Add 1 1/2 cups water, potato, salt, and pepper. Bring to boil, reduce heat, and simmer, covered, 10 minutes or until potato slices are fork-tender.

3 Bring soup to boil. Stir in salmon, reduce heat, and simmer 3 minutes or until fish flakes easily when tested with fork. Stir in milk and simmer until soup is heated through (do not boil). Sprinkle with dill or parsley and serve.

CLAM CHOWDER WITH TOMATOES AND CORN

New Englanders traditionally make their clam chowder with cream, but New Yorkers love this spicy clam and vegetable soup.

SERVES 6

1 pint shucked hard-shell clams or 2 cans (6 ounces each) minced clams

2 strips lean bacon, chopped

1/2 cup finely sliced leek or 4 large scallions with tops, finely sliced

1 celery stalk, finely chopped

2 garlic cloves, minced

3 cups low-sodium vegetable juice cocktail

2 medium potatoes, peeled and chopped

1 can (14 1/2 ounces) low-sodium tomatoes, undrained, cut up

1 can (11 ounces) whole-kernel corn with bell peppers

2 bay leaves

2 teaspoons dried thyme

2 teaspoons low-sodium Worcestershire sauce

1 teaspoon dried marjoram

1/4 teaspoon salt

1/8 teaspoon hot red pepper sauce

1 Coarsely chop fresh clams (or drain canned clams), reserving juice. Strain fresh juice to remove bits of shell.

2 In a soup pot or Dutch oven over medium heat, cook bacon until crisp. Remove from pan, reserving drippings, and transfer to paper towels to drain.

3 Add leek, celery, and garlic to pan and sauté in drippings until leek is tender, about 5 minutes. Add vegetable juice, potatoes, tomatoes, corn, bay leaves, thyme, Worcestershire, marjoram, salt, and hot pepper sauce. Bring to boil, reduce heat, and simmer, covered, until potatoes are tender, about 50 minutes.

4 Stir in clams, juice, and bacon and cook, stirring occasionally, until heated through. Remove bay leaves.

MANHATTAN CLAM CHOWDER

It's the tomatoes that distinguish Manhattan-style clam chowder from creamy New England-style chowder.

SERVES 4

2 teaspoons unsalted butter
    or margarine

1 medium yellow onion, chopped

1 small carrot, peeled and diced

1 small celery stalk, diced

1/8 teaspoon salt

1/4 teaspoon black pepper

1 medium potato, peeled and diced

1 can (14 1/2 ounces) low-sodium tomatoes,
    undrained, pureed

1 cup minced fresh or canned clams, undrained

1 bottle (8 ounces) clam juice

2 tablespoons minced fresh parsley

1 In a large saucepan over low heat, melt butter. Add onion, carrot, celery, salt, and pepper. Cover and cook, stirring occasionally, 5 minutes or until vegetables are soft.

2 Add 1 cup water, potato, and tomatoes and bring to boil. Reduce heat, cover, and simmer 15 minutes or until potato is just tender.

3 Stir in clams and clam juice and bring to boil. Reduce heat, cover, and simmer 5 minutes or until flavors are blended. Sprinkle with parsley.

SLOW-COOK MANHATTAN CLAM CHOWDER

Fill the slow cooker in the morning and come home to the aroma of a ready-to-eat dinner.

SERVES 9

3 celery stalks, sliced

1 large onion, chopped

1 can (14 1/2 ounces) sliced potatoes,
    drained

1 can (14 1/2 ounces) sliced carrots,
    drained

2 cans (6 1/2 ounces each) chopped
    clams

2 cups tomato juice

1/2 cup tomato puree

1 tablespoon parsley flakes

1 1/2 teaspoons dried thyme

1 teaspoon salt *(optional)*

1 bay leaf

2 whole black peppercorns

1 In a slow cooker, combine 1 1/2 cups water, celery, onion, potatoes, carrots, clams, tomato juice, tomato puree, parsley, thyme, salt, if desired, bay leaf, and peppercorns. Cover and cook on low 8 to 10 hours or until vegetables are tender. Remove bay leaf and peppercorns before serving.

NEW ENGLAND CLAM CHOWDER

Curl up on a chilly evening with a cozy bowl of this creamy chowder—just as New Englanders have done for centuries.

SERVES 4

24 cherrystone or chowder clams
    (about 2 pounds), scrubbed

4 slices turkey bacon,
    cut into 1/2-inch pieces

1 large onion, chopped

2 tablespoons all-purpose flour

1 pound all-purpose potatoes,
    peeled and cut into 1/2-inch cubes

2 cups reduced-fat (2%) milk

2 teaspoons fresh thyme leaves

1 bay leaf

Pinch of ground red pepper

1/4 cup chopped flat-leaf parsley

1 Bring clams and 2 cups water to boil in a large saucepan over high heat. Reduce heat, cover, and simmer 5 minutes. Uncover and transfer clams with tongs or a slotted spoon to bowl as they open. Strain clam broth, adding enough water to equal 1 1/2 cups, and set aside. Wipe out saucepan.

2 Lightly coat saucepan with nonstick cooking spray and set over medium heat. Sauté bacon and onion until onion is golden, about 7 minutes. Sprinkle in flour and cook, stirring constantly, just until bubbling but not browned, about 1 minute.

3 Add potatoes, milk, reserved clam broth, thyme, bay leaf, and pepper. Bring to simmer over medium heat and cook, stirring occasionally, until potatoes are tender, about 10 minutes (do not boil).

4 Meanwhile, remove clams from shells and cut into bite-size pieces if necessary. Stir in clams and cook until heated through, about 2 minutes longer. Discard bay leaf. Ladle into bowls and sprinkle with parsley.

NEW ENGLAND CLAM CHOWDER WITH CORN

Crisp corn kernels and a touch of rosemary set this chowder apart. If you can't find fresh clams, use 2 cans (6 1/2 ounces each) minced clams, drained. Add them in Step 3, cooking for a minute or so, until heated through. Either way you'll love the taste.

SERVES 4

2 ounces bacon, finely chopped

1 small onion, finely chopped

1 red bell pepper, cut into 1/2-inch squares

3/4 pound all-purpose potatoes, peeled
    and cut into 1/2-inch chunks

1 cup bottled clam juice or chicken stock

1/2 teaspoon salt

1/2 teaspoon black pepper

1/4 teaspoon dried rosemary, crumbled

1 cup low-fat (1%) milk

2 tablespoons flour

1 cup frozen whole-kernel corn

1 cup shucked clams (from 2 dozen littlenecks),
    coarsely chopped

1 In a large saucepan, cook bacon with 2 tablespoons water over low heat 3 minutes or until bacon has rendered its fat and is lightly crisped. Add onion and bell pepper, and cook, stirring frequently, 5 minutes or until onion is soft. Add potatoes, tossing to coat.

2 Stir in clam juice, 1 1/4 cups water, salt, black pepper, and rosemary, and bring to boil. Reduce to simmer, cover, and cook 10 minutes or until potatoes are tender.

3 In a small bowl, whisk milk into flour until well combined. Stir into the saucepan along with corn and clams, and cook, stirring frequently, 5 minutes or until soup is slightly thickened and clams are cooked through.

LOW-FAT CLAM CHOWDER

The work preparing fresh clams is worth it—not only do they taste better than canned, but they are less salty.

SERVES 6

1 dozen littleneck or cherrystone clams or
    1 can (10 ounces) whole baby clams,
    drained and rinsed

6 cups fish stock

1 turkey bacon slice, coarsely chopped

2 large onions, coarsely chopped

1 pound all-purpose potatoes,
    peeled and diced

2 cups low-fat (1%) milk

1/8 teaspoon salt

1/8 teaspoon black pepper

2 tablespoons chopped parsley

1 Scrub clam shells under cold water to remove sand and grit. Place in a large saucepan with 1/4 cup fish stock. Cover and bring to boil. Lower heat and simmer 5 minutes or until shells open. Remove clams with a slotted spoon and let cool. Remove cooled clams from their shells, discarding any shells that have not opened, and coarsely chop.

2 Cook bacon in a 4-quart saucepan over medium heat about 3 minutes, until it is crisp and the fat is rendered. With a slotted spoon, remove bacon and reserve on paper towels for garnish.

3 Add onions to pan with 1/4 cup of stock. Sauté about 5 minutes or until softened but not browned.

4 Stir in potatoes and remaining fish stock and bring to boil. Reduce heat and simmer, partially covered, stirring occasionally, about 10 minutes or until potatoes are very tender.

5 Remove from heat and puree about 2 cups of the vegetables in a blender or food processor until smooth. Add puree to soup and return to the heat.

6 Add milk and chopped clams and simmer about 5 minutes to blend flavors. Season with salt and pepper and stir in parsley. Garnish with bacon.

HASTY CLAM CHOWDER

Here's a quick chowder that's great for potluck dinners.

SERVES 5

6 bacon strips, diced

1/2 cup finely chopped onion

2 cans (10 3/4 ounces each) condensed
    cream of potato soup

1 1/2 cups milk

3 cans (6 1/2 ounces each) minced
    clams, undrained

1 tablespoon lemon juice

1/4 teaspoon dried thyme

1/4 teaspoon black pepper

Minced fresh parsley

1 In a large saucepan over medium heat, cook bacon until crisp and transfer to paper towels to drain. Drain pan, reserving 1 tablespoon drippings.

2 Return drippings to pan, add onion, and sauté over medium heat 3 minutes or until tender. Stir in soup and milk. Add clams, lemon juice, thyme, pepper, and bacon and heat through. Garnish with parsley.

CLAM CHOWDER WITH MUSHROOMS

This is a very rich chowder, made more delicious by the addition of mushrooms.

SERVES 10

2 cans (6 1/2 ounces each) minced clams

6 potatoes, peeled and diced

6 carrots, diced

1/2 cup chopped onion

1/2 cup butter

2 cans (10 3/4 ounces each) cream of mushroom soup, condensed

2 cans (12 ounces each) evaporated milk

1 teaspoon salt

1/2 teaspoon black pepper

1 Drain clams, reserving liquid. Set clams aside. In a large soup pot, combine clam juice, potatoes, carrots, onion, butter, and 1 1/2 cups water. Bring to boil, reduce heat, and simmer, covered, 15 minutes or until vegetables are tender.

2 Stir in soup, evaporated milk, salt, and pepper, and simmer 4 minutes or until heated through. Stir in clams.

NEW ENGLAND CLAM CHOWDER IN-A-HURRY

This creamy chowder is a year-round favorite across the United States.

SERVES 4

1 1/2 ounces salt pork, diced

1 medium yellow onion, chopped

1/4 cup celery, chopped

2 medium potatoes, peeled and diced

1 bottle (8 ounces) clam juice

1 cup cooked clams, chopped, or 2 cans (6 1/2 ounces each) chopped clams, drained

1 1/2 cups milk

1 cup half-and-half

1/8 teaspoon ground white pepper

Salt

1 In a large saucepan over medium heat, lightly brown salt pork. Add onion and celery, and sauté 5 minutes or until onion is soft. Stir in potatoes, clam juice, and 1/2 cup water. Bring to boil, reduce

heat, and simmer, covered, 10 minutes or until potatoes are fork-tender.

2 Stir in clams, milk, half-and half, and pepper, and season with salt to taste. Cook over medium heat until soup is hot (do not boil).

LOBSTER BISQUE

This rich, party first-course soup deserves to be made with real lobster if you can get it.

SERVES 4

1 large yellow onion, finely chopped

1 celery stalk, finely chopped

1/4 cup low-sodium chicken broth

2 3/4 cups low-fat (1%) milk

1 cup half-and-half

3 tablespoons all-purpose flour

1/2 teaspoon salt

1/2 teaspoon ground mace

1/4 teaspoon white or black pepper

8 ounces coarsely flaked lobster or 1 package (8 ounces) frozen lobster-flavored, chunk-style fish, thawed

1/4 cup dry sherry, dry white wine, or half-and-half

1 In a large saucepan over medium heat, combine onion, celery, and broth. Bring to boil, reduce heat, and simmer, covered, until vegetables are tender, about 5 minutes. Stir in milk.

2 In a small bowl, whisk together half-and-half, flour, salt, mace, and pepper. Stir into pan and cook, stirring constantly over medium heat until thickened and bubbly, about 10 minutes. Stir in lobster and sherry and simmer, uncovered, until heated through, about 5 minutes.

CLASSIC LOBSTER BISQUE

SERVES 4

1 small cooked lobster, about 14 ounces

2 tablespoons butter

1 large onion, finely chopped

1 leek, finely chopped

1 carrot, finely chopped

1 celery stalk, finely chopped

1/2 cup dry white wine or dry vermouth

1 bay leaf

1/2 cup long-grain rice

1/2 pound plum tomatoes, skinned, seeded, and chopped

1 tablespoon lemon juice

2 tablespoons cream

Few drops hot red pepper sauce to taste

Salt and pepper

1 1/2 tablespoons snipped fresh chives to garnish

This recipe makes the most of a lobster—it even uses the shell—so it is a good way to stretch a luxury ingredient.

1 Pull and twist off lobster claws and set aside. With a sharp knife cut body in half lengthwise, from tail end through head. Scoop out creamy greenish-gray liver (tomalley) and, if it is a female lobster, red-orange coral or roe. Reserve these together, covered and chilled. Remove lobster meat from claws and body-tail shell. Discard all inedible parts. Cut meat into bite-size pieces and set aside. Chop shell into large pieces.

2 In a large saucepan over medium heat, melt 1 tablespoon butter. Add pieces of lobster shell and sauté until brown bits begin to stick on bottom of the pan. Add about one-third of the onion, leek, carrot, and celery, and cook, stirring constantly, 1 minute. Add wine and let bubble 1 minute. Add 3 1/2 cups water and bay leaf and bring to boil. Reduce heat and simmer, uncovered, 30 minutes. Strain lobster stock through a fine sieve, discarding shell and vegetables, and spooning off any fat.

3 In a large saucepan over medium heat, melt remaining butter. Add remaining onion, leek, carrot, and celery. Cover and cook, stirring frequently, 5 minutes or until vegetables are soft and just starting to color. Stir in rice. Add tomatoes and lobster stock and bring almost to boil. Reduce heat and simmer, covered, 25 minutes or until rice and vegetables are tender.

4 Add tomalley with any coral, pressing them through a sieve if any pieces of lobster shell are evident. Puree soup with a hand blender, food processor, or blender, until very smooth.

5 Return soup to saucepan over low heat. Add lemon juice and simmer 2 minutes or until heated through. Stir in cream, season with salt and pepper to taste, and add a few drops of hot pepper sauce. Ladle soup into warm bowls, add reserved lobster meat, and garnish with chives.

SHRIMP CHOWDER

Here's a super-simple recipe that shrimp lovers will devour, thanks to its creamy yet spicy flavor.

SERVES 4

1 large yellow onion, finely chopped

1/4 cup low-sodium chicken broth

12 ounces peeled and deveined fresh or thawed frozen medium shrimp

1/2 teaspoon salt

1/8 teaspoon cayenne pepper

1 3/4 cups low-fat (1%) milk

1 cup half-and-half

1/2 teaspoon low-sodium Worcestershire sauce *(optional)*

1 In a large saucepan over medium heat, combine onion and broth. Bring to boil, reduce heat, and simmer, covered, until onion is tender, about 5 minutes. Add shrimp, salt, and cayenne and cook until shrimp are pink and opaque, about 3 minutes.

2 Add milk, half-and-half, and Worcestershire, if desired. Cook, stirring often, over medium heat until heated through.

MANHATTAN SHRIMP CHOWDER

Shrimp are served to delicious effect in a classic Manhattan-style chowder, made with tomatoes, corn, and chunks of potato. (Photograph on page 21)

SERVES 4

2 teaspoons olive oil

1 medium onion, finely chopped

4 garlic cloves, minced

12 ounces all-purpose potatoes, cut into 1/2-inch dice

1 cup bottled clam juice

1/2 teaspoon fennel seed

1 teaspoon grated orange zest

1 can (14 1/2 ounces) stewed tomatoes, chopped, undrained

1/2 teaspoon salt

1/2 teaspoon hot red pepper sauce

8 ounces medium shrimp, peeled, deveined, and cut into bite-size pieces

1/2 cup frozen whole-kernel corn

1 Heat oil in a large nonstick saucepan over medium heat. Add onion and garlic and sauté 7 minutes or until onion is softened.

2 Stir in potatoes, clam juice, 1 cup water, fennel seed, and orange zest. Bring to boil. Reduce to simmer, cover, and cook 10 minutes or until potatoes are almost tender.

3 Stir in tomatoes, salt, and hot pepper sauce. Return to boil. Add shrimp and corn. Cover and cook 3 minutes or until shrimp are just opaque and corn is hot.

SHRIMP AND CORN CHOWDER

For an even richer chowder, add 8 ounces fresh mussels or clams along with the shrimp and simmer until they open.

SERVES 8

1 1/2 tablespoons olive or canola oil

2 large onions, diced

2 large carrots, diced

2 celery stalks, diced

1 pound all-purpose potatoes, peeled and diced

5 cups fish stock

8 ounces medium shrimp, peeled and deveined

2 cups fresh or frozen whole-kernel corn

2 cups low-fat (1%) milk

1/8 teaspoon salt

1/8 teaspoon black pepper

Pinch of paprika

1 In a 4-quart saucepan, heat oil over medium heat. Add onions, carrots, and celery and sauté 5 minutes or until softened but not browned.

2 Stir in potatoes with fish stock and bring to boil. Reduce heat and simmer, partially covered, stirring occasionally, 10 to 15 minutes or until vegetables are tender.

3 Puree 2 cups of the vegetables in a blender or food processor until smooth. Add puree to saucepan with shrimp, corn, and milk. Return to boil, reduce heat, and simmer 3 minutes. Season with salt, pepper, and paprika.

SHRIMP, CORN, AND PEPPER CHOWDER

This soup has complementary flavors that make it a very popular dish for company.

SERVES 6

2 tablespoons olive or vegetable oil

1 large yellow onion, finely chopped

1 large all-purpose potato,
    peeled and diced

1 bay leaf

1/2 teaspoon dried marjoram, crumbled

1/8 teaspoon ground nutmeg

1 3/4 cups chicken stock

1 can (17 ounces) cream-style corn

1 package (10 ounces) frozen
    whole-kernel corn, thawed

1 3/4 cups milk

1/4 teaspoon black pepper

1 jar (7 ounces) roasted red peppers,
    drained and thinly sliced

1 pound large shrimp,
    peeled and deveined

1 In a large saucepan over medium heat, heat oil. Add onion and sauté 5 minutes or until translucent.

2 Add potato, bay leaf, marjoram, nutmeg, and stock and bring to boil. Reduce heat, cover, and simmer 10 minutes or until potato is just tender.

3 Add cream-style corn, whole-kernel corn, milk, and black pepper and bring to boil. Reduce heat to medium and add red peppers and shrimp. Simmer, uncovered, 3 minutes or until shrimp are just cooked through and pink. Remove bay leaf before serving.

SHRIMP BISQUE WITH CROUTONS

A bisque usually derives its richness from heavy cream. This version is rendered "creamy" with low-fat milk and flour.

SERVES 4

4 slices (1/2 inch thick) French
    or Italian bread

1 garlic clove, halved

1 cup bottled clam juice or chicken stock

1 pound medium shrimp,
    peeled and deveined

1 can (8 ounces) low-sodium tomato sauce

2 cups low-fat (1%) milk

2 tablespoons flour

1/2 teaspoon dried tarragon

1/2 teaspoon salt

1/2 teaspoon black pepper

1/4 cup chopped parsley

1 Preheat oven to 400°F. Rub bread with the cut sides of halved garlic, then cut bread into 1/2-inch cubes. Place on a baking sheet and bake 5 minutes or until lightly toasted. Remove and set aside.

2 In a medium saucepan, bring clam juice and 1/4 cup water to simmer. Add shrimp and cook 3 minutes or until just done. With a slotted spoon, transfer shrimp to a bowl. Stir tomato sauce into the saucepan.

3 In a medium bowl, whisk milk into flour, then whisk mixture into saucepan. Cook over medium heat, stirring constantly, 5 minutes or until mixture is slightly thickened and no floury taste remains. Stir in tarragon, salt, pepper, and parsley.

4 Return shrimp to pan and simmer 1 minute or until they are just heated through. Serve topped with croutons.

SHRIMP AND TOMATO BISQUE

This lighter version of a bisque substitutes fish stock and milk for most of the heavy cream.

SERVES 6

1 tablespoon unsalted butter

1 tablespoon vegetable oil

3/4 cup yellow onion, finely chopped

1/2 cup celery, finely chopped

1/3 cup carrot, finely chopped

2 tablespoons all-purpose flour

3 cups homemade fish stock or canned
     low-sodium chicken broth

1 can (14 1/2 ounces) low-sodium whole
     tomatoes, drained and chopped

1/2 cup dry white wine or fish stock

1 bay leaf

1 teaspoon dried marjoram

1/8 teaspoon ground nutmeg

1 pound medium shrimp, shelled, deveined,
     and cut into 1/2-inch pieces

1 cup low-fat (1%) milk

2 tablespoons heavy cream or low-fat milk

1/2 teaspoon salt

2 tablespoons fresh lemon juice

Fresh marjoram sprigs *(optional)*

1 In a large saucepan, melt butter and heat oil over medium-high heat. Stir in onion, celery, and carrot and sauté 5 minutes or until tender. Add flour and cook, stirring constantly, until bubbly.

Stir in stock, tomatoes, wine, bay leaf, marjoram, and nutmeg and bring to boil. Reduce heat and simmer, covered, 15 minutes, then discard bay leaf.

2 In a food processor or blender, puree soup, in batches if necessary, until smooth. Return soup to saucepan. Add shrimp and cook, uncovered, over medium heat 1 minute. Blend in milk and cream and cook until soup is heated through and shrimp are firm and pink. Remove from heat and season with salt and lemon juice. Garnish with marjoram sprigs, if desired.

CREAMY SHRIMP BISQUE

Rich and delicious, this soup is a wonderful first course for a festive dinner celebration.

SERVES 6

2 tablespoons unsalted butter

1 medium onion, finely chopped

1 celery stalk, finely chopped

1/3 cup finely chopped carrot

2 tablespoons all-purpose flour

2 cups homemade fish stock
     or canned chicken broth

1 can (14 1/2 ounces) whole tomatoes,
     drained and chopped

1/2 cup dry white wine or fish stock

1 bay leaf

1 teaspoon dried marjoram

1/8 teaspoon ground nutmeg

1 pound medium shrimp, shelled,
     deveined, and cut into 1/2-inch pieces

2 cups heavy cream

1/2 teaspoon salt

2 tablespoons fresh lemon juice

1 In a large saucepan, melt butter over medium-high heat. Stir in onion, celery, and carrot and sauté 5 minutes or until tender. Add flour and cook, stirring constantly, until bubbly. Stir in stock, tomatoes, wine, bay leaf, marjoram, and nutmeg and bring to boil. Reduce heat and simmer, covered, 15 minutes, then discard bay leaf.

2 In a food processor or blender, puree soup, in batches if necessary, 45 seconds or until smooth. Return soup to saucepan. Add shrimp and cook, uncovered, over medium heat 1 minute. Blend in cream and cook 2 minutes or just until soup is heated through and shrimp are firm and pink. Remove from heat and season with salt and lemon juice.

SHRIMP AND FENNEL BISQUE

This classic seafood soup is ideal for a holiday first course. The last-minute addition of chopped red bell pepper adds a flourish of flavor and texture. (Photograph on page 11)

SERVES 6

1 pound raw shrimp

4 tablespoons dry white wine

4 slices of lemon

4 black peppercorns, lightly crushed

2 sprigs parsley

1 fennel bulb, 2/3 coarsely chopped,
    1/3 finely chopped

1 teaspoon lemon juice

1 tablespoon butter

1 tablespoon sunflower oil

1 shallot, finely chopped

1/4 cup fine white breadcrumbs,
    made from day-old bread

Pinch of paprika

1 red bell pepper, cored, seeded,
    and finely diced

Salt and pepper

Fennel leaves, chopped

1 Peel shrimp and set aside. Place shells in a large saucepan. Pour in 4 cups cold water and add white wine, lemon, peppercorns, and parsley. Bring to boil, reduce heat, and simmer, uncovered, 20 minutes. Skim foam that rises during cooking.

2 Make a shallow slit along the curved back of each shrimp with a small, sharp knife and remove and discard black vein. Cover and chill shrimp until required.

3 Let stock cool slightly and discard lemon. Process stock in blender or food processor until shells are finely ground. Strain through cheesecloth-lined sieve into large bowl. Discard shells.

4 Place finely chopped fennel in bowl, add lemon juice, toss, cover, and set aside.

5 Melt butter and heat oil over medium heat in rinsed saucepan. Add coarsely chopped fennel and shallot. Sauté 8 minutes or until vegetables are soft but not browned. Stir in breadcrumbs, paprika, and stock. Add shrimp. Bring to boil, reduce heat, and simmer 3 minutes.

6 Set aside 6 shrimp. Simmer soup 15 minutes and season with salt and pepper to taste.

7 Puree soup in blender or food processor until smooth. Return to pan and add finely chopped fennel and red pepper. Heat soup without boiling. Garnish each bowl with shrimp and chopped fennel leaves.

SHE-CRAB SOUP

In Charleston, South Carolina, cooks traditionally used the roe and meat from female crabs in a creamy, delicately flavored soup. This lighter version substitutes milk and half-and-half for heavy cream. To simulate the roe, you can sprinkle sieved, hard-cooked egg yolk on top.

SERVES 4

Large yellow onion, finely chopped

1 celery stalk, finely chopped

1/4 cup low-sodium chicken broth

2 3/4 cups low-fat (1%) milk

1 cup half-and-half

3 tablespoons all-purpose flour

1/2 teaspoon salt

1/2 teaspoon ground mace

1/4 teaspoon white or black pepper

8 ounces lump crabmeat, picked over and flaked, or 1 package (8 ounces) thawed frozen crab-flavored, salad-style fish, chopped

1/4 cup dry sherry, dry white wine, or half-and-half

1 In a large saucepan over medium heat, combine onion, celery, and broth. Bring to boil, reduce heat, and simmer, covered, until vegetables are tender, about 5 minutes. Stir in milk.

2 In a small bowl, whisk together half-and-half, flour, salt, mace, and pepper. Stir into pan and cook, stirring constantly, over medium heat until thickened and bubbling, about 10 minutes. Stir in crab and sherry and simmer, uncovered, until heated through, about 5 minutes.

CREOLE CRAB BISQUE

The zesty seasonings in this bisque nicely complement the subtle flavor of crab.

SERVES 4

1/4 cup (1/2 stick) butter

1/2 cup chopped celery

2 tablespoons chopped onion

1/4 cup all-purpose flour

2 1/2 cups milk

2 beef bouillon cubes

1 cup half-and-half

1 can (6 ounces) crabmeat, drained

1/2 cup sliced fresh mushrooms

1/2 teaspoon dried basil

1/4 teaspoon garlic powder

1/2 teaspoon Creole seasoning

1/4 teaspoon black pepper

1 In a 3-quart saucepan over medium heat, melt butter. Add celery and onion and sauté until tender. Stir in flour and cook 2 minutes, then gradually whisk in milk. Bring to boil and cook 2 minutes, stirring constantly.

2 Add bouillon, half-and-half, crab, mushrooms, basil, garlic powder, 1/4 teaspoon Creole seasoning and 1/8 teaspoon pepper. Reduce heat and simmer, covered, 45 minutes, stirring frequently. Season to taste with remaining Creole seasoning and pepper, if desired.

CRAB AND BELL PEPPER BISQUE

This sweet, creamy crab soup is a special treat, suitable for your best china and most beloved guests.

SERVES 4

1 tablespoon butter

2 large celery stalks, finely chopped

1 large red bell pepper, cored, seeded, and finely chopped

2 tablespoons chopped pimiento

1 1/2 tablespoons all-purpose flour

1 bottle (8 ounces) clam juice

1/4 cup dry sherry

1 cup heavy cream

1 cup half-and-half

1/4 teaspoon salt

1/4 teaspoon black pepper

6 ounces lump crabmeat, well picked over (or canned or imitation crabmeat)

1 In a medium saucepan, over medium heat, melt butter. Add celery and sauté 5 minutes. Add red pepper and pimiento and sauté 10 minutes or until pepper is softened.

2 Blend in flour, then gradually whisk in clam juice, stirring constantly, until smooth. Add sherry and cook, stirring, 2 to 3 minutes.

3 Add heavy cream, half-and-half, salt, and pepper. Reduce heat to low and cook, uncovered, 30 minutes. Do not overheat or soup may curdle.

4 Add crabmeat and simmer 2 minutes or until heated through.

CURRIED CRAB BISQUE

One of the delicacies of Maryland—and the base of this soup—is blue crab, which is abundant from May through October.

SERVES 6

1/2 cup (1 stick) butter

1/2 cup all-purpose flour

1 tablespoon seafood seasoning

1 teaspoon salt

1/2 teaspoon curry powder

4 cups milk

1 pound cooked crabmeat

2 tablespoons minced fresh parsley

Additional milk and parsley *(optional)*

1 In a 3-quart saucepan over medium-low heat, melt butter. Stir in flour, seafood seasoning, salt, and curry powder. Cook until thickened and bubbling. Gradually add milk and cook, stirring, until mixture is hot (do not boil).

2 Remove cartilage from crab if necessary. Add crab and parsley and cook, stirring, just until heated through. If desired, thin with additional milk and garnish with parsley.

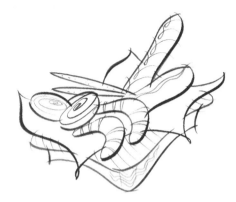

HAM AND BEAN CHOWDER

Cheesy and nicely seasoned with bay leaves and cloves, this chowder is a satisfying dish.

SERVES 12

1 pound dried great Northern beans, sorted and rinsed

3 tablespoons butter

2 cups chopped onion

1 cup sliced celery

2 garlic cloves, minced

1 meaty hambone

1 can (14 1/2 ounces) chicken broth

1 can (14 1/2 ounces) stewed tomatoes

2 bay leaves

2 whole cloves

1/2 teaspoon black pepper

2 cups milk

2 cups (8 ounces) shredded cheddar cheese

1 Place beans in a Dutch oven or soup pot and add water to cover by 2 inches. Bring to boil and cook 2 minutes. Remove from heat, cover, and let stand 1 hour. Drain beans and set aside.

2 In rinsed-out pot, melt butter over medium heat. Add onion, celery, and garlic and sauté 5 minutes or until tender. Add 2 cups water, beans, hambone, broth, tomatoes, bay leaves, cloves, and pepper. Bring to boil, reduce heat, and simmer, covered, 2 hours.

3 Remove hambone, bay leaves, and cloves. When cool enough to handle, remove meat from bone, cut into small pieces, and add to pot.

4 Cool soup, then refrigerate 8 hours or overnight. Remove congealed fat. Stir in milk and cook on low until heated through. Just before serving, stir in cheese and cook until melted.

HAM AND CORN CHOWDER

You can put this appetite-satisfying, tasty one-dish meal together in less than 30 minutes.

SERVES 4

4 ears fresh corn or 2 cups frozen whole-kernel corn

1 3/4 cups low-sodium chicken broth

1 large yellow onion, chopped

1 medium potato or parsnip, peeled and cubed

1 cup chopped green, red, and/or yellow bell pepper

1 tablespoon minced fresh marjoram or 1 teaspoon dried marjoram

1/4 teaspoon salt

1/4 teaspoon white or black pepper

1/2 cup low-fat (1%) milk

2 tablespoons all-purpose flour

1 cup bite-size pieces cooked low-sodium ham

1 In a large saucepan over medium heat, combine corn, broth, onion, potato, bell pepper, marjoram, salt, and white pepper. Bring to boil, then reduce heat, cover, and simmer, stirring occasionally, until potato is almost tender, about 10 minutes.

2 In a small bowl, whisk together milk and flour. Stir into pan and cook, stirring constantly, until thickened and bubbly, about 2 minutes. Stir in ham and cook until heated through, about 2 minutes.

HAM CONFETTI CHOWDER

The many bright-colored vegetables in this chowder make it look like it was sprinkled with confetti.

3 tablespoons butter

1 cup diced carrots

1 cup diced zucchini

1 cup broccoli florets

1/2 cup chopped onion

1/2 cup chopped celery

1/4 cup all-purpose flour

1/2 teaspoon salt

1/2 teaspoon black pepper

1/4 teaspoon sugar

3 cups milk

1 cup chicken stock

1 cup whole-kernel corn

1 cup diced fully cooked ham

1/2 cup peas

1 jar (2 ounces) sliced pimiento, drained

1 cup (4 ounces) shredded cheddar cheese

1 In a Dutch oven over medium heat, melt butter. Add carrots, zucchini, broccoli, onion, and celery and sauté for 5 minutes or until crisp-tender. Sprinkle flour, salt, pepper, and sugar over vegetables and mix well.

2 Stir in milk and chicken stock and cook until thickened and bubbly. Add corn, ham, peas, and pimiento and cook until heated through, stirring often. Remove from heat, add cheese, and stir until melted.

HAM AND VEGETABLE CHOWDER

A meaty hambone and leftover mashed potatoes are key ingredients in this cauliflower-rich soup.

1 meaty hambone

1/2 cup (1 stick) butter

1 large onion, chopped

1 medium green bell pepper, cored, seeded, and chopped

3/4 cup all-purpose flour

1 1/2 teaspoons salt

1/4 teaspoon black pepper

4 cups milk

4 cups cauliflower florets, cooked and drained

2 cups mashed potatoes, prepared with milk and butter

Minced fresh parsley *(optional)*

1 In a Dutch oven or soup pot over medium heat, combine hambone and 8 cups water. Bring to boil, reduce heat, and simmer, uncovered, 1 1/2 hours. Remove bone. When cool enough to handle, remove meat from bone and add to pot.

2 In a large saucepan over medium heat, melt butter. Add onion and bell pepper and sauté 5 minutes or until tender. Stir in flour, salt, and black pepper until blended. Gradually add milk, bring to boil, and cook, stirring, until thickened, about 2 minutes. Add to ham pot, stir in cauliflower and potatoes, and cook until heated through. Sprinkle with parsley, if desired.

SCHOOL-DAY CHOWDER

This hotdog soup is a change-of-pace lunch for brown baggers, who almost always have sandwiches.

SERVES 5

1/4 cup (1/2 stick) butter

1/2 pound hotdogs, halved lengthwise and sliced

1 cup sliced celery

1/2 cup sliced carrot

1/2 cup chopped seeded green bell pepper

1/4 cup chopped onion

1/4 cup all-purpose flour

1/8 teaspoon black pepper

3 cups milk

2 cups (8 ounces) shredded cheddar cheese

1 In a large saucepan over medium heat, melt butter. Add hotdogs, celery, carrot, bell pepper, and onion and sauté 5 minutes or until vegetables are tender.

2 Stir in flour and pepper until blended. Gradually add milk, bring to boil, and cook, stirring, until thickened, about 2 minutes. Add cheese and stir until melted.

HAM AND CAULIFLOWER CHOWDER

This creamy chowder has plenty of vegetable, meat, and cheese.

SERVES 6

1 cup thinly sliced celery

2 cups cauliflower florets, fresh or frozen

1 can (13 ounces) chicken broth

1 cup half-and-half or evaporated milk

1 can (10 3/4 ounces) cream of potato soup

2 tablespoons cornstarch

1/8 teaspoon white pepper

2 cups cooked ham, diced

1/2 cup shredded cheddar cheese

Fresh chopped parsley

1 In a large saucepan, combine celery, cauliflower, and chicken broth. Bring to boil over medium heat, reduce heat, and simmer, covered, 10 minutes or until vegetables are almost tender. Set aside without draining.

2 In a mixing bowl, gradually stir half-and-half into undiluted potato soup. Blend in 1/4 cup water, cornstarch, and pepper.

3 Stir the milk-potato mixture into the cauliflower-broth mixture. Stir in the ham. Cook over low heat, 10 minutes. Just before serving, stir in cheese. Garnish with fresh parsley.

SIMPLE SAUSAGE CHOWDER

This creamy soup, flavored with fresh basil, makes a hearty lunch or first course for dinner.

SERVES 12

1 pound fully cooked smoked sausage, halved and thinly sliced

1 medium onion, quartered and thinly sliced

4 cups diced potatoes

2 tablespoons minced fresh parsley or 2 teaspoons parsley flakes

1 tablespoon minced fresh basil or 1 teaspoon dried basil

1 teaspoon salt

1/8 teaspoon black pepper

1 can (15 1/4 ounces) whole-kernel corn, drained

1 can (14 3/4 ounces) cream-style corn

1 can (12 ounces) evaporated milk

1 In a Dutch oven or soup pot over medium heat, brown sausage and onion. Drain off fat. Add 3 cups water, potatoes, parsley, basil, salt, and pepper. Bring to boil, reduce heat, and simmer, covered, 15 minutes or until potatoes are tender.

2 Add whole-kernel and cream-style corn and milk and cook 5 minutes or until heated through.

SAUSAGE AND CORN CHOWDER

This creamy mélange of fresh corn, spicy sausage, potatoes, heavy cream, onions, and jalapeño peppers is one of life's great indulgences.

SERVES 8

3 ears fresh corn, husked and cleaned

4 cups heavy whipping cream

2 cups chicken stock

4 garlic cloves, minced

10 fresh thyme sprigs

1 bay leaf

1 1/2 medium onions, finely chopped, divided

1/2 pound hot Italian sausage links

2 tablespoons butter

2 teaspoons minced jalapeño peppers with seeds (wear gloves when handling; they burn)

1/2 teaspoon ground cumin

2 tablespoons all-purpose flour

2 medium potatoes, peeled and cut into 1/2-inch cubes

Salt and black pepper to taste

1 1/2 teaspoons snipped fresh chives

1 Using a small, sharp knife, cut corn from cobs and set corn aside. In a large saucepan, combine corncobs, cream, stock, garlic, thyme, bay leaf, and one-third of onions. Bring almost to boil, reduce heat, and simmer, covered, 1 hour, stirring occasionally. Remove and discard corncobs.

2 Strain corn-cream mixture through a sieve set over a large bowl, pressing solids with back of spoon, and set aside. Meanwhile, in a large skillet over medium heat, brown sausage. Cool and cut into 1/2-inch slices.

3 In a large saucepan, melt butter. Add jalapeños, cumin, and remaining onions and sauté 5 minutes. Stir in flour and cook 2 minutes, stirring often. Gradually add corn-cream mixture. Add sausage and potatoes. Bring almost to boil, reduce heat, and simmer, covered, 25 minutes or until potatoes are tender.

4 Add corn and cook 5 minutes or just until tender. Remove bay leaf. Season with salt and pepper. For a thinner chowder, add additional chicken stock. Sprinkle with chives before serving.

SAUSAGE-BROCCOLI CHOWDER FOR A CROWD

Mushrooms combine with sausage and broccoli to make this creamy soup a popular crowd pleaser.

SERVES 12

1 pound bulk Italian sausage

2 tablespoons butter

1 medium onion, chopped

3 garlic cloves, minced

8 ounces fresh mushrooms, sliced

2 cans (14 1/2 ounces each) chicken broth

2 cups broccoli florets

2-3 carrots, diced

1 can (10 3/4 ounces) condensed cream of mushroom soup

9 ounces cheese tortellini, cooked and drained

1/2 teaspoon black pepper

1/2 teaspoon dried basil

1/2 teaspoon dried thyme

2 quarts half-and-half

1/2 cup grated Romano cheese

1 In a skillet over medium heat, crumble and cook sausage until no longer pink. Remove to paper towels to drain and set aside. Drain off fat from skillet.

2 In the same skillet, over low heat, melt butter. Add onion, garlic, and mushrooms and sauté 5 minutes or until tender and set aside.

3 In a Dutch oven, bring chicken broth to boil, add broccoli and carrots, reduce heat, and simmer, covered, 10 minutes or until tender.

4 Stir in sausage and mushroom mixture. Add soup, tortellini, pepper, basil, and thyme and heat through. Stir in half-and-half and Romano cheese and heat through.

REUBEN CHOWDER

If you like Reuben sandwiches, you'll like this soup. Rye croutons top a mix of sauerkraut, corned beef, and mozzarella cheese in a creamy mushroom and nacho cheese base.

SERVES 8

1 tablespoon butter, softened
3 slices rye bread
1 can (11 ounces) condensed
    nacho cheese soup
1 can (10 3/4 ounces) condensed
    cream of mushroom soup
3 cups milk
1 can (14 ounces) sauerkraut,
    drained and rinsed
12 ounces deli corned beef, diced
1 cup (4 ounces) shredded mozzarella cheese

1 Preheat oven to 375°F. Butter bread on both sides and cut into cubes. Place on ungreased baking sheet and bake until browned, about 6 minutes.

2 Meanwhile, in a large saucepan over medium heat, combine cheese soup, mushroom soup, milk, sauerkraut, and corned beef. Cook, stirring, 8 minutes or until heated through. Add cheese and stir until melted. Top with croutons.

BEEF, BROCCOLI, AND CHEESE CHOWDER

A happy combination of meat, vegetables, and tasty sauce, this soup is easy to make as well as easy to eat.

SERVES 4

1/2 pound ground beef
1/2 cup chopped onion
1/4 cup chopped green bell pepper
1 can (11 ounces) cheddar soup
1 soup can milk
1 teaspoon Worcestershire sauce
1 cup chopped broccoli
2 potatoes, peeled and diced

1 In a large saucepan over medium heat, sauté beef with onion and green pepper 5 minutes or until beef is browned and vegetables are tender. Drain off fat.

2 Stir in cheddar soup, milk, and Worcestershire sauce. Add broccoli and potatoes. Bring to boil, reduce heat, and simmer, covered, about 30 minutes or until potatoes are tender.

CHICKEN CHOWDER

This satisfying chowder can be made in minutes from a well-stocked pantry.

SERVES 4

1 package (10 ounces) frozen mixed
    vegetables
2 cans (10 3/4 ounces) condensed,
    reduced-sodium cream of chicken soup
1 1/2 cups milk
1 can (5 ounces) white chicken
    packed in water, drained

1 In a medium saucepan, combine 1 cup water and mixed vegetables. Bring to boil and stir in cream of chicken soup, milk, and chicken.

2 Return to boil, stirring occasionally. Pour into bowls and serve.

CHICKEN-CORN CHOWDER

Typical of New England chowders, this one is hearty, creamy, and chock-full of chicken and vegetables.

SERVES 6

3 strips lean bacon, diced
1 large yellow onion, chopped
1 celery stalk, chopped
4 medium all-purpose potatoes,
    peeled and cut into 1/4-inch cubes
3 cups homemade chicken stock or canned
    low-sodium chicken broth
3 cups low-fat (1%) milk
12 soda crackers, crumbled
3 cups fresh whole-kernel corn (from 6 ears)
    or frozen kernels
3 skinless, boneless chicken breast halves
    (12 ounces), cut into bite-size pieces
1/2 teaspoon salt
1/4 teaspoon paprika

1 In a 6-quart Dutch oven, sauté bacon over medium-high heat 3 minutes or until crisp, then transfer to paper towels to drain. Pour off all but 2 teaspoons of the bacon drippings.

2 Add onion and celery and sauté 5 minutes or until tender. Stir in potatoes and stock and bring to boil. Reduce heat and simmer, uncovered, 10 minutes or until potatoes are tender.

3 Meanwhile, in a medium bowl, stir milk with crackers and let stand 5 minutes or until crackers are thoroughly soaked. Stir this cracker mixture into the chowder, then add corn, chicken, salt, and paprika. Cook 10 minutes or until chicken is cooked through. Ladle into large soup bowls and garnish with bacon.

CHICKEN-POTATO CHOWDER

The simple, delicious flavors of this soup will make it popular with the entire family. Try it for a weekend lunch, served with plenty of crusty bread and fresh fruit for dessert.

SERVES 4

1 tablespoon extra-virgin olive oil
2 slices bacon, finely chopped
1 chicken thigh (about 5 ounces), skinned
2 onions, peeled and finely chopped
1 pound potatoes, peeled and diced
2 1/2 cups chicken stock
1/2 teaspoon dried thyme
10 fluid ounces low-fat (1%) milk
Salt and pepper
Chopped parsley, or chopped parsley
    and fresh thyme leaves

1 In a large saucepan over low heat, heat oil. Add bacon, chicken, onions, and sauté 3 minutes. Increase heat to medium and cook, stirring often and turning chicken once, 5 minutes or until chicken is golden.

2 Add potatoes and cook 2 minutes, stirring. Pour in stock, add thyme, and season with salt and pepper to taste. Bring to boil, reduce heat, and simmer, covered, 30 minutes.

3 Transfer chicken to plate. Remove and discard bone. Chop meat and return to soup. Stir in milk and heat soup through without boiling.

4 Ladle soup into bowls and garnish with parsley or parsley and thyme.

CHICKEN CHOWDER WITH CHEESE

A lovely cheddar flavor embraces the chicken and vegetables in this scrumptious chowder.

SERVES 6

3 cups chicken stock
2 cups diced peeled potatoes
1 cup diced carrots
1 cup diced celery
1/2 cup diced onion
1 1/2 teaspoons salt
1/4 teaspoon black pepper
1/4 cup (1/2 stick) butter
1/3 cup all-purpose flour
2 cups milk
2 cups (about 8 ounces) shredded
    cheddar cheese
2 cups diced cooked chicken

1 In a 4-quart saucepan, bring chicken stock to boil. Add potatoes, carrots, celery, onion, salt, and pepper. Reduce heat, cover, and simmer 15 minutes or until vegetables are tender.

2 Meanwhile, in a medium saucepan over medium-low heat, melt butter and add flour and mix well. Gradually stir in milk, cooking over low heat until slightly thickened. Stir in cheese and cook until melted. Add cheese sauce to stock along with chicken. Cook over low heat until heated through, stirring often.

CHICKEN-TORTILLA CHOWDER

This thick, creamy chowder mixes Mexican and American ingredients to fine effect.

SERVES 8

1 can (14 1/2 ounces) chicken broth
1 can (10 3/4 ounces) condensed
    cream of chicken soup
1 can (10 3/4 ounces) condensed
    cream of potato soup
1 1/2 cups milk
2 cups cubed cooked chicken
1 can (11 ounces) Mexican-style corn
1 jar (4 1/2 ounces) sliced mushrooms,
    drained
1 can (4 ounces) chopped green chiles
1/4 cup thinly sliced scallions
4 flour tortillas (6 to 7 inches),
    cut into 1/2-inch strips
1 1/2 cups (6 ounces) shredded
    cheddar cheese

1 In a Dutch oven or soup pot, combine broth, chicken soup, potato soup, and milk. Add chicken, corn, mushrooms, chiles, and scallions and mix well. Bring to boil.

2 Add tortilla strips. Reduce heat and simmer, uncovered, 8 minutes or until heated through. Add cheese and stir just until melted.

HARVEST CORN CHOWDER

Easy to put together, this is a wonderful, warming soup to share with family and friends.

SERVES 12

1 tablespoon butter

1 medium onion, chopped

1 can (14 1/2 ounces) cream-style corn

4 cups whole-kernel corn

4 cups diced peeled potatoes

1 can (10 3/4 ounces) condensed
    cream of mushroom soup

1 jar (6 ounces) sliced mushrooms, drained

3 cups milk

1/2 medium green bell pepper, chopped

3/4 medium red bell pepper, chopped

Black pepper to taste

1/2 pound bacon, cooked and crumbled

1 In a saucepan over low heat, melt butter. Add onion and sauté 4 minutes or until tender. Add cream-style corn, kernel corn, potatoes, soup, and mushrooms. Stir in milk. Add green and red peppers. Season with black pepper.

2 Bring to boil, reduce heat, and simmer, covered, 30 minutes or until vegetables are tender. Garnish with bacon.

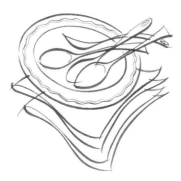

CORN CHOWDER WITH PANCETTA

Substantial and warming, this soup was inspired by a traditional recipe from New England.

SERVES 4

1 can (12 ounces) whole-kernel corn

1 tablespoon sunflower oil

5 slices pancetta or bacon, chopped

1 large onion, sliced

3 medium potatoes, cubed

1 1/4 cups light cream

1 1/4 cups milk

Salt and black pepper

Fresh parsley, chopped, to garnish

1 Put a kettle of water on to boil. Drain corn kernels and in a blender or food processor, puree into a chunky paste, reserving a few whole kernels for garnish.

2 In a saucepan over medium heat, heat oil and cook pancetta or bacon until crisp and brown. Set aside on paper towels.

3 Add onion to fat remaining in pan and sauté over medium heat 5 minutes or until softened. Stir in corn, potatoes, and 2 1/2 cups boiling water. Reduce heat and simmer, covered, 15 minutes.

4 Meanwhile, in a saucepan over medium heat, heat cream and milk without boiling. When potatoes are cooked but still retain their shape, stir in cream and milk, and heat to just below boiling point. Stir in pancetta or bacon and add salt and pepper to taste. Garnish with chopped parsley and corn kernels.

CORN CHOWDER WITH SODA CRACKERS

When it's blustery and cold outside, nothing's more warming inside than a bowlful of chowder, particularly corn chowder. (Photograph on page 7)

SERVES 6

3 slices turkey bacon

1 large onion, chopped

1 pound small red potatoes, quartered

2 1/2 cups reduced-sodium chicken broth

6 large ears corn, shucked,
   or 2 packages (10 ounces each)
   frozen whole-kernel corn

18 (2-inch-square) soda crackers,
   crumbled (1 cup)

2 1/2 cups reduced-fat (2%) milk

1/2 teaspoon salt

1/2 teaspoon hot red pepper sauce

1 tablespoon chopped parsley

1 Cook bacon in a large heavy nonstick saucepan over medium-high heat until crisp. Transfer to paper towels with slotted spatula to drain and crumble it. Sauté onion in pan drippings 5 minutes or until soft. Stir in potatoes and broth and bring to boil. Reduce heat and simmer, uncovered, 20 minutes or until potatoes are tender.

2 If using fresh ears of corn, stand cobs upright and cut off kernels with serrated knife. If using frozen corn, put kernels in colander, rinse with warm water, and drain. Put cracker crumbs into medium bowl and stir in milk. Let stand 5 minutes or until crackers are soft.

3 Meanwhile, use a handheld blender to puree about half of the potato mixture while still in saucepan on range. Or transfer half of potato mixture to a food processor and puree and return to saucepan. Stir in cracker mixture, corn, salt, and red pepper sauce. Cook 10 minutes or until flavors are blended. Top with parsley and bacon.

CORN CHOWDER WITH PEPPERS AND CHILES

Sweet peppers and mild chiles pump up the flavor and healthiness of this hearty favorite. (Photograph on page 5)

SERVES 6

3 slices turkey bacon

1 tablespoon olive oil

1 large onion, finely chopped

1/2 pound all-purpose potatoes,
   unpeeled and cut into 1/2-inch cubes

2 cans (14 1/2 ounces each) reduced-sodium,
   fat-free chicken broth

1 can (15 1/4 ounces) whole-kernel corn,
   drained

1 red bell pepper, cored, seeded,
   and finely chopped

2 cups low-fat (1%) milk

1/2 teaspoon salt

1 tablespoon canned chopped mild green chiles

1 In a large saucepan over medium heat, cook bacon 6 minutes or until crisp. Transfer to paper towel to drain.

2 Heat oil in same pan over medium heat. Add onion. Sauté 5 minutes or until softened. Add potatoes and broth. Bring to boil, reduce heat, and simmer, partially covered, 20 minutes or until potatoes are tender. Stir in corn. Simmer 5 minutes.

3 Transfer half of potatoes and corn with a little liquid to food processor. Puree. Return to saucepan. Add red pepper, milk, and salt. Cover and simmer 10 minutes.

4 Finely chop bacon. Stir into chowder with chiles and heat through.

CORN AND BACON CHOWDER

This rich chowder is popular for community or family get-togethers.

SERVES 6 TO 8

4 bacon strips
1 cup chopped onion
1 1/2 cups diced peeled potatoes
1 teaspoon chicken bouillon granules
1/4 cup all-purpose flour
2 cups milk
1 cup half-and-half
1 package (16 ounces) frozen corn
8 ounces process American cheese,
    cut into cubes
Salt and black pepper to taste

1 In a large saucepan over medium heat, cook bacon until crisp. Transfer to paper towels to drain, then crumble and set aside.

2 Add onion to pan and sauté in drippings 3 minutes or until tender. Add 2 cups water, potatoes, and bouillon and bring to boil. Reduce heat, cover, and simmer 10 minutes or until potatoes are tender.

3 In a small bowl, combine flour and 1/4 cup milk until smooth. Add flour mixture, half-and-half, corn, and remaining milk to pan and bring to boil. Cook, stirring, until thickened, about 2 minutes. Reduce heat, add cheese and bacon and cook, stirring, until cheese is melted. Season with salt and pepper.

LOW-FAT CORN CHOWDER

Creamy but healthy, this version of corn chowder gets its rich taste from pureed potatoes and low-fat milk.

SERVES 8

2 ounces turkey bacon, coarsely chopped
2 large onions, diced
2 large carrots, diced
2 celery stalks, diced
12 ounces all-purpose potatoes,
    peeled and diced
6 cups chicken stock
2 cups fresh or frozen whole-kernel corn
2 cups low-fat (1%) milk
1/8 teaspoon salt
1/8 teaspoon black pepper
Cayenne pepper

1 In a 4-quart saucepan, cook bacon over medium heat about 4 minutes or until it is browned and the fat is rendered. Remove bacon with a slotted spoon and reserve on paper towels for garnish.

2 Add onions, carrots, and celery to saucepan and sauté 5 minutes or until softened. Stir in potatoes and chicken stock and bring to boil. Reduce heat and simmer, partially covered, stirring occasionally, 10 minutes or until vegetables are tender.

3 Add corn kernels and return soup to boil. Reduce heat and simmer, uncovered, 5 minutes. Remove from heat and cool. Using slotted spoon, transfer 2 1/2 cups of vegetables to a blender or food processor. Puree until smooth.

4 Add puree and milk to saucepan and simmer 3 minutes. Season with salt, pepper, and a pinch of cayenne. Serve garnished with bacon.

POTATO-CORN CHOWDER

Here's a rare soup: filled with interesting and diverse ingredients, and made entirely in a microwave oven!

2 ounces thick-sliced bacon, diced

1 pound white potatoes, peeled and cubed

1/2 cup chopped onion

2 garlic cloves, minced

1 cup chicken stock

1/2 teaspoon crushed red pepper flakes (optional)

4 cups milk, room temperature

1 tablespoon cornstarch

1 tablespoon salt

3 cups corn, fresh or canned

1/3 cup diced green bell pepper

1/3 cup diced red bell pepper

2 tablespoons diced scallion

2 tablespoons chopped fresh parsley

1 In a 4-quart microwave-safe bowl, cook bacon at full power 2 minutes or until crisp. Add potatoes, onion, and garlic and stir to coat with bacon drippings. Cover bowl with wax paper and microwave at full power 5 minutes.

2 Add stock and pepper flakes, if desired. Cover, return to microwave, and cook 8 minutes or until potatoes are tender.

3 In separate bowl, stir 2 tablespoons milk into cornstarch and add to potato mixture with remaining milk, salt, corn, green pepper, and red pepper. Stir well. Cover and cook, stirring twice, 6 minutes or until vegetables are tender. Just before serving, stir in scallion and parsley.

POTATO BACON CHOWDER

It's easy to make a good supper soup based on ingredients you are likely to have on hand, such as onions, potatoes, parsnips, bacon, and milk.

3 1/2 cups whole milk

1 tablespoon extra-virgin olive oil

2 slices bacon, chopped

1 large onion, chopped

2 tablespoons flour

3 medium potatoes, scrubbed and diced

1 parsnip, grated

Freshly grated nutmeg

4 ounces baby spinach leaves

Salt and black pepper

1 In a medium saucepan, bring milk just to boil. In another large saucepan over medium-high heat, heat oil. Add bacon and onion and sauté 2 minutes. Add flour, stir to combine, then slowly add one-quarter of hot milk, stirring and scraping bottom of pan to mix in flour. When mixture thickens, stir in remaining hot milk.

2 Add potatoes and parsnip. Season with salt, pepper, and nutmeg to taste. Bring to boil, reduce heat, and simmer, partially covered, stirring occasionally, 10 minutes or until vegetables are nearly tender.

3 Stir in spinach and simmer 2 minutes or until spinach has wilted. Taste soup, adjust seasoning, if necessary, and serve.

IDAHO POTATO CHOWDER

This richly flavored chowder uses just enough bacon to give it an old-fashioned taste.

SERVES 6

2 strips lean bacon, chopped

1 cup finely sliced leeks or 8 large scallions with tops, finely sliced

2 garlic cloves, minced

3 medium potatoes, peeled and cubed

1 3/4 cups low-sodium chicken broth

1/2 teaspoon salt

1/4 teaspoon white or black pepper

2 cups low-fat (1%) milk

3 tablespoons all-purpose flour

1 teaspoon dried basil

1 In a large saucepan over medium heat, cook bacon until crisp. Remove from pan, reserving drippings, and transfer to paper towels to drain.

2 Add leeks and garlic to pan and sauté in drippings until tender, about 3 minutes. Add potatoes, broth, salt, and pepper and bring to boil. Reduce heat, cover, and simmer until potatoes are tender, about 20 minutes. Using a fork, slightly mash potatoes against side of pan.

3 In a medium bowl, whisk together milk, flour, and basil, then stir into pan. Cook over medium heat, stirring constantly, until starting to thicken. Continue to cook, stirring, until thickened, about 2 minutes. Ladle into bowls and top with bacon.

MIXED POTATO CHOWDER

Red and sweet potatoes hold their shape, while baking potatoes fall apart and thicken the broth.

SERVES 4

2 teaspoons vegetable oil

1 onion, finely chopped

3 garlic cloves, minced

1 pound baking potatoes, peeled and thinly sliced

3/4 pound red potatoes, cut into 1/2-inch chunks

1/2 pound sweet potatoes, peeled and cut into 1/2-inch chunks

1 cup chicken stock

3/4 teaspoon salt

1/2 teaspoon dried sage

1 cup reduced-fat (2%) milk

2/3 cup frozen whole-kernel corn

1/2 cup chopped parsley

1 In a medium saucepan, heat oil over medium heat. Add onion and garlic, and sauté 7 minutes or until onion is soft.

2 Add baking potatoes, red potatoes, and sweet potatoes, stirring to coat. Add stock, 2 cups water, salt, and sage, and bring to boil. Reduce heat and simmer, covered, 25 minutes or until red potatoes and sweet potatoes are tender, and baking potatoes are soft and creamy.

3 Stir in milk and corn, and simmer 4 minutes or until corn is heated through. Stir in parsley and serve.

POTATO-VEGETABLE CHOWDER

This chowder gets some of its flavor from root vegetables, making it more interesting and more nutritious than plain potato chowder.

SERVES 6

2 strips lean bacon, chopped

1 cup finely sliced leeks or 8 large scallions with tops, finely sliced

2 garlic cloves, minced

1 1/2 cups cubed peeled potatoes

1 1/2 cups cubed peeled turnips, parsnips, or rutabagas

1 3/4 cups low-sodium chicken broth

1/2 teaspoon salt

1/4 teaspoon white or black pepper

2 cups low-fat (1%) milk

3 tablespoons all-purpose flour

1 teaspoon dried basil

1 In a large saucepan over medium heat, cook bacon until crisp. Remove from pan, reserving drippings, and transfer to paper towels to drain.

2 Add leeks and garlic to pan and sauté in drippings until tender. Add potatoes, turnips, broth, salt, and pepper and bring to boil. Reduce heat, cover, and simmer until vegetables are tender, about 20 minutes. Using a fork, slightly mash vegetables against side of pan.

3 In a medium bowl, whisk together milk, flour, and basil, then stir into pan. Cook over medium heat, stirring constantly, until starting to thicken. Continue to cook, stirring, until thickened, about 2 minutes. Ladle into bowls and top with bacon.

CREAMY ASPARAGUS CHOWDER

This can be a rich full meal or an elegant starter, depending on the size of the serving.

SERVES 5 OR 10

1/4 cup butter

2 medium onions, chopped

2 cups chopped celery

1 garlic clove, minced

1/2 cup all-purpose flour

1 large potato, peeled and cut into 1/2-inch cubes

4 cups milk

4 cups chicken stock

1/2 teaspoon dried thyme

1/2 teaspoon dried marjoram

4 cups chopped fresh asparagus, cooked and drained

Salt and pepper to taste

Sliced almonds

Shredded cheddar cheese

Chopped fresh tomato

1 In a Dutch oven over medium heat, melt butter and sauté onions, celery, and garlic 4 minutes or until tender. Stir in flour and cook 2 minutes.

2 Add potato, milk, stock, and herbs. Cook over low heat, stirring occasionally, 30 minutes or until potato is tender and soup is thickened.

3 Add asparagus, salt, and pepper and heat through. To serve, sprinkle with almonds, cheese, and chopped tomato.

ASPARAGUS AND SWEET POTATO BISQUE

A surprising combination of vegetables makes a lovely first-course or lunch soup.

SERVES 4

1 1/2 pounds asparagus, trimmed and cut into 1-inch lengths, reserving trimmings

1 large sweet potato (8 ounces), peeled and cut into 1/2-inch cubes

2 teaspoons olive oil

1 onion, halved and thinly sliced

2 tablespoons flour

1 cup chicken stock

1/2 teaspoon dried marjoram

1/8-1/4 teaspoon cayenne pepper

1/2 teaspoon salt

3/4 cup low-fat (1%) milk

3 ounces baked ham, finely diced

1 In a medium pot, bring 2 1/2 cups water to boil. Add 8 of the asparagus tips and cook 2 minutes to blanch. Remove with a slotted spoon and set aside for garnish.

2 Add sweet potato to the boiling water and cook 10 minutes or until tender. Remove with a strainer or slotted spoon. Add asparagus trimmings, reduce heat and simmer, covered, 10 minutes. Reserving liquid, strain and discard asparagus trimmings. You should have 2 cups liquid.

3 Meanwhile, in a medium saucepan, heat oil over medium-low heat. Add onion and sauté 7 minutes or until light golden. Stir in flour until onion is well coated. Add reserved cooking liquid, stock, remaining asparagus, marjoram, cayenne, and salt, and bring to boil. Reduce heat and simmer, covered, 7 minutes or until asparagus is tender.

4 Transfer mixture to a food processor and process to a smooth puree. Return puree to pan and stir in milk, ham, and sweet potato. Cook 2 minutes or until heated through. Serve soup garnished with reserved asparagus tips.

BROCCOLI CHOWDER

Nutmeg seasons the creamy broth that holds the broccoli florets and diced potatoes in this rich, satisfying soup.

SERVES 6

3 cups broccoli florets

2 cups diced peeled potatoes

1/3 cup sliced scallions

1 teaspoon salt

1/2 teaspoon black pepper

3 tablespoons butter

3 tablespoons all-purpose flour

1/8 teaspoon ground nutmeg

2 cups milk

1/2 cup (2 ounces) shredded cheddar cheese

1 In a large saucepan, combine 2 cups water, broccoli, potatoes, scallions, salt, and pepper. Bring to boil, reduce heat, and simmer, covered, 12 minutes or until vegetables are tender.

2 Meanwhile, in a medium saucepan over low heat, melt butter. Stir in flour and nutmeg until smooth. Gradually add milk, bring to boil, and cook, stirring, until thickened, about 2 minutes. Stir into vegetable mixture and heat through. Sprinkle each serving with cheese.

CABBAGE CHOWDER

This creamy cabbage soup is seasoned with caraway seeds and slices of your favorite smoked sausage.

SERVES 6

2 tablespoons butter

2 cups diagonally sliced carrots

1/4 teaspoon caraway seed

2 cans (10 3/4 ounces each) condensed cream of celery soup

1 soup can milk

3 cups shredded cabbage

1 pound smoked sausage, cut into 1/2-inch diagonal slices

1 In a large soup pot over low heat, melt butter. Add carrots and caraway seeds and sauté 5 minutes or until carrots are just crisp-tender.

2 Add soup, milk, 1 soup can water, cabbage, and sausage. Bring to boil, reduce heat, and simmer, covered, 15 minutes or until cabbage is tender.

BUTTERNUT BISQUE

The lovely winter squash flavor of this creamy soup is given some extra zip by jalapeño pepper.

SERVES 8

1/4 cup (1/2 stick) butter

2 medium carrots, sliced

2 celery stalks with leaves, chopped

2 medium leeks (white portion only), sliced

1 jalapeño pepper, seeded, deveined, and minced (wear gloves when handling; they burn)

2 pounds butternut squash, peeled, seeded, and cut into cubes (about 6 cups)

2 cans (14 1/2 ounces each) chicken broth

1/2 teaspoon ground ginger

1/2 cup half-and-half

1/2 teaspoon salt

1/4 teaspoon white pepper

1/2 cup chopped pecans, toasted

1 In a large saucepan over low heat, melt butter. Add carrots, celery, leeks, and jalapeño and sauté 10 minutes.

2 Add squash, broth, and ginger. Bring to boil, reduce heat, and simmer, covered, 25 minutes or until squash is tender. Cool until lukewarm.

3 Transfer soup in batches to a blender or food processor, cover, and puree until smooth. Return to pan, stir in half-and-half, salt, and pepper, and heat through without boiling. Garnish with pecans.

PUMPKIN BISQUE

With a lacy garnish that's unbelievably easy to make, this rich bisque is the perfect starter for Thanksgiving dinner. (Photograph on page 10)

SERVES 4

2 teaspoons olive oil

1 small onion, finely chopped

3 garlic cloves, minced

1 small sweet potato (about 6 ounces), peeled and thinly sliced

1 can (15 ounces) pumpkin puree

1 tablespoon light brown sugar

1 teaspoon salt

3/4 teaspoon ground pepper

1/2 teaspoon rubbed sage

1 cup fat-free half-and-half

2 tablespoons grated Parmesan cheese

4 pinches of cracked pepper

1 Heat oil in a large nonstick saucepan over low heat. Add onion and garlic and sauté 5 minutes or until onion is tender. Add sweet potato and 1 1/2 cups water. Bring to boil. Reduce heat and simmer, covered, 10 minutes or until sweet potato is tender.

2 Stir in pumpkin puree, brown sugar, salt, ground pepper, sage, and 1 cup water, and bring to boil. Reduce heat and simmer, covered, 5 minutes or until flavors have blended. Working in batches if necessary, transfer to food processor and puree until smooth.

3 Return to saucepan and stir in 3/4 cup half-and-half. Cook 2 minutes or until heated through. Spoon into soup bowls. With a spoon, drizzle remaining half-and-half over soup. Use the tip of a knife to create a pattern. Sprinkle Parmesan and cracked pepper on top.

SPINACH BISQUE

Not only is this soup hearty and filling, it's elegant and easy to prepare.

SERVES 5 TO 6

2 tablespoons butter

1/2 cup chopped onion

1/3 cup all-purpose flour

1 teaspoon salt

1/8 teaspoon ground nutmeg

2 1/2 cups milk

3/4 cup cubed process American cheese

1 package (10 ounces) frozen
   chopped spinach, thawed and drained

Oyster crackers *(optional)*

1 In a 3-quart saucepan over low heat, melt butter. Add onion and sauté 3 minutes or until tender. Add flour, salt, and nutmeg and stir until smooth. Gradually whisk in milk and 1 cup water.

2 Add cheese and cook, stirring, over medium heat until melted. Add spinach, cover, and simmer 4 minutes. Serve with oyster crackers, if desired.

ROOT VEGETABLE CHOWDER WITH BACON BITS

How many helpful vitamins and minerals can you squeeze into one serving of soup? Plenty, when the soup is a blend of nutritional powerhouses like sweet potatoes, carrots, onions, peppers, and potatoes. (Photograph on page 14)

SERVES 4

2 teaspoons olive oil

1 large onion, finely chopped

2 celery stalks, coarsely chopped

1 1/4 teaspoons dried thyme, crumbled

2 medium carrots, peeled
   and coarsely chopped

1 large yam or sweet potato,
   peeled and coarsely chopped

1 medium parsnip, peeled
   and coarsely chopped

1 large red potato, peeled
   and coarsely chopped

1/2 green bell pepper, cored, seeded,
   and coarsely chopped

1 can (14 1/2 ounces) reduced-sodium,
   low-fat chicken broth or vegetable broth

1/2 teaspoon salt

1 2/3 cups reduced-fat (2%) milk

1 tablespoon balsamic vinegar

3 strips turkey bacon, cooked
   and coarsely chopped

1 In a large saucepan over medium heat, heat oil. Add onion, celery, and thyme. Sauté 5 minutes or until softened. Add carrots, yam, parsnip, potato, green pepper, chicken broth, and salt. Add just enough water to cover ingredients. Bring to boil, reduce heat, and simmer, covered, 30 minutes or until vegetables are tender.

2 In a blender, puree half the soup until smooth. Return puree to saucepan. Stir in milk. Gently heat. Stir in vinegar. Sprinkle with bacon before serving.

SUCCOTASH CHOWDER

The combination of corn, lima beans, and milk gives this chowder lots of good protein with very little fat.

SERVES 9

1 1/2 tablespoons olive or canola oil
2 large onions, diced
2 carrots, diced
2 celery stalks, diced
6 cups chicken or vegetable stock
2 cups fresh or frozen whole-kernel corn
2 cups fresh or frozen baby lima beans
2 cups low-fat (1%) milk
1 tablespoon cornstarch
1/2 teaspoon dry mustard
1/2 teaspoon finely grated lemon zest
1/8 teaspoon salt
1/8 teaspoon black pepper

1 In a 4-quart saucepan, heat oil over medium heat. Add onions, carrots, celery, and 1/4 cup of the stock, and sauté 5 minutes or until softened.

2 Stir in corn kernels and lima beans. Add remaining stock and bring the mixture to boil. Reduce heat and simmer, partially covered, stirring occasionally, 10 minutes or until vegetables are tender.

3 In a small bowl, combine 1/2 cup milk with cornstarch and mustard and whisk until smooth. Stir into soup with remaining milk and lemon zest. Return soup to boil, reduce heat, and simmer about 3 minutes. Season with salt and pepper.

ZUCCHINI GARDEN CHOWDER

When your zucchini plants outdo themselves toward the end of the summer, this is the recipe to pull out.

SERVES 8

1/3 cup butter
2 medium zucchini, chopped
1 medium onion, chopped
2 tablespoons minced fresh parsley
1 teaspoon dried basil
1/3 cup all-purpose flour
1 teaspoon salt
1/4 teaspoon black pepper
3 chicken bouillon cubes
1 teaspoon lemon juice
1 can (14 1/2 ounces) diced
    tomatoes, undrained
1 can (12 ounces) evaporated milk
1 package (10 ounces) frozen corn
1/4 cup grated Parmesan cheese
2 cups (8 ounces) shredded cheddar cheese
Pinch of sugar *(optional)*
Chopped parsley *(optional)*

1 In a Dutch oven or soup pot over medium heat, melt butter. Add zucchini, onion, parsley, and basil and sauté 4 minutes or until vegetables are tender.

2 Stir in flour, salt, and pepper, then gradually stir in 3 cups water. Add bouillon and lemon juice and mix well. Bring to boil and cook, stirring, 2 minutes.

3 Add tomatoes, milk, and corn and bring to boil. Reduce heat, cover, and simmer 5 minutes or until corn is tender. Just before serving, stir in Parmesan and cheddar cheese until melted. Add sugar and garnish with parsley, if desired.

VERMONT CHEDDAR CHEESE SOUP

SERVES 6

3 tablespoons unsalted butter

1 celery stalk, chopped (1/2 cup)

6 scallions, thinly sliced (3/4 cup)

1 small yellow onion, chopped (1/2 cup)

3 tablespoons all-purpose flour

1/8 teaspoon ground nutmeg

1/8 teaspoon black pepper

2 cups homemade chicken stock or
    canned low-sodium chicken broth

2 cups light cream

2 cups whole milk

3/4 teaspoon salt

1/8 teaspoon cayenne pepper

12 ounces sharp Vermont cheddar cheese,
    shredded (3 cups)

Vermont cheddar cheese is a pale color but has a distinctive flavor and bite that enhance this rich soup.

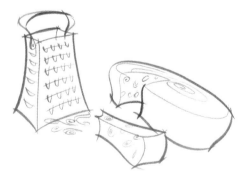

1 In a large saucepan, melt butter over medium-high heat. Add celery, 1/2 cup scallions and onion. Sauté 5 minutes or until tender. Stir in flour, nutmeg, and black pepper and cook 2 minutes, stirring constantly.

2 Whisk in stock and bring to boil. Reduce heat, cover, and simmer 15 minutes, stirring occasionally. Stir in cream, milk, salt, and cayenne. Heat just until soup begins to bubble.

3 Add cheese, one handful at a time, and whisk constantly until melted. Do not let it boil. Ladle into bowls and garnish with the remaining 1/4 cup scallions.

SAVORY CHEESE SOUP

This creamy soup is great for parties. Let guests serve themselves and choose from fun garnishes such as popcorn, croutons, and scallions.

SERVES 6 TO 8

3 cans (14 1/2 ounces each) chicken broth

1 small onion, chopped

1 large carrot, chopped

1 celery stalk, chopped

1/4 cup chopped seeded red bell pepper

2 tablespoons butter

1 teaspoon salt

1/2 teaspoon black pepper

1/3 cup all-purpose flour

1 package (8 ounces) cream cheese,
    cut into cubes and softened

2 cups (8 ounces) shredded cheddar cheese

1 can (12 ounces) beer *(optional)*

Croutons *(optional)*

Popcorn *(optional)*

Sliced scallions *(optional)*

1 In a slow cooker, combine broth, onion, carrot, celery, bell pepper, butter, salt, and black pepper. Cover and cook on low 7 hours.

2 In a small bowl, whisk flour into 1/3 cup cold water until smooth. Stir into soup, cover, and cook on high until thickened, about 30 minutes longer.

3 Stir in cream cheese and cheddar until blended. Stir in beer, if desired. Cover and cook on low until heated through, about 20 minutes. Serve with desired toppings.

FOUR-CHEESE SOUP

This rich, smooth starter soup is a surprising blend of four diverse cheese flavors. Sautéed onion is the only other seasoning, while potato and cream keep it thick and velvety.

SERVES 6

2 tablespoons butter

1 onion, chopped

2 cans (14 1/2 ounces) low-sodium chicken broth

1 medium potato, peeled and diced

2 cups half-and-half, regular or no-fat

3/4 cup freshly shredded provolone cheese

3/4 cup freshly shredded parmesan cheese

3/4 cup freshly shredded mozzarella cheese

3/4 cup freshly grated cheddar cheese

Croutons *(optional)*

1 In a large saucepan over medium heat, melt butter. Add onion and sauté 5 minutes or until golden. Add stock and potato and bring to boil. Reduce heat and simmer, covered, 15 minutes, stirring occasionally

2 Remove from heat and let cool slightly. Puree soup, in batches, in blender or food processor and return to saucepan. Add half-and-half and bring to

simmer. Gradually whisk cheeses into soup until melted. Ladle soup into bowls. Sprinkle with croutons, if desired.

VERMONT CHEDDAR-APPLE SOUP

This is a hearty fall soup that should appeal to everyone. If you can't get Vermont cheddar, which is pale in color, use a sharp yellow cheddar.

SERVES 4

2 tablespoons unsalted butter

4 cups peeled, cored, and chopped tart apples

1 cup peeled diced potatoes

1 stalk celery, diced

1 small onion, chopped

1/2 teaspoon dried thyme

1/4 cup white wine

4 cups chicken stock

3 cups shredded Vermont cheddar cheese

Salt

White pepper

1/8 teaspoon ground nutmeg

1/4 cup heavy cream

1 In a large heavy-bottomed saucepan over medium heat, melt butter. Add apples, potatoes, celery, onion, and thyme and sauté 10 minutes or until softened. Add white wine and scrape up residue from sautéing.

2 Add chicken stock and bring to boil. Reduce heat and simmer, covered, 30 minutes. Remove from heat and let cool slightly. In blender or food processor, puree soup and return to pan.

3 Reheat soup over medium heat. Gradually stir in cheese, salt and pepper to taste, nutmeg, and cream. Cook until cheese is melted without boiling.

GOLDEN CHEESE SOUP

This healthier version of cheese soup calls for less cheese and butter and low-fat milk in place of cream and whole milk.

SERVES 6

2 tablespoons unsalted butter
1 celery stalk, chopped (1/2 cup)
6 scallions, thinly sliced (3/4 cup)
1 small yellow onion, chopped (1/2 cup)
3 tablespoons all-purpose flour
1/8 teaspoon ground nutmeg
1/8 teaspoon black pepper
2 cups homemade chicken stock or
    canned low-sodium chicken broth
1 quart (4 cups) low-fat (1%) milk
1/8 teaspoon cayenne pepper
8 ounces sharp cheddar cheese,
    shredded (2 cups)

1 In a large saucepan, melt butter over medium-high heat. Add celery, 1/2 cup scallions, and onion. Sauté 5 minutes or until tender. Stir in flour, nutmeg, and black pepper and cook 2 minutes.

2 Whisk in stock and bring to boil. Reduce heat, cover, and simmer 15 minutes, stirring occasionally. Stir in milk and cayenne and heat just until soup bubbles.

3 Gradually add cheese and whisk constantly until melted. Do not let it boil. Ladle into bowls and garnish with remaining 1/4 cup scallions.

CHEESE AND HOT PEPPER SOUP

This is a very thick and cheesy soup that you can make as hot as you like with cayenne pepper.

SERVES 12

1/3 cup finely chopped carrots
1/3 cup finely chopped celery
1 cup thinly sliced scallions
3/4 cup butter
1 medium onion, chopped
1 cup plus 2 tablespoons flour
4 cups milk
4 cups chicken stock
1 jar (16 ounces) process
    American cheese spread
1/8 teaspoon cayenne pepper or to taste
Salt and black pepper to taste
1 tablespoon prepared mustard

1 In a large saucepan, combine carrots, celery, and scallions with 2 cups water. Bring to boil, reduce heat, and simmer 3 minutes or until tender. Set aside without draining.

2 In a large saucepan, over medium heat, melt butter. Add onion and sauté 3 minutes or until transparent. Stir in flour and blend well without browning.

3 In another saucepan, combine milk and stock. Bring to boil and reduce heat to simmer. Whisk in onion-flour mixture. Add process American cheese spread, cayenne, salt, pepper, and mustard.

4 Slowly stir in vegetables and water they were cooked in. Bring just to boil and remove from heat.

SPICY CHEESE AND BEER SOUP

Bring the cheese to room temperature before you add it to soup and it will melt more quickly. Serve with pumpernickel bread.

SERVES 4

1 tablespoon butter
1 medium yellow onion, finely chopped
1 medium carrot, shredded
2 cups low-fat (1%) milk
1/4 cup all-purpose flour
1/4 teaspoon cayenne pepper
1 1/2 cups (6 ounces) shredded
    sharp American cheese
1 can (12 ounces) light beer
1 cup shredded cabbage

1 In a large saucepan over medium heat, melt butter. Add onion and carrot and sauté until tender, about 5 minutes.

2 In a small bowl, whisk together milk, flour, and cayenne. Stir into onion mixture and cook, stirring constantly, until thickened and bubbling, about 7 minutes. Gradually add cheese. Reduce heat to low and cook, stirring constantly, until cheese melts (do not boil). Stir in beer and cabbage and heat through.

OVEN CHEESE CHOWDER

This hearty soup, with its vegetables, chickpeas, and cheese, is rich and delicious. (Photograph on page 32)

SERVES 10

1/2 pound zucchini, cut into
    1-inch chunks
2 medium onions, chopped
1 can (15 ounces) chickpeas,
    drained and rinsed
1 can (14 1/2 ounces) diced
    tomatoes, undrained

1 can (11 ounces) Mexican-style corn,
    drained
1 can (14 1/2 ounces) chicken broth
2 teaspoons salt
1/4 teaspoon black pepper
1 garlic clove, minced
1 teaspoon dried basil
1 bay leaf
1 cup (4 ounces) shredded
    Monterey Jack cheese
1 cup grated Romano cheese
1 1/2 cups half-and-half
Additional Monterey Jack cheese *(optional)*

1 Preheat oven to 400°F. In a 3-quart baking dish, combine zucchini, onions, chickpeas, tomatoes, corn, broth, salt, pepper, garlic, basil, and bay leaf. Cover and bake 1 hour, stirring once.

2 Stir in Jack and Romano cheeses and half-and-half and bake, uncovered, 10 minutes. Remove bay leaf. Top with additional Jack cheese, if desired.

CALIFORNIA CHEESE SOUP

Here is a simply made cheese soup, brimming with vegetables.

SERVES 10

2 chicken bouillon cubes
1 cup diced celery
1/2 cup diced onion
2 1/2 cups diced peeled potatoes
1 cup diced carrots
1 bag (16 ounces) frozen
    California Blend vegetables
2 cans (10 3/4 ounces each) condensed
    cream of chicken soup
1 pound process cheese, cut into cubes

1 In a large soup pot, bring 1 quart water to boil and add bouillon, celery, onion, potatoes, carrots, and frozen vegetables. Reduce heat and simmer, covered, 30 minutes or until all vegetables are tender.

2 Stir in chicken soup and cheese and cook until soup is heated through and cheese is melted.

MONTEREY JACK CHEESE SOUP

This soup combines a Western cheese with some Western seasonings to make a wonderful meal.

SERVES 5

1 cup chicken stock
1 large tomato, peeled, seeded, and diced
1/2 cup finely chopped onion
2 tablespoons chopped green chiles
1 garlic clove, minced
2 tablespoons butter
2 tablespoons all-purpose flour
Salt and black pepper to taste
3 cups milk
1 1/2 cups (6 ounces) shredded Monterey Jack cheese

1 In a 3-quart saucepan over medium-high heat, combine broth, tomato, onion, chiles, and garlic. Bring to boil, reduce heat, and simmer, covered, 10 minutes or until vegetables are tender. Remove from heat.

2 In a medium saucepan over medium heat, melt butter. Stir in flour, salt, and pepper and cook, stirring, until smooth. Gradually stir in 1 1/2 cups milk. Bring to boil and cook 1 minute, stirring constantly. Slowly stir into vegetable mixture. Add cheese and remaining milk. Cook, stirring, over low heat until cheese is melted.

SOUTH OF THE BORDER CHOWDER

Chiles and Monterey Jack cheese distinguish this Tex-Mex chowder.

SERVES 4

2 tablespoons (1/4 stick) butter
1 small yellow onion, chopped
1 tablespoon all-purpose flour
2 cups reduced-sodium chicken broth
2 small zucchini, diced
2 cups fresh or frozen corn kernels
1/4 cup canned, chopped green chiles
1/4 teaspoon ground black pepper
1 cup milk
2 ounces Monterey Jack cheese, coarsely shredded

1 In a large saucepan over medium heat, melt butter. Add onion and sauté 5 minutes or until soft. Stir in flour until well mixed.

2 Stir in broth, zucchini, corn, chiles, and pepper. Bring to boil, reduce heat, and simmer, covered, stirring occasionally, 5 minutes.

3 Add milk and heat over medium heat, stirring, until soup is hot (do not boil). Ladle into bowls, top with shredded cheese, and serve.

CHEESY WILD RICE SOUP

Packaged and prepared ingredients speed up preparation of this rich, creamy soup.

SERVES 6 TO 8

1 package (6 ounces) quick-cooking long-grain and wild rice mix
4 cups milk
1 can (10 3/4 ounces) condensed cream of potato soup
8 ounces process American cheese, cut into cubes

1/2 pound sliced bacon,
    cooked and crumbled (*optional*)

1 In a large saucepan, cook rice according to package directions.

2 Add milk, soup, and cheese to pan and stir to combine. Cook and stir over medium heat until cheese is melted. Garnish with bacon if desired.

CHEESY VEGETABLE SOUP

This rich cheese soup is made with Swiss cheese, which gives it a delightful nutty flavor.

SERVES 8

3 tablespoons butter
3 tablespoons all-purpose flour
2 cans (14 1/2 ounces each) chicken broth
2 cups coarsely chopped broccoli
3/4 cup chopped carrots
1/2 cup chopped celery
1 small onion, chopped
1/2 teaspoon salt
1/4 teaspoon garlic powder
1/4 teaspoon dried thyme
1 egg yolk
1 cup heavy whipping cream
1 1/2 cups (6 ounces) shredded Swiss cheese

1 In a heavy 4-quart saucepan over medium heat, melt butter. Add flour. Cook and stir until thick and bubbly and remove from heat. Gradually blend in broth.

2 Add broccoli, carrots, celery, onion, and seasonings. Return to heat and bring to boil. Reduce heat, cover, and simmer 20 minute or until vegetables are tender.

3 In a small bowl, blend egg yolk and cream. Gradually blend in several tablespoonfuls hot soup. Then return the egg-cream mixture to the saucepan, stirring until slightly thickened. Simmer 15 to 20 minutes. Stir in cheese and cook over medium heat until melted.

BLUE CHEESE VEGETABLE SOUP

It's a happy surprise to combine vegetables with blue cheese rather than cheddar for a lovely first course or lunch soup.

SERVES 4

1/2 cup broccoli florets
1/2 cup cauliflower florets
3 tablespoons butter
1 small onion, chopped
1 teaspoon dried herbes de Provence
1/4 cup flour
4 cups milk
1 cup crumbled blue cheese
Salt and white pepper to taste
Croutons (*optional*)

1 Prepare a large pan or bowl of cold water. In a large saucepan over high heat, bring 2 quarts water to boil. Add broccoli and cauliflower and cook 2 minutes. Remove vegetables with slotted spoon and plunge into pan of cold water to stop cooking. Drain and set aside.

2 In heavy saucepan over medium heat, melt butter. Add onion and herbes de Provence and sauté 5 minutes or until onions are soft. Add flour and cook 2 minutes, stirring. Gradually stir in milk. Bring to simmer and cook 5 minutes, stirring, or until soup begins to thicken.

3 Add cheese and stir until melted. Add broccoli and cauliflower and simmer 5 minutes to heat through without boiling. Season with salt and white pepper. Garnish with croutons, if desired.

CHEDDAR CHEESE SOUP WITH VEGETABLES

This is a rich, creamy soup that will be welcomed on chilly days.

SERVES 4

2 stalks celery, sliced

1 small green bell pepper, cored, seeded, and chopped

2 medium carrots, diced

1 cup cauliflower florets

2 cups canned, reduced-sodium chicken broth

4 tablespoons (1/2 stick) butter

1/2 cup all-purpose flour

3 cups milk

6 ounces sharp cheddar cheese, coarsely shredded (1 1/2 cups)

1 teaspoon Worcestershire sauce

Paprika

1 Combine celery, bell pepper, carrots, cauliflower, and broth in a large saucepan. Bring to boil, reduce heat, and simmer, covered, 10 minutes or until vegetables are tender.

2 In a medium saucepan over medium heat, melt butter. Stir in flour, cook 1 minute or until just bubbly. Remove pan from heat. Gradually whisk in milk.

3 Cook milk mixture over medium heat without boiling, stirring constantly, 5 minutes or until slightly thickened. Stir in cheese until it is melted.

4 Thoroughly stir cheese mixture and Worcestershire sauce into vegetable mixture. Ladle into bowls, sprinkle with paprika, and serve.

CHEESY ASPARAGUS SOUP

When fresh asparagus is in season, there is no better way to enjoy it than in a cheese-filled soup.

SERVES 8

3 pounds fresh asparagus, trimmed and cut into 2-inch pieces

1 small onion, chopped

2 cans (10 3/4 ounces each) condensed cream of asparagus soup

2 soup cans milk

1 jar (4 1/2 ounces) sliced mushrooms, drained

3 cups (12 ounces) shredded Cheddar cheese

1 In a large soup pot, combine asparagus and onion with enough water to cover. Bring water to boil, reduce heat, and simmer, covered, 8 minutes or until tender. Drain liquid.

2 Add soup, milk, mushrooms, and cheese and cook, stirring, over medium heat until cheese is melted and soup is hot.

ASPARAGUS-BRIE SOUP

Make this rich, elegant soup when fresh asparagus is in season.

SERVES 4

1/2 cup (1 stick) butter

1/2 pound fresh asparagus, cut into 2-inch pieces

1/4 cup all-purpose flour

3 cups chicken stock

1 cup heavy whipping cream

1/2 cup white wine or chicken stock

4-6 ounces Brie, rind removed

Dash of salt and black pepper

1 In a large saucepan over low heat, melt butter. Add asparagus and sauté 5 minutes or until crisp-tender.

2 Stir in flour until blended, then cook, stirring, 2 minutes or until golden brown. Gradually add stock, cream, and wine. Bring to boil, reduce heat, and simmer, covered, 10 minutes or until asparagus is tender.

3 Transfer to a blender or food processor, in 2 batches if necessary, cover, and puree until smooth. Return to pan. Cut cheese into cubes, add to pan, and simmer, uncovered, 5 minutes or until melted. Season with salt and pepper.

TWO-CHEESE BROCCOLI SOUP

Swiss and cheddar cheese complement each other when they're combined with broccoli.

SERVES 8

4 teaspoons chicken bouillon granules
2 packages (10 ounces each) frozen chopped broccoli
4 cups milk
1/2 teaspoon salt
1/4 teaspoon black pepper
1/8 teaspoon ground nutmeg
1/2 cup all-purpose flour
1 1/4 cups (5 ounces) shredded Swiss cheese
3/4 cup (3 ounces) shredded cheddar cheese

1 In a large saucepan, bring 3 cups water to boil. Add bouillon and stir until dissolved. Add broccoli and return to boil. Reduce heat, cover, and simmer 8 minutes or until tender. Stir in milk, salt, pepper and nutmeg.

2 In a small bowl, combine flour and 1 cup water and stir until smooth. Stir into pan and cook, stirring, over medium heat until thick and bubbling, about 3 minutes. Remove from heat, add Swiss and cheddar cheeses, and stir until melted.

GOLDEN CHEESE-BROCCOLI CHOWDER

Here is a filling chowder that combines broccoli, ham, and lots of cheddar.

SERVES 12

1 cup celery, chopped
1 cup carrots, chopped
1/2 cup onion, chopped
1 pound fresh broccoli, washed and chopped
1/2 cup butter
1/2 cup flour
2 teaspoons salt or to taste
1/4 teaspoon white pepper
4 cups milk
Hot red pepper sauce *(optional)*
1 pound process cheese spread, cut in 1/2-inch cubes or 4 cups shredded cheddar cheese
2 cups ham, cut in 1/2-inch cubes

1 In a large saucepan, combine 2 cups water, celery, carrots, and onion. Bring to boil, reduce heat, and simmer, covered, 5 minutes or until vegetables are crisp-tender.

2 Add broccoli and simmer 5 minutes or until it is crisp-tender. (To keep broccoli bright green, leave the cover slightly ajar.) Do not drain vegetables.

3 Melt butter in a large saucepan over medium heat and blend in flour, salt, and pepper. Cook, stirring, 2 minutes. Add milk and cook, stirring, until mixture thickens. Add several drops hot pepper sauce if desired.

4 Stir in cheese and cook until melted. Then add ham cubes and combine cheese mixture with undrained vegetables, stirring to blend, and serve in soup bowls.

CHEDDAR CHEESE AND BROCCOLI SOUP

With 496 milligrams of calcium per serving, this satisfying soup is healthy comfort food. (Photograph on page 8)

SERVES 6

1 pound broccoli
1 tablespoon olive oil
1 onion, chopped
1 celery rib, chopped
2 tablespoons all-purpose flour
1 can (14 1/2 ounces) reduced-sodium chicken broth
1 can (12 ounces) evaporated fat-free milk
1 1/2 cups shredded low-fat cheddar cheese (12 ounces)
1/2 teaspoon black pepper
1/4 teaspoon nutmeg
1/4 teaspoon salt

1 Trim and peel broccoli stems. Cut off 12 small florets. Coarsely chop enough remaining broccoli to equal 2 cups.

2 In a pot of boiling water, blanch chopped broccoli and florets 2 minutes or just until bright green. Drain and set aside.

3 Heat olive oil in a medium saucepan over medium heat. Sauté onion and celery 5 minutes or until soft. Whisk in flour and cook 1 minute. Add broth and milk. Cook, stirring constantly, until mixture simmers and thickens, about 5 minutes.

4 Add chopped broccoli, cheddar, pepper, nutmeg, and salt. Stir until cheese melts and soup is heated through, about 3 minutes. Serve 1 cup per person, garnished with broccoli florets.

SPINACH-CHEESE SOUP

A nutritious, calcium-packed soup that is likely to please youngsters as well as adults. Try it for family gatherings.

SERVES 14

1 tablespoon olive oil
1 large onion, chopped
4 garlic cloves, minced
6 cups chicken stock
8 ounces linguine
1 package (10 ounces) frozen chopped spinach, thawed and well drained
2 cups cubed cooked chicken
6 cups milk
3 cups (12 ounces) shredded Swiss cheese
3 cups (12 ounces) shredded Monterey Jack cheese

1 In a Dutch oven or soup pot over medium heat, heat oil. Add onion and garlic and sauté 4 minutes or until tender.

2 Add stock and bring to boil. Add pasta and cook 8 minutes or until tender. Reduce heat, add spinach and chicken, and heat through without boiling. Stir in milk and heat through. Add Swiss and Jack cheeses and stir just until melted.

NACHO-POTATO SOUP

How easy is this? Five basic ingredients add up to a surprisingly yummy bowl of food.

1 package (5 1/4 ounces) au gratin potatoes
1 can (11 ounces) whole-kernel corn, drained
1 can (10 ounces) diced tomatoes and green chiles, undrained
2 cups milk
2 cups cubed process American cheese
Dash of hot red pepper sauce *(optional)*
Minced fresh parsley *(optional)*

1 In a 3-quart saucepan over medium-high heat, combine 2 cups water, potatoes and sauce mix, corn, and tomatoes and mix well. Bring to boil, reduce heat, and simmer, covered, 15 minutes or until potatoes are tender.

2 Add milk, cheese, and red pepper sauce, if desired, and simmer, stirring, until cheese is melted. Garnish with parsley, if desired.

WISCONSIN POTATO-CHEESE SOUP

This rich, velvety soup takes some peeling and chopping, but cooks quickly for a hearty, satisfying meal.

2 tablespoons butter
1/3 cup chopped celery
1/3 cup chopped onion
4 cups diced peeled potatoes
3 cups chicken stock
2 cups milk
1 1/2 teaspoons salt
1/4 teaspoon black pepper
Dash of paprika

2 cups (8 ounces) shredded cheddar cheese
Croutons
Chopped fresh parsley

1 In a large saucepan, melt butter over medium-high heat. Sauté celery and onion 3 minutes or until tender. Add potatoes and stock. Bring to boil, lower heat, and simmer, covered, 12 minutes or until potatoes are tender.

2 In batches, puree potato mixture in a blender or food processor. Return to saucepan. Stir in milk and seasonings. Add cheese and heat only until melted. Garnish with croutons and parsley.

CHUNKY CHEESE-POTATO SOUP

This soup will warm you up on icy winter nights.

SERVES 6

2 cups diced peeled potatoes
1/2 cup diced carrot
1/2 cup chopped celery
1/4 cup chopped onion
1 1/2 teaspoons salt
1/4 teaspoon black pepper
1 cup cubed fully cooked ham
1/4 cup (1/2 stick) butter
1/4 cup all-purpose flour
2 cups milk
2 cups (8 ounces) shredded cheddar cheese

1 In a large saucepan, combine 2 cups water, potatoes, carrot, celery, onion, salt, and pepper. Bring to boil, reduce heat, and simmer, covered, 15 minutes or until vegetables are tender. Add ham.

2 In a medium saucepan, melt butter, then stir in flour until smooth. Gradually add milk, bring to boil, and cook, stirring, until thickened, about 2 minutes. Add cheese and stir until melted. Stir into soup.

CREAM CHEESE-CHICKEN SOUP

Cream cheese gives this soup a silky-smooth texture.

SERVES 8

1 tablespoon butter

1 small onion, chopped

3 cups chicken stock

3 medium carrots, cut into 1/4-inch slices

2 medium potatoes,
    peeled and cut into cubes

2 cups cubed cooked chicken

2 tablespoons minced fresh parsley

Salt and black pepper to taste

1/4 cup all-purpose flour

1 cup milk

1 package (8 ounces) cream cheese,
    cut into cubes

1 In a large saucepan over medium heat, melt butter. Add onion and sauté 3 minutes. Add stock, carrots, and potatoes and bring to boil. Reduce heat, cover, and simmer 15 minutes or until tender. Add chicken, parsley, salt, and pepper and heat through.

2 In a small bowl, combine flour and milk until smooth. Add to pan and bring to boil. Cook, stirring, until thickened, about 2 minutes. Reduce heat, add cream cheese, and cook, stirring, until melted.

CHEDDAR AND CHICKEN CHOWDER

Cheddar's robust bite is balanced in this soup by chicken breasts, vegetables, and milk.

SERVES 4

1 1/2 cups chicken stock

3/4 pound red potatoes,
    cut into 1/2-inch chunks

1 large carrot, thinly sliced

1 green bell pepper, cut into 1/2-inch squares

1 teaspoon paprika

1/2 teaspoon black pepper

1/4 teaspoon salt

3/4 pound skinless, boneless chicken breasts,
    cut into 1-inch chunks

1/2 cup low-fat (1%) milk

2 tablespoons flour

6 ounces cheddar cheese, shredded

1 In a large saucepan, bring stock and 2 1/2 cups water to boil. Add potatoes, carrot, bell pepper, paprika, black pepper, and salt. Reduce heat and simmer, covered, 10 minutes or until potatoes are firm-tender. Add chicken and cook 5 minutes or until it is cooked through.

2 In a small bowl, whisk milk into flour until smooth. Whisk milk mixture into soup and simmer 3 minutes or until soup is lightly thickened. Remove from heat and stir in cheese until melted.

MOZZARELLA-HAM SOUP

A simple soup, put together in a trice, this can make a quick lunch into a memorable one.

SERVES 4

4 cups beef stock

1 stalk celery, sliced

2 slices cooked ham, diced

2 ounces mozzarella cheese, diced

Salt and black pepper

Croutons *(optional)*

Fresh basil leaves, chopped *(optional)*

1 In a large saucepan over medium-high heat, bring stock to boil. Add celery. Reduce heat and simmer, uncovered, 1 minute. Add ham and simmer 1 minute.

2 Season with salt and pepper to taste. Divide cheese among serving bowls, ladle soup over it, garnish with croutons and fresh basil, if desired.

Vegetable SOUPS

VEGETABLE SOUPS
recipe list

EASY: 10 minutes to prepare

QUICK: Ready to eat in 30 minutes

ONE-DISH: contains protein, vegetables, and good carbohydrates (beans, whole-grains, etc.) for a complete healthy meal

HEALTHY: High in nutrients, low in bad fats and empty carbohydrates

SLOW COOKER: Easily adapted for slow cooker by cutting down on liquids

VEGETABLE SOUPS

recipe list CONTINUED

SUMMER GARDEN SOUP

A mélange of vegetables in this beautiful soup ensures you're getting the best summer flavors as well as a variety of vitamins and minerals in every spoonful. (Photograph on page 15)

SERVES 6

2 teaspoons olive oil

1 medium onion, finely chopped

1 large celery stalk, finely chopped

2 teaspoons finely chopped peeled fresh ginger

1/4 pound green beans, cut into 1/2-inch pieces

2 medium all-purpose potatoes, cut into 1/2-inch cubes

1 large carrot, peeled and cut into 1/2-inch cubes

1 medium yellow squash, quartered lengthwise, seeded, and cut into 1/2-inch cubes

1 bay leaf

3/4 teaspoon salt

3/4 cup fresh or frozen green peas

2 plum tomatoes, seeded and coarsely chopped

2 tablespoons finely chopped fresh basil

1 1/2 teaspoons finely chopped fresh thyme

1 Heat oil in a large soup pot over medium heat. Add onion, celery, and ginger and sauté 10 minutes or until tender. Add 8 cups water, beans, potatoes, carrot, squash, bay leaf, and salt. Bring to boil, reduce heat, and simmer, covered, 20 minutes.

2 Uncover pot and simmer 15 minutes, adding peas, tomatoes, basil, and thyme during last 5 minutes. Remove bay leaf before serving.

GARDEN SOUP IN TOMATO BROTH

This delightful vegetable soup is easy to make, pretty to look at, and quite fresh tasting.

SERVES 4

1 vegetable stock cube or 2 teaspoons vegetable bouillon powder or paste

2 1/2 cups tomato juice

2 garlic cloves, crushed

4 scallions, sliced

1 large all-purpose potato, peeled and diced

1 large carrot, diced

3 1/2 ounces broccoli florets

3 1/2 ounces shredded cabbage

2 ounces frozen cut green beans

2 ounces frozen peas

2 ounces frozen broad beans

8 basil sprigs

Salt and black pepper

1 In a medium saucepan, bring 1 1/4 cups water to boil. Add stock cube, tomato juice, garlic, scallions, potato, and carrot and return to boil. Reduce heat, cover, and simmer, stirring occasionally, 10 minutes.

2 Add broccoli, cabbage, green beans, peas, and broad beans. Return to boil, reduce heat, and simmer 5 minutes or until crisp-tender.

3 Season to taste with salt and pepper. Shred 4 basil sprigs and add to soup. Ladle into bowls and garnish each serving with a whole basil sprig.

GARDEN SOUP WITH YOGURT

Yogurt gives this colorful soup extra bite.

SERVES 4

1 tablespoon unsalted butter

4 small white onions, peeled

3 tablespoons all-purpose flour

2 1/2 cups chicken stock

1 medium carrot, peeled and cut diagonally into 1/2-inch-thick slices

1 1/2 teaspoons dried tarragon, crumbled

1 teaspoon fresh lemon juice

1/4 teaspoon black pepper

1/2 cup broccoli florets

1/2 cup quartered small mushrooms

1 small yellow squash, cut into 1/2-inch-thick slices

1/2 cup low-fat plain yogurt

1 In a large heavy saucepan over medium heat, melt butter. Add onions and sauté 8 minutes or until browned on all sides. Transfer to a plate lined with paper towels.

2 Blend flour into pan drippings and cook, stirring, over medium heat 2 minutes. Gradually whisk in stock and cook, stirring constantly, until slightly thickened, about 3 minutes.

3 Add carrot, tarragon, lemon juice, and pepper and bring to boil. Reduce heat and simmer, covered, 8 minutes. Add broccoli, mushrooms, and squash and simmer, covered, 5 minutes or until tender.

4 Gradually whisk in yogurt and heat about 1 minute (do not boil).

CREAM OF VEGETABLE SOUP

Carrots, onions, and potatoes are the vegetables that flavor this creamy, satisfying starter soup.

SERVES 4

1 tablespoon unsalted butter

1 large carrot, peeled and sliced

1 medium yellow onion, sliced

1 large all-purpose potato, peeled and sliced

3 garlic cloves, crushed

1 bay leaf

1/4 teaspoon dried thyme, crumbled

2 1/2 cups canned low-sodium chicken broth

2 cups low-fat (1%) milk

1/8 teaspoon salt

1/8 teaspoon black pepper

1 In a heavy saucepan over low heat, melt butter. Add carrot, onion, potato, garlic, bay leaf, and thyme and toss to coat. Stir in 1/2 cup broth and cook, covered, 15 minutes or until almost all liquid has evaporated.

2 Increase heat to medium, stir in milk and remaining broth, and cook, stirring occasionally, 30 minutes or until vegetables are tender and flavors well blended.

3 Let cool slightly and strain, reserving vegetables and stock. Discard bay leaf. Transfer vegetables and 1 cup stock to a food processor or blender and puree until smooth. Return puree and remaining stock to pan. Add salt and pepper and bring to serving temperature over medium heat, about 3 minutes.

FINNISH SUMMER VEGETABLE SOUP

Traditionally, this thick, creamy soup, called kesakeitto, is made with the first vegetables of summer. It's usually accompanied by open-face cold meat sandwiches.

SERVES 6

2 large carrots, sliced

1 cup fresh or frozen peas

1 cup fresh green beans, cut into bite-size pieces

1 cup fresh cauliflower florets

1 medium all-purpose potato, peeled and diced

4 large scallions with tops, finely sliced, or 1/2 cup sliced leeks

6 small radishes, quartered

3/8 teaspoon salt, divided

1 cup bite-size pieces fresh spinach

2 tablespoons butter

2 tablespoons all-purpose flour

1 tablespoon finely chopped fresh dill or 1 teaspoon dill weed

1/4 teaspoon black pepper

2 cups low-fat (1%) milk

1 large egg yolk, lightly beaten

1 In a large saucepan over medium heat, combine 2 cups water, carrots, peas, beans, cauliflower, potato, scallions, radishes, and 1/8 teaspoon salt. Bring to boil, then reduce heat and simmer, covered, 10 minutes or just until crisp-tender. Stir in spinach. Drain, reserving 1 cup cooking liquid, and transfer vegetables to a bowl.

2 Add butter to pan and melt over medium heat. Whisk in flour, dill, 1/4 teaspoon salt, and pepper and cook 1 minute. Add cooking liquid and milk and cook, whisking constantly, until beginning to thicken. Continue to cook, whisking, 2 minutes.

3 In a small bowl, slowly stir 1 cup soup into egg yolk, then return to pan. Cook, stirring constantly, 3 minutes or until thickened (do not boil). Stir in vegetables and cook 1 to 2 minutes or until heated through.

GOLDEN AUTUMN SOUP

This soup uses the freshest, most beautiful fall produce. Celebrate the season by serving this bounty to friends.

SERVES 12

5 medium parsnips, peeled and chopped

5 medium carrots, sliced

2 medium onions, chopped

1 medium sweet potato, peeled and chopped

1 medium turnip, peeled and chopped

2 celery stalks, sliced

2 bay leaves

3 cans (14 1/2 ounces each) chicken broth

2 cups half-and-half or fat-free evaporated milk

1 teaspoon dried tarragon

1/4 teaspoon black pepper

1 In a Dutch oven or soup pot, combine parsnips, carrots, onions, sweet potato, turnip, celery, bay leaves, and broth. Bring to boil, then reduce heat and simmer, covered, 30 minutes or until tender. Remove from heat, remove bay leaves, and let cool 20 minutes.

2 Transfer in small batches to a blender or food processor, cover, and puree until smooth. Return to pot, add half-and-half, tarragon, and pepper, and heat through.

VEGETABLE SOUP FOR A CROWD

With a big pot of homemade vegetable soup on hand, you can easily entertain a mob of people. Serve crusty bread on the side.

SERVES 14

1 tablespoon olive oil

8 medium carrots, sliced

2 large onions, chopped

4 celery stalks, chopped

1 large green bell pepper, cored, seeded, and chopped

1 garlic clove, minced

1 can (28 ounces) diced tomatoes, undrained

2 cups vegetable juice

2 cups chopped cabbage

2 cups frozen cut green beans

2 cups frozen peas

1 cup frozen whole-kernel corn

1 can (15 ounces) chickpeas, drained and rinsed

2 teaspoons chicken bouillon granules

1 1/2 teaspoons parsley flakes

1 teaspoon salt

1 teaspoon dried marjoram

1 teaspoon dried thyme

1 bay leaf

1/2 teaspoon dried basil

1/4 teaspoon black pepper

1 Heat oil in a Dutch oven or soup pot over medium heat. Add carrots, onions, celery, bell pepper, and garlic and sauté 7 minutes or until crisp-tender.

2 Stir in 4 cups water, tomatoes, vegetable juice, cabbage, beans, peas, corn, chickpeas, bouillon, parsley, salt, marjoram, thyme, bay leaf, basil, and pepper. Bring to boil, then reduce heat and simmer, covered, 1 hour or until tender. Remove bay leaf before serving.

PICKUP CREAMY VEGETABLE SOUP

Here's a lovely way to clean out the refrigerator; in this velvety soup, the leftovers won't be recognized.

SERVES 8

3/4 cup butter

1 medium onion, chopped

1/2 cup all-purpose flour

4 1/2 cups homemade chicken stock or 3 cans (10 1/2 ounces each) chicken broth

2 cups milk

2 cups half-and-half

1 teaspoon dried basil

1/2 teaspoon salt

1/2 teaspoon black pepper

1/4 teaspoon garlic powder

5 cups chopped cooked mixed vegetables, such as broccoli, carrots, and cauliflower

1 In a large soup pot or Dutch oven over medium heat, melt butter. Add onion and sauté 4 minutes or until tender.

2 Add flour and cook, stirring, until bubbling. Gradually add stock, cooking and stirring 5 minutes or until thickened. Stir in milk, half-and-half, basil, salt, pepper, and garlic powder.

3 Add vegetables and cook over low heat until heated through.

EVERYDAY VEGETABLE SOUP

Years ago, women often heated soup plates in the oven so the soup would stay hot longer at the table. Today, you can warm bowls quickly under hot tap water.

SERVES 8

3 1/2 cups beef stock

6 large carrots, cut into 1-inch-thick slices

3 medium turnips or all-purpose potatoes, peeled and cut into 1-inch cubes

12 ounces fresh green or wax beans, trimmed and cut into bite-size pieces, or 1 package (9 ounces) frozen cut green beans

1 tablespoon low-sodium Worcestershire sauce

1 teaspoon dry mustard

1/4 teaspoon salt

1/4 teaspoon black pepper

2 cans (8 ounces each) low-sodium tomato sauce

1 cup frozen peas

2 cups sliced fresh mushrooms

2 tablespoons minced fresh parsley

1 In a soup pot or Dutch oven over medium heat, combine broth, carrots, turnips, beans, Worcestershire sauce, mustard, salt, and pepper. Bring to boil, then reduce heat and simmer, covered, 25 minutes or until crisp-tender.

2 Stir in tomato sauce and peas and cook, stirring occasionally, 5 minutes. Stir in mushrooms and cook 2 minutes. Sprinkle with parsley.

OLD-FASHIONED VEGETABLE-BEEF SOUP

Here is an easy and delicious one-dish meal you can make with leftover roast beef or steak.

SERVES 8

3 1/2 cups beef stock

6 large carrots, cut into 1-inch-thick slices

3 medium turnips or potatoes, peeled and cut into 1-inch cubes

12 ounces fresh green or wax beans, trimmed and cut into bite-size pieces, or 1 package (9 ounces) frozen cut green beans

1 tablespoon low-sodium Worcestershire sauce

1 teaspoon dry mustard

1/4 teaspoon salt

1/4 teaspoon black pepper

3 cups bite-size pieces cooked beef

2 cans (8 ounces each) low-sodium tomato sauce

1 cup frozen peas

2 cups sliced fresh mushrooms

2 tablespoons minced fresh parsley

1 In a soup pot or Dutch oven over medium heat, combine broth, carrots, turnips, beans, Worcestershire sauce, mustard, salt, and pepper. Bring to boil, then reduce heat and simmer, covered, 25 minutes or until crisp-tender.

2 Stir in meat, tomato sauce, and peas and cook, stirring occasionally, 5 minutes. Stir in mushrooms and cook 2 minutes. Sprinkle with parsley.

VEGETABLE SOUP WITH RED LENTILS

Hearty and satisfying, this delicious soup calls for an accompaniment of biscuits or French bread.

SERVES 4

2 tablespoons olive oil

1 medium yellow onion, chopped

1 stalk celery, chopped

1 large carrot, chopped

1 cup dry split red lentils, sorted and rinsed

2 cups vegetable stock

1 bay leaf

1/2 teaspoon dried thyme, crumbled

1 medium ripe tomato, cored, seeded, and chopped

1 scallion, thinly sliced

1 Heat oil in a large saucepan over medium heat. Add onion, celery, and carrot and sauté 1 minute. Stir in 2 cups water, lentils, stock, bay leaf, and thyme and bring to boil. Reduce heat and simmer, covered, 15 minutes or until vegetables are tender.

2 Stir in tomato and simmer, covered, 10 minutes or until lentils are tender. Remove bay leaf, ladle soup into bowls, and sprinkle with scallion.

QUICK VEGETABLE SOUP

You'll have this nourishing soup on the table in half an hour or less, and your family may cheer!

SERVES 6

4 cups chicken stock

1 can (16 ounces) tomatoes, undrained

1/2 cup chopped onion

1/2 cup chopped cabbage

1 package (10 ounces) frozen mixed vegetables, thawed

1/2 teaspoon dried basil

1/8 teaspoon black pepper

Dash of sugar

1/4 cup elbow macaroni

1 cup cubed cooked chicken or beef

1 In a large saucepan or Dutch oven over high heat, bring stock, tomatoes, onion, cabbage, mixed vegetables, basil, pepper, and sugar to boil.

2 Add macaroni, reduce heat, and simmer, covered, 10 to 15 minutes or until tender. Add meat and heat through.

QUICK VEGETABLE-BEEF SOUP

The trick to this easy, one-dish soup is using ground beef instead of chunks of beef and adding canned and frozen vegetables.

SERVES 6

1 pound lean ground beef

1 medium yellow onion, sliced

4 cups beef stock

1 can (14 1/2 or 16 ounces) stewed tomatoes

1 package (16 ounces) frozen mixed vegetables

1 cup fresh or frozen whole-kernel corn

1/2 teaspoon dried basil, crumbled

Salt and black pepper to taste

1 In a large saucepan over medium heat, sauté beef and onion 10 minutes or until beef is browned and onion is tender. Drain off fat.

2 Stir in stock, tomatoes, mixed vegetables, corn, basil, salt, and pepper. Cover and bring to boil over high heat. Reduce heat and simmer, covered, 10 minutes or until vegetables are tender.

VEGETABLE SOUP WITH PESTO

Fragrant basil pesto lends a taste of summer's bounty to this variation on a classic French soup. (Photograph on page 21)

SERVES 4

1 onion, chopped

1 carrot, chopped

1 celery stalk, sliced

2 garlic cloves, finely chopped

1 pound plum tomatoes, peeled, seeded, and chopped

1 medium yellow squash, sliced

1 medium zucchini, sliced

1 can (14 1/2 ounces) low-sodium chicken broth

1 can (14 1/2 ounces) vegetable broth

1 cup loosely packed fresh basil leaves

2 1/2 tablespoons prepared pesto sauce

1 Coat a large saucepan with cooking spray and set over medium-high heat. Add onion, carrot, celery, and garlic and sauté 5 minutes or until soft. Add tomatoes, squash, and zucchini and sauté 8 minutes or until tender. Stir in chicken and vegetable broths and bring to boil. Reduce heat and simmer, uncovered, 20 minutes or until flavors are blended.

2 In a food processor or blender, process basil and pesto sauce with on-off pulses until basil is chopped. Process again until pesto is thick and creamy. Ladle soup into bowls and top with pesto.

MEDITERRANEAN ROASTED VEGETABLE SOUP

Roasting vegetables brings out their tantalizing sweetness. Carrot juice in place of broth also intensifies the flavor. (Photograph on page 6)

SERVES 4

1 tablespoon olive oil

5 garlic cloves, peeled

12 ounces all-purpose potatoes, cut into 1/2-inch chunks

2 bell peppers (green and yellow), cored, seeded, and cut into 1/2-inch squares

1/2 teaspoon fresh rosemary, chopped

1 yellow squash, halved lengthwise and cut crosswise into 1/2-inch pieces

1 large red onion, cut into 1/2-inch chunks

1 1/2 cups carrot juice

12 ounces plum tomatoes, seeded and diced

1 teaspoon fresh tarragon

3/4 teaspoon salt

1 Preheat oven to 450°F. In a roasting pan, combine oil and garlic and roast until oil begins to sizzle, about 5 minutes. Add potatoes, bell peppers, and rosemary and toss to coat. Roast 15 minutes or until potatoes begin to color and soften. Add squash and onion and roast 15 minutes or until squash is tender.

2 In a medium Dutch oven, combine carrot juice, tomatoes, tarragon, and salt and bring to boil over medium heat. Add roasted vegetables.

3 Pour 3/4 cup water into roasting pan and scrape up any brown bits. Pour pan juices into Dutch oven and cook 2 minutes or until heated through.

ROASTED VEGETABLE SOUP WITH EGGPLANT

Roasting adds a smoky flavor to all the vegetables in this soup, including the eggplant.

SERVES 6

1 large eggplant, halved lengthwise

2 large yellow onions, quartered

1 tablespoon olive oil

1 large red bell pepper, cored, seeded, and quartered

3 plum tomatoes, halved and seeded

3 garlic cloves

1/2 teaspoon dried thyme, crumbled

1/2 teaspoon dried basil, crumbled

1/4 teaspoon salt

1/8 teaspoon black pepper

6 cups chicken stock

1 Preheat oven to 400°F. Arrange eggplant and onions in a large shallow baking pan, brush cut sides with 1 1/2 teaspoons oil, and bake 20 minutes. Add bell pepper, tomatoes, and garlic and brush cut sides with remaining oil. Sprinkle thyme, basil, salt, and black pepper over vegetables and bake 20 minutes or until very tender.

2 Transfer bell pepper and half of eggplant to a plate. Chop onions, tomatoes, garlic, and remaining eggplant and transfer to a large saucepan. Add stock and bring to boil, then reduce heat and simmer, stirring occasionally, 20 minutes. Meanwhile, peel and dice bell pepper. Dice reserved eggplant.

3 Working in batches if necessary, transfer tomato mixture to a blender or food processor, cover, and puree until smooth. Return to pan, stir in bell pepper and eggplant, and simmer 5 minutes or until heated through.

TEXAS VEGETABLE SOUP

Texans like their peppers—both hot and sweet— and no dish with "Texas" in its name is likely to be without either of them.

SERVES 6

1 tablespoon olive or canola oil

1-2 jalapeño peppers, finely chopped (wear gloves when handling; they burn)

1 large onion, coarsely chopped

1 red bell pepper, cored, seeded, and diced

2 carrots, diced

1 tablespoon all-purpose flour

1/2 teaspoon dry mustard

8 cups vegetable stock

2 cups fresh or frozen whole-kernel corn

1/8 teaspoon salt

1/8 teaspoon black pepper

2 ounces reduced-fat cheddar cheese, shredded

1 Heat oil in a large saucepan over medium heat. Add jalapeño, onion, bell pepper, and carrots and sauté 7 minutes or until softened.

2 Stir in flour and mustard until vegetables are coated and cook 2 minutes. Add stock and bring to boil, then reduce heat and simmer 8 minutes or until vegetables are tender.

3 Add corn and return to boil. Reduce heat and simmer 5 minutes or until tender. Add salt and pepper. Sprinkle cheese on each serving.

VEGETABLE SOUP
WITH DUMPLINGS

SERVES 12

Soup:

2-3 beef soup bones with meat

2 small onions, 1 whole and 1 chopped

1 bay leaf

4 medium all-purpose potatoes,
    peeled and cubed

2 carrots, cubed

1 1/2 cups canned whole tomatoes,
    undrained, cut up

2 cups shredded cabbage

2 celery stalks, sliced

2 cups cut green beans

3/4 cup pearl barley

Chopped fresh parsley

Salt and black pepper

Dumplings:

1 cup all-purpose flour

2 teaspoons baking powder

Pinch of salt

1/2 cup milk

1 For soup, combine soup bones, 12 cups water, whole onion, and bay leaf in a soup pot. Bring to boil and skim off foam. Reduce heat and simmer, covered, 3 hours or until meat falls off bones.

2 Remove bones, onion, and bay leaf. Remove meat from bones and dice. Skim fat from stock. Add meat, chopped onion, potatoes, carrots, tomatoes, cabbage, celery, beans, barley, and parsley to the pot and season to taste with salt and pepper. Bring to boil, then reduce heat and simmer, covered, 1 hour or until barley is done and vegetables are tender.

3 For dumplings, combine flour, baking powder, and salt in a medium bowl. Add milk and stir until moistened, then drop by teaspoons into soup. Cover and cook 10 minutes or until heated through.

This is a scrumptious old fashioned vegetable soup that will stick to the ribs and healthfully satisfy the biggest appetite.

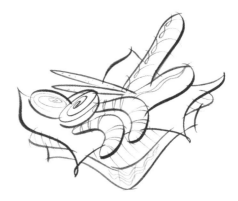

MUSHROOM AND WINTER VEGETABLE SOUP

Cabbage and mushrooms, two nutrient-rich foods, team up in this hearty, healthy vegetarian soup that goes well with thin dark rye or pumpernickel toast. (Photograph on page 5)

SERVES 4

1/2 cup dried shiitake mushrooms
2 tablespoons olive oil
1 large onion, finely chopped
4 garlic cloves, minced
1 large carrot, peeled and thinly sliced
1 large parsnip, peeled and thinly sliced
1 small head green cabbage, shredded
1 1/4 cups frozen baby lima beans
1/3 cup chopped fresh dill
1/3 cup tomato paste
1/4 cup red wine vinegar
3/4 teaspoon salt

1 In a small bowl, combine shiitakes and 1 1/2 cups boiling water. Let stand until softened, about 20 minutes, then remove mushrooms, reserving liquid. Trim stems from mushrooms and coarsely chop caps. Strain liquid through a fine-mesh sieve or coffee filter into a small bowl.

2 Heat oil in large saucepan or Dutch oven over medium heat. Add onion and garlic and sauté at least 5 minutes or until onion is golden. Add carrot and parsnip and sauté 5 minutes or until carrot is crisp-tender.

3 Stir in cabbage and cook, covered, 5 minutes or until beginning to wilt. Stir in 3 cups water, mushrooms, soaking liquid, lima beans, dill, tomato paste, vinegar, and salt. Bring to boil, then reduce heat and simmer, covered, 25 minutes or until soup is richly flavored.

FRENCH VEGETABLE SOUP

This elegant combination of fresh spring vegetables, cooked together and added to a rich, tomato-flavored broth, makes a hearty soup that can serve as a main course for lunch or supper.

SERVES 4

2 tablespoons butter
2 garlic cloves, chopped
2 shallots, chopped
1 can (28 ounces) chopped tomatoes, undrained
1 3/4 cups chicken or vegetable stock
1 teaspoon dried sweet basil
Salt and black pepper to taste
8 ounces baby new potatoes, quartered
12 baby or 4 small carrots, cut up
6 large radishes, diced
12 asparagus tips
3 1/2 ounces snow peas or sugar snap peas, halved
1/2 cup light cream
8 large basil leaves, chopped
Grated Parmesan or shredded cheddar cheese

1 Put a pot of water on to boil. In a large saucepan over medium heat, melt butter. Add garlic and shallots and sauté 3 minutes, stirring occasionally.

2 Add tomatoes, stock, basil, salt, and pepper to pan and bring to boil. Reduce heat, cover, and simmer 15 minutes.

3 Place potatoes in another saucepan over high heat and cover with boiling water. Return to boil, then reduce heat and simmer 5 minutes. Add carrots, radishes, asparagus, and peas. Cook 10 to 12 minutes or until just tender; drain Add to tomato mixture, then stir in cream and basil. Serve immediately, passing cheese separately to sprinkle on top.

ARTICHOKE SOUP WITH CARAWAY

Jerusalem artichokes are the base of this creamy, aromatic root vegetable soup.

SERVES 6

1 teaspoon fresh lemon juice

1 pound 2 ounces Jerusalem artichokes

2 tablespoons butter

1 celery stalk, sliced

1 small onion, chopped

2 carrots, chopped

1 garlic clove, minced

4 cups chicken stock

1 teaspoon caraway seed

1/2 cup low-fat (1%) milk

1/4 cup light cream

Salt and black pepper

1 small carrot, julienned

2 tablespoons chopped parsley

1 Add lemon juice to a bowl of cold water. Peel and slice artichokes and add to water to prevent discoloration.

2 In a large saucepan over medium heat, melt butter. Drain artichokes and add to pan, then add celery, onion, carrots, and garlic. Cover and cook, stirring occasionally, 10 minutes or until softened.

3 Add stock and caraway seed and bring to boil. Reduce heat and simmer, covered, 20 minutes or until vegetables are tender. Remove from heat and let cool slightly, then transfer to a blender or food processor, cover, and puree until smooth.

4 Return soup to pan, stir in milk and cream, and season to taste with salt and pepper. Cook over low heat until heated through (do not boil). Garnish each serving with carrots and parsley.

ASPARAGUS SOUP

Asparagus doesn't just taste good, it's also a top source of folate, a B vitamin that helps prevent heart disease and birth defects.
(Photograph on page 11)

SERVES 6

2 pounds asparagus, trimmed

1 teaspoon butter

1 tablespoon vegetable oil

2 leeks, pale green and white parts only, rinsed and finely chopped

1/2 onion, finely chopped

2 garlic cloves, minced

3 tablespoons long-grain white rice

Grated zest of 1 lemon

3 cans (14 1/2 ounces each) fat-free low-sodium chicken broth

1/2 teaspoon salt

1/4 teaspoon black pepper

1/2 teaspoon dried tarragon, crumbled

3 tablespoons plain yogurt

1 Slice tips from asparagus. In a medium saucepan, blanch in boiling water 1 minute; drain. Coarsely chop remaining asparagus.

2 In a large saucepan over medium heat, melt butter and heat oil. Add leeks, onion, and garlic and sauté 5 minutes or until softened. Add chopped asparagus and cook, covered, 10 minutes.

3 Add rice, lemon zest, broth, salt, and pepper. Bring to boil, then reduce heat and simmer, partially covered, 30 minutes. Remove from heat and let cool slightly.

4 Transfer soup in batches to a food processor or blender, cover, and puree until smooth. Return to pan, stir in tarragon and asparagus tips, and simmer 3 minutes. Remove from heat and stir in yogurt.

ASPARAGUS-HAZELNUT SOUP

This elegant soup is actually very easy to make. Toasting the hazelnuts gives the soup a richer flavor and makes it possible to remove the skins. If you prefer, you can substitute blanched almonds for the hazelnuts.

SERVES 6

1/2 cup shelled hazelnuts

1 tablespoon vegetable oil

1 large leek, cut into 1/2-inch cubes

3 garlic cloves, thinly sliced

1 medium all-purpose potato, peeled and thinly sliced

1/4 cup firmly packed fresh parsley leaves

1 1/2 pounds asparagus, trimmed, or 2 packages (10 ounces each) frozen asparagus, cut into 1-inch pieces

1/2 teaspoon salt

1/2 teaspoon dried marjoram or savory, crumbled

1 scallion with top, thinly sliced

1 Preheat oven to 400°F. Spread hazelnuts on a baking sheet and toast 10 minutes or until skins have loosened and nuts are fragrant. Place on a clean kitchen towel and rub vigorously to remove skins (a few will remain). Coarsely chop a third of nuts.

2 Heat oil in a soup pot or 5-quart Dutch oven over low heat. Add leek and sauté 7 minutes or until softened. Add garlic and sauté 1 minute. Add potato and parsley, cover, and cook, stirring occasionally, 5 minutes.

3 Set aside 1 cup asparagus tips. Add remaining tips and stalks, 4 1/2 cups water, whole nuts, salt, and marjoram to pan. Increase heat to medium and bring to boil, then reduce heat and simmer, covered, 20 minutes or until asparagus and potato are tender. Remove from heat and let cool slightly.

4 Working in batches if necessary, transfer soup to a blender or food processor, cover, and puree until smooth. Return to pan, add reserved asparagus, and heat through. Garnish with chopped hazelnuts and scallion.

CREAMY ASPARAGUS SOUP

Pureed potatoes thicken this soup, while olive oil and low-fat milk supply creaminess without using cream. (Photograph on page 15)

SERVES 4

1 1/4 pounds asparagus, tough ends trimmed

1 1/2 teaspoons olive oil

4 scallions, thinly sliced

8 ounces all-purpose potatoes, peeled and thinly sliced

1 teaspoon tarragon

3/4 teaspoon salt

1/4 teaspoon black pepper

1/2 cup low-fat (1%) milk

1 Cut 10 thin asparagus stalks into 3 pieces each. Cut remaining asparagus into 1/2-inch lengths.

2 Heat oil in a medium nonstick saucepan over low heat. Add scallions and sauté 2 minutes or until tender. Add potatoes and 1/2-inch asparagus pieces to pan and stir to combine. Add 1 3/4 cups water, tarragon, salt, and pepper and bring to boil. Reduce heat and simmer, covered, 10 minutes or until potatoes and asparagus are tender.

3 Transfer soup to a food processor or blender, cover, and puree until smooth. Return to saucepan and stir in milk and 3-inch asparagus pieces. Cook over low heat 3 minutes or until soup is heated through and asparagus pieces are tender.

ASPARAGUS SOUP WITH PEAS

This pretty spring soup makes the most of fresh asparagus. A garnish of bacon pieces and croutons adds savoriness, while a swirl of whipped cream provides a decorative touch.

SERVES 4

2 1/2 cups chicken or vegetable stock

8-9 scallions, chopped

1 pound frozen peas

12 small asparagus spears, tips removed and stems chopped

Salt and black pepper

3 bacon slices

1-2 tablespoons vegetable oil *(optional)*

2 slices day-old white bread, cut into 1/2-inch cubes

3 tablespoons whipped cream

1 In a medium saucepan over medium-high heat, bring stock to boil. Add scallions, peas, asparagus stems, and a pinch of salt. Reduce heat and simmer, covered, 10 to 15 minutes or until asparagus is tender.

2 Meanwhile, in a skillet over medium heat, cook bacon until crisp and golden. Transfer to paper towels.

3 If there isn't enough fat in pan to fry croutons, add oil and heat over medium-high heat. Add bread and sauté, turning frequently, 2 to 3 minutes or until golden. Transfer to paper towels.

4 Transfer soup to a blender or food processor, cover, and puree until smooth. Return to pan, bring to boil, and add asparagus tips. Reduce heat and simmer, covered, 5 minutes or until asparagus is tender.

5 Pour soup into warm serving bowls, swirl a little whipped cream into each, and sprinkle with bacon, croutons, and freshly ground black pepper.

ASPARAGUS-POTATO SOUP

This comforting soup features tender potatoes and asparagus topped with cheddar cheese.

SERVES 6

2 cups diced peeled all-purpose potatoes

8 ounces fresh asparagus, chopped

1/2 cup chopped onion

2 celery stalks, chopped

1 tablespoon chicken bouillon granules

1/4 cup (1/2 stick) butter

1/2 cup all-purpose flour

1 cup heavy whipping cream

1/2 cup milk

1/2 teaspoon salt

Dash of black pepper

3/4 cup (3 ounces) shredded cheddar cheese

1 In a Dutch oven or soup pot over medium-high heat, combine 4 cups water, potatoes, asparagus, onion, celery, and bouillon. Bring to boil, then reduce heat and simmer, covered, 15 minutes or until tender. Stir in butter.

2 In a medium bowl, combine flour, cream, milk, salt, and pepper until smooth. Add to pot, increase heat, and bring to boil. Cook, stirring, 2 minutes or until thickened. Garnish each serving with cheese.

LEMON ASPARAGUS SOUP

Lemon and nutmeg add surprising accents to the taste of fresh asparagus in this soup.

SERVES 4

1/4 cup (1/2 stick) butter

1 medium onion, chopped

1/2 cup chopped celery

2 tablespoons cornstarch

2 chicken bouillon cubes

12 ounces fresh asparagus, trimmed and cut into 1-inch pieces

2 cups milk

1/2 teaspoon grated lemon zest

1/8 teaspoon ground nutmeg

Dash of salt

1 In a 2-quart saucepan over medium heat, melt butter. Add onion and celery and sauté 4 minutes or until tender. In a small bowl, dissolve cornstarch in 1 cup water and add to pan. Add bouillon, bring to boil, and cook, stirring, 2 minutes. Add asparagus, reduce heat, and simmer, covered, 4 minutes or until crisp-tender.

2 Stir in milk, lemon zest, nutmeg, and salt and bring just to boil. Reduce heat, cover, and simmer, stirring occasionally, 25 minutes.

BEET SOUP WITH MASHED POTATOES

Guaranteed to ward off winter blues, this hearty beet soup, served with creamy mashed potatoes, is enlivened with crunchy, raw vegetables.

SERVES 4

1 tablespoon extra-virgin olive oil

1 onion, chopped

1 large carrot, peeled, 3/4 chopped and 1/4 grated

1/2 teaspoon fresh lemon juice

1 fennel bulb, quartered, 3 quarters chopped

1 pound beets, peeled and diced

7 1/2 cups vegetable stock

1 3/4 pounds baking potatoes, peeled and cubed

1/2 cup low-fat (1%) milk

4 tablespoons Greek-style yogurt

2 scallions, sliced

Salt and black pepper

Chopped fresh fennel leaves or parsley

1 Heat oil in a large saucepan over medium heat. Add onion and chopped carrot and cook, covered, 5 minutes or until onion is softened.

2 Pour lemon juice into a small bowl. Grate a quarter of fennel and add to bowl, then add grated carrot and toss. Cover and set aside.

3 Add chopped fennel, beets, and stock to pan and bring to boil. Reduce heat and simmer, covered, 30 minutes or until vegetables are tender.

4 Bring another saucepan of water to boil over medium-high heat. Add cubed potatoes and cook 10 minutes or until tender. Drain, return to pan, and place over low heat 1 minute to dry, shaking pan occasionally to prevent sticking. Remove from heat and cover.

5 Transfer soup to a blender or food processor, cover, and puree until smooth (or use a handheld blender to puree in pan). Return to pan, heat through, and season to taste with salt and pepper.

6 Meanwhile, over medium heat, mash potatoes, gradually adding milk. Stir in yogurt, grated fennel and carrot, and scallions and season to taste with salt and pepper. Divide mashed potatoes among 4 bowls, piling them in center. Ladle soup around potatoes and sprinkle with fennel.

EASY BORSCHT

A beautiful and delicious first course, this soup can be ready in minutes. (Photograph on page 12)

SERVES 4

1 can (8 1/4 ounces) sliced beets, undrained
1 cup chicken stock
3/4 cup sour cream
2 tablespoons fresh lemon juice
2 tablespoons chopped yellow onion
2 teaspoons sugar
1/2 teaspoon dill weed
Salt

1 In a food processor or blender, puree beets and liquid 1 minute. Add broth, 1/2 cup sour cream, lemon juice, onion, sugar, and dill. Season to taste with salt and puree until smooth, stopping occasionally to scrape container with a rubber spatula.

2 Pour into a medium saucepan over medium heat and simmer 5 minutes or until heated through (do not boil). Ladle into bowls and swirl a dollop of remaining sour cream into each serving, if desired.

BROCCOLI PUREE SOUP

A pretty and healthy first course, this soup is welcome at lunch or dinner.

SERVES 4

2 teaspoons olive oil
1 small onion, chopped
1 1/2 cups chicken stock
1 package (10 ounces) frozen broccoli
1/4 teaspoon dried marjoram or oregano
Pinch of cayenne pepper
1 cup low-fat (1%) milk

1 Heat oil in a medium saucepan over medium heat. Add onion and sauté until softened.

2 Add stock, broccoli, marjoram, and cayenne and bring to boil. Reduce heat and simmer 5 minutes or until broccoli is tender. Remove from heat and let cool slightly. Transfer to a food processor or blender, add milk, cover, and puree until smooth. Return to pan and cook until heated through.

CREAMY BROCCOLI SOUP

This delicious soup is thickened with pureed potato rather than heavy cream, making it lower in fat and calories.

SERVES 8 TO 10

1 pound broccoli
1 tablespoon olive or canola oil
3 leeks, trimmed and sliced, or 1 onion, sliced
2 garlic cloves, finely chopped
1 pound all-purpose potatoes, peeled and diced
6 cups chicken stock
1 cup low-fat (1%) milk
1/8 teaspoon salt
1/8 teaspoon black pepper

1 Cut broccoli florets from stems. Using a vegetable peeler, peel stems, then slice.

2 Heat oil in a 4-quart saucepan over medium heat. Add leeks and garlic and sauté 3 minutes or until softened. Add 1/2 cup water and cook 5 minutes. Add broccoli stems, potatoes, stock, and milk. Bring to boil, then reduce heat and simmer, partially covered, 8 minutes or until tender. Stir in broccoli florets and simmer 5 minutes or until tender.

3 Remove from heat and let cool slightly. Using a slotted spoon, transfer vegetables to a blender or food processor, cover, and puree until very smooth. Return to pan and cook until heated through. Add salt and pepper.

CREAM OF BROCCOLI SOUP WITH BASIL AND NUTMEG

Enjoy all the richness of cream soup with none of the fat and excess calories.

SERVES 6

1 tablespoon olive or vegetable oil

1 medium yellow onion, coarsely chopped

5 garlic cloves, slivered

1 bunch broccoli (1 1/4 pounds), heads cut into florets and stalks trimmed, peeled, and thinly sliced, or 2 packages (10 ounces each) frozen broccoli

3 medium all-purpose potatoes, peeled and thinly sliced

1/2 teaspoon dried basil, crumbled

1/8 teaspoon ground nutmeg

5 cups chicken stock

2 cups low-fat (1%) milk

1/4 teaspoon salt

1/4 teaspoon black pepper

Garnishes:

3 tablespoons minced fresh parsley (*optional*)

2 scallions, sliced (*optional*)

3 tablespoons fat-free plain yogurt (*optional*)

1 Heat oil in a soup pot or 5-quart Dutch oven over low heat. Add onion and garlic and sauté 5 minutes or until softened.

2 Add broccoli, potatoes, basil, nutmeg, and stock, increase heat to medium, and bring to boil. Reduce heat, cover, and simmer 20 minutes or until broccoli and potatoes are very tender. Remove from heat and let cool slightly.

3 Working in batches if necessary, transfer to a blender or food processor, cover, and puree until smooth. Return to pot, stir in milk, salt, and pepper, and cook 4 minutes or just until heated through. Garnish with parsley, scallions, or yogurt, if desired.

BRUSSELS SPROUT SOUP

This unusual, delicious pureed soup is thickened with potatoes, heavy cream, and egg yolk and flavored with curry.

SERVES 4

2 tablespoons butter

1 medium onion, chopped

1 medium all-purpose potato, peeled and cut into cubes

1 pound fresh Brussels sprouts, quartered

3 cups chicken stock

1/2-1 teaspoon salt

1/4-1/2 teaspoon curry powder

1/8 teaspoon black pepper

1 egg yolk

1/4 cup heavy whipping cream

Sour cream (*optional*)

Paprika (*optional*)

1 In a large saucepan over medium heat, melt butter. Add onion and potato and sauté 5 minutes or until onion is tender. Add Brussels sprouts, stock, salt, curry powder, and pepper and bring to boil. Reduce heat, and simmer, covered, 10 minutes or until vegetables are tender. Remove from heat and let cool to room temperature.

2 Working in batches if necessary, transfer to a blender or food processor, cover, and puree until smooth. Return to pan.

3 In a small bowl, combine egg yolk and cream. Add to pan and cook, stirring, over medium heat 5 minutes (do not boil). Garnish with sour cream and paprika, if desired.

CREAM OF CABBAGE SOUP

This unusual cabbage soup has a creamy base and is flavored with other vegetables, herbs, and lots of cheese.

SERVES 12

2 tablespoons chicken bouillon granules

3 cups diced peeled all-purpose potatoes

1 cup finely chopped onion

1 cup diced peeled rutabaga

1/2 cup diced peeled carrots

6 cups chopped cabbage

1 cup chopped celery

1/2 cup chopped seeded green bell pepper

1 garlic clove, minced

1 teaspoon salt

1 teaspoon dill weed

1 cup (2 sticks) butter

1 cup all-purpose flour

2 cups milk

2 cups chicken stock

8 ounces process American cheese, cut into cubes

1/2 teaspoon dried thyme

Black pepper

1 In a Dutch oven or soup pot over medium heat, bring 4 cups water and bouillon to boil. Add potatoes, onion, rutabaga, and carrots and return to boil. Reduce heat and simmer, covered, 5 minutes.

2 Add cabbage, celery, and bell pepper and simmer, uncovered, 5 minutes or until crisp-tender. Stir in garlic, salt, and dill.

3 In a medium saucepan over low heat, melt butter. Increase heat to medium, stir in flour, and cook, stirring, until golden. Gradually add milk and stock, stirring until smooth. Reduce heat to low, add cheese, thyme, and pepper, and cook until cheese is melted. Stir into pot and simmer 5 minutes. Thin with additional milk if necessary.

CABBAGE SOUP FOR A CROWD

There are many variations on cabbage soup. This one emphasizes tomatoes and beef as foils for the cabbage.

SERVES 16

1 cup chopped celery

1 cup chopped onion

1 medium head cabbage, shredded

1 beef bouillon cube

1 teaspoon salt

2 teaspoons black pepper

1 1/2 pounds ground beef, browned and drained

2 cans (15 ounces each) tomato sauce

1 tablespoon brown sugar

1/4 cup ketchup

1 In a large Dutch oven or soup pot, combine 8 cups water, celery, onion, and cabbage. Bring to boil, then reduce heat and simmer, covered, 6 minutes or until tender.

2 Add bouillon, salt, pepper, beef, and tomato sauce and bring to boil. Reduce heat and simmer, covered, 10 minutes. Stir in brown sugar and ketchup and simmer 10 minutes or until heated through.

CABBAGE AND CARROT SOUP

You can make this soup with crinkly Savoy cabbage, which is rich in beta-carotene.

SERVES 4

1 tablespoon olive oil

1 large onion, finely chopped

4 garlic cloves, minced

2 carrots, thinly sliced

8 cups shredded green cabbage

2 1/2 cups chicken stock

3/4 cup snipped fresh dill

1/3 cup low-sodium tomato paste

3/4 teaspoon ground ginger

1/4 teaspoon salt

1/4 teaspoon black pepper

1/3 cup reduced-fat sour cream

1 Heat oil in a large Dutch oven or flameproof baking dish over medium heat. Add onion and garlic and sauté 7 minutes or until onion is soft. Add carrots and sauté 5 minutes or until crisp-tender.

2 Stir in cabbage, cover, and cook, stirring occasionally, 10 minutes or until wilted.

3 Add 2 1/2 cups water, stock, dill, tomato paste, ginger, salt, and pepper. Bring to boil, then reduce heat and simmer, covered, 15 minutes or until cabbage is very tender. Stir in sour cream just before serving.

CABBAGE SOUP WITH DILL

To make this a main-dish meal, add 3 cups cooked noodles and 2 cups diced cooked chicken or ham along with the vinegar in Step 2.

SERVES 8

1 teaspoon vegetable or olive oil

1 small yellow onion, finely chopped

4 garlic cloves, minced

6 cups chicken stock

2 pounds green or red cabbage, cored and shredded

3 medium carrots, peeled, halved lengthwise, and thinly sliced

2 medium tomatoes, cored, seeded, and chopped

2 tablespoons tomato paste

1/3 cup snipped fresh dill or 1 1/2 tablespoons dill weed

2 tablespoons red wine vinegar

1 1/2 teaspoons sugar

1/4 teaspoon salt

1 Heat oil in a soup pot or 5-quart Dutch oven over low heat. Add onion and garlic and sauté 2 minutes. Add 1/3 cup stock, cover, and cook, stirring occasionally, 5 minutes.

2 Stir in 3 cups water, remaining stock, cabbage, carrots, tomatoes, tomato paste, and dill. Increase heat to medium and bring to boil, then reduce heat and simmer, covered, 35 minutes. Stir in vinegar, sugar, and salt and simmer, covered, 5 minutes.

CREAMY CARROT SOUP

This good soup, with its bright color and velvety texture, is often a favorite of children.

SERVES 4

3 1/2 cups chicken stock

4 medium carrots, sliced

1 medium yellow onion, cut into thick slices

1 medium celery stalk, sliced

3 tablespoons long-grain white rice

1/2 teaspoon sugar

1/8 teaspoon cayenne pepper

1/2 cup milk

1/2 cup sour cream

Salt

Diced pimientos *(optional)*

1 In a large saucepan over high heat, combine 3 cups stock, carrots, onion, celery, rice, sugar, and cayenne. Cover and bring to boil, then reduce heat and simmer 15 to 20 minutes or until rice and carrots are tender.

2 Stir in milk and sour cream. Working in batches if necessary, transfer to a food processor or blender, cover, and puree until smooth. If a thinner soup is desired, blend in remaining stock.

3 Return soup to a medium saucepan over medium heat. Stir in salt and additional cayenne, if desired, and cook until hot but not boiling. Ladle into bowls and top each serving with pimientos, if desired.

SPICY CARROT SOUP

Carrots and ginger bring out the best in each other, and in this thick vegetable soup, they are boosted with a fresh green chile and Eastern spices.

SERVES 4 TO 6

4 cups vegetable stock or water
1 medium all-purpose potato, cut into chunks
1 medium onion, cut into chunks
1 pound carrots, cut into chunks
2 large garlic cloves, quartered
Salt
2 tablespoons olive oil
1 fresh green chile, chopped (wear gloves when handling; they burn)
2-inch piece fresh ginger, chopped
1 teaspoon garam masala or Chinese five-spice powder
Juice of 1 lemon or lime
1 teaspoon toasted sesame oil
Black pepper

1 In a large saucepan, bring stock to boil. Stir in potato, onion, carrots, garlic, and salt. Return to boil, reduce heat, and simmer, partially covered, 15 to 20 minutes.

2 Meanwhile, heat oil in a small skillet over medium heat. Add chile and ginger and sauté 1 minute (do not burn). Stir in garam masala and lemon juice and cook 1 minute. Add sesame oil and stir until thickened. Remove from heat.

3 When vegetables are tender, stir in ginger sauce. Transfer to a blender or food processor, cover, and puree until smooth. Return to pan, add pepper, and cook until heated through.

MOROCCAN CARROT SOUP

The warming flavors of Moroccan spices, tempered by the sweetness of carrots, carrot juice, and tomato paste, add interesting complexity to this thick, creamy soup.

SERVES 4

1 tablespoon olive oil
1 medium onion, thinly sliced
3 garlic cloves, thinly sliced
1 pound carrots, thinly sliced
3/4 teaspoon ground cinnamon
3/4 teaspoon ground ginger
3/4 teaspoon turmeric
1/2 teaspoon paprika
1 cup carrot juice
2 tablespoons tomato paste
3 tablespoons rice
3/4 teaspoon salt
1/2 teaspoon black pepper
1/2 cup fresh cilantro, chopped

1 Heat oil in a medium saucepan over medium heat. Add onion and garlic and sauté 5 minutes or until onion is golden.

2 Add carrots, cinnamon, ginger, turmeric, and paprika and sauté 1 minute. Stir in 2 cups water, carrot juice, tomato paste, rice, salt, and pepper. Bring to boil, then reduce heat and simmer, covered, 20 minutes or until carrots and rice are tender. Remove from heat and let cool slightly.

3 Transfer to a food processor or blender, cover, and puree until smooth. Return to pan and cook until heated through. Pour into bowls and sprinkle with cilantro.

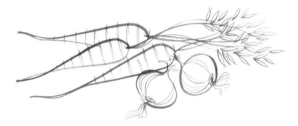

CREAMY CARROT AND MINT SOUP

Mint gives this lovely starter soup extra fresh zing.

SERVES 4

3 cups thinly sliced carrots
1 tablespoon rice
1 cup chicken stock
1 teaspoon sugar
1/2 teaspoon salt
1/4 teaspoon cayenne pepper
1 cup low-fat (1%) milk
1/3 cup chopped fresh mint

1 In a large saucepan over medium heat, combine carrots, rice, stock, sugar, salt, and cayenne. Bring to boil, then reduce heat and simmer, covered, 17 minutes or until rice is tender. Remove from heat and let cool slightly.

2 Transfer soup to a food processor or blender, add milk, cover, and puree until smooth. Return to pan, stir in mint, and cook until heated through.

CARROT SOUP WITH TOMATOES

This thick, creamy soup is delicately spiced with ginger and studded with chunks of plum tomatoes.

SERVES 6

1 tablespoon vegetable oil
1 large yellow onion, coarsely chopped
9 medium carrots, peeled and thinly sliced
3 tablespoons minced fresh ginger
4 cups chicken stock
1/4 teaspoon salt
1/4 teaspoon sugar
1/8 teaspoon black pepper
1 bay leaf
1 pound plum tomatoes, peeled, seeded, and diced
2 tablespoons minced fresh basil, dill, or parsley

1 Heat oil in a large heavy saucepan over medium-low heat. Add onion, carrots, and ginger, then cover and cook, stirring occasionally, 5 minutes or until onion is tender. Add stock, salt, sugar, pepper, and bay leaf and bring to boil. Reduce heat and simmer, covered, 25 minutes or until carrots are tender. Remove bay leaf.

2 Working in batches if necessary, transfer to a blender or food processor, cover, and puree until smooth. Return to pan, stir in tomatoes, and simmer 5 minutes, stirring occasionally, until heated through. Garnish each serving with basil.

CARROT-PARSNIP SOUP

Although this soup is made with winter vegetables, it tastes just as delicious served chilled in summer.

SERVES 8

1 tablespoon olive or canola oil

1 large onion, coarsely chopped

1 tablespoon chopped fresh ginger
    or 1/2 teaspoon ground ginger

1 pound carrots, coarsely chopped

8 ounces parsnips, coarsely chopped

8 cups chicken or vegetable stock

1/2 cup low-fat (1%) milk

1/8 teaspoon salt

1/8 teaspoon black pepper

1 Heat oil in a 4-quart saucepan over medium heat. Add onion and ginger and sauté 5 minutes or until softened. Add carrots and parsnips and sauté 5 minutes or until slightly softened.

2 Add stock and bring to boil. Reduce heat and simmer, partially covered, 20 to 25 minutes or until carrots and parsnips are very soft. Remove from heat and let cool slightly.

3 Working in batches if necessary, transfer vegetables to a blender or food processor, cover, and puree until very smooth. Return to pan, add milk, salt, and pepper, and simmer 5 minutes or until heated through.

CARROT-PARSNIP SOUP WITH HORSERADISH

This creamy soup has fresh-from-the-garden flavor. Subtle hints of horseradish and ginger give it zest.

SERVES 12

8 cups chopped peeled carrots

6 cups chopped peeled parsnips

4 cups chicken stock

2 teaspoons sugar

1 teaspoon salt

3 tablespoons butter

1 medium onion, chopped

4 garlic cloves, minced

1 teaspoon grated fresh horseradish

1 teaspoon grated fresh ginger

2 cups buttermilk

2 tablespoons sour cream

Dill sprigs *(optional)*

1 In a Dutch oven or soup pot over medium-high heat, combine 3 cups water, carrots, parsnips, stock, sugar, and salt. Bring to boil, then reduce heat and simmer, covered, 25 minutes or until tender.

2 In a skillet over low heat, melt butter. Add onion, garlic, horseradish, and ginger and sauté until tender. Stir into pot.

3 Working in batches, transfer soup to a blender or food processor, cover, and puree until smooth. Return to pot, stir in buttermilk, and cook until heated through (do not boil). Garnish each serving with sour cream and dill, if desired.

CREAM OF CAULIFLOWER SOUP

This is an elegant soup made from a humble vegetable.

SERVES 8

1/4 cup (1/2 stick) plus 6 tablespoons butter
2 medium onions, chopped
2 medium carrots, grated
2 celery stalks, sliced
2 garlic cloves, minced
1 medium head cauliflower, chopped
5 cups chicken stock
1/4 cup minced fresh parsley
1 teaspoon salt
1 teaspoon coarsely ground black pepper
1/2 teaspoon dried basil
1/2 teaspoon dried tarragon
6 tablespoons all-purpose flour
1 cup milk
1/2 cup heavy whipping cream
1/4 cup sour cream
Fresh tarragon *(optional)*

1 In a Dutch oven or soup pot over low heat, melt 1/4 cup butter. Add onions, carrots, celery, and garlic and sauté until tender, about 6 minutes.

2 Add cauliflower, stock, parsley, salt, pepper, basil, and dried tarragon. Bring to boil, then reduce heat and simmer, covered, 30 minutes or until vegetables are tender.

3 Meanwhile, in a saucepan over low heat, melt remaining butter. Add flour and stir until smooth. Gradually stir in milk and cream, bring to boil, and cook, stirring, until thickened, about 2 minutes.

4 Add cream sauce to pot and cook, stirring frequently, 10 minutes or until soup is thickened. Remove from heat and stir in sour cream. Garnish each serving with fresh tarragon, if desired.

CAULIFLOWER-YOGURT SOUP

You can just as easily make this soup with fresh cauliflower in season.

SERVES 4

1 bag (20 ounces) frozen cauliflower
2 tablespoons butter or margarine
2 tablespoons slivered almonds
1 small yellow onion, chopped
1 tablespoon all-purpose flour
1/2 teaspoon salt
1/2 teaspoon black pepper
1/8 teaspoon ground nutmeg
1 cup low-fat plain yogurt
1 cup milk
Chopped fresh parsley

1 In a large saucepan over high heat, combine 2 1/4 cups water and cauliflower and bring to boil. Reduce heat to low, cover, and simmer 7 minutes or until tender. Drain over a medium bowl, reserving 2 cups liquid. Transfer cauliflower to another bowl.

2 In the same saucepan over medium heat, melt butter. Add almonds and sauté 1 to 2 minutes or until browned. Using a slotted spoon, transfer to a plate. Add onion to remaining butter in pan and sauté 5 minutes or until softened.

3 Add flour, salt, pepper, and nutmeg to pan and stir 1 minute. Add reserved cooking water and stir until thickened and bubbling. Remove from heat and stir in cauliflower. Working in batches, transfer soup to a food processor or blender, add yogurt, cover, and puree until smooth.

4 Pour puree into a medium saucepan over medium heat, add milk, and cook until heated through (do not boil). Ladle into bowls and sprinkle each serving with almonds and a pinch of parsley.

CAULIFLOWER SOUP WITH GRUYÈRE

Satisfy your daily requirement for vitamin C with a single serving of this soup.

SERVES 4

1 tablespoon vegetable oil

1 small leek, white part only, rinsed and coarsely chopped

1 medium onion, finely chopped

2 cans (14 1/2 ounces) fat-free low-sodium chicken broth

1/2 head cauliflower, coarsely chopped

1/2 teaspoon dried thyme, crumbled

1/2 teaspoon ground cumin

1/4 teaspoon ground white pepper

2/3 cup shredded Gruyère cheese

1 Heat oil in a large saucepan over medium-high heat. Add leek and onion and sauté 5 minutes or until softened. Add broth, cauliflower, thyme, and cumin and simmer, uncovered, 30 minutes or until cauliflower is tender.

2 Add pepper, ladle into bowls, and sprinkle cheese over each serving.

CAULIFLOWER SOUP WITH CHEDDAR AND MOZZARELLA

Combining cheddar with a mild Italian cheese gives this soup an interesting and unusual taste.

SERVES 6

2 tablespoons butter

1/2 cup shredded carrots

1/4 cup chopped onion

2 cans (10 3/4 ounces each) condensed cream of potato soup

2 cups milk

1 can (7 ounces) whole-kernel corn, drained

1-2 cups fresh or frozen cauliflower florets, cooked just until tender

1 cup (4 ounces) shredded cheddar cheese

1/2 cup (2 ounces) shredded mozzarella or provolone cheese

1/8 teaspoon black pepper

1 In a medium saucepan over medium heat, melt butter. Add 1/4 cup water, carrots, and onion and cook until carrots are tender, about 4 minutes.

2 Stir in soup, milk, corn, and cauliflower and heat through. Just before serving, stir in cheddar, mozzarella, and pepper.

CURRIED CAULIFLOWER SOUP

This simple soup has rice to give it heft and tomato juice to give it color.

SERVES 4

1 tablespoon unsalted butter

1 medium yellow onion, coarsely chopped

2 teaspoons curry powder

1/2 teaspoon ground ginger

2 cups chicken stock

1/3 cup long-grain white rice

3 cups fresh cauliflower florets or 2 packages (10 ounces each) frozen cauliflower florets

1/4 teaspoon salt

1/4 teaspoon black pepper

1/2 cup tomato juice

Parsley sprigs *(optional)*

1 scallion, sliced *(optional)*

1 In a large heavy saucepan over medium heat, melt butter. Add onion and sauté 3 minutes or until softened. Stir in 2 cups water, curry powder, ginger, stock, rice, and cauliflower and bring to boil. Reduce heat, cover, and simmer 20 minutes. Stir in salt and pepper.

2 Set a large sieve over a bowl and drain vegetables, reserving liquid. Working in batches if necessary, transfer vegetables to a blender or food processor, add tomato juice, cover, and puree until smooth. Return to pan, stir in reserved liquid, and cook over medium heat until heated through. Garnish with parsley or scallion, if desired.

CURRIED CAULIFLOWER-POTATO SOUP

Indian cooks often combine cauliflower with curry; the lime juice adds refreshing zest to the soup.

SERVES 10

1 1/2 tablespoons olive or canola oil

2 large onions, coarsely chopped

2 garlic cloves, finely chopped

2 teaspoons curry powder

Pinch of ground ginger (optional)

Pinch of turmeric (optional)

1 1/2 pounds cauliflower florets

8 ounces all-purpose potatoes, peeled and diced

8 cups chicken stock

1 tablespoon fresh lime juice

1/8 teaspoon salt

1/8 teaspoon black pepper

1 Heat oil in a 4-quart saucepan over medium heat. Add onions and garlic and sauté 3 minutes or until softened. Stir in curry powder, ginger, if desired, and turmeric, if desired, and sauté 3 minutes.

2 Coarsely chop cauliflower florets. Add cauliflower, potatoes, and stock to pan and bring to boil. Reduce heat and simmer, partially covered, 20 to 25 minutes or until softened. Remove from heat and let cool slightly.

3 Using a slotted spoon, transfer vegetables in batches to a blender or food processor, cover, and puree until smooth. Return to pan and cook until heated through. Stir in lime juice, salt, and pepper.

CELERY ROOT-SPINACH SOUP

Celery root by itself makes a rich, creamy soup. Baby spinach gives the soup color and fresh flavor.

SERVES 4

2 tablespoons extra-virgin olive oil

1 large onion, thinly sliced

1 garlic clove, crushed

1 large celery root, peeled and grated

1 vegetable stock cube, crumbled, or 2 teaspoons vegetable bouillon powder or paste

1 pound baby spinach leaves

Grated nutmeg

Salt and black pepper

4 tablespoons cream

Fresh chives

1 Heat oil in a large saucepan over medium heat. Add onion and garlic and sauté 5 minutes or until onion is softened but not browned. Add celery root. Pour in 3 1/2 cups boiling water, add stock cube, and stir to dissolve. Bring to boil, then reduce heat and simmer, covered, 10 minutes.

2 Add spinach, stir well, and bring to boil. Remove from heat and let cool slightly. Working in batches, transfer to a blender or food processor, cover, and puree until smooth (or use a handheld blender to puree in pan).

3 Cook until heated through and season to taste with nutmeg, salt, and pepper. Ladle into warm bowls, swirl a tablespoon of cream into each serving, and garnish with chives.

CELERY ROOT-POTATO SOUP

Celery root has a slightly stronger flavor than celery. If it's not available, you can use sliced celery.

SERVES 8

1 tablespoon olive or canola oil

2 large onions, coarsely chopped

8 cups chicken or vegetable stock

12 ounces celery root, diced, or celery, thickly sliced

1 large all-purpose potato, peeled and diced

1/4 teaspoon dried thyme

1 bay leaf

1/2 cup buttermilk or low-fat (1%) milk

1/8 teaspoon salt

1/8 teaspoon black pepper

1/2 cup watercress or torn spinach leaves

1 Heat oil in a 4-quart saucepan over medium heat. Add onions and 3/4 cup stock and sauté until softened but not browned.

2 Stir in celery root and potato. Add remaining stock, thyme, and bay leaf and bring to boil. Reduce heat, partially cover, and simmer, stirring occasionally, 20 to 25 minutes or until vegetables are very soft. Remove from heat and let cool slightly.

3 Remove bay leaf. Using a slotted spoon, transfer vegetables in batches to a blender or food processor, cover, and puree until very smooth.

4 Return puree to pan and bring to simmer. Add buttermilk, salt, and pepper and simmer 5 minutes. Stir in watercress, then remove from heat and let stand until wilted.

PEPPERY CORN SOUP

Hot Mexican jalapeños add bite to what otherwise would be a humdrum corn soup.

SERVES 4

6 bacon slices

2 tablespoons vegetable oil

I large yellow onion, finely chopped

2 medium celery stalks, thinly sliced

2 medium carrots, peeled and diced

1 pound all-purpose potatoes, peeled and diced

3/4 teaspoon salt

1/4 teaspoon black pepper

2 cups chicken stock

2 cups milk

2 cups fresh corn or 1 package (10 ounces) frozen whole-kernel corn, thawed

1 tablespoon minced and seeded canned jalapeño peppers (wear gloves when handling; they burn)

1/2 cup (2 ounces) shredded low-fat cheddar or Monterey Jack cheese

1 tablespoon minced fresh cilantro, flat-leaf parsley, or chives

1 In a deep 12-inch skillet or large saucepan over medium heat, cook bacon until crisp. Transfer to paper towels to drain, then crumble. Drain fat from skillet.

2 Add oil and heat over medium heat. Add onion, celery, and carrots and sauté until softened, about 10 minutes. Add potatoes, salt, pepper, and stock and bring to boil. Reduce heat and simmer, covered, until tender, about 15 minutes.

3 Add milk and corn and simmer, covered, 5 minutes. Stir in jalapeños and cheese until cheese is melted. Garnish each serving with cilantro and bacon.

ROASTED EGGPLANT SOUP

SERVES 4

3 small eggplants

1 tablespoon olive oil

1 large yellow onion, sliced

2 garlic cloves, crushed

1 tablespoon minced fresh ginger
   or 1/2 teaspoon ground ginger

1/4 teaspoon hot red pepper flakes

2 medium red bell peppers, cored,
   seeded, and sliced

1/4 teaspoon salt

3 cups canned low-sodium chicken broth

4 teaspoons red wine vinegar

1/4 cup low-fat plain yogurt

1 Preheat oven to 375°F. Pierce eggplants in several places with a fork and place on an ungreased baking sheet. Bake 40 minutes or until very soft when pierced with a fork. Let cool.

2 Heat oil in a medium heavy saucepan over low heat. Add onion, garlic, ginger, and red pepper flakes and sauté 10 minutes or until onion is softened.

3 Stir in bell peppers and salt and cook, covered, 10 minutes or until softened. Add broth and bring to boil, then reduce heat and simmer, uncovered, 20 minutes or until peppers are very soft. Remove from heat and strain into a medium bowl, reserving liquid. Transfer vegetables to another medium bowl.

4 When eggplants are cool enough to handle, remove skins and halve lengthwise. Using a small spoon, remove seeds, then cut flesh into 1-inch cubes.

5 Working in batches if necessary, transfer eggplants, reserved vegetables, and 1 cup cooking liquid to a food processor or blender. Cover and puree until smooth. Return to pan, add remaining liquid and vinegar, and cook, uncovered, over medium heat 5 minutes or until heated through. Ladle into bowls and top each serving with a tablespoon of yogurt.

Roasting the eggplant gives this soup a deep, smoky flavor and removes any bitterness the eggplant may have.

GREEN BEAN SOUP

An old country recipe, this soup is best with fresh-from-the-farmers'-market beans, carrots, onions, and potatoes.

SERVES 6

2 cups fresh green beans,
cut into 2-inch pieces

1 1/2 cups cubed peeled all-purpose
potatoes

1 cup cubed fully cooked ham

1/2 cup thinly sliced carrot

1 medium onion, diced

1 bay leaf

1 parsley sprig

1 savory sprig or 1/4 teaspoon dried savory

1 beef bouillon cube

1/4 teaspoon black pepper

1/2 teaspoon salt *(optional)*

1 In a 2-quart saucepan, combine 4 cups water, beans, potatoes, ham, carrot, onion, bay leaf, parsley, savory, bouillon, pepper, and salt, if desired. Bring to boil, then reduce heat and simmer, covered, 20 minutes or until vegetables are tender. Remove bay leaf, parsley, and savory before serving.

GREEN BEAN SOUP WITH PESTO

This dish is based on soupe au pistou, a classic French soup from Provence.

SERVES 4

1 tablespoon extra-virgin olive oil

1 leek, thinly sliced

1 large zucchini, diced

5 1/2 ounces French green beans,
cut into short lengths

2 garlic cloves, minced

5 cups vegetable stock

9 ounces tomatoes, cored, seeded,
and chopped

Black pepper

4 ounces vermicelli, broken into small pieces

2 tablespoons pesto sauce

4 tablespoons freshly grated Parmesan
cheese *(optional)*

1 Heat oil in a large saucepan over medium heat. Add leek, zucchini, beans, and garlic and sauté 5 minutes or until softened and beginning to brown.

2 Add stock, tomatoes, and pepper and bring to boil. Reduce heat and simmer, covered, 10 minutes or until vegetables are tender.

3 Stir in pasta and simmer 5 minutes or until al dente. Ladle into bowls and stir 1 1/2 teaspoons pesto into each serving. Pass cheese separately, if desired.

GREEN BEAN AND TOMATO SOUP

A lovely vegetable soup, fortified with pasta, to make a lunch or begin a dinner.

MAKES 9 CUPS

8 cups chicken stock

1 cup small pasta shells or bowties

1 large carrot, diced

2 celery stalks, diced

1/4 teaspoon dried oregano

1/4 teaspoon dried basil

4 ounces green beans, cut crosswise
into 1/2-inch slices

1 cup canned crushed tomatoes

1/8 teaspoon salt

1/8 teaspoon black pepper

2 tablespoons chopped fresh basil

1 In a 4-quart saucepan over high heat, bring stock to boil. Add pasta, reduce heat, and simmer 5 minutes, stirring occasionally.

2 Add carrot, celery, oregano, and basil. Simmer, stirring occasionally, 5 minutes or until pasta and vegetables are almost cooked through. Add beans, tomatoes, salt, and pepper and simmer, stirring occasionally, 5 minutes. Stir in basil.

CREAMY GREENS SOUP

Mild-flavored collard greens and Swiss chard add a powerful blast of beta-carotene to every spoonful of this smooth, creamy soup.

SERVES 8

2 teaspoons olive oil

2 leeks, pale green and white parts only, rinsed and coarsely chopped

1 medium onion, coarsely chopped

2 garlic cloves, minced

1 small bunch collard greens, trimmed and coarsely chopped

1 small bunch Swiss chard, trimmed and coarsely chopped

2 medium Yukon Gold or all-purpose potatoes, coarsely chopped

1 carrot, peeled and coarsely chopped

2 cans (14 1/2 ounces each) fat-free low-sodium chicken broth

1 teaspoon salt

1/2 cup half-and-half

1 Heat oil in a large soup pot over medium heat. Add leeks and onion and sauté 5 minutes or until softened. Add garlic and sauté 2 minutes. Add collards, chard, potatoes, and carrot. Stir in 4 cups water, broth, and salt. Simmer, partially covered, 50 minutes. Remove from heat and let cool slightly.

2 Working in batches, transfer soup to a blender or food processor, cover, and puree until smooth. Return to pot, stir in half-and-half, and cook just until heated through.

LEAFY GREENS SOUP WITH HERBS

Hearty but not heavy, this is a soup for summer and autumn. Use any greens you like—simply adjust the cooking time.

SERVES 4

2 tablespoons extra-virgin olive oil

1 leek, white part only, cut into thin strips

1 small onion, chopped

1/2 carrot, thinly sliced

4 garlic cloves, chopped

1/2 teaspoon fennel seed

2 tablespoons chopped fresh parsley

2 slices prosciutto, trimmed of fat and cut into thin strips or chopped

5 1/2 ounces Swiss chard, spinach, spring greens, or a mixture, very finely shredded

3 small ripe tomatoes, cored, seeded, and diced

6 cups chicken or vegetable stock

Pinch of crushed dried red chiles *(optional)*

Salt and black pepper

8 ounces small pasta shapes, such as conchigliette (shells) or ditalini (small thimbles)

Garnishes:

1/4 cup fresh basil leaves, chopped

4 tablespoons grated Parmesan cheese

4 tablespoons chopped young arugula *(optional)*

1 Heat oil in a large saucepan over medium heat. Add leek and onion and sauté 5 minutes or until slightly softened. Add carrot, garlic, fennel seed, parsley, and prosciutto and sauté 5 minutes.

2 Stir in greens and tomatoes and cook, covered, 2 minutes or until slightly softened. Add stock and chiles, if desired, and season to taste with salt and pepper. Bring to boil, then reduce heat and simmer 5 minutes or until greens are just tender.

3 Meanwhile, cook pasta in boiling water for 10 to 12 minutes or according to package directions until al dente; drain.

4 Divide pasta among 4 bowls. Ladle soup over pasta and sprinkle with basil, Parmesan, and arugula, if desired.

LEEK SOUP WITH HAM

This is a lovely soup with subtle flavors that will use up an Easter ham in an elegant way.

SERVES 8

1 pound leeks, cleaned and cut into
    1/2-inch pieces
1/2 cup (1 stick) butter
1/2 cup all-purpose flour
4 cups chicken stock
2 cups half-and-half
1/2 teaspoon salt
1/4 teaspoon black pepper
1 cup diced cooked all-purpose potato
1 cup diced cooked ham

1 In a covered container in a microwave oven, steam leeks with 1/2 cup water until tender, about 6 minutes. Do not drain.

2 In a large saucepan over medium heat, melt butter. Add flour, stirring constantly, and cook 2 minutes. Gradually whisk in stock and bring to boil, then reduce heat and simmer. Add half-and-half, salt, pepper, leeks and cooking liquid, potato, and ham and cook 3 minutes or until heated through (do not boil).

LEEK AND POTATO SOUP WITH SOUR CREAM

The whole family will enjoy this soup, a low-fat version of classic French vichyssoise.

SERVES 6

1 tablespoon olive or canola oil
8 ounces leeks, white part only, thickly sliced
1 large onion, coarsely chopped
6 cups chicken or vegetable stock
1 pound all-purpose potatoes, peeled
    and diced
1/8 teaspoon salt
1/8 teaspoon ground white pepper
1/3 cup reduced-fat sour cream
Chopped fresh chives

1 Heat oil in a 4-quart saucepan over medium heat. Stir in leeks, onion, and 3/4 cup stock. Cover and cook, stirring frequently, 10 minutes or until vegetables are soft but not browned.

2 Add potatoes and stir to coat. Pour in half of remaining stock and bring to boil, then reduce heat and simmer, partially covered, 15 to 20 minutes or until potatoes are soft. Remove from heat and let cool slightly. Working in batches if necessary, transfer to a blender or food processor, cover, and puree until smooth.

3 Pour remaining stock into pan. Add puree and simmer, stirring constantly, 2 to 3 minutes. Add salt and pepper, remove from heat, and stir in sour cream. Ladle into bowls and garnish with chives.

LEEK AND POTATO SOUP WITH MILK

You can serve this easy-to-make soup hot or cold, depending on the weather.

SERVES 4

2 tablespoons butter

2 medium leeks, white part only, rinsed and sliced

1 small yellow onion, chopped

1 large baking potato, peeled and diced

1/2 cup milk

1/2 teaspoon salt

1/2 teaspoon chopped fresh chives

Black pepper

1 In a large saucepan over medium heat, melt butter. Add leeks, onion, and potato and sauté 5 minutes. Add 2 cups water and bring to boil over high heat. Reduce heat and simmer, covered, 15 minutes or until potatoes are soft. Remove from heat and let cool slightly.

2 Working in batches if necessary, transfer soup to a blender or food processor, cover, and puree until smooth. Pour into a medium saucepan. Stir in milk and salt and cook over medium heat until hot (do not boil). Ladle into bowls and sprinkle each serving with chives and a pinch of pepper.

CURRIED LEEK SOUP

This is a beautiful, subtle soup with a touch of curry in a delicate leek and cream base.

SERVES 4

2 tablespoons butter

3 medium leeks, white parts only, thinly sliced

1 garlic clove, minced

1 can (14 1/2 ounces) chicken broth

1 1/2 cups thinly sliced carrots

2 celery stalks, thinly sliced

2 teaspoons chicken bouillon granules

1/2 teaspoon curry powder

1/8 teaspoon black pepper

1 can (12 ounces) fat-free evaporated milk

1 In a 3-quart saucepan over low heat, melt butter. Add leeks and garlic, increase heat to medium, and sauté until tender. Add 3/4 cup water, broth, carrots, celery, bouillon, curry powder, and pepper. Bring to boil, then reduce heat and simmer, covered, until vegetables are tender, about 20 minutes. Remove from heat and let cool slightly.

2 Transfer 1 cup soup to a blender or food processor, cover, and puree until smooth. Return to pan, add milk, and cook until heated through (do not boil).

MUSHROOM SOUP

The earthy flavor of the large, dark mushrooms in this soup is given a lift by garlic, parsley, and mace. It has a deep, smoky color and a rich taste that needs no cream to enhance it.

SERVES 4 TO 6

5 cups vegetable stock
3 slices country-style bread
2 tablespoons olive oil
1/2 small onion or 1 shallot, chopped
1/2 small garlic clove, minced
1 1/2 pounds portobello mushrooms, cleaned and chopped
3 parsley sprigs, chopped
Pinch of ground or freshly grated nutmeg
Salt and black pepper

1 In a large saucepan over medium-high heat, bring stock to boil. Meanwhile, in a medium bowl, soak bread in a small amount of cold water.

2 Heat oil in another large saucepan over medium heat. Add onion and sauté 3 minutes or until golden. Add garlic and sauté 1 minute. Add mushrooms and sauté 3 minutes or until they release their liquid. Stir in parsley.

3 Squeeze as much water as possible from bread and add to mushroom mixture. Add stock and nutmeg and bring to boil. Reduce heat and simmer, partially covered, 15 to 20 minutes.

4 Working in batches if necessary, transfer soup to a blender or food processor, cover, and puree until creamy but still slightly grainy. Return to pan, add salt and pepper, and cook until heated through.

CREAM OF MUSHROOM SOUP

This is a superb, creamy mushroom soup that can start off a festive dinner party or holiday celebration.

SERVES 4 TO 6

2 tablespoons butter
1/4 cup chopped onion
3 cups sliced fresh mushrooms
6 tablespoons all-purpose flour
2 cans (14 1/2 ounces each) chicken broth
1 cup half-and-half
1/2 teaspoon salt
1/8 teaspoon black pepper

1 In a large saucepan over medium heat, melt butter. Add onion and sauté 3 minutes or until tender. Add mushrooms and sauté 7 minutes or until tender.

2 In a small bowl, whisk flour into a small amount of broth until smooth, then stir into pan. Add remaining broth, bring to boil, and cook, stirring, until thickened, about 2 minutes. Reduce heat and stir in half-and-half, salt, and pepper. Simmer, uncovered, 15 minutes, stirring frequently.

GOLDEN STATE MUSHROOM SOUP

Fresh mushrooms—now available in many varieties at supermarkets—make all the difference in this luscious soup.

SERVES 4

1/4 cup (1/2 stick) butter
1 pound fresh mushrooms, sliced
1 medium onion, chopped
1/4 cup all-purpose flour
1/2 teaspoon salt
1/8 teaspoon black pepper
1 1/2 cups milk

1 can (14 1/2 ounces) chicken broth
1 teaspoon chicken bouillon granules
1 cup sour cream
Minced fresh parsley *(optional)*

1 In a large saucepan over medium heat, melt butter. Add mushrooms and onion and sauté until tender, about 6 minutes. Add flour, salt, and pepper and stir to combine.

2 Gradually stir in milk, broth, and bouillon, bring to boil, and cook, stirring, 2 minutes. Reduce heat, stir in sour cream, and cook until heated through (do not boil). Garnish each serving with parsley, if desired.

MUSHROOM SOUP WITH PEPPERS

This lovely one-pan soup is on the table in minutes.

SERVES 4

2 tablespoons butter
1 large yellow onion, finely chopped
1/2 cup chopped seeded green bell pepper
1 small garlic clove, minced
4 ounces fresh mushrooms, sliced
2 tablespoons all-purpose flour
2 cups canned low-sodium chicken broth
1/2 cup milk
Salt and black pepper
1 tablespoon chopped fresh parsley

1 In a large saucepan over medium heat, melt butter. Add onion, bell pepper, and garlic and sauté 5 minutes or until onion is softened. Stir in mushrooms and sauté 3 minutes or until just wilted.

2 Add flour and stir until well mixed. Add broth and bring to boil over high heat, stirring until thickened, about 5 minutes.

3 Reduce heat to medium, add milk, and season to taste with salt and black pepper. Cook, stirring frequently, until heated through (do not boil). Stir in parsley.

MUSHROOM AND CHIVE SOUP

This delightful and refreshing vegetarian soup is a wonderful starter for a special dinner or a festive lunch.

MAKES 9 CUPS

5 cups vegetable stock
1/2 ounce dried porcini mushrooms
2 teaspoons olive or canola oil
1 shallot or small onion, finely chopped
1 celery stalk, coarsely chopped
8 ounces fresh mushrooms, trimmed and sliced
1 tablespoon chopped fresh or frozen chives
1/8 teaspoon salt
1/8 teaspoon black pepper
2 tablespoons reduced-fat sour cream

1 In a small saucepan, bring 1 cup stock to boil. Remove from heat and add porcini mushrooms. Let stand at least 10 minutes or until softened. Drain, reserving liquid, and chop mushrooms.

2 Heat oil in a 4-quart saucepan over medium heat. Add shallot and celery and sauté 4 minutes or until softened and golden.

3 Add porcini and fresh mushrooms and sauté 5 minutes. Add remaining stock and soaking liquid and bring to boil. Reduce heat and simmer, partially covered, 10 minutes or until mushrooms are soft. Stir in chives, salt, and pepper and simmer 3 minutes. Garnish each portion with sour cream.

FRESH AND DRIED MUSHROOM SOUP

Dried porcini mushrooms are a smart substitute for pricy fresh porcini in this flavorful soup.

SERVES 4

1/2 cup dried porcini or other imported
    dried mushrooms
2 teaspoons vegetable oil
1 large onion, finely chopped
4 garlic cloves, minced
8 ounces fresh shiitake mushrooms,
    trimmed, halved, and thinly sliced
1 pound fresh button mushrooms,
    thinly sliced
1/4 cup dry sherry or chicken stock
1 1/2 cups chicken stock
1 large tomato, cored, seeded,
    and finely chopped
1/2 teaspoon dried tarragon
1/2 teaspoon black pepper

1 In a small bowl, combine dried mushrooms and 1 cup boiling water and let stand 10 minutes or until softened. Using a slotted spoon, remove mushrooms, then coarsely chop. Strain soaking liquid through a coffee filter or a sieve lined with paper towels.

2 Heat oil in a large saucepan over medium heat. Add onion and garlic and sauté 5 minutes or until onion is softened. Stir in dried mushrooms, add shiitakes, and sauté 5 minutes or until softened. Add button mushrooms and sauté 5 minutes or until they begin to release their liquid.

3 Add soaking liquid and bring to boil. Add sherry and cook 5 minutes or until reduced by half. Add 1 1/2 cups water, stock, tomato, tarragon, and pepper. Bring to boil, then reduce heat and simmer, covered, 10 minutes.

MUSHROOM SOUP WITH ONIONS

Nowadays it's possible to buy an assortment of mushrooms at the grocery store to make a soup like this more interesting.

SERVES 4

2 cups fresh mushrooms
3 tablespoons butter
2 medium onions, chopped
2 tablespoons all-purpose flour
5 cups chicken stock
1/2 teaspoon salt *(optional)*
Dash of black pepper
1/3 cup long-grain rice
1 bay leaf
2 tablespoons chopped fresh parsley

1 Remove mushroom stems level with caps, then finely chop stems and thinly slice caps.

2 In a large saucepan over medium heat, melt butter. Add mushrooms and onions and sauté 5 minutes. Add flour and stir well.

3 Add stock, salt, and pepper and bring to boil, stirring constantly. Add rice and bay leaf. Reduce heat and simmer, covered, 15 to 20 minutes or until rice is tender. Remove bay leaf. Sprinkle each serving with parsley.

WILD MUSHROOM SOUP

A mixture of fresh mushrooms, widely available at farmers' markets and supermarkets, is good for making this quick, woodsy-tasting soup. Ciabatta bread is available at many supermarkets and all Italian markets. You can substitute Italian or peasant bread. (Photograph on page 1)

SERVES 6

3 tablespoons extra-virgin olive oil

1 small onion, chopped

1 small fennel bulb, chopped

1 garlic clove, minced

1 pound mixed fresh mushrooms, cleaned and coarsely chopped

1 tablespoon vegetable bouillon granules or paste

8 thin slices ciabatta bread

2 tablespoons chopped fresh parsley

2 tablespoons chopped fresh mint

Salt and black pepper

1 Heat 2 tablespoons oil in a large saucepan over medium heat. Add onion and fennel and sauté 5 minutes or until slightly softened. Add garlic and mushrooms and sauté 5 minutes. Add 3 1/2 cups boiling water and stir in bouillon. Return to boil; reduce heat and simmer, uncovered, 10 minutes.

2 Preheat grill or broiler. Brush bread lightly on both sides with remaining oil and toast until golden, about 1 minute per side. Cut into cubes and place in a medium bowl. Add parsley and mint and toss.

3 Season soup to taste with salt and pepper. Ladle into bowls and sprinkle with croutons.

EIGHT-ONION SOUP WITH PUFF-PASTRY HAT

With its festive puffed hat, this soup delectably mingles flavors from many onion family members.

SERVES 8

2 tablespoons butter

5 medium yellow onions, thinly sliced

20 pearl onions, peeled

1 red onion, thinly sliced

2 leeks, rinsed and thinly sliced

2 shallots, thinly sliced

5 garlic cloves, crushed

1 tablespoon sugar

8 scallions, thinly sliced

7 cups beef stock

2 sheets frozen puff pastry, 9 1/2 x 9 1/4 x 1/8 inches, thawed in the refrigerator

1/4 cup snipped fresh chives

1 Preheat oven to 400°F. In a 5-quart Dutch oven or soup pot over medium-high heat, melt butter. Add yellow, pearl, and red onions, leeks, shallots, garlic, and sugar and sauté over high heat until onions are golden, about 10 minutes. Reduce heat to medium-low and sauté, stirring occasionally, 15 minutes.

2 Add scallions and stock and bring to boil. Reduce heat and simmer, uncovered, 1 hour. Meanwhile, on a lightly floured work surface, spread out puff pastry and cut into 8 rounds slightly larger than the circumference of serving bowls.

3 Divide soup among 8 ovenproof bowls and sprinkle each portion with 1 tablespoon chives. Fit pastry on top of bowls, crimping edges to seal. Place bowls on a heavy-duty baking sheet in middle of oven and bake, uncovered, until puffed and golden, about 20 minutes.

CLASSIC ONION SOUP

This is the rich, aromatic soup that used to be served at Les Halles, the famous Paris food market, many years ago.

SERVES 4

2 tablespoons butter
5 medium yellow onions, thinly sliced
2 tablespoons sugar
3 1/2 cups beef stock
1/2 teaspoon salt
1/2 teaspoon black pepper
1/4 cup brandy *(optional)*
4 slices French bread, 1/2 inch thick, toasted
4 tablespoons shredded Gruyère cheese

1 Preheat oven to 400°F. In a 5-quart Dutch oven or soup pot over medium-high heat, melt butter. Increase heat to high, add onions and sugar, and sauté until onions are golden, about 10 minutes. Reduce heat to medium-low and sauté 10 minutes.

2 Increase heat to high, add stock and 5 cups water, and bring to boil. Reduce heat and simmer, uncovered, 20 minutes. Increase heat to high, add salt, pepper, and brandy, if desired, and return to boil.

3 Ladle soup into four 8-ounce ovenproof ramekins or soup bowls and place on a heavy-duty baking sheet or ovenproof metal tray. Top each serving with bread and sprinkle with 1 tablespoon cheese. Bake 5 minutes or until cheese is melted.

OVEN-ROASTED ONION SOUP

Here's a soup that delivers all the rich flavor of the French classic with a fraction of the fat—the onions are roasted, not sautéed. (Photograph on page 8)

SERVES 4

2 1/2 pounds large onions, thinly sliced
1 tablespoon chopped fresh thyme
1 tablespoon sugar
1/2 teaspoon salt
1/2 teaspoon black pepper
1/2 cup dry white wine
3 cans (14 1/2 ounces each) low-sodium
  chicken broth
4 thick slices French bread
2/3 cup shredded Gruyère cheese

1 Preheat oven to 425°F. In a large bowl, toss onions, thyme, sugar, salt, and pepper. Spread onions in a large roasting pan, lightly coat with olive oil cooking spray, and drizzle with 1/4 cup water. Cover with foil and roast 30 minutes. Uncover and roast, stirring often, until browned and tender, about 40 minutes longer.

2 Set roasting pan across two burners over high heat. Add wine and stir with a wooden spoon, scraping onions and browned bits from bottom of pan, until wine is syrupy, about 2 minutes.

3 Transfer onions and pan juices to a large saucepan. Stir in broth and bring to boil over high heat. Reduce heat and simmer, covered, until flavors are blended, about 15 minutes.

4 Meanwhile, preheat broiler. Place bread on a baking sheet and broil until lightly toasted, about 2 minutes on each side. Ladle soup into four ovenproof bowls, float a bread slice in each, and sprinkle with cheese. Place bowls in a broiler pan or shallow baking pan and broil until cheese melts, about 2 minutes.

CREAMY ONION AND SCALLION SOUP

The combination of onions and scallions gives a lively boost to this first-course soup.

SERVES 4

2 teaspoons olive oil

3 cups diced onions

6 scallions, sliced

1 garlic clove, minced

1 teaspoon sugar

1/2 teaspoon dried thyme

1/4 teaspoon salt

3/4 cup chicken stock

1 cup low-fat (1%) milk

1 Heat oil in a nonstick saucepan over medium heat. Add onions, scallions, garlic, sugar, thyme, and salt and sauté 5 minutes or until onions are tender.

2 Add stock and 3/4 cup water and bring to boil. Reduce heat and simmer, covered, 5 minutes.

3 Working in batches if necessary, transfer soup to a food processor or blender, add milk, cover, and puree until smooth. Return to pan and heat through.

QUICK FRENCH ONION SOUP

By making the bread coated with melted cheese separately from the soup, you will save time in putting this classic dish together.

SERVES 4

3 tablespoons butter

4 large yellow onions, sliced

1 tablespoon all-purpose flour

2 cups beef stock

1 teaspoon Worcestershire sauce

4 slices French bread, 1/2 inch thick

4 slices Swiss cheese

1 In a large saucepan over medium heat, melt butter. Add onions and cook, covered, 10 minutes, shaking pan frequently to prevent sticking. Stir in flour until well mixed.

2 Increase heat to high and add stock, 2 cups water, and Worcestershire sauce. Bring to boil, reduce heat, and simmer, covered, 10 minutes or until onions are very soft.

3 Preheat broiler. Place bread on baking sheet and toast on both sides. Cover each slice with a cheese slice and broil until cheese is browned and melted, about 2 seconds.

4 Place 1 bread slice in each bowl and ladle in soup.

BUTTERY ONION SOUP

The surprise in this rich, creamy onion soup is the choice of mozzarella cheese as the final flavoring.

SERVES 6

1/2 cup (1 stick) butter

2 cups thinly sliced onions

1/4 cup all-purpose flour

2 cups chicken stock

2 cups milk

1 1/2-2 cups (6-8 ounces) shredded mozzarella cheese

Salt and black pepper

1 In a large soup pot over low heat, melt butter. Add onions and sauté until tender and transparent, about 20 minutes. Blend in flour and cook 2 minutes.

2 Gradually add stock and milk and cook, stirring, over medium heat until bubbling. Continue to cook, stirring, 1 minute. Reduce heat to low, add cheese, and stir constantly until melted (do not boil). Season to taste with salt and pepper.

FRENCH ONION-TOMATO SOUP

This is a twist on traditional French onion soup. The tomato juice gives the onions a different flavor.

SERVES 6

2 tablespoons butter
4 cups thinly sliced onions
1 garlic clove, minced
1 can (46 ounces) tomato juice
2 teaspoons beef bouillon granules
3 tablespoons fresh lemon juice
2 teaspoons parsley flakes
2 teaspoons brown sugar
6 slices French bread, toasted
2 cups (8 ounces) shredded mozzarella cheese

1 In a large saucepan over low heat, melt butter. Add onions and garlic and sauté 7 minutes or until tender.

2 Add tomato juice, bouillon, lemon juice, parsley, and brown sugar. Bring to boil, then reduce heat and simmer, uncovered, 10 minutes, stirring occasionally.

3 Preheat broiler. Ladle soup into 10-ounce ovenproof soup bowls or ramekins. Top with toasted bread and sprinkle with cheese. Broil 4 to 6 inches from heat until cheese is bubbling, about 2 minutes.

CREAMY SWISS ONION SOUP

Individual bowls of this soup are topped with buttered croutons, sprinkled with Swiss cheese, and browned under the broiler.

SERVES 4

7 tablespoons butter
1 1/2 cups day-old bread cubes
3 large onions, quartered and thinly sliced
4 1/2 teaspoons chicken bouillon granules
1/4 cup all-purpose flour
1 3/4 cups milk
1 1/2 cups (6 ounces) shredded Swiss cheese
Black pepper
Minced fresh chives or parsley

1 Preheat oven to 350°F. Lightly grease a baking sheet.

2 In a small saucepan over low heat, melt 3 tablespoons butter. Pour into a small bowl, add bread, and toss. Place bread on baking sheet and bake 7 minutes, then turn and bake 7 minutes or until toasted.

3 Meanwhile, in a large saucepan over low heat, melt remaining butter. Add onions and sauté until golden, about 12 minutes. Stir in 1 1/2 cups water and bouillon. Bring to boil, reduce heat, and simmer, covered, 15 minutes.

4 In a small bowl, combine flour and 1/2 cup milk until smooth, then gradually stir into pan. Add remaining milk, bring to boil, and cook, stirring, until thickened, about 2 minutes. Reduce heat to low and stir in 3/4 cup Swiss cheese and pepper.

5 Ladle into 4 ovenproof bowls and sprinkle with croutons and remaining cheese. Broil 4 inches from heat until cheese is melted and bubbling. Garnish with chives.

MEXICAN RED ONION SOUP

Serve this delicately spiced soup plain or topped with shredded Monterey Jack cheese. To save preparation time, slice the onions in a food processor using the slicing attachment. You can substitute 8 large yellow onions or 4 Spanish onions for the red onions.

SERVES 8

3 tablespoons olive oil

6 large red onions, thinly sliced

1 tablespoon sugar

1 teaspoon dried oregano, crumbled

3/4 teaspoon ground coriander

3/4 teaspoon ground cumin

1/4 teaspoon ground allspice

1/4 teaspoon ground cinnamon

1/2 cup red wine vinegar

1/3 cup orange juice

1 1/2 tablespoons all-purpose flour

7 cups chicken stock

1/2 teaspoon salt

1/4 teaspoon black pepper

1 Heat oil in a soup pot or 5-quart Dutch oven over low heat. Add onions and cook, stirring frequently, until soft and golden. Sprinkle with sugar, oregano, coriander, cumin, allspice, and cinnamon and cook, stirring occasionally, 20 minutes.

2 Stir in vinegar and orange juice and cook 4 minutes. Sprinkle with flour and cook, stirring constantly, 1 minute. Increase heat to medium, stir in stock, and bring to boil. Reduce heat, cover, and simmer 20 minutes. Stir in salt and pepper.

AROMATIC PARSNIP SOUP

This fragrant, warming winter soup has a sweet undertone of apple.

SERVES 4 TO 6

3 1/2 cups vegetable stock

1 tablespoon sunflower oil

1 medium onion, chopped

1 garlic clove, chopped

2 teaspoons ground coriander

1 teaspoon ground cumin

1 teaspoon turmeric

1 large cooking apple,
    cored and cut into chunks

1 pound parsnips, cut into chunks

Salt

1 1/2 cups milk

Cilantro sprigs

4-6 tablespoons plain yogurt

1 In a large saucepan over low heat, warm stock.

2 In another large saucepan over medium heat, heat oil. Add onion and sauté 3 minutes. Add garlic, coriander, cumin, and turmeric and sauté 1 minute.

3 Pour stock into pan and add apple, parsnips, and salt. Bring to boil, then reduce heat, cover, and simmer 15 minutes. Remove from heat and stir in milk.

4 Transfer to a food processor or blender, cover, and puree until smooth. Return to pan and cook until heated through. Ladle into bowls and garnish with cilantro. Pass yogurt separately.

CREAMY PARSNIP SOUP

This is a spicy root vegetable soup with ginger, cinnamon, allspice, and apples as well as parsnips, turnips, onions, potatoes, and carrots.

SERVES 6

1 tablespoon vegetable oil

1 medium yellow onion, thinly sliced

3 garlic cloves, slivered

1 tablespoon minced fresh ginger
    or 1 teaspoon ground ginger

1 medium McIntosh apple, peeled,
    cored, and thinly sliced

1 pound parsnips, peeled and
    thinly sliced

1 white turnip, peeled, halved,
    and thinly sliced

1 medium all-purpose potato, peeled,
    halved, and thinly sliced

2 small carrots, peeled and thinly sliced

3/4 teaspoon salt

1/2 teaspoon ground cinnamon

1/8 teaspoon ground allspice

3 cups low-fat (1%) milk

1/4 teaspoon black pepper

Parsley sprigs (*optional*)

Thin apple slices (*optional*)

1 Heat oil in a large heavy saucepan or 5-quart Dutch oven over low heat. Add onion and sauté 5 minutes or until soft. Add garlic and ginger and sauté 2 minutes. Add apple and sauté 5 minutes or until soft.

2 Stir in 1 cup water, parsnips, turnip, potato, carrots, salt, cinnamon, and allspice. Bring to boil, then reduce heat, and simmer, covered, 20 minutes. Add 3 cups water and simmer, covered, 20 minutes or until vegetables are tender.

3 Working in batches if necessary, transfer soup to a blender or food processor and puree until smooth. Return to pan and stir in milk and pepper.

Increase heat to medium and cook, stirring, 5 minutes or until heated through. Garnish each serving with parsley or apple, if desired.

GREEN PEA SOUP

Green peas, lettuce, and scallions make a delightful, refreshing spring soup.

SERVES 4

4 cups vegetable stock

2 cups fresh or frozen peas

1 small head Boston lettuce, cored, halved,
    and cut into shreds

3 scallions, chopped

1/2 teaspoon dried tarragon, crumbled

1/4 teaspoon ground white pepper

Salt to taste

Croutons (*optional*)

1 In a large saucepan, combine stock, peas, lettuce, scallions, and tarragon and bring to boil over high heat. Reduce heat, cover, and simmer for 5 minutes.

2 Transfer soup in 3 batches to a food processor or blender, cover, and puree until smooth. Return to pan and cook until heated through (do not boil).

3 Stir in pepper and salt. Ladle into bowls and top each serving with a few croutons, if desired.

CREAM OF PEA SOUP

This velvety soup is comforting on chilly nights.

SERVES 4

1 can (15 ounces) peas

1/4 cup (1/2 stick) butter

2 tablespoons chopped onion

1/4 cup all-purpose flour

1 teaspoon sugar

1/2 teaspoon salt

1/8 teaspoon black pepper

1/8 teaspoon rubbed sage

1 can (12 ounces) evaporated milk

1 Drain peas, reserving 1/3 cup liquid. Place peas and liquid in a blender or food processor, cover, and puree until smooth.

2 In a saucepan over low heat, melt butter. Add onion and sauté until tender, about 3 minutes. Stir in flour, sugar, salt, pepper, and sage until smooth. Gradually add 2 cups water, bring to boil, and cook, stirring, 2 minutes. Stir in milk and puree and heat through.

FRESH GREEN PEA SOUP

When buying fresh peas, look for plump, bright green pods with medium-size peas. Large pods are likely to be old and tough.

SERVES 4

1 3/4 cups canned low-sodium chicken broth

2 pounds fresh peas, shelled, or 1 package (10 ounces) frozen peas

1/2 cup finely sliced leek

1 celery stalk, chopped

1 large carrot, chopped

1 can (12 ounces) fat-free evaporated milk

1 teaspoon dried mint

1/4 teaspoon salt

1/8 teaspoon white or black pepper

1 In a large saucepan over medium heat, combine broth, peas, leek, celery, and carrot. Bring to boil, then reduce heat and simmer, covered, 15 minutes or until tender. Remove from heat and let cool 10 minutes.

2 Transfer in 2 batches to a food processor or blender, cover, and puree until smooth. Push

through a sieve, discarding solids. Return soup to pan and stir in milk, mint, salt, and pepper. Cook, uncovered, over low heat until heated through, about 10 minutes.

RED PEPPER SOUP

Red bell peppers give this soup its color and flavor, and rice makes it filling.

SERVES 10

1 tablespoon olive oil

6 medium red bell peppers, cored, seeded, and chopped

2 medium carrots, chopped

2 medium onions, chopped

1 celery stalk, chopped

4 garlic cloves, minced

2 cans (one 49 1/2 ounces, one 14 1/2 ounces) chicken broth

1/2 cup long-grain rice

2 tablespoons minced fresh thyme or 2 teaspoons dried thyme

1 1/2 teaspoons salt

1/4 teaspoon black pepper

1/8 teaspoon cayenne pepper

1/8 teaspoon crushed hot red pepper flakes

1 Heat oil in a Dutch oven or soup pot over medium heat. Add bell peppers, carrots, onions, celery, and garlic and sauté until tender, about 7 minutes.

2 Stir in broth, rice, thyme, salt, black pepper, and cayenne and bring to boil. Reduce heat and simmer, covered, 20 minutes or until rice is tender. Remove from heat and let cool 30 minutes.

3 Transfer in batches to a blender or food processor, cover, and puree until smooth. Return to pot, add red pepper flakes, and cook until heated through.

PEPPER AND ORANGE SOUP

A soup to delight the senses, this dish gets stunning color from red peppers and a heady aroma and fruity flavor from orange flower water and freshly squeezed orange juice.

SERVES 4

2 tablespoons olive oil

2 pounds red bell peppers, cored, seeded, and sliced

Salt

Grated zest of 1 orange

3/4 cup fresh orange juice

1 tablespoon orange flower water

Garnishes *(optional)*:

Orange zest

Chopped fresh parsley

Croutons

1 Heat oil in a large saucepan over medium heat. Add bell peppers and sauté 2 to 3 minutes. Season to taste with salt.

2 Add orange zest, cover, increase heat to high, and cook until steam starts to escape from under lid. Reduce heat and simmer, covered, 15 to 18 minutes, shaking pan occasionally, letting peppers cook in their own juice.

3 When peppers are soft, transfer to a food processor or blender, cover, and puree until smooth. (It doesn't matter if some of the peppers caramelize; this just adds flavor.) Add orange juice and orange flower water, cover, and puree. Return to pan and cook until heated through. Garnish with orange zest, parsley, and croutons, if desired.

YELLOW PEPPER SOUP

This sunny-looking soup is superb when served warm with a dollop of sour cream, but you can also chill it for a refreshing starter in summer.

SERVES 12

1 tablespoon butter *(optional)*

1 tablespoon olive oil

6 medium yellow bell peppers, cored, seeded, and cut into 1-inch pieces

1 large onion, diced

1 medium all-purpose potato, peeled and quartered

1 garlic clove, minced

6 cups chicken stock

1 bay leaf

1/2 teaspoon salt *(optional)*

1/4 teaspoon black pepper

1 cup buttermilk

Sour cream *(optional)*

Snipped fresh chives *(optional)*

1 In a Dutch oven or soup pot over medium heat, melt butter, if desired, and heat oil. Add bell peppers, onion, potato, and garlic and sauté until onion is tender, about 5 minutes.

2 Add stock, bay leaf, salt, if desired, and black pepper and bring to boil. Reduce heat and simmer, covered, until vegetables are tender, about 20 minutes. Remove from heat, remove bay leaf, and let cool slightly.

3 Transfer soup in batches to a blender or food processor, cover, and puree until smooth. Return to pot, stir in buttermilk, and heat through. Garnish with sour cream and chives, if desired.

PEPPER *PASSATA* SOUP

Passata, or sieved fresh tomatoes, is a popular cooking ingredient in the United Kingdom, where it is sold in jars at most markets. Americans can put fresh or canned tomatoes through a food mill or food processor to get the same effect. Serve this soup with garlic or pesto bread. (Photograph on page 17)

SERVES 6

2 tablespoons extra-virgin olive oil

1 onion, coarsely chopped

1 garlic clove, chopped

1 1/2 pounds red bell peppers, cored, seeded, and coarsely chopped

1 1/4 cups vegetable stock

1 1/4 cups *passata*

1 teaspoon fresh thyme, chopped, or 1/2 teaspoon dried thyme

1/4 teaspoon ground cinnamon

1 teaspoon sugar

Salt and black pepper

6 tablespoons crème fraîche

6 basil sprigs

1 Heat oil in a saucepan over medium heat. Add onion and garlic and sauté 5 minutes or until softened. Stir in bell peppers and sauté 5 minutes. Add stock, stir, and remove from heat.

2 Transfer soup to a blender or food processor, cover, and puree until smooth. Return to pan and stir in *passata*, thyme, cinnamon, and sugar. Cook over low heat until heated through (do not boil). Season to taste with salt and black pepper.

3 Ladle soup into warm bowls and garnish each serving with a spoonful of crème fraîche and a basil sprig.

RED PEPPER AND TOMATO SOUP

This very red soup is beautiful to behold, very tasty, and packed with vitamins and phytonutrients that fight disease.

MAKES 8 CUPS

2 tablespoons olive or canola oil

2 large red bell peppers, cored, seeded, and coarsely chopped

1 pound fresh plum tomatoes, halved and cored

2 garlic cloves, sliced

1 large onion, coarsely chopped

4 cups chicken stock

1/4 cup packed cilantro or parsley, coarsely chopped

1/8 teaspoon salt

1/8 teaspoon black pepper

1 Preheat oven to 375°F. Coat bottom of a roasting pan with half of oil. Add peppers, tomatoes, and garlic and toss to coat. Roast, stirring once, 25 to 30 minutes.

2 Heat remaining oil in a 4-quart saucepan over medium heat. Add onion and sauté 3 minutes or until softened. Add 2 cups water, vegetables, and stock and bring to boil. Reduce heat and simmer, partially covered, 20 to 25 minutes or until vegetables are soft.

3 Remove from heat. Using a slotted spoon, transfer vegetables to a blender or food processor. Strain liquid into a clean saucepan. Add 1 cup liquid to processor, cover, and puree until smooth. Stir puree into pan and simmer 5 minutes, then stir in cilantro, salt, and black pepper.

RED PEPPER SOUP WITH RICOTTA DUMPLINGS

SERVES 4

Soup:

2 tablespoons olive or vegetable oil

1 large yellow onion, thinly sliced

4 garlic cloves, crushed

1 medium carrot,
    peeled and thinly sliced

1 large all-purpose potato,
    peeled and thinly sliced

3 red bell peppers, cored, seeded,
    and cut into thin slices

3/4 cup canned crushed tomatoes

3 strips orange rind, 3 x 1/2 inch

1/2 teaspoon ground ginger

1/2 teaspoon salt

1 1/4 cups fresh orange juice

Dumplings:

1 cup low-fat ricotta cheese

2 tablespoons butter, softened

1 large egg plus 1 large egg white

1/2 cup sifted all-purpose flour

1/4 teaspoon salt

1/8 teaspoon black pepper

3 tablespoons minced fresh parsley

1 For soup, heat 1 tablespoon oil in a large saucepan over medium heat. Add onion and garlic and sauté until limp, about 5 minutes. Add carrot, potato, bell peppers, and remaining oil. Reduce heat to low and cook, covered, until peppers are tender, about 8 minutes.

2 Stir in 2 cups water, tomatoes, orange rind, ginger, salt, and 3/4 cup orange juice. Bring to boil, then reduce heat to low and simmer, partially covered, until potatoes are tender, about 25 minutes.

3 For dumplings, combine cheese, butter, egg, egg white, flour, salt, pepper, and parsley in a medium bowl. Bring a large saucepan of water to simmer over low heat and drop in dough by tablespoons. Cook, covered, until set and no longer doughy, about 8 minutes. Using a slotted spoon, transfer to a plate.

4 Working in batches if necessary, transfer soup to a blender or food processor and puree 1 minute, then push through a sieve. Return to pan, stir in remaining orange juice, and cook over low heat until heated through (do not boil). Place dumplings on top before serving.

It's definitely worth the time to make fresh orange juice for this splendid but unusual soup.

TWO-PEPPER SOUP

Like a hot gazpacho, this easy soup perks up the taste buds for the meal to follow.

SERVES 4

3 red bell peppers, cored,
    seeded, and diced

1 green bell pepper, cored,
    seeded, and diced

1 small onion, diced

1 garlic clove, minced

1 cup chopped tomatoes

1 cup chicken stock

1 teaspoon ground coriander

1/2 teaspoon salt

Chopped fresh parsley

1 In a covered saucepan, bring bell peppers, onion, garlic, tomatoes, stock, coriander, and salt to boil. Reduce heat and simmer 5 minutes. Stir in parsley.

STUFFED BELL PEPPER SOUP

This soup incorporates all the ingredients and seasonings you might use to stuff bell peppers and bake them.

SERVES 14

2 pounds ground beef

1/2 medium onion, chopped

8 beef bouillon cubes

2 cans (28 ounces each) tomatoes,
    undrained, cut up

1 cup rice

2 teaspoons salt

1/2 teaspoon black pepper

1/2 teaspoon paprika

3 green, yellow, or red bell peppers, cored,
    seeded, and chopped

1 In a large Dutch oven or soup pot over medium heat, cook beef and onion until beef is browned and onion is tender. Drain off fat.

2 Add 6 cups water, bouillon, tomatoes, rice, salt, black pepper, and paprika. Bring to boil, then reduce heat and simmer, covered, 1 hour. Add peppers and cook, uncovered, 10 minutes or just until tender.

POTATO AND CUCUMBER SOUP

This soup is a perfect starter hot or, in the summer, cold.

SERVES 8

6 medium all-purpose potatoes,
    peeled and cubed

1 1/2 teaspoons salt

1/4 teaspoon black pepper

1 cup heavy whipping cream

1 cup milk

1 teaspoon grated onion

1 large or 2 medium cucumbers,
    peeled, seeded, and diced

1 tablespoon finely chopped fresh dill
    or 1 teaspoon dill weed

1 In a large saucepan over high heat, bring 3 cups cold water, potatoes, salt, and pepper to boil. Reduce heat and simmer, uncovered, 10 minutes or until tender. Remove from heat and let cool.

2 Working in batches if necessary, transfer to a food processor or blender, cover, and puree until smooth. Return to pan and stir in cream, milk, onion, and cucumber, adding more milk if necessary. Simmer over low heat, stirring occasionally, 5 minutes. Season with dill.

CHUNKY POTATO SOUP

This chunky soup, seasoned with sage, sends out a hearty "Welcome home!" on a chilly evening.

SERVES 4

1 tablespoon olive oil

1 large onion, finely chopped

3 garlic cloves, minced

1 small green bell pepper, cored, seeded, and cut into 1/2-inch squares

10 ounces cremini or white mushrooms, thickly sliced

1 pound small red potatoes, thinly sliced

1 teaspoon salt

3/4 teaspoon liquid smoke

3/4 teaspoon rubbed sage

1/2 teaspoon black pepper

1 cup frozen whole-kernel corn

1/2 cup fat-free half-and-half

1/4 cup chopped fresh parsley *(optional)*

1 Heat oil in a large nonstick saucepan over medium heat. Add onion and garlic and sauté 10 minutes or until onion is golden.

2 Add bell pepper and mushrooms and sauté 5 minutes or until pepper is tender.

3 Add 2 cups water, potatoes, salt, liquid smoke, sage, and black pepper and bring to boil. Reduce heat and simmer, covered, 15 minutes or until potatoes are tender. Stir in corn and half-and-half and cook 3 minutes or until heated through. Garnish with parsley, if desired.

CREAMY POTATO SOUP

This lovely soup can start an elegant dinner or serve as a lunch partner for ham salad.

SERVES 4

2 chicken bouillon cubes

3 cups cubed peeled all-purpose potatoes

1/2 cup chopped onion

1/2 cup thinly sliced celery

3/4 teaspoon salt

1/2 teaspoon black pepper

2 cups milk

2 tablespoons all-purpose flour

1 cup sour cream

2 tablespoons chopped fresh parsley

1 tablespoon chopped fresh chives

1 In a 3-quart saucepan over medium heat, combine 2 cups water, bouillon, potatoes, onion, celery, salt, and pepper. Bring to boil, then reduce heat and simmer, covered, until potatoes are tender, about 15 minutes. Add 1 3/4 cups milk.

2 In a small bowl, combine flour with remaining milk and stir to form a smooth paste. Gradually add to pan, stirring constantly. Bring to boil and cook, stirring, until thickened and bubbling, about 2 minutes.

3 In another small bowl, add a small amount of hot liquid to sour cream and stir to combine. Gradually add to pan, stirring constantly, and cook until heated through (do not boil). Add parsley and chives just before serving.

LUNCH POTATO SOUP

Leftover mashed potatoes never tasted so good!

 SERVES 3

8 bacon slices, diced
1 small onion, chopped
1 1/2 cups mashed potatoes
1 can (10 3/4 ounces) condensed cream
    of chicken soup
2 cups milk
1/2 teaspoon salt *(optional)*
1/8 teaspoon black pepper
2 tablespoons chopped fresh parsley

1 In a 3-quart saucepan over medium heat, cook bacon until crisp. Transfer to paper towels to drain. Drain all but 1 tablespoon fat from pan.

2 Add onion to pan and sauté until tender. Add potatoes and soup and stir until smooth. Gradually stir in milk and cook, stirring, until heated through. Stir in bacon, salt, if desired, and pepper. Garnish each serving with parsley.

DANISH POTATO SOUP

Other vegetables and cream make this potato soup rich in flavor and texture.

 SERVES 6

1 hambone
2 all-purpose potatoes,
    peeled and diced
6 scallions, sliced
3 celery stalks, chopped
1/4 cup minced fresh parsley
2 cups chopped cabbage
2 carrots, diced
3 tablespoons all-purpose flour
1 cup light cream
Ground nutmeg

1 In a soup pot, bring hambone and 8 cups water to boil. Reduce heat and simmer, covered, 1 hour or until meat pulls away from bone.

2 Transfer hambone to a plate. When cool enough to handle, remove meat and dice. Add ham, potatoes, scallions, celery, parsley, cabbage, and carrots to pot and bring to boil. Reduce heat and simmer, covered, 40 minutes.

3 In a small bowl, stir together flour and 1/4 cup cold water. Slowly pour into soup, stirring constantly. Bring to boil and cook 2 minutes, then reduce heat and stir in cream.

4 Ladle into bowls and sprinkle each serving with nutmeg.

POTATO-CHEESE SOUP

This soup is a smooth combination of potatoes and sharp cheese.

 SERVES 4

2 cups chicken stock
3 garlic cloves, minced
4 scallions, sliced
1 1/2 pounds all-purpose potatoes,
    peeled and sliced
1 cup (4 ounces) shredded white cheddar
    cheese

1 In a saucepan over medium-high heat, combine 2 cups water, stock, garlic, and all but 1/4 cup scallions. Bring to boil, add potatoes, and cook until tender, about 12 minutes. Using a potato masher, partially mash potatoes.

2 Stir in cheese until melted. Garnish each serving with remaining scallions.

PRONTO POTATO SOUP

A great way to use leftover mashed potatoes, this soup can be ready in no time flat.

SERVES 3

8 bacon slices, cut up
1 small onion, chopped
1 1/2-2 cups mashed potatoes
1 can (10 3/4 ounces) condensed cream of chicken soup
1-2 soup cans milk
1/2 teaspoon salt
Dash of black pepper
2 tablespoons chopped fresh parsley

1 In a small skillet over medium heat, cook bacon until crisp. Transfer to paper towels to drain. Drain all but 2 teaspoons fat from pan. Add onion and sauté 2 to 3 minutes.

2 Meanwhile, in a 3-quart saucepan over medium heat, combine mashed potatoes and soup until smooth. Add milk gradually, stirring constantly, until soup reaches desired consistency. Add bacon, onions, salt, pepper, and parsley and cook until heated through.

GERMAN POTATO SOUP

This is a thick, filling soup that's topped with dumplings, butter, and parsley.

SERVES 6

Soup:
6 cups cubed peeled all-purpose potatoes
1 1/4 cups sliced celery
1/2 cup chopped onion
1/2 teaspoon salt
1/8 teaspoon black pepper
Butter
Chopped fresh parsley

Dumplings:
1 egg, beaten
1/2 teaspoon salt
3/4 cup all-purpose flour

1 For soup, combine 5 cups water, potatoes, celery, onion, salt, and pepper in a soup pot over medium-high heat. Bring to boil, then reduce heat and simmer, covered, 1 hour or until tender. Using a potato masher, puree most of vegetables in pot.

2 For dumplings, combine 1/3 cup water, egg, salt, and flour in a medium bowl and stir until smooth and stiff. Return soup to boil and drop in dough by teaspoons. Reduce heat and simmer, covered, 10 to 15 minutes or until dumplings are cooked through. Top each serving with a pat of butter and a sprinkling of parsley.

POTATO AND KALE SOUP

This is a good, hearty lunch soup for cold weather.

SERVES 4

4 teaspoons olive oil
1 medium yellow onion, chopped
3 garlic cloves, minced
3 medium all-purpose potatoes, peeled and sliced
8 ounces kale, trimmed and shredded
1/4 teaspoon black pepper

1 Heat oil 1 minute in a large heavy saucepan over medium heat. Add onion and sauté 5 minutes or until softened.

2 Add 4 cups water, garlic, and potatoes and bring to boil. Reduce heat and simmer, uncovered, 20 minutes or until tender.

3 Mash potatoes in pan. Add kale and pepper, cover, and simmer 15 minutes or until kale is tender.

MEXICAN POTATO SOUP

SERVES 4

3 tablespoons chopped canned
   green chiles or 1 dried ancho
   or pasilla chile, about 6 inches long
   (wear gloves when handling; they burn)

3 tablespoons unsalted butter

1 large yellow onion, coarsely chopped

4 medium all-purpose potatoes,
   peeled and cut into 1/2-inch cubes

2 small bell peppers (red, green,
   or 1 of each), cored, seeded,
   and diced

2 garlic cloves, minced

4 cups chicken stock

1 bay leaf

1/4 teaspoon salt

1 1/2 teaspoons ground cumin

1 cup milk

1/2 cup sour cream or low-fat plain yogurt

2 cups (8 ounces) shredded low-fat
   Monterey Jack or cheddar cheese

1/4 cup minced fresh cilantro or flat-leaf
   parsley *(optional)*

1 Set chopped chiles aside. If using a dried chile, preheat oven to 350°F. Place chile in a small baking pan and roast, uncovered, 10 minutes. Transfer to a small bowl, break in half, and cover with 1/2 cup boiling water. Let stand 15 minutes, then drain and remove stem, seeds, and veins.

2 In a large saucepan over medium heat, melt butter. Add onion and sauté 5 minutes or until limp. Add potatoes, bell peppers, and garlic and sauté 2 minutes. Add stock, bay leaf, and salt and bring to boil. Reduce heat, cover, and simmer until potatoes are tender, about 20 minutes. Remove bay leaf.

3 Stir in chiles and cumin. Working in batches if necessary, transfer to a blender or food processor, cover, and puree until smooth. Strain soup through a sieve back into pan.

4 Reduce heat to medium-low and stir in milk and sour cream. Bring to simmer and cook, stirring constantly, 5 minutes (do not boil). Add 1 cup cheese, a little at a time, stirring until melted. Top each serving with 1 tablespoon cheese and cilantro, if desired. Pass remaining cheese.

If you want more zip in this rich, creamy soup, add a sprinkling of chili powder or increase the amount of chiles. You can cool it down with a dollop or two of sour cream.

IBERIAN POTATO SOUP

This combination of potatoes, onions, sausage, and greens is a favorite across southern Europe, and no wonder: It's filling and delicious.

SERVES 4

2 tablespoons olive oil

1 large yellow onion, chopped

2 garlic cloves, minced

2 medium baking potatoes, peeled and diced

3 cups canned low-sodium chicken broth

1 bay leaf

2 chorizo sausages or 8 ounces kielbasa, cut into 1/2-inch slices

2 cups kale, stems removed and leaves thinly sliced

1 Heat oil in a large saucepan over medium heat. Add onion and garlic and sauté 2 minutes. Increase heat to high, add potatoes, broth, and bay leaf, and bring to boil. Reduce heat and simmer, covered, 20 minutes or until potatoes are very tender.

2 Remove bay leaf. Mash some of potatoes to thicken soup slightly, if desired. Stir in sausage and kale and simmer 5 minutes or until sausage is heated through and kale is tender.

NEW ENGLAND POTATO SOUP

This is comfort food, New England-style—creamy potato soup with ham, peas, and onion, infused with rosemary and thyme.

SERVES 6

2 tablespoons butter

1 medium onion, chopped

1 celery stalk, thinly sliced

1 can (14 1/2 ounces) chicken broth

3 medium all-purpose potatoes, peeled and cubed

1 1/2 teaspoons sugar

1 teaspoon salt

1/2 teaspoon dried rosemary, crushed

1/2 teaspoon dried thyme

1/4 teaspoon black pepper

1/3 cup all-purpose flour

2 1/2 cups milk

1 1/2 cups cubed fully cooked ham

1 cup frozen peas

1 In a saucepan over medium heat, melt butter. Add onion and celery and sauté until tender, about 4 minutes. Add broth, potatoes, sugar, salt, rosemary, thyme, and pepper. Bring to boil, then reduce heat and simmer, covered, until potatoes are tender, about 15 minutes.

2 In a small bowl, combine flour and 1/2 cup milk until smooth. Stir into pan, bring to boil, and cook, stirring, 2 minutes. Stir in ham, peas, and remaining milk and cook until heated through.

POTATO MINESTRONE

The aroma of this savory soup will waft through the house as it cooks slowly, making everyone ravenous. For thicker soup, mash half of the chickpeas before adding them.

SERVES 12

2 cans (14 1/2 ounces each) chicken broth

1 can (28 ounces) crushed tomatoes

1 can (16 ounces) kidney beans, drained and rinsed

1 can (15 ounces) chickpeas, drained and rinsed

1 can (14 1/2 ounces) beef broth

2 cups thawed frozen cubed hash brown potatoes

1 tablespoon dried minced onion

1 tablespoon parsley flakes

1 teaspoon salt

1 teaspoon dried oregano

1/2 teaspoon garlic powder

1/2 teaspoon dried basil

1/2 teaspoon dried marjoram

1 package (10 ounces) frozen chopped spinach, thawed and drained

2 cups frozen peas and carrots, thawed

1 In a 5-quart slow cooker, combine chicken broth, tomatoes, beans, chickpeas, beef broth, potatoes, onion, parsley, salt, oregano, garlic powder, basil, and marjoram. Cover and cook on low 8 hours.

2 Stir in spinach and peas and carrots and cook, covered, until heated through, about 20 minutes.

BAKED POTATO SOUP

This is a hearty potato soup with scallions and cheese.

SERVES 8

4 large baking potatoes

2/3 cup butter

2/3 cup all-purpose flour

3/4 teaspoon salt

1/4 teaspoon ground white pepper

6 cups milk

1 cup sour cream

1/4 cup thinly sliced scallions

1 cup (4 ounces) shredded cheddar cheese

1 Bake potatoes at 350°F until tender, about 65 minutes. Let cool completely, then peel and cube.

2 In a large saucepan over low heat, melt butter. Stir in flour, salt, and pepper until smooth. Gradually add milk, bring to boil, and cook, stirring, until thickened, about 2 minutes. Remove from heat, whisk in sour cream, and add potatoes and scallions. Garnish with cheese.

PUMPKIN SOUP

Pumpkin was one of the first foods introduced to colonists by Native Americans. Throughout the country's history, pumpkin dishes have remained a part of our tradition.

SERVES 6

1 tablespoon unsalted butter

1 tablespoon vegetable oil

1 cup diced onion

1/2 cup diced celery

1/2 cup rinsed, sliced leeks with tops

1 garlic clove, minced

1 tablespoon minced fresh ginger or 1 teaspoon ground ginger

4 cups chicken stock

3 cups peeled pumpkin chunks or 2 cups plain canned pumpkin puree

1/2 teaspoon salt

2 teaspoons light brown sugar

1/8 teaspoon freshly grated or ground nutmeg

6 tablespoons low-fat plain yogurt or reduced-fat sour cream

1 In a large heavy saucepan over medium-high heat, melt butter and heat oil. Add onion, celery, leeks, garlic, and ginger and sauté 5 minutes or until tender.

2 Add stock, pumpkin, and salt and bring to boil. Reduce heat, cover, and simmer 20 minutes or until soup is thickened and flavors are blended.

3 Working in batches if necessary, transfer soup to a blender or food processor, cover, and puree 45 seconds or until smooth. Return to pan, stir in sugar and nutmeg, and cook over medium-high heat, stirring occasionally, 5 minutes or until heated through. Ladle into bowls and garnish each serving with 1 tablespoon yogurt.

PUMPKIN SOUP WITH MUFFINS

(Photograph on page 20)

SERVES 4

Soup:

1 tablespoon extra-virgin olive oil

1 onion, chopped

1 1/2 pounds fresh pumpkin,
    peeled and diced

1 all-purpose potato, peeled and diced

2 garlic cloves, minced

1 tablespoon fresh rosemary, chopped

3 cups vegetable stock

3/4 cup low-fat (1%) milk

4 ounces cream cheese

Salt and black pepper

Garnishes:

4 ounces cream cheese

Paprika

4 rosemary sprigs

Muffins:

3 1/2 ounces hazelnuts, coarsely
    chopped and toasted

2 cups all-purpose flour

2 teaspoons baking powder

6 tablespoons butter, melted

2 tablespoons chopped fresh rosemary

2 eggs, beaten

1 cup low-fat (1%) milk

This richly colored, ultra-smooth soup is enhanced by the flavor of rosemary. Crunchy hazelnut, pumpkin, and rosemary muffins complement the soup perfectly.

1 For soup, heat oil in a large saucepan over medium heat. Reserve 1/3 cup each onion and pumpkin for muffins. Add remaining onion to pan and sauté until softened, about 5 minutes. Add remaining pumpkin and sauté until softened but not browned, about 5 minutes.

2 Add potato, garlic, and rosemary and sauté 2 minutes. Pour in stock and season to taste with salt and pepper. Bring to boil, then reduce heat and simmer, covered, 30 minutes. Remove from heat and let cool slightly.

3 For muffins, preheat oven to 425°F and coat a 12-cup muffin pan with cooking spray or line with paper liners. In a medium bowl, combine reserved pumpkin, reserved onion, hazelnuts, flour, baking powder, butter, rosemary, eggs, and milk. Mix with a fork until moistened. Spoon into muffin cups and bake 15 minutes or until a toothpick inserted in center of a muffin comes out clean. Cool on a wire rack 5 minutes, then remove from pan and wrap in a towel to keep warm.

4 Transfer soup to a blender or food processor, cover, and puree until smooth (or use a handheld blender to puree in pan). Return to pan, stir in milk and cream cheese, and cook until heated through (do not boil). Season to taste with salt and pepper.

5 Ladle soup into warm bowls and garnish with cream cheese, paprika, and rosemary. Serve with warm muffins.

CREAMY PUMPKIN SOUP

This is the kind of comforting, delicious pumpkin soup that gives pumpkin pie a run for its money.

SERVES 6

2 tablespoons butter

1 medium onion, chopped

2 cans (14 1/2 ounces each) chicken broth

2 cups sliced peeled all-purpose potatoes

2 cups canned pumpkin

2-2 1/2 cups milk

1/2 teaspoon ground nutmeg

1/2 teaspoon salt

1/4 teaspoon black pepper

1 cup sour cream

1 tablespoon chopped fresh parsley

3 bacon slices, cooked and crumbled *(optional)*

1 In a large saucepan over medium heat, melt butter. Add onion and sauté until tender, about 4 minutes.

2 Add broth, potatoes, and pumpkin and bring to boil. Reduce heat, cover, and simmer until potatoes are tender, about 15 minutes. Remove from heat and let cool slightly. Transfer in 2 batches to a blender or food processor, cover, and puree until smooth. Return to pan, add milk, nutmeg, salt, and pepper, and heat through.

3 Meanwhile, in a small bowl, combine sour cream and parsley. Top each serving with a dollop of parsleyed sour cream and sprinkle with bacon, if desired.

PUMPKIN AND SWEET POTATO SOUP

Both pumpkin and sweet potatoes are very high in disease-fighting beta-carotene, as well as good taste.

SERVES 8

2 ounces reduced-sodium bacon or turkey bacon, coarsely chopped

2 shallots or small onions, finely chopped

8 cups chicken or vegetable stock

12 ounces sweet potatoes, peeled and cut into 1/2-inch pieces

1 can (16 ounces) solid-pack pumpkin or 2 cups cooked pumpkin or winter squash

1/8 teaspoon salt

1/8 teaspoon black pepper

Pinch of ground nutmeg

2 tablespoons chopped fresh parsley

1 In a 4-quart saucepan over medium heat, cook bacon 3 minutes or until crisp. Using a slotted spoon, transfer to paper towels.

2 Add shallots and 1/4 cup stock to pan and sauté 3 minutes or until softened. Add sweet potatoes and sauté 3 minutes. Pour in remaining stock and bring to boil. Reduce heat and simmer, partially covered, 10 minutes or until sweet potatoes are very soft.

3 Using a slotted spoon, transfer vegetables to a blender or food processor, cover, and puree until smooth. Add pumpkin and process to combine.

4 Return puree to pan and cook until heated through (do not boil). Stir in salt, pepper, and nutmeg. Garnish each serving with crumbled bacon and parsley.

PUMPKIN SOUP WITH RICE

When pureed, the pumpkin and rice become so silky that the soup has a velvety texture. Curry adds a touch of heat.

SERVES 6

2 tablespoons extra-virgin olive oil

2 onions, chopped

1 teaspoon mild curry powder

2 1/4 pounds fresh pumpkin, peeled and cubed

2 garlic cloves, finely chopped

1 hot green chile, seeded and finely chopped (wear gloves when handling; they burn)

3 1/4 cups vegetable stock

6 1/4 ounces rice

Pumpkin seeds

1 tablespoon chopped fresh cilantro

Salt and black pepper

1 Heat oil in a large saucepan over low heat. Add onions and curry powder and sauté 15 minutes or until onions soften and start to caramelize.

2 Add pumpkin, garlic, and chile and stir to coat. Pour in stock and 5 tablespoons rice. Bring to boil, then reduce heat and simmer, covered, 25 minutes or until pumpkin and rice are tender. Remove from heat and let cool slightly.

3 Meanwhile, bring a saucepan of water to boil and add remaining rice. Reduce heat and simmer for 15 minutes or until just tender. Drain in a sieve, rinse under cold water, and place over a bowl to continue draining.

4 Preheat grill to medium-high. Spread pumpkin seeds in a single layer on a baking sheet and toast under grill for 3 minutes, turning several times, until golden and aromatic. Set aside.

5 Transfer pumpkin mixture to a blender or food processor, cover, and puree until smooth.

Return to pan, stir in cooked rice, and season to taste with salt and pepper. Cook over low heat until heated through (if soup seems too thick, add a small amount of hot vegetable stock or water). Stir in cilantro and serve sprinkled with toasted pumpkin seeds.

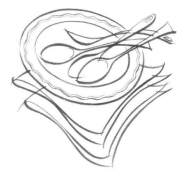

PUMPKIN AND PEACH SOUP

You may not have thought of this combination, but you'll be hooked after one taste.

SERVES 4

1 can (16 ounces) juice-packed sliced cling peaches, undrained

1 can (16 ounces) pumpkin puree

1 can (14 1/2 ounces) low-sodium chicken broth

1/2 teaspoon dried thyme

1/8 teaspoon ground white pepper

3/4 cup milk

1 In a food processor or blender, puree peaches and juice until smooth.

2 In a medium saucepan over medium-high heat, combine puree, pumpkin, broth, thyme, and pepper and bring to boil, stirring occasionally. Stir in milk and cook 2 minutes or until heated through.

SPINACH AND ONION SOUP WITH TOMATO CROSTINI

This is a colorful vegetarian version of French onion soup. Its rich flavor depends on sautéing onions very slowly until they are browned, caramelized, and sweet. (Photograph on page 21)

SERVES 4

Soup:

2 tablespoons butter

1 tablespoon extra-virgin olive oil

1 pound large onions, thinly sliced

1 teaspoon superfine sugar

2 garlic cloves, chopped

7 cups vegetable stock

4 ounces broccoli, finely chopped

4 ounces spinach leaves, torn

Salt and black pepper

Crostini:

8 thick slices French bread

1 garlic clove, halved

2 teaspoons tomato puree

2 tomatoes, each cut into 8 wedges

Salt and black pepper

2 tablespoons grated Parmesan cheese

1 For soup, melt butter and heat oil in a large saucepan over medium-low heat. Add onions and sauté 10 minutes or until softened and golden. Stir in sugar and garlic and sauté 10 minutes or until onions are browned and caramelized.

2 Stir in stock and season to taste with salt and pepper. Bring to boil, then reduce heat and simmer, covered, 30 minutes. Add broccoli and simmer 3 minutes. Remove from heat, stir in spinach, cover, and let stand.

3 For crostini, preheat grill to high and lightly toast bread on both sides. Rub one side of each slice with cut garlic and spread with tomato puree.

Add 2 tomato wedges to each slice, season to taste with salt and pepper, and sprinkle with cheese. Grill 2 minutes or until cheese is just bubbling.

4 Meanwhile, cook soup until heated through and ladle into 4 warm bowls. Float 2 crostini in each bowl.

CREAM OF SPINACH SOUP

If you like, use a 10-ounce package of frozen chopped spinach, thawed, in place of the fresh spinach.

SERVES 4

2 tablespoons butter

1 cup sliced leeks or yellow onion

2 celery stalks, sliced

6 cups chopped fresh spinach

1 3/4 cups chicken stock

1 teaspoon dried mint

1 teaspoon dried marjoram

1/2 teaspoon salt

1/4 teaspoon black pepper

1 cup low-fat (1%) milk

3 tablespoons all-purpose flour

1 In a large saucepan over medium-high heat, melt butter. Add leeks and celery and sauté 5 minutes or until tender. Add spinach, stock, mint, marjoram, salt, and pepper and bring to boil. Reduce heat, cover, and simmer 5 minutes. Remove from heat and let cool slightly.

2 Transfer in 2 batches to a food processor or blender, cover, and puree until smooth. Return to pan. In a small bowl, whisk together milk and flour, then whisk into pan. Cook over medium heat, whisking constantly, until starting to thicken. Continue to cook, whisking, until thickened, about 2 minutes.

SUMMER SQUASH SOUP WITH LEEKS

You can make this delectable blend of garden vegetables with either yellow summer squash or zucchini.

SERVES 4

2 tablespoons vegetable oil

2 large leeks or 1 large yellow onion,
    coarsely chopped

2 medium all-purpose potatoes,
    peeled and cut into cubes

4 cups chicken stock

1/2 teaspoon dried thyme, crumbled

1 bay leaf

1/4 teaspoon salt

1/8 teaspoon black pepper

1 large red bell pepper, cored, seeded,
    and cut into 1-inch squares

8 ounces fresh mushrooms, sliced

2 garlic cloves, minced

2 medium yellow squash,
    cut into 1-inch cubes

3 tablespoons snipped fresh chives

1 Heat 1 tablespoon oil in a large heavy saucepan over medium-low heat. Add leeks, cover, and cook, stirring occasionally, until softened, about 3 minutes. Add potatoes, stock, thyme, bay leaf, salt, and black pepper and bring to boil. Reduce heat, cover, and simmer until potatoes are tender, about 15 minutes.

2 Meanwhile, heat remaining oil in a 10-inch nonstick skillet over medium-low heat. Add bell pepper and mushrooms, cover, and cook, stirring occasionally, 3 minutes. Stir in garlic and cook 1 minute. Remove from heat.

3 Working in batches if necessary, transfer potato mixture to a blender or food processor, cover, and puree until smooth. Return to pan and stir in mushroom mixture and squash. Reduce heat to medium-low, cover, and simmer, stirring occasionally, until squash is tender, about 5 minutes. Remove bay leaf. Sprinkle each serving with chives.

GRATED SUMMER SQUASH AND POTATO SOUP

This fast and healthy vegetable soup is flavored with garlic, which has strong antifungal and antiviral powers said to help prevent colds and flu.

SERVES 4

1 1/2 pounds all-purpose potatoes,
    peeled and cut into 1/2 inch-thick slices

2 large garlic cloves, chopped

Salt and black pepper

1 yellow squash, coarsely grated

2 zucchini, coarsely grated

Extra-virgin olive oil

4 large mint or basil leaves, torn

Cayenne pepper

1 In a large saucepan over medium-high heat, bring 3 1/2 cups water and potatoes to boil, skimming off foam. Add garlic, reduce heat, and simmer until potatoes are soft enough to mash, about 10 minutes.

2 Remove from heat, mash potatoes and garlic in cooking water, and season to taste with salt and pepper.

3 Add squash and zucchini and simmer until soft, about 5 minutes. Ladle into bowls, top each with a splash of oil, and garnish with mint and cayenne.

YELLOW SQUASH SOUP

Lemon and orange zest and a healthy dash of lemon juice give this soup its delightfully fresh flavor.

SERVES 4

1 tablespoon unsalted butter

2 medium yellow onions, chopped

3 garlic cloves, minced

3 strips lemon rind, 2 x 1/2 inch

3 strips orange rind, 2 x 1/2 inch

1 bay leaf

1/2 teaspoon dried marjoram, crumbled

2 medium yellow squash,
    cut into 1/2-inch cubes

3 cups canned low-sodium chicken broth

1/4 teaspoon salt

5 teaspoons fresh lemon juice

1 In a heavy saucepan over low heat, melt butter. Add onions, garlic, lemon and orange rind, bay leaf, and marjoram. Sauté 10 minutes or until onion is softened.

2 Add squash and stir to coat. Add broth and salt and bring to boil. Reduce heat and simmer, covered, until squash is soft when pierced with a fork, about 20 minutes.

3 Remove from heat and remove rind and bay leaf. Stir in lemon juice and ladle into 4 bowls.

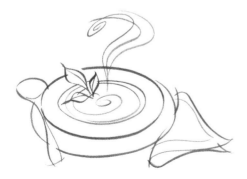

SUMMER SQUASH SOUP

A simple soup turns all those ripening young squash into a perfect first course for any lunch or dinner.

SERVES 8

1 tablespoon olive or canola oil

1 large onion, coarsely chopped

2 garlic cloves, finely chopped

8 cups chicken stock

8 ounces all-purpose potatoes,
    peeled and coarsely chopped

8 ounces zucchini, sliced

8 ounces yellow squash, sliced

1/2 cup packed basil leaves,
    finely shredded

1/8 teaspoon salt

1/8 teaspoon black pepper

1 Heat oil in a 4-quart saucepan over medium heat. Add onion, garlic, and 2 tablespoons stock and sauté until softened but not browned.

2 Add potatoes and remaining stock and bring to boil. Reduce heat and simmer, partially covered, about 5 minutes or until potatoes are softened.

3 Stir in zucchini and squash and return to boil. Reduce heat and simmer 10 minutes or until potatoes and squash are tender. Remove from heat and let cool slightly.

4 Using a slotted spoon, transfer vegetables to a blender or food processor, cover, and puree until smooth. Return to pan and cook until heated through. Stir in basil, salt, and pepper.

BUTTERNUT SQUASH SOUP

Rich, creamy, and nicely seasoned, this savory soup takes the chill off a winter day.

SERVES 6

1 tablespoon unsalted butter

1 medium yellow onion, chopped

1 garlic clove, minced

1 small celery stalk, chopped

1 medium butternut squash, peeled, seeded, and cubed

4 cups chicken stock

1/2 teaspoon dried marjoram, crumbled

1 bay leaf

1/4 teaspoon black pepper

1 cup buttermilk

Parsley sprigs *(optional)*

1 In a large heavy saucepan over medium heat, melt butter. Add onion, garlic, and celery and sauté 5 minutes or until onion is softened.

2 Add squash, stock, marjoram, bay leaf, and pepper and bring to boil. Reduce heat and simmer, covered, 20 minutes or until squash is tender when pierced with a fork. Remove from heat, remove bay leaf, and let cool 5 minutes.

3 Transfer soup in 4 batches to a blender or food processor, cover, and puree until smooth. Return to pan, stir in buttermilk, and cook until heated through (do not boil). Ladle into bowls and garnish with parsley, if desired.

SPICED BUTTERNUT SQUASH SOUP

Curry powder and ginger lend an Indian air to this healthy soup. Not only is it delicious, it also provides a hefty shot of beta-carotene as well as potassium, calcium, and magnesium. (Photograph on page 8)

SERVES 4

2 teaspoons olive oil

1 large onion, finely chopped

4 red apples

2 pounds butternut squash, peeled and thinly sliced

1 large baking potato, peeled and thinly sliced

2 teaspoons curry powder

1 teaspoon ground ginger

1 teaspoon salt

1/2 teaspoon ground cinnamon

1 cup low-fat (1%) milk

1/4 cup roasted cashews, coarsely chopped

1 Heat oil in a large saucepan over medium heat. Add onion and sauté 5 minutes or until golden.

2 Peel, core, and slice 3 1/2 apples and add to pan. Stir in squash, potato, curry powder, ginger, salt, and cinnamon until combined. Add 3 cups water and bring to boil, then reduce heat and simmer, covered, until squash is tender, about 30 minutes.

3 Working in batches if necessary, transfer soup to a food processor or blender, cover, and puree until smooth. Return to pan, add milk, and whisk to combine. Cook over low heat until heated through.

4 Thinly slice remaining apple. Spoon soup into 4 mugs or bowls and top with cashews and apple slices.

SQUASH SOUP WITH CHEDDAR CHEESE

Here's a rich winter squash soup that is treated with French bread and cheese as if it were onion soup. It is a lovely variation that will surprise and delight guests.

SERVES 4

2 medium butternut or acorn squash

1/4 teaspoon salt

1/4 teaspoon black pepper

1 teaspoon vegetable oil

4 shallots, finely chopped

1/4 cup dry white wine or water

1/4 cup chicken stock

1 cup fat-free milk

4 slices French or Italian bread, 1/2 inch thick

1 cup (4 ounces) shredded low-fat cheddar or Gruyère cheese

2 tablespoons snipped fresh chives or minced fresh parsley *(optional)*

1 Preheat oven to 400°F. Halve squash lengthwise and sprinkle with 1/8 teaspoon salt and 1/8 teaspoon pepper. Place on a baking sheet, cover loosely with foil, and bake 50 minutes or until tender. Scoop pulp from shells and transfer to a blender or food processor.

2 Heat oil in a small saucepan over medium heat. Add shallots and sauté 3 minutes or until softened. Add wine and cook, uncovered, 2 minutes or until reduced to 2 tablespoons. Stir in stock, milk, and remaining salt and pepper. Transfer to blender with squash, cover, and puree until smooth.

3 Divide half of soup among four 1 1/2-cup ovenproof bowls or baking dishes. Place 1 slice bread on top of each and sprinkle with 2 tablespoons cheese. Pour in remaining soup and sprinkle with remaining cheese. Place bowls on a baking sheet and bake until bubbling, about 25 minutes. If desired, place briefly under a preheated broiler until cheese is browned, then sprinkle with chives.

SQUASH AND APPLE SOUP

You can garnish this autumnal puree with very thin, unpeeled apple slices.

SERVES 4

1 tablespoon olive oil

1 small onion, halved and thinly sliced

3 garlic cloves, crushed

1 tablespoon minced fresh ginger

1 pickled jalapeño pepper, seeded, deveined, and finely chopped (wear gloves when handling; they burn)

1 1/2 pounds butternut squash, peeled, seeded, and thinly sliced

2 teaspoons sugar

1 pound McIntosh apples, cored, peeled, and thinly sliced

1 pound Granny Smith apples, cored, peeled, and thinly sliced

1 1/2 teaspoons chili powder

1/2 teaspoon salt

1/4 teaspoon dried thyme

1 1/2 cups chicken stock

1 Heat oil in a Dutch oven over medium heat. Add onion, garlic, ginger, and jalapeño and sauté 5 minutes or until onion is softened. Add squash, sprinkle with sugar, and sauté 5 minutes or until crisp-tender.

2 Add apples, chili powder, salt, and thyme and stir to coat. Add stock and 1 1/2 cups water and bring to boil. Reduce heat and simmer, partially covered, 30 minutes or until squash is tender. Working in batches, transfer to a blender or food processor, cover, and puree until smooth. Return to pan and cook until heated through.

CURRIED ACORN SQUASH SOUP

Curry powder gives this lovely squash soup extra warmth and flavor.

SERVES 4

3 medium acorn squash, halved and seeded
2 tablespoons butter
1/2 cup chopped onion
3 teaspoons curry powder
3 cups chicken stock
1 cup half-and-half
1/2 teaspoon ground nutmeg
Salt and black pepper
Crumbled cooked bacon *(optional)*

1 Preheat oven to 350°F. Grease a shallow baking pan. Place squash cut side down in pan and bake 35 minutes or until almost tender.

2 Meanwhile, in a medium saucepan over low heat, melt butter. Add onion and curry powder and sauté until onion is tender, about 3 minutes. Remove from heat.

3 Carefully scoop pulp from squash and add to pan. Return to heat, gradually add stock, and bring to boil. Reduce heat and simmer, covered, until very tender, about 15 minutes.

4 Working in batches if necessary, transfer soup to a blender or food processor, cover, and puree until smooth. Return to pan, stir in half-and-half and nutmeg, and season to taste with salt and pepper. Reduce heat to low and cook until heated through (do not boil). Garnish with bacon, if desired.

CURRIED WINTER SQUASH SOUP

Native Americans found squash growing wild and quickly learned to love it. We have shortened the Narragansett name—askutasquash—to squash.

SERVES 8

3 tablespoons unsalted butter or margarine
1 medium yellow onion, chopped
1 large butternut squash, peeled, seeded, and cut into 1/2-inch pieces
2 large red cooking apples, such as McIntosh or Rome Beauty, cored, peeled, and diced
1 tablespoon curry powder
1/2 teaspoon ground ginger
1/4 teaspoon ground allspice
4 cups chicken stock
1/2 cup low-fat plain yogurt

1 In a 6-quart Dutch oven over medium heat, melt butter. Add onion and sauté 5 minutes or until tender. Stir in squash, apples, curry powder, ginger, and allspice and sauté 10 minutes.

2 Stir in stock, increase heat to medium-high, and bring to boil. Reduce heat and simmer, covered, 30 minutes or until squash is tender.

3 Working in batches if necessary, transfer soup to a blender or food processor, cover, and puree 45 seconds or until smooth. Return to Dutch oven and cook over medium heat, stirring frequently, 5 minutes or until heated through. Ladle into bowls and garnish each serving with 1 tablespoon yogurt.

SWEET POTATO SOUP

Old-fashioned sweet potato soup was delightfully thick and rich because it was made with lots of heavy cream and butter. This more healthful version has less cream, more potatoes, and just a hint of butter for flavor.

SERVES 4

1 tablespoon butter

1 large yellow onion, chopped

1 large carrot, chopped

1/4 cup minced fresh parsley

2 medium sweet potatoes,
    peeled and cut into chunks

1 3/4 cups canned low-sodium chicken broth

1 teaspoon ground cinnamon

1/4 teaspoon salt

1/4 teaspoon black pepper

1/4 teaspoon ground nutmeg

1 cup low-fat (1%) milk

1/3 cup fat-free half-and-half

1 In a large saucepan over medium-high heat, melt butter. Add onion, carrot, and parsley and sauté until tender, about 5 minutes. Add sweet potatoes, broth, cinnamon, salt, pepper, and nutmeg and bring to boil. Reduce heat, cover, and simmer until sweet potatoes are tender, about 20 minutes. Remove from heat and let cool slightly.

2 Transfer in 2 batches to a food processor or blender, cover, and puree until smooth. Return to pan and stir in milk and half-and-half. Cook, uncovered, until heated through, about 5 minutes.

SWEET POTATO SOUP WITH MAPLE SYRUP

This spicy orange-colored soup is a delicious way to fill up on disease-fighting beta-carotene.

SERVES 6

1 tablespoon unsalted butter

1 tablespoon vegetable oil

1 cup diced onion

1/2 cup diced celery

1/2 cup rinsed sliced leeks with tops

1 garlic clove, minced

1 cinnamon stick, 3 inches

Pinch of ground cloves

1 tablespoon minced fresh ginger
    or 1 teaspoon ground ginger

4 cups chicken stock

3 cups peeled sweet potato chunks or 2 cups
    plain canned pureed sweet potatoes

1/2 teaspoon salt

1 teaspoon maple syrup

1/8 teaspoon freshly grated or ground nutmeg

6 tablespoons low-fat plain yogurt or reduced-
    fat sour cream

1 In a large heavy saucepan over medium-high heat, melt butter and heat oil. Add onion, celery, leeks, garlic, cinnamon, cloves, and ginger and sauté 5 minutes or until vegetables are tender.

2 Add stock, sweet potatoes, and salt and bring to boil. Reduce heat and simmer, covered, 20 minutes or until soup is thickened and flavors are blended.

3 Using a slotted spoon, remove cinnamon stick. Working in batches if necessary, transfer soup to a blender or food processor, cover, and puree 45 seconds or until smooth. Return to pan and stir in syrup and nutmeg. Cook over medium-high heat, stirring occasionally, 5 minutes or until heated through. Ladle into bowls and garnish each serving with 1 tablespoon yogurt.

HARVEST SWEET POTATO SOUP

You may want to double this super-easy recipe, since leftovers are delicious. Serve soup warm or chilled.

SERVES 4

1 tablespoon vegetable oil

1 cup chopped celery

1/2 cup chopped onion

3 medium sweet potatoes, peeled and cut into cubes

3 cups chicken stock

1 bay leaf

1/2 teaspoon dried basil

1/4 teaspoon salt *(optional)*

1 Heat oil in a Dutch oven or soup pot over medium heat. Add celery and onion and sauté until tender, about 5 minutes. Add sweet potatoes, stock, bay leaf, basil, and salt, if desired. Bring to boil, then reduce heat and simmer, covered, until tender, about 25 minutes. Remove from heat, remove bay leaf, and let cool slightly.

2 Transfer in batches to a blender or food processor, cover, and puree until smooth. Return to pot and cook until heated through.

SWEET POTATO-PEANUT BUTTER SOUP

This unique, velvety smooth soup is delicious hot or cold.

SERVES 4

1 3/4 cups chicken stock

1 large yellow onion, coarsely chopped

2 medium celery stalks, coarsely chopped

1/2 teaspoon minced garlic

2 medium sweet potatoes, peeled and cut into 1/2-inch cubes

1 bay leaf

1/4 teaspoon dried thyme, crumbled

1/4 teaspoon hot red pepper sauce

3 tablespoons creamy peanut butter

2 teaspoons rice vinegar or white wine vinegar

1/4 cup chopped dry-roasted peanuts *(optional)*

1/4 cup chopped scallions *(optional)*

1 In a large saucepan or 4-quart Dutch oven over medium heat, combine 1 cup water, stock, onion, celery, garlic, sweet potatoes, bay leaf, thyme, and red pepper sauce. Bring to boil, then reduce heat, cover, and simmer until potatoes are tender, 20 to 25 minutes. Remove from heat, remove bay leaf, and stir in peanut butter and vinegar.

2 Working in batches if necessary, transfer to blender or food processor, cover, and puree until smooth. Garnish each serving with peanuts or scallions, if desired.

SWEET POTATO AND CARROT VICHYSSOISE

A colorful take on the original potato and leek soup, this version is high in beta-carotene and other disease-fighting elements typical of orange foods.

SERVES 6

3 tablespoons butter

2 small leeks, halved lengthwise, rinsed, and sliced

1/2 teaspoon ground nutmeg

2 medium sweet potatoes, peeled and cut into 2-inch chunks

2 medium carrots, peeled and cut into 2-inch chunks

4 cups chicken stock

1 1/2 cups buttermilk

Salt and black pepper

2 tablespoons snipped fresh chives *(optional)*

1 In a saucepan over medium heat, melt butter. Add leeks and nutmeg and sauté 5 minutes or until tender.

2 Add sweet potatoes, carrots, and stock and bring to boil. Reduce heat and simmer, uncovered, until tender, 15 to 20 minutes. Remove from heat and let cool 10 minutes.

3 Working in batches, transfer to a blender or food processor, cover, and puree until smooth. Return to saucepan and stir in buttermilk, salt, and pepper (if soup seems too thick, thin with a small amount of additional stock or buttermilk). Cook over low heat until heated through. Sprinkle each serving with chives, if desired.

FRESH TOMATO SOUP

This wonderful summer soup can be a first course at dinner or part of a great soup-and-sandwich lunch.

SERVES 9

1/4 cup (1/2 stick) butter
2 cups sliced carrots
1 cup chopped celery
1 small onion, finely chopped
1/2 cup chopped seeded green bell pepper
4 1/2 cups chicken stock
4 medium tomatoes, peeled, cored, seeded, and chopped
4 teaspoons sugar
1/2 teaspoon curry powder
1/2 teaspoon salt *(optional)*
1/4 teaspoon black pepper
1/4 cup all-purpose flour

1 In a Dutch oven or soup pot over medium heat, melt butter. Add carrots, celery, onion, and bell pepper and sauté 7 minutes or until tender.

2 Add 4 cups stock, tomatoes, sugar, curry powder, salt, if desired, and pepper. Bring to boil, then reduce heat and simmer, covered, 20 minutes.

3 In a small bowl, stir flour into remaining broth until smooth. Gradually add to soup, bring to boil, and cook, stirring, 2 minutes.

PICKLED TOMATO SOUP

This unusual soup is a great way to use up the extra tomatoes in your garden at the end of summer.

SERVES 8

5 pounds fresh tomatoes, quartered
3/4 cup sugar
2 tablespoons salt
1 tablespoon mixed pickling spice, tied in a cheesecloth bag
3 large onions, chopped
1 bunch parsley, chopped
1 celery stalk, sliced
2 tablespoons butter
2 tablespoons all-purpose flour
5 bacon slices, cooked and crumbled
Unsweetened whipped cream
Toasted slivered almonds

1 In a large soup pot, bring 2 cups water, tomatoes, sugar, salt, spice bag, onions, parsley, and celery to boil. Reduce heat and simmer, covered, 1 1/2 hours.

2 Remove from heat and let cool slightly. Remove spice bag, press mixture through a food mill, and return liquid to pot.

3 In a small saucepan over medium heat, melt butter. Add flour and cook, stirring, 2 minutes or until browned and bubbling. Stir into soup. Add bacon and cook until heated through. Top each serving with a dollop of whipped cream and sprinkle with almonds.

TOMATO SOUP WITH CROSTINI

SERVES 8

Soup:

1/2 cup (1 stick) butter

2 tablespoons olive oil

1 large onion, sliced

2 thyme sprigs or
    1/2 teaspoon dried thyme

4 fresh basil leaves or
    1/2 teaspoon dried basil

1 teaspoon salt

1/4 teaspoon black pepper

2 1/2 pounds ripe tomatoes, diced,
    or 2 cans (16 ounces each) Italian-style
    tomatoes, undrained

3 tablespoons tomato paste

1/4 cup all-purpose flour

3 3/4 cups chicken stock

1 teaspoon sugar

1 cup heavy whipping cream

Crostini:

8 slices day-old French or Italian bread

1 large garlic clove, halved lengthwise

2 tablespoons olive oil

1 For soup, melt butter and heat oil in a large soup pot over medium heat. Add onion, thyme, basil, salt, and pepper and sauté 4 minutes or until onion is softened. Stir in tomatoes and tomato paste until blended and cook 10 minutes.

2 In a small bowl, combine flour and 1/4 cup stock. Stir into tomato mixture, add remaining stock, and bring to boil. Reduce heat, cover, and simmer, stirring frequently, 30 minutes. Remove from heat and let cool slightly.

3 Transfer soup to a food processor or blender, cover, and puree until smooth. Return to pot, add sugar and cream, and cook until heated through, stirring occasionally.

4 For crostini, preheat oven to 350°F. Rub cut side of garlic over both sides of bread and brush both sides with oil. Place on a baking sheet and bake 10 minutes or until toasted. Turn and toast other side 2 to 3 minutes. Just before serving, top each serving with 1 or 2 crostini.

This is a rich Italian tomato soup served with its own floating garlic bread.

ALPHABET TOMATO SOUP

Kids will have fun spelling their names with the alphabet pasta they find in their bowls.

SERVES 4

1 can (10 1/2 ounces) condensed
   cheddar cheese soup
1 can (10 3/4 ounces) condensed
   tomato soup
1/2 cup finely chopped seeded green
   bell pepper
1 teaspoon dried basil
1/8 teaspoon black pepper
1/3 cup alphabet pasta

1 In a large saucepan over medium heat, combine 2 cups water, cheese soup, tomato soup, bell pepper, basil, and black pepper. Bring to boil, then reduce heat and stir in pasta. Cover and simmer, stirring frequently, until tender, 10 to 12 minutes.

SPICY TOMATO-RICE SOUP

This is a fast lunch soup for busy families to enjoy on the run.

SERVES 4

1 can (14 1/2 ounces) low-sodium
   stewed tomatoes
1 cup chicken stock
1 tablespoon tomato paste
3/4 teaspoon ground ginger
1/2 teaspoon salt
1/4 teaspoon cayenne pepper
2 cups cooked rice

1 In a large saucepan, combine 1 cup water, tomatoes, stock, tomato paste, ginger, salt, and cayenne. Bring to boil, stir in rice, and cook 2 to 3 minutes or until heated through.

ROSY TOMATO SOUP

Here is a modern, healthier version of cream of tomato soup, just as tasty as the original but much lower in fat, cholesterol, and sodium.

SERVES 6 ☼

1 tablespoon vegetable oil
1 medium yellow onion, chopped
3 garlic cloves, minced
2 tablespoons all-purpose flour
1 can (28 ounces) low-sodium whole
   peeled tomatoes, undrained
1 cup beef stock
1 teaspoon sugar
1/2 teaspoon salt
1/4 teaspoon baking soda
1/4 teaspoon black pepper
1/4 teaspoon ground mace or nutmeg
3 cups low-fat (1%) milk

Garnishes:
1 medium tomato, cored, seeded,
   and finely chopped
2 tablespoons snipped fresh chives
Low-fat plain yogurt (*optional*)

1 Heat oil in a large saucepan over medium heat. Add onion and garlic and sauté 5 minutes or until tender. Stir in flour and cook, stirring constantly, until bubbling. Add tomatoes, stock, sugar, salt, baking soda, pepper, and mace. Bring to boil, then reduce heat and simmer, uncovered, 10 minutes. Transfer to a food processor or blender, cover, and puree until smooth.

2 Add milk to pan and cook over medium heat until just beginning to bubble. Stir in puree and cook until heated through (do not boil). Ladle into bowls and garnish with tomato and chives. Top each serving with a swirl of yogurt, if desired.

TOMATO EGG DROP SOUP

An infusion of garlic adds rich flavor to this Cuban-style broth. (Photograph on page 11)

SERVES 6

1 tablespoon olive oil

1 small onion, finely chopped

6 garlic cloves, minced

4 ripe tomatoes, cored, seeded, and finely chopped

2 cans (14 1/2 ounces each) fat-free low-sodium chicken broth

1 bay leaf

1 teaspoon salt

2 large eggs, lightly beaten

6 slices Italian semolina bread, 1 inch thick, toasted

3 tablespoons coarsely chopped fresh parsley

1 Heat oil in a large saucepan over medium heat. Add onion and sauté 5 minutes or until softened. Add garlic and sauté 30 seconds. Stir in tomatoes and sauté 1 minute.

2 Add broth, bay leaf, and salt and bring to boil. Reduce heat and simmer, uncovered, 10 minutes. Remove from heat, remove bay leaf, and stir in eggs. Place 1 bread slice in each serving bowl, ladle in soup, and sprinkle with parsley.

CREAM OF TOMATO SOUP

This is an American classic that's all the better when made in your own kitchen. The touch of baking soda rounds out the flavors by neutralizing the acid in the tomatoes.

SERVES 6

2 tablespoons unsalted butter

1 medium yellow onion, chopped

3 garlic cloves, minced

2 cans (28 ounces each) whole peeled tomatoes, undrained

1/2 cup beef stock

1 teaspoon sugar

1 teaspoon salt

1/4 teaspoon baking soda

1/4 teaspoon black pepper

1/4 teaspoon ground mace or nutmeg

1 1/2 cups heavy cream

Garnishes:

1 medium tomato, cored, seeded, and finely chopped

Chopped fresh parsley

Heavy cream *(optional)*

1 In a large saucepan over medium heat, melt butter. Add onion and garlic and sauté 5 minutes or until tender. Stir in tomatoes, stock, sugar, salt, baking soda, pepper, and mace. Bring to boil, then reduce heat and simmer, uncovered, 10 minutes.

2 Transfer soup to a food processor or blender, cover, and puree until smooth. Return to pan and stir in cream. Cook over medium-low heat 5 minutes or just until heated through (do not boil). Ladle into bowls and garnish with chopped tomato, parsley, and a swirl of cream, if desired.

SOUTHWESTERN TOMATO SOUP

This smooth soup is unbeatable when the ripest and most flavorful tomatoes are available from your farmers' market or home garden.

SERVES 6

10 plum tomatoes, halved lengthwise
1-2 Anaheim peppers, halved and seeded
1 tablespoon olive oil
1/2 cup chopped onion
2 garlic cloves, minced
2 cans (14 1/2 ounces each) chicken broth
1 tablespoon minced fresh cilantro
2 teaspoons ground cumin
1/2 teaspoon sugar
1/2 teaspoon salt
1/4 teaspoon black pepper
8 corn tortillas (6 inches), cut into 1/4-inch strips
Sour cream *(optional)*

1 Preheat broiler. Place tomatoes cut side down on a broiler pan and broil 4 inches from heat 15 minutes. Transfer to a plate. Broil peppers 5 minutes and transfer to plate. When cool enough to handle, remove skins from both.

2 Heat oil in a skillet over medium heat. Add onion and garlic and sauté until tender, about 3 minutes. Transfer to a blender or food processor, add tomatoes and peppers, cover, and puree until smooth. Pour into a large saucepan over medium heat and cook, stirring, 2 minutes. Remove from heat and let cool.

3 Place mixture in a strainer over a bowl and press with a spoon, discarding seeds. Return to pan and add broth, cilantro, cumin, sugar, salt, and pepper. Bring to boil, then reduce heat and simmer, uncovered, until heated through, about 15 minutes.

4 Meanwhile, add 1/2 inch of oil to an electric skillet set at 375°F. Add tortillas in batches and fry until golden, about 3 minutes. Transfer to paper towels to drain. Garnish each serving of soup with tortilla strips and serve with sour cream, if desired.

TOMATO-GARLIC SOUP

Grandmothers often said garlic was good for what ails you, and we now know they were right. This soup uses 10 cloves, but because garlic mellows as it cooks, it has a mild, slightly sweet flavor.

SERVES 6

1 tablespoon butter
1 tablespoon olive or vegetable oil
2 large yellow onions, quartered and thinly sliced
10 garlic cloves, minced
4 medium tomatoes, cored, peeled, seeded, and chopped
1 3/4 cups canned low-sodium beef broth
1 can (8 ounces) low-sodium tomato sauce
1 teaspoon dried thyme
1 bay leaf
1/2 teaspoon sugar
1/4 teaspoon salt
1/4 teaspoon black pepper
1/4 cup minced fresh parsley

1 In a large nonstick saucepan over medium-low heat, melt butter and heat oil. Add onions and garlic and sauté 25 minutes or until onions are very soft and golden.

2 Stir in tomatoes, broth, tomato sauce, thyme, bay leaf, sugar, salt, and pepper. Bring to boil, then reduce heat and simmer, covered, 15 minutes. Remove bay leaf and stir in parsley.

TOMATO-GARLIC SOUP FOR A CROWD

You can expect lots of compliments when you serve this soup to dinner guests.

SERVES 18

10 whole garlic heads

3/4 cup olive oil

4 cans (one 14 1/2 ounces, three 28 ounces) diced tomatoes, undrained

1 medium onion, diced

3 cans (14 1/2 ounces each) stewed tomatoes

2/3 cup heavy whipping cream

1-3 tablespoons chopped pickled jalapeño peppers (wear gloves when handling; they burn)

2 teaspoons garlic pepper

2 teaspoons sugar

1 1/2 teaspoons salt

Croutons

Grated Parmesan cheese *(optional)*

1 Preheat oven to 375°F. Remove papery outer skin from garlic heads (do not peel or separate cloves). Cut off tops and place cut side up in an ungreased 8-inch square baking dish. Pour oil over garlic and bake, uncovered, until softened, about 45 minutes. Let cool 10 to 15 minutes.

2 Squeeze softened garlic into a blender or food processor. Add 14 1/2-ounce can diced tomatoes, cover, and puree until smooth.

3 Transfer 1/4 cup oil from baking dish to a Dutch oven or soup pot and heat over medium heat (discard remaining oil or save for another use). Add onion and sauté until soft, about 3 minutes. Stir in stewed tomatoes, cream, jalapeños, garlic pepper, sugar, salt, pureed tomato mixture, and remaining diced tomatoes. Bring to boil, then reduce heat and simmer, covered, 1 hour. Garnish with croutons and cheese, if desired.

MIDDLE EASTERN TOMATO SOUP

A touch of mint gives this soup its distinctive and refreshing flavor.

SERVES 4

1 tablespoon olive oil

1 small zucchini, julienned

1/2 cup bulgur

4 cups canned low-sodium chicken broth

2 teaspoons dried mint, crumbled

2 large ripe tomatoes, peeled, cored, seeded, and chopped

1 scallion, sliced

2 pita breads, toasted and cut into 12 triangles

1 Heat oil in a medium saucepan over medium heat. Add zucchini and sauté 2 minutes. Add bulgur and stir to coat, then add broth and mint, increase heat to high, and bring to boil. Reduce heat and simmer, covered, 5 minutes.

2 Stir in tomatoes, cover, and simmer 5 minutes. Garnish each serving with scallion and serve with pita triangles.

TOMATO-SPINACH SOUP

This nutritious soup combines tomatoes and spinach with Italian seasonings.

SERVES 8

2 tablespoons olive oil

2 large yellow onions, cut into cubes

1 can (28 ounces) diced tomatoes, undrained

4 beef bouillon cubes

1 cup sliced fresh mushrooms

3/4 teaspoon Italian seasoning

1/2 teaspoon dried basil

1/2 teaspoon salt

1/8 teaspoon black pepper

4 cups loosely packed spinach leaves

Grated Parmesan or shredded cheddar cheese

1 Heat oil in a Dutch oven or soup pot over medium heat. Add onions and sauté until tender, about 7 minutes.

2 Add 4 cups water, tomatoes, bouillon, mushrooms, Italian seasoning, basil, salt. and pepper. Bring to boil, then reduce heat and simmer, covered, 30 minutes. Stir in spinach and simmer until heated through, about 4 minutes. Garnish with cheese.

WATERCRESS SOUP

To keep watercress fresh for up to a week, place the stems in a container of cold water, place the container in a sealed plastic bag, and refrigerate.

SERVES 6

3 1/2 cups canned low-sodium
   beef broth
2 cups thinly sliced fresh mushrooms
1/2 cup shredded carrot
2 large scallions with tops, cut into
   1/2-inch pieces
1 tablespoon minced fresh basil
   or 1 teaspoon dried basil
1 tablespoon fresh lemon juice
1 garlic clove, minced
1/4 teaspoon salt
1/8 teaspoon black pepper
2 cups bite-size pieces watercress

1 In a large saucepan over medium heat, combine broth, mushrooms, carrot, scallions, basil, lemon juice, garlic, salt, and pepper. Bring to boil, then reduce heat and simmer, covered, until vegetables are just crisp-tender, about 3 minutes.

2 Stir in watercress and cook, uncovered, until just starting to wilt, about 30 seconds.

WATERCRESS AND PARSLEY SOUP

This light, elegant soup is rich in vitamin A. Serve it for lunch with a sandwich or as a first course for a special dinner.

SERVES 4

2 tablespoons unsalted butter
1 small yellow onion, coarsely chopped
1/4 cup all-purpose flour
2 1/4 cups chicken stock
1 can (12 ounces) fat-free evaporated milk
2 1/2 cups flat-leaf parsley
2 cups watercress leaves
1/8 teaspoon ground nutmeg
1/8 teaspoon salt
1/4 teaspoon black pepper

1 In a large heavy saucepan over medium-low heat, melt butter. Add onion and cook, covered, until softened, about 5 minutes. Add flour and cook, stirring, until smooth and straw colored, about 3 minutes. Gradually stir in stock and milk, increase heat to medium, and bring to boil, whisking constantly. Reduce heat, add 2 cups parsley, watercress, nutmeg, salt, and pepper, and simmer, covered, 5 minutes.

2 Set a large sieve over a bowl and drain vegetables, reserving liquid. Transfer vegetables, 1 cup liquid, and remaining parsley to a blender or food processor and puree until smooth. Return to pan, stir in remaining liquid, and cook until heated through.

ZUCCHINI AND WATERCRESS SOUP

The mellow smoothness of the zucchini provides a foil for the sharp, peppery taste of watercress.

SERVES 4

2 tablespoons unsalted butter
2 medium onions, chopped
3 cups chicken or vegetable stock
2 pounds firm zucchini, thinly sliced
Large bunch watercress, chopped
Grated zest of 1 lemon
Salt and black pepper
4 watercress sprigs

1 In a large saucepan over medium heat, melt butter. Add onions and sauté 5 minutes or until transparent. Add stock, cover, and bring to boil.

2 Add zucchini, reduce heat, and simmer, covered, 15 minutes. Stir in watercress, then remove from heat and let stand, covered, 5 minutes.

3 Transfer soup to a food processor or blender, cover, and puree until smooth. Add lemon zest and season to taste with salt and pepper. Cook until heated through and serve garnished with watercress.

ZUCCHINI-POTATO SOUP

This delightful soup is finished with egg and lemon, in the Greek way, and just a touch of dill.

SERVES 8

5 cups chicken stock
4 small zucchini, thinly sliced
1 large potato, peeled, halved,
    and thinly sliced
1 large onion, thinly sliced
3 eggs

2 tablespoons fresh lemon juice
2 teaspoons dill weed
Salt and black pepper to taste

1 In a saucepan over medium heat, bring stock to boil. Stir in zucchini, potato, and onion. Reduce heat and simmer, covered, 15 minutes or until tender.

2 In a small bowl, beat eggs, then blend in lemon juice and 1/2 cup stock. Add to pan and cook over medium heat 1 minute, stirring constantly (do not boil). Stir in dill and season to taste with salt and pepper.

CREAM OF BASIL SOUP

Fresh basil has a flavor that's rich enough to carry its own cream sauce. This soup may happily surprise you.

SERVES 8

3 cups chicken stock
1 cup minced fresh basil
1/4 cup (1/2 stick) butter
3 tablespoons all-purpose flour
Ground white pepper to taste
3 cups milk
1/2 cup sour cream

1 In a medium saucepan over medium-high heat, combine stock and basil. Bring to boil, then reduce heat and simmer, uncovered, 15 minutes.

2 In another medium saucepan over medium heat, melt butter. Add flour and pepper and stir until smooth. Gradually add milk, bring to boil, and cook, stirring, until thickened, about 2 minutes. Reduce heat and gradually stir in stock mixture and sour cream.

GARLIC SOUP

This very tasty cream soup is a great meal starter, whetting appetites for the main attraction.

SERVES 4

1/2 cup (1 stick) butter
2 small onions, chopped
3 garlic cloves, minced
6 tablespoons all-purpose flour
6 cups chicken stock
1/2 teaspoon cayenne pepper

1 In a large saucepan over medium heat, melt butter. Add onions and garlic and sauté until tender, about 3 minutes.

2 Stir in flour until blended. Gradually add stock, bring to boil, and cook, stirring, until thickened, about 2 minutes. Reduce heat and simmer, uncovered, 15 minutes. Stir in cayenne.

CREAMY GARLIC SOUP WITH HERBED CROUTONS

To ease the task of peeling the garlic, first blanch the unpeeled cloves in boiling water for 1 to 2 minutes.

SERVES 4

Croutons:
3 slices (1 ounce each) firm-textured
    white sandwich bread
1 tablespoon olive oil
1 tablespoon grated Parmesan cheese
1/4 teaspoon dried thyme
1/4 teaspoon dried sage

Soup:
1 1/2 cups chicken stock
3 heads garlic, peeled
1/4 teaspoon dried thyme
1/4 teaspoon dried sage

12 ounces all-purpose potatoes,
    peeled and thinly sliced
1/4 teaspoon salt
3 tablespoons reduced-fat mayonnaise
1/4 cup chopped fresh parsley

1 For croutons, preheat oven to 375°F. Brush bread with oil and cut into 1/2-inch squares. In a small bowl, toss with Parmesan, thyme, and sage. Spread on a baking sheet and bake 5 minutes or just until crisp.

2 For soup, combine stock, garlic, thyme, and sage in a medium saucepan over medium heat. Simmer, covered, 25 minutes or until garlic is very soft.

3 Meanwhile, in another medium saucepan over medium-high heat, bring 2 cups water to boil. Add potatoes and cook 12 minutes or until tender.

4 Transfer garlic mixture to a food processor or blender, cover, and puree until smooth. Return to pan, add potatoes, cooking liquid, and salt, and bring to boil. Reduce heat, add mayonnaise, and simmer, whisking, 2 minutes or until slightly thickened. Top each serving with croutons and parsley.

CARAWAY-SOUR CREAM SOUP

Caraway's sharp, nutty flavor makes this rich soup unique.

SERVES 6 TO 8

3 tablespoons butter

2 medium onions, diced

1 cup diced celery

1 cup diced carrots

1 tablespoon caraway seed

1/2 cup all-purpose flour

4 cups chicken stock

1 cup sour cream

1/2 cup milk

Salt and black pepper

1 In a large saucepan over low heat, melt butter. Add onions, celery, carrots, and caraway seed and sauté until tender, about 5 minutes.

2 Remove from heat and stir in flour until well blended. Gradually stir in stock. Return to heat, bring to boil, and cook, stirring, 2 minutes. Reduce heat and simmer, covered, 10 minutes.

3 In a medium bowl, combine sour cream and milk, then add about 1 cup stock mixture. Return to pan and cook until heated through (do not boil). Season to taste with salt and pepper.

VEGETABLE STEW

This dish is great for using up summer crops from the garden and will please many palates. If you use vegetable broth instead of chicken broth, vegetarians will love it too.

SERVES 8

1 small eggplant, peeled and cut into 3/4-inch cubes

1 3/4 cups canned low-sodium chicken broth

1 can (14 1/2 ounces) low-sodium tomatoes, undrained, cut up

2 cans (5 1/2 ounces each) hot-style vegetable juice cocktail

1 can (8 ounces) low-sodium tomato sauce

1 large yellow onion, chopped

1 medium green, red, or yellow bell pepper, cored, seeded, and chopped

2 garlic cloves, minced

1 teaspoon dried oregano

1/4 teaspoon salt

1/4 teaspoon black pepper

1/3 cup minced fresh parsley

Grated Parmesan cheese

1 In a large saucepan over medium heat, combine eggplant, broth, tomatoes, vegetable juice, tomato sauce, onion, bell pepper, garlic, oregano, salt, and black pepper. Bring to boil, then reduce heat and simmer, covered, until vegetables are crisp-tender, about 25 minutes. Stir in parsley and serve with cheese.

SWEET AND SPICY VEGETABLE STEW

With turmeric, ginger, and cinnamon, this lovely stew has an affinity for the Middle East. It is also strictly vegetarian.

SERVES 4

3 cups cauliflower florets

1 tablespoon olive oil

1 small yellow onion, finely chopped

3 garlic cloves, minced

1 can (35 ounces) low-sodium tomatoes, drained and chopped

1 cinnamon stick

3/4 teaspoon ground turmeric

3/4 teaspoon ground ginger

1/2 teaspoon paprika

1/2 teaspoon black pepper

1 medium red bell pepper, cored, seeded, and cut into 1-inch pieces

1 medium carrot, peeled, halved lengthwise, and thinly sliced

5 pitted prunes, chopped

1 cup fresh green beans, trimmed and halved

1 cup cooked drained chickpeas

1 cup couscous

1 In a large saucepan, combine cauliflower and 6 cups water. Bring to boil and cook 4 minutes or until just tender; drain.

2 Heat oil in a heavy 12-inch skillet over medium heat. Add onion and garlic and sauté until onion is softened, about 5 minutes. Add tomatoes, cinnamon, turmeric, ginger, paprika, and black pepper. Bring to boil, then reduce heat and simmer, covered, 10 minutes. Stir in 1/2 cup cold water, bell pepper, carrot, and prunes. Bring to boil, then reduce heat and simmer, covered, 15 minutes. Add another 1/2 cup cold water, beans, and cauliflower and simmer, covered, 20 minutes. Stir in chickpeas and simmer, covered, 5 minutes.

3 As soon as chickpeas are added to skillet, place couscous in a medium bowl and add 1 1/2 cups boiling water. Cover and let stand 5 minutes, then fluff with a fork and mound onto a platter. Remove cinnamon stick from stew and ladle stew over couscous.

VEGETABLE STEW WITH SWISS CHARD

Here's a healthy mix of vegetables in a vegetarian stew that you can cook up quickly. Cheese biscuits would complement it well.

SERVES 4

2 tablespoons butter

1 tablespoon olive oil

4 scallions, cut into 1/2-inch pieces

8 ounces Swiss chard, stems cut into 1-inch lengths and leaves cut into 1/2-inch-wide ribbons

4 ounces fresh mushrooms, halved

12 baby carrots, halved lengthwise

1 garlic clove, chopped

1 package (10 ounces) frozen baby lima beans

4 ounces snow peas, strings removed

Salt and black pepper

1 tablespoon chopped parsley

1 In a 5-quart Dutch oven over medium heat, melt butter and heat oil. Add scallions and sauté 30 seconds. Stir in 1 cup water, chard stems, mushrooms, carrots, garlic, and lima beans and bring to boil, stirring to thaw beans. Reduce heat, cover, and simmer 8 minutes or until carrots are almost tender.

2 Add chard leaves and snow peas. Cook until vegetables are crisp-tender, about 4 minutes. Season to taste with salt and pepper and sprinkle with parsley.

SPANISH-STYLE VEGETABLE STEW

With its colorful vegetables, this zesty meal can be made ahead and reheated for a party.

SERVES 4

1 tablespoon olive oil

1 medium yellow onion, chopped

1 garlic clove, minced

1 medium tomato, cored, seeded, and chopped

1 medium red or green bell pepper, cored, seeded, and chopped

1 small all-purpose potato, peeled and diced

1/2 teaspoon paprika

1/4 teaspoon cayenne pepper

1 cup long-grain rice

2 cups canned low-sodium chicken broth

1 medium zucchini, quartered lengthwise and cut into 3-inch pieces

2 medium carrots, peeled, halved lengthwise, and cut into 3-inch pieces

2 cups fresh or frozen peas

1 Heat oil in a large heavy saucepan over medium heat. Add onion and garlic and sauté 1 minute. Add tomato and bell pepper and sauté 3 minutes. Add potato, paprika, and cayenne and sauté 2 minutes.

2 Stir in rice and broth and bring to boil. Reduce heat and simmer, covered, 15 minutes or until most of liquid is absorbed. Stir in zucchini, carrots, and peas and simmer, covered, 10 minutes. Serve on a large heated platter.

INDIAN CORN, PEPPER, TOMATO, AND SQUASH STEW

Pueblo Indians often simmered large pots of meat stew over an open fire, adding fresh vegetables such as corn and squash to the pot before serving.

SERVES 6

1 tablespoon vegetable oil

1 1/2 pounds lean ground beef

1 1/2 cups chopped seeded green bell peppers

1 large yellow onion, chopped

2 garlic cloves, minced

8 large ears corn, kernels cut off, or 4 cups frozen whole-kernel corn

1 can (14 ounces) crushed tomatoes

4 teaspoons Worcestershire sauce

1/2 teaspoon black pepper

1/2 teaspoon chili powder

1/4 teaspoon salt

1/8 teaspoon cayenne pepper

1 medium zucchini or yellow squash, thinly sliced crosswise

1 Heat oil in a 6-quart Dutch oven or soup pot over medium-high heat. Add beef and cook, stirring frequently, 8 minutes or until browned. Reduce heat, stir in bell peppers, onion, and garlic, and simmer, uncovered, 5 minutes or until tender, stirring occasionally.

2 Stir in corn, tomatoes, Worcestershire sauce, black pepper, chili powder, salt, and cayenne. Bring to boil, then reduce heat and simmer, covered, 15 minutes. Add zucchini and simmer 5 minutes or until tender.

CARIBBEAN SQUASH AND CORN STEW

Butternut squash has a lovely firm texture, making it ideal for stews. This stew combines it with black-eyed peas, corn, and red bell pepper in a vegetarian delight.

SERVES 4

1 tablespoon extra-virgin olive oil

1 onion, sliced

2 garlic cloves, crushed

1 butternut squash, peeled and cut into 1/2-inch cubes

1 red bell pepper, cored, seeded, and sliced

1 bay leaf

1 can (14 1/2 ounces) chopped tomatoes, undrained

1 can (15 ounces) black-eyed peas, drained and rinsed

1 cup canned or frozen whole-kernel corn

1 1/4 cups vegetable stock

1 tablespoon Worcestershire sauce

1 teaspoon hot red pepper sauce

1 tablespoon dark brown sugar

2 teaspoons balsamic vinegar

Minced fresh parsley

1 Heat oil in a large saucepan over medium-low heat. Add onion, garlic, squash, bell pepper, and bay leaf. Stir well, cover, and cook, stirring occasionally, 5 minutes.

2 Stir in tomatoes, peas, and corn. Add stock, Worcestershire sauce, red pepper sauce, brown sugar, and vinegar and stir to combine. Bring to boil, then reduce heat and simmer, covered, until squash is tender, about 15 minutes. Remove bay leaf before serving. Garnish with parsley.

CORN AND BROCCOLI STEW

This is a nice change-of-pace main dish that features broccoli, corn, potatoes, and onions. A touch of bacon adds flavor, and milk adds protein.

SERVES 4

1 bacon slice, chopped

1 small yellow onion, chopped

1 small all-purpose potato, peeled and cut into 1/2-inch cubes

1/2 cup fat-free milk

1/8 teaspoon black pepper

3 cups broccoli florets

1 1/4 cups fresh or frozen whole-kernel corn

1 In a 12-inch nonstick skillet over low heat, cook bacon until beginning to brown, about 3 minutes. Increase heat to medium-low, add onion and cook, covered, 5 minutes.

2 Add potato, 1/4 cup milk, and pepper. Cover and cook until potato is almost tender, about 7 minutes. Add broccoli and remaining milk and cook, uncovered, 5 minutes. Add corn and cook until heated through, about 3 minutes.

INDIAN VEGETABLE STEW

SERVES 4

Soup:

3 1/2 cups vegetable stock

1 onion, chopped

2 carrots, peeled and chopped

2 celery stalks, sliced

1 parsnip, peeled and chopped

2 all-purpose potatoes,
   peeled and chopped

2 ounces fresh mushrooms, sliced

1 garlic clove, minced

2 large cilantro sprigs, chopped

Salt and black pepper

4 plain naan or pita breads

Curried Onion:

1 tablespoon sunflower oil

1 onion, thinly sliced

1 garlic clove, crushed

1 tablespoon mild curry paste

Raita:

1 small zucchini, grated

1 piece cucumber, 3 inches long, grated

1 tart apple, cored and grated

6 ounces low-fat plain yogurt

2 tablespoons chopped fresh parsley

Handful of fresh mint leaves

Salt and black pepper

1 For soup, bring stock to boil in a large saucepan. Add onion, carrots, celery, parsnip, potatoes, mushrooms, and garlic. Return to boil, then reduce heat and simmer, covered, until soft, about 30 minutes.

2 For curried onion, heat oil in a small skillet over medium-low heat. Add onion and sauté until softened and beginning to caramelize, about 10 minutes. Add garlic and sauté 2 minutes. Stir in curry paste and 1 tablespoon water and cook, stirring, 2 minutes. Remove from heat.

3 For raita, combine zucchini, cucumber, and apple in a medium bowl. Stir in yogurt and parsley. Using scissors, shred mint, then fold into zucchini mixture. Season to taste with salt and pepper and transfer to a serving bowl.

4 Transfer half of soup to a blender or food processor, cover, and puree until smooth (or use a handheld blender to coarsely puree in pan, leaving some vegetables diced). Return to pan and cook until heated through (if soup is too thick, add a small amount of boiling water). Stir in curried onion and cilantro, season to taste with salt and pepper, and ladle into warm bowls. Serve raita separately. Guests can add spoonfuls to soup or spread on bread as an accompaniment.

Cool, crunchy fresh raita offers a nice contrast in flavor and texture, while curried onions offer just a touch of sweet heat to this spiced stew.

VEGETABLE HOTPOT WITH CHESTNUTS AND DUMPLINGS

Stews and hotpots have always been popular in British cuisine, especially in winter, when root vegetables provide warming, sustaining nourishment.

SERVES 4

Soup:

1 tablespoon olive oil

1 tablespoon butter

8 ounces baby or pickling onions, peeled

2 carrots, peeled and cut into wedges

1 small parsnip, peeled and cut into chunks

1 small turnip, peeled and cut into chunks

12 ounces all-purpose potatoes, peeled and halved or quartered

8 ounces frozen chestnuts

2 cups vegetable stock

1 thyme sprig

8 ounces fresh green beans, trimmed

Salt and black pepper

Dumplings:

3/4 cup self-rising flour

2 tablespoons chopped fresh parsley

3 tablespoons butter

1 For soup, heat oil and melt butter in a large Dutch oven over medium heat. Add onions and sauté until just beginning to brown, about 2 minutes.

2 Reduce heat to low, add carrots, parsnip, and turnip, and sauté 2 minutes. Cover and cook 6 to 8 minutes.

3 Add potatoes, chestnuts, stock, and thyme. Bring to boil, reduce heat, and simmer, covered, 30 minutes. Add beans and cook 5 minutes. Season to taste with salt and pepper.

4 For dumplings, combine flour and parsley in a medium bowl. Add a pinch of salt and cut in

butter. Stir in enough water to make a soft dough, then shape into 8 small dumplings.

5 Arrange dumplings on top of vegetables, cover tightly, and simmer until dumplings are puffed and cooked through, about 10 minutes.

SPICY CAULIFLOWER AND POTATO STEW

Indian spices enliven this classic vegetarian stew.

SERVES 4

2 teaspoons olive oil

2 scallions, thinly sliced

2 tablespoons minced fresh ginger

2 pounds all-purpose potatoes, peeled and cut into 1-inch chunks

1 head cauliflower, cut into florets

1 tablespoon curry powder

1 teaspoon ground coriander

1 teaspoon cumin

1/2 teaspoon salt

1 cup canned low-sodium chopped tomatoes

1/3 cup low-fat plain yogurt

2 teaspoons all-purpose flour

1 Heat oil in a large nonstick skillet over medium heat. Add scallions and ginger and sauté 2 minutes or until scallions are tender. Add potatoes, cauliflower, curry powder, coriander, cumin, and salt and stir to combine. Add 1 1/2 cups water and bring to boil. Reduce heat and simmer, covered, 15 minutes or until potatoes are almost tender.

2 Add tomatoes and simmer, covered, 10 minutes or until potatoes and cauliflower are tender. In a small bowl, combine yogurt and flour. Whisk into pan and cook 1 minute or until slightly thickened.

SQUASH STEW WITH POLENTA

This colorful stew on a base of polenta is an excellent way to use up a glut of ripe summer vegetables.

SERVES 4

6 ounces instant polenta

3 tablespoons olive oil

1 small onion, finely chopped

1 garlic clove, finely chopped

1 pound mixed summer squash,
   such as pattypan, yellow crookneck,
   and zucchini, trimmed and sliced

4 thyme sprigs

Salt and black pepper to taste

6 ounces cheddar cheese, shredded

1 1/2 tablespoons butter

2 beefsteak tomatoes, cored, seeded,
   and diced

Grated zest of 1 lemon

Chopped parsley sprigs

1 In a medium saucepan, combine polenta and 3 cups water. Bring to boil, then reduce heat and simmer 8 minutes, stirring occasionally to remove any lumps.

2 Heat oil in a skillet over medium heat. Add onion and garlic and sauté 5 minutes or until soft. Add squash, thyme, salt, and pepper and cook, covered, 10 minutes.

3 When polenta comes away cleanly from sides of pan, remove from heat. Transfer to a medium bowl and beat in cheese and butter. Season to taste with salt and pepper, cover, and let stand in a warm place.

4 Add tomatoes, lemon zest, and parsley to skillet and cook, stirring, until heated through, about 2 minutes. Remove thyme. Serve stew with polenta.

Bean and Lentil SOUPS

recipe list

 EASY: 10 minutes to prepare

QUICK: Ready to eat in 30 minutes

ONE-DISH: contains protein, vegetables, and good carbohydrates (beans, whole-grains, etc.) for a complete healthy meal

HEALTHY: High in nutrients, low in bad fats and empty carbohydrates

SLOW COOKER: Easily adapted for slow cooker by cutting down on liquids

BEAN AND LENTIL SOUPS

recipe list CONTINUED

EIGHT-BEAN SOUP

This party dish has everybody's favorite beans and then some!

SERVES 20

1/2 cup great Northern beans
1/2 cup dry kidney beans
1/2 cup dry navy beans
1/2 cup dry lima beans
1/2 cup dry butter beans
1/2 cup dry split green or yellow peas
1/2 cup dry pinto beans
1/2 cup dry lentils
1 hambone
2 chicken bouillon cubes
1 can (28 ounces) tomatoes,
    undrained, quartered
1 can (6 ounces) tomato paste
1 large onion, chopped
3 celery stalks, chopped
4 carrots, sliced
2 garlic cloves, minced
1/4 cup dried chives
3 bay leaves
2 tablespoons parsley flakes
1 teaspoon dried thyme
1 teaspoon dry mustard
1/2 teaspoon cayenne pepper

1 In a 4-quart saucepan over medium-high heat, bring beans and 5 cups water to boil. Cook 2 minutes, then remove from heat and let stand, covered, 1 hour.

2 Meanwhile, in an 8-quart soup pot over medium-high heat, bring hambone and 2 cups water to boil. Reduce heat and simmer 1 hour.

3 Drain beans and add to stock. Add bouillon, tomatoes, tomato paste, onion, celery, carrots, garlic, chives, bay leaves, parsley, thyme, mustard, and cayenne. Bring to boil, then reduce heat and

simmer 2 hours or until beans are tender. Remove hambone and bay leaves; add more water if desired.

THREE-BEAN SOUP WITH SPINACH

This bean soup showcases an appealing assortment of fresh produce—onions, potatoes, carrots, and spinach.

SERVES 12

1 tablespoon vegetable oil
1 medium onion, chopped
3 small potatoes, peeled and cut
    into cubes
2 medium carrots, sliced
3 cans (14 1/2 ounces each) chicken broth
2 tablespoons parsley flakes
2 teaspoons dried basil
1 teaspoon dried oregano
1 garlic clove, minced
1/2 teaspoon black pepper
1 can (15 1/2 ounces) great Northern beans,
    drained and rinsed
1 can (15 ounces) pinto beans,
    drained and rinsed
1 can (15 ounces) chickpeas,
    drained and rinsed
3 cups chopped fresh spinach

1 Heat oil in a Dutch oven or soup pot over medium heat. Add onion and sauté 4 minutes or until tender.

2 Add 3 cups water, potatoes, carrots, broth, parsley, basil, oregano, garlic, and pepper. Bring to boil, then reduce heat and simmer, covered, 20 minutes or until vegetables are tender. Add great Northern beans, pinto beans, chickpeas, and spinach and simmer 5 minutes or until heated through.

TUSCAN THREE-BEAN SOUP

Tuscan cuisine focuses on fresh, healthful ingredients and uncomplicated cooking techniques to make traditionally delicious fare like this main-dish bean soup. (Photograph on page 25)

SERVES 6

1 tablespoon olive oil

2 medium onions, coarsely chopped

2 medium carrots, coarsely chopped

2 celery stalks, chopped

2 cans (14 1/2 ounces each) low-sodium chicken broth

1 can (28 ounces) crushed tomatoes in puree

1/2 cup chopped fresh basil

2 tablespoons chopped fresh oregano or 1 teaspoon dried oregano

1 can (15 1/2 ounces) red kidney beans, drained and rinsed

1 can (15 1/2 ounces) cannellini beans, drained and rinsed

1 can (15 1/2 ounces) chickpeas, drained and rinsed

6 tablespoons freshly grated Parmesan cheese

1 Heat oil in a large nonstick Dutch oven or soup pot over medium-high heat. Add onions, carrots, and celery and sauté 5 minutes or until soft. Add broth, tomatoes, basil, and oregano and bring to boil. Reduce heat and simmer, partially covered, 10 minutes

2 Stir kidney beans, cannellini beans, and chickpeas into pot and simmer 10 minutes. Remove from heat.

3 Using a handheld blender, coarsely puree about a quarter of soup (or transfer 2 cups to a food processor or blender, cover, puree coarsely, and return to pot). Garnish each 2-cup serving with 1 tablespoon Parmesan.

THREE-BEAN BEEF SOUP

The three very different beans—green beans, red kidney beans, and lima beans—each add a separate taste and texture to this soup.

SERVES 8

1 pound ground beef

1 can (28 ounces) tomatoes, undrained, cut up

1 can (10 1/2 ounces) beef consommé

1/2 cup pearl barley

1/4 cup chopped onion

1 teaspoon salt

1/4 teaspoon dried marjoram

1/4 teaspoon dried thyme

1 can (16 ounces) cut green beans or Italian-style green beans, drained

1 can (16 ounces) dark red kidney beans, drained and rinsed

1 can (16 ounces) lima beans, drained and rinsed

Grated Parmesan or Romano cheese *(optional)*

1 In a large soup pot over medium heat, cook beef until browned. Drain off fat. Add 1 cup water, tomatoes, consommé, barley, onion, salt, marjoram, and thyme. Bring to boil, then reduce heat and simmer, covered, 50 minutes.

2 Stir in green beans, kidney beans, and lima beans and bring to boil. Reduce heat and simmer, covered, 10 minutes. Garnish each serving with cheese, if desired.

PRAIRIE BEAN SOUP

Sausage and spicy seasonings make this three-bean soup lively, and brown sugar and vinegar give it a sweet-sour taste.

SERVES 12

1 pound ground beef

1 pound bulk pork sausage

2 large onions, chopped

1/2 cup packed brown sugar

1 tablespoon ground cumin

1/2 teaspoon garlic powder

1 tablespoon prepared mustard

1 cup ketchup

1/3 cup vinegar

4 cups cooked and drained pinto beans

2 cans (15 ounces each) chili beans

2 cans (16 ounces each) pork and beans

1 tablespoon salt

1 1/2 teaspoons black pepper

1 In a large Dutch oven or soup pot over medium heat, cook beef, sausage, and onions until meat is browned and onions are tender. Drain off fat.

2 Stir in 1/2 cup water, sugar, cumin, garlic powder, mustard, ketchup, vinegar, and mix well. Stir in beans, salt, and pepper. Bring to boil, then reduce heat and simmer, covered, 2 hours.

TACO SOUP

Three kinds of beans and hominy make this tasty soup a popular meal for those with healthy appetites.

SERVES 10

2 pounds lean ground beef

1 small onion, chopped

3 cans (4 ounces each) chopped green chiles

1 teaspoon salt

1 teaspoon black pepper

1 can (15-16 ounces) pinto beans, drained and rinsed

1 can (16 ounces) lima beans, drained and rinsed

1 can (15-16 ounces) red kidney beans, drained and rinsed

1 package (1 1/4 ounces) taco seasoning

1 package (1 ounce) ranch dressing mix

1 can (14 1/2 ounces) hominy, drained

3 cans (14 1/2 ounces each) stewed tomatoes

Shredded cheddar cheese *(optional)*

Tortilla chips *(optional)*

1 In a large Dutch oven or soup pot over medium heat, cook beef and onion until browned. Drain off fat. Add 1 1/2 cups water, chiles, salt, pepper, pinto beans, lima beans, kidney beans, taco seasoning, dressing mix, hominy, and tomatoes. Bring to boil, then reduce heat and simmer, covered, 30 minutes.

2 Top with cheese and serve with chips, if desired.

TUSCAN WHITE BEAN SOUP

This simple, wholesome soup is typical of the cooking of Tuscany. It can be a starter or make a meal.

SERVES 4

1 tablespoon extra-virgin olive oil

2 bacon slices, chopped

1 onion, chopped

2 garlic cloves, chopped

1 red bell pepper, cored, seeded, and chopped

3 1/2 ounces dry cannellini beans, soaked at least 8 hours

5 cups chicken or vegetable stock

2 sprigs fresh rosemary or 1 teaspoon dried rosemary

3 1/2 ounces Savoy cabbage, finely shredded

Salt and black pepper

1 Heat oil in a large saucepan over medium heat. Add bacon and onion and sauté 5 minutes or until onion is softened and bacon is crisp. Add garlic and bell pepper and sauté 2 minutes.

2 Drain beans and rinse under cold running water. Add beans and stock to pan, bring to boil, and boil rapidly 10 minutes. Reduce heat and simmer, skimming off any foam. Add rosemary and simmer, partially covered, 45 minutes or until beans are tender.

3 Using a slotted spoon, transfer 3 tablespoons beans to a bowl, then mash with a fork.

4 Add cabbage to pan and simmer 5 minutes. Remove any rosemary twigs, then stir in mashed beans until slightly thickened. Season to taste with salt and black pepper.

TUSCAN VEGETABLE SOUP

This is a classic Italian soup, tasty and filling at any time of year.

SERVES 6

1 tablespoon olive oil

4 ounces thick-sliced bacon,
    cut into 1/2-inch dice

1 large red onion, diced

5 garlic cloves, minced

2 large carrots, peeled, halved lengthwise,
    and thinly sliced

1 can (28 ounces) tomatoes, drained
    and chopped

5 cups vegetable stock or canned
    low-sodium vegetable broth

1 pound new potatoes,
    peeled and cut into 1/2-inch dice

2 1/2 cups cooked drained dry cannellini
    beans or 1 can (19 ounces)
    cannellini beans, drained and rinsed

3/4 teaspoon salt

1/2 teaspoon dried sage, crumbled

1/2 teaspoon dried thyme, crumbled

4 cups shredded Savoy cabbage

4 cups tightly packed trimmed, rinsed,
    and torn spinach

3 slices Italian bread, toasted and torn
    into 1-inch chunks

1 Heat oil 1 minute in a 5-quart Dutch oven or soup pot over medium heat. Add bacon and cook, stirring frequently, until lightly crisp, 4 to 6 minutes. Remove all but 2 tablespoons drippings, add onion and garlic, and sauté 5 minutes or until softened. Add carrots and sauté 5 minutes or until softened.

2 Increase heat to high and add tomatoes, stock, potatoes, beans, salt, sage, and thyme. Bring to boil, then reduce heat and simmer, covered, 12 minutes or until potatoes are firm-tender.

3 Add cabbage and simmer, covered, 12 minutes or until tender. Add spinach and bread and cook, uncovered, 1 minute or until spinach wilts.

WHITE BEAN AND PASTA SOUP WITH BASIL

Small shell pasta works very well in this Italian-influenced soup. Try to find fresh basil for the garnish.

SERVES 9

2 cups dry white kidney beans

1 tablespoon olive or canola oil

2 carrots, sliced

4 garlic cloves, coarsely chopped

8 cups vegetable stock

1 tablespoon chopped fresh basil or
    1 teaspoon dried basil

1 can (16 ounces) sliced plum tomatoes

1 zucchini, sliced

1/2 cup small pasta shapes or broken spaghetti

1 tablespoon grated Parmesan cheese

1/8 teaspoon black pepper

1 teaspoon chopped fresh basil or parsley

1 Place beans in a large saucepan with enough water to cover generously. Bring to boil and cook 2 minutes, then remove from heat and let stand, covered, at least 1 hour or overnight.

2 Drain beans, rinse under cold water, and drain again.

3 Heat oil in a 4-quart saucepan over medium heat. Add carrots, garlic, and 2 tablespoons stock and sauté 5 minutes or until softened but not browned.

4 Add basil and sauté 2 minutes. Add beans and remaining stock and bring to boil. Reduce heat, partially cover, and simmer, stirring occasionally, 1 hour 20 minutes or until beans and vegetables are very tender.

5 Add tomatoes, zucchini, and pasta and return to boil. Reduce heat and simmer, partially covered, 10 minutes or until zucchini and pasta are tender.

6 Add cheese and season to taste with pepper. Garnish with basil.

FRENCH WHITE BEAN SOUP

You can serve this hearty vegetable soup either with or without the robust garlic and cheese pesto.

SERVES 4

Pesto:

1 garlic clove, minced

1 tablespoon minced fresh basil or
    1 teaspoon dried basil, crumbled

1 tablespoon minced fresh parsley

1 tablespoon grated Parmesan cheese

1 tablespoon olive oil

Soup:

2 teaspoons olive oil

1 medium yellow onion, finely chopped

8 ounces fennel or celery, finely chopped

2 medium carrots, peeled and diced

1/8 teaspoon salt

1/8 teaspoon black pepper

1 can (14 1/2 ounces) low-sodium tomatoes, undrained, pureed

2 1/2 cups chicken stock

1/4 teaspoon dried basil, crumbled

1/4 teaspoon fennel seed, crushed

1 can (19 ounces) cannellini beans, drained and rinsed

1 For pesto, combine garlic, basil, parsley, cheese, and oil in a small bowl. Using the back of a spoon, mash into a paste.

2 For soup, heat oil in a large saucepan over medium heat. Add onion, fennel, carrots, salt, and pepper and sauté 5 minutes. Add tomatoes, stock, basil, and fennel seed and bring to boil. Reduce heat and simmer, covered, 10 minutes. Add beans and simmer 3 minutes or until heated through. Garnish each serving with pesto.

WHITE BEAN SOUP WITH SPINACH

This is a healthy, low-fat version of a classic European soup that tastes rich and satisfying. (Photograph on page 18)

SERVES 4

1 tablespoon vegetable oil

4 ounces mild or hot Italian-style turkey
    sausage, casings removed

2 garlic cloves, minced

1 teaspoon dried sage, crumbled

1 can (19 ounces) cannellini beans,
    drained and rinsed

1 can (14 1/2 ounces) fat-free low-sodium
    chicken broth

4 cups torn spinach or 1/2 package (10 ounces)
    chopped frozen spinach

1/4 teaspoon salt

1/8 teaspoon black pepper

2 tablespoons finely chopped fresh parsley

1 tablespoon fresh lemon juice

1/4 cup grated Parmesan cheese

1 Heat oil in large nonstick saucepan over medium heat. Add sausage and cook, stirring to break up clumps, 3 minutes or until browned. Transfer to paper towels.

2 Add garlic and sage to pan and sauté 30 seconds. Add 1 1/2 cups water, beans, and broth and bring to boil, then reduce heat and simmer, uncovered, 10 minutes.

3 Transfer half of beans and a few spoonfuls of broth to a food processor or blender, cover, and puree until smooth. Return to pan, add sausage, spinach, salt, and pepper, and simmer, uncovered, 10 minutes. Stir in parsley and lemon juice. Garnish with cheese.

TUSCAN SOUP WITH ESCAROLE

Adding good, tart greens to bland bean soup is an old Tuscan cooking trick.

SERVES 4

1 tablespoon olive oil

1 small onion, chopped

1 small carrot, sliced

2 cans (14 1/2 ounces each) chicken broth

3/4 teaspoon salt

1/4 teaspoon black pepper

1 can (16 ounces) white kidney or great
    Northern beans, drained and rinsed

2/3 cup small spiral pasta

3 cups thinly sliced fresh escarole or spinach

1 Heat oil in a 2-quart saucepan over medium-high heat. Add onion and carrot and sauté 5 minutes or until onion is golden.

2 Add 1 cup water, broth, salt, and pepper and bring to boil. Stir in beans and pasta and return to boil. Reduce heat, cover, and simmer, stirring occasionally, 15 minutes or until pasta and vegetables are tender. Add escarole and cook until heated through.

TWO-BEAN GARDEN VEGETABLE SOUP

This is a perfect vegetarian soup, with beans for protein and lots of vegetables for vitamins and minerals.

SERVES 8

3 medium all-purpose potatoes,
    peeled and diced

3 medium carrots, peeled and sliced

1 large yellow onion, coarsely chopped

1 teaspoon salt

2 cups cooked dry great Northern beans or
    1 can (16 ounces) cannellini beans,
    drained and rinsed

8 ounces green beans, cut into 1/2-inch lengths

2 medium zucchini, diced

2 large tomatoes, cored, peeled, seeded,
and diced, or 2 cans (16 ounces each)
tomatoes, undrained, chopped

1 cup 1-inch pieces thin spaghetti

3 garlic cloves, minced

1/2 cup minced fresh basil or parsley

1/4 teaspoon black pepper

1 1/4 cups grated Parmesan cheese

1/4 cup extra-virgin olive oil

Salt and black pepper

1 In a 5-quart Dutch oven or soup pot over medium-high heat, bring 12 cups water, potatoes, carrots, onion, and salt to boil. Reduce heat to low, partially cover, and cook until potatoes are tender, about 20 minutes.

2 Add great Northern beans, green beans, zucchini, tomatoes, and spaghetti. Cover and simmer, stirring occasionally, 10 minutes. Remove from heat.

3 Stir in garlic, basil, and pepper. Sprinkle with 1/2 cup cheese, drizzle with oil, and season to taste with salt and pepper. Pass remaining cheese.

PEASANT BEAN SOUP

This is a basic soup in which the beans absorb many melded vegetable and herb flavors to good effect.

SERVES 8

1 pound dry great Northern beans,
sorted and rinsed

3 carrots, sliced

3 celery stalks, sliced

2 medium onions, chopped

1 garlic clove, minced

1 can (16 ounces) stewed tomatoes,
cut up

1-2 bay leaves

2 tablespoons olive oil

Salt and black pepper

1 Soak beans overnight in 8 cups water; drain. Add 2 cups fresh water and bring to boil, then reduce heat and simmer, covered, 30 minutes.

2 Add carrots, celery, onions, garlic, tomatoes, bay leaves, and oil and simmer 1 hour or until beans are tender. Remove bay leaves and season to taste with salt and pepper.

SHAKER BEAN SOUP

This is a classic and very tasty bean soup.

SERVES 12

1 pound dry great Northern beans,
rinsed and sorted

1 meaty hambone or 2 smoked ham hocks

1 large onion, chopped

3 celery stalks, diced

2 carrots, shredded

1/4 teaspoon salt

1/2 teaspoon black pepper

1/2 teaspoon dried thyme

1 can (28 ounces) crushed tomatoes in puree

2 tablespoons brown sugar

1 1/2 cups finely shredded fresh spinach leaves

1 In a Dutch oven or soup pot, bring beans and enough water to cover to boil. Cook 2 minutes, then remove from heat and let stand 1 hour; drain.

2 Add 12 cups water, hambone, and beans to pot and bring to boil. Reduce heat and simmer, covered, 1 1/2 hours or until meat easily falls from bone. Transfer bone to a plate.

3 When cool enough to handle, remove meat from bone. Add ham, onion, celery, carrots, salt, pepper, and thyme to pot and bring to boil. Reduce heat and simmer, covered, 1 hour or until beans are tender. Add tomatoes and brown sugar and cook 10 minutes. Add spinach just before serving.

WHITE BEAN AND CABBAGE SOUP

SERVES 4

1 teaspoon dried thyme, crumbled

4 whole cloves

12 parsley sprigs

1 bay leaf, crumbled

1 cup dry navy or pea beans, sorted, soaked, and drained

2 smoked ham hocks (about 1 pound)

3 tablespoons olive or vegetable oil

1 large yellow onion, finely chopped

2 medium carrots or 2 small parsnips, peeled and cut into 1/4-inch-thick slices

1 medium celery stalk, cut into 1/4-inch-thick slices

4 garlic cloves, minced

1 large all-purpose potato or white turnip, peeled and cut into 1-inch cubes

1/2 small head cabbage, shredded

1/4 teaspoon salt

1/8 teaspoon black pepper

1/4 cup minced fresh parsley

1/4 cup grated Parmesan cheese (optional)

1 Tie thyme, cloves, parsley, and bay leaf into a cheesecloth bag or bouquet garni. In a large saucepan over medium-high heat, bring beans, ham, 7 cups water, and bouquet garni to boil. Reduce heat and simmer, covered, 20 minutes.

2 Meanwhile, heat oil in a 10-inch skillet over medium heat. Add onion, carrots, celery, and garlic and sauté 5 minutes or until onion is softened.

3 Stir vegetables, potato, cabbage, salt, and pepper into pan and simmer, covered, 20 minutes or until beans and potato are tender. Remove bouquet garni. Sprinkle each serving with parsley and serve with cheese, if desired.

If you don't have time to soak beans overnight, use the quick method: Place the beans in a saucepan and add enough water to cover by 3 inches. Boil 2 minutes, remove from heat, cover, and let stand 1 hour, then drain.

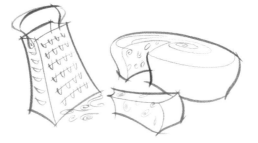

KIELBASA-BEAN SOUP

Here is an easy soup to make as a meal.

SERVES 6

1 medium all-purpose potato,
    peeled and diced
2 carrots, peeled and sliced
1 medium onion, chopped
1/3 cup chopped celery
8 ounces smoked kielbasa, thinly sliced
1 can (11 1/2 ounces) condensed bean
    with bacon soup
Chopped fresh parsley *(optional)*

1 In a large saucepan over medium-high heat, bring 2 cups water, potato, carrots, onion, and celery to boil. Reduce heat and simmer, covered, 10 minutes or until tender.

2 Add kielbasa and soup and cook until heated through. Garnish with parsley, if desired.

WHITE BEAN AND PASTA SOUP

This hearty soup is a real stick-to-your-ribs meal, thanks to the mix of sausage, beans, and pasta.

SERVES 12

1 1/2 cups dry great Northern beans,
    sorted and rinsed
12 ounces Italian sausage links,
    casings removed
1 large onion, chopped
1 large carrot, chopped
3 garlic cloves, minced
6 cups chicken stock
2 tablespoons dried currants
1 teaspoon dried basil
1 can (14 1/2 ounces) diced
    tomatoes, undrained
1 cup small shell pasta
Grated Parmesan cheese

1 Place beans in a Dutch oven or soup pot and add enough water to cover by 2 inches. Bring to boil and cook 2 minutes, then remove from heat and let stand, covered, 1 hour; drain.

2 Add sausage, onion, carrot, and garlic to pot and cook over medium heat until sausage is no longer pink. Drain off fat. Add 3 cups water, stock, currants, basil, and beans and bring to boil. Reduce heat, cover, and simmer, stirring occasionally, 1 1/2 hours or until beans are tender.

3 Add tomatoes and pasta and bring to boil. Reduce heat and simmer, covered, 15 minutes or until pasta is tender. Serve with cheese.

SPEEDY BEAN SOUP

Nothing could be easier than putting this hearty bean soup together and heating it up, to plaudits from family and friends.

SERVES 12

2 cans (11 1/2 ounces each) condensed
    bean with bacon soup
3 cans (15 1/2 ounces each) great Northern
    or navy beans, undrained
1 can (15 ounces) jalapeño pinto
    beans, undrained
1 medium onion, finely chopped
1 teaspoon salt
1/2 teaspoon garlic powder
1/4 teaspoon black pepper

1 In a large Dutch oven or soup kettle, combine 2 cups water, soup, great Northern beans, pinto beans, onion, salt, garlic powder, and pepper. Bring to boil, then reduce heat and simmer, covered, 20 minutes.

WHITE BEAN SOUP
WITH CARROTS

It's always a good idea to cook with dry beans. They have better flavor and texture and much less sodium than canned.

SERVES 6

2 cups dry white beans, such as
    great Northern or navy beans,
    sorted and rinsed
1 tablespoon olive oil
1 large onion, sliced
6 garlic cloves, coarsely chopped
6 cups vegetable stock
2 large carrots, sliced
1 tablespoon chopped fresh sage or
    1/2 teaspoon dried sage, crumbled
1/8 teaspoon salt
1/8 teaspoon black pepper

1 In a large saucepan, bring beans and enough water to cover to boil. Cook 2 minutes, then remove from heat and let stand, covered, at least 1 hour or overnight. Drain, rinse thoroughly under cold water, and drain again.

2 Heat oil in a 4-quart saucepan over medium heat. Add onion, garlic, and 2 tablespoons stock and sauté 5 minutes or until softened but not browned. Add carrots and sage and sauté 2 minutes. Add beans and remaining stock and bring to boil. Reduce heat, partially cover, and simmer, stirring occasionally, 1 1/2 hours or until beans are tender. Remove from heat.

3 Transfer 1 1/2 cups beans and vegetables to a blender or food processor, cover, and puree until smooth. Add 1/2 cup broth and process until combined. Return puree to pan and add salt and pepper. Return to heat and simmer 3 minutes.

NAVY BEAN SOUP

This is a great soup to make for a hungry crowd.

SERVES 10

3 cups (1 1/2 pounds) dry navy beans,
    sorted and rinsed
1 can (16 ounces) tomatoes,
    undrained, chopped
1 large onion, chopped
1 meaty ham hock or 1 cup diced cooked ham
2 cups chicken stock
Salt and black pepper to taste
Chopped fresh parsley

1 Place beans in a large bowl with enough cold water to cover and let stand overnight. Drain and place in a large soup pot or Dutch oven, then add 2 1/2 cups water, tomatoes, onion, ham, stock, salt, and pepper. Bring to boil, then reduce heat and simmer, covered, 1 1/2 hours, adding more water if necessary. Transfer ham hock to a plate.

2 When ham hock is cool enough to handle, remove meat, add to pot, and cook until heated through. (For thicker soup, puree beans in a food processor or blender and return to pot before adding meat.) Garnish with parsley.

NAVY BEAN-SQUASH SOUP

On a chilly day, this ham, bean, and squash combination is a savory way to warm up.

SERVES 12

1 pound dry navy beans, sorted and rinsed
2 cans (14 1/2 ounces each) chicken broth
1 meaty hambone
2 1/4 pounds butternut squash, peeled,
    seeded, and cut into cubes
1 large onion, chopped
1/2 teaspoon salt
1/2 teaspoon black pepper

1 Place beans in a Dutch oven or soup pot and add enough water to cover by 2 inches. Bring to boil and cook 2 minutes, then remove from heat and let stand, covered, 1 hour. Drain and return beans to pot.

2 Add 2 cups water, broth, hambone, squash, onion, salt, and pepper. Bring to boil, then reduce heat and simmer, covered, 1 1/2 hours or until beans are tender. Transfer hambone to a plate.

3 Mash beans and vegetables, leaving some chunks, if desired. When hambone is cool enough to handle, remove meat and cut into chunks. Add to pot and cook until heated through.

COUNTRY BEAN SOUP

Serve this soup the old-fashioned way—over a thick slice of cornbread.

SERVES 4

1 cup dry navy, great Northern,
   or lima beans, sorted and rinsed
5 cups canned low-sodium chicken broth
2 cups shredded cabbage
2 medium carrots, shredded
1 medium yellow onion, chopped
3 garlic cloves, minced
3 bay leaves
2 teaspoons dried oregano
1 teaspoon dried sage
1/2 teaspoon salt
1/2 teaspoon black pepper
1/4 cup minced fresh parsley

1 In a large saucepan, combine beans and 16 cups water and bring to boil. Reduce heat and simmer, uncovered, 2 minutes, then remove from heat and let stand, covered, 1 hour. Drain beans and rinse thoroughly.

2 Return beans to pan and add broth, cabbage, carrots, onion, garlic, bay leaves, oregano, sage, salt, and pepper. Bring to boil, then reduce heat and simmer, covered, 2 hours or until beans are tender. Remove bay leaves. Using a fork, slightly mash some of beans against side of pan to thicken soup. Stir in parsley.

U.S. SENATE BEAN SOUP

A resolution was passed that requires bean soup to be served every day in the U.S. Senate Dining Room. Several recipes exist, but we like this one best.

SERVES 6

1 pound dry navy or great Northern
   beans, sorted, rinsed, soaked
   overnight, and drained
2 meaty smoked ham hocks
3 cups chopped onions
2 cups chopped celery
1 cup mashed potatoes
3 garlic cloves, minced
1/2 teaspoon black pepper
1/2 cup chopped fresh parsley

1 In an 8-quart soup pot over high heat, bring 12 cups cold water, beans, and ham hocks to boil. Reduce heat, cover, and simmer, stirring occasionally and skimming off foam, 1 hour.

2 Stir in onions, celery, potatoes, and garlic and bring to boil. Reduce heat, cover, and simmer, stirring occasionally, 1 hour or until vegetables are tender. Season to taste with pepper.

3 Using a slotted spoon, transfer ham hocks to a cutting board. When cool enough to handle, remove meat from bones and cut into bite-size pieces. Return to pot and add parsley.

BACON-BEAN SOUP

Hearty and flavorful, this soup will please everyone.

SERVES 4

4 bacon slices
3/4 cup chopped onion
3/4 cup chopped celery
1/8 teaspoon garlic powder
1 can (16 ounces) refried beans
1/4 cup salsa
1 can (14 1/2 ounces) chicken broth
1 tablespoon chopped fresh parsley
Hot red pepper sauce *(optional)*
Shredded cheddar cheese
Tortilla chips

1 In a medium saucepan over medium heat, cook bacon until crisp, then transfer to paper towels to drain. Crumble and set aside.

2 Add onion and celery to pan and sauté briefly in drippings, then sprinkle with garlic powder. Reduce heat and simmer, covered, 5 minutes or until tender.

3 Add beans, salsa, broth, parsley, and bacon and bring to boil. Reduce heat and simmer, uncovered, 10 minutes. Season to taste with red pepper sauce, if desired. Garnish each serving with cheese and serve with tortilla chips.

LIMA BEAN SOUP

Easy, quick, and filling, this soup was made for busy-day lunches.

SERVES 4

4 cups chicken stock
1 medium onion, chopped
2 bratwurst or other mild cooked
    sausage, sliced

1 can (16 ounces) lima beans,
    drained and rinsed
1 garlic clove, crushed

1 In a large saucepan, bring stock to boil. Add onion, sausage, lima beans, and garlic. Reduce heat and simmer, uncovered, 5 minutes or until onion is tender and sausage is heated through. Season to taste with salt and pepper.

BEAN AND BEEF CUBE SOUP

Grandma knew how to tell when beans were done. She'd press one between her fingers, and if it was soft all the way to the center, it was cooked.

SERVES 8

1 1/2 cups dry lima beans,
    sorted and rinsed
1 tablespoon vegetable oil
12 ounces boneless beef chuck roast,
    trimmed and cut into 3/4-inch cubes
1 large yellow onion, chopped
2 garlic cloves, minced
3 1/2 cups low-sodium beef broth
 1 3/4 cups dry red wine or low-sodium
    beef broth
2 bay leaves
1/2 teaspoon salt
1/2 teaspoon black pepper
3 cups baby carrots
2 teaspoons dried marjoram
2 teaspoons dried oregano
1 medium green bell pepper, cored,
    seeded, and chopped

1 In a soup pot or 6-quart Dutch oven, combine beans with 6 cups water and bring to boil. Reduce heat and simmer, uncovered, 2 minutes, then remove from heat and let stand, covered, 1 hour. Drain beans and rinse thoroughly.

2 Heat oil in a large skillet over medium heat. Add half of beef and sauté 5 minutes or until browned. Transfer to a plate. Add remaining beef, onion, and garlic and sauté 5 minutes or until beef is browned and onion is tender.

3 Return beans to pot and add 2 cups water. Stir in beef mixture, reserved beef, broth, wine, bay leaves, salt, and black pepper. Bring to boil, then reduce heat and simmer, covered, 40 minutes. Add carrots, marjoram, and oregano and simmer, covered, 15 minutes or until beans are almost tender. Add bell pepper and simmer 5 minutes. Remove bay leaves before serving.

GREEN BEAN SOUP

A trio of beans—green, lima, and flageolet—add their individual flavors to this delicate pale green soup.

SERVES 4 TO 6

4 cups vegetable stock

2 tablespoons olive oil

1 medium onion, chopped

1 large garlic clove, minced

8 ounces thin green beans,
    cut into 1-inch pieces

12 ounces frozen lima beans

15 ounces canned flageolet beans,
    undrained

Salt and black pepper

1 small bunch fresh chives, chopped

1 In a medium saucepan over medium heat, bring stock to boil. Heat oil in a large saucepan over medium heat. Add onion and garlic and sauté 2 to 3 minutes.

2 Add green beans and lima beans and sauté 3 minutes. Add stock and cook 5 minutes, then reduce heat and simmer, covered, 10 minutes.

3 Remove from heat, add flageolet beans, and stir well. Transfer half of soup to a blender or food processor, cover, and puree until smooth. Return to pan and cook until heated through. Season with salt and pepper. Garnish with chives.

MEXICAN BEAN-BARLEY SOUP

Wonderfully warming, this lovely vegetarian soup is always a hit after a chilly day outdoors.

SERVES 7

2 tablespoons vegetable oil

2 medium onions, chopped

3 garlic cloves, minced

1 medium turnip, peeled and diced

1 medium carrot, diced

2 tablespoons finely chopped seeded and
    deveined jalapeño pepper (wear gloves
    when handling; they burn)

1 1/2 teaspoons ground cumin

1/2 teaspoon ground coriander

3 cans (14 1/2 ounces each) vegetable broth

2 cups cooked barley

1 can (15 ounces) pinto beans,
    drained and rinsed

2 teaspoons fresh lemon juice

1 Heat oil in a large saucepan over medium heat. Add onions and garlic and sauté 3 minutes or until tender. Add turnip, carrot, and jalapeño and sauté until tender. Add cumin and coriander and cook, stirring, 2 minutes.

2 Add broth and bring to boil, then reduce heat and simmer, covered, 20 minutes. Add barley, beans, and lemon juice and simmer, uncovered, 10 minutes or until slightly thickened.

PINTO BEAN AND HAM SOUP

Hungarian csipetke, featured in this soup, are considered the missing link between noodles and dumplings.

SERVES 16

Soup:

1 pound dry pinto beans,
    sorted and rinsed

6 large carrots, cut into 1/2-inch-thick
    slices

1 large onion, chopped

6 celery stalks, cut diagonally into
    1/2-inch-thick slices

1 large garlic clove

3 1/2-4 pounds ham hocks

2 teaspoons paprika

Csipetke:

1 cup all-purpose flour

1/2 teaspoon salt

1 egg

1 tablespoon vegetable oil

1 For soup, place beans in a large soup pot with enough water to cover and let stand overnight; drain.

2 In an 8-quart soup pot, combine beans, carrots, onion, celery, garlic, ham hocks, paprika, and enough water to cover by 2 inches. Bring to boil, then reduce heat and simmer, partially covered, 2 1/2 hours or until beans are tender, adding more water if needed. Transfer ham hocks to a plate.

3 For *csipetke,* mix flour, salt, egg, and oil into a stiff dough in a medium bowl. Let stand 30 minutes and divide into 4 pieces. Flatten each piece and pinch off cherry-pit-size pieces, then roll each between your fingers and drop into soup, using all dough. Simmer, covered, 30 minutes. When ham hocks are cool enough to handle, remove meat from bones, cut into bite-size pieces, and stir into pot.

PORTUGUESE KALE SOUP WITH BEANS

Vitamin-rich kale tastes great teamed with sausage, potatoes, and kidney beans. If you don't have kale, you can substitute spinach or chard. (Photograph on page 9)

SERVES 6

4 ounces spicy turkey sausage
    or Italian sausage

1 1/2 ounces sliced pepperoni, slivered

1 large yellow onion, quartered
    and thinly sliced

1 medium celery stalk, coarsely chopped

4 cups chicken stock combined with
    4 cups water

8 ounces kale, thick stems removed and leaves
    sliced, or 2 packages (10 ounces each)
    frozen kale, thawed and squeezed dry

1/2 teaspoon minced garlic

12 ounces red potatoes, halved and sliced

1/2 teaspoon hot red pepper sauce

1/4 teaspoon salt

1 1/2 cups cooked red kidney beans
    or cannellini beans

1 Remove casings from sausage and crumble meat. In a soup pot or 5-quart Dutch oven over medium-low heat, cook sausage, stirring, 4 minutes. Add pepperoni and cook 2 minutes or until fat is rendered. Transfer to paper towels to drain. Drain off all but 1 teaspoon drippings from pot.

2 Add onion and celery to pot. Reduce heat, cover, and cook, stirring occasionally, 8 minutes or until softened. Return meat to pot and add stock, kale, and garlic. Bring to boil, then reduce heat and simmer, covered, 10 minutes.

3 Stir in potatoes, red pepper sauce, and salt and simmer, covered, 20 minutes or until potatoes and kale are tender. Add beans and cook just until heated through.

TUSCAN RED BEAN SOUP

You can bring out the best flavor in this soup by using fresh oregano and basil.

SERVES 6 TO 8

2 cups dry red kidney beans, sorted and rinsed

1 tablespoon olive or canola oil

2 leeks or small onions, rinsed and coarsely chopped

2 celery stalks, coarsely chopped

2 carrots, coarsely chopped

6 cups vegetable stock

1 can (28 ounces) crushed tomatoes

1/4 teaspoon dried oregano

1/4 teaspoon dried basil

1 bay leaf

1 cup shredded cabbage

4 ounces green beans, cut crosswise into 1-inch pieces

1/8 teaspoon salt

1/8 teaspoon black pepper

2 tablespoons grated Parmesan cheese

1 In a large saucepan, bring beans and enough water to cover generously to boil. Cook 2 minutes, then remove from heat and let stand, covered, at least 1 hour or overnight.

2 Drain beans, rinse under cold water, and drain again.

3 Heat oil in a 4-quart saucepan over medium heat. Add leeks, celery, and carrots and sauté 5 minutes or until softened but not browned.

4 Add stock, tomatoes, oregano, basil, bay leaf, and beans. Bring to boil and cook 10 minutes, then reduce heat, partially cover, and simmer, stirring occasionally, 45 minutes or until tender.

5 Add cabbage and green beans and simmer 10 minutes or until tender. Remove bay leaf.

6 Add salt and pepper and sprinkle with cheese.

ITALIAN BEAN SOUP WITH PASTA AND BASIL

You can make this soup with kidney beans, chickpeas, or cannellini beans and any small or medium pasta.

SERVES 6

1 tablespoon olive oil

1 medium yellow onion, finely chopped

1 medium celery stalk, finely chopped

1 small carrot, peeled and finely chopped

2 garlic cloves, minced

1/4 teaspoon salt

1/8 teaspoon black pepper

1 can (28 ounces) crushed tomatoes

4 cups chicken stock

1/2 teaspoon dried thyme, crumbled

1/2 teaspoon dried basil, crumbled

2/3 cup small shells, elbow macaroni, or wagon wheel pasta

1 can (15 1/2 ounces) red kidney beans, cannellini beans, or chickpeas, drained and rinsed

1/4 cup minced fresh basil or parsley

1 Heat oil in a large heavy saucepan over medium-low heat. Add onion, celery, carrot, garlic, salt, and pepper and sauté 5 minutes. Increase heat to medium and stir in tomatoes, stock, thyme, and basil. Bring to boil, then reduce heat and simmer, covered, 15 minutes.

2 Return to boil, add pasta, and cook, stirring occasionally, 5 minutes. Add beans and cook 5 minutes or until pasta is tender and beans are heated through. Stir in basil.

MEXICAN HOMINY-BEAN SOUP

This is a delicious, filling soup that easily handles a hungry crowd. Serve it with cornbread.

SERVES 10

2 pounds ground beef

1 medium onion, chopped

3 cans (14 1/2 ounces each) diced tomatoes, undrained

2 cans (15 1/2 ounces each) hominy, drained

2 cans (15 ounces each) ranch-style or chili beans

1 can (16 ounces) kidney beans, drained and rinsed

1 can (4 ounces) chopped green chiles

2 envelopes taco seasoning

1 envelope original ranch dressing mix

2 tablespoons brown sugar

1/4 teaspoon cayenne pepper

Shredded cheddar cheese

Sour cream

1 In a Dutch oven or soup pot over medium heat, cook beef and onion until beef is browned and onion is tender. Drain off fat.

2 Add 4 cups water, tomatoes, hominy, beans, chiles, taco seasoning, dressing mix, brown sugar, and cayenne. Bring to boil, then reduce heat and simmer, covered, 30 minutes. Garnish with cheese and sour cream.

QUICK CASSOULET

This French country stew traditionally requires some 20 ingredients and days to cook. Here's a simplified version for today's cook. (Photograph on page 24)

SERVES 4

4 skinless, boneless chicken thighs (3 ounces each)

4 garlic cloves, minced

1/2 teaspoon dried thyme

1/2 teaspoon salt

1/4 teaspoon black pepper

2 teaspoons olive oil

1 small onion, finely chopped

2 carrots, halved lengthwise and thinly sliced

1 cup canned low-sodium tomatoes, undrained, chopped

3 cups cooked cannellini beans

6 ounces kielbasa or other fully cooked garlic sausage, thinly sliced

3 tablespoons plain dry bread crumbs

1 In a large bowl, toss chicken with garlic, thyme, salt, and pepper. Cover and refrigerate at least 1 hour.

2 Heat oil in a small Dutch oven or flameproof baking dish over medium heat. Add chicken and cook 4 minutes or until lightly browned on both sides. Transfer to a plate.

3 Preheat oven to 400°F. Meanwhile, add onion and carrots to baking dish and sauté 7 minutes or until onion is softened. Add tomatoes, beans, and kielbasa. Bring to boil, reduce heat, and return chicken to baking dish. Cover and bake 20 minutes or until chicken is cooked through.

4 Sprinkle bread crumbs on top, drizzle with 3 tablespoons cooking liquid to moisten crumbs, and bake, uncovered, 20 minutes or until crumbs are golden.

CLASSIC CASSOULET

Cassoulet:

5 1/2 ounces dry cannellini beans,
    soaked at least 8 hours

1 tablespoon extra-virgin olive oil

10 ounces pork tenderloin,
    cut into 1-inch chunks

3 ounces dry-cured garlicky French
    or Italian sausage, diced

1 onion, chopped

2 celery stalks, chopped

2 carrots, thickly sliced

1 turnip, chopped

1 can (14 1/2 ounces) chopped
    tomatoes, undrained

5 ounces dry white wine

1 can (14 1/2 ounces) low-sodium
    chicken broth

1 tablespoon tomato paste

2 bay leaves

4 thyme sprigs

Salt and black pepper

Crust:

1 tablespoon extra-virgin olive oil

3 ounces fresh white bread crumbs

1 tablespoon chopped fresh parsley

1 For cassoulet, drain beans and rinse under cold running water. Place in a large saucepan, cover with cold water, and bring to boil over high heat. Boil rapidly 10 minutes, then reduce heat and simmer, partially covered, 50 minutes or until tender; drain.

2 Heat oil in a large flameproof baking dish over medium heat. Add pork and cook 5 minutes or until browned. Using a slotted spoon, transfer to a plate. Add sausage to baking dish and cook until browned, then transfer to plate.

3 Add onion, celery, carrots, and turnip to baking dish and sauté 5 minutes or until softened and lightly browned.

4 Return meat to baking dish and add beans, tomatoes, wine, broth, tomato paste, bay leaves, and thyme. Bring to boil, then reduce heat and simmer, covered, 1 1/2 hours or until tender. Remove bay leaves.

5 For crust, heat oil in a skillet over medium heat. Add bread crumbs and parsley and sauté 3 minutes or until crumbs are golden and dry. Season cassoulet to taste with salt and pepper and scatter bread-crumb mixture evenly over top.

A warming combination of beans, sausage, and vegetables makes this classic French country dish a real winner.

WHITE BEAN STEW WITH CHICKEN AND WINTER SQUASH

This hearty, satisfying stew is definitely a comfort during cold weather thanks to ample amounts of colorful, healthy squash.

SERVES 6

1 tablespoon olive oil

3 pounds chicken parts

1/4 teaspoon black pepper

1/2 teaspoon salt

1 medium onion, coarsely chopped

4 garlic cloves, peeled and halved

1 cup white wine

2 tablespoons tomato paste

2 bay leaves

1/2 teaspoon dried thyme, crumbled

1 can (15 1/2 ounces) cannellini beans, drained and rinsed

1 1/2 pounds butternut squash, seeded, peeled, and cut into 1 1/2-inch pieces

1 Preheat oven to 350°F.

2 Heat oil in a large flameproof baking dish over medium-high heat. Season chicken with pepper and 1/4 teaspoon salt. Working in batches if necessary, add chicken to baking dish in a single layer and cook until browned. Transfer to a plate.

3 Reduce heat to medium, add onion and garlic to baking dish, and sauté 3 minutes or until slightly softened. Add wine and stir to scrape up any browned bits. Stir in tomato paste, bay leaves, thyme, and remaining 1/4 teaspoon salt. Add chicken and bring to boil.

4 Cover and bake 20 minutes. Stir in beans and squash and bake, covered, 20 minutes or until tender. Remove bay leaves.

WHITE BEAN, YELLOW SQUASH, AND TOMATO STEW

This hearty main dish is equally good made with great Northern beans or smaller navy beans.

SERVES 4

1 tablespoon olive oil

2 large yellow onions, chopped

2 garlic cloves, minced

2 large celery stalks, finely chopped

1 can (16 ounces) low-sodium tomatoes, undrained, chopped

1 medium yellow squash, thinly sliced

1 cup fresh or frozen lima beans

1/2 cup dry white wine or low-sodium chicken broth

1 bay leaf

3/4 teaspoon dried thyme, crumbled

3/4 teaspoon dried basil, crumbled

3/4 teaspoon dried marjoram, crumbled

1/4 teaspoon black pepper

1/8 teaspoon cayenne pepper

2 cups cooked drained great Northern beans or navy beans

1 teaspoon fresh lemon juice

2 tablespoons minced fresh parsley

1 Heat oil in a heavy 6-quart Dutch oven over medium heat. Add onions, garlic, and celery and sauté 5 minutes or until onion and celery are softened.

2 Add tomatoes, squash, lima beans, wine, bay leaf, thyme, basil, marjoram, black pepper, and cayenne. Bring to boil, then reduce heat and simmer, uncovered, 10 minutes.

3 Stir in great Northern beans and simmer 5 minutes, then stir in lemon juice and parsley. Remove bay leaf before serving.

MICROWAVE PORTUGUESE BEAN STEW

For this lovely microwave stew, you can use canned red kidney beans, chickpeas, or black-eyed peas in place of the cannellini if you like.

SERVES 4

1 1/2 ounces pepperoni, finely chopped

1 large yellow onion, coarsely chopped

1 medium green bell pepper, cored, seeded, and coarsely chopped

1 garlic clove, minced

1 tablespoon olive oil

1 can (14 1/2 ounces) stewed tomatoes, undrained

2 medium carrots, peeled and thinly sliced on the diagonal

1 large all-purpose potato, peeled and cut into 1/2-inch cubes

1 bay leaf

1 can (15 1/2 ounces) cannellini beans, drained and rinsed

1 package (10 ounces) frozen chopped kale or spinach, thawed and squeezed dry

2/3 cup finely diced boiled or baked ham

1 tablespoon cornstarch combined with 2 tablespoons chicken broth or water

1/8 teaspoon black pepper

Pinch of cayenne pepper

1/3 cup minced fresh parsley

1 In an ungreased 2 1/2-quart microwavable baking dish with a lid, combine pepperoni, onion, bell pepper, garlic, and oil. Cover with wax paper and microwave on high 5 minutes or until onion is glassy, stirring midway.

2 Stir in tomatoes, carrots, potato, and bay leaf. Cover with lid and microwave 10 minutes or until potatoes and carrots are tender.

3 Stir in beans, kale, and ham, cover, and microwave on medium 10 minutes. Stir in cornstarch, black pepper, and cayenne. Cover and

microwave on high just until boiling, 2 1/2 to 3 minutes. Remove bay leaf and stir in parsley.

BEAN AND ROASTED VEGETABLE STEW

This easy, one-pot dish of pinto beans and root vegetables makes a nourishing and delectable winter main course.

SERVES 4

1 acorn squash (about 1 1/2 pounds)

1 pound new potatoes, scrubbed and cut into 1 1/2-inch chunks

8 ounces carrots, cut into 1 1/2-inch chunks

8 ounces parsnips, cut into 1 1/2-inch chunks

2 large zucchini, cut into 1 1/2-inch chunks

2 tablespoons extra-virgin olive oil

1 garlic clove, finely chopped

Salt and black pepper

8 large rosemary sprigs

2 cans (15 1/2 ounces each) pinto beans, drained and rinsed

1 cup apple cider

1 cup vegetable stock

1 Preheat oven to 400°F. Halve squash and remove seeds and fibers, then peel and cut flesh into 1 1/2-inch chunks. In a medium bowl, combine squash, potatoes, carrots, parsnips, and zucchini. Drizzle with oil and toss to coat evenly. Stir in garlic and season to taste with salt and pepper.

2 Lay 4 rosemary sprigs in a large roasting pan and spread vegetables on top in a single layer. Roast, turning once, 30 minutes or until vegetables are lightly browned.

3 Remove from oven and stir in beans, cider, and stock. Cover with foil and bake 20 minutes or until vegetables are tender. Remove cooked rosemary sprigs and garnish with remaining fresh rosemary.

KIDNEY BEAN, RICE, AND VEGETABLE STEW

Raisins, chiles, and fresh herbs add interesting flavors to a vegetarian stew of rice, vegetables, and beans topped with Parmesan cheese.

SERVES 4

3 tablespoons olive oil

1 medium onion, finely chopped

2 medium celery stalks, chopped

2 garlic cloves, chopped

1 medium red bell pepper, cored, seeded, and chopped

2/3 cup seedless raisins

Pinch of dried oregano

Pinch of dried crushed red chile

1 teaspoon ground cumin

1 can (19 ounces) chopped tomatoes

Salt and black pepper

8 ounces broccoli, cut into florets

1 can (19 ounces) kidney beans, drained and rinsed

3 cups cooked rice

4 ounces frozen whole-kernel corn

4 tablespoons chopped fresh cilantro

2 1/2 ounces Parmesan cheese, grated

2/3 cup Greek yogurt

1 Bring a saucepan of water to boil. Heat oil in a large ovenproof skillet over medium heat. Add onion, celery, and garlic and sauté 5 minutes.

2 Add bell pepper, raisins, oregano, dried chile, and cumin and sauté 2 minutes. Add 5 tablespoons water, tomatoes, and salt and black pepper to taste. Bring to boil, then reduce heat and simmer, covered, 5 minutes.

3 In a small saucepan, cover broccoli with boiling water. Return to boil and cook, covered, 2 minutes; drain.

4 Preheat broiler to medium. Add beans, rice, and corn to skillet. Return to boil, then reduce heat and simmer 2 minutes. Add broccoli and simmer 1 minute.

5 Remove from heat, stir in cilantro, and sprinkle with cheese. Broil 5 to 6 minutes or until cheese is melted. Serve with yogurt.

TACO STEW WITH THREE BEANS

This is a very quick recipe for a one-dish meal with a Mexican flavor.

SERVES 5

1 pound ground beef

1 envelope (1 1/4 ounces) taco seasoning

1 can (14 1/2 ounces) stewed tomatoes

1 can (15 ounces) kidney beans, undrained

1 1/4 cups (6 ounces) shredded cheddar cheese

Garnishes *(optional):*

Sliced scallions

Corn or tortilla chips

Sour cream

1 In a large Dutch oven over medium heat, cook beef until browned. Drain off fat.

2 Add 1 cup water, taco seasoning, tomatoes, and beans and bring just to boiling. Ladle into individual bowls and top with cheese. Garnish with scallions, corn chips, and sour cream, if desired.

SIMPLE BLACK BEAN SOUP

Despite its quick and easy preparation, this classic soup has a depth of flavor thanks to its mix of herbs and spices.

SERVES 4

2 teaspoons olive oil

1 large yellow onion, chopped

2 cloves garlic, minced

1/2 teaspoon dried oregano, crumbled

1/4 teaspoon dried thyme, crumbled

1/4 teaspoon ground cumin

1/8 teaspoon cayenne pepper

1 1/2 cups cooked and drained black beans

1 1/2 cups low-sodium chicken broth

4 teaspoons fresh coriander or parsley *(optional)*

1 In a large heavy saucepan, heat olive oil over medium heat, 1 minute. Add onion and garlic and cook, uncovered, 5 minutes or until onion is soft. Stir in oregano, thyme, cumin, and cayenne pepper, and cook, stirring 1 minute longer.

2 Meanwhile, place half of black beans in an electric blender or food processor and puree by whirling, 30 seconds. Add bean puree, remaining beans, and chicken broth to saucepan, reduce heat to low, and cook, uncovered, 15 minutes. Ladle soup into bowls and garnish with coriander, if desired.

BLACK BEAN SOUP WITH PORK

This is an easy-to-prepare soup that packs a wallop in the taste department.

SERVES 6

2 cups dry black beans, sorted and rinsed

1 medium onion, chopped

8 ounces lean cubed pork

2 teaspoons salt

3 garlic cloves, minced

1 teaspoon dried oregano

1 can (6 ounces) tomato paste

Garnishes *(optional)*:

Thinly sliced radishes

Finely shredded cabbage

Minced fresh chiles (wear gloves when handling; they burn)

Sour cream

1 In a Dutch oven, bring beans and 8 cups water to boil. Reduce heat and simmer, covered, 1 1/2 hours or until beans wrinkle and crack.

2 Add onion, pork, salt, garlic, and oregano and simmer, covered, 1 1/2 to 2 hours, or until beans and pork are tender. Stir in tomato paste and cook until heated through. Ladle into soup bowls and top each serving with radishes, cabbage, chiles, and sour cream, if desired.

BLACK BEAN SOUP WITH CHICKEN

This is a filling soup for a hungry group after sports or a long walk.

SERVES 10

1 tablespoon canola oil

3/4 cup chopped celery

1 medium onion, chopped

3 garlic cloves, minced

3 cans (14 1/2 ounces each) chicken broth

2 cans (15 ounces each) black beans, drained and rinsed

1 jar (16 ounces) salsa

1 cup cubed cooked chicken breast

1 cup cooked long-grain rice

1 tablespoon fresh lime juice

1 teaspoon ground cumin

1 Heat oil in a large saucepan over medium heat. Add celery, onion, and garlic and sauté until tender.

2 Stir in broth, beans, salsa, chicken, rice, lime juice, and cumin and cook until heated through.

BLACK BEAN SOUP WITH BEEF

Here's a rich, warming soup that cooks and becomes more flavorful while you are doing other things.

SERVES 10

1 pound ground beef

2 cans (14 1/2 ounces each) chicken broth

1 can (14 1/2 ounces) diced tomatoes, undrained

8 scallions, thinly sliced

3 medium carrots, thinly sliced

2 celery stalks, thinly sliced

2 garlic cloves, minced

1 tablespoon sugar

1 1/2 teaspoons dried basil

1/2 teaspoon salt

1/2 teaspoon dried oregano

1/2 teaspoon ground cumin

1/2 teaspoon chili powder

2 cans (15 ounces each) black beans, drained and rinsed

1 1/2 cups cooked rice

1 In a skillet over medium heat, cook beef until browned. Drain off fat. Transfer to a slow cooker and add broth, tomatoes, scallions, carrots, celery, garlic, sugar, basil, salt, oregano, cumin, and chili powder. Cover and cook on high 1 hour.

2 Reduce heat to low and cook 4 hours or until vegetables are tender. Add beans and rice and cook 1 hour or until heated through.

BLACK BEAN AND TURKEY SOUP WITH WINTER SQUASH

The black beans add a rich, almost smoky flavor and dark purple hue to this soup. Corn and butternut squash provide a sweet counterpoint to the earthy taste of the turkey and beans.

SERVES 8

1 1/2 cups dry black beans, sorted and rinsed

3 1/2 pounds turkey drumsticks, skin removed

1 green bell pepper, cored, seeded, and cut into 1/2-inch squares

1 cup chopped fresh cilantro

4 scallions, thinly sliced

1 tablespoon grated lemon zest

1 tablespoon chili powder

2 1/2 teaspoons ground cumin

2 1/2 teaspoons ground coriander

1 teaspoon ground ginger

5 cups diced butternut squash

1 package (10 ounces) frozen whole-kernel corn

2 1/4 teaspoons salt

1/4 cup fresh lemon juice

1 In a large saucepan or soup pot, cover beans with 3 inches of water and bring to boil. Add drumsticks, bell pepper, 1/2 cup cilantro, scallions, lemon zest, chili powder, cumin, coriander, and ginger. Return to boil, then reduce heat and simmer, partially covered, 1 1/4 hours.

2 Add squash, corn, and salt and simmer, uncovered, 15 minutes or until beans and turkey are tender. Remove from heat and transfer turkey to a plate.

3 When turkey is cool enough to handle, remove meat from bones and cut into bite-size pieces. Return to pan, add lemon juice and remaining cilantro, and cook 3 minutes or until heated through.

CUBAN BLACK BEAN SOUP

Rich and aromatic, black bean soup is a wonderful centerpiece for lunch or dinner on a cold, wintry day.

SERVES 9

2 cups dry black beans, sorted and rinsed

1 ounce lean salt pork or turkey bacon, coarsely chopped

2 garlic cloves, coarsely chopped

1 large onion, coarsely chopped

1 large green bell pepper, cored, seeded, and coarsely chopped

1/4 teaspoon ground cumin

1/4 teaspoon dried thyme

4 cups vegetable stock

1 can (28 ounces) crushed tomatoes

1 tablespoon fresh lime juice

1/8 teaspoon pepper

Dash of hot red pepper sauce

1/3 cup reduced-fat sour cream

Chopped fresh thyme or parsley

1 In a large saucepan, bring beans and enough water to cover to boil. Cook 2 minutes, then remove from heat and let stand, covered, at least 1 hour or overnight. Drain beans, rinse under cold water, and drain again.

2 In a 4-quart saucepan over medium heat, cook pork, stirring frequently, until meat is crisp and fat is rendered. Using a slotted spoon, remove and discard pork.

3 Add garlic, onion, and bell pepper to pan and sauté 5 minutes or until softened and lightly browned. Add cumin and thyme and sauté 2 minutes. Stir in 1 cup water, stock, tomatoes, and beans and bring to boil. Reduce heat, partially cover, and simmer, stirring occasionally, 1 hour or until tender. Remove from heat.

4 Transfer 2 cups beans and vegetables to a blender or food processor, cover, and puree until very smooth. Add half of liquid and process until combined. Return to pan, stir in lime juice, pepper, and red pepper sauce, and cook until heated through. Garnish each serving with a spoonful of sour cream and some thyme.

BLACK BEAN SOUP WITH GREEN PEPPER

Nutritious, tasty, and easy, this soup is sure to become a favorite. (Photograph on page 24)

SERVES 4

2 teaspoons vegetable oil

1 green bell pepper, cored, seeded, and diced

2 scallions, sliced

3 garlic cloves, minced

1 can (19 ounces) black beans, drained and rinsed

1 1/2 cups chicken stock

1 teaspoon ground coriander

1 teaspoon ground cumin

2 tablespoons reduced-fat sour cream

1/4 cup diced tomato

1 Heat oil in a medium saucepan over medium heat. Add bell pepper, scallions, and garlic and sauté 2 minutes or until softened. Add beans, stock, coriander, and cumin. Bring to boil, reduce heat, and simmer 5 minutes.

2 Transfer half of soup to a food processor or blender, cover, and puree until smooth. Return to pan and cook until heated through. Ladle into bowls and top each serving with sour cream and tomato.

BLACK BEAN SOUP WITH CORN AND CINNAMON

This delicious black bean soup is seasoned with cinnamon, marjoram, cilantro, and lime juice.

SERVES 8

2 cups dry black beans, sorted and rinsed

1 large yellow onion, coarsely chopped

1 large green bell pepper, cored, seeded, and coarsely chopped

4 garlic cloves, slivered

2 teaspoons mild chili powder

2 bay leaves

1 cinnamon stick, split lengthwise

3/4 teaspoon dried marjoram, crumbled

1 package (10 ounces) frozen whole-kernel corn

1 teaspoon salt

1/2 cup minced fresh cilantro or 1/2 cup minced fresh parsley mixed with 3 teaspoons ground coriander

2 tablespoons fresh lime juice

1 teaspoon hot red pepper sauce (*optional*)

Low-fat plain yogurt (*optional*)

Chopped scallions (*optional*)

1 In a large soup pot or 5-quart Dutch oven over medium heat, bring beans and enough cold water to cover to boil. Cook 2 minutes, remove from heat and let stand 1 hour, then drain and rinse.

2 Return beans to pot and add 7 cups water, onion, bell pepper, garlic, chili powder, bay leaves, cinnamon, and marjoram. Bring to boil, then reduce heat and simmer, covered, 1 hour or until beans are tender.

3 Remove bay leaves and cinnamon. Stir in corn, salt, cilantro, lime juice, and red pepper sauce, if desired, and cook 4 minutes or until corn is heated through. Garnish with yogurt and scallions, if desired.

CARIBBEAN EGGPLANT AND BLACK BEAN SOUP

You can turn this soup into a one-dish meal by adding 2 cups diced cooked pork, chicken, or shrimp along with the beans.

SERVES 4

1 tablespoon canola or olive oil

1 medium green bell pepper, cored, seeded, and coarsely chopped

1 medium celery stalk, coarsely chopped

1 garlic clove, minced

2 small carrots, peeled and thinly sliced

1 1/2 teaspoons ground cumin

3/4 teaspoon ground allspice

3/4 teaspoon dried oregano, crumbled

1/4 teaspoon salt

1 can (28 ounces) tomatoes in puree

2 tablespoons dry sherry, orange juice, or water

1 tablespoon honey

1/2 teaspoon grated lime zest

1 small eggplant, peeled and cut into 1/2-inch cubes

1 cup cooked black beans

6 drops hot red pepper sauce

1 Heat oil in a soup pot or 5-quart Dutch oven over medium-low heat. Add bell pepper, celery, garlic, and carrots. Cover and cook, stirring occasionally, 8 minutes or until softened. Stir in cumin, allspice, oregano, and salt and cook 2 minutes.

2 Add tomatoes and break up with a spoon. Increase heat to medium, add sherry, honey, lime zest, and bring to boil. Reduce heat and simmer, covered, 15 minutes. Add eggplant and cook, covered, 10 minutes or until tender. Stir in beans and red pepper sauce and cook just until heated through.

LENTIL SOUP WITH ROOT VEGETABLES

These delicious little legumes meld perfectly with the flavors of root vegetables for a rich, satisfying soup.

SERVES 6 TO 8

1 tablespoon olive oil
1 large onion, diced
2 celery stalks, diced
2 garlic cloves, finely chopped
8 ounces turnip or parsnip, diced
2 large carrots, diced
8 cups beef or vegetable stock
2 cups dry brown lentils, sorted and rinsed
1 tablespoon tomato paste
1/4 teaspoon dried thyme
1 bay leaf
1/8 teaspoon salt
1/8 teaspoon black pepper

1 Heat oil in a 4-quart saucepan over medium heat. Add onion, celery, and garlic and sauté 6 minutes or until softened and golden. Add turnip, carrots, and 1/4 cup stock and sauté until softened. Add lentils, tomato paste, thyme, remaining stock, and bay leaf and stir until combined.

2 Bring to boil, then reduce heat, partially cover, and simmer, stirring occasionally, 50 minutes or until lentils and vegetables are tender. Add salt and pepper. Remove bay leaf before serving.

BEEF-LENTIL SOUP

This wonderful main-dish soup is as rich in flavor as it is in beneficial nutrients.

SERVES 6

1 pound ground beef
1 cup dried lentils, sorted and rinsed
2 cups chopped cabbage
1 cup sliced carrots
1 cup sliced celery
1 cup chopped onion
1/2 cup diced seeded green bell pepper
1/2 teaspoon black pepper
1/2 teaspoon dried thyme
1 bay leaf
1 teaspoon salt *(optional)*
2 beef bouillon cubes *(optional)*
1 package (10 ounces) frozen chopped spinach, thawed

1 In a large soup pot over medium heat, cook beef until browned. Drain off fat.

2 Add 4 cups water, lentils, cabbage, carrots, celery, onion, bell pepper, black pepper, thyme, bay leaf, and salt and bouillon, if desired. Bring to boil, then reduce heat and simmer, uncovered, 1 to 1 1/2 hours or until lentils and vegetables are tender.

3 Add spinach and cook until heated through. Remove bay leaf before serving.

TOMATO-LENTIL SOUP WITH MUSHROOMS

Lentils supply robust, earthy flavor when you cook them in mushroom broth and add ginger and tarragon to the mix.

SERVES 4

1/4 cup dried porcini or shiitake mushrooms
1 tablespoon olive oil
1 large onion, finely chopped
3 garlic cloves, minced
1 can (15 ounces) diced tomatoes, undrained
1 teaspoon ground ginger
1 teaspoon tarragon
3/4 teaspoon salt
1/2 cup dried lentils, sorted and rinsed

1 In a small bowl, combine mushrooms and 1 cup hot water. Let stand 20 minutes or until softened, then, using a slotted spoon, remove from liquid. Strain liquid through a fine-mesh sieve into another small bowl and coarsely chop mushrooms.

2 Meanwhile, heat oil in a large saucepan over medium heat. Add onion and garlic and sauté 7 minutes or until onion is golden.

3 Stir in 2 cups water, mushrooms, soaking liquid, tomatoes, ginger, tarragon, and salt. Add lentils and bring to boil, then reduce heat and simmer, covered, 30 minutes or until lentils are tender.

CREAM OF RED LENTIL SOUP

Red lentils and red peppers—bell and hot—make a soup with lively color and taste.

SERVES 4

1 cup red lentils
2 red bell peppers, cored, seeded, and chopped
3 garlic cloves, minced
3/4 teaspoon salt
3/4 teaspoon ground cumin
1/8 teaspoon cayenne pepper
1/2 cup evaporated milk
2 tablespoons diced seeded red bell pepper

1 In a medium saucepan, combine 2 1/2 cups water, lentils, bell peppers, garlic, salt, cumin, and cayenne. Bring to boil, then reduce heat and simmer 20 minutes or until lentils are soft.

2 Transfer to a food processor or blender and add milk, then cover and puree until smooth. Ladle into bowls and top each serving with diced red pepper.

RED LENTIL AND CELERY SOUP WITH MELTED STILTON AND CHIVES

Carrots give a slightly sweet edge to this thick, smooth soup with its delicious pockets of melted blue cheese.

SERVES 4

1 1/2 tablespoons extra-virgin olive oil
1 large mild onion, coarsely chopped
10 1/2 ounces split red lentils
6 cups vegetable stock
4 large carrots, sliced
1 bunch celery, sliced and some leaves reserved
3 1/2 ounces Stilton cheese, crumbled
4 tablespoons snipped fresh chives
Salt and black pepper

1 Heat oil in a large saucepan over medium heat. Add onion and sauté 10 minutes or until softened. Add lentils and stock and bring to boil. Add carrots and celery and return to boil. Reduce heat and simmer, covered, 40 minutes or until lentils and vegetables are tender.

2 Transfer soup to a blender or food processor, cover, and puree until smooth (or use a handheld blender to puree in pan). Return to pan, season to taste with salt and pepper, and cook until heated through (do not boil). Remove from heat.

3 Scatter crumbled Stilton over soup and stir in chives. Ladle into bowls and garnish with celery leaves.

LENTIL SOUP WITH SPINACH

Brown lentils have the most flavor, but you can use yellow or red ones if you prefer.

SERVES 8

1 tablespoon olive or canola oil

2 celery stalks, coarsely chopped

2 garlic cloves, finely chopped

1 large onion, coarsely chopped

1/4 teaspoon curry powder

Pinch of ground coriander *(optional)*

Pinch of ground cumin *(optional)*

Pinch of cayenne pepper

2 cups dried brown lentils, sorted and rinsed

8 cups vegetable stock

2 cups packed fresh spinach, washed and trimmed, or 1/2 package (10 ounces) frozen spinach, thawed

1/8 teaspoon salt

1/2 cup fat-free plain yogurt

1 Heat oil in a 4-quart saucepan over medium heat. Add celery, garlic, onion, curry powder, coriander and cumin, if desired, and cayenne and sauté 5 minutes or until softened. Add lentils and stock and bring to boil. Reduce heat, partially cover, and simmer, stirring occasionally, 50 minutes or until lentils and vegetables are tender.

2 Stir in spinach and salt and simmer 5 minutes. Ladle into bowls and top each serving with a spoonful of yogurt.

GOLDEN LENTIL SOUP

This velvety soup owes its color to lentils, parsnips, and carrots. Dry sherry and horseradish cream add to its flavor.

SERVES 6

2 tablespoons butter

1 large onion, finely chopped

1 pound parsnips, cut into small cubes

12 ounces carrots, cut into small cubes

2/3 cup dry sherry

3 ounces red lentils

4 cups vegetable stock

Salt and black pepper

2 teaspoons grated horseradish

6 tablespoons *crème fraîche*

Minced fresh chives

1 In a large saucepan over medium heat, melt butter. Reduce heat to low, add onion, and stir well. Cook, covered, 10 minutes or until softened. Stir in parsnips, carrots, and sherry and bring to boil. Reduce heat and simmer, covered, 40 minutes.

2 Add lentils, stock, and salt and pepper to taste. Bring to boil, then reduce heat and simmer, covered, 15 minutes or until lentils are tender. Transfer to a blender or food processor, cover, and puree until smooth (or use a handheld blender to puree in pan). Return to pan and bring to boil (if soup seems too thick, add a little stock or water).

3 In a small bowl, stir horseradish into *crème fraîche*. Ladle soup into warm bowls and top each serving with a spoonful of horseradish cream and chives.

MINTED LENTIL SOUP

This hearty soup can be served chunky or pureed.
It also can be frozen for up to 3 months.

SERVES 6

2 tablespoons olive oil

4 medium yellow onions,
  coarsely chopped

1 garlic clove, minced

4 medium carrots, peeled and coarsely
  chopped

1/4 cup mint flakes, crumbled

1 cup dried brown lentils,
  sorted and rinsed

2 cups chicken stock

1/4 teaspoon salt

1/4 teaspoon black pepper

1/2 cup low-fat plain yogurt *(optional)*

1 Heat oil in a large heavy saucepan over medium heat. Add onions, garlic, and carrots and sauté 2 to 3 minutes. Stir in 3 cups water, mint, lentils, and stock and bring to boil, then reduce heat and simmer, covered, 35 minutes or until lentils are tender. Stir in salt and pepper. Serve chunky style garnished with yogurt, if desired, or puree as directed in Step 2.

2 To puree, set a sieve over a bowl and strain mixture, reserving liquid. Transfer mixture and 1/2 cup liquid to a blender or food processor, cover, and puree until smooth. Return to pan, stir in remaining liquid, and cook until heated through. Garnish each serving with yogurt, if desired.

LENTIL SOUP WITH KNOCKWURST

The combination of spicy sausage and mild-flavored lentils makes a comforting soup.

SERVES 4

2 tablespoons vegetable oil

1 pound knockwurst or kielbasa,
  cut into 1/4-inch-thick slices

2 medium carrots, peeled and finely
  chopped

1 large yellow onion, finely chopped

1 medium celery stalk, finely chopped

1 garlic clove, minced

1/4 cup minced fresh parsley

8 ounces dried lentils, sorted and rinsed

1 cup canned tomatoes, undrained,
  chopped

1 bay leaf

3 cups beef stock

1/2 teaspoon salt

1/8 teaspoon black pepper

1 Heat oil in a 4-quart saucepan over medium heat. Add knockwurst and sauté 5 minutes or until golden, then transfer to paper towels to drain. Drain all but 1 tablespoon drippings from pan. Add carrots, onion, celery, garlic, and parsley and sauté 5 minutes or until onion is tender.

2 Add 1 1/2 cups water, lentils, tomatoes, bay leaf, stock, and knockwurst and bring to boil. Reduce heat and simmer, partially covered, 40 minutes or until lentils are tender. Season with salt and pepper and remove bay leaf.

LENTIL-BARLEY SOUP

Lentils and barley complement each other in taste and texture, making this a very satisfying one-dish meal.

SERVES 8 TO 10

2 tablespoons butter
2 celery stalks, thinly sliced
1 medium onion, chopped
1 garlic clove, minced
1 can (28 ounces) diced tomatoes, undrained
3/4 cup dried lentils, sorted and rinsed
3/4 cup medium pearl barley
2 tablespoons chicken bouillon granules
1/2 teaspoon dried oregano
1/2 teaspoon dried rosemary, crushed
1/4 teaspoon black pepper
1 cup thinly sliced carrots
1 cup (4 ounces) shredded Swiss cheese (*optional*)

1 In a Dutch oven or soup pot over low heat, melt butter. Add celery, onion, and garlic and sauté 4 minutes or until tender.

2 Add 6 cups water, tomatoes, lentils, barley, bouillon, oregano, rosemary, and pepper. Bring to boil, then reduce heat and simmer, covered, 40 minutes or until lentils and barley are almost tender. Add carrots and simmer 15 minutes or until carrots, lentils, and barley are tender. Sprinkle each serving with cheese, if desired.

LENTIL-BARLEY SOUP WITH CHICKEN

This is a warm, rib-sticking soup with lots of flavor that can chase the chill out of a winter evening.

SERVES 8

1 tablespoon butter
1 medium onion, chopped
1/2 cup chopped seeded green bell pepper
3 garlic cloves, minced
1 can (49 1/2 ounces) chicken broth
3 medium carrots, chopped
1/2 cup dried lentils, sorted and rinsed
1 1/2 teaspoons Italian seasoning
1 teaspoon salt
1/4 teaspoon black pepper
1 cup cubed cooked chicken or turkey
1/2 cup quick-cooking barley
2 medium fresh mushrooms, chopped
1 can (28 ounces) crushed tomatoes, undrained

1 In a Dutch oven or soup pot over medium heat, melt butter. Add onion, bell pepper, and garlic and sauté until tender.

2 Add broth, carrots, lentils, Italian seasoning, salt, and black pepper. Bring to boil, then reduce heat and simmer, covered, 25 minutes.

3 Add chicken, barley, and mushrooms and return to boil. Reduce heat and simmer, covered, 10 minutes or until lentils, barley, and carrots are tender. Add tomatoes and cook until heated through.

TOMATO AND RED LENTIL SOUP

A dollop of basil-flavored cream cheese adds a rich touch to this simple soup.

SERVES 4

2 1/2 cups chicken or vegetable stock
2 tablespoons olive oil
3 shallots, chopped
2-3 garlic cloves, chopped
1/2 cup drained and rinsed split red lentils
1 can (19 ounces) chopped tomatoes
1 tablespoon chopped fresh basil
1 package (4 1/2 ounces) cream cheese
Salt and black pepper
Fresh basil leaves

1 In a large saucepan over medium heat, bring stock to boil.

2 Heat oil in another large saucepan over medium heat. Add shallots and garlic and sauté 3 minutes or until softened.

3 Add lentils, tomatoes, and stock and bring to boil, then reduce heat and simmer, covered, 15 minutes. Add half of chopped basil after 10 minutes.

4 In a small bowl, beat cream cheese until softened. Stir in remaining chopped basil.

5 Transfer soup to a blender or food processor, cover, and puree until smooth. Season to taste with salt and pepper, return to pan, and cook until heated through. Ladle into bowls and top with spoonfuls of cream cheese mixture and basil leaves.

LENTIL PREACHING SOUP

Among the Pennsylvania Dutch, serving this hearty soup between their two Sabbath services satisfies both preacher and the faithful.

SERVES 8

1 tablespoon vegetable oil
2 medium yellow onions, chopped
3 large leeks, white parts only, sliced
3 garlic cloves, minced
1 tablespoon ground cumin
2 teaspoons fresh thyme or 1/2 teaspoon dried thyme
1/2 teaspoon black pepper
5 cups homemade chicken stock or canned low-sodium chicken broth
1 pound dried lentils, sorted and rinsed
12 ounces baked ham, cut into bite-size pieces
4 large carrots, peeled and chopped
2 celery stalks, chopped
1 bay leaf
1/4 cup chopped parsley
2 tablespoons cider vinegar
1/4 teaspoon salt

1 Heat oil in a 6-quart Dutch oven over medium-high heat. Add onions, leeks, garlic, cumin, thyme, and pepper and sauté 10 minutes or until tender.

2 Stir in 4 cups cold water, stock, lentils, ham, carrots, celery, and bay leaf. Increase heat to high and bring to boil. Reduce heat, partially cover, and simmer, stirring occasionally, 1 hour or until lentils are tender. Remove bay leaf and stir in parsley, vinegar, and salt.

CHICKEN, BUTTERNUT SQUASH, AND LENTIL STEW

To cut up the butternut squash, you'll need a large sturdy chef's knife. To make the procedure easier, first cut off the neck of the squash, then halve the thicker bottom part.

SERVES 4

2 tablespoons olive oil

1 onion, finely chopped

3 garlic cloves, minced

1/2 cup dried lentils, sorted and rinsed

1 small butternut squash, peeled, halved, seeded, and cut into 1/2-inch chunks

1 cup drained canned tomatoes, chopped

2 teaspoons chili powder

1 teaspoon ground coriander

1/2 teaspoon salt

1/8 teaspoon ground cloves

1 1/2 pounds skinless, boneless chicken thighs, cut into 1-inch chunks

1 Preheat oven to 350°F. Heat oil in a Dutch oven or soup pot over medium heat. Add onion and garlic and sauté 7 minutes or until onion is golden.

2 Stir in 1/2 cup water, lentils, squash, tomatoes, chili powder, coriander, salt, and cloves and bring to boil. Add chicken, cover, and bake 45 minutes or until chicken and lentils are cooked through and squash is tender.

LENTIL-RICE STEW

Here's a delicious, inexpensive dish to serve a crowd; both meat eaters and vegetarians will like it.

SERVES 20

2 cups dried lentils, sorted and rinsed

3/4 cup brown rice

1 can (28 ounces) tomatoes, undrained, chopped

1 can (48 ounces) tomato or vegetable juice

3 garlic cloves, minced

1 large onion, chopped

2 celery stalks, sliced

3 carrots, sliced

1 bay leaf

1 teaspoon dried basil

1 teaspoon dried oregano

1 teaspoon dried thyme

1/2 teaspoon black pepper

3 tablespoons minced fresh parsley

1 zucchini, sliced

2 medium all-purpose potatoes, peeled and diced

2 tablespoons fresh lemon juice

1 teaspoon dry mustard

Salt

1 In a 6-quart Dutch oven or soup pot over medium-high heat, combine 4 cups water, lentils, rice, tomatoes, tomato juice, garlic, onion, celery, carrots, bay leaf, basil, oregano, thyme, pepper, and parsley. Bring to boil, then reduce heat and simmer, covered, 45 minutes or until rice and lentils are tender (if soup is too thick, add more water or tomato juice).

2 Stir in zucchini, potatoes, lemon juice, and mustard and simmer, covered, 45 minutes or until vegetables are tender. Add salt to taste.

LEAN LENTIL STEW

A favorite for blustery winter days, this stew will satisfy skaters and sledders. Serving it with rice increases the amount of protein by more than 3 grams per serving.

SERVES 8

1 cup dried lentils, sorted and rinsed

4 cups canned low-sodium beef broth

1 medium yellow onion, chopped

2 garlic cloves, minced

2 large celery stalks, diced

4 medium carrots, peeled and cut into 1-inch pieces

2 cans (16 ounces each) low-sodium tomatoes, undrained, chopped

1 teaspoon dried rosemary, crumbled

1/4 teaspoon black pepper

8 small white onions

2 tablespoons unsalted butter

4 ounces small mushrooms, halved

4 medium all-purpose potatoes, peeled and cut into 1-inch cubes

1 In a 6-quart Dutch oven or soup pot over medium heat, bring lentils, broth, yellow onion, garlic, celery, half of carrots, tomatoes, rosemary, and pepper to boil. Reduce heat and simmer, covered, 35 minutes.

2 Meanwhile, in a heavy 12-inch skillet over medium-high heat, melt butter. Add white onions and remaining carrots and sauté 5 minutes or until golden. Add mushrooms and sauté 3 minutes.

3 Add vegetables and potatoes to pot and simmer, covered, 20 minutes or until lentils and potatoes are tender.

SPANISH LENTIL AND RICE STEW

This traditional stew comes from the Valencia province of Spain. Feel free to vary the vegetables.

SERVES 6 TO 8

1 cup dried lentils, rinsed and sorted

1 1/2 pounds Swiss chard, trimmed of stalks and chopped

1 large potato, peeled and cut into 10 pieces

1 large turnip, peeled and cut into 10 pieces

2 1/4 cups hot water

Salt

Freshly ground black pepper

1/2 cup extra-virgin olive oil

1 red bell pepper, chopped

3 cloves garlic, finely chopped

1 large, ripe tomato, peeled, seeded, and chopped (or substitute 1/2 cup canned tomatoes)

1 cup medium-grain rice

1 In a medium casserole or stockpot, cover lentils, Swiss chard, potato, and turnip with the hot water. Season with salt and pepper and bring to simmer over medium heat. Cook 20 minutes, then reduce heat to low.

2 Meanwhile, heat olive oil in a small skillet over medium heat and add bell pepper, garlic, and tomato. Cook 8 to 10 minutes or until peppers are soft and tomatoes are broken down, shaking skillet occasionally. Transfer tomato, garlic, and pepper to casserole.

3 Cook stew another 40 minutes over low heat, then add rice and cook until rice has absorbed liquid and is tender, about 20 more minutes (add water as needed if stew is becoming dry while cooking). Serve immediately.

GRANDMA'S PEA SOUP WITH *SPAETZLE*

SERVES 16

Soup:

8 ounces dried whole peas, sorted and rinsed

8 ounces dried split peas, sorted and rinsed

1 hambone

1 large onion, chopped

1 carrot, chopped

2 celery stalks, chopped

Leaves from 6 celery stalks, chopped

1 teaspoon mixed herbs

1 tablespoon minced fresh parsley

1 bay leaf

1 teaspoon salt

1/4 teaspoon black pepper

8 ounces smoked cooked Thuringer sausage, chopped *(optional)*

Spaetzle:

1 cup all-purpose flour

1 egg, beaten

1 For soup, place whole peas and split peas in a medium bowl, add enough water to cover, and let stand overnight. Drain, rinse, and transfer to a large Dutch oven or soup pot over high heat. Add 3 quarts water, hambone, onion, carrot, celery, celery leaves, herbs, parsley, bay leaf, salt, and pepper. Bring to boil, then reduce heat and simmer, covered, 2 to 2 1/2 hours. Remove from heat and let cool.

2 Remove hambone and skim any fat from soup. When bone is cool enough to handle, remove and dice meat. Add ham and sausage, if desired, to pot.

3 For *spaetzle,* place flour in a small bowl and make a depression in center. Add egg and 1/3 cup water and stir until smooth. Place a colander with 3/16-inch-diameter holes over pot, pour in batter, and press through holes with a wooden spoon. Cook, uncovered, 10 to 15 minutes. Remove bay leaf before serving.

The spaetzle cooked in this soup are a German specialty (spaetzle means "little sparrow"): noodles formed by pushing dough through the holes in either a colander or a tool called a spaetzle hex.

SPLIT PEA SOUP
WITH MEATBALLS

Tender meatballs add a nice fillip to ordinary split pea soup. It's a great dish for potluck suppers.

SERVES 10

Soup:

1 pound dried green split peas,
　sorted and rinsed

3 medium carrots, cut into
　1/2-inch-thick slices

3/4 cup diced celery

1 medium onion, diced

3 medium all-purpose potatoes,
　cut into 1/2-inch cubes

2 1/2 teaspoons salt

1/4 teaspoon black pepper

Meatballs:

4 tablespoons vegetable oil

3/4 cup finely chopped celery

1 medium onion, finely chopped

1 1/2 cups soft bread crumbs

1 teaspoon salt

1/2 teaspoon rubbed sage, crushed

1 egg

1 pound ground pork

1 For soup, combine 8 cups water, peas, carrots, celery, and onion in a Dutch oven or soup pot over medium heat. Bring to boil, then reduce heat and simmer, covered, 1 hour. Add potatoes, salt, and pepper and simmer, covered, 30 minutes.

2 For meatballs, heat 2 tablespoons oil in a large skillet over medium heat. Add celery and onion and sauté until tender, about 3 minutes. Transfer to a medium bowl and add 2 tablespoons water, bread crumbs, salt, sage, and egg. Crumble pork over mixture, mix well, and form into 3/4-inch balls.

3 Heat remaining oil in skillet over medium heat, then add meatballs and cook until browned. Add to pot and simmer, covered, 15 minutes.

SPLIT PEA AND HAM SOUP

Split peas are just what their name implies: peas that have been dried until they split in two.

SERVES 8

1 medium yellow onion, studded
　with 3 whole cloves

1 medium yellow onion, chopped

1 meaty smoked ham hock (about 1 pound)

4 large carrots, peeled and chopped

2 cups dried green split peas,
　sorted and rinsed

2 celery stalks, finely chopped

3 garlic cloves, minced

1 bay leaf

1/4 teaspoon salt

1/4 teaspoon hot red pepper sauce

Carrot curls

1 In a 6-quart Dutch oven or soup pot, combine 6 cups cold water, studded onion, chopped onion, ham hock, carrots, peas, celery, garlic, and bay leaf. Bring to boil, then reduce heat and simmer, covered, 1 1/4 hours or until peas are tender.

2 Using a slotted spoon, transfer ham to a cutting board. When cool enough to handle, remove meat from bone, cut into bite-size pieces, and return to pot. Remove bay leaf and studded onion. Stir in salt and red pepper sauce and garnish with carrot curls.

SPLIT PEA-VEGETABLE SOUP

Healthy additions to venerable split pea soup are potatoes, carrots, onions, and cabbage.

SERVES 16

1 1/2 cups dried split peas,
  sorted and rinsed

7-8 whole allspice,
  tied in a cheesecloth bag

2 teaspoons salt

1/2 teaspoon pepper

6 large all-purpose potatoes, peeled
  and cut into 1/2-inch cubes

6 carrots, chopped

2 medium onions, chopped

2 cups cubed cooked ham

1/2 medium head cabbage, shredded

1 In a large soup pot, combine 10 cups water, peas, spice bag, salt, and pepper. Bring to boil, reduce heat, and simmer, covered, 1 hour.

2 Stir in potatoes, carrots, onions, ham, and cabbage and return to boil. Reduce heat, cover, and simmer, stirring occasionally, 30 minutes or until vegetables are tender. Remove spice bag before serving.

SPLIT PEA AND POTATO SOUP

For a lunch or supper that's a real treat, serve this delicious soup with a Waldorf salad.

SERVES 4

1 tablespoon unsalted margarine

1 medium yellow onion, chopped

2 cups canned low-sodium beef broth

1/2 cup dried green split peas,
  sorted and rinsed

2 medium all-purpose potatoes,
  peeled and quartered

1/4 teaspoon black pepper

1 In a large heavy saucepan over medium heat, melt margarine. Add onion and cook, uncovered, until softened, about 5 minutes. Stir in broth and 2 cups water, bring to boil, and cook 4 minutes. Add peas and potatoes, reduce heat, and simmer gently, covered, 30 minutes or until tender. Remove from heat and let stand 10 minutes.

2 Transfer soup in 5 batches to a blender or food processor, cover, and puree 15 seconds. Return to pan, set over low heat, and cook, stirring, until heated through. Add pepper.

SPLIT PEA AND SAUSAGE SOUP

The affinity of kielbasa sausage and split peas is legendary. This soup demonstrates why.

SERVES 8

1 pound fully cooked kielbasa or
  Polish sausage, halved lengthwise
  and cut into 1/4-inch slices

1 pound dried split peas,
  sorted and rinsed

1 cup chopped carrots

1 cup chopped onion

1 cup chopped celery

1 tablespoon minced fresh parsley

1 teaspoon salt

1/2 teaspoon coarsely ground black pepper

2 bay leaves

1 In a Dutch oven or soup pot, combine 6 cups water, kielbasa, peas, carrots, onion, celery, parsley, salt, pepper, and bay leaves. Bring to boil, then reduce heat and simmer, covered, 1 1/4 hours or until peas are tender. Remove bay leaves before serving.

SPLIT PEA SOUP WITH CARAWAY

A small ham hock adds rich, smoky flavor to soup, and cutting off all the visible fat keeps the soup lean.

SERVES 8

1 tablespoon olive or canola oil

4 ounces shallots or small white onions, finely chopped

2 celery stalks, coarsely chopped

1/4 teaspoon caraway seed

7 cups chicken stock

1 small ham hock (8 ounces)

2 1/2 cups dried yellow or green split peas, sorted and rinsed

2 carrots, diced

Parsley stems

1 bay leaf

1 tablespoon chopped parsley

1/8 teaspoon black pepper

1 Heat oil in a 4-quart saucepan over medium heat. Add shallots, celery, caraway seed, and about 2 tablespoons stock and sauté 5 minutes or until softened.

2 Meanwhile, trim as much fat as possible from ham. Stir peas into pan and add ham, stock, and carrots. Tie parsley stems and bay leaf together with string to make a bouquet garni and add to pan. Bring to boil, then reduce heat, partially cover, and simmer, stirring occasionally, 1 hour or until peas are tender and ham comes easily off bone. Remove from heat.

3 Remove bouquet garni and transfer ham hock to a plate. When cool enough to handle, remove meat from bone, reserving any juices.

4 Add ham and juices to soup, return to heat, and simmer 5 minutes. Stir in chopped parsley and pepper.

SPLIT PEA AND SAUSAGE SOUP WITH TOMATO

Here's the basic soup dating back to Colonial times.

SERVES 4

3 1/2 cups canned low-sodium chicken broth

1 cup dried green split peas, sorted and rinsed

1 teaspoon ground cumin

1/2 teaspoon salt

1/4-1/2 teaspoon cayenne pepper

2 large yellow onions, chopped

1 can (14 1/2 ounces) low-sodium tomatoes, undrained, cut up

2 large carrots, chopped

6 ounces turkey kielbasa, sliced

1 In a large saucepan over medium heat, combine broth, peas, cumin, salt, and cayenne. Bring to boil, then reduce heat, cover, and simmer, stirring occasionally, 1 hour.

2 Stir in 1/2 cup water, onions, tomatoes, carrots, and kielbasa. Increase heat and return to boil. Reduce heat, cover, and simmer, stirring occasionally, 25 minutes or until vegetables are tender.

SPLIT PEA AND GREEN PEA SOUP

You can use fresh green peas in season, adding them to the soup about 5 minutes earlier than you would frozen peas.

SERVES 4

2 teaspoons vegetable oil

6 scallions, thinly sliced

3 garlic cloves, minced

1 1/4 cups dried split peas, sorted and rinsed

1 cup shredded iceberg lettuce

1/3 cup fresh mint leaves

3/4 teaspoon salt

1/4 teaspoon dried marjoram

1 1/2 cups frozen green peas

1 can (12 ounces) fat-free evaporated milk

1 Heat oil in a large saucepan over medium heat. Add scallions and garlic and sauté 2 minutes or until scallions are tender. Add 3 cups water, split peas, lettuce, mint, salt, and marjoram and bring to boil. Reduce heat and simmer, covered, 25 minutes or until peas are tender. Stir in green peas and cook 5 minutes.

2 Transfer soup to a food processor or blender, add milk, cover, and puree until smooth. Return to pan and cook 3 minutes or until heated through.

LOW-FAT SPLIT PEA SOUP

Split pea soup can be savory and satisfying without being heavy. A few drops of liquid smoke can give it a meaty flavor. (Photograph on page 5)

SERVES 6

2 teaspoons olive oil

1 large onion, finely chopped

3 garlic cloves, minced

2 carrots, halved lengthwise and
    thinly sliced crosswise

3/4 cup dried split peas, sorted and rinsed

2 tablespoons tomato paste

1 teaspoon salt

1/2 teaspoon black pepper

1/2 teaspoon rubbed sage

1/2 teaspoon liquid smoke

1/3 cup small pasta shapes

1/4 cup grated Parmesan cheese

1 Heat oil in nonstick Dutch oven or soup pot over medium heat. Add onion and garlic and sauté 7 minutes or until onion is golden. Add carrots and sauté 5 minutes or until crisp-tender.

2 Stir in 4 1/2 cups water, peas, tomato paste, salt, pepper, sage, and liquid smoke and bring to boil. Reduce heat and simmer, covered, 30 minutes.

3 Add pasta and simmer, uncovered, 15 minutes or until pasta and peas are tender. Serve sprinkled with cheese.

DOUBLE PEA SOUP WITH GINGER

A hint of mint and ginger gives this creamy soup a new, fresh taste. To add crunch, you can sprinkle each serving with toasted sesame seeds.

SERVES 8

2 tablespoons olive or vegetable oil

1 can (7 ounces) Vienna sausages,
    cut into 1/4-inch-thick slices

3 medium yellow onions, finely chopped

3 garlic cloves, minced

4 scallions with tops, thinly sliced

2 cups chopped lettuce (Boston, iceberg,
    or red leaf)

1/4 cup minced fresh mint or 2 teaspoons
    mint flakes, crumbled

1 teaspoon ground ginger

1 1/2 cups dried green split peas,
    sorted and rinsed

1 teaspoon salt

1 package (10 ounces) frozen
    green peas, thawed

2 cups milk

3/4 cup grated Parmesan cheese

1 Heat oil in a large saucepan or 5-quart Dutch oven over medium heat. Add sausages and sauté 2 minutes or until golden. Transfer to paper towels to drain. Add onions and garlic to pan and sauté 5 minutes or until softened.

2 Add scallions and toss to coat, then stir in lettuce, mint, and ginger and cook, covered, 5 minutes. Add 6 cups water, split peas, and salt and bring to boil. Reduce heat and simmer, covered, 30 minutes. Add green peas and simmer, covered, 5 minutes or until all peas are tender.

3 Working in batches if necessary, transfer to a blender or food processor, cover, and puree 20 seconds. Return to pan, stir in milk, and add sausages. Cover, set over medium heat, and cook until heated through, 3 to 5 minutes. Sprinkle each serving with cheese.

LONDON SPLIT PEA SOUP

Named after the dense "pea-soup" fogs that were once regular occurrences in London, this thick pea soup is sustaining, nutritious, and very tasty.

SERVES 4

2 bacon slices, coarsely chopped
1 onion, coarsely chopped
1 carrot, coarsely chopped
1 celery stalk, coarsely chopped
4 cups chicken stock
8 ounces dried green split peas,
    sorted and rinsed
Salt and black pepper
2 slices white bread, crusts removed
1 garlic clove, crushed
Minced fresh parsley

1 In a heavy saucepan over medium heat, cook bacon 2 minutes or until lightly browned. Add onion, carrot, and celery and sauté 2 minutes.

2 Add stock and peas and bring to boil, then reduce heat and simmer, covered, 30 minutes or until tender. Transfer to a blender or food processor, cover, and puree (or use a handheld blender to puree in pan). Return to pan and season to taste with salt and pepper.

3 Preheat broiler. Cut bread into 1/2-inch cubes. In a large bowl, toss bread with garlic until evenly coated. Spread on baking sheet and toast under broiler, turning until golden. Cook soup until heated through and serve sprinkled with croutons and parsley.

PUREE OF YELLOW SPLIT PEAS

You can use green split peas if yellow ones are not available.

SERVES 8

1 ounce turkey bacon, coarsely chopped
1 onion, coarsely chopped
2 large carrots, coarsely chopped
4 celery stalks, coarsely chopped and
    leaves reserved
1 garlic clove, finely chopped
Parsley stems
1 bay leaf
Thyme sprigs
2 cups dried yellow split peas,
    sorted and rinsed
8 cups vegetable or chicken stock
1/8 teaspoon black pepper

1 In a 4-quart saucepan over medium heat, cook bacon 3 minutes or until crisp and fat is rendered. Using a slotted spoon, transfer to paper towels to drain.

2 Add onion, carrots, celery, and garlic to pan and sauté until softened. Tie parsley, bay leaf, and thyme together with string to make a bouquet garni and add to pan. Stir in peas and stock and bring to boil. Reduce heat, partially cover, and simmer, stirring occasionally, 45 minutes or until tender. Remove from heat.

3 Remove bouquet garni. Working in batches if necessary, transfer soup to a blender or food processor, cover, and puree until smooth. Return to pan.

4 Return pan to heat, stir in bacon, and simmer 3 minutes. Season to taste with pepper and garnish with reserved celery leaves.

YELLOW SPLIT PEA SOUP WITH PISTACHIOS

A new twist on traditional split pea recipes, this soup has a sunny yellow color, a touch of lemon, and pistachio nuts.

SERVES 6

1 tablespoon butter
1 tablespoon olive oil
1 large onion, coarsely chopped
1 large celery stalk with leaves, chopped
6 cups chicken stock
1 pound dried yellow split peas,
    sorted and rinsed
2 tablespoons fresh lemon juice
1/2 teaspoon ground cumin
1/2 teaspoon black pepper
2 tablespoons minced fresh parsley
1/4 cup pistachios

1 In a large saucepan over medium heat, melt butter and heat oil. Add onion and celery and sauté 5 minutes or until tender.

2 Add stock and bring to boil. Add peas and return to boil, then reduce heat and simmer, covered, 1 hour or until tender. Stir in lemon juice, cumin, and pepper and simmer 5 minutes. Let cool slightly.

3 Working in small batches, transfer to a blender or food processor, cover, and puree until smooth, Return to pan and cook 4 minutes or until heated through. Garnish each serving with parsley and pistachios.

SPLIT PEA AND CAULIFLOWER SOUP

This is a rich, well-spiced vegetarian soup that can be a meal.

SERVES 4

1 tablespoon olive oil
2 medium yellow onion, finely chopped
1 medium celery stalk, finely chopped
1 tablespoon minced garlic
1 tablespoon minced fresh ginger
    or 1 teaspoon ground ginger
2 teaspoons ground cumin
2 teaspoons ground coriander
1/4 teaspoon red pepper flakes
1/4 teaspoon ground turmeric
3/4 cup dried green or yellow split peas,
    sorted and rinsed
1 bay leaf
1/2 teaspoon salt
1 head cauliflower, broken into florets
2 tablespoons minced fresh cilantro or
    2 tablespoons minced fresh parsley mixed
    with 1 teaspoon ground coriander
Low-fat plain yogurt *(optional)*

1 Heat oil in a large heavy saucepan over medium-low heat. Add onion and celery and sauté 5 minutes. Add garlic, ginger, cumin, coriander, red pepper flakes, and turmeric and sauté 1 minute.

2 Add 4 cups water, peas, bay leaf, and salt and bring to boil. Reduce heat and simmer, covered, 30 minutes or until peas are tender. Remove bay leaf.

3 Working in batches if necessary, transfer to a blender or food processor, cover, and puree until smooth. Return to pan, increase heat to medium, and bring to boil, then add cauliflower. Reduce heat and simmer, covered, 20 minutes or until cauliflower is tender. Garnish each serving with cilantro and yogurt, if desired.

SCANDINAVIAN YELLOW
PEA SOUP

Yellow split peas are like green split peas in everything but color. Marjoram, thyme, and ginger spice this soup.

SERVES 4

3 1/2 cups canned low-sodium chicken broth

1 cup dried yellow split peas, sorted and rinsed

1 meaty hambone (1 to 1 1/2 pounds)

1 teaspoon dried marjoram

1 teaspoon dried thyme

2 large yellow onions, halved crosswise and thinly sliced

2 celery stalks, finely chopped

1/2 teaspoon ground ginger

1/4 teaspoon black pepper

1 In a large saucepan over medium heat, combine broth, peas, hambone, marjoram, and thyme. Bring to boil, then reduce heat and simmer, covered, 1 hour. Using a slotted spoon, transfer hambone to a plate. When cool enough to handle, remove meat from bone, cut into bite-size pieces, and add to pan.

2 Add onions, celery, ginger, and pepper and bring to boil. Reduce heat, cover, and simmer, stirring occasionally, 25 minutes or until tender.

BLACK-EYED PEA SOUP
WITH GREENS

A fine soup for New Year's Day, when black-eyed peas are a traditional must.

SERVES 8

1 pound dried black-eyed peas, sorted and rinsed

1 1/2 teaspoons salt

6 thick bacon slices

2 large yellow onions, coarsely chopped

2 celery stalks, coarsely chopped

2 medium carrots, peeled and chopped

2 garlic cloves, minced

2 bay leaves

1 teaspoon dried thyme, crumbled

5 cups homemade chicken stock or canned low-sodium chicken broth

2 cups trimmed, rinsed, and chopped collards, kale, or mustard or turnip greens

3 tablespoons fresh lemon juice

1/2 teaspoon hot red pepper sauce

1 Place peas in a 5-quart Dutch oven or soup pot over high heat, add cold water to cover, and bring to boil. Cook 2 minutes, then remove from heat and let stand, covered, 1 hour.

2 Drain and rinse peas and return to pot. Add 8 cups water and salt and bring to boil, then reduce heat and simmer, covered, 30 minutes. Drain, reserving 1 cup liquid and set aside. Transfer 1 cup peas to a blender or food processor, cover, and puree until smooth, adding 1 to 2 tablespoons cooking liquid if necessary.

3 Stack bacon slices and, using sharp kitchen scissors, cut crosswise into 1/2-inch strips. (This step is easiest if you place bacon in freezer for 30 minutes before cutting.) Add to pot over medium-high heat and cook, stirring occasionally, until crisp, 5 to 8 minutes. Using a slotted spoon, transfer to paper towels to drain. Reduce heat to medium, add onions, celery, carrots, garlic, bay leaves, and thyme to pan, and sauté 8 minutes or until softened.

4 Add cooking liquid, stock, peas, and pea puree and bring to boil. Reduce heat and simmer, covered, 30 minutes. Stir in greens and simmer, covered, 15 minutes or until wilted. Stir in lemon juice, red pepper sauce, and bacon and heat through. Remove bay leaves before serving.

MEXICAN BLACK-EYED PEA SOUP

The creamy texture of black-eyed peas works particularly well in warming, spicy soups meant as a main course.

SERVES 6

1 tablespoon sunflower oil

1 large fresh green chile, seeded and finely chopped (wear gloves when handling; they burn)

2 green bell peppers, cored, seeded, and chopped

1 teaspoon ground cumin

1 can (14 1/2 ounces) chopped tomatoes, undrained

1 teaspoon sun-dried tomato paste

2 1/2 cups vegetable stock

1 bay leaf

2 cans (15 1/2 ounces) black-eyed peas, drained and rinsed

6 ounces frozen whole-kernel corn

3 tablespoons chopped fresh cilantro

Salt and black pepper

12 large flour tortillas

3 ounces Monterey Jack cheese, coarsely grated

Cilantro sprigs *(optional)*

Thinly sliced fresh green chile *(optional)*

1 Heat oil in a large saucepan over medium heat. Add chile and bell peppers and sauté 5 minutes or until almost softened. Stir in cumin and sauté a few seconds.

2 Add tomatoes, tomato paste, 2 cups stock, bay leaf, and 1 1/2 cans black-eyed peas. Bring to boil, then reduce heat and simmer, covered, 15 minutes. Remove bay leaf.

3 Working in batches, transfer soup to a blender or food processor, cover, and puree until smooth (or use a handheld blender to puree in pan). Stir in remaining peas, corn, and cilantro. Add enough remaining stock to thin soup to desired consistency. Season to taste with salt and pepper and cook until heated through.

4 Meanwhile, heat tortillas in oven or microwave according to package directions. Ladle soup into bowls and sprinkle cheese on each. Garnish with cilantro sprigs and green chiles, if desired, and serve with tortillas.

BLACK-EYED PEA SOUP

Here's a quick way to prepare black-eyed peas for New Year's Day, when they are said to bring good luck.

SERVES 9

1 pound bacon

1 cup chopped celery

1 cup chopped onion

1 cup chopped seeded green bell pepper

2 cans (16 ounces each) black-eyed peas, drained and rinsed

1 can (10 1/2 ounces) beef consommé

2 cans (14 1/2 ounces each) stewed tomatoes

1 In a medium saucepan over medium heat, cook bacon until crisp. Transfer to paper towels to drain. Drain all but 2 tablespoons drippings from pan.

2 Add celery, onion, and bell pepper and sauté over medium heat 4 minutes or until tender. Crumble bacon and add to pan, then add black-eyed peas, consommé, and tomatoes and cook until heated through.

BLACK-EYED PEA STEW

This meatless one-dish meal brings you good luck on New Year's Day and good nutrition the rest of year.

SERVES 2

4 ounces dried black-eyed peas, soaked overnight

1 large yellow onion, finely chopped

2 medium carrots, peeled and chopped

2 medium tomatoes, peeled, cored, seeded, and chopped

1/2 teaspoon dried savory, crumbled

1/2 teaspoon dried marjoram, crumbled

1/4 teaspoon crushed red pepper flakes

2 bay leaves

1 cinnamon stick

1/3 cup fresh or frozen whole-kernel corn

1/4 teaspoon black pepper

1/8 teaspoon salt

2/3 cup low-fat plain yogurt

1 Drain black-eyed peas and place in a heavy medium saucepan with onion, carrots, tomatoes, savory, marjoram, red pepper flakes, bay leaves, and cinnamon. Stir in 3 cups water and bring to boil, then reduce heat and simmer, partially covered, 50 minutes or until peas are tender.

2 Add corn, pepper, and salt and cook, uncovered, 5 minutes. Remove bay leaves and cinnamon stick. Ladle into bowls and top each serving with 1/3 cup yogurt.

PORTUGUESE KALE SOUP WITH CHICKPEAS

The combination of fresh kale, carrots, and red bell pepper in this soup guarantees a rich variety of important vitamins and minerals.

SERVES 8

8 ounces hot Italian-style turkey sausages

1 tablespoon vegetable oil

1 small onion, coarsely chopped

2 garlic cloves, minced

1 teaspoon ground cinnamon

1/2 teaspoon ground allspice

1 1/4 teaspoon salt

4 ounces kale, trimmed, washed, and torn into small pieces

2 carrots, peeled, halved lengthwise, and thinly sliced crosswise

1 small red bell pepper, cored, seeded, and diced

2 cans (14 1/2 ounces each) fat-free low-sodium chicken broth

1 can (19 ounces) chickpeas, drained and rinsed

1/4 cup grated Parmesan cheese

1 Prick sausages with a knife and place in a small skillet with 1/4 inch water. Bring to boil, then reduce heat and simmer, uncovered and turning occasionally, 8 minutes or until water evaporates. Sauté 5 minutes or until browned. Remove from skillet and let stand 5 minutes. Trim off any loose casing and cut sausages into 1/2-inch-thick slices.

2 Heat oil in a large saucepan over medium heat. Add onion and sauté 7 minutes or until softened and golden. Stir in garlic, cinnamon, allspice, and salt and sauté 1 minute. Stir in kale, carrots, bell pepper, and broth. Add sausage and bring to boil, then reduce heat and simmer, partially covered, 30 minutes or until vegetables are tender.

3 Stir in chickpeas and cook until heated through. Garnish each serving with cheese.

CHICKPEA AND GREENS SOUP WITH CARROTS

You can substitute Swiss chard, watercress, or kale for the spinach and red kidney beans or black beans for the chickpeas.

SERVES 4

3/4 cup chicken stock

2 carrots, quartered lengthwise
and thinly sliced

3 garlic cloves, minced

1/2 teaspoon dried sage

1/4 teaspoon black pepper

2 cups cooked chickpeas

4 cups packed torn spinach

1 In a large saucepan, bring stock to boil over medium heat. Add carrots, garlic, sage, and pepper and cook 5 minutes or until carrots are tender. Add 1 cup water and chickpeas and return to boil. Reduce heat and simmer, covered, 7 minutes or until soup is flavorful and chickpeas are hot.

2 Stir in spinach and cook 1 minute or just until wilted.

CHICKPEA, PASTA, AND SPINACH SOUP

You can also use 1 pound of fresh escarole or Swiss chard for this quick-cooking Italian soup.

SERVES 4

2 tablespoons olive oil

1 large yellow onion, finely chopped

2 garlic cloves, minced

1/2 teaspoon dried marjoram, crumbled

1/4 teaspoon dried rosemary

1 pound fresh spinach, trimmed and rinsed,
or 1 package (10 ounces) frozen
chopped spinach

1 can (15 ounces) chickpeas, drained and rinsed

6 cups beef stock

1 cup small tube-shaped pasta,
such as tubettini or ditalini

1/4 teaspoon salt

1/8 teaspoon black pepper

1/2 cup grated Parmesan cheese *(optional)*

1 Heat oil in a large saucepan over medium heat. Add onion and sauté 10 minutes or until browned. Stir in garlic, marjoram, and rosemary and sauté 2 minutes. Add spinach and cook, covered, 5 minutes or until tender.

2 Add chickpeas and stock and bring to boil. Reduce heat, add pasta, and cook, uncovered, 10 minutes or until just tender. Stir in salt and pepper. Serve with cheese, if desired.

CHICKPEA SOUP WITH ASPARAGUS

This filling soup is easy to make, tasty, and virtually fat-free.

SERVES 4

1 can (14 1/2 ounces) chickpeas,
drained and rinsed

1 onion, coarsely chopped

2 garlic cloves, chopped

4 cups vegetable stock

6 ounces asparagus, trimmed and cut
into bite-size pieces

6 ounces orzo or other soup pasta

Salt and black pepper

Garnishes:

Rind of 1 lemon, cut into thin strips

2 tablespoons fresh flat-leaf parsley, chopped

1 lemon, cut into wedges

1 In a large saucepan, combine chickpeas, onion, garlic, and stock. Bring to boil, then reduce heat and simmer 20 minutes or until onion and chickpeas are tender. If mixture is too thick, add some stock or water.

2 Transfer a third of soup to a blender or food processor, cover, and puree until smooth. Return to pan, bring to simmer, and add asparagus. Simmer, covered, 5 minutes or until just tender.

3 Meanwhile, cook pasta according to package directions until al dente. Drain and add to soup. Season to taste with salt and pepper.

4 In a small bowl, combine lemon rind and parsley, then spoon onto each serving of soup. Pass lemon wedges so guests can add juice to taste.

CHICKPEA SOUP WITH SAUSAGE

This soup is hearty enough to serve as a main dish. You can substitute black-eyed peas for chickpeas. Allow extra time to soak beans or peas using either the overnight or quick soaking method.

SERVES 8

2 tablespoons olive oil

1 large yellow onion, coarsely chopped

1 large red bell pepper, cored, seeded, and coarsely chopped

2 medium carrots, peeled, halved, and thinly sliced

3 garlic cloves, minced

1 tablespoon paprika

4 ounces chorizo sausage, pepperoni, or kielbasa, halved lengthwise and thinly sliced

8 cups chicken stock

1 pound dried chickpeas or black-eyed peas, sorted, rinsed, and soaked

2 bay leaves

1/2 cup minced fresh parsley

1/2 teaspoon black pepper

1 Heat oil in a soup pot or 5-quart Dutch oven over low heat. Add onion and sauté 5 minutes or until softened. Stir in bell pepper, carrots, and garlic and sauté 5 minutes.

2 Add paprika and cook 1 minute. Add chorizo, stock, chickpeas, and bay leaves and bring to boil. Reduce heat and simmer, covered, 1 1/2 hours or until chickpeas are tender. Skim off fat, remove bay leaves, and stir in parsley and black pepper.

CHICKPEA STEW WITH PORK

Chickpeas, fresh and dried mushrooms, and Marsala wine combine with lean pork to make a very tasty and substantial stew.

SERVES 4

1/2 ounce dried mushrooms

12 ounces boneless lean pork butt, cut into 1-inch cubes

2 tablespoons all-purpose flour

1 small yellow onion, chopped

2 cloves garlic, minced

3 tablespoons Marsala, port, or other sweet red wine

1/2 cup canned low-sodium chicken broth

1 bay leaf

1/2 teaspoon dried rosemary, crumbled

1/4 teaspoon black pepper

1 cup drained cooked chickpeas

8 ounces fresh mushrooms, quartered

1 tablespoon fresh lemon juice

1 In a small bowl, soak dried mushrooms in 1/2 cup warm water 30 minutes. Transfer mushrooms to another small bowl, reserving liquid. (Note: If mushrooms are gritty, strain liquid through a coffee filter or layered cheesecloth before setting aside.)

2 Coat a heavy 10-inch skillet with cooking spray. Place flour in a shallow dish and dredge pork, shaking off any excess. Add pork to skillet over medium heat and cook 10 minutes or until browned on all sides. Transfer to a bowl.

3 Add onion and garlic to skillet and sauté 5 minutes or until softened. Return pork to skillet and add wine, broth, bay leaf, rosemary, pepper, soaked mushrooms, and 1/4 cup soaking liquid. Bring to boil, then reduce heat and simmer, covered, 20 minutes.

4 Add chickpeas and simmer 35 minutes. After 30 minutes, coat a heavy 7-inch skillet with cooking spray and heat over medium heat. Add fresh mushrooms and sauté 2 minutes.

5 Add mushrooms to stew and simmer 10 minutes, then stir in lemon juice.

CHICKPEA AND WINTER SQUASH STEW

This is a meatless stew with plenty of beta-carotene—a plant pigment that's a potent disease fighter—and protein.

SERVES 4

1 tablespoon olive oil

1 large onion, halved and thinly sliced

3 garlic cloves, minced

1 pound butternut squash,
    peeled and cut into 1-inch chunks

1 1/2 teaspoons curry powder

1 teaspoon ground coriander

3/4 teaspoon salt

1 cup canned tomatoes, coarsely chopped

1 cup canned chickpeas, drained and rinsed

1/4 cup raisins

1/4 cup chopped fresh cilantro

1 Preheat oven to 350°F. Heat oil in a nonstick Dutch oven over medium heat. Add onion and garlic and sauté 7 minutes or until onion is golden.

2 Add 1/2 cup water, squash, curry powder, coriander, and salt and stir to coat. Add tomatoes, chickpeas, and raisins and bring to boil.

3 Cover and bake 20 minutes or until squash is tender. Stir in cilantro just before serving.

CHICKPEA-PUMPKIN STEW WITH PEANUT BUTTER

Thickening a stew with peanut butter is a wonderful West African technique.

SERVES 4

1 tablespoon olive oil

1 large onion, finely chopped

3 garlic cloves, minced

2 1/2 pounds fresh pumpkin or butternut
    squash, peeled and cut into 1-inch chunks

12 ounces small red potatoes, halved

1 cup chicken stock

1 can (14 1/2 ounces) low-sodium
    stewed tomatoes, undrained, chopped

3/4 teaspoon dried oregano

3/4 teaspoon salt

1 can (16 ounces) chickpeas,
    drained and rinsed

2 tablespoons creamy peanut butter

1 Heat oil in a nonstick Dutch oven or large saucepan over medium heat. Add onion and garlic and sauté 5 minutes or until onion is softened.

2 Add pumpkin and potatoes and stir to coat. Add stock, tomatoes, oregano, and salt, then bring to boil, reduce heat, and simmer, covered, 20 minutes.

3 Add chickpeas, stir in peanut butter, and simmer 10 minutes or until pumpkin and potatoes are tender.

VIRGINIA PEANUT SOUP

George Washington Carver first created soup from peanuts in the early 1900s. Today peanut soup is prized throughout the United States.

SERVES 8

1 tablespoon unsalted butter

1 large carrot, peeled and chopped

1 celery stalk, chopped

1 small onion, chopped

1 garlic clove, minced

1/3 cup all-purpose flour

6 cups homemade chicken stock or canned low-sodium chicken broth

1 cup unsalted creamy peanut butter

1/3 cup chopped dry-roasted peanuts

2 tablespoons fresh lemon juice

1/4 teaspoon celery seed

1/4 teaspoon salt

1/8 teaspoon black pepper

1/8 teaspoon hot red pepper sauce

1 In a large saucepan over medium-high heat, melt butter. Add carrot, celery, onion, and garlic and sauté 5 minutes or until tender. Stir in flour and cook 2 minutes (do not brown).

2 Gradually whisk in stock and bring to boil. Reduce heat and simmer, uncovered, 30 minutes. Whisk in peanut butter, peanuts, lemon juice, celery seed, salt, and pepper and heat through. Season with red pepper sauce.

CREAMY PEANUT SOUP

A wonderfully flavorful and hearty dish, this soup is a meal in itself.

SERVES 4

1 tablespoon vegetable oil

1 medium yellow onion, finely chopped

1 garlic clove, finely chopped

2 medium all-purpose potatoes, peeled and chopped

2 medium carrots, sliced

1 medium celery stalk, sliced

3 1/2 cups canned low-sodium chicken broth

1/2 cup smooth peanut butter

1/4 teaspoon cayenne pepper

1/4 cup sour cream

1 Heat oil in a large saucepan over medium heat. Add onion and garlic and sauté 1 minute. Stir in potatoes, carrots, and celery, then add broth and bring to boil. Reduce heat and simmer, covered, 15 minutes or until vegetables are tender.

2 Remove from heat and stir in peanut butter and cayenne. Transfer in 2 batches to a food processor or blender, cover, and puree until smooth.

3 Return soup to pan and cook until heated through (do not boil). Ladle into bowls and swirl a spoonful of sour cream into each serving.

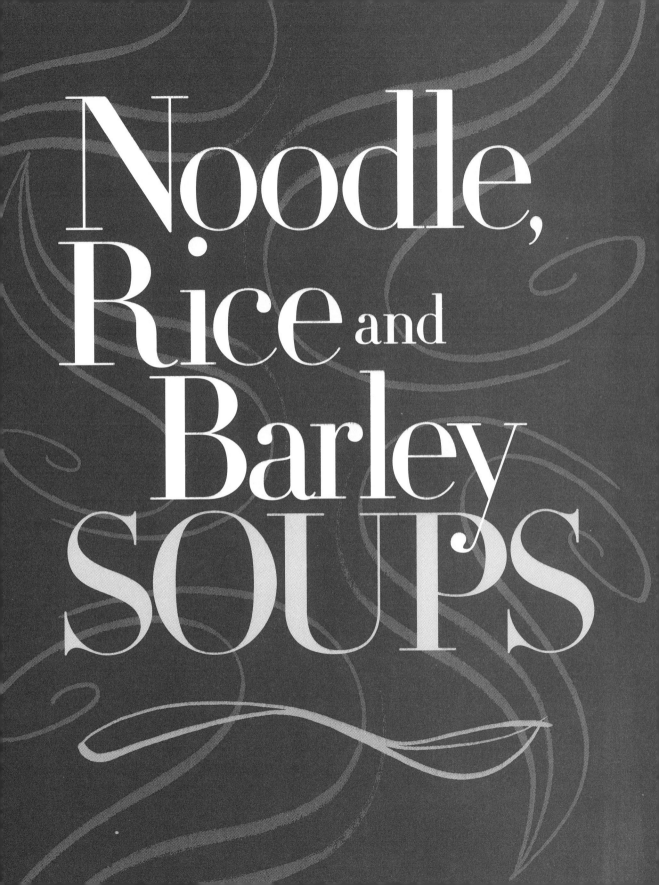

Noodle, Rice and Barley SOUPS

NOODLE, RICE, AND BARLEY SOUPS

recipe list

 EASY: 10 minutes to prepare

QUICK: Ready to eat in 30 minutes

ONE-DISH: contains protein, vegetables, and good carbohydrates (beans, whole-grains, etc.) for a complete healthy meal

HEALTHY: High in nutrients, low in bad fats and empty carbohydrates

SLOW COOKER: Easily adapted for slow cooker by cutting down on liquids

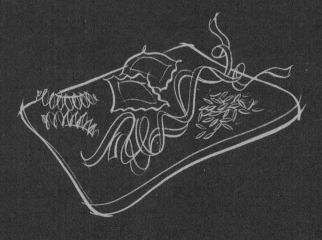

VEGETABLE LO MEIN

This simple Chinese dish has tofu for protein, noodles for carbohydrates, and plenty of vegetables for vitamins and minerals.

SERVES 4

4 ounces Asian egg noodles or
    thin egg noodles

1 tablespoon peanut or vegetable oil

3 scallions, finely chopped, with tops
    sliced and reserved

2 garlic cloves, minced

1 teaspoon minced fresh ginger or
    1/4 teaspoon ground ginger

2 celery stalks, sliced thin

2 medium carrots, peeled and sliced thin

1/4 pound mushrooms, sliced thin

1 cup low-sodium chicken broth or water

2 cups broccoli florets

1 tablespoon cornstarch

1 tablespoon low-sodium soy sauce

1 tablespoon dry sherry

1 teaspoon Asian sesame or peanut oil

1/2 teaspoon sugar

1/2 pound firm tofu, cut into 3/4-inch cubes

1 Cook noodles according to package directions, omitting salt, and then drain and set aside.

2 In a heavy 12-inch skillet over medium-high heat, heat peanut oil. Add scallions, garlic, and ginger and stir-fry 30 seconds. Add celery, carrots, and mushrooms and stir-fry 2 minutes. Stir in 1/2 cup chicken broth, cover, and simmer 3 minutes. Add broccoli, cover, and simmer 2 minutes.

3 In a small bowl, combine remaining chicken broth with cornstarch, soy sauce, sherry, sesame oil, and sugar. Add to skillet and cook, stirring constantly, over medium heat until thick, about 4 minutes. Add noodles and tofu, cover, and simmer 2 minutes or until tofu is heated through. Transfer to a bowl, toss gently, and sprinkle with sliced scallion tops.

GINGERED TOFU AND NOODLE SOUP

Ginger and scallions add pizzazz to this otherwise delicate soup.

SERVES 4

8 ounces fine egg noodles

2 tablespoons olive oil

5 scallions, with tops, cut diagonally into
    1-inch-thick slices

3 tablespoons minced fresh ginger

5 cups chicken stock

1 small head cabbage, finely sliced

12 ounces firm tofu, cut into 1/2-inch cubes

1/4 teaspoon salt

1/8 teaspoon black pepper

1 Cook noodles according to package directions. Drain, transfer to a bowl, and toss with 1 tablespoon oil.

2 In a large saucepan over medium heat, heat remaining oil. Add scallions and ginger and stir-fry 2 minutes or until crisp-tender. Increase heat to high, add stock, and bring to boil. Add cabbage, reduce heat and simmer, uncovered, 2 minutes or until crisp-tender. Stir in noodles, tofu, salt, and pepper.

VIETNAMESE SOUP WITH RICE NOODLES

Aromatic ingredients transform this broth into an exotic dish that makes a substantial starter or a light meal.

SERVES 2

1 ounce dried shiitake mushrooms

2 ounces fine rice noodles,
　　such as vermicelli

6 ounces lean rump steak, diced

1 can (17 ounces) beef broth

2 tablespoons fish sauce

1 heaped teaspoon fresh ginger, grated

1 ounce bean sprouts

1/2 small onion, thinly sliced

2 scallions, thinly sliced

1 medium red chile pepper, seeded and
　　finely chopped (wear gloves when
　　handling; they burn)

1 tablespoon fresh mint, shredded

1 tablespoon fresh cilantro, shredded

1 tablespoon fresh basil, shredded

Garnishes:

Lime wedges

Soy sauce *(optional)*

1 Rinse mushrooms and put in a small bowl. Place rice noodles in a large bowl. Cover mushrooms with boiling water and leave to soak 20 minutes. Cover rice noodles with boiling water and soak 4 minutes, or according to package directions. Drain noodles and set aside.

2 Drain mushrooms and pour soaking liquid into a large saucepan. Trim off and discard any tough stalks from mushrooms, then slice and add to pan. Add steak, broth, fish sauce, and ginger. Bring to boil, then reduce heat and simmer 10 to 15 minutes or until steak is tender. Skim off any scum that rises to surface during cooking.

3 Divide noodles, bean sprouts, and sliced onion between 2 large, deep soup bowls. Use slotted spoon to remove steak and mushrooms from broth and divide them between bowls. Ladle broth into bowls, then scatter scallions, chiles, mint, cilantro, and basil over the top.

4 Serve with lime wedges. Lime juice can be squeezed into broth to taste. Soy sauce can also be added.

TASTY REUBEN SOUP

The ingredients in this soup will remind you of the famous delicatessen sandwich.

SERVES 10

4 cans (14 1/2 ounces each)
　　chicken broth

4 cups shredded cabbage

2 cups medium egg noodles

1 pound fully cooked kielbasa or Polish
　　sausage, halved and cut into 1-inch slices

1/2 cup chopped onion

1 teaspoon caraway seed

1/4 teaspoon garlic powder

1 cup (4 ounces) shredded Swiss cheese

1 In a large saucepan over medium-high heat, combine broth, cabbage, noodles, kielbasa, onion, caraway seed, and garlic powder.

2 Bring to boil, reduce heat, and simmer, covered, 15 minutes or until cabbage and noodles are tender. Garnish with cheese.

CHUNKY BEEF SOUP WITH NOODLES

This satisfying, rich-tasting soup will become a family favorite.

SERVES 8

1 tablespoon vegetable oil

1 pound boneless round steak,
cut into 1/2-inch cubes

1 medium onion, chopped

2 garlic cloves, minced

1 can (14 1/2 ounces) diced tomatoes,
undrained

1 can (10 1/2 ounces) condensed
beef consommé

1 teaspoon chili powder

1 teaspoon salt

1/2 teaspoon dried oregano

1 cup spiral pasta

1 medium green bell pepper, cored,
seeded, and chopped

1/4 cup minced fresh parsley

1 In a large saucepan over medium heat, heat oil. Add meat, onion, and garlic and sauté 5 minutes or until meat is browned and onion is tender.

2 Stir in 2 cups water, tomatoes, consommé, chili powder, salt, and oregano. Bring to boil, reduce heat, and simmer, covered, 1 1/2 hours or until meat is tender.

3 Stir in pasta and bell pepper. Simmer, uncovered, 8 minutes or until noodles are tender. Add parsley.

PASTA-SAUSAGE SOUP

The sausage adds a spicy note to this well-flavored soup.

SERVES 12

1 1/2 pounds hot or sweet
Italian sausage

1 medium onion, chopped

1 medium green bell pepper, cored,
seeded, and cut into strips

1 garlic clove, minced

1 can (28 ounces) tomatoes, chopped,
liquid reserved

2-2 1/2 cups uncooked bow tie pasta

1 tablespoon sugar

1 tablespoon Worcestershire sauce

2 chicken bouillon cubes

1 teaspoon dried basil

1 teaspoon dried thyme

1 teaspoon salt

1 Remove casing from sausages and cut into 1-inch pieces. In a Dutch oven, brown sausage over medium heat. Remove sausage to paper towels and drain off all but 2 tablespoons of the drippings.

2 Sauté onion, pepper, and garlic 3 minutes or until tender. Add sausage, 6 cups water, tomatoes, pasta, sugar, Worcestershire sauce, bouillon cubes, basil, thyme, and salt. Bring to boil, reduce heat, and simmer, uncovered, stirring occasionally, 15 minutes or until pasta is tender.

PASTA AND BEAN SOUP

This popular soup—known as pasta e fagioli in Italian—is closely related to minestrone, but its taste and texture are entirely different.

SERVES 4

2 tablespoons olive oil

1 large yellow onion, finely chopped

1 celery stalk, finely chopped

1 can (8 ounces) tomato sauce

1 garlic clove, minced

2 tablespoons minced parsley

1/2 teaspoon dried rosemary, crumbled

4 cups cooked great Northern beans or
   2 cans (1 pound each) cannellini
   (white kidney beans), drained and rinsed

4 cups beef stock or canned beef broth

1 cup small elbow pasta

1/2 cup grated Parmesan cheese (2 ounces)

1/2 teaspoon salt

1/8 teaspoon black pepper

1 In a 4-quart saucepan over medium heat, heat oil 1 minute. Add onion and celery, and sauté 10 minutes or until very soft.

2 Stir in tomato sauce, garlic, parsley, and rosemary. Cover and cook 5 minutes.

3 Add beans and stock and bring to boil. Reduce heat and simmer. Stir in pasta and cook, uncovered, stirring frequently, 10 minutes or until tender. Stir in cheese, salt, and pepper, then taste and adjust seasonings.

VEGETABLE SOUP WITH MACARONI

Many, many vegetables flavor this healthy macaroni soup with an Italian accent.

SERVES 12

1 pound ground beef

1 cup diced onion

1 cup sliced celery

1 cup sliced carrots

2 garlic cloves, minced

1 can (16 ounces) tomatoes

1 can (15 ounces) tomato sauce

1 can (15 ounces) red kidney beans,
   undrained

5 teaspoons beef bouillon granules

1 tablespoon dried parsley flakes

1/2 teaspoon oregano

1/2 teaspoon sweet basil

1/4 teaspoon black pepper

2 cups shredded cabbage

1 cup frozen or fresh green beans,
   cut in 1-inch pieces *(optional)*

1/2 cup small elbow macaroni

Parmesan cheese, grated

1 In a large, heavy soup pot over medium heat, brown beef, then drain off fat. Add onion, celery, carrots, garlic, tomatoes, tomato sauce, kidney beans, 2 cups water, beef bouillon granules, parsley, oregano, basil, and pepper. Bring to boil, reduce heat, and simmer, covered, 20 minutes.

2 Add cabbage, green beans, if desired, and macaroni. Return to boil, reduce heat, and simmer, covered, until vegetables are tender. If you prefer a thinner soup, add additional water or broth. Sprinkle with Parmesan cheese before serving.

MACARONI SOUP WITH HAM

Leftover ham is the basis for many good soups; this one combines beans and macaroni for substance.

SERVES 10

3 tablespoons olive oil

2 1/2 cups chopped fully cooked ham

1 large onion, finely chopped

3 garlic cloves, minced

2 cans (28 ounces each) crushed tomatoes

2 cans (14 1/2 ounces each) beef broth

1/2 teaspoon salt

1/2 teaspoon dried basil

1/4 teaspoon fennel seed

3 cans (16 ounces each) great Northern beans, drained and rinsed

8 cups cooked macaroni

Grated Parmesan cheese *(optional)*

1 In a Dutch oven or soup pot over medium heat, heat oil. Add ham, onion, and garlic and sauté 5 minutes or until onion is tender.

2 Add 3 1/4 cups water, tomatoes, broth, salt, basil, and fennel seed. Bring to boil, reduce heat, and simmer, covered, 1 hour. Add beans and simmer 30 minutes.

3 Add macaroni and simmer 10 minutes or until heated through. Garnish each serving with cheese, if desired.

MACARONI SOUP WITH BEEF

A chili-macaroni mix provides this dish with some spice, but a can of chopped green chiles makes it really hot.

SERVES 8

1 pound ground beef

1 medium onion, chopped

1 can (15 ounces) pinto beans, drained and rinsed

1 can (14 1/2 ounces) diced tomatoes, undrained

1 can (7 ounces) whole-kernel corn, drained

1 can (4 ounces) chopped green chiles *(optional)*

1/2 teaspoon coarse-grain mustard

1/2 teaspoon salt

1/8 teaspoon black pepper

1 package (7 1/2 ounces) chili-macaroni dinner mix

Salsa con queso dip

1 In a saucepan over medium heat, cook beef and onion until meat is no longer pink and then drain off fat. Stir in 5 cups water, beans, tomatoes, corn, and chiles, if desired. Stir in mustard, salt, pepper, and contents of macaroni dinner sauce packet. Bring to boil, reduce heat, and simmer, covered, 10 minutes.

2 Stir in contents of macaroni packet. Cover and simmer, stirring once, 10 minutes or until macaroni is tender. Serve with salsa con queso dip.

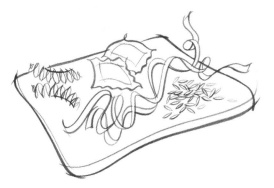

CLASSIC MINESTRONE

You can vary minestrone's ingredients to suit your own tastes by using any fresh, seasonal vegetables, any small pasta shapes, and your own choice of canned beans.

SERVES 4

3 tablespoons olive oil

1 small leek, sliced

1 garlic clove, minced

2 celery stalks, finely sliced

2 medium zucchini, halved lengthwise and cut into half-moon slices

1 parsley sprig, chopped

1 can (19 ounces) cannellini beans, drained and rinsed

1 can (19 ounces) chopped tomatoes

1 bay leaf

2/3 cup dry white wine

1/4 cup soup-pasta shapes

1 strip lemon zest

1 tablespoon grated Parmesan cheese

1 cup Savoy or other green cabbage, shredded

Salt and black pepper

To serve:

1 loaf crusty bread

4 tablespoons pesto sauce (*optional*)

1 Put a kettle of water on to boil. In a large saucepan over medium heat, heat oil and sauté leek 1 minute. Add garlic and cook 1 minute. Add celery and zucchini and cook another 3 minutes.

2 Add parsley, beans, tomatoes, bay leaf, wine, pasta, lemon zest, and 2 1/2 cups boiling water. Cover, bring back to boil, then reduce heat and simmer 7 minutes.

3 Add half Parmesan cheese and cabbage and simmer 5 minutes. Season to taste with salt and pepper. Remove bay leaf, transfer minestrone into four bowls, and shake remaining cheese over each bowl. Serve soup with crusty bread and a small, separate bowl of pesto sauce.

MINESTRONE

Italian cooks have no definite rules for what goes into minestrone. It just has to be a hearty mix of vegetables, white beans, and pasta or rice. To make it vegetarian, substitute vegetable broth for the beef broth.

SERVES 6

1 tablespoon olive oil

1 large yellow onion, chopped

2 garlic cloves, minced

3 1/2 cups low-sodium beef broth

1 can (15 ounces) great Northern beans, drained and rinsed

1 3/4 cups chopped tomatoes or 1 can (14 1/2 ounces) Italian-style tomatoes, undrained, cut up

2 cups coarsely shredded cabbage

2 large carrots, thinly sliced

1 teaspoon dried oregano

1 teaspoon dried basil

1/2 teaspoon salt

1/2 teaspoon black pepper

2 ounces vermicelli or thin spaghetti, broken

1 small zucchini, halved lengthwise and sliced

Grated Parmesan cheese

1 In a large nonstick saucepan over medium-high heat, heat oil. Add onion and garlic and sauté until onion is tender, about 5 minutes. Stir in broth, beans, tomatoes, cabbage, carrots, oregano, basil, salt, and pepper.

2 Bring to boil and stir in vermicelli. Reduce heat, cover, and simmer, until vegetables and pasta are tender, about 15 minutes. Stir in zucchini and cook, uncovered, 3 minutes. Serve with cheese.

MINESTRONE WITH WINTER VEGETABLES

SERVES 6

1 tablespoon extra-virgin olive oil

1 large onion, peeled and finely chopped

3 garlic cloves, minced

1/2 pound dried cannellini or borlotti beans, soaked overnight and drained

1 can plum tomatoes in juice, about 14 ounces

2 tablespoons tomato paste

1/2 pound carrots, peeled and diced

1 large rutabaga, diced

1 celeriac bulb, diced

1/2 pound fresh pumpkin, peeled and diced

1 teaspoon fresh thyme leaves

1 bay leaf

3 allspice berries, crushed

1/2 pound all-purpose potatoes, peeled and diced

1/3 pound green beans cut into short lengths

3 1/2 ounces small pasta shapes, such as farfallini (bows) or conchigliette (shells), or broken spaghetti

1/4 pound spinach, chopped

4 tablespoons shredded fresh basil

Salt and pepper

2 ounces Parmesan cheese, freshly grated

1 In a large saucepan over medium heat, heat oil. Add onion and garlic and sauté 4 minutes or until onion is translucent. Add dry beans and 7 cups water. Bring to boil and boil 10 minutes. Reduce heat, and simmer, covered, 30 minutes.

2 Add tomatoes with juice (break them up with a fork), tomato paste, carrots, rutabaga, celeriac, and pumpkin. Stir in thyme, bay leaf, and crushed allspice. Return to boil, reduce heat, and simmer, covered, for 20 minutes.

3 Stir in potatoes and green beans. Simmer, covered, 15 minutes. Stir in pasta and cook, covered, 10 minutes or until dry beans are tender and pasta is cooked.

4 Add spinach and basil. Season to taste with salt and pepper. Simmer uncovered 2 minutes or until spinach wilts. Ladle into warm bowls and sprinkle with Parmesan cheese.

This minestrone makes the most of winter vegetables. Beans and pasta give it heft.

VEGETABLE MINESTRONE

This meal-in-a-bowl soup keeps well, so refrigerate what you don't eat the first time around and serve it later in the week.

SERVES 8

4 teaspoons olive oil

2 yellow onions, chopped

4 garlic cloves, minced

2 carrots, peeled, halved lengthwise, and thinly sliced

1 all-purpose potato, peeled and cut into 1/2-inch cubes

1 medium zucchini, cut into 1/2-inch cubes

1/4 cup minced fresh basil or 1 tablespoon dried basil, crumbled

1 teaspoon dried oregano, crumbled

2 large bay leaves

4 medium tomatoes, peeled, cored, seeded, and chopped, or 1 large can (28 ounces) crushed low-sodium tomatoes, with juice

5 cups low-sodium chicken broth

1/4 pound green beans, trimmed and cut into 1-inch pieces

4 ounces rotelle or other tubular pasta

2 cups cooked and drained pinto or white kidney beans

1/2 cup grated Parmesan cheese

3 tablespoons minced parsley

1 In a large heavy soup pot, heat olive oil over low heat 1 minute. Add onions and garlic and sauté 5 minutes or until soft. Increase heat to medium and add carrots, potato, zucchini, basil, oregano, and bay leaves. Cook, uncovered, 5 minutes, stirring occasionally.

2 Add tomatoes and chicken broth, and bring to boil. Then reduce heat, and simmer, uncovered, 20 minutes. Add green beans, cover, and simmer 10 minutes or until beans are tender but still crisp. Remove bay leaves.

3 Cook rotelle according to package directions, omitting salt. Drain and add to soup along with pinto beans. Cook until heated through, about 3 minutes. Ladle into bowls and sprinkle with cheese and parsley.

SPINACH MINESTRONE

This flavorful soup offers beans and pasta to satisfy your appetite plus spinach, tomatoes, onion, and carrots to meet your vitamin quotas.

SERVES 8

1 large onion, chopped

1 garlic clove, minced

4 cups reduced-sodium chicken broth

1 can (16 ounces) kidney beans, drained and rinsed

1 can (14 1/2 ounces) no-salt-added diced tomatoes, undrained

2 medium carrots, sliced

1/2 cup elbow macaroni

1/4 teaspoon dried oregano

1 package (10 ounces) frozen chopped spinach, thawed

Grated Parmesan cheese

1 Coat a large saucepan with cooking spray. Add onion and garlic and sauté over medium heat 3 minutes or until tender.

2 Add broth, beans, tomatoes, carrots, macaroni, and oregano. Bring to boil, reduce heat, and simmer, covered, 20 minutes or until vegetables and macaroni are tender.

3 Stir in spinach and bring to boil. Remove from heat and let stand 5 minutes. Sprinkle with cheese.

MINESTRONE FOR A CROWD

Here is a version of this Italian soup, designed to feed a hungry mob very well indeed.

SERVES 24

1 beef chuck roast (4 pounds)

2 bay leaves

2 medium onions, diced

2 cups sliced carrots

2 cups sliced celery

1 can (28 ounces) tomatoes with liquid, cut up

1 can (15 ounces) tomato sauce

1/4 cup chopped fresh parsley

4 teaspoons dried basil

1 teaspoon garlic powder

Salt and black pepper

2 packages (9 ounces each) frozen Italian or cut green beans

1 package (16 ounces) frozen peas

2 cans (15 1/2 ounces each) kidney beans, rinsed and drained

2 boxes (7 ounces each) shell macaroni, cooked and drained

Grated Parmesan cheese

1 Place beef, 1 gallon water, and bay leaves in a large soup pot. Bring to boil, reduce heat, and simmer, covered, 3 hours or until meat is tender.

2 Remove meat from stock and let cool. Add onions, carrots, and celery to stock. Bring to boil, reduce heat, and simmer, covered, 20 minutes or until vegetables are tender.

3 Cut meat into bite-size pieces and add to stock. Add tomatoes, tomato sauce, parsley, basil, garlic powder, and salt and pepper to taste. Then add green beans, peas, and kidney beans. Simmer 10 minutes or until vegetables are done. Add macaroni and heat through. Remove bay leaves. Ladle into bowls and sprinkle with cheese.

INSTANT MINESTRONE

A well-stocked pantry can combine with fresh ground beef for an easy, almost instant main-dish soup.

SERVES 10

2 pounds ground beef, browned and drained

2 cans (10 3/4 ounces each) minestrone soup, undiluted

2 cans (15 ounces each) chili beans with gravy

1 can (16 ounces) Mexican-style or regular stewed tomatoes

1/2-1 cup mild, medium, or hot salsa

1 In a large saucepan, combine all ingredients. Mix well and bring to boil. Reduce heat and simmer, covered, 20 to 30 minutes.

MICROWAVE MINESTRONE

This hearty soup is packed with vegetables and pasta, and it takes only minutes to make.

SERVES 5

1 cup sliced carrots

1 cup sliced celery

1 cup sliced zucchini

1/2 cup diced yellow bell pepper

1 small onion, chopped

1 tablespoon olive oil

1 can (15 ounces) cannellini or white kidney beans, drained and rinsed

1 can (14 1/2 ounces) beef broth

1 can (14 1/2 ounces) diced tomatoes, undrained

1 cup medium pasta shells, cooked and drained

1/2 teaspoon dried basil

1/2 teaspoon salt

1/4 teaspoon black pepper

1 In a 2-quart microwavable bowl, combine carrots, celery, zucchini, bell pepper, and onion. Drizzle with oil and toss to coat.

2 Cover and microwave on high 5 minutes. Stir in beans, broth, tomatoes, pasta, basil, salt, and pepper. Cover and microwave on high 15 minutes.

MINESTRONE WITH TORTELLINI

This is a rich, savory minestrone that's ready in minutes: Just what you need on a busy day.

SERVES 6

2 tablespoons (1/4 stick) butter

1 medium red onion, sliced

2 small yellow squashes, sliced

1 garlic clove, chopped

5 cups canned beef broth

2 ounces day-old Italian bread, cubed

8 ounces refrigerated or frozen
  meat-filled tortellini

1 package (10 ounces) frozen chopped
  broccoli, partially thawed under warm
  running water

Salt and black pepper

12 cherry tomatoes, halved

1 In a large saucepan over medium heat, melt butter. Add sliced onion and sauté 5 minutes or until soft. Stir in squash and garlic and sauté 2 minutes

2 Add broth and bread. Increase heat and bring to boil, stirring occasionally. Reduce heat and simmer, covered, 2 minutes.

3 Add tortellini and simmer 7 minutes. Increase heat and bring to boil. Add broccoli and cook 3 minutes or until tender. Season with salt and pepper to taste, stir in cherry tomatoes, and serve.

SAUSAGE-TORTELLINI SOUP

This hearty Italian-flavored soup is great for winter get-togethers.

SERVES 14

1 pound bulk Italian sausage

6 cups beef stock

1 can (28 ounces) stewed tomatoes

1 can (15 ounces) tomato sauce

2 cups sliced zucchini

1 large onion, chopped

1 cup sliced carrots

1 cup sliced fresh mushrooms

1 medium green bell pepper, cored,
  seeded, and chopped

1/4 cup minced fresh parsley

2 teaspoons sugar

1 teaspoon dried oregano

1 teaspoon dried basil

1 garlic clove, minced

2 cups frozen cheese tortellini

Grated Parmesan cheese *(optional)*

1 In a skillet over medium heat, cook sausage until no longer pink and drain off fat. Transfer to a 5-quart slow cooker.

2 Add stock, tomatoes, tomato sauce, zucchini, onion, carrots, mushrooms, bell pepper, parsley, sugar, oregano, basil, and garlic. Cover and cook on high until vegetables are tender, 3 to 4 hours.

3 Cook pasta according to package directions and drain. Stir into slow cooker, cover, and cook 30 minutes. Serve with cheese, if desired.

CREAMY TORTELLINI SOUP

Unexpected company? Keep frozen tortellini on hand, and you can have this elegant dish on the table in minutes.

SERVES 4

1 package (1 pound) frozen cheese
    or meat tortellini

3 tablespoons olive or vegetable oil

1 medium yellow onion, coarsely chopped

5 garlic cloves, minced

4 cups chicken stock

1 package (10 ounces) frozen green peas,
    thawed and drained

2 cups low-fat plain yogurt, well stirred,
    or sour cream

1/4 teaspoon black pepper

1/3 cup minced fresh parsley

1/2 cup grated Parmesan cheese *(optional)*

1 Cook tortellini according to package directions. Drain, transfer to a bowl, add 1 tablespoon oil, and toss.

2 In a large saucepan over medium heat, heat remaining oil. Add onion and garlic and sauté until soft, about 3 minutes. Increase heat to high, add stock and peas, cover, and bring to boil. Reduce heat to low and whisk in yogurt. Add tortellini and pepper and cook until heated through without boiling. Stir in parsley. Serve with cheese, if desired.

TORTELLINI-BEAN SOUP

Packaged ingredients make this soup a snap to assemble.

SERVES 6

4 cups chicken stock

1 package (9 ounces) refrigerated
    cheese tortellini

1 can (15 ounces) cannellini or white kidney
    beans, drained and rinsed

1 can (14 1/2 ounces) Italian diced
    tomatoes, undrained

1 1/2 teaspoons dried basil

1 tablespoon red wine vinegar

Grated Parmesan cheese *(optional)*

Coarsely ground black pepper *(optional)*

1 In a large saucepan over medium-high heat, bring stock to boil. Stir in pasta, then reduce heat, cover, and simmer, stirring occasionally, 4 minutes.

2 Stir in beans, tomatoes, and basil and simmer 4 minutes or until pasta is tender. Stir in vinegar. Sprinkle with cheese and pepper, if desired.

RAVIOLI SOUP

This soup has a rich tomato base to hold tender, cheese-filled ravioli.

SERVES 8

1 pound ground beef

1 can (28 ounces) crushed tomatoes

1 can (14 1/2 ounces) beef broth

1 can (6 ounces) tomato paste

1 1/2 cups chopped onion

1/4 cup minced fresh parsley

2 garlic cloves, minced

3/4 teaspoon dried basil

1/2 teaspoon dried oregano

1/2 teaspoon onion salt

1/2 teaspoon sugar

1/2 teaspoon salt

1/4 teaspoon black pepper

1/4 teaspoon dried thyme

1/4 cup grated Parmesan cheese

1 package (9 ounces) refrigerated
    cheese ravioli

1 In a Dutch oven or soup pot over medium heat, cook beef until no longer pink and drain off fat from surface.

2 Add 2 cups water, tomatoes, broth, tomato paste, onion, parsley, garlic, basil, oregano, onion salt, sugar, salt, pepper, and thyme. Bring to boil, reduce heat, and simmer, covered, 30 minutes. Stir in cheese.

3 Cook ravioli according to package directions and drain. Add to pot and heat through.

BEEF RAVIOLI SOUP

Floating stuffed pasta in soup is part of Italian as well as Chinese cooking. This can be an easy starter.

SERVES 4

2 tablespoons vegetable oil

1 cup sliced celery

1/2 cup chopped onion

1 cup sliced carrots

4 cups beef stock

1/8 teaspoon black pepper

1/4 teaspoon crushed red pepper flakes

1 can (15 ounces) beef ravioli

Garnish:

1/4 cup chopped fresh parsley

Grated Parmesan cheese

1 In a large soup pot over medium heat, heat oil. Add celery, onion, and carrots, and sauté for 3 minutes.

2 Add stock and seasonings. Bring to boil, reduce heat, and simmer, covered, 15 minutes or until vegetables are tender. Stir in ravioli and heat through. Garnish with parsley and Parmesan cheese.

LASAGNA SOUP

Some packaged ingredients make this recipe easy and quick to make. Fresh zucchini adds nutrients and a little crunch.

SERVES 10

1 pound ground beef

1/2 cup chopped onion

1 package (7 3/4 ounces) lasagna
    dinner mix

1 can (14 1/2 ounces) diced
    tomatoes, undrained

1 can (7 ounces) whole-kernel corn,
    undrained

2 tablespoons grated Parmesan cheese

1 small zucchini, chopped

1 In a Dutch oven or soup pot over medium heat, cook beef and onion until meat is no longer pink and drain off fat.

2 Add 5 cups water, contents of lasagna sauce packet, tomatoes, corn, and cheese. Bring to boil, reduce heat, and simmer, covered, 10 minutes, stirring occasionally. Add lasagna and zucchini. Cover and simmer until noodles are tender, about 10 minutes. Serve immediately.

PASTA PIZZA SOUP

Oregano adds the pizza flavor to this tasty combination of tender vegetables, pasta spirals, and ground beef.

SERVES 8

1 pound ground beef
4 ounces fresh mushrooms, sliced
1 medium onion, chopped
1 celery stalk, thinly sliced
1 garlic clove, minced
1 can (14 1/2 ounces) Italian diced
   tomatoes, undrained
2 medium carrots, chopped
4 teaspoons beef bouillon granules
1 bay leaf
1 1/2 teaspoons dried oregano
1 1/2 cups cooked tricolor spiral pasta

1 In a large saucepan over medium heat, cook beef, mushrooms, onion, celery, and garlic until beef is no longer pink and vegetables are tender. Then drain off fat.

2 Stir in 4 cups water, tomatoes, carrots, bouillon, bay leaf, and oregano. Bring to boil, reduce heat, and simmer, covered, 20 minutes or until carrots are tender. Stir in pasta and heat through. Remove bay leaf before serving.

CHUNKY VEGETABLE SOUP WITH PASTA

Here is a tasty, filling vegetarian soup to delight everyone for lunch or supper.

MAKES 11 CUPS

2 tablespoons olive or canola oil
2 leeks or onions, trimmed and thinly sliced
2 large carrots, cut into 1/2-inch dice
8 ounces rutabaga, cut into 1/2-inch dice

8 ounces fennel or celery, cut into 1/2-inch dice
6 cups vegetable stock
2 cups canned crushed tomatoes
4 ounces orzo or any small pasta
1/8 teaspoon salt
1/8 teaspoon black pepper
1/4 cup shredded fresh basil
2 tablespoons grated Parmesan cheese

1 In a large saucepan, heat oil over medium heat. Sauté leeks until softened but not browned.

2 Sauté remaining vegetables until softened. Stir in stock. Bring to boil, reduce heat, and simmer, partially covered, 5 minutes or until vegetables are almost soft.

3 Stir in tomatoes and return to boil. Add orzo and cook 8 minutes. Add salt, pepper, and basil. Serve with cheese sprinkled on each portion.

PENNSYLVANIA DUTCH DUMPLING SOUP

This soup is a speedy, but hearty, appetizer for lunch or dinner.

SERVES 4

Soup:
3 cups canned reduced-sodium
   chicken or beef broth
2 cups fresh or frozen whole-kernel corn

Dumplings:
2/3 cup all-purpose flour
1/2 teaspoon salt
2 large eggs

1 In a large saucepan, bring broth, 3 cups water, and corn to boil over high heat.

2 Meanwhile, for the dumplings, combine flour and salt in a small bowl. In another small bowl, whisk eggs thoroughly. Stir beaten eggs into flour mixture until a soft dough forms. Dip a teaspoon into cold water and use it to spoon up dough. With a knife, push off half-teaspoon-size pieces of dough into boiling broth. Use all dough.

3 Reduce heat, cover, and simmer 15 minutes or until dumplings are puffy and cooked through.

WILD RICE SOUP

This creamy, aromatic soup helps you spread the pleasure from a small amount of wild rice to the maximum number of eaters.

SERVES 8

1/3 cup uncooked wild rice
1 tablespoon vegetable oil
1/2 cup butter
1 medium onion, chopped
1 celery stalk, finely chopped
1 carrot, finely chopped
1/2 cup all-purpose flour
3 cups chicken stock
2 cups half-and-half
1/2 teaspoon dried rosemary
1 teaspoon salt

1 Rinse rice and drain. In a medium saucepan, combine rice, oil, and 1 quart water. Bring to boil, reduce heat, and simmer, covered, 30 minutes.

2 Meanwhile, in a large soup pot over medium heat, melt butter. Sauté onion, celery, and carrot until vegetables are almost tender.

3 Blend in flour, cook, and stir for 2 minutes. Add stock and rice. Bring to boil, cook, and stir until slightly thickened. Stir in half-and-half, rosemary, and salt. Reduce heat and simmer, uncovered, 20 minutes or until rice is tender.

WILD RICE SOUP WITH HAM

This is a luxurious soup for guests, thanks to its ultra-rich mix of butter, cream, egg yolks, and mushrooms.

SERVES 12

1 large meaty ham bone
1 large onion, chopped
1 1/2 cups uncooked wild rice, rinsed
6 tablespoons butter or margarine
6 tablespoons all-purpose flour
2 cups heavy whipping cream
3 egg yolks
3 jars (4 1/2 ounces each) sliced mushrooms
1 can (14 1/2 ounces) chicken broth
1/2 teaspoon white pepper
1 teaspoon dried thyme
1 tablespoon chopped parsley
Milk

1 Place ham bone, onion, and 3 quarts water in an 8-quart soup pot. Bring to boil, reduce heat, and simmer, covered, 2 1/2 hours. Remove ham bone. When cool enough to handle, remove meat from bone and set aside. Discard bone.

2 Add wild rice to stock. Simmer 1 hour or until tender. Remove from heat, drain, and reserve stock. Set rice and onion aside. Add enough water to stock to make 2 quarts and set aside.

3 In the same pot, melt butter over medium heat. Stir in flour and cook for 2 minutes. Do not brown. Gradually stir in reserved stock. Bring to rapid boil over high heat and boil 3 minutes, stirring constantly. Remove from heat.

4 In a mixing bowl, combine cream and egg yolks. Add 1 cup stock to egg mixture, then stir into pot. Return soup to heat and heat over medium-low (do not boil). Add reserved rice, onion, and ham along with mushrooms, chicken broth, pepper, thyme, and parsley. Thin with milk if necessary.

BEEFY WILD RICE SOUP

This rich-in-flavor soup helps stave off the chill on a wintry night.

SERVES 10

1 pound ground beef

1/2 teaspoon Italian seasoning

2 large onions, chopped

3 celery stalks, chopped

1 cup wild rice

2 teaspoons beef bouillon granules

1/2 teaspoon black pepper

1/4 teaspoon hot red pepper sauce

3 cans (10 3/4 ounces each) condensed
    cream of mushroom soup

1 can (4 ounces) mushroom stems
    and pieces, drained

1 In a Dutch oven or soup pot over medium heat, cook beef and Italian seasoning until beef is no longer pink and drain off fat.

2 Add 2 cups water, onions, celery, rice, bouillon, pepper, and red pepper sauce. Bring to boil, reduce heat, and simmer, covered, 45 minutes.

3 Stir in soup, mushrooms, and 4 cups water. Cover and simmer 30 minutes.

RICE-STUFFED BELL PEPPER SOUP

Instead of baking stuffed bell peppers, you can make this soup, with all the ingredients simmered together in a tasty broth.

SERVES 16

1 pound ground beef

4 cups tomato juice

3 medium red or green bell peppers,
    cored, seeded, and diced

1 1/2 cups chili sauce

1 cup long-grain rice

2 celery stalks, diced

1 large onion, diced

3 chicken bouillon cubes

2 garlic cloves, minced

1/2 teaspoon salt

2 teaspoons browning sauce *(optional)*

1 In a Dutch oven or soup pot over medium heat, cook beef until no longer pink and drain off fat.

2 Add 8 cups water, tomato juice, peppers, chili sauce, rice, celery, onion, bouillon, garlic, salt, and browning sauce, if desired. Bring to boil, reduce heat, and simmer, uncovered, 1 hour or until rice is tender.

TOMATO AND RED RICE SOUP

Canned tomatoes have more color and flavor than most fresh ones, particularly during the colder months.

SERVES 4

2 tablespoons extra virgin olive oil

6 shallots, finely chopped

3 ounces red rice

5 ounces dry white wine

1 can (14 1/2 ounces) vegetable broth

1 can (14 1/2 ounces) chopped tomatoes

3 tablespoons fresh oregano or basil, finely chopped

Salt and black pepper

To serve:

4 tablespoons *crème fraîche*

Fresh basil or oregano leaves

1 In a large saucepan over medium heat, heat oil. Add shallots and sauté 4 minutes or until softened.

2 Add rice and stir to coat all grains with oil, then cook 30 seconds. Stir in wine, raise heat, and boil rapidly 30 seconds. Add broth and tomatoes with their juice. Bring to boil, reduce heat, and simmer, covered, 35 minutes or until rice is just tender.

3 Stir in chopped oregano or basil, and season with salt and pepper to taste. Ladle into serving bowls, add 1 tablespoon of *crème fraîche* to each one, and top with a few basil or oregano leaves.

LEMON RICE SOUP

This lemony soup can be made in a flash and served hot or cold.

SERVES 4

8 cups chicken stock

3/4 cup long-grain white rice

6 scallions, with tops, sliced

1/2 cup minced fresh parsley

1 teaspoon grated lemon zest

1/3 cup lemon juice

1 In a soup pot or 5-quart Dutch oven over medium heat, bring stock to boil. Add rice, scallions, parsley, and lemon zest. Return to boil, then reduce heat and simmer, covered, 20 minutes or until rice is tender. Remove from heat and stir in lemon juice.

GREEK SPINACH, EGG, AND LEMON SOUP WITH RICE

A traditional Greek combination is made healthier with fewer egg yolks, reduced-fat broth, and brown rice without compromising the rich flavor and velvety texture. (Photograph on page 5)

SERVES 4

3 cups reduced-sodium, fat-free chicken broth

3 scallions, thinly sliced

3 garlic cloves, minced

1 package (10 ounces) frozen chopped spinach

1/2 teaspoon oregano

1 cup cooked brown rice

1 teaspoon grated lemon zest

3 tablespoons fresh lemon juice

1/2 teaspoon salt

1 large egg plus 2 egg whites

1 In a medium saucepan, combine 1/4 cup broth, scallions, and garlic. Cook over medium heat 2 minutes or until scallions are tender.

2 Add remaining 2 3/4 cups broth, spinach, and oregano, and bring to boil. Reduce heat and simmer, covered, 5 minutes or until spinach is tender.

3 Stir in rice, lemon zest, lemon juice, and salt, and return to simmer. Remove 1/2 cup hot liquid and whisk into whole egg and egg whites in medium bowl. Whisking constantly, pour warmed egg mixture into simmering soup.

SPANISH MEATBALL STEW

SERVES 4

1 pound lean ground beef
1 large egg, lightly beaten
1/3 cup dried bread crumbs
4 garlic cloves, minced
1/2 teaspoon salt
1/2 teaspoon black pepper
1/2 teaspoon dried basil, crumbled
1/2 teaspoon dried thyme, crumbled
2 tablespoons olive oil
1 medium yellow onion, finely chopped
1 medium red bell pepper, cored, seeded,
    and cut into 1-inch-square pieces
1 cup canned tomatoes,
    drained and chopped
1 1/2 cups beef stock
2 tablespoons tomato paste
1/3 cup long-grain white rice
1 cup frozen green peas
1/2 cup pimiento-stuffed green olives
1 tablespoon minced fresh cilantro or
    flat-leaf parsley *(optional)*
1 tablespoon drained small capers *(optional)*

1 In a large bowl, combine beef, egg, bread crumbs, half of garlic, 1/4 teaspoon salt, 1/4 teaspoon black pepper, 1/4 teaspoon basil, and 1/4 teaspoon thyme. Shape into 16 balls about 1 1/2 inches in diameter.

2 Arrange meatballs around edge of an ungreased 10- to 12-inch microwavable plate and cover with wax paper. Microwave on high 5 minutes or until golden brown. At midway point, move meatballs in center to outer edge and those on outer edge to center. Set aside.

3 In an ungreased 3-quart microwavable baking dish with a lid, combine oil, onion, bell pepper, and remaining garlic, salt, black pepper, basil, and thyme. Cover and microwave 4 minutes or until onion is glassy, stirring once midway.

4 Stir in tomatoes, stock, tomato paste, and meatballs. Cover and microwave 5 minutes, stirring once midway. Stir in rice, cover, and microwave 3 minutes.

5 Cover, reduce power to medium high, and microwave until rice is just tender, 8 to 10 minutes. Stir in peas and olives, cover, increase power to high, and microwave 5 minutes or until peas are cooked. Let stand, covered, in microwave oven 5 minutes. Just before serving, garnish with cilantro and capers, if desired.

Here is a stew to make in a microwave oven. In this adaptation of a Spanish recipe, olives add some unexpected zip.

BEEF-BARLEY SOUP

This is a rich, filling soup that takes the chill off winter evenings for a family or a crowd.

SERVES 10

4 pounds meaty cross-cut beef shanks, about 1 inch thick

3/4 teaspoon salt

3/4 teaspoon black pepper

1/4 cup all-purpose flour

3 tablespoons vegetable oil

1 pound mushrooms, sliced

3 large carrots, peeled and thinly sliced

1 large yellow onion, chopped

1 celery stalk, chopped

3 garlic cloves, minced

3 cups homemade beef stock or canned low-sodium beef broth

3 cups homemade chicken stock or canned low-sodium chicken broth

1 can (14 ounces) low-sodium whole tomatoes, undrained

1/3 cup medium pearl barley

1 bay leaf

1 teaspoon chopped fresh thyme or 1/4 teaspoon dried thyme leaves

1/4 cup chopped parsley

1 Season beef shanks with salt and pepper, then coat with flour, shaking off any excess. In a 6-quart Dutch oven, heat 2 tablespoons oil over medium-high heat. Add beef shanks and cook, turning occasionally, 10 minutes or until evenly browned. Add 8 cups cold water, increase heat to high, and bring to boil. Reduce heat, cover partially, and simmer 1 1/2 hours, skimming surface occasionally.

2 In a large heavy skillet, heat remaining 1 table-spoon of oil over medium-high heat. Add mushrooms, carrots, onion, celery, and garlic and sauté 5 minutes.

3 To the Dutch oven, add vegetables, beef and chicken stocks, tomatoes and their juices, barley, bay leaf, and thyme. Return to boil, stirring to break up tomatoes. Reduce heat and simmer, uncovered, 45 minutes or until beef is tender.

4 With a slotted spoon, transfer beef to cutting board. When cool enough to handle, cut meat into bite-size pieces and return to soup, discarding bones. Reheat soup until steaming. Discard bay leaf and stir in parsley.

EASY-BEEF BARLEY SOUP

This is a delicious and healthy way to use up leftovers from a beef roast and to add vegetables to your diet.

SERVES 12 TO 14

2 cups beef stock

2 cups chopped cooked roast beef

1/2 cup chopped carrots

3 celery stalks, chopped

1/2 cup chopped onion

1 can (14 1/2 ounces) diced tomatoes, undrained

1 cup quick-cooking barley

1 teaspoon dried oregano

1/2 teaspoon black pepper

1 can (10 3/4 ounces) condensed tomato soup

1/2 cup frozen or canned peas

1/2 cup frozen or canned cut green or wax beans

Seasoned salt to taste

1 In a Dutch oven or soup pot, combine 8 cups water, stock, beef, carrots, celery, onion, tomatoes, barley, oregano, and pepper. Bring to boil, reduce heat, and simmer, covered, 25 minutes, stirring occasionally.

2 Add soup, peas, and beans and simmer, uncovered, 10 minutes. Add seasoned salt.

BEEF-BARLEY SOUP
WITH POTATOES

Potatoes plus barley make a filling and thoroughly satisfying soup.

SERVES 8

2 meaty beef soup bones

2 beef bouillon cubes or 2 teaspoons
   beef bouillon granules

1 pound ground beef

1/4-1/2 cup medium pearl barley

1 large carrot, diced

1 small onion, chopped

3-4 all-purpose potatoes,
   peeled and diced

2 teaspoons garlic salt

1 teaspoon onion powder

2 teaspoons dried parsley

1 teaspoon salt

1 teaspoon black pepper

1 In a large Dutch oven or soup pot, bring 2 quarts water and soup bones to rapid boil and add bouillon. Stir in ground beef in small amounts. Reduce heat and simmer, covered, 1 1/2 hours or until meat comes easily off the bones.

2 Remove bones. Strain stock. Cool and then chill stock. Scrape off fat. Remove meat from bones, dice, and return to broth with barley, carrot, onion, potatoes, and seasonings. Bring to boil. Reduce heat and simmer, covered, about 1 hour or until vegetables are tender.

BEEF-BARLEY SOUP
WITH CABBAGE

Cabbage and spinach give this beef-barley soup a new twist.

SERVES 10

1 pound ground beef

2 cups cubed, peeled potatoes

1 cup shredded cabbage

1 cup chopped onion

2 beef bouillon cubes

1 cup sliced celery

1 cup sliced carrot

1 can (28 ounces) tomatoes with
   liquid, cut up

1 can (16 ounces) cut green beans,
   undrained

1/3 cup pearl barley

1 1/2 teaspoons salt

1/2 teaspoon dried basil

1/2 teaspoon dried thyme

1/4 teaspoon pepper

1 bay leaf

1 package (10 ounces) frozen
   spinach, chopped

1 In a Dutch oven or soup pot over medium heat, brown meat. Drain off fat.

2 Stir in 5 cups water, potatoes, cabbage, onion, bouillon cubes, celery, carrot, tomatoes, green beans, barley, and seasonings. Bring to boil, reduce heat, and simmer, covered, 40 minutes. Add spinach, cover, and simmer 15 minutes.

3 Stir to blend spinach into soup. Remove bay leaf before serving.

BROCCOLI AND BARLEY SOUP

Filling and delicious, this soup offers welcome sustenance on a chilly day.

SERVES 4

1 tablespoon olive oil

1 onion, finely chopped

3 garlic cloves, minced

2 carrots, thinly sliced

2/3 cup quick-cooking barley

1/2 cup chicken stock

1 can (14 1/2 ounces) low-sodium stewed tomatoes

3/4 teaspoon salt

1/2 teaspoon pepper

1/2 teaspoon dried tarragon

4 cups small broccoli florets

1 In a large saucepan or Dutch oven, heat oil over medium heat. Add onion and garlic, and sauté 5 minutes or until softened. Add carrots and sauté 4 minutes.

2 Add barley, stirring to coat. Stir in 3 1/2 cups water, stock, tomatoes, salt, pepper, and tarragon. Bring to boil, breaking up tomatoes with a spoon. Reduce to simmer, cover, and cook 20 minutes or until barley is tender.

3 Add broccoli and cook 5 minutes or until just tender.

BARLEY BORSCHT

Barley gives this authentic borscht a nutty flavor and the added heft of a healthy whole grain.

SERVES 16

2 pounds beef bones

1 medium onion, chopped

1 bay leaf

1 teaspoon salt

10 whole peppercorns

1 medium rutabaga, diced

3 cups fresh diced beets

2 cups chopped celery

1 small head cabbage, shredded

2 1/2 cups diced carrots

2 1/2 cups diced peeled potatoes

3/4 cup pearl barley

1 can (14 1/2 ounces) tomatoes with liquid, cut up

1/4 cup vinegar

Sour cream (*optional*)

Fresh dill

1 In a Dutch oven, combine beef bones, onion, bay leaf, salt, peppercorns, and 6 cups water. Bring to boil, reduce heat, and simmer, covered, 2 hours. Strain stock, discard bones, onion, and seasonings. Skim fat and return stock to pot.

2 Add rutabaga, beets, celery, cabbage, carrots, potatoes, and barley. Return to boil, reduce heat, and simmer, covered, 50 minutes or until vegetables are almost tender and barley is cooked.

3 Stir in tomatoes with liquid and vinegar and heat through. Ladle into serving bowls. Top with a dollop of sour cream, if desired. Sprinkle with dill.

MUSHROOM-BARLEY SOUP

This nutritious soup is even more flavorful if made ahead of time and reheated just before serving. (Photograph on page 24)

SERVES 4

2 large yellow onions, chopped
3 carrots, peeled and sliced
1/2 pound mushrooms, sliced thin
4 cups low-sodium beef broth
1/4 cup parsley, chopped
1/2 cup medium pearl barley
1/4 teaspoon black pepper

1 In a large heavy saucepan over medium-high heat, combine onions, carrots, mushrooms, broth, parsley, barley, and pepper. Bring to boil, reduce heat, and simmer, partly covered, 40 minutes or until barley is tender.

MUSHROOM-BARLEY SOUP WITH RED BELL PEPPER

This soup has celery and red bell pepper instead of carrot for a slightly sharper taste.

SERVES 4

2 large yellow onions, chopped
2 celery stalks, sliced
1/2 red bell pepper, cored, seeded, and chopped
1/2 pound mushrooms, sliced thin
4 cups low-sodium beef broth
1/4 cup parsley, chopped
1/2 cup medium pearl barley
1/4 teaspoon black pepper

1 In a large heavy saucepan over medium-high heat, combine onions, celery, bell pepper, mushrooms, broth, parsley, barley, and pepper. Bring to boil, reduce heat, and simmer, partly covered, 40 minutes or until barley is tender.

BEEF-BARLEY SOUP WITH LEEKS AND RED WINE

This is a soup with a hearty aroma and a satisfying combination of hunger-slaking ingredients.

SERVES 6

2 tablespoons olive or canola oil
8 ounces lean beef stew meat, cut into thin 1/2-inch strips
2 leeks or onions, trimmed and sliced
8 ounces mushrooms, sliced
1/2 cup pearl barley
7 cups beef stock
1 cup red wine or beef stock
2 teaspoons lemon juice
1/8 teaspoon salt
1/8 teaspoon black pepper

1 In a 4-quart saucepan, heat 1 tablespoon oil over medium heat. Add beef and sauté, stirring, until browned. Using a slotted spoon, transfer beef to a plate lined with paper towels and reserve.

2 Heat remaining oil in saucepan. Add leeks and sauté until softened. Add mushrooms and sauté until softened.

3 Return beef to saucepan with barley, stock, and red wine. Bring to boil, then reduce heat and simmer, partially covered, 45 minutes, or until beef and barley are tender. Season with lemon juice, salt, and pepper.

GRANDMA'S BARLEY SOUP

This thick, robust soup—full of vegetables and meat—is a hearty meal all by itself.

SERVES 6

3 1/2 cups low-sodium beef broth

12 ounces fresh green or wax beans, trimmed and cut into bite-size pieces, or 1 package (9 ounces) frozen cut green beans

1 large potato, peeled and cubed

1 large yellow onion, chopped

2 large carrots, sliced

3 bay leaves

1/4 teaspoon salt

1/4 teaspoon black pepper

1 1/2 cups bite-size pieces cooked beef or pork

1 can (14 1/2 ounces) low-sodium tomatoes, undrained, cut up

1/2 cup quick-cooking barley

1 teaspoon dried rosemary

1 In a large saucepan over medium heat, combine broth, beans, potato, onion, carrots, bay leaves, salt, and pepper. Bring to boil, reduce heat, and simmer, covered, until vegetables are almost tender, about 20 minutes.

2 Stir in meat, tomatoes, barley, and rosemary, increase heat and bring to boil. Reduce heat and simmer, covered, until barley is tender, about 15 minutes. Remove bay leaves.

BARLEY SOUP WITH LEAN BEEF

It's easy to understand why robust one-dish recipes have withstood the test of time: They're easy to fix and delicious. (Photograph on page 18)

SERVES 6

12 ounces lean beef chuck, cut into 1-inch cubes

3 onions, coarsely chopped

10 ounces mushrooms, sliced

3 large carrots, sliced

1/2 cup pearl barley

7 cups reduced-sodium beef stock

1 cup dry red wine or low-sodium tomato juice

1/2 teaspoon salt

1/2 teaspoon freshly ground black pepper

1 cup frozen green peas

2 teaspoons fresh lemon juice

1 Coat soup pot or large heavy saucepan with nonstick cooking spray and set over medium-high heat until hot but not smoking. Sauté beef until brown, about 5 minutes. Transfer with slotted spoon to double layer of paper towels to drain.

2 Sauté onions and mushrooms in pan drippings 7 minutes or until onions are golden. Return beef to pot. Stir in carrots, barley, stock, wine, salt, and pepper, and bring to boil.

3 Reduce heat and simmer, partially covered, 45 minutes or until beef and barley are tender. Stir in peas and cook, uncovered, 5 minutes or until tender. Remove from heat and stir in lemon juice.

CHINESE BEEF SOUP WITH BARLEY AND SPINACH

Ordinary herbs and spices used in cooking often make their own contribution to good health. Both the ginger and fennel seeds in this meaty soup, for example, help soothe the digestive tract.
(Photograph on page 24)

SERVES 4

1 1/2 pounds beef stew meat, trimmed and cut into 1-inch cubes

1 onion, finely chopped

4 garlic cloves, minced

1 can (14 1/2 ounces) reduced-sodium, fat-free beef broth

1/4 cup soy sauce

1 piece fresh ginger (2 inches), peeled and cut into 4 pieces

1 teaspoon fennel seed

1/2 teaspoon salt

1 cup pearl barley

12 cups stemmed spinach leaves

2 scallions, thinly sliced, to garnish *(optional)*

1 In a large saucepan, combine beef, onion, garlic, 6 cups water, broth, soy sauce, ginger, fennel seeds, and salt. Bring to boil over medium heat.

2 Stir in barley. Reduce heat and simmer, covered, 1 1/2 hours or until beef is very tender. Stir in spinach. Simmer 2 minutes. Remove ginger pieces. Garnish with scallions, if desired.

BARLEY-MUSHROOM RAGOUT

More filling than a barley-mushroom soup, this is a stick-to-the-ribs vegetarian stew.

SERVES 4

1/2 ounce dried porcini mushrooms

4 teaspoons olive oil

1 large yellow onion, finely chopped

4 garlic cloves, minced

1 tablespoon minced fresh ginger

1 carrot, peeled, quartered, and thinly sliced

1 red bell pepper, cored, seeded, and chopped

6 ounces shiitake mushrooms, stemmed, wiped clean, and thinly sliced

6 ounces button mushrooms, stemmed, wiped clean, and thinly sliced

1/2 cup canned tomatoes, chopped

1/3 cup medium pearl barley

1 cup homemade vegetable stock or canned reduced-sodium vegetable broth

1/2 teaspoon salt

1/4 teaspoon dried rosemary, crumbled

1 Place dried porcini mushrooms in a small bowl and pour in 1 cup boiling water. Let stand until softened, about 40 minutes. Drain mushrooms, reserving liquid, and coarsely chop. Strain liquid and set aside.

2 Meanwhile, in a heavy saucepan over medium heat, heat oil 1 minute. Add onion, garlic, and ginger and cook, stirring frequently, about 7 minutes. Stir in carrot and bell pepper and cook, stirring occasionally, until tender, about 5 minutes.

3 Add reserved mushrooms, 2 tablespoons mushroom liquid, and shiitake and button mushrooms, and sauté 5 minutes or until tender. Stir in tomatoes and barley.

4 Add remaining mushroom liquid, broth, salt, and rosemary and bring to boil. Reduce heat to medium low, cover, and simmer 45 minutes or until barley is tender.

LAMB-BARLEY SOUP

Lamb and barley have a savory affinity for one another, as this soup proves.

SERVES 6

3 1/2 cups low-sodium beef broth

12 ounces fresh green or wax beans, trimmed and cut into bite-size pieces, or 1 package (9 ounces) frozen cut green beans

1 large potato, peeled and cubed

1 large yellow onion, chopped

2 large carrots, sliced

3 bay leaves

1/4 teaspoon salt

1/4 teaspoon black pepper

2 cups bite-size pieces cooked lamb

1 can (14 1/2 ounces) low-sodium tomatoes, undrained, cut up

1/2 cup quick-cooking barley

1 teaspoon dried rosemary

1 In a large saucepan over medium heat, combine broth, beans, potato, onion, carrots, bay leaves, salt, and pepper. Bring to boil, reduce heat, and simmer, covered, until vegetables are almost tender, about 20 minutes.

2 Stir in lamb, tomatoes, barley, and rosemary, increase heat, and bring to boil. Reduce heat and simmer, covered, until barley is tender, about 15 minutes. Remove bay leaves.

BULGUR PILAF WITH MUSHROOMS

Bulgur simmered in stock is mixed with fresh mushrooms, nuts, and parsley for a wonderful and filling vegetarian main dish or side dish for lamb or beef.

SERVES 4

1/4 pound butter

1 onion, finely chopped

12 ounces bulgur

3 1/4 cups vegetable stock

1 tablespoon olive oil

1/2 pound mixed mushrooms, cleaned and sliced

Salt and black pepper

4 tablespoons slivered almonds

4 tablespoons chopped hazelnuts

Small bunch parsley, chopped

1 In a flameproof casserole over medium heat, melt half the butter. Add onion and sauté 3 minutes or until translucent.

2 Add bulgur and cook, stirring frequently, 3 minutes. Add stock, bring to boil, then reduce heat, and simmer, covered, 10 to 15 minutes, or until all stock has been absorbed.

3 In a skillet over medium heat, heat oil. Add mushrooms, and sauté until they are lightly browned. Season with salt and pepper. Pour mushrooms and any juice on top of the partially cooked bulgur, cover casserole, and let cook.

4 Add slivered almonds to skillet and shake over medium heat 1 minute, then add chopped hazelnuts and sauté both until lightly browned. When stock is absorbed and bulgur is cooked, stir in remaining butter, toasted nuts, and parsley. Taste for seasoning and serve.

VEGETABLE COUSCOUS

Sweet winter vegetables and legumes mix with dried apricots and hot spices to make a Middle Eastern stew to serve on a bed of couscous.

SERVES 2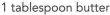

1 tablespoon butter

1 tablespoon olive oil

1 small onion, chopped

2 small carrots, cut into chunks

1/2 small turnip, cut into chunks

1 medium parsnip, cut into chunks

Pinch of cayenne pepper

Pinch of turmeric

1/2 teaspoon ground ginger

1/2 teaspoon ground cinnamon

Pinch of saffron threads *(optional)*

Salt and black pepper

12 ready-to-eat dried apricots, chopped

2 ounces frozen baby peas

3 tablespoons canned chickpeas, drained and rinsed

3/4 cup couscous

2 fresh cilantro sprigs

1 Put a kettle of water on to boil. In a large, heavy, flameproof casserole over medium heat, heat butter and olive oil. Add onion and sauté until soft, 4 or 5 minutes.

2 Add carrots, turnip, and parsnip. Stir in cayenne pepper, turmeric, ginger, cinnamon, and saffron threads, if using, and season to taste with salt and pepper.

3 Add apricots, peas, and chickpeas. Add 1 1/4 cups boiling water and bring back to boil. Reduce heat, cover, and simmer 15 minutes.

4 Meanwhile, pour 1 cup boiling water into a saucepan, add couscous and stir, then turn off heat and let stand, covered, 5 minutes or until vegetables are ready. Meanwhile, rinse and dry cilantro and set aside. Check couscous and season to taste. Break grains apart with a fork and transfer couscous to serving dish.

5 Taste and adjust seasoning of vegetables and their broth, then ladle over couscous. Garnish with cilantro.

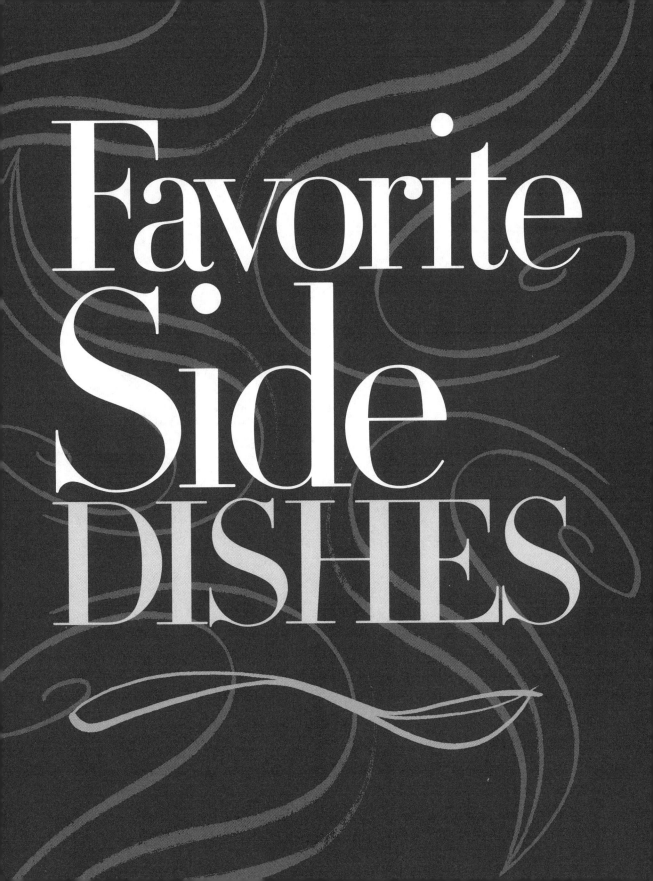

Favorite Side DISHES

FAVORITE SIDE DISHES

recipe list

 EASY: 10 minutes to prepare

QUICK: Ready to eat in 30 minutes

ONE-DISH: contains protein, vegetables, and good carbohydrates (beans, whole-grains, etc.) for a complete healthy meal

HEALTHY: High in nutrients, low in bad fats and empty carbohydrates

SLOW COOKER: Easily adapted for slow cooker by cutting down on liquids

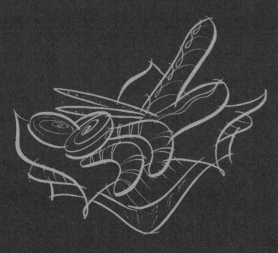

BUTTERMILK BISCUITS

Here are delicious scratch biscuits that you can turn out in a matter of minutes.

MAKES 16 BISCUITS

2 cups all-purpose flour
3 teaspoons baking powder
1 teaspoon sugar
1/2 teaspoon baking soda
1/2 teaspoon salt
1/4 cup (1/2 stick) butter, cut up
2 tablespoons vegetable shortening
1 cup buttermilk

1 Preheat oven to 450°F. In a large bowl, combine flour, baking powder, sugar, baking soda, and salt. Using a pastry blender or 2 knives, cut in butter and shortening until mixture resembles coarse meal. Add buttermilk and stir lightly with a fork just until a soft dough forms.

2 Turn dough out onto a lightly floured surface and knead gently 6 to 8 times.

3 Drop by heaping tablespoons 1 inch apart on ungreased baking sheets and bake until golden, 12 to 15 minutes. Serve hot.

TOMATO BISCUITS

Tomatoes add health and flavor to these biscuits.

MAKES 12 BISCUITS

1 medium tomato, cored, seeded, and finely chopped
2 cups all-purpose flour
1 tablespoon baking powder
1/2 teaspoon salt
1 cup low-fat plain yogurt
1/3 cup olive oil
2 tablespoons finely chopped scallion
1 tablespoon finely chopped sun-dried tomato

1 Preheat oven to 450°F. Lightly coat a baking sheet with cooking spray. Drain fresh tomato on paper towels.

2 In a medium bowl, combine flour, baking powder, and salt. In a small bowl, combine yogurt and oil. Stir into flour mixture just until evenly moistened.

3 Stir in fresh tomato, scallion, and sun-dried tomato. Drop dough 1/4 cup at a time onto baking sheet, making a total of 12 biscuits.

4 Bake 12 minutes or until tops are golden. Serve warm.

SWEET POTATO BISCUITS

These delicious biscuits are low in saturated fat because they're made with oil instead of butter. (Photograph on page 5)

MAKES 12 BISCUITS

1 3/4 cups all-purpose flour
1/4 teaspoon salt
4 teaspoons baking powder
Pinch of ground nutmeg
1 cup mashed sweet potato or yam
1/4 cup vegetable oil
1/4 cup low-fat (1%) milk
1 large egg, lightly beaten
2 tablespoons light brown sugar

1 Preheat oven to 425°F.

2 In a small bowl, sift together flour, salt, baking powder, and nutmeg. In a medium bowl, stir together sweet potato, oil, milk, egg, and sugar. Stir in flour mixture just until evenly moistened.

3 Turn dough out onto a lightly floured surface and pat into a 3/4-inch-thick circle. Using a 2 1/2-inch biscuit cutter, cut into rounds. Place on baking sheet about 1 inch apart. Gather scraps, gently pat into a circle, and cut out remaining biscuits.

4 Bake until biscuits are golden, 12 to 15 minutes. Serve warm.

CHEDDAR SCONES

With the addition of cheese, these scones make a perfect foil for soups and stews of all kinds.

MAKES 8 SCONES

2 cups all-purpose flour
1 tablespoon sugar
3 teaspoons baking powder
1/2 teaspoon salt
1/4 cup (1/2 stick) butter, cut up
1/2 cup (2 ounces) shredded cheddar cheese
2 eggs
1/3 cup heavy cream

1 Preheat oven to 425°F. In a large bowl, combine flour, sugar, baking powder, and salt. Using a pastry blender or 2 knives, cut in butter until mixture resembles coarse meal. Using a fork, blend in cheese.

2 In a medium bowl, beat eggs and cream with a fork until well blended. Stir lightly into flour mixture, adding 1 to 2 tablespoons more cream if necessary, to make a soft but manageable dough.

3 Turn dough out onto a lightly floured work surface, knead gently 5 or 6 times, and roll to 1/2-inch thickness. Using a floured 3-inch biscuit cutter, cut into 8 rounds, gathering scraps and rerolling as necessary.

4 Place 2 inches apart on an ungreased baking sheet and bake until golden, 10 to 15 minutes. Serve hot.

PERFECT POPOVERS

For no-fail popovers, start with a piping-hot pan. Steady the pan with a potholder and pour the batter from a pitcher.

MAKES 12 POPOVERS

2 large egg whites
1 large egg, lightly beaten
1 cup low-fat (1%) milk
1 tablespoon olive or vegetable oil
1 cup all-purpose flour
1/2 teaspoon parsley flakes or dried oregano
1/8 teaspoon salt

1 Preheat oven to 400°F. Generously grease a 12-cup muffin pan and place in oven to heat.

2 Meanwhile, in a medium bowl, combine egg whites, egg, milk, and oil. Add flour, parsley, and salt. Using a rotary beater or whisk, beat until smooth.

3 Fill each cup of muffin pan about half full and bake on lowest oven rack until very brown and crusty, about 25 minutes. Remove from oven and immediately pierce each popover with a sharp knife to release steam. Serve immediately.

PARKER HOUSE ROLLS

MAKES 64 ROLLS

2 tablespoons sugar

2 packets (1/4 ounce each)
    active dry yeast

1 cup milk

2 teaspoons salt

1/2 cup (1 stick) plus 3 tablespoons
    butter, melted

1 large all-purpose potato, peeled,
    diced, boiled, and riced

6 1/2-7 cups all-purpose flour

1 egg, lightly beaten

These lunch or dinner rolls
are an American classic,
beloved by many generations
for their light, buttery flavor.

1 In a small bowl, combine sugar, 1/2 cup luke-warm water (105°-115°F), and yeast. Stir to dissolve and set aside until foamy, about 10 minutes.

2 In a small saucepan over medium-high heat, bring 1 cup water and milk to boil. Transfer to a large bowl. Using a wooden spoon or an electric mixer with paddle attached, add salt and 3 table-spoons melted butter, then let cool 10 minutes. At medium speed, mix in potato, 2 cups flour, and egg, beating for 1 minute after each addition. Add yeast mixture and beat 1 minute. If using an electric mixer, insert dough hook. Add 4 1/2 cups remaining flour and beat 3 to 5 minutes, adding as much of remaining flour as necessary to make a soft, manageable dough.

3 Butter a 5-quart bowl. Shape dough into a ball, add to bowl, and turn to coat. Cover with a kitchen towel and let rise in a warm, draft-free place 50 minutes or until doubled in bulk.

4 Punch down dough, turn out onto a lightly floured work surface, and divide into 4 equal pieces. Working with 1 piece at a time, roll into an 8 x 10-inch rectangle 1/4 inch thick. Using a floured 2 1/2-inch biscuit cutter, cut into 12 rounds, then gather scraps, roll out, and cut 4 more rounds. Brush each with melted butter and then, using a ruler or the blunt side of a knife, crease each along the center and fold, stretching the top half so it covers the bottom half. Pinch edges to seal.

5 Lightly grease baking sheets. Place rolls on baking sheets and brush tops with remaining butter. Cover with towel and let rise 30 minutes. Preheat oven to 350°F. Bake 30 minutes or until golden. Serve warm or transfer to a wire rack to cool.

SANTA FE CORNBREAD

Tex-Mex ingredients give this cornbread more spiciness than traditional recipes.

SERVES 8

5 tablespoons olive oil or bacon drippings

2 scallions, thinly sliced

2 garlic cloves, minced

1 small red bell pepper, cored, seeded, and chopped

1/2 cup minced fresh cilantro

1 pickled jalapeño pepper, cored, deveined, seeded, and minced (wear gloves when handling; they burn)

1 1/3 cups stone-ground yellow cornmeal

3/4 cup all-purpose flour

2 tablespoons sugar

3 teaspoons baking powder

1 teaspoon salt

1/2 teaspoon baking soda

1 1/4 cups buttermilk

2 eggs

1 Preheat oven to 450°F. Brush a 10-inch cast-iron or ovenproof nonstick skillet with oil.

2 Heat 1 tablespoon oil 1 minute in a small skillet over medium heat. Add scallions and garlic and sauté 2 minutes or until softened. Add bell pepper and sauté 4 minutes or until softened. Stir in cilantro, jalapeño, and remaining oil. Remove from heat.

3 Place cast-iron skillet in oven to heat. Meanwhile, in a large bowl, stir together cornmeal, flour, sugar, baking powder, salt, and baking soda. In a small bowl, whisk together buttermilk and eggs. Stir in scallion mixture.

4 Make a well in center of cornmeal mixture, pour in buttermilk mixture, and stir until just combined (do not overmix). Pour into hot skillet, smoothing top. Bake 20 minutes or until a toothpick inserted in center comes out clean. Cut into wedges and serve hot.

RED PEPPER AND GREEN CHILE SPOON BREAD

This Southwestern corn pone has plenty of peppers as well as corn.

SERVES 6

1 cup yellow cornmeal

1 cup low-fat (1%) milk

1 teaspoon salt

1 tablespoon butter

1 can (4 1/2 ounces) green chiles, drained and rinsed

1 red bell pepper, cored, seeded, and cut into small chunks

1 cup fresh, drained canned, or thawed frozen whole-kernel corn

3 large egg yolks, lightly beaten

3 large egg whites

1 Preheat oven to 375°F. Coat a 2-quart baking dish with vegetable oil.

2 In a small saucepan, bring 1 1/2 cups water and cornmeal to boil. Reduce heat and simmer, stirring frequently, 3 minutes. Transfer to a medium bowl and stir in milk, salt, butter, chiles, bell pepper, and corn until butter melts. Let cool, then stir in egg yolks.

3 In a medium bowl, beat egg whites until stiff peaks form. Fold into cornmeal mixture and pour into baking dish.

4 Bake 50 minutes or until center is firm and top is browned. Serve warm.

LEMON-WALNUT BREAD

This lively flavor combination depends on plenty of lemon juice and zest. If you heat a lemon in the microwave for 30 seconds, you can squeeze out the juice more easily.

SERVES 8

1 cup all-purpose flour
1/2 cup whole wheat flour
2 tablespoons brown sugar
2 teaspoons baking powder
1/2 teaspoon baking soda
1/4 teaspoon salt
1 teaspoon vanilla extract
1 egg
2 egg whites
1/3 cup fat-free plain yogurt
1/4 cup chopped walnuts
2 tablespoons honey
2 teaspoons finely grated lemon zest
6 tablespoons fresh lemon juice

1 Preheat oven to 350°F. Lightly coat an 8 1/4 x 4 1/2-inch loaf pan with cooking spray. In a large bowl, stir together all-purpose flour, whole wheat flour, brown sugar, baking powder, baking soda, and salt.

2 In a medium bowl, lightly beat vanilla with egg and egg whites. Stir in yogurt, walnuts, 1 tablespoon honey, 1 teaspoon lemon zest, and 3 tablespoons lemon juice. Add to flour mixture and beat quickly until just mixed.

3 Transfer batter to pan and spread evenly with spatula. Bake 30 minutes or until a toothpick inserted in center comes out clean and dry.

4 In a small saucepan, heat remaining lemon zest, lemon juice, and honey 3 minutes or until zest is tender and syrup is thick. Turn baked bread out of pan. While still warm, poke holes in top with a skewer or toothpick and brush syrup on top, repeating until all syrup is used.

CARROT AND ZUCCHINI BREAD

Here is a delicious quick bread that uses yogurt instead of butter and whole wheat flour as well as vegetables to make it more nourishing.

SERVES 8

1 cup all-purpose flour
1/2 cup whole wheat flour
2 tablespoons brown sugar
2 teaspoons baking powder
1/4 teaspoon salt
1 teaspoon vanilla extract
1 egg
2 egg whites
1/2 cup shredded zucchini
1/2 cup shredded carrot
1/3 cup fat-free plain yogurt
1/4 cup chopped walnuts
1 tablespoon honey
2 teaspoons finely grated lemon zest

1 Preheat oven to 350°F. Lightly coat an 8 1/4 x 4 1/2-inch loaf pan with cooking spray. In a large bowl, stir together all-purpose flour, whole wheat flour, brown sugar, baking powder, and salt.

2 In a medium bowl, lightly beat vanilla with egg and egg whites. Stir in zucchini, carrot, yogurt, walnuts, honey, and lemon zest. Add to flour mixture and beat quickly until just mixed.

3 Transfer batter to pan and spread evenly with a spatula. Bake 35 minutes or until a toothpick inserted in center comes out clean and dry.

WINTER SQUASH BREAD

This moist, spicy bread is a perfect foil for almost any soup, from cream of tomato to fish chowder.

MAKES 1 LOAF (ABOUT 16 SLICES)

1 packet (1/4 ounce) active dry yeast

1 tablespoons light brown sugar

2 tablespoons unsalted butter

1 large egg, lightly beaten

1 1/2 teaspoons grated orange zest

1/2 teaspoon ground cinnamon

1/4 teaspoon salt

1/8 teaspoon ground mace

1/8 teaspoon ground cloves

1/2 cup mashed cooked acorn squash, butternut squash, or pumpkin

2 3/4 cups sifted all-purpose flour

1 large egg white, lightly beaten

1 In a large bowl, combine yeast, 1/3 cup lukewarm water (105°-115°F), and sugar. Let stand 5 minutes, then stir until yeast dissolves.

2 In a small saucepan over low heat, melt butter, then remove from heat and let cool until warm. Add egg, orange zest, cinnamon, salt, mace, cloves, squash, and butter to yeast mixture and stir until thoroughly mixed. Add flour 1 cup at a time to make a firm but not dry dough.

3 Turn dough out onto a lightly floured surface and knead vigorously 6 minutes. Coat a large bowl with cooking spray. Shape dough into a ball, add to bowl, and turn to coat. Cover with a clean kitchen towel and let rise in a warm, draft-free place 1 1/2 hours or until doubled in bulk.

4 Lightly coat a 9 1/4 x 5 1/4 x 2 3/4-inch loaf pan with cooking spray. Punch down dough and knead 1 minute. Shape into a loaf and place in pan seam side down. Cover with towel and let rise 45 minutes or until dough extends 1 inch above rim of pan.

5 Toward end of rising, preheat oven to 375°F. Brush top of loaf with egg white and bake 35 minutes or until loaf is golden and sounds hollow when tapped on bottom.

POPPY SEED LOAF

Whole wheat flour adds nutrition and flavor to this bread that, when toasted, goes well with any soup.

MAKES 20 SLICES

2 cups all-purpose flour

1 cup whole wheat flour

1 packet (1/4 ounce) active dry yeast

1 teaspoon sugar

1/2 teaspoon salt

1 cup low-fat (1%) milk

2 tablespoons butter

1 egg white

1 tablespoon poppy seeds

1 In a large bowl, combine all-purpose flour, whole wheat flour, yeast, sugar, and salt. In a small saucepan, heat milk and butter over low heat until warm. Add gradually to flour mixture and mix until a dough begins to form. Add egg white and mix until dough is fairly firm.

2 Turn dough out onto a lightly floured surface, knead 10 minutes, and shape into a ball. Lightly coat a large bowl with cooking spray, add dough, and turn to coat. Cover with a kitchen towel and let rise in a warm place 2 hours or until doubled in bulk.

3 Preheat oven to 400°F. Lightly grease a baking sheet. Punch down dough and shape into a large oval, tapering the ends. Place on baking sheet. Using a sharp knife, cut 4 to 6 diagonal slashes in top, then brush with milk and sprinkle with poppy seeds. Bake 30 minutes or until loaf sounds hollow when tapped on bottom. Transfer to a wire rack to cool.

MULTIGRAIN SEEDED BREAD

Along with adding flavor to this loaf, the seeds are a good source of potassium, vitamin E, protein, and iron.

MAKES 18 SLICES

1 1/2 cups whole wheat flour

3/4 cup all-purpose flour

1 packet (1/4 ounce) active dry yeast

1/2 teaspoon salt

3 tablespoons sunflower seeds

3 tablespoons sesame seeds

3 tablespoons pumpkin seeds

1/3 cup rolled oats

2 tablespoons molasses

1 egg white

Low-fat (1%) milk

1 In a large bowl, combine whole wheat flour, all-purpose flour, yeast, and salt. In a small bowl, combine sunflower seeds, sesame seeds, pumpkin seeds, and oats.

2 In a small saucepan, heat 1 cup water and molasses over low heat until very warm (120°- 130°F). Gradually stir into flour mixture, then stir in egg white until a soft dough forms. Turn dough out onto a lightly floured surface and knead 10 minutes, then shape into a ball. Lightly coat a large bowl with cooking spray. Add dough and turn to coat. Cover with a kitchen towel and let rise in a warm place 2 hours or until doubled in bulk.

3 Lightly grease a 9 x 5-inch loaf pan. Punch down dough and work in seed mixture, reserving 2 tablespoons. Transfer to a lightly floured surface and roll into a 12 x 8-inch rectangle. Roll up tightly from the shortest end, then pinch ends together and tuck underneath. Place seam side down in pan.

4 Cover with towel and let dough rise in a warm place 1 hour or until doubled in bulk. Preheat oven

to 350°F. Brush top of loaf with milk and sprinkle with reserved seeds. Bake 30 minutes or until loaf sounds hollow when tapped on bottom. Transfer to a wire rack to cool.

CRISPY SEED-TOPPED FLATBREADS

These Near Eastern-style "crackers" are sprinkled with pumpkin seeds, sunflower seeds, and grated Parmesan. (Photograph on page 31)

SERVES 12

2 1/4 cups all-purpose flour

3/4 teaspoon salt

1/4 teaspoon cayenne pepper

1 tablespoon unsalted butter

1 tablespoon vegetable shortening

1 egg white, lightly beaten with
    2 teaspoons water

1/4 cup shelled pumpkin seeds

1/4 cup shelled dry-roasted sunflower seeds

2 tablespoons plus 2 teaspoons grated
    Parmesan cheese

1 In a medium bowl, combine flour, salt, and cayenne. With a pastry blender or 2 knives, cut in butter and shortening until mixture resembles coarse meal. Gradually add 2/3 cup water to make a soft, smooth dough. Knead 5 minutes or until smooth and elastic. Coat a large bowl with cooking spray, add dough, cover, and let rest 1 hour.

2 Preheat oven to 425°F. Spray 2 large baking sheets with cooking spray (or use nonstick pans). Cut dough into 4 pieces and roll each into a 9-inch round 1/16 inch thick. Transfer to baking sheets and brush with egg white mixture. Sprinkle pumpkin and sunflower seeds on each round, then sprinkle with 2 teaspoons cheese. Bake 12 minutes or until lightly puffed, golden, and crisp.

SOURDOUGH BREAD

MAKES 2 LOAVES, 10 SLICES EACH ☼

Starter:
1 packet (1/4 ounce) active dry yeast
1 1/2 cups bread flour

Dough:
1 1/2 cups starter
2 tablespoons sugar
1 tablespoon salt
5-6 cups bread flour
1/4 cup (1/2 stick) butter, melted

Sourdough breads and rolls have a distinct flavor and are a tangy addition to any meal.

1 For starter, whisk together 2 cups lukewarm water (105°-115°F), yeast, and flour in a medium glass or ceramic bowl. Cover loosely with wax paper and set in a warm, draft-free place 12 hours or overnight.

2 For dough, place starter in a large bowl. Using a wooden spoon or an electric mixer with paddle attached, mix in 1 cup water, sugar, salt, and 2 1/2 cups flour. Beat at medium speed 15 seconds or until smooth. If using electric mixer, remove paddle and insert dough hook. Add 3 tablespoons melted butter and another 2 1/2 cups flour, 1/2 cup at a time. Beat about 10 minutes, adding as much of remaining flour as necessary to make a smooth, elastic dough. (If mixing by hand, you will probably have to knead in the last of the flour.)

3 Butter a 5-quart bowl. Shape dough into a ball, add to bowl, and turn to coat. Cover with a kitchen towel and let rise in a warm, draft-free place 1 to 1 1/2 hours or until doubled in bulk. Punch down dough, cover, and let rise 1 1/2 hours.

4 Lightly grease an 8-inch round layer cake or springform pan. Punch down dough, turn out onto a lightly floured surface, and knead gently 2 to 3 minutes or until smooth. Divide in half and form each half into a ball. Place balls in pan, cover with towel, and let rise 45 minutes to 1 hour or until doubled in bulk. Preheat oven to 350°F.

5 Brush loaves with remaining butter. Using a sharp knife, make a diagonal slash in top of each. Bake 45 to 50 minutes or until loaves are golden and sound hollow when tapped on bottom. Transfer to wire racks to cool.

CRUSTY FRENCH LOAVES

This bread has a chewy crust and is soft inside, just the way Grandma used to make it.

MAKES 3 LOAVES (24 SERVINGS)

3 packets (1/4 ounce each)
   active dry yeast
1 tablespoon sugar
3/4 teaspoon salt
4 3/4-5 1/4 cups all-purpose flour
Cornmeal
1 large egg white

1 In a large bowl, combine 1/2 cup lukewarm water (105°-115°F), yeast, and sugar and let stand until foamy, about 10 minutes. Stir in 1 1/3 cups water and salt. Using a wooden spoon, beat in enough flour 1 cup at a time to make a soft dough.

2 Butter a large bowl. Turn dough out onto a lightly floured surface and knead 8 to 10 minutes or until smooth and elastic, adding only as much of remaining flour as needed. Transfer to bowl and turn to coat. Cover with a kitchen towel and let rise in a warm place 45 minutes to 1 1/4 hours or until doubled in bulk.

3 Lightly grease 3 baking sheets and sprinkle with cornmeal. Punch down dough and divide into thirds. Cover and let stand 10 minutes, then roll each piece into a 13 x 8-inch rectangle. Starting at a long side, roll up jelly-roll style and taper ends. Place on baking sheets seam side down, then cover and let rise 30 to 45 minutes or until doubled in bulk.

4 Preheat oven to 450°F and place a pan of boiling water on bottom rack. In a small bowl, combine egg white and 1 tablespoon water. Brush on loaves and, using a sharp knife, make a slash in top of each.

5 Place 1 or 2 loaves on middle oven rack (refrigerate remaining loaf or loaves until ready to bake). Bake 16 to 18 minutes or until bread is golden and sounds hollow when tapped on bottom. (If loaves seem to be browning too quickly, lay pieces of foil loosely over them.) Transfer to wire racks to cool.

HOMEMADE POTATO CHIPS

Feel free to indulge yourself with these fabulous, guilt-free munchies. They're best when served hot.

SERVES 4 TO 6

2 medium russet potatoes,
   cut into 1/16-inch-thick slices
1 tablespoon grated Parmesan cheese
1 teaspoon paprika

1 Preheat oven to 350°F. Lightly grease a nonstick baking sheet. Arrange potatoes in 1 layer on baking sheet and bake, turning occasionally, until golden, about 45 minutes.

2 In a small bowl, combine cheese and paprika and sprinkle over potatoes. Bake 5 minutes, let cool slightly, and transfer to serving dish.

CROSTINI WITH ARTICHOKES AND TOMATO

You'll love the fresh, bold flavor of this simple, sun-drenched treat. (Photograph on page 12)

SERVES 4

1 jar (6 ounces) marinated artichokes, drained and coarsely chopped

1 large tomato, cored, seeded, and coarsely chopped

1/4 cup pitted black olives, coarsely chopped

2 tablespoons chopped parsley

1 tablespoon olive oil

1 small garlic clove, passed through a garlic press

1/4 teaspoon salt

1/8 teaspoon black pepper

8 thin slices Italian bread, lightly toasted

1 In a medium bowl, combine artichokes, tomato, olives, parsley, oil, garlic, salt, and pepper.

2 Divide equally among toast slices.

GRILLED VEGETABLE BRUSCHETTA

Grilling brings out all the sweet flavors of an assortment of Mediterranean vegetables that are piled on top of toasted bread slices rubbed with garlic and tomato.

SERVES 4

1 medium red bell pepper, cored, seeded, and cut into strips

1 medium yellow bell pepper, cored, seeded, and cut into strips

2 small zucchini, sliced diagonally

1 medium fennel bulb, sliced

1 red onion, sliced

5 tablespoons olive oil

2 garlic cloves, halved

1 small tomato, halved

1 loaf ciabatta bread or 1 French baguette

Salt and black pepper

6 large basil leaves, torn

1 Preheat grill to high. Cover grill rack with a single layer of vegetables, placing peppers skin side down. Brush with oil and grill on one side only until lightly browned but still firm. If necessary, cook in batches and keep first batch warm in the oven.

2 Meanwhile, cut bread lengthwise and then crosswise into quarters and toast on both sides. Rub tops of slices with cut garlic and tomato and pile vegetables on top. Drizzle with remaining oil and season to taste. Scatter basil leaves over the top.

CHILE-CHEESE QUESADILLAS WITH TOMATOES

Chiles are not just delicious, they also contain phytonutrients that protect against cancer and other chronic diseases. (Photograph on page 14)

SERVES 4

6 flour tortillas (8 inches)

1 large tomato, cored, seeded, and finely chopped

1 cup (4 ounces) shredded Monterey Jack or cheddar cheese

1 can (4 1/2 ounces) chopped mild chiles

1 tablespoon chopped fresh cilantro

1/4 teaspoon salt

1/8 teaspoon black pepper

1 Preheat oven to 200°F.

2 Place 3 tortillas on a work surface and sprinkle with equal amounts of tomato, cheese, chiles, cilantro, salt, and pepper. Place remaining tortillas on top and press gently to flatten.

3 Coat a large nonstick skillet with cooking spray and heat over medium-high heat. Working with 1 quesadilla at a time, place in skillet and cook until lightly browned on both sides and cheese is melted, about 2 minutes per side. Transfer to a baking sheet and place in oven to keep warm. To serve, cut each quesadilla into 4 wedges.

CORNED BEEF AND CABBAGE CALZONES

Compared to a sandwich on rye, these corned beef and cabbage pies are easier on the calories. They're a fine accompaniment to a bowl of soup.

MAKES 12 CALZONES

2 teaspoons vegetable oil
1 large onion, finely chopped
3 cups shredded green cabbage
1 carrot, peeled and chopped
2 teaspoons Dijon mustard
1/4 teaspoon salt
1/8 teaspoon black pepper
1 cup (4 ounces) shredded part-skim
    Jarlsberg cheese
1/4 cup chopped deli corned beef
1/2 package (32 ounces) frozen pizza
    dough, thawed

1 Preheat oven to 400°F.

2 Heat oil in a large nonstick skillet over medium heat. Add onion and sauté 3 minutes or until slightly softened. Stir in cabbage, carrot, mustard, salt, and pepper. Cover, reduce heat to low, and cook until cabbage is wilted, 10 to 15 minutes, adding water if necessary to prevent sticking. Uncover and cook, stirring, 1 minute. Let cool slightly, then stir in cheese and corned beef.

3 Place pizza dough on a lightly floured board and shape into a 12-inch-long log, adding flour as needed to prevent sticking. Divide into 12 equal pieces. Working with 1 piece at a time, roll or pat out into a 6-inch circle. Spoon 1/4 cup filling over lower half and fold dough over to enclose filling. Press edges firmly to seal and crimp with a fork. Transfer to an ungreased baking sheet.

4 Bake until heated through and golden, about 20 minutes. Transfer to a wire rack and let cool 15 minutes. (You can make calzones ahead, wrap unbaked pies in plastic wrap, and refrigerate up to 3 days before baking.)

HERBED CHEESE BAGELS

A little parsley adds a hint of freshness and color to recipes. When used in quantity, its unique flavor can really be appreciated.

SERVES 4

3 1/2 ounces reduced-fat cream cheese
2 scallions, thinly sliced
1/2 cup fresh parsley, finely chopped
2 tablespoons chopped fresh dill
1 tablespoon chopped fresh tarragon
Salt and black pepper
4 bagels
1/2 cucumber, thinly sliced
3 tomatoes, thinly sliced
1 red onion, thinly sliced

1 In a medium bowl, combine cream cheese, scallions, parsley, dill, and tarragon. Add salt and pepper to taste and mix until well blended.

2 Slice bagels in half horizontally and spread cheese mixture on bottom halves. Layer cucumber, tomato, and onion slices on top of cheese and cover with tops of bagels.

FRENCH-TOASTED CHEESE SANDWICHES

Originally, these sandwiches were coated in egg like French toast and then deep-fried. Today's lighter version is coated with egg whites and pan-fried to make the same golden crust and creamy center with less fat.

SERVES 4

1 tablespoon butter

1/2 cup chopped fresh mushrooms

1/4 cup chopped onion

1/8 teaspoon black pepper

8 slices home-style white bread

4 slices process American cheese or 2 slices cheddar cheese, halved crosswise

2 slices part-skim mozzarella cheese, halved crosswise

1 large egg

1 large egg white

3 tablespoons low-fat (1%) milk

1 In a 10-inch nonstick skillet over medium heat, melt butter. Add mushrooms, onion, and pepper and sauté until tender, about 5 minutes. Transfer to a small bowl and wipe out skillet.

2 For each sandwich, layer 1 slice American cheese, some of mushroom mixture, and 1/2 slice mozzarella on 1 bread slice, then top with another bread slice.

3 In a shallow bowl, whisk together egg, egg white, and milk. Dip sandwiches, coating on both sides. Coat skillet with cooking spray. Add sandwiches 2 at a time and cook, turning once, over medium heat until bread is golden and cheese begins to melt.

APPLE AND CHEESE GRILLS

Use fresh whole wheat bread for this fruity version of cheese on toast.

SERVES 4

4 thick slices whole wheat bread cut from a large loaf

Butter

2 small red dessert apples, peeled, cored, and finely sliced

5 ounces cheddar, Cheshire, or Emmental cheese, shredded

8 sage leaves, chopped

Black pepper

1 Preheat grill to high. Toast bread on 1 side under grill.

2 Spread untoasted side with butter, arrange apple slices on top, and cover with cheese. Grill 4 to 5 minutes or until cheese melts and apples are heated through.

3 Sprinkle with sage and pepper and serve immediately.

HOT HAM SANDWICHES

This combination of ham, mayonnaise, cheddar, and dill pickle comes straight out of the 1940s, but it still tastes wonderful with a bowl of hot soup.

SERVES 4

4 slices white sandwich bread, toasted

1 tablespoon plus 1/4 cup reduced-fat mayonnaise

8 thin slices cooked low-sodium ham

1/4 cup (1 ounce) shredded low-fat cheddar cheese

1 tablespoon finely chopped dill pickle or dill pickle relish

1 Preheat broiler. Spread bread slices with 1 tablespoon mayonnaise and place 2 slices ham on each. Cut each in half diagonally.

2 In a small bowl, stir together cheese, pickle, and remaining mayonnaise until well mixed. Spread evenly over ham. Broil 4 inches from heat until cheese melts and starts to brown, about 4 minutes. Serve hot.

PORK ON A BUN

As a sandwich, this barbecue complements a bowl of good soup. You can also serve the barbecue pork and vegetable combination over rice.

SERVES 4

1 pound sliced boneless smoked
     pork butt, cut into thin strips
1 cup barbecue sauce
1 small yellow onion, finely chopped
1 package (10 ounces) frozen cut
     green beans, thawed
1 package (10 ounces) frozen whole-kernel
     corn, thawed
4 hamburger buns or large rolls,
     split and toasted

1 In a 12-inch nonstick skillet over medium heat, cook pork, stirring frequently, until browned, about 10 minutes.

2 Stir in barbecue sauce, onion, beans, and corn. Cover, reduce heat to low, and simmer until beans are tender, about 15 minutes. Spoon over buns.

THAI-STYLE BEEF SANDWICHES

These delicious sandwiches include a large layer of spicy, refreshing slaw. They're the perfect companion to vegetable soups.

SERVES 4

2 tablespoons tomato paste
1/2 cup fresh lime juice
1 1/2 teaspoons ground coriander
1 pound well-trimmed flank steak
1 teaspoon sugar
3/4 teaspoon salt
3/4 teaspoon red pepper flakes
3 cups packed shredded green cabbage
2 carrots, shredded
1 large red bell pepper, cored, seeded,
     and cut into matchsticks
1/2 cup chopped fresh cilantro
1/3 cup chopped fresh mint
4 hard rolls, halved crosswise

1 In a shallow nonreactive (not aluminum) pan, stir together tomato paste, 1/4 cup lime juice, and coriander. Add steak and turn to coat. Cover and refrigerate 30 minutes.

2 In a large bowl, whisk together remaining lime juice, sugar, salt, and red pepper flakes. Add cabbage, carrots, bell pepper, cilantro, and mint and toss well to combine. Refrigerate until ready to serve.

3 Preheat broiler. Transfer steak to a broiler pan (reserve marinade) and broil 6 inches from heat 4 minutes per side for medium-rare, brushing with marinade after turning. Let stand 10 minutes, then thinly slice diagonally across grain.

4 To serve, place slaw on bottom half of each cut roll, then top with ribbons of sliced steak and top half of roll.

COUNTRY MEAT LOAF SANDWICHES

Great picnic fare, these old-fashioned sandwiches are just the right follow-up to a bowl of gazpacho or other light starter soup.

SERVES 8

1 tablespoon olive oil

1 medium yellow onion, finely chopped

1 small green bell pepper, cored, seeded, and finely chopped

1 small red bell pepper, cored, seeded, and finely chopped

1 garlic clove, minced

1/2 teaspoon dried basil, crumbled

1/2 teaspoon dried thyme, crumbled

1 large egg

1 pound lean ground beef

4 ounces lean ground veal or pork

1 cup frozen whole-kernel corn

1/2 cup rolled oats

2 ounces part-skim mozzarella cheese, cut into 1/4-inch cubes

1/4 cup grated Parmesan cheese

1/2 teaspoon salt

1/8 teaspoon black pepper

1/4 cup ketchup

2 loaves crusty Italian bread, split lengthwise

1 Preheat oven to 375°F. Lightly grease a 9 x 5 x 3-inch loaf pan.

2 Heat oil in a 10-inch skillet over medium heat. Add onion and sauté 3 minutes. Add bell peppers, garlic, basil, and thyme and sauté until limp, about 5 minutes.

3 In a large bowl, beat egg until frothy. Add beef, veal, corn, oats, mozzarella, Parmesan, salt, pepper, and bell pepper mixture. With clean hands, mix well and pat into pan.

4 Bake, uncovered, 25 minutes. Brush top with ketchup and bake until no longer pink inside, about 25 minutes. Let stand 10 minutes, then cut into 1/4-inch slices, arrange along bottom half of each loaf of bread, and cover with tops. Cut each loaf into 4 pieces.

TURKEY CLUB SANDWICHES

There are two theories about how this perennial sandwich favorite got its name. Some say it was dubbed a club sandwich because it was served in club cars on trains, while others insist it was because the double-decker was a must on country club menus.

SERVES 4

4 lean bacon slices, halved

12 slices home-style white or whole wheat sandwich bread, toasted

1/2 cup reduced-fat mayonnaise

8 lettuce leaves

1 large tomato, thinly sliced

8 ounces thinly sliced cooked turkey breast or chicken breast

8 tiny sweet pickles *(optional)*

8 pimiento-stuffed green olives *(optional)*

1 In a 10-inch skillet over medium heat, cook bacon until crisp. Transfer to paper towels to drain.

2 Spread 1 side of each bread slice with some of mayonnaise. For each sandwich, top 1 bread slice with a lettuce leaf, one-quarter of tomato slices, and 2 half-slices bacon. Add another bread slice, mayonnaise side up, then another lettuce leaf and 1/4 of turkey. Finally, top with another bread slice, mayonnaise side down. Cut in half diagonally.

3 If desired, thread 1 pickle and 1 olive onto each of 8 wooden picks and place a pick into each sandwich half.

PIROZHKIS

You can make this quick adaptation of an Eastern European favorite using store-bought bread dough. Pirozhkis are tiny meat-and-potato turnovers, a perfect accompaniment to soup. Serve them warm with brown mustard.

MAKES 30

4 ounces lean ground beef
1/4 cup finely chopped raw potato
2 tablespoons finely chopped yellow onion
1/2 teaspoon dried basil
1/8 teaspoon salt
1/8 teaspoon black pepper
1 loaf (16 ounces) frozen white bread
    dough, thawed

1 In a medium skillet over medium-high heat, sauté beef, potato, and onion until beef is no longer pink, about 5 minutes. Using a slotted spoon, transfer to a bowl. Stir in basil, salt, and pepper.

2 Preheat oven to 375°F. Lightly grease a large baking sheet. On a lightly floured surface, roll bread dough into a circle 3/16 inch thick. Using a 2 1/2-inch biscuit cutter, cut into 30 circles, gathering and rerolling scraps to use all dough.

3 Place 1 rounded teaspoon of meat mixture onto each circle. Fold in half over filling to make a semicircle and seal edges tightly with floured tines of a fork. Place on baking sheet and bake until golden, about 15 minutes.

CHICKEN FAJITAS

This popular Mexican dish is a perfect foil for a vegetable soup. To save time, chop the vegetables while the chicken is marinating.

SERVES 4 TO 8

2 tablespoons fresh lime juice
1 tablespoon vegetable oil
1 large garlic clove, minced
1/4 teaspoon salt
1/8 teaspoon black pepper
1 pound skinless boneless chicken breasts
8 flour tortillas (8 inches)
2 cups salsa
1 small avocado, peeled, pitted,
    and thinly sliced
2 cups coarsely shredded lettuce
1/2 cup low-fat plain yogurt or sour cream

1 Preheat broiler and set rack 5 inches from heat. In a medium bowl, combine lime juice, oil, garlic, salt, and pepper. Add chicken, turn to coat, and let stand 10 minutes.

2 Drain chicken and broil until no longer pink inside, about 3 minutes on each side. Meanwhile, wrap tortillas in foil, place on sides of broiler pan, and heat 5 minutes, turning once.

3 Cut chicken into thin slices. Unwrap tortillas and place some of chicken in center of each. Top with salsa, avocado, lettuce, and yogurt, then roll up.

SPINACH-RICOTTA ROLL-UPS

SERVES 3

Roll-Ups:

1 package (10 ounces) frozen chopped
    spinach, thawed

1 tablespoon olive or canola oil

1 tablespoon all-purpose flour

1/3 cup low-fat (1%) milk

1/8 teaspoon ground nutmeg

Salt and black pepper

3 egg whites

Filling:

1 cup part-skim ricotta cheese

2 tablespoons chopped herbs,
    such as parsley, basil, or thyme

Salt and black pepper

1 tablespoon grated Parmesan cheese

1 For roll-ups, preheat oven to 375°F. Line a 15 1/2 x 10 1/2 x 3/4-inch baking pan with parchment paper. In a food processor or with a knife, chop spinach, then transfer to a medium bowl.

2 In a small saucepan over medium-low heat, combine oil and flour and cook, stirring constantly, about 2 minutes. Remove from heat and stir in milk, nutmeg, and a pinch of salt and pepper. Return to heat, bring to boil, and cook, stirring, about 1 minute or until thickened and smooth. Scrape into a medium bowl, stir in spinach, and let cool.

3 Meanwhile, in a medium bowl, whisk egg whites until soft peaks form. Spoon one-quarter into spinach mixture and gently fold to combine. Stir back into remaining egg whites and carefully combine. Spread mixture in pan and bake about 10 minutes, until risen and firm. Turn out onto a clean kitchen towel and let cool. Remove parchment paper.

4 For filling, combine ricotta, herbs, Parmesan, and a pinch of salt and pepper in a small bowl until smooth. When spinach mixture is cool, spoon on filling and spread to edges. Starting with a short side, roll up so seam is underneath, then cut crosswise into 9 equal slices. Serve at room temperature.

These cheesy spinach treats are a perfect accompaniment to a bowl of chicken noodle soup or a similar light main dish.

LOBSTER SALAD ROLLS

Maine is famous for these simple but luxurious sandwiches—the highlight of many a New England summer vacation.

SERVES 4

1/4 cup finely chopped celery

2 tablespoons lemon juice

1/4 cup mayonnaise

1/4 cup finely chopped fresh parsley

Pinch of cayenne pepper

1/4 teaspoon salt

1 pound cooked lobster meat, cut into 1/2-inch cubes (about 6 lobster tails or four 1 1/4-pound lobsters)

4 teaspoons unsalted butter, softened

4 soft rolls, split and toasted

4 romaine lettuce leaves, cut to fit rolls

1 In a medium bowl, combine celery, lemon juice, mayonnaise, parsley, cayenne, and salt. Add lobster and toss to mix.

2 Spread 1 teaspoon butter on bottom half of each roll and divide salad equally among them. Top with lettuce and cover with tops of rolls.

AVOCADO, JICAMA, AND ORANGE SALAD

A true health salad, this Southwestern-style combination is sweet and tangy.

SERVES 6

3 tablespoons olive oil

1 tablespoon fresh lime juice

1 garlic clove, minced

1 1/2 teaspoons white wine vinegar

1/4 teaspoon ground cumin

1/8 teaspoon salt

Pinch of chili powder

8 ounces jicama, peeled and cut into 3 x 1/4-inch strips

2 oranges, peeled and cut into sections

1 avocado, pitted, peeled, and cut into chunks

1/2 small red onion, thinly sliced crosswise

8 cups torn romaine lettuce

1 In a small bowl, whisk together oil, lime juice, garlic, vinegar, cumin, salt, and chili powder. In a large bowl, combine jicama, oranges, avocado, and onion. Add dressing and toss to coat. Refrigerate 15 minutes.

2 Serve on a bed of romaine leaves.

ENDIVE, PEAR, AND ROQUEFORT SALAD

This simple but elegant salad is a mixture of orchard fruit, blue cheese, fresh nuts, and bitter leaves.

SERVES 4 TO 6

6 whole fresh walnuts or 12 shelled walnut halves

3 bunches endive

2 Bartlett, Bosc, or Oriental pears

3 ounces Roquefort cheese

1 small bunch chervil or 4 tarragon sprigs *(optional)*
1 tablespoon white wine vinegar
Salt
2 tablespoons virgin olive oil
3 tablespoons walnut oil

1 If using fresh walnuts, crack shells and remove nutmeats. Roughly chop whole or half nutmeats and set aside.

2 Rinse, dry, and separate endive leaves and arrange on individual plates. Rinse, dry, quarter, and core pears. Cut each quarter into 3 slices and lay over endive.

3 Crumble cheese and scatter with walnuts over pears. If using chervil, rinse and dry it, strip off leaves, and set aside.

4 Pour vinegar into a small bowl, add salt and olive and walnut oils, and whisk. Pour a little over each salad and scatter chervil on top, if desired.

SPINACH AND ORANGE SALAD

This is a wonderful salad to serve with soups. Its ingredients contrast surprisingly with each other and add a bright, light note to a creamy soup.

 SERVES 4

2 teaspoons olive, vegetable, or hazelnut oil
1/2 teaspoon dried marjoram, crumbled
Pinch of black pepper
Pinch of ground nutmeg
1/2 cup coarsely chopped orange sections
2 medium radishes, trimmed and thinly sliced
1 scallion with top, chopped
8 ounces fresh spinach, trimmed
1 1/4 teaspoons rice vinegar or white wine vinegar

1 In a medium bowl, combine oil, marjoram, pepper, and nutmeg. Add oranges, radishes, and scallion and toss. Cover and refrigerate 2 hours, tossing occasionally.

2 Rinse spinach, pat dry with paper towels, and tear into bite-size pieces. Just before serving, add spinach and vinegar to chilled mixture and toss.

SPINACH AND BABY CORN SALAD

A smooth avocado dressing combines with tender spinach, sharp arugula, and tiny cobs of crunchy corn.

SERVES 4

8 cobs baby corn
Salt
3 ounces arugula
1 package baby spinach leaves
1 avocado
1 garlic clove, minced
3 tablespoons extra-virgin olive oil
1 tablespoon white wine vinegar
1 teaspoon sugar
1 teaspoon hot red pepper sauce
Salt

1 Bring a small saucepan of water to boil. Halve corn crosswise, add to pan with some salt, and simmer 1 minute; drain.

2 Rinse arugula and spinach leaves and let drain.

3 Halve avocado, remove pit, and use a spoon to scoop flesh into a large salad bowl. Add garlic, oil, vinegar, sugar, and red pepper sauce. Season to taste with salt, then stir until mostly smooth, with some small chunks of avocado.

4 Add corn, arugula, and spinach and toss well.

WILTED SPINACH SALAD

An old favorite is updated: Lower-fat turkey bacon replaces regular bacon, whole grain bread is used to make croutons, and nutrient-rich tomato juice spikes the dressing.

SERVES 4

8 cups fresh spinach leaves

2 tablespoons olive oil

1 red onion, thinly sliced

1/4 cup tomato juice

1 tablespoon fresh lemon juice

1 teaspoon Dijon mustard

1 small garlic clove, minced

1/4 teaspoon salt

1/8 teaspoon black pepper

2 turkey bacon slices, cooked and crumbled

2 slices multigrain bread, trimmed, toasted, and cut into 1/2-inch cubes

1 Place spinach in a large bowl. Heat oil in a large nonstick skillet over medium heat. Add onion and sauté 1 minute. Stir in tomato juice, lemon juice, mustard, garlic, salt, and pepper. Bring just to boil and remove from heat.

2 Pour dressing over spinach and toss to coat. Top with bacon and bread cubes and serve warm.

WARM GOAT CHEESE SALAD

A beautiful and delicious salad like this can finish off a meal centered on a one-dish soup.

SERVES 4

1/4 cup olive or canola oil

3 tablespoons white wine vinegar

1 garlic clove, finely chopped

2 tablespoons chopped fresh herbs, such as parsley or chives

1/8 teaspoon black pepper

Dash of hot red pepper sauce

1 log (8 ounces) goat cheese

1 French baguette

4 cups red and green leaf lettuce, torn into large pieces

1 In a large bowl, combine oil, vinegar, garlic, herbs, pepper, and red pepper sauce. Cut cheese crosswise into 12 slices. Add to marinade and toss to coat, then cover and let stand at least 1 hour.

2 Preheat broiler. Cut baguette into twelve 3/4-inch slices and place on a broiler pan. Broil on 1 side until browned, 2 to 3 minutes.

3 Drain cheese, reserving marinade. Turn toasts, place a slice of cheese on each, and broil 1 to 2 minutes.

4 Place toasts on lettuce leaves and spoon on remaining marinade.

WARM SNOW PEA SALAD WITH MUSHROOMS AND GOAT CHEESE

This delicious salad can fill out any soup-based meal with nutrition and good taste.

SERVES 4

2 teaspoons olive oil

8 ounces fresh mushrooms, thinly sliced

2 garlic cloves, minced

1 pound snow peas, strings removed

1 small red bell pepper, cored, seeded, and cut into 2 x 1/4-inch strips

1/2 teaspoon salt

3 tablespoons rice vinegar

2 teaspoons honey

4 cups watercress leaves

4 ounces mild goat cheese

2 tablespoons pecans, roasted and chopped

1 Heat 1 teaspoon oil in a large nonstick skillet over medium heat. Add mushrooms and sauté 4 minutes or until tender and golden. Add garlic and cook 1 minute. Add snow peas, bell pepper, and salt and sauté 4 minutes or until crisp-tender.

2 Transfer to a large bowl, add vinegar, honey, and remaining oil, and toss to combine. Let stand 20 minutes.

3 Divide watercress among 4 salad plates and top with snow pea mixture. Sprinkle with goat cheese and pecans.

RAINBOW COLESLAW

This colorful slaw features spinach, carrots, and bell peppers as well as three kinds of cabbage.

SERVES 12

Slaw:

1/4 small head white cabbage

1/4 small head green cabbage

1/4 small head red cabbage

1 cup shredded carrots

1 cup shredded spinach

1 red bell pepper, cored, seeded, and thinly sliced

1 red onion, thinly sliced

Dressing:

1/4 cup fat-free plain yogurt

3 tablespoons olive oil

2 tablespoons reduced-fat mayonnaise

1 tablespoon chopped fresh mint

2 teaspoons wine vinegar

1/8 teaspoon salt

1/8 teaspoon black pepper

Pinch of curry powder

1 For slaw, trim stem ends from cabbages and remove any wilted outer leaves. Using a long sharp knife, cut cabbages lengthwise in half and then into quarters.

2 Cut out cores from quarters. Thinly shred leaves, cutting lengthwise or crosswise across cabbage depending on size of shred desired.

3 In a large bowl, combine cabbage with carrots, spinach, bell pepper, and onion.

4 For dressing, combine yogurt, oil, mayonnaise, mint, vinegar, salt, pepper, and curry powder in a small bowl. Pour over cabbage mixture and toss until well coated. Cover and refrigerate for at least 30 minutes.

ROMAINE LETTUCE WITH CHUNKY TOMATO VINAIGRETTE

Rarely will dressing boost the vitamin content of a salad as much as this one made with chopped fresh tomatoes.

SERVES 6

2 large ripe tomatoes, halved, cored, seeded, and coarsely chopped

1/3 cup loosely packed fresh basil

2 tablespoons ketchup

2 tablespoons olive oil

1 tablespoon balsamic vinegar

1 small garlic clove, minced

1/2 teaspoon salt

1 large head romaine lettuce, torn into bite-size pieces

1/4 cup crumbled feta cheese

1 In a food processor or blender, combine tomatoes, basil, ketchup, oil, vinegar, garlic, and salt. Process with on/off pulses until blended but still chunky. In a large bowl, toss with lettuce and sprinkle with cheese.

CAESAR SALAD

Created in 1924 at Caesar's Place in Tijuana, Mexico, this salad has since become a runaway favorite. Because of salmonella concerns, our version uses a cooked egg instead of the traditional raw one.

SERVES 4

1 large egg

2 tablespoons fresh lemon juice

2 tablespoons olive oil

1 teaspoon Worcestershire sauce

2 garlic cloves, roasted

1/2 teaspoon salt

1/2 teaspoon black pepper

1/4 teaspoon dry mustard

16 cups washed and coarsely chopped romaine lettuce

2 cups garlic croutons

1/2 cup freshly grated Parmesan cheese

1 Half-fill a small saucepan with water and bring to a simmer over medium heat. Slide in egg and cook 5 minutes. Using a slotted spoon, plunge egg into cold water. When cool enough to handle, peel it.

2 In a food processor or blender, puree egg, lemon juice, oil, Worcestershire sauce, garlic, salt, pepper, and mustard 1 minute or until smooth.

3 In a large salad bowl, toss together lettuce, croutons, and cheese. Add dressing and toss to coat well. Serve immediately while still crisp.

GREEK SALAD

Even though this salad has only a small amount of dressing, the combination of greens, mint, olives, and cheese makes it exceptionally tasty.

SERVES 4

1/2 small head romaine lettuce, rinsed and torn into bite-size pieces

2 cups trimmed spinach, rinsed and torn into bite-size pieces

2 tablespoons chopped peeled and seeded cucumber

3 tablespoons low-fat dry-curd cottage cheese or farmers cheese

2 tablespoons minced fresh mint or 1 1/2 teaspoon mint flakes

1 tablespoon crumbled rinsed feta cheese

2 medium pitted black olives, finely chopped

1 teaspoon olive oil

1 teaspoon lemon juice

1 clove garlic, minced

1/8 teaspoon black pepper

1 In a large bowl, combine lettuce, spinach, cucumber, cottage cheese, mint, and cheese.

2 In a small bowl, combine olives, oil, lemon juice, garlic, and pepper and whisk until blended. Pour over salad and toss to combine.

LENTIL, PEAR, AND GOAT CHEESE SALAD

While the lentils cook, toast the pecans for 8 to 10 minutes at 350°F for extra flavor.

SERVES 4

1 1/2 cups lentils
1 teaspoon salt
1/2 teaspoon black pepper
1/4 cup fresh lime juice
2 tablespoons honey
1/2 teaspoon ground ginger
2 pears, cut into 1/2-inch chunks
1 bunch watercress, large stems trimmed
4 ounces mild goat cheese, crumbled
2 tablespoons coarsely chopped pecans

1 Bring a medium saucepan of water to boil. Add lentils, 1/4 teaspoon salt, and 1/4 teaspoon pepper and cook 20 to 25 minutes or until tender; drain.

2 Meanwhile, in a medium bowl, whisk together lime juice, honey, ginger, and remaining salt and pepper. Add lentils and let cool to room temperature.

3 Add pears and watercress and toss to combine. Serve sprinkled with goat cheese and pecans.

MOZZARELLA WITH TOMATO DRESSING

A simple salad of mozzarella cheese and lettuce is given character with a rich tomato and fresh herb dressing.

SERVES 4

4 ounces mixed salad greens, washed and dried
1 pound fresh mozzarella cheese, drained and sliced
5 1/2 ounces sun-dried tomatoes in oil
1 small bunch basil
1 small bunch parsley
1 small bunch marjoram or oregano
1 tablespoon balsamic vinegar
1 tablespoon capers
1 garlic clove *(optional)*
Black pepper

1 Arrange greens and cheese on 4 plates.

2 Remove tomatoes from jar and place in a food processor or blender. Pour 2/3 cup oil from jar into a measuring cup (if necessary, top up with olive oil). Add basil, parsley, marjoram, vinegar, capers, and garlic to food processor, then pour in tomato oil and puree until thick. (Or process ingredients in a bowl with a handheld mixer.) Season to taste with pepper (salt isn't necessary since capers are salty).

3 Spoon over salads.

GRILLED VEGETABLE SALAD WITH MOZZARELLA

SERVES 4

2 tablespoons olive oil

2 tablespoons fresh lemon juice

1 garlic clove, minced

1/2 teaspoon dried thyme, crumbled

1/2 teaspoon dried marjoram, crumbled

1/2 teaspoon salt

1/4 teaspoon black pepper

2 small Japanese eggplants, trimmed and halved lengthwise

1 small yellow squash, cut lengthwise into 1/4-inch-thick slices

1 small zucchini, cut lengthwise into 1/4-inch-thick slices

1 medium red bell pepper, cored, seeded, and quartered lengthwise

4 ounces fresh or smoked part-skim mozzarella cheese, thinly sliced

8 pitted black olives

2 tablespoons minced fresh basil or parsley

1 tablespoon balsamic vinegar

1 In a small bowl, combine oil, lemon juice, garlic, thyme, marjoram, salt, and black pepper. Using a pastry brush, coat eggplants, squash, zucchini, and bell pepper with some of mixture.

2 On a grill rack set 4 inches from heat, cook eggplants 3 to 4 minutes on each side or until tender. Cook squash, zucchini, and bell pepper 2 minutes on each side or until tender.

3 Cut bell pepper into strips and arrange on a serving platter with eggplants, squash, zucchini, cheese, and olives. Whisk basil and vinegar into remaining oil mixture and drizzle over all.

If you prefer to broil rather than grill the vegetables, set the rack 6 inches from the heat and broil until crisp-tender, 1 or 2 minutes longer than directed for grilling.

MINTED BARLEY WITH PEAS SALAD

To prepare this salad ahead of time, complete Step 1, then cover and refrigerate the ingredients for up to 6 hours. Add cheese, nuts, tomatoes, and garnish right before serving.

SERVES 4

3/4 cup medium pearled barley

1 package (10 ounces) frozen petite green peas

1 small red onion, finely diced

2 medium celery stalks, finely diced

1/4 cup olive or vegetable oil

3 tablespoons red wine vinegar

1 tablespoon minced fresh mint

1/4 teaspoon salt

1/4 teaspoon black pepper

2 cups cubed cheddar cheese

3/4 cup coarsely chopped roasted peanuts or walnuts

2 medium tomatoes, cored, seeded, and diced

4 mint sprigs (*optional*)

1 In a large saucepan over medium heat, cook barley according to package directions, adding peas, onion, and celery during last 3 minutes of cooking. Drain well and transfer to a large bowl. Add oil, vinegar, chopped mint, salt, and pepper and toss well.

2 Add cheese, peanuts, and tomatoes and toss well. Garnish with mint sprigs, if desired. Serve cold or at room temperature on a bed of lettuce.

WARM WINTER SALAD

This substantial first course or side dish is a perfect companion to light soups.

SERVES 4

Salad:

8 ounces small red potatoes, quartered

1 container (10 ounces) Brussels sprouts, quartered

1 red apple, cut into 1/2-inch chunks

2 celery stalks, thinly sliced

3 scallions, thinly sliced

Dressing:

1/2 cup apple juice

1/3 cup distilled white vinegar

2 tablespoons all-purpose flour

1 tablespoon spicy brown mustard

1 tablespoon drained white horseradish

1 teaspoon olive oil

1/2 teaspoon caraway seed

1/2 teaspoon salt

1 For salad, cook potatoes 5 minutes in a large saucepan of boiling water. Add Brussels sprouts and cook 5 to 8 minutes or until firm-tender. Drain and place in a large salad bowl, then add apple, celery, and scallions.

2 For dressing, whisk together apple juice, vinegar, flour, mustard, horseradish, oil, caraway seed, and salt in a small saucepan. Bring to a simmer, whisking, over medium heat and cook 2 minutes. Pour over vegetables and toss to combine. Serve warm or at room temperature.

PANZANELLA SALAD

Bread salad can add a little heft to a soup-based meal.

SERVES 4

2 tablespoons red wine vinegar

3 tablespoons olive oil

1 cup coarsely chopped fresh basil

1/2 teaspoon salt

1/2 teaspoon black pepper

1 small loaf (about 10 ounces) day-old or
toasted Italian or French bread, sliced
1/2 inch thick and cubed

8 ripe plum tomatoes,
cut into 1/2-inch cubes

1 medium red onion, diced

1 In a large bowl, whisk together vinegar, oil, basil, salt, and pepper.

2 Add bread, tomatoes, and onion and toss until well coated.

PANZANELLA WITH OLIVES

This variation on plain bread salad uses balsamic vinegar, sourdough bread, and olives.

SERVES 4

1/4 cup balsamic vinegar

3 tablespoons olive oil

1 tablespoon chopped fresh oregano

1/4 teaspoon salt

1/2 teaspoon black pepper

1 small loaf (about 10 ounces) day-old or
toasted sourdough bread, sliced
1/2 inch thick and cubed

8 ripe plum tomatoes,
cut into 1/2-inch cubes

1 medium red onion, diced

1/2 cup halved and pitted kalamata olives

1 In a large bowl, whisk together vinegar, oil, oregano, salt, and pepper.

2 Add bread, tomatoes, onion, and olives and toss until well coated.

Index

Note: Page references in italics indicate photographs.

Illustrations: ©Heather Holbrook

Photography Credits: The Reader's Digest Association, Inc. Cover: Brian Hagiwana, Foodpix/Getty.
Photodisc/Getty: page 7 *right center,* page 8 *right center,* page 9 *right,* page 11 *bottom right,* page 12 *left center,*
page 14 *left center,* page 15 *right center,* page 16 *right,* page 17 *top left,* page 24 *right center,* page 28 *top left.*
Creatas: page 7 *upper right,* page 14 *right bottom.* Corbis: page 8 *bottom center.* PhotoAlto: page 22 *top left.*
Digital Vision/Getty: page 26 *top center,* page 27 *bottom center.* Imagesoure: page 26 *upper right.*
Pixland/Getty: page 32 *top center.*

METRIC
CONVERSION CHARTS

Abbreviations

mm = millimeter
cm = centimeter
m = meter
in = inch
ft = foot
ml = milliliter
l = liter
tsp = teaspoon
tbsp = tablespoon
oz = ounce
fl oz = fluid ounce
qt = quart
gal = gallon
g = gram
kg = kilogram
lb = pound
C = Celsius
F = Fahrenheit

Cooking Equivalents U.S., U.K./Australia *All numbers have been rounded.*

Volume

U.S.	U.K./Australia
1/8 teaspoon = 0.5 ml	
1/4 teaspoon = 1 ml	
1/2 teaspoon = 2 ml	
1 teaspoon = 5 ml	
1 tablespoon = 15 ml	
1/4 cup = 2 tablespoons = 2 fluid ounces = 60 ml	
1/3 cup = 1/4 cup = 3 fluid ounces = 90 ml	
1/2 cup = 1/3 cup = 4 fluid ounces = 120 ml	
1 cup = 3/4 cup = 8 fluid ounces = 240 ml	
1 1/4 cups = 1 cup	
2 cups = 1 pint	
1 quart = 1 liter – 3 tablespoons	
1 gallon = 4 liters – 1 1/2 cups	

Weight

U.S.	U.K./Australia
1/4 ounce = 7 grams	
1/2 ounce = 14 grams	
3/4 ounce = 21 grams	
1 ounce = 28 grams	
8 ounces = 1/2 pound = 225 gr	
12 ounces = 3/4 pound = 341 g	
16 ounces = 1 pound = 454 gram	
35 ounces = 2.2 pounds = 1 kilo	

Temperature

Fahrenheit	Celsius	
0°F =	-18°C	(freezer temperature)
32°F =	0°C	(water freezes)
180°F =	82°C	(water simmers)
212°F =	100°C	(water boils)
250°F =	120°C	(low oven)
350°F =	175°C	(moderate oven)
425°F =	220°C	(hot oven)
500°F =	260°C	(very hot oven)

Length

U.S.	U.K./Australia
1/2 inch = 1.3 centimeters	
1 inch = 2.5 centimeters	
12 inches = 1 foot = 30 centimeters	
39 inches = 1 meter	